Interpersonal Communication

Why You Need This New Edition

This new edition of *Interpersonal Communication: Competence and Contexts* presents communication challenges—and also gives you the tools you need to learn to overcome them. You have the opportunity to engage in the critical evaluation of real-life, ethically challenging communication situations that are presented throughout the text. This book will help you succeed in interpersonal communication and in your class by clarifying the associations between communication concepts and the competence model components to which they relate.

The second edition also reflects the latest research and trends in the field. This new edition provides:

1. New **chapter opening objective questions** and corresponding chapter summary prompts that outline the ways the chapter information will help you, what you will learn, and what skills you will acquire. These questions are placed adjacent to chapter information and are answered in each chapter review.
2. An **updated competence icon** that visually illustrates text material as it relates to motivation, knowledge, and skill. You will learn at-a-glance whether a section of chapter information can help motivate you to communicate competently, can add to your knowledge of communication, and/or can instruct you to skillfully interact with others.
3. **More in-class activities than any interpersonal text on the market.** Each chapter features a variety of boxed activities, color-coded to the communication competence model, that enable you to apply what you've learned. Individual activities, group activities, and role-playing scenarios are related to the motivation to communicate, the knowledge of communication, and interpersonal communication skills. These in-class activities are found in sidebars and may also include URL addresses for online activities, assessments, and additional information about chapter topics.
4. Updated **information about technology and new media** included in every chapter. Specifically, new research about communication in virtual reality environments such as "Second Life" is included in the text.
5. Cutting-edge research that you can apply to your life and presents modern-day topics to which you can relate. **Information about computer-mediated communication (CMC)** includes online identity, the communication of emotion, the generation of new CMC-oriented words, conversing via computers, flaming, and relationship initiation and maintenance.
6. Additional material about **workplace communication,** including research on workplace romances, friendships, and communication patterns.
7. A **full length transcript** illustrating communication theories, concepts, and skills integrated into every chapter. Each transcript can be viewed as a video clip on the MyCommunicationLab website and is accompanied by questions for analysis.
8. **Updated chapter opening photos, examples, and reflection questions** included to encourage you to begin thinking about chapter information. For example, "pop culture" celebrities such as magician David Copperfield, actor Angelina Jolie, and talk-show host Oprah Winfrey are used to introduce you to perception and communication, verbal communication, and listening and confirming responses.

PEA

Interpersonal Communication

Competence and Contexts

SECOND EDITION

Shelley D. Lane
University of Texas at Dallas

Allyn & Bacon
Boston ▪ New York ▪ San Francisco
Mexico City ▪ Montreal ▪ Toronto ▪ London ▪ Madrid ▪ Munich ▪ Paris
Hong Kong ▪ Singapore ▪ Tokyo ▪ Cape Town ▪ Sydney

Editor-in-Chief: *Karon Bowers*
Acquisitions Editor: *Jeanne Zalesky*
Editorial Assistant: *Megan Lentz*
Assistant Development Manager: *David B. Kear*
Assistant Development Editor: *Angela Pickard*
Marketing Manager: *Blair Tuckman*
Production Supervisor: *Roberta Sherman*
Editorial Production Service: *TexTech/Stratford Publishing Services*
Manufacturing Buyer: *JoAnne Sweeney*
Electronic Composition: *TexTech/Stratford Publishing Services*
Interior Design: *Gina Hagen*
Photo Researcher: *Jessica Riu*
Cover Administrator: *Joel Gendron*

Library of Congress Cataloging-in-Publication Data

Lane, Shelley D.
Interpersonal communication : competence and contexts / Shelley D. Lane — 2nd ed.
p. cm.
includes bibliographical references and index.
ISBN-13: 978-0-205-66302-6
ISBN-10: 0-205-66302-8
1. Interpersonal communication. I. Title.
P94.7.L36 2010
302.2—dc22 2008055983

10 9 8 7 6 5 4 3 2 1 Q-TAU 13 12 11 10 09

Allyn & Bacon is an imprint of

www.pearsonhighered.com

ISBN-10: 0-205-66302-8
ISBN-13: 978-205-66302-6

Brief Contents

PART 1 Basics of Competent Communication

PART 2 Creating Competent Messages

PART 3 Communication Competency in Relationships

Contents

Chapter 2 Perception and Communication 34

Chapter 3
The Self-Concept and Communication 62

Chapter 4 Emotion and Communication 92

PART 2 Creating Competent Messages

Chapter 5 Verbal Communication 118

Chapter 6 Nonverbal Communication 146

Chapter 7
Conversation and Communication Style 178

Chapter 8
Listening and Confirming Responses 204

PART 3 Communication Competency in Relationships

Chapter 9

Disconfirming Communication and Setting Boundaries 230

Chapter 10
Interpersonal Relationships 256

Chapter 11 Interpersonal Conflict 290

Preface

For many years, my colleagues and I have lamented that many interpersonal communication textbooks fail to present theories, concepts, and skills in a unified and thematic manner. Many textbooks deliver a smattering of theory, a dollop of concepts, and a hodgepodge of skills. *Interpersonal Communication: Competence and Contexts,* on the other hand, provides the theories, concepts, and applications in a pedagogically sound format based on a model of communication competence that includes motivation, knowledge, and skill. Studying interpersonal communication through this distinct framework will boost students' *motivation* to communicate competently, increase their *knowledge* about communication, and enhance their acquisition and performance of communication *skills.* This unique approach to the study and application of interpersonal communication will also prepare students to communicate civilly amidst the numerous communication challenges we encounter in today's fast-paced, diverse, and complex society.

The Second Edition of *Interpersonal Communication: Competence and Contexts* strengthens the associations between text material and components of the communication competence model. The communication competence model is represented in the text by a visual icon that identifies to which model component the chapter material relates. Nearly all of the material in the text including chapter opening questions, textual headings, feature boxes, and the chapter review questions are labeled to illustrate their relation to the *motivation, knowledge,* or *skill* components of the communication competence model.

Unique Features

The Second Edition of *Interpersonal Communication: Competence and Contexts* offers a distinctly different approach to the presentation of various contexts that affect interpersonal communication. Rather than relegated to a sidebar, box, or included as a brief addition, information concerning culture, relationships (with family, friends, and coworkers), gender, and the individual is fully integrated into each chapter of the text. Additionally, *Interpersonal Communication: Competence and Contexts* explores research concerning civility and communication—such as our "rights" versus the "right" to say anything we want, the use of profanity and curse words, road rage, the (un)civil use of cell phones, and whether manners matter. This research empowers students to make informed choices regarding the communication of civility.

In addition, the Second Edition provides cutting-edge research that students can apply to their lives and present modern-day topics to which students can relate. Information about computer-mediated communication (CMC) that will resonate with today's computer-savvy students is included in every chapter. CMC material includes online identity, the communication of emotion, the generation of new CMC-oriented words, conversing with computers, flaming, and relationship initiation and maintenance. Furthermore, not all of our communication encounters are easy in today's complicated world. Therefore, the Second Edition presents communication challenges and how we can overcome them. Students also have the opportunity to engage in the critical evaluation of real-life, ethically challenging communication situations that are presented throughout the text.

Chapter Organization

To make the themes and concepts in this text come alive, I have organized the second edition of *Interpersonal Communication: Competence and Contexts* using a student-friendly, unifying framework that will help them become competent communicators. Each chapter begins with a series of features designed to spark students' interest in the theories, concepts, and skills they will encounter as they explore that chapter:

- Every chapter begins with a quotation by and a reference to a noted scholar, historical figure or pop culture celebrity to encourage students to begin thinking about chapter information and how the material may relate to their lives.
- Learning objective questions are organized by the motivation, knowledge, and skills that students will gain as they progress through the chapter.

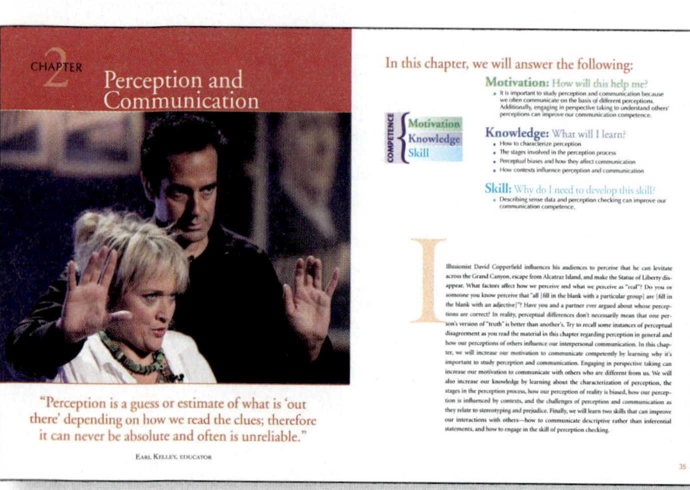

CHAPTER 2 Perception and Communication

"Perception is a guess or estimate of what is 'out there' depending on how we read the clues; therefore it can never be absolute and often is unreliable."

EARL KELLEY, EDUCATOR

In this chapter, we will answer the following:

COMPETENCE Motivation Knowledge Skill

Motivation: How will this help me?

- It is important to study perception and communication because we often communicate on the basis of different perceptions. Additionally, engaging in perspective taking to understand others' perceptions can improve our communication competence.

Knowledge: What will I learn?

- How to characterize perception
- The stages involved in the perception process
- Perceptual biases and how they affect communication
- How contexts influence perception and communication

Skill: Why do I need to develop this skill?

- Describing sense data and perception checking can improve our communication competence.

Illusionist David Copperfield influences his audiences to perceive that he can levitate across the Grand Canyon, escape from Alcatraz Island, and make the Statue of Liberty disappear. What factors affect how we perceive and what we perceive as "real"? Do you or someone you know perceive that "all [fill in the blank with a particular group] are [fill in the blank with an adjective]"? Have you and a partner ever argued about whose perceptions are correct? In reality, perceptual differences don't necessarily mean that one person's version of "truth" is better than another's. Try to recall some instances of perceptual disagreement as you read the material in this chapter regarding perception in general and how our perceptions of others influence our interpersonal communication. In this chapter, we will increase our motivation to communicate competently by learning why it's important to study perception and communication. Engaging in perspective taking can increase our motivation to communicate with others who are different from us. We will also increase our knowledge by learning about the characterization of perception, the stages in the perception process, how our perception of reality is biased, how our perception is influenced by contexts, and the challenges of perception and communication as they relate to stereotyping and prejudice. Finally, we will learn two skills that can improve our interactions with others—how to communicate descriptive rather than inferential statements, and how to engage in the skill of perception checking.

35

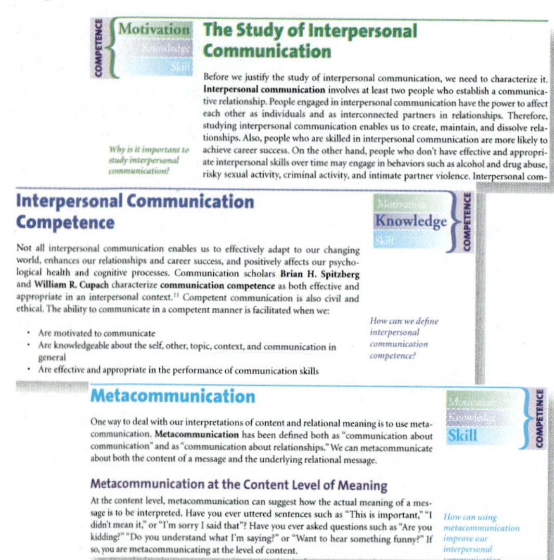

COMPETENCE Motivation Knowledge Skill

The Study of Interpersonal Communication

Why is it important to study interpersonal communication?

Before we justify the study of interpersonal communication, we need to characterize it. **Interpersonal communication** involves at least two people who establish a communicative relationship. People engaged in interpersonal communication have the power to affect each other as individuals and as interconnected partners in relationships. Therefore, studying interpersonal communication enables us to create, maintain, and dissolve relationships. Also, people who are skilled in interpersonal communication are more likely to achieve career success. On the other hand, people who don't have effective and appropriate interpersonal skills over time may engage in behaviors such as alcohol and drug abuse, risky sexual activity, criminal activity, and intimate partner violence. Interpersonal com-

Interpersonal Communication Competence

Motivation Knowledge Skill COMPETENCE

Not all interpersonal communication enables us to effectively adapt to our changing world, enhances our relationships and career success, and positively affects our psychological health and cognitive processes. Communication scholars **Brian H. Spitzberg** and **William R. Cupach** characterize **communication competence** as both effective and appropriate in an interpersonal context.[11] Competent communication is also civil and ethical. The ability to communicate in a competent manner is facilitated when we:

How can we define interpersonal communication competence?

- Are motivated to communicate
- Are knowledgeable about the self, other, topic, context, and communication in general
- Are effective and appropriate in the performance of communication skills

Metacommunication

Motivation Knowledge Skill COMPETENCE

One way to deal with our interpretations of content and relational meaning is to use metacommunication. **Metacommunication** has been defined both as "communication about communication" and as "communication about relationships." We can metacommunicate about both the content of a message and the underlying relational message.

Metacommunication at the Content Level of Meaning

At the content level, metacommunication can suggest how the actual meaning of a message is to be interpreted. Have you ever uttered sentences such as "This is important," "I didn't mean it," or "I'm sorry I said that"? Have you ever asked questions such as "Are you kidding?" "Do you understand what I'm saying?" or "Want to hear something funny?" If so, you are metacommunicating at the level of content.

How can using metacommunication improve our interpersonal

Students will explore the varied theories, concepts, and skills that make up the heart of the new edition of *Interpersonal Communication: Competence and Contexts* in the main text of each chapter. The second edition includes several special features:

- The three versions of the competence icon visually illustrate text material as it relates to motivation, knowledge, and skill. Students will learn at-a-glance whether a section of chapter information can help motivate them to communicate competently, can add to their knowledge of communication, and/or can instruct them to skillfully interact with others.

- **Knowledge on the Cutting Edge** research that illustrates various theories and concepts is presented in a series of boxes. Topics include biocommunication, workplace incivility, linguistic profiling, Asperger's Syndrome, how Deaf people listen, and conversing with computers.

KNOWLEDGE ON THE CUTTING EDGE

Words without English Equivalents

You most likely know that languages differ in terms of symbols (words) and syntax (grammar). What you may not realize is that languages also differ in regard to the availability and variety of words that communicate meaning. Some words in other languages do not have English equivalents. For example, what English word would you use to describe an object, such as a teacup, that is museum-quality but has a crack running down its side? The crack is considered to be an aesthetic flaw that represents the spirit of the moment in which the teacup is created. You probably cannot think of a word because there is no word in English that encompasses all of these characteristics. However, the Japanese word *wabi* (which rhymes with "bobby") describes such a treasured cultural object. Have you ever attempted to describe your feelings about someone you once loved but now do not? Maybe you used the word *like* to describe your feelings but realized that while you "like" your roommate, the "like" you feel for your ex-lover is something quite different. Perhaps you tried to describe your current feelings by using the phrase "but we're still friends." Once again, your "friends" are people with whom you socialize and whose company you enjoy; however, you may no longer meet with your former lover. There is no word in English that describes the feeling a person has for someone once loved. However, the Russian language includes such a word, *razbliuto* (pronounced ros-blee-OO-tow). Other words that have no English equivalents include *Farpotshket* and *Bilita mpatshi*. *Farpotshket* (Yiddish; pronounced "far-POTCH-ket") refers to a bad situation that becomes worse after someone tries to fix it. For example, if water flows from the faucet in a heavy stream after you try to repair a slight drip, you can say your faucet is "farpotshket." *Bilita mpatshi* (Bantu; pronounced bee-LEE-tah mm-POT-she) refers to blissful dreams. Although the English language includes a word for terrible dreams, "nightmares," English lacks a word for dreams that are glorious, legendary, and blissful.[29]

- The Second Edition of *Interpersonal Communication: Competence and Contexts* provides students with more in-class activities than any interpersonal text on the market. Each chapter features a variety of activities that enable students to apply what they learn. Individual activities, group activities, and role-playing scenarios are related to the motivation to communicate, knowledge of communication, and **Motivation & Mindwork, Knowledge Power, and Skill Practice**. The color of the box and title clearly relates each activity to a component of the competence model.
- Short video clips available on the MyCommunicationLab website provide an opportunity for students to carefully observe and learn about interpersonal communication theories, concepts, and skills. Each chapter features a transcript of a video clip entitled, **Competence & Critical Thinking** that students can analyze in terms of chapter material. Accompanying questions based on the transcript help students focus on the chapter information to be used in their analyses.
- A section related to **Overcoming Communication Challenges** is included near the end of each chapter. Communication challenges include the interpersonal problems that result from inflated self-esteem, workplace bullying and mobbing, stalking, conversational dilemmas, and relational transgressions.
- Each chapter concludes with a true-life **Case Study in Ethics**, such as the teacher who required her students to write, "I'm a loser . . ." when they forgot their homework, the "Meet the F*ckers" tee-shirt that some considered offensive, the cell phone alibi club members who made lying phone calls on behalf of others, and the conflict concerning the father who refused to pay for his son's college education unless he changed political parties. Questions for analysis accompany each case study.

Special features located at the end of each chapter are designed to help students organize their study of communication theories, concepts, and skills:

- A chapter review provides answers to the objective questions presented at the beginning of the chapter by exploring the motivation, knowledge, and skills students have acquired. The appropriate competence visual icon reinforces the competency involved.

KNOWLEDGE power • Love Is Blind

With a partner or in a group, recall instances when you or someone you know was subject to perception based on selectivity. For example, in terms of selective attention, can you think of a time when you or someone else "heard" some parts of a message and ignored others? Has someone

message that you communicated and missed the rest of it? Have your friends ever perceived some bad qualities in a relational partner that you had not noticed (selective perception)? After you share your examples of selectivity and its influence on perception, discuss ways we can prevent

MOTIVATION & mindwork • Managing My Debilitative Emotions

Think about some situations in which you can use REBT to change the thoughts that cause your debilitative emotions. Such situations may include a first date, asking

asking someone to change her or his behavior. With a partner or in a group, practice changing your irrational thoughts to those that are rational using the

SKILL practice • Using Specific and Concrete Words

Reword the following statements to make them more specific. Use words located at the bottom of the ladder of abstraction, that is, sense data, concrete words (those that appeal to the senses), examples, and precise words such as names and titles.

- "I like going to concerts."
- "You should be more careful next time."
- "He's a reckless driver."
- "She's always late."
- "Why can't we talk about anything interesting?"

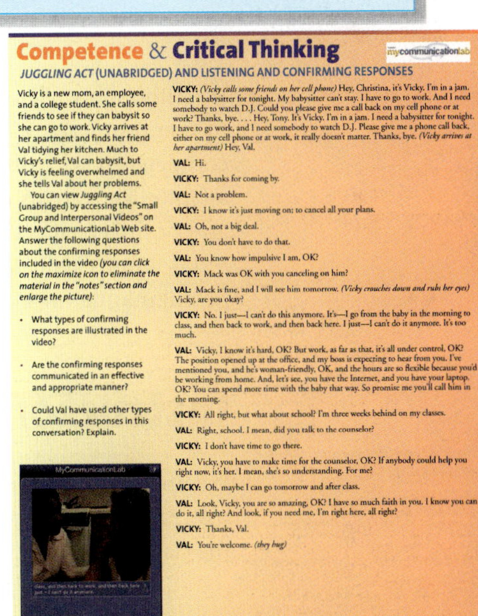

Competence & Critical Thinking mycommunicationlab

JUGGLING ACT (UNABRIDGED) AND LISTENING AND CONFIRMING RESPONSES

Vicky is a new mom, an employee, and a college student. She calls some friends to see if they can babysit so she can go to work. Vicky arrives at her apartment and finds her friend Val tidying her kitchen. Much to Vicky's relief, Val can babysit, but Vicky is feeling overwhelmed and she tells Val about her problems.

You can view *Juggling Act* (unabridged) by accessing the "Small Group and Interpersonal Videos" on the MyCommunicationLab Web site. Answer the following questions about the confirming responses included in the video *(you can click on the maximize icon to eliminate the material in the "notes" section and enlarge the picture)*:

- What types of confirming responses are illustrated in the video?
- Are the confirming responses communicated in an effective and appropriate manner?
- Could Val have used other types of confirming responses in this conversation? Explain.

VICKY: *(Vicky calls some friends on her cell phone)* Hey, Christina, it's Vicky. I'm in a jam. I need a babysitter for tonight. My babysitter can't stay. I have to go to work. And I need somebody to watch D.J. Could you please give me a call back on my cell phone or at work? Thanks, bye. . . . Hey, Tony. It's Vicky. I'm in a jam. I need a babysitter for tonight. I have to go work, and I need somebody to watch D.J. Please give me a phone call back, either on my cell phone or at work, it really doesn't matter. Thanks, bye. *(Vicky arrives at her apartment)* Hey, Val.

VAL: Hi.

VICKY: Thanks for coming by.

VAL: Not a problem.

VICKY: I know it's just moving on; to cancel all your plans.

VAL: Oh, not a big deal.

VICKY: You don't have to do that.

VAL: You know how impulsive I am, OK?

VICKY: Mack was OK with you canceling on him?

VAL: Mack is fine, and I will see him tomorrow. *(Vicky crouches down and rubs her eyes)* Vicky, are you okay?

VICKY: No. I just—I can't do this anymore. It's—I go from the baby in the morning to class, and then back to work, and then back here. I just—I can't do it anymore. It's too much.

VAL: Vicky, I know it's hard, OK? But work, as far as that, it's all under control, OK? The position opened up at the office, and my boss is expecting to hear from you. I've mentioned you, and he's woman-friendly, OK, and the hours are so flexible because you'd be working from home. And, let's see, you have the Internet, and you have your laptop, OK? You can spend more time with the baby that way. So promise me you'll call him in the morning.

VICKY: All right, but what about school? I'm three weeks behind on my classes.

VAL: Right, school. I mean, did you talk to the counselor?

VICKY: I don't have time to go there.

VAL: Vicky, you have to make time for the counselor, OK? If anybody could help you right now, it's her. I mean, she's so understanding. For me?

VICKY: Oh, maybe I can go tomorrow and after class.

VAL: Look, Vicky, you are so amazing, OK? I have so much faith in you. I know you can do it, all right? And look, if you need me, I'm right here, all right?

VICKY: Thanks, Val.

VAL: You're welcome. *(they hug)*

A CASE STUDY IN ETHICS

Cell Phone Subterfuge

Competent communication includes an ethical dimension of well-based standards of right and wrong. To help us make decisions and select communication strategies that are effective and appropriate, we can ask ourselves a series of questions: Have I practiced any virtues today (e.g., have I demonstrated integrity, trustworthiness, honesty, and responsibility)? Have I done more good than harm (e.g., have I shown appreciation and gratitude to others)? Have I treated people with dignity and respect? Have I been fair and just? Have I made my community stronger because of my actions? Read the following case study about cell phone subterfuge and consider whether staged phone calls, alibi clubs, and fake noises are ethical ways to engage in conversations with others.

James E. Katz, professor of communication at Rutgers University, suggests that some people use cell phones to indirectly communicate with people who surround them. For example, some people stage fake phone calls as explanations for their behavior, such as scolding a pretend child for invading a wallet when they find themselves without cash in a checkout line. Others pretend to be talking on their cell phone when they are actually trying to get a good angle to take a photo on it. Still others create fake phone calls for reasons of safety. Loudly saying, "I'll meet you in a few minutes!" may be helpful when we think we're being followed.

In addition to using cell phones to stage fake phone calls, some people, with the help of other cell phone users, use their cell phones to lie. "Cell phone alibi clubs" are flourishing in many parts of the globe as a way to help callers make excuses and hide their whereabouts. People pay a fee to join a club and are subsequently linked to thousands of members to whom they can send text messages en masse that ask for help. When a potential collaborator indicates her or his willingness to phone a "victim," the caller and collaborator create a lie, and the collaborator phones with the excuse. Similar to alibi clubs, companies offer audio recordings that can be played in the background of such phone calls. Sounds such as honking horns, a dentist's drill, and ambulance sirens can be used to make a phone call sound realistic.

Although fake cell phone calls, cell phone alibi clubs, and background audio recordings may reflect questionable ethics, some individuals find nothing wrong with their use. Harry Kargman, founder of a company that sells audio background sounds, says that using background sounds is "not necessarily malicious or nefarious." Michelle Logan, founder of an alibi club based in San Diego, suggests that such clubs spare others' feelings with "white lies."[50]

Do you think it's ethical to stage fake phone calls? Is it ethical to use alibi clubs and/or background audio recordings? Do you agree with Michelle Logan that alibi clubs spare others' feelings?

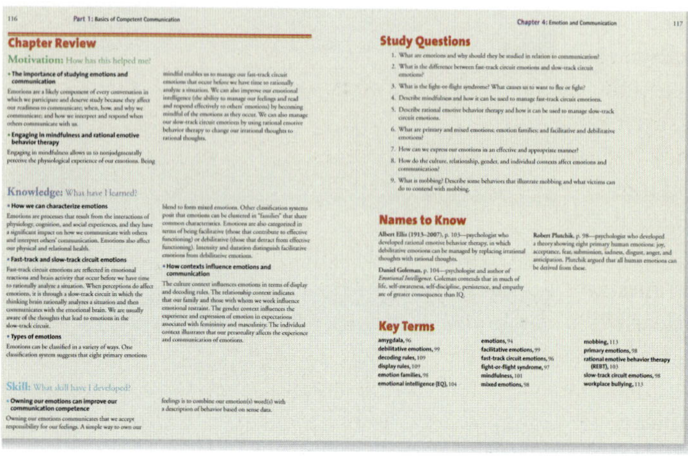

116 Part 1: Basics of Competent Communication

Chapter Review

Motivation: How has this helped me?

- **The importance of studying emotions and communication**

Emotions are a likely component of every conversation in which we participate and deserve study because they affect our readiness to communicate; when, how, and why we communicate; and how we interpret and respond when others communicate with us.

- **Engaging in mindfulness and rational emotive behavior therapy**

Engaging in mindfulness allows us to nonjudgmentally perceive the physiological experience of our emotions. Being mindful enables us to manage our fast-track circuit emotions that occur before we have time to rationally analyze a situation. We can also improve our emotional intelligence (the ability to manage our feelings and read and respond effectively to others' emotions) by becoming mindful of the emotions as they occur. We can also manage our slow-track circuit emotions by using rational emotive behavior therapy to change our irrational thoughts to rational thoughts.

Knowledge: What have I learned?

- **How we can characterize emotions**

Emotions are processes that result from the interactions of physiology, cognition, and social experiences, and they have a significant impact on how we communicate with others and interpret others' communication. Emotions also affect our physical and relational health.

- **Fast-track and slow-track circuit emotions**

Fast-track circuit emotions are reflected in emotional reactions and brain activity that occur before we have time to rationally analyze a situation. When perceptions do affect emotions, it is through a slow-track circuit in which the thinking brain rationally analyzes a situation and then communicates with the emotional brain. We are usually aware of the thoughts that lead to emotions in the slow-track circuit.

- **Types of emotions**

Emotions can be classified in a variety of ways. One classification system suggests that eight primary emotions blend to form mixed emotions. Other classification systems posit that emotions can be clustered in "families" that share common characteristics. Emotions are also categorized in terms of being facilitative (those that contribute to effective functioning) or debilitative (those that detract from effective functioning). Intensity and duration distinguish facilitative emotions from debilitative emotions.

- **How contexts influence emotions and communication**

The culture context influences emotions in terms of display and decoding rules. The relationship context indicates that our family and those with whom we work influence emotional restraint. The gender context influences the experience and expression of emotion in expectations associated with femininity and masculinity. The individual context illustrates that our personality affects the experience and communication of emotions.

Skill: What skill have I developed?

- **Owning our emotions can improve our communication competence**

Owning our emotions communicates that we accept responsibility for our feelings. A simple way to own our feelings is to combine our emotion(s) word(s) with a description of behavior based on sense data.

Chapter 4: Emotion and Communication 117

Study Questions

1. What are emotions and why should they be studied in relation to communication?
2. What is the difference between fast-track circuit emotions and slow-track circuit emotions?
3. What is the fight-or-flight syndrome? What causes us to want to flee or fight?
4. Describe mindfulness and how it can be used to manage fast-track circuit emotions.
5. Describe rational emotive behavior therapy and how it can be used to manage slow-track circuit emotions.
6. What are primary and mixed emotions; emotion families; and facilitative and debilitative emotions?
7. How can we express our emotions in an effective and appropriate manner?
8. How do the culture, relationship, gender, and individual contexts affect emotions and communication?
9. What is mobbing? Describe some behaviors that illustrate mobbing and what victims can do to contend with mobbing.

Names to Know

Albert Ellis (1913–2007), p. 103—psychologist who developed rational emotive behavior therapy, in which debilitative emotions can be managed by replacing irrational thoughts with rational thoughts.

Daniel Goleman, p. 104—psychologist and author of *Emotional Intelligence*. Goleman contends that in much of life, self-awareness, self-discipline, persistence, and empathy are of greater consequence than IQ.

Robert Plutchik, p. 98—psychologist who developed a theory showing eight primary human emotions: joy, acceptance, fear, submission, sadness, disgust, anger, and anticipation. Plutchik argued that all human emotions can be derived from these.

Key Terms

amygdala, 96
debilitative emotions, 99
decoding rules, 109
display rules, 109
emotion families, 98
emotional intelligence (EQ), 104
emotions, 94
facilitative emotions, 99
fast-track circuit emotions, 96
fight-or-flight syndrome, 97
mindfulness, 101
mixed emotions, 98
mobbing, 113
primary emotions, 98
rational emotive behavior therapy (REBT), 103
slow-track circuit emotions, 98
workplace bullying, 113

- A "Names-to-Know" section includes brief biographies of the classic and modern communication scholars included in each chapter. The names are in boldface type in the main text of the chapter.
- A list of key terms at the end of the chapter (in boldface type when they are introduced in the chapter) can help students review before a test. Definitions are available in an end-of-book glossary.
- Study questions can be used to spark classroom discussion, serve as homework assignments, or can be used as a study tool for students as they review or prepare for exams.

Although we live in a dynamic and complex society that sometimes makes it difficult to communicate, it is possible to be motivated, knowledgeable, and skillful to interact competently with others. Competent and civil interpersonal communication enables us to adapt effectively to our changing world, enhances our relationships and career success, and positively affects our psychological health. The second edition of *Interpersonal Communication: Competence and Contexts* is designed to help students communicate in a competent manner in a diverse, fast-paced, and technology-oriented society.

Instructor Supplements

We provide a complete and integrated package of resources to help the new or experienced instructor use *Interpersonal Communication: Competence and Contexts* most effectively in the classroom.

Print Resources

Instructor's Manual. The printed Instructor's Manual, written by the text author, is designed to complement the communication competence theme featured in the book. Communication competence icons, like the ones in the student text, appear next to content that is designed to develop your students' competence in each of the three elements of competence: knowledge, motivation, and skill. The manual begins with a variety of features that faciliate course organization. The IM includes sample syllabi, ideas for term projects and assignments, and instructions for the creation and administration of an oral skills mastery assessment. The chapter-by-chapter materials are designed to help you make the most out of every class meeting and assignment. Features include:

- learning objectives
- a detailed chapter outline
- a summary of chapter information
- discussion questions
- additional activities and homework assignments
- the analysis of the video transcript included in the text chapter

- additional skill practice scenarios
- URL addresses and information about additional assessments
- descriptions of professionally produced videos and accompanying discussion questions located in the accompanying MyCommunicationLab
- a "Do you want to show a film clip?" Feature that describes a scene in a popular film related to the chapter topic (DVD counter numbers are provided)

Test Bank. Prepared by Gary Kuhn, Chemeketa Community College, the test bank contains more than 100 test questions per chapter. Questions are classified by the type of competence being tested: knowledge, motivation, or skill. Therefore, you can test your students' communication competence by choosing test questions that relate to the competence you wish to test. You can choose from multiple choice, true/false, fill-in, short answer, and essay questions, all of which are listed with answers. Each question is associated with a difficulty level making question selection easy, and every question includes a page reference where the answer can be located in the text.

The Blockbuster Approach: Teaching Interpersonal Communication with Video, Third Edition. This guide by Thomas E. Jewell, Marymount College, provides lists and descriptions of commercial videos that can be used in the classroom to illustrate interpersonal concepts and complex interpersonal relationships. Sample activities are also included.

Electronic Resources

MyCommunicationLab. MyCommunicationLab is an interactive and instructive online solution designed to be used as a supplement to a traditional lecture course or to completely administer an online course. MyCommunicationLab gives you and your students access to a wealth of resources geared to meet your teaching needs and to help students learn to communicate more effectively.

MyCommunicationLab for *Interpersonal Communication: Competence and Contexts* includes a full e-book including embedded video and audio Web site links, digital flashcards, quizzes, and tests. You'll also find an array of enrichment resources including videos, blogs, and interactive activities to complement those in the text. The printed IM contains teaching resources to help you make the most of the entire package in your class. Available on the web at www.MyCommunicationLab.com (access code required).

MyTest Computerized Test Bank. The printed test bank that accompanies this text is also available in electronic format. The user-friendly interface enables instructors to view, edit, and add questions, transfer questions into tests, and print tests in a variety of fonts. Search and sort features allow instructors to locate questions quickly and arrange them in preferred order. Available online at www.pearsonmytest.com/irc (access code required).

PowerPoint Presentation Package. Prepared by the author, this text-specific comprehensive package consists of a collection of lecture outlines and graphic images keyed to every chapter in the text. It is downloadable through our Instructor's Resource Center at http://www.pearsonhighered.com/irc (access code required).

VideoWorkshop for Interpersonal Communication Instructor's Teaching Guide. This guide by Christine North, Ohio Northern University, provides teaching suggestions, quiz questions and answers, and discussion starters that will help you use the VideoWorkshop for Interpersonal Communication CD-ROM in class. The complete CD-ROM and Student Learning Guide are included in this guide.

Allyn & Bacon's Interpersonal Communication Video Library. This library contains a range of videos from which adopters can choose. Each of the videos features a variety of scenarios that illustrate interpersonal concepts and relationships, including topics such as nonverbal communication, perception, conflict, and listening. Please contact your Pearson Allyn & Bacon representative for details and a complete list of videos and their contents to choose which would be most useful to in your class. Each video has its own ISBN and must be ordered separately.

Communication Digital Media Archive, Version 3.0. The Digital Media Archive CD-ROM contains electronic images of charts, graphs, maps, tables, and figures, along with media elements such as video, audio clips, and related web links. These media assets are fully customizable to use with our pre-formatted PowerPoint ™ outlines or to import into instructor's own lectures. (Available in Windows and Mac formats.)

Lecture Questions for Clickers: Interpersonal Communication by Keri Moe, El Paso Community College. An assortment of questions and activities covering the principles and axioms of interpersonal communication, self concept, listening, nonverbal, and more are presented in PowerPoint. These slides will help liven up your lectures and can be used along with the Personal Response System to get students more involved in the material. Available on the Web at www.pearsonhighered.com/irc.

Student Supplements

We also offer an array of study and enrichment resources in print and electronic format to help your students become competent communicators.

Print Resources

Study Card for Interpersonal Communication. Colorful, affordable, and packed with useful information, Allyn & Bacon's Study Cards make studying easier, more efficient, and more enjoyable. Course information is distilled down to the basics, helping you quickly master the fundamentals, review a subject for understanding, or prepare for an exam. Because they're laminated for durability, you can keep these Study Cards for years to come and pull them out whenever you need a quick review.

Electronic Resources

MyCommunicationLab. MyCommunicationLab is an interactive and instructive online solution designed to be used as a supplement to a traditional lecture course or to completely administer an online course. MyCommunicationLab gives you and your students access to a wealth of resources geared to meet your teaching needs and to help students learn to communicate more effectively.

MyCommunicationLab for *Interpersonal Communication: Competence and Contexts* includes a full E-book including video and audio resources, Web site links, digital flash-cards, quizzes, and tests. You'll also find an array of enrichment resources including videos, blogs and interactive activities to complement those in the text. Available on the web at www.MyCommunicationLab.com (access code required).

Interpersonal Communication Study Site. Accessed at www.abinterpersonal.com, this site contains a fully expanded set of practice tests for all major topics in the course, flash-cards, and links to other valuable Web sources.

VideoWorkshop for Interpersonal Communication Student Learning Guide. Video-Workshop for Interpersonal Communication, by Christine North, Ohio Northern University, is a new way to bring video into your course for maximized learning! This total teaching and learning system includes quality video footage on an easy-to-use CD-ROM, plus a Student Learning Guide. The result? A program that brings textbook concepts to life with ease and helps your students understand, analyze, and apply the objectives of the course.

Acknowledgments

Interpersonal Communication: Competence and Contexts would not be a reality without the support and encouragement of a number of people who deserve recognition. I thank everyone at Pearson Education/Allyn & Bacon who made this book possible: Karon Bowers—Editor-in-Chief, Jeanne Zalesky—Acquisitions Editor, Blair Tuckman—Marketing Manager, Roberta Sherman—Production Supervisor, and Megan Lentz—Editorial Assistant. I especially want to thank Carol Alper, Development Editor for the first edition, for her hard work, enthusiasm, and good nature. Stephanie Ricotta and Kristen D. LeFevre deserve praise for their efforts in making the Second Edition of *Interpersonal Communication: Competence and Contexts* a reality.

My gratitude extends to the reviewers who provided excellent suggestions and insightful comments about this second edition:

Rhonda R. Buckley, Ph.D., Texas Woman's University
Nanci M. Burk—Glendale Community College
Carolyn Clark—Salt Lake Community College
Louisa A. Eckert—Central Oregon Community College
Katrina Eicher—Elizabethtown Community and Technical College
Lucy Evelyn—Howard Community College
Chris Kennedy—Western Wyoming Community College
Gary D. Kuhn—Chemetaka Community College
Shawn Miklaucic—DeSales University
Randall R. Mueller—Gateway Technical College
Nancy Nichols—Linn Benton Community College
Patricia R. Palmerton, Hamline University
Leesha M. Thrower-Camera, Ph.D., Northern Kentucky University

I would also like to express my appreciation to the reviewers of the first edition of *Interpersonal Communication: Competence and Contexts*:

Cheryl A. Baugh, Fontbonne University
Polly A. Begley, Fresno City College
Francesca Bishop, El Camino College
Edward C. Brewer, Murray State University
Tammala Bulger, University of North Carolina at Wilmington
Nanci Burk, Glendale Community College
Lori A. Byers, University of North Texas
Joyce Clohessy, Westmoreland County Community College
Jean L. DeHart, Appalachian State University
Duane Alan Dowd, Louisiana Tech University
Donald B. Egolf, University of Pittsburgh
Diane Ferrero-Paluzzi, Iona College
Annette L. Folwell, University of Idaho
Jo Anna Grant, California State University at San Bernardino
Sandy H. Hanson, University of North Carolina at Charlotte
Anneliese Harper, Scottsdale Community College
Susan A. Holmes, Northwest Arkansas Community College
Patricia Islas, El Paso Community College
James A. Katt, University of Central Florida
Chris Kennedy, Western Wyoming Community College
Chris Kernion, Portland Community College
Karen Lada, Delaware County Community College
Carol Leeman, University of North Carolina at Charlotte
Alan Lerstrom, Luther College
Robin McGehee, College of Sequoias
Lynnea McHenry, Hawkeye Community College
Jody Dee Morrison, Salisbury University
Nan Peck, Northern Virginia Community College
Mary-Jo Popovici, Monroe Community College
C. Thomas Preston, Jr., University of Texas at Brownsville
Paul C. Schleifer, Southern Wesleyan University
Suzanne L. Stangl-Erkens, St. Cloud State University
Marceline Thompson-Hayes, Arkansas State University
Terry L. West, Southern Utah University
Richard L. Wiseman, California State University at Fullerton

I also appreciate my colleagues and friends who played an important role in the creation of *Interpersonal Communication: Competence and Contexts*. Dr. Brian Spitzberg, Professor of Communication at San Diego State University, and Dr. Gust Yep, Professor of Communication at San Francisco State University, generously shared their research and willingly offered their sage counsel. Eric Carlson, Professor of Communication at Collin College, provided emotional support and enthusiasm, honest and supportive critique, and insight about the machinations of academic textbook publishing. Helene Cohen-Gilbert, founder of the ASL interpreter education consulting firm "Hand-in-Hand" and my best friend, deserves praise and appreciation for her wisdom, advice, and her inspiring survival and escape from "life in the trenches" that we once shared. And last but certainly not least, my heartfelt gratitude extends to my family. I thank Simon M. Lane, M.S.ed., D.P.M., and Rita A. Lane, my parents, for their unflagging confidence in my ability to author an interpersonal communication textbook. I thank my children, Ethan, Elizabeth, and Ariana, for understanding why Mom spent such long hours on the computer. And I thank my husband, Lawrence W. Miller, Ph.D., for his loving encouragement, proofreading services, and his willingness to take on the increased household and childcare duties that enabled me to complete *Interpersonal Communication: Competence and Contexts.*

About the Author

Shelley D. Lane (B.A., Communication Studies, University of California at Los Angeles; M.A. and Ph.D., Communication Arts and Sciences, University of Southern California) has approximately 30 years of university and college experience that combines publication, teaching, and administration. Lane was selected as the outstanding professor in her academic division and college and was named a Minnie Stevens Piper Professor, the highest university teaching award in Texas. She is currently involved in the development of the "Emerging Media and Communication" major at the University of Texas at Dallas.

Do you have questions, comments, and/or suggestions regarding *Interpersonal Communication: Competence and Contexts?* If so, please feel free to email at Shelley.Lane@utdallas.edu.

Interpersonal Communication

CHAPTER 1 Introduction to Interpersonal Communication

"Communication is a fundamental skill for building connection and contact, communion and community."

DEAN ORNISH, M.D., PROFESSOR OF MEDICINE AND AUTHOR

In this chapter, we will answer the following:

Motivation: How will this help me?

- It is important to study interpersonal communication because interpersonal communication affects our thoughts, feelings, and interactions with others; enables us to create, maintain, and dissolve relationships; and helps us achieve career success.
- We can use intrapersonal communication and goal setting to reduce social anxiety that can rob us of our confidence and motivation to communicate in a competent manner.

Knowledge: What will I learn?

- How to define interpersonal communication competence
- The contexts that influence interpersonal communication
- The types of communication that are related to interpersonal communication competence
- Principles of communication
- The components involved in a transactional model of communication

Skill: Why do I need to develop these skills?

- Metacommunication can improve our interpersonal communication competence at the content and relational levels of communication.

Have you ever experienced a day in which you conducted research on the Internet, text-messaged a friend, answered emails, and sent a fax? Maybe you or someone you know attends classes, works, is involved in a relationship, and ends the day too tired to speak with anyone. Perhaps you communicate with people from a variety of cultures and work hard to maintain your relationships with intimate partners, friends, and colleagues. You may even work with others to rebuild your community, similar to the people who worked together to revitalize New Orleans after Hurricane Katrina. Although we live in a dynamic and complex society that sometimes makes it difficult to communicate with others, it is possible to be motivated, knowledgeable, and skillful to interact competently with our conversation partners. This book is written to help you communicate in a competent manner in a fast-paced, technology-oriented, and diverse society. In this chapter, we will learn that our motivation to communicate competently can be enhanced by understanding why it's important to study interpersonal communication, using intrapersonal communication and goal setting to reduce social anxiety, and engaging in perspective taking and other techniques in which we use our imagination. We will also increase our knowledge of communication by learning about interpersonal communication competence and contexts that affect others' perceptions of competent interaction; types and principles of communication; and components associated with a transactional model of the communication process. Finally, we will learn to use the skill of metacommunication, or "communication about communication," when we interact with others.

The Study of Interpersonal Communication

Before we justify the study of interpersonal communication, we need to characterize it. **Interpersonal communication** involves at least two people who establish a communicative relationship. People engaged in interpersonal communication have the power to affect each other as individuals and as interconnected partners in relationships. Therefore, studying interpersonal communication enables us to create, maintain, and dissolve relationships. Also, people who are skilled in interpersonal communication are more likely to achieve career success. On the other hand, people who don't have effective and appropriate interpersonal skills over time may engage in behaviors such as alcohol and drug abuse, risky sexual activity, criminal activity, and intimate partner violence. Interpersonal communication also has the power to affect physical health. Studies conducted by researchers

Why is it important to study interpersonal communication?

KNOWLEDGE ON THE CUTTING EDGE

Technology Update: Communication and Our Changing World

Think about the diverse people you interact with, those you read about in the newspaper, and those you see on TV and in the movies. Globalization of the economy, population migration, and technology developments have transformed the world into a "global village" in which we can communicate with people almost anywhere on Earth.[1] Multinational corporations are increasingly moving operations overseas, and many people work in organizations that conduct business in many countries. More than 175 million migrants have left their countries for economic reasons, to escape war and civil conflict, or for family reunification. And through computer-mediated communication (CMC), we may come in contact with people who are very different from ourselves, often in ways we may not understand.[2] Globalization, population migration, and technological developments make it imperative, yet challenging, to understand interpersonal communication.

Is technology part of your daily life? Surveys in early 2006 revealed that 147 million U.S. adults are Internet users, an increase of 14 million over 2005. Twelve million people share information by posting material on a Web log (blog) or by using other content-creating applications, and 39% of Internet users read blogs.[3] Similarly, wireless technology is changing the nature of 21st-century communication. Approximately 71% of all U.S. households own at least one cell phone, and wireless technology is changing how people interact. For example, social plans are made later in the day, and conversations tend to be shorter and more frequent.[4] The explosion of CMC makes it necessary to study interpersonal communication.

Think about your daily activities. Are you often pressed for time? You're not alone; 95% of Americans believe they don't have enough time to accomplish all they need to do.[5] A 2005 survey of U.S. workers found that 39% said they'd forgo a $5,000 raise for more time off.[6] In a 2006 Associated Press-Ipsos poll, 20% of respondents admit they're rude to employees if they are made to wait too long for service. We become impatient after five minutes "on hold" on the phone and won't tolerate a wait of fifteen minutes in line.[7] Our hectic and stressed-filled lifestyles make knowledge about interpersonal communication essential.

This book offers information about how to engage in competent interpersonal communication in our diverse, technology-oriented, fast-paced society. This information can help us improve our interpersonal communication and adapt to the changing world we live in.

at Yale, Harvard, Johns Hopkins, Stanford, and UCLA reveal that individuals who experience competent communication in intimate relationships have less coronary artery blockage and less stress and are less likely to develop cancer than individuals who lack intimate relationships.[8] Moreover, scientists at the University of Michigan Institute for Social Research found that communication with others improves memory and everyday decision making. The researchers suggest that talking with family and friends preserves and enhances mental functioning.[9] Even modest improvements in our interpersonal communication are related to physical and psychological well-being in this research.[10]

Interpersonal Communication Competence

Not all interpersonal communication enables us to effectively adapt to our changing world, enhances our relationships and career success, and positively affects our psychological health and cognitive processes. Communication scholars **Brian H. Spitzberg** and **William R. Cupach** characterize **communication competence** as both effective and appropriate in an interpersonal context.[11] Competent communication is also civil and ethical. The ability to communicate in a competent manner is facilitated when we:

How can we define interpersonal communication competence?

- Are motivated to communicate
- Are knowledgeable about the self, other, topic, context, and communication in general
- Are effective and appropriate in the performance of communication skills

It's important to note that perceptions of interpersonal communication competence are situational. There is no guarantee that a conversation partner will perceive as competent someone who is effective and appropriate, civil, ethical, motivated, knowledgeable, and skillful. As discussed later, our culture(s); family, friends, and coworkers; gender; and/or individual characteristics affect our perceptions of communication competence. Because interpersonal communication competence is situational, it's best to develop a repertoire of communication behaviors and to choose the behaviors that best fit a particular situation.[12]

Effectiveness and Appropriateness

Recall that competent communication is both effective and appropriate. **Effectiveness** refers to achieving our goals, and **appropriateness** refers to conforming to the expectations or communication rules of a particular situation. **Communication rules** are prescriptions that tell us what we should or shouldn't say or do in certain situations. We can tell that we've broken an interpersonal communication rule when we receive a negative sanction.[13] A dirty look, a poke in the ribs, unexpected laughter, and even a verbal admonition (e.g., "That type of language is unacceptable!") are examples of negative sanctions.

To illustrate effectiveness and appropriateness, consider the following situations. Suppose a classmate wishes to borrow your notes on the day before a test. Your classmate yells, "Gimme!" while walking past your desk and grabs the notes without asking for them. Although meeting the goal of "borrowing" your notes, your classmate's behavior violates the expectations of the situation by taking your notes without asking permission. In other

KNOWLEDGE power • Is Your Communication Effective and Appropriate?

With a partner or in a group, recall a time when your interpersonal communication was effective but not appropriate. When did you realize that your communication was perceived as inappropriate? Did you receive negative sanctions for breaking communication rules? Discuss what you could have done differently to be perceived as appropriate. After sharing your experiences, recall a time when you were appropriate but not effective. What could you have done differently to meet your goals? Finally, talk about an experience when you were both effective and appropriate in your communication. Decide which of the three situations was most rewarding for yourself and for the other person(s) involved.

words, your classmate's behavior is effective but it isn't appropriate. Some time later, another classmate stops by your desk. With downcast eyes and a barely audible voice, your classmate nervously stammers, "uhm . . . er . . . if you don't need to study, do you think I could use your notes for tomorrow's test. Well . . . ahh . . . I understand if you can't let me borrow them; you have to study for the test too. So it's OK, I guess, if I can't borrow them." Of course, your answer is "No!" Although this classmate doesn't violate the expectations of the situation and requests your permission before taking your notes, the goal isn't achieved because you refuse the request. In other words, your classmate's behavior is appropriate, but it isn't effective. These situations show that both effectiveness and appropriateness are necessary to be a competent communicator.

Communication Competence and Civility

Interpersonal communication competence and the appropriateness criterion, in particular, promote the social values of respect and civility. **Civility** can be characterized as a sacrifice that we make for others. We engage in civil behavior when we discipline our passions for the sake of cooperating with others and limit our language to create community. Civility also requires us to express ourselves in ways that communicate respect for others. Unfortunately, many people believe that uncivil communication characterizes contemporary life. An Associated Press-Ipsos poll found that many people believe that today's fast-paced and high-tech existence causes uncivil communication.[14] Rudeness seems to be increasing in modern society. According to a study by Public Agenda, a nonprofit, nonpartisan polling organization, respondents cite foul language in public, loud and aggravating cell phone conversations, and incidents of road rage as examples of rude behavior. Many study respondents admitted they also behave rudely. The most surprising survey result was that almost 80% of the respondents suggested that incivility is a serious national problem. The *San Francisco Chronicle* editorialized Public Agenda's findings with the assertion that "such incivility is insidious, painful and dangerous, inciting violence and weakening communities."[15]

Fortunately, we can reduce uncivil behavior by becoming communicatively competent.[16] One way to promote civil communication is to engage in **perspective taking,** considering a situation from the point of view of someone else. We can imagine ourselves being influenced by the situations or contexts that affect others to understand their thoughts and feelings. We will learn more about perspective taking in the next chapter about perception and communication. We can also strive to be appropriate as well as

KNOWLEDGE power • Uncivil Communication

With a partner or in a group, discuss a situation in which you witnessed or were the target of uncivil communication. Relate how you felt during the uncivil episode and whether you believe you responded in an effective and appropriate manner. When you are finished, discuss a situation in which *you* communicated in an uncivil manner, the emotions you felt during the episode, and how others responded to your incivility. Could you (and the persons involved in the examples) have expressed thoughts and feelings in a more civil manner? Did you find that your emotions were more negative and intense in the uncivil communication situations than they were in the civil communication situations? How can this knowledge motivate you to communicate and respond more civilly in future interactions?

effective in our behavior so as not to break communication rules and to demonstrate respect. Overall, we can strive to be competent communicators and include "sacrifice, respect, and consideration" in our conversations with others.[17]

Communication Competence and Ethics

Someone who is perceived as communicatively competent is also likely to be perceived as ethical. **Ethics** can be characterized as "well based standards of right and wrong that prescribe what humans ought to do." We create our personal code of ethics when we ask ourselves, "How am I doing at 'the art of being human'?"[18] Ethics are critical to the study of communication because "questions of right or wrong arise whenever people communicate."[19]

Communication that meets our goals and that others judge to be legitimate is likely to be perceived as ethical.[20] Consider the student who asks to borrow your notes in a manner that is effective and appropriate. Suppose, without your permission, the student photocopies the notes and makes a hefty profit selling them to members of your class. Will you continue to perceive that the student is communicatively competent? Probably not, because the student acted in an unethical manner.

Because we all have a choice about being ethical in our communication, some may take the easy way out by disregarding the need to be ethical communicators. We may think that our own small attempts at respecting others won't make a difference in the larger scheme of things. We may worry that people will reject us when we communicate in an ethical manner. We may also excuse our unethical behavior by referring to the fast pace of modern life in which everything happens so quickly that we don't have time to think about ethics.[21] However, we should ask ourselves how we would respond to these excuses from the classmate who photocopied our notes and sold them without our knowledge. Not only would we not accept the excuses but also we wouldn't think that our classmate's actions were effective and appropriate. Clearly, ethical communication is necessary for the perception of communication competence.

We can become ethical communicators by considering our answers to the following questions that deal with everyday ethical behavior:[22]

1. "Have I practiced any virtues today?" Consider whether you have shown integrity (consistency of belief and action), trustworthiness, honesty, or responsibility. For example, if you believe that stereotyping is wrong, do you laugh when a friend tells

MOTIVATION & mindwork • Are You an Ethical Communicator?

With a partner or in a group, think about a situation in which a person communicated in an unethical manner (e.g., a character in a film, TV show, or novel; a historical or political figure; or someone you know). Describe what the person did or said and why you believe the behavior was unethical. When you are finished, discuss a situation in which you believe someone communicated in an ethical manner. Describe the behavior and why you consider it ethical. After your discussion, consider whether you believe you can communicate like the ethical communicators. Can the ethical communicators and their behavior motivate you to practice virtues, do more good than harm, treat people with dignity and respect, act in a fair and just manner, and/or make your community stronger?

Photocopying someone's notes to sell to others without her/his permission is an example of unethical behavior.

a sexist or racist joke (integrity)? If someone tells you a secret, do you disclose the confidential information if the disclosure can bring you personal benefit (trustworthiness)? Do you cheat on a romantic partner without telling her or him about it (honesty)? Do you bad-mouth a professor for refusing to accept a late assignment? Do you realize that you are accountable for completing an assignment by the due date (responsibility)?

2. "Have I done more good than harm today?" Consider the consequences of your actions. For example, do you make it a point to show appreciation and gratitude for your relationship partner(s)? Do you compliment people close to you, knowing that your compliments have the ability to bolster their self-esteem?
3. "Have I treated people with dignity and respect?" Respect refers to showing consideration to people's beliefs, attitudes, values, and rights. For example, do you call people names or needlessly yell when angered? Do you belittle or contradict beliefs, attitudes, and values that differ from your own?
4. "Have I been fair and just today?" "Fairness" refers to treating everyone the same; "justice" refers to being fair in the way we distribute benefits and burdens. Do you ask your relationship partner to engage in activities such as cleaning the apartment or taking care of the car merely because of her or his sex? Do you communicate to those with less power than yourself (e.g., a little brother or sister) the same way that you communicate to someone with equal power (e.g., a friend)?
5. "Have I made my community stronger because of my actions?" Consider whether you go beyond the self to take into consideration the members of your community. Your community can be your neighborhood, apartment building, family, company, or place of worship. For example, do you help others in need without expecting anything in return? Do you consider others' thoughts and feelings when listening to music, using a cell phone, or talking in a public place?

Motivation, Knowledge, and Skill

In addition to effectiveness, appropriateness, civility, and ethics, perceptions of interpersonal communication competence also depend on three facilitating factors: an individual's motivation to communicate; knowledge of self, others, topic, context, and communication; and communication skill in performing behaviors. All three facilitating factors must function together for a person to be perceived as a competent communicator. Moreover, these facilitating factors are interconnected. For example, *knowing* why it's important to study interpersonal communication (i.e., it affects our thoughts, feelings, and interactions with others; enables us to create, maintain, and dissolve relationships; and affects our psychological and physical health) can *motivate* us to perform various communication *skills* to increase the likelihood of being perceived as a competent communicator. Spitzberg and Cupach use a dramatistic metaphor to illustrate motivation, knowledge, and skill. They suggest that people engaged in interpersonal communication should have, like actors, an impetus to act, should know their lines, and should give a good performance.[23]

Motivation **Motivation** refers to the desire to communicate. We are likely to be motivated if we are confident and interested in our conversation partners and if we see the interaction as potentially rewarding. Unfortunately, anxiety can rob us of our confidence and motivation to communicate in a competent manner. Consider an actor about to appear on the stage. The actor may be interested in her or his fellow players and may perceive the situation as potentially rewarding in terms of fame and salary. However, the actor may suddenly fall victim to an overwhelming bout of stage fright. The racing heart, sweaty palms, constricted breathing, and chaotic thought processes may become unbearable. Therefore, to reduce the physiological symptoms of stage fright, the motivation to perform well is supplanted by the motivation to escape the theater! An actor overcome by stage fright is unlikely to be perceived as communicatively competent. Similarly, an individual in conversation who is overcome by social anxiety will most likely be perceived as an incompetent communicator. In such situations, intrapersonal communication such as self-talk and goal setting can reduce our anxiety and increase and sustain our motivation to communicate in a competent manner. Similarly, we can motivate ourselves to communicate competently by engaging in perspective taking and other techniques that use our imagination and by learning what drives us to communicate. We can also increase our motivation by discovering how these drives influence our communication in settings such as the classroom and the workplace. These techniques and additional methods designed to increase and sustain our motivation to communicate competently will be presented throughout this textbook.

Lauren Caitlin, contestant for Miss Teen USA 2007, suggested that stage fright caused her to flub her answer about why some Americans can't locate the United States on a map.

Knowledge Motivation isn't the only characteristic that affects the perception of communication competence. **Knowledge**, as related to communication competence, includes knowledge about ourselves, our conversation partner(s), our topic, the situation, and the communication process itself. Suppose that our actor has learned techniques to manage stage fright and has also diligently studied the lines for Shakespeare's *Macbeth*. The actor now confidently strides upon the stage, and just as he or she is about to recite the required lines, his or her mind goes blank. The rest of the cast looks on in horror. The only sounds that escape the actor's mouth are "ahhhhh, ohhhhhh," and "oh, #$%&!" An actor who doesn't know the lines for a particular performance will most likely not be perceived as communicatively competent. Similarly, an individual in conversation who doesn't know what to say or says "the wrong thing" will most likely be perceived as an incompetent communicator.

Skill The third characteristic that influences the perception of communication competence is skill. **Skills** are goal-oriented actions or action sequences that we can master and repeat in appropriate situations. The more skills you have, the more likely you are to be able to structure your messages effectively and appropriately.[24] Skill refers to the actual performance of action sequences. This characteristic of competence goes beyond knowing about skills to actually putting them into practice. To illustrate, let's return to the actor who has now successfully managed stage fright and has most definitely learned Shakespeare's words. The actor once again strides upon the stage and begins to recite the lines. Unfortunately, the actor speaks very softly and the audience cannot hear the lines, plus the actor continuously mispronounces words by placing "the 'em-PHA-sis' on the wrong 'syll-AH-ble.'" An actor who isn't skilled in acting will most likely not be perceived as communicatively competent. Similarly, an individual in conversation who isn't skilled in performing communication action sequences will most likely be perceived as an incompetent communicator.

Becoming a Competent Communicator

Interpersonal Communication: Competence and Contexts will help you learn to be a competent communicator by presenting theories, concepts, research, and applications within the framework of the communication competence model; that is, motivation, knowledge, and skill. Studying interpersonal communication through this distinct framework will enable you to realize how theory, concept, research, and skill are related and will ignite your motivation to communicate competently, increase your knowledge about communication, and enhance your acquisition and performance of communication skills.

The communication competence model is represented in the text by an icon that identifies to which component major chapter sections relate. Chapter opening questions and Chapter reviews are also keyed to the components of the communication competence model. Special features such as the "Knowledge Power" boxes relate directly to the Knowledge component of the communication competence model. Application activities such as "Skill Practice" boxes are linked to the Skill component of the model, while the "Motivation & Mindwork" boxes are linked to the motivation component.

Recall that the appropriateness criterion associated with interpersonal communication competence promotes the social values of respect and civility. Each chapter of this text relates *civil communication* to the specific chapter topic and asks you to consider whether or not you communicate in a civil manner. In addition, you have read that competent communicators are ethical. Each chapter of this text includes a *Case Study in Ethics* that asks you to consider everyday ethical behavior, specifically, whether the behavior illustrated in the case study is ethical. "Knowledge on the Cutting Edge" boxes cover computer-mediated communication, providing cutting-edge research that students can apply to their own lives. In addition, the "Competence and Critical Thinking" boxes provide a full-length transcript of a communication situation, putting theories, concepts and skills into action. Each transcript is accompanied by questions for analysis, and can be viewed as a video clip on the MyCommunicationLab Web site.

Although we live in a dynamic and complex society that sometimes makes it difficult to communicate with each other, it is still possible to interact competently with others by being motivated, knowledgeable, and skillful. *Interpersonal Communication: Competence and Contexts* is designed to help you communicate in a competent manner in a diverse, fast-paced, and technology-oriented society.

Contexts and Interpersonal Communication

Motivation
Knowledge
Skill
COMPETENCE

Recall that our perceptions of communication competence are situational. **Context** is a synonym for "situation" and can be characterized as a physical location or environment that affects communication.[25] Look around the room where you are reading this book. What aspects of the room facilitate the communication and interpretation of messages? What aspects of the room hinder your ability to communicate? If you are reading this book in your quiet bedroom, you may want to strike up a conversation when your roommate knocks on your door. On the other hand, if you are reading this book in the quiet campus library, you may not want to communicate for fear of distracting others. Similarly, our interpretations of a particular situation can be characterized as a context. Our communication will most likely be influenced by our perceptions of the formality or informality and the intimacy or nonintimacy of a situation (e.g., upon being introduced to others, do we say, "Pleased to meet you" or "Hey, howya' doin'"?).[26] Context also refers to our frame of reference or the historical and psychological fields of experience that each person brings to an interaction. The historical context includes our past history with a topic and/or conversation partner, and the psychological context includes our values, beliefs, and attitudes.[27] Our interpersonal communication and perceptions of communication competence are also significantly affected by our culture(s); our relationships with others; our gender; and our roles, needs, background, and history. Learning about the culture, relationships, gender, and individual contexts and how they influence interaction will increase the likelihood that we will be perceived as competent communicators.

What are the contexts that influence interpersonal communication?

Culture Context

Culture can be defined as "the shared assumptions, values, and beliefs of a group of people which result in characteristic behaviors."[28] We perceive the world based on **cultural patterns**, or the particular beliefs and values associated with our specific culture.[29] Social scientists create cultural pattern taxonomies to understand cultural similarities and differences. Such taxonomies, or "belief systems," are typically represented by a grid with a cultural belief or value at one end and an opposing cultural belief or value at the other end. Although there are many cultural pattern taxonomies, this book concentrates on two: collectivist and individualist cultures and high-context and low-context cultures. Remember that no culture is 100% individualist or collectivist. Both patterns exist in all cultures, although one pattern usually dominates. The next sections compare

Our perception of the world is influenced by the beliefs and values associated with our culture.

Table 1.1 Individualist/Low-Context Cultures and Collectivist/High-Context Cultures

Individualist/Low-Context Cultures	Collectivist/High-Context Cultures
• Individual needs come before group needs	• Group needs come before individual needs
• Individuals are expected to take care of themselves	• Groups are expected to take care of their members
• Communication is direct	• Communication is indirect
• Meaning comes primarily through the spoken word	• Meaning comes primarily from nonverbal communication

individualist/low-context and collectivist/high-context cultures. We will learn that not everyone agrees which groups of people constitute a "culture" and that intercultural communication research can be problematic.

Individualist/Low-Context and Collectivist/High-Context Cultures As shown in Table 1.1, "Individualist/Low-Context Cultures and Collectivist/High-Context Cultures," cultures can be placed on a continuum that ranges from individualistic to collectivistic. **Individualist cultures** focus more on the individual than on the group. Individual needs come before group needs, and people take care of themselves before they take care of others, if at all.[30] The dominant cultures in Australia, the Netherlands, Belgium, and the

KNOWLEDGE power • The Squeaky Wheel or the Nail Hammered Down?

First come, first served. Time waits for no one. All is fair in love and war. These proverbs reflect values, specifically individuality, time, and equality associated with an individualistic culture. Proverbs teach us cultural values and guide our thoughts and actions. With a partner or in a group, identify proverbs associated with your culture(s) that illustrate the following values:

- Individualism or collectivism
- Communication
- Money
- Time
- Action (doing, controlling, affecting change)

Web sites such as Creative Proverbs from Around the World (http://creativeproverbs.com/) can help you find proverbs and the cultures with which they are associated.

When you have completed your list, discuss how these proverbs and their cultural values can influence communication with others. What might the consequences be if highly individualistic culture-based communication were to be exchanged with members of highly collectivistic cultures?

United States are highly individualistic and tend to be low context. In **low-context cultures**, communication is direct, and most of the meaning comes from the spoken word.[31] Individualist and low-context cultures value independence, privacy, equality, and informality; are oriented toward change, progress, and the future; are focused on time, achievement, competition, and action; and value directness and assertiveness.[32] Because most Americans in the dominant culture assume that "the individual comes first," this cultural value can influence them to disregard the consequences to others in their communication choices. Specific examples of such behavior include individuals who in public talk loudly on their cell phones and people who berate employees, children, and partners in front of others. In contrast, **collectivist cultures** focus more on the group (e.g., the family, village, or organization) than on the individual. Decisions are based on what is best for the group, and the group is expected to take care of its members. The dominant cultures in Indonesia, West Africa, Guatemala, and Pakistan are primarily collectivistic. Collectivist cultures are typically high context. In **high-context cultures**, much of the meaning of communication is indirect, implicit, and derived from nonverbal communication. For example, members of collectivist cultures may avoid conflict or ask a third-party mediator to resolve conflict situations because of the cultural emphasis on group harmony.[33]

Intercultural Communication Research Some researchers argue that we shouldn't make generalizations about communication and behavior based on the influence of individualist and collectivist cultures because culture should not be studied apart from the influence of race, class, socioeconomic status, sexual orientation, and gender.[34] Similarly, not everyone agrees on what constitutes a culture or **co-culture**, a group with its own particular values that influence behavior, along with the values associated with the dominant culture. For example, many communication researchers suggest that a gay co-culture influences the communication and overall behavior of its members. However, other scholars assert that bisexuals, gays, lesbians, and transgenders cannot be grouped into a single category because sexual identities are fluid. Similarly, members of Deaf (with a capital "D") culture ascribe to the following values: respect for and use of American Sign Language (ASL), the passing of Deaf values from generation to generation in stories and folklore, the importance of participation in social events, and the use of direct personal comments or "straight talk." However, not all deaf (nonhearing) and hearing persons believe in the existence of a Deaf culture and instead view deafness as a physical disability or handicap that should be corrected if at all possible.[35] Finally, the dominant U.S. culture is often presented as the standard by which other cultural groups are measured. This means that cultures and co-cultures that aren't similarly individualist and low context are somehow "exotic, unnatural, deviate from the norm, and do not change."[36] However, no culture is the "ideal" culture. Cultures are social categories that are created by people who are influenced by politics and history.

Relationship Context

Just as culture provides us with underlying assumptions and expectations that guide communication, the relationship context of family, friends, and coworkers influences how we communicate with others.

Family The term "family" can be defined in many ways, and a widely agreed-upon definition doesn't exist. In the broadest sense of the word, **family** can be defined as "a group

KNOWLEDGE power • What Are Your Family Rules and Stories?

How have your family's rules and stories affected your communication with others? With a partner or in a group, describe the communication rules created by your family. Mention the particular topics you are and are not allowed to discuss with family members and with individuals outside your family. Similarly, recall some stories or "family folklore" that tends to be repeated and discussed at family gatherings. What do these stories teach members of your family, and how do they influence your communication with others?

of people with a past history, a present reality, and a future expectation of interconnected, mutually influencing relationships."[37] Our beliefs, attitudes, and values are molded by our family, and our relationships with family members are the most influential in our lives.[38] Many of our friends can be considered a "voluntaristic family." Because we depend on these friends for companionship and social support, they may be even more important than family based on blood ties.[39]

Voluntaristic or not, all families establish rules that affect communication. **Family rules** concern "shoulds and oughts," and they range on a continuum from explicit to implicit.[40] Explicit family rules may concern freedom of expression, that is, what we can talk about, when and where we can talk about it, and to whom we can talk. Explicit family rules may be communicated with the sentence, "We don't discuss such subjects/use those words in our family!" Similarly, family stories illustrate rules that affect communication. Family stories communicate history, expectations, and identity; they instruct, warn, and communicate issues that matter to a specific family.[41] Stories about births and deaths, immigration and foreign travel, and triumphs and tragedies can communicate implicit rules about helping others, what it means to live a moral life, and how to deal with adversity. These implicit rules also influence how we communicate with others.

Friends We expect to invest time, energy, and effort into our friendships, and our friendships enable us to feel close to others. Whether we are female or male, old or young, homosexual or heterosexual, we expect our friends to accept us, to be dependable and reliable, and to trust us.[42] In general, friendships become increasingly important as we grow up. High school and college students may find themselves surrounded by friends and potential friends, yet it becomes more difficult to make new friends as we age.[43] However, modern friendship is changing as Web-based social networking sites such as MySpace and Facebook make it easier to develop online friendships that can develop into face-to-face relationships. Today's computer-savvy young adults are changing the nature of friendships in other ways as well. Young adults who live in urban areas far from their families are often members of "urban tribes," or groups of friends that meet members' needs. Urban tribes are like extended families in which members establish rituals and take on roles such as the "advice-giver, comedian, and worrier." Some urban tribes form

KNOWLEDGE power • Communication Competence at Work

With a partner or in a group, create a hypothetical organization and pretend that you have been hired as a communication consultant. Your task is to provide recommendations regarding the competent communication concepts and skills needed for successful interactions within the organization and with the public. You can begin by recalling a communication episode in a business setting (e.g., restaurant, store, or fitness club) that you perceive as effective and appropriate. Discuss this episode with your partner or group, and explain why you believe the interaction reflects interpersonal communication competence. When you are finished, consider whether your recommendations are similar to the qualities that employers look for in new employees, according to the NACE "Job Outlook Survey."

because of mutual interests and specific activities, and others form because of happenstance. However, all tribes are social entities that take the place of a traditional family and are sustained with interpersonal communication.[44]

Coworkers Various studies of businesses and professions illustrate that communicating well with others is critical for success. In particular, workplace relationships can positively influence productivity and morale. By contrast, alienated and isolated workers may contribute to a negative organizational climate, cause workplace dissatisfaction, and result in poor information sharing.[45] According to the 2006 National Association of Colleges and Employers (NACE) "Job Outlook Survey," the five qualities employers seek most when hiring employees reflect concepts and skills associated with competent interpersonal communication. In order of ranked importance, these concepts and skills include:[46]

1. Verbal and written communication skills
2. Honesty and integrity
3. Teamwork (working well with others)
4. Interpersonal skills (relating well to others)
5. Motivation

In all, effective workplace communication and relationships are just as important as communication in family and friendship relationships. In fact, competent communication is important to every career, not just those that are essentially "people-oriented." Highly trained professionals in the sciences, math, and computer technology must assume duties traditionally performed by managers and often find themselves in interactive team environments. Scientific and technical professionals also find themselves communicating with external customers and nontechnical peers.[47] In her book *The Hard Truth about Soft Skills,* corporate trainer Peggy Klaus summarizes the need for competent workplace communication and relationships when she writes that employees derail their careers and miss opportunities not because of a shortfall in professional or technical expertise. Instead, problems on the job stem from a shortcoming of "soft skills" such as communication, self-awareness, empathy, and likeability.[48]

Gender Context

Just as the culture context and the relationship context affect our communication, the gender context influences communication with others. While "sex" is based on anatomy, endocrinology, and neurology, **gender** refers to the influence of the environment and socially constructed meaning. Surprisingly, the idea that there are only two distinct gender categories has never been scientifically studied, and differences *within* the gender categories tend to be ignored in favor of research that compares women to men.[49] According to communication scholar **Julia T. Wood**, growing up "masculine" in Western cultures means learning that females are not as important as males and that men are judged in terms of what they do and their financial success. Growing up masculine also means learning that the male role is to be aggressive, sexually active, self-reliant, and emotionally reserved. Although there is no longer one consensual characterization of what it means to be "feminine," current views of femininity include at least four themes: women should be attractive, should take care of others, are devalued in society, and should "do and have it all."[50] These gender expectations are illustrated in the "Zits" cartoon and influence how we communicate and interpret communication from others.

ZITS/ by Jerry Scott and Jim Borgman

Gender expectations suggest that men should be emotionally reserved and that women should take care of others and maintain relationships.

Gender and Communication Elements of what it means to be masculine and what it means to be feminine play a role in how we communicate. For example, women may find it easier to talk in private settings, such as on the phone at home, and men may find it easier to talk in public settings, such as in meetings at work.[51] Talking in private settings reflects the assumption that femininity means taking care of others and maintaining relationships; talking in public settings reflects the assumption that masculinity means behaving in an aggressive and competitive manner. These examples illustrate that the assumptions about masculinity and femininity influence communication behavior.

Gender Communication Research Not all communication researchers believe that socialization and gender roles create substantial differences in communication behavior between women and men. Empirical research that is based on tests of statistical significance indicates that women and men are more similar than different in their communication behavior. The gender differences that have been found in empirical studies are small and inconsistent. Some communication scholars argue that proponents of gender-based communication differences support their conclusions with nonempirical data that is not credible and has little value. However, both empirical and nonempirical research of gender similarities and differences are "ways of knowing" that provide us with interesting and provocative conclusions about gender communication.[52]

Individual Context

The individual context is based on our roles and our needs, backgrounds, and histories. Although many people share similar individual attributes, we all have personalities that are influenced by these specific aspects of the individual context.

KNOWLEDGE ON THE CUTTING EDGE

Putting It in Context: Sex and Communication Behavior

In 2005, former Harvard University President Lawrence Summers suggested that differences in male-female brain biology may explain why fewer women than men flourish in scientific careers. A flood of criticism ensued because such a statement could reinforce gender stereotypes and indirectly legitimize gender discrimination. Although men outnumber women in the study of science and in scientific careers, the reason is not due to sex differences. Gender-based expectations for women to stay home to raise children (which results in the loss of career momentum) and the combative and cutthroat culture of science (a culture more conducive to masculinity than femininity) are just some of the barriers to scientific achievement for women. To date, no one has discovered any anatomical or biological disparities between males and females that influence women's achievement in the areas of math, physics, or engineering. However, Summers is not the only person to mistakenly equate sex, which is based on genetics, anatomy, hormones, and brain type, with gender and gender-based expectations.

Although sex is not related to achievement in the sciences, recent research illustrates that brain differences can influence how men and women communicate. In PET scans, which provide physiological images of the brain, there are male-female differences in the hippocampus (activated in memory storage), the cerebellum (neurons involved in complex tasking), and the corpus callosum (the nerves that connect right and left hemispheres and affect emotional expression). Women typically have smaller brains with more gray matter than male brains. This finding is used to explain why women tend to excel in language use and communication and why men are typically better than women at spatial tasks. In addition, imaging studies indicate that neurons on both sides of the brain are activated when women listen to others but neurons in the male brain are activated on only one side of the brain. This finding can explain why women may be distracted by the conversation of others and why men tend to perceive only one stimulus at a time.

The development of imaging techniques that illustrate male and female brain differences occurred in the mid-1990s, but communication textbooks since this time have been in "biological denial." Some scholars fear that sex-based communication research may be used to support beliefs like Lawrence Summers's. However, we cannot ignore the influence of sex on behavior, as research increasingly points to the brain as the basis for female-male communication differences. Knowing that sex differences can affect how people communicate will help us become competent communicators.[53]

We cannot ignore the influence of sex on behavior as research increasingly points to the brain as the basis for a number of communication differences between females and males.

Roles A **role** can be defined as learned behaviors that we use to meet the perceived demands of specific situations. We may identify with many roles, such as star athlete, good parent, and conscientious student. Role expectations can influence how we communicate with others. For example, one assumption with an impact on our communication in the role of a helpful employee may be "the customer is always right." This assumption will guide how we communicate with a customer who complains about the service in our establishment. However, this assumption will probably not influence how

> **KNOWLEDGE power • Student and Worker and Child, Oh My!**
>
> Think about the variety of roles you fulfill, such as child, parent, sibling, student, and/or employee. With a partner or in a group, describe your roles and the communication expectations associated with those roles. Provide your partner or group with specific examples of how your role expectations have affected your communication. Discuss whether your roles and the communication expectations associated with them influence your ability to communicate in a competent manner.

we communicate at home because we are no longer in the role of an employee. The assumption that may influence our communication in our role of parent, child, or sibling is "it's OK to argue!"

Needs, Background, and History Our individual needs, background, and history affect our communication with others. For example, if we assume that we need to be in an intimate relationship with another person, we will most likely communicate in a manner that will facilitate the development of a close, personal relationship. We may make it a point to flirt, pay special attention to our appearance, and communicate with individuals we perceive to be attractive. Similarly, if our religious background teaches us that we must proselytize our religion, this assumption will probably influence us to talk about our religion and try to convert those who do not share our religious beliefs. If we have a history of failed relationships, we may (incorrectly) assume that we'll never experience a successful relationship and therefore decline to participate in social events.

To summarize, the assumptions and expectations associated with a variety of contexts affect perceptions of interpersonal communication competence. The cultural context, comprised of beliefs and values; the relationship context, which includes the rules and assumptions we have learned from family, friends, and coworkers; the gender context, which influences communication in terms of societal expectations; and the individual context, made up of our roles and unique needs, background, and history, act together to influence how we communicate with others.

Types of Communication

Recall that the knowledge component of the communication competence model suggests that it's necessary to understand the communication process. Consider whether you are perceived as a competent communicator as you read the following information about

What types of communication are related to interpersonal communication competence?

> **KNOWLEDGE power • Are You a Good Communicator?**
>
> Do you believe that you're a good communicator? To discover how well you communicate in different situations and what habits you may have that are barriers to effective communication, you can access the thirty-four item Communication Skills Test at: www.psychtests.com/tests/relationships/ communication_skills_r_access.html. When you are finished, think about how you can use the results of this assessment to improve your communication competence.

Figure 1.1: Intrapersonal and Interpersonal Communication

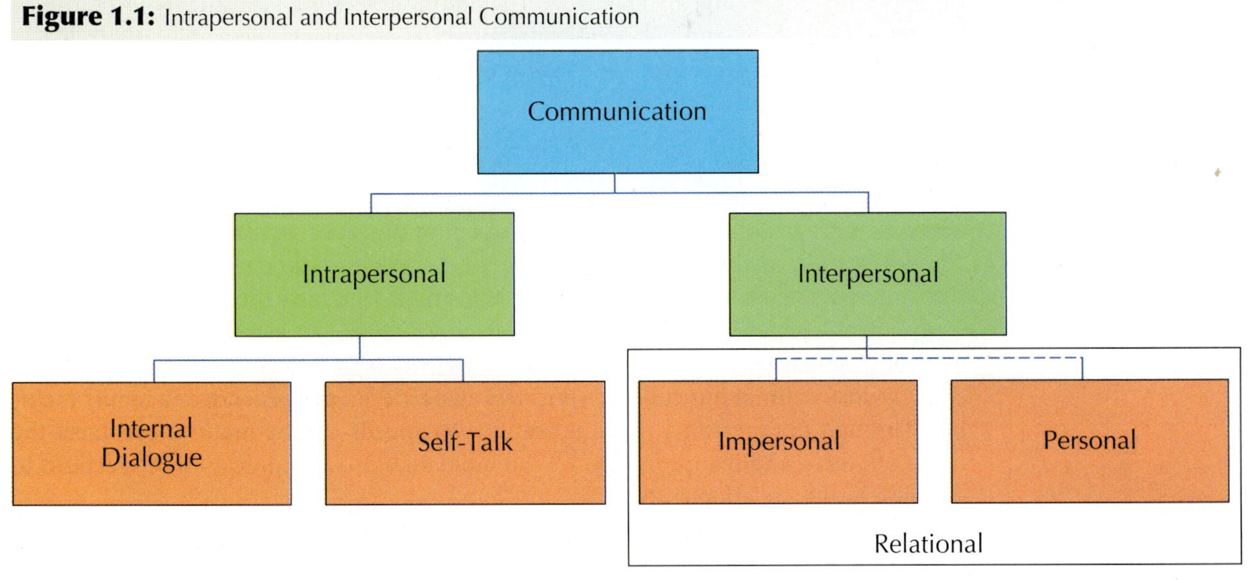

types of communication, metacommunication, principles of communication, and elements involved in the communication process.

Intrapersonal Communication

Communication is a broad and multifaceted phenomenon that can be characterized in a variety of ways. We've learned that communication can take place verbally, nonverbally, in public, or mediated through the use of technology. Figure 1.1, "Intrapersonal and Interpersonal Communication," helps us focus on the types of communication included in this book.

Intrapersonal communication takes place within us. As illustrated in the "Intrapersonal and Interpersonal Communication" figure, our internal dialogue and self-talk are examples of this form of communication.

Internal Dialogue Suppose you are searching for your new friend's house and feel frustrated because you are lost. As you search, you are likely to have a conversation with yourself: "I'll never find this place. I have directions, but I don't see any house numbers. She told me to go to the third house." This kind of intrapersonal communication is called **internal dialogue**. It's a natural and normal form of intrapersonal communication that helps us solve problems and work out our feelings.

Self-Talk A second kind of intrapersonal communication is **self-talk**, or communication within us that is specifically about ourselves. Positive self-talk offers us encouragement, support, reassurance, and sometimes a pat on the back. As a student, you've probably used positive self-talk when you've performed well on a test, written a thoughtful essay, or solved a difficult problem. An example of positive self-talk is: "I didn't do as well as I would have liked on that test, but I know what the instructor wants. I'll do better next time," and "I did great on that essay, and I knew I could solve that problem. I'm so relieved!" Negative self-talk is critical, evaluative, and devaluing. This form of self-talk occurs when we end a relationship, fail to master a skill, or feel we are unworthy of friendship or love. Some examples of negative self-talk are: "I knew I'd be dumped; no one wants to spend time with me," "I'm so stupid I'll never find a boyfriend/girlfriend," and "There must be something wrong with me." Negative self-talk can be extremely destructive, and we will learn that it can affect our self-concept and our relationships.

Interpersonal Communication

Whereas intrapersonal communication is communication within us, interpersonal communication involves at least two people who establish a communicative relationship. Interpersonal communication involves partners who have the power to simultaneously affect each other through their behavior, either positively or negatively. For example, we may communicate interpersonally with a salesclerk at a local department store, an instructor at our college, a business associate, a casual friend, or a family member. Through interpersonal communication, our needs can be met, we can meet the needs of others, and if appropriate, we can build on our communication interactions to establish healthy relationships.

As illustrated in the "Intrapersonal and Interpersonal Communication" figure, interpersonal communication can be further characterized along a continuum from impersonal to personal, depending on how we perceive our conversation partners. As you read about the following types of communication, think about your typical interactions and where you might place them on the impersonal-personal continuum.

Impersonal Communication At one end of the continuum is impersonal communication. When we communicate with others as if they are "objects" or roles or we communicate in stereotypic ways, we engage in **impersonal communication**. For example, suppose we decide to go to a restaurant one evening. At the beginning of the meal, we interact with the server for the sole purpose of meeting our immediate needs—obtaining the food we desire. The server introduces herself or himself, asks how we're doing, and attempts to interact with us through small talk. We answer with a curt "fine" and turn away, only to acknowledge the server when she or he returns with our meal. This behavior meets the criteria for impersonal communication. In this situation, we are treating this person as a role (i.e., a server) rather than a unique individual with distinct characteristics.

We have also probably been the recipient of impersonal communication. Suppose we receive a sales call at home. The salesperson calls us by our first name, which suggests that we may have a personal relationship, and then begins the sales pitch. We respond by saying that we're not interested in the product. However, the salesperson is

KNOWLEDGE power • Treated as an Object

With a partner or in a group, recall a few instances when an interaction partner communicated to you in an impersonal manner. What roles were you engaged in fulfilling (e.g., server, salesperson, parent, child, student)? How did you feel when your uniqueness was ignored? How did you handle the situation? Next, discuss those times when you communicated in an impersonal manner to an interaction partner. How can you improve your communication when you find yourself in a similar situation?

We need not be completely impersonal or completely personal when we interact with others.

trained to override our objections and continues to talk, even though we have expressed a desire to end the conversation. We might find ourselves feeling uncomfortable at first and then angry because we believe that we are being treated as an object, a means to an end.

Obviously, we cannot engage in personal communication with everyone we meet, either face-to-face, via the phone, or on a computer. However, disregarding a person's individuality and uniqueness has the potential to foster ineffective communication interactions.

Personal Communication At the other end of the continuum in the "Intrapersonal and Interpersonal Communication" figure is personal communication. **Personal communication** occurs when we interact with others on the basis of their uniqueness. At the extreme end of the impersonal-personal continuum, personal communication within an intimate relationship entails a high degree of self-disclosure. However, personal communication can also occur among friends and acquaintances. For example, suppose your best friend asks, "What's up?" You respond that you feel stupid because you just flunked your chemistry test. "I'll never understand chemistry!" you exclaim. Your friend says, "Come on, I know how smart you are. You usually do well in your science classes; I bet you'll do better on your next test." This exchange can be characterized as personal communication because of your self-disclosure (feeling stupid; flunking the chemistry test) and your best friend's acknowledgment of your unique characteristics (being smart; usually doing well on science tests).

Would it be appropriate to communicate about our feelings or the chemistry test at a restaurant to a server who asks, "How are you doing today?" Of course not. But it would be appropriate to move from the highly impersonal response "Fine. I'm ready to order now" to the more personal response "I've had better days. How about you?" As illustrated in the photo above, the second response demonstrates that we need not be completely impersonal or completely personal in our communication interactions; we can choose to communicate at an effective and appropriate midpoint on the impersonal-personal continuum.

Relational Communication

Another type of interpersonal communication illustrated in the "Intrapersonal and Interpersonal Communication" figure is **relational communication**. Whether we're primarily engaged in personal or impersonal communication, relational communication demonstrates that we not only interact about the content of communication but also interact about our association with a conversation partner. Without our realizing it and without explicit mention, a single message can communicate information about a topic and about a relationship. Characterized by psychotherapists **Paul Watzlawick, Janet Beavin**, and **Dan Jackson**, relational communication includes the subject of an interaction and the implicit information about the participants' relationship. These messages are described as occurring at the content and relational levels of communication.[54]

Content and Relational Levels of Communication The **content-level meaning** of a message refers simply to the content of the words and sentences that are communicated. The **relational-level meaning** of a message concerns the unspoken meaning that can be ascertained, in part, from nonverbal communication. The way something is said (interpreted by a speaker's eye contact, facial expression, and/or gestures) is an example of nonverbal behavior that influences meaning at the relational level of communication. In addition, the interpretation of relational messages can be influenced by the past experience and personal associations that we bring to a conversation. For example, suppose our partner says, "Please get off the computer." The meaning on the content level is obvious; our partner wants us to get off the computer. But what about the meaning at the relational level where relationships are defined and negotiated? If our partner communicates this message with a smile and a calm tone of voice and places a hand on our shoulder, our partner may be communicating that our relationship is based on respect and affection. Similarly, we are more likely to construe the relational meaning as positive if our partner has made previous requests to spend time with us away from the computer. On the other hand, if our partner communicates this message with a frown and an angry tone of voice and crosses her or his arms, our partner may be communicating that the relationship is based on control and a power differential. In addition, we are more likely to construe the relational meaning as being negative if our partner has previously demanded that we cease engaging in particular activities. Even though people typically interpret relational meanings based on nonverbal communication and past experiences, we should remember that our perceptions of others' nonverbal messages and intentions may be incorrect.[55] For instance, the sharp tone of voice our partner uses to tell us to get off the

KNOWLEDGE power • Is it Control or Connection?

Think of at least three messages uttered by various conversation partners that you believe were attempts to control you. Write the messages on a piece of paper and form a group with your classmates. All group members should exchange messages, read them aloud, and suggest how these messages may also reflect the communication of care or affection. Reconsider your interpretations of relational control as they relate to your three messages. Based on your classmates' analysis, could your control messages actually be messages of connection?

computer may have nothing to do with us and just reflect a hard day at school or tiredness. It may even be that a relational meaning interpreted as control (e.g., "Drive carefully!" or "Put on your jacket") may be an expression of affection and an attempt to establish connection.

Relational-Level Messages Have you ever found yourself feeling angry with a conversation partner and not knowing exactly why? Maybe you've been in arguments and realized you didn't understand what you were actually arguing about. It may be that the reason for your anger and the disagreement rests on the relational level of meaning.

What exactly about a relationship is communicated at the relational level? Every relationship and every conversation can be considered a blend of affection (or "connection") and control. **Affection**, the force to become close with a relational partner, and **control**, the force to gain dominance, are communicated at the relational level. In addition to affection and control, respect is sometimes included as a relational message. **Respect** concerns valuing a person's right to life and expression, and whether or not we are taken seriously is often a source of relational conflict. In fact, respect can be a predictor of relational success or failure. Think about the role "respect" plays in your relationships. Have you experienced relational conflict because you thought your partner hadn't taken you seriously? Have you ended relationships or conversations because you thought you were disrespected?

Even though our strongest reactions to messages tend to occur at the relational level, we aren't typically aware of the multitude of relational messages that confront us each day. Sometimes we're unaware of relational messages because they match our expectations about the amount and type of affection and control in our relationships. However, conflicts can arise at the relational level when we or someone with whom we're close feels uncomfortable about relational meanings.[56] For example, do you become upset when your partner, roommate, or family member tells you to put out the dog, pick up the mess, or turn off the light? You don't become upset at the particular request (whether or not it deals with the dog, the mess, or the light); however, you become upset because that particular someone feels entitled to tell you what to do. As a result, you say, "Don't tell me what to do!" and you begin to fight not about the request itself but about whether this person has the power to control your actions.

Metacommunication

Motivation
Knowledge
Skill
COMPETENCE

One way to deal with our interpretations of content and relational meaning is to use metacommunication. **Metacommunication** has been defined both as "communication about communication" and as "communication about relationships." We can metacommunicate about both the content of a message and the underlying relational message.

Metacommunication at the Content Level of Meaning

How can using metacommunication improve our interpersonal communication competence?

At the content level, metacommunication can suggest how the actual meaning of a message is to be interpreted. Have you ever uttered sentences such as "This is important," "I didn't mean it," or "I'm sorry I said that"? Have you ever asked questions such as "Are you kidding?" "Do you understand what I'm saying?" or "Want to hear something funny?" If so, you are metacommunicating at the level of content.

We can deal with uncertainty on the content level of communication by using metacommunication. Specifically, we can attempt to ascertain meaning, ask for additional information, and acknowledge our opinion(s) and the opinion(s) of others. For example:

- "I guess what you're saying is that you don't want to go out tonight."
- "I don't understand what you're trying to tell me. Can you explain that again?"
- "I understand why you said those things but I don't agree with you. Can I ask you a few questions about it?"

You may be thinking that these examples appear too "stilted" or formal for the way you usually communicate. However, metacommunication doesn't require you to speak in any particular way or to change the manner in which you typically communicate. And metacommunication at the content level can be nonverbal in nature. For example, we can tilt our head and scrunch our nose to communicate that we don't understand what a conversation partner is saying.

Metacommunication at the Relational Level of Meaning

Recall that metacommunication on the relational level is often based on nonverbal behavior and may occur in response to past conversations and events. Similarly, metacommunication on the relational level can make clear our perception of how we and our relationships are perceived in terms of affection, control, and respect. The Sally Forth cartoon below illustrates that Sally's nonverbal behavior is associated with her perception of relational control ("... you darn well better be early"). Her husband, Ted, metacommunicates when he says he feels "a cold chill." Let's return to the example of your partner asking you to turn off the computer. If you respond to the request with "Do you want me to spend time with you?" you are metacommunicating about a relational-level interpretation of affection. If you respond to the request with "Stop ordering me around!" you are metacommunicating about a relational-level interpretation of control. In addition to affection and control, our verbal communication can also suggest where we see ourselves and our relationship in terms of "respect." For example, content-level metacommunication, such as saying, "I can understand why you say that, but I disagree with your opinion," suggests our respect for others on the relational level. Attempting to ascertain a conversation partner's meaning on the content level simultaneously communicates on the relational level that we respect our partner and her or his viewpoints.

Metacommunication at the relational level of meaning communicates our perceptions of affection, control, and/or respect.

Source: © SALLY FORTH – KING FEATURES SYNDICATE.

In addition to verbal communication, we also metacommunicate our perceptions of affection, control, and respect through our nonverbal communication. Nonverbal metacommunication can communicate our affection and respect with focused eye contact, head nods, and vocalizations ("uh-huh") that suggest understanding and acknowledgment. However, we need to be sure that our nonverbal communication doesn't contradict our verbal communication. Even the best attempt at metacommunication may be perceived as insulting if it's accompanied by a sarcastic tone of voice, rolling eyes, or laughter.

It's important to remember that the knowledge and skills presented in this book are not guaranteed to make us competent communicators. In fact, our use of communication skills may result in unexpected outcomes. An underlying assumption associated with interpersonal communication skills is that people are rational beings. Unfortunately, this isn't always the case. For example, using metacommunication to check our understanding of relational communication (e.g., "Are you telling me what to do because you don't think I can do this on my own?") may result in an irate partner who completely loses control. Similarly, metacommunication may not lead to our desired result if our conversation partner is more powerful than we are. Such metacommunication may prompt a supervisor to sarcastically respond, "I'm telling you what to do because I am your boss!" It may be best to remain silent in such situations because nothing we can say or do will convince an irrational or more powerful partner that we are trying to communicate in a competent manner. Flexibility and strategy are integral to communication competence. Knowing that communication skills won't always "work" can help us plan for and anticipate situations that would otherwise be unexpected.

SKILL practice • Metacommunication

With a partner or in a group, engage in metacommunication to interpret and communicate meaning. On the content level, you can attempt to clarify perceptions, ask for information, or acknowledge the opinions of a conversation partner. On the relational level, you can use nonverbal communication (e.g., tone of voice, eye contact, and gestures) to suggest how you perceive your partner and/or relationship in terms of affection/connection, respect, and control:

- You're discussing a controversial topic with a friend. Although you think you understand why your friend believes as he or she does, you are not sure that your friend understands the basis of your viewpoint.
- You believe that your intimate partner has stopped asking for your opinion and has started to order you around. Your partner makes comments such as "Turn off the lights when you leave the room" and "Clean up the dishes before you watch TV."
- A coworker is explaining how to use the new office computer. She uses jargon that you don't understand and appears to speak a mile a minute.
- Your parents complain that you're "always going out." You believe they nag you when they ask, "Why don't you ever stay home anymore?" and "Are you leaving *again*?"
- A sibling tells you that she needs to provide you with some constructive criticism for your own good. She comments that she loves you and only wants to see you succeed, and subsequently she lists a number of character flaws and problematic behaviors.

Competence & Critical Thinking

THE SWITCH AND RELATIONAL COMMUNICATION

Sarah's roommate and her friend Mark rearrange the furniture in the room that Sarah shares with her roommate. Sarah is on her cell phone complaining to a friend when her roommate returns and suggests that Sarah is upset because of the changes. Although Sarah denies being upset, her roommate can tell that Sarah is angry. Sarah finally admits that she is upset and emphasizes that it's not the changes that bother her; it's the fact that her roommate made the changes without checking with her first.

You can view scene one in the video *The Switch* by accessing the "Small Group and Interpersonal Videos" on the MyCommunication-Lab Web site (*note*: click on the maximize icon to eliminate the material in the "notes" section and enlarge the picture). Answer the following questions about the relational communication featured in the scene:

- Even though Sarah says that "nothing" is wrong, how can Sarah's roommate tell that Sarah is upset?
- On what level of meaning does Sarah's roommate perceive the argument to be? What does the conflict concern at this level?
- On what level of meaning does Sarah perceive the argument to be? What does the conflict concern at this level?
- Analyze the relational level meanings in terms of affection, control, and respect.
- Identify examples of metacommunication used in this video and relate the metacommunication to the expression of affection, control, and/or respect.

MARK: Yeah, your father is ridiculous when he does that magic show. I can't believe the stuff that he can do.

ROOMMATE: So why don't you ask him to do a show for you, trust me.

MARK: Yeah, I bet he can. But you know what, we're juggling the subject. We've got to do something about this room. What do you want to do here?

ROOMMATE: Yeah, we do. These bunk beds definitely have to move. The top one is probably going to go over there.

MARK: OK.

ROOMMATE: Since the bed's going there, that desk . . . I'm probably going to want to put it over here on this wall? And I guess the dresser, I'll probably want to put at the end of that bed since they are with hers.

MARK: OK.

ROOMMATE: Uhm, that chair, I guess put it at the end of this bed.

MARK: OK.

ROOMMATE: You think it would look good there?

MARK: Yeah, definitely good. However, what are we going to do about this TV?

ROOMMATE: Minor detail.

MARK: And Sarah's going to be OK with this?

ROOMMATE: Oh, yeah, sure. As long as it's done by the time she gets back, we're good.

MARK: All right. Not a problem. All right, well, let's get to moving then.

ROOMMATE: All right. Oh, let me go first so I can get the door for you.

MARK: Please. It's not . . . *(grunting)*

SARAH: *(On cell phone)* I can't even begin to tell you how angry I am right now. It's not even that she did that. It's she didn't even ask. She didn't even ask. She had no right to do that. Again. Yeah, I, I don't know. *(Sarah's roommate enters the room)*

ROOMMATE: Hey.

SARAH: Hey. Can I call you back? OK.

ROOMMATE: What's wrong?

SARAH: Nothing.

ROOMMATE: Yeah, OK, what's wrong?

SARAH: Nothing.

ROOMMATE: OK, fine. You want to play that game, you don't have to tell me what's wrong. I know you. You hate the room.

SARAH: The room is fine. I don't hate the room.

ROOMMATE: OK.

SARAH: Whatever.

ROOMMATE: You don't like the room, we'll change it.

SARAH: The room is fine. Just leave it the way it is.

ROOMMATE: So then what's wrong?

SARAH: Do you want to know what's wrong?

ROOMMATE: Mm-hmm.

SARAH: The fact that you have the audacity to come in here and change the room when I'm gone, and then you're not even here when I get back. You're never here. Never. So why do you care how the room is arranged?

ROOMMATE: 'Told you something was wrong.

SARAH: You don't get it, do you?

ROOMMATE: You don't like the room. I saw the—I saw your face when as soon as I walked in. I knew you didn't like it.

SARAH: Well, then, here. Take another look. 'Cause I like the room just fine. You could put the desk on the ceiling if you really want to. I don't care. But at least check and make sure it's OK to put the desk on the ceiling. Just give me a heads-up, let me know. We're in this together. Take me into consideration.

Principles of Communication

Read the following statements and consider whether they are true or false:

- People communicate simultaneously during a conversation.
- The statement "Disregard what I've just said" makes us ignore or forget an utterance.
- It is easy to pinpoint when communication begins and ends.
- "One cannot *not* communicate."

What are some principles of communication?

These statements correspond to four principles that can increase our knowledge of communication and the likelihood that we will be perceived as competent communicators. We will learn whether the statements are true and false when we read that communication is transactional, irreversible, an ongoing process, and inevitable.

Communication Is Transactional

Communication as **transaction** means that individuals who participate in face-to-face conversation simultaneously communicate and listen as a conversation unfolds. You may be wondering how two or more people can communicate in a simultaneous manner. Consider the following example: as a student, you are probably accustomed to listening to your instructor's lecture or comments. However, at the same time and without realizing it, you are probably communicating with the instructor as well. Suppose you are unclear about your instructor's explanations. As the lecture continues, you look down at your notes, shake your head, and make a slight "tsk" sound. Even though your instructor is verbally communicating with you, you are simultaneously communicating with your instructor on the basis of your nonverbal communication (lack of eye contact, shaking head, and "tsk"). Your instructor asks if you understand her or his comments, and the process reverses. As you explain your confusion, you notice that your instructor looks you in the eyes, shakes her or his head up and down, and murmurs, "Uh-huh." Once again, while you are verbally communicating your confusion to your instructor, your instructor is simultaneously nonverbally communicating interest in your concerns.

Communication Is Irreversible

"I'm sorry; please forget that I ever said it!" How often have you or someone you know uttered a similar wish? No matter how sincerely we apologize, our communication may be forgiven but probably not forgotten. Communication is irreversible; we can't take it back once a listener interprets it. This principle is particularly applicable to computer-mediated communication (CMC). It's impossible to take back our thoughts and feelings when we engage in instant messaging, and email may provide someone with a permanent message that we wish we had never sent.

Communication Is an Ongoing Process

Communication is an ongoing **process** because communication is not static. Although communication occurs in distinct episodes with various individuals, it is difficult, if not impossible, to determine when communication begins and when it ends. We may think communication begins when we initiate interaction by speaking to a conversation partner, but "communication" is more than verbal interaction. It can be argued that communication begins in the intrapersonal domain, that is, with a thought or a feeling. Similarly, a communication episode can be said to begin on the basis of a previous interaction. For example, have you ever become angry at someone and taken it out on someone else? Suppose you have an argument with a coworker in the morning and replay the argument in your mind while driving home in the late afternoon. Preoccupied, you don't respond to your partner's question, "How was your day?" when you arrive home. Annoyed, your partner sarcastically asks, "What's the matter with you?" You respond with an angry "Give me a break!" Even though you're mad at your coworker for the morning's argument, you direct your anger at your partner. When did this communication episode with your partner begin? Did it begin when you responded with silence to "How was your day?" Did it begin with the intrapersonal communication in the car? Did it begin with the argument with your coworker? Or did it begin with your thoughts prior to the argument? Clearly, this example illustrates that communication is ongoing and process oriented.

Communication Is Inevitable

All communication has the potential to convey meaning to someone else. Actually, we "cannot *not* communicate." Even when we think we are not communicating, we are. As human beings, we are constantly perceiving and interpreting other people's behavior. Whether we are frowning or laughing, speaking or being silent, expressing joy or showing anger, we are still communicating. Take a moment to think about a time when you were riding in a car with a friend. Perhaps your friend talked for several miles and then stopped talking. After a few moments, you may have begun to feel uncomfortable because you were not sure why he or she stopped talking. You may have turned to your friend and asked, "What's wrong?" Surprised, your friend may have answered, "Nothing." She or he may have merely been "paying attention to the road," while you interpreted the silence quite differently. This is an example of how a person's silence can convey meaning even though it's not intended to communicate.

Components in a Transactional Model of Communication

Communication models are pictures of the structure and key components of communication. They define and isolate specific elements in the communication process and show their relationship to each other and to the communication process itself. Specifically, communication models are useful because they enable us to locate the particular components of a communication exchange and determine how their relationship to each other can affect the outcome of a communication episode. Think about how each component can affect others as you read the information about the elements involved in the communication process. Consider as well how the relationships between the components can positively or negatively affect the outcome of a conversation.

What are some components involved in a transactional model of communication?

Elements Involved in the Communication Process

A transactional model of communication illustrates the various components in the communication process. As you can see in Figure 1.2, "A Transactional Model of Communica-

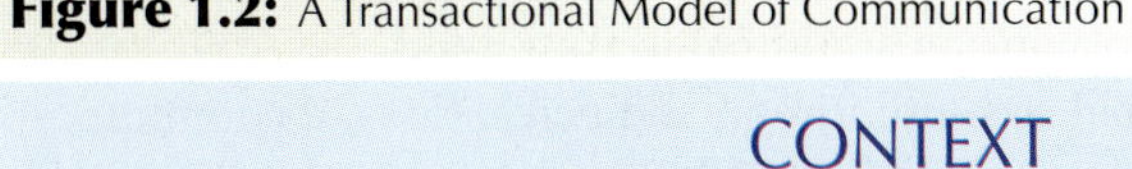

Figure 1.2: A Transactional Model of Communication

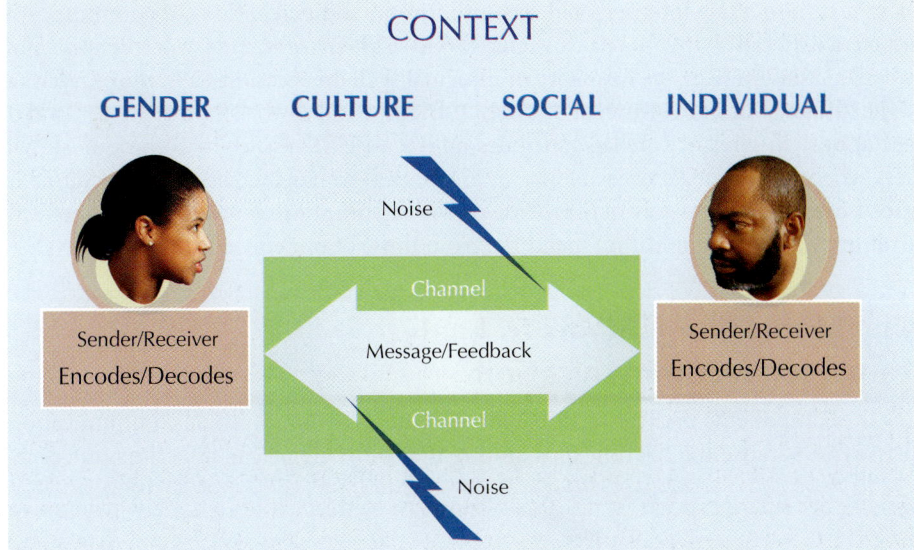

tion," face-to-face communication occurs simultaneously with two or more individuals sending and receiving messages. In terms of the components of a transactional model of communication, the **sender** is the person who conveys thoughts, feelings, or ideas to others. To be perceived as communicatively competent, senders should select the most effective and appropriate verbal and nonverbal behaviors to represent their thoughts, feelings, and ideas. They should also attempt to uncover, acknowledge, and understand the hidden assumptions that influence their and others' communication. The process of translating thoughts, feelings, and ideas into symbols (words and nonverbal cues) is called **encoding**. This is a mental process generated by the sender to convey meaning to the receiver of the communication.

The **receiver** is the person who receives the message conveyed by the sender. The receiver is responsible for interpreting or assigning meaning to the message and for responding to the sender. The mental process of interpreting the message is called **decoding**.

The **message** contains the information (e.g., thoughts, feelings, ideas) the sender wishes to convey to the receiver. Both verbal (words) and nonverbal (e.g., "body language" and vocal behavior) communication are used to convey meaning.

The response to the sender's message is called **feedback**. The response can be verbal, nonverbal, or both. It is through feedback that the sender learns whether her or his message has been received as intended.

A **channel** is the pathway used to convey the message between the sender and the receiver. Usually our five senses assist us in the transfer and interpretation of the message. However, technology such as telephones, intercoms, the instant-messaging function of personal computers, or the text-messaging function of cell phones also provides channels used to convey messages.

Noise is any force that can interfere with the communication process in any communication context or situation. Noise can occur anytime during an interaction and can be external or internal. Distractions such as loud voices at another table in a restaurant, a jet plane flying overhead, or a student arriving late to class are examples of external noise. Internal noise can be physiological or psychological. Physiological factors include illness, fatigue, pain, and even hunger. Psychological factors are mental or emotional distractions such as daydreaming about upcoming weekend events, feeling bored by the speaker's message, and feeling annoyed while replaying an argument in your mind.

Contexts also affect interpersonal communication and perceptions of communication competence. Recall that contexts can refer to physical environments, interpretations of a particular situation (e.g., the formality or informality of an occasion), a frame of reference, and the influence of our culture, of our family, friends, and coworkers, our gender, and our expectations, past history, beliefs, attitudes, and values. It's easier to communicate with others when our contexts overlap, and interaction becomes increasingly difficult as our contexts diverge because they may provide us with assumptions and standards for effective and appropriate communication that differ from those of our conversation partner(s).

Using Model Components to Analyze Interpersonal Communication

Using the components in a transactional model to analyze interpersonal communication is constructive because the relationships among the components can affect the outcome of communication episodes. Consider the following example: How might a *sender* perceive a *receiver* who constantly fidgets, coughs, and glances downward as the *sender* communicates a *message*? The *receiver's* nonverbal *feedback* may influence the *sender* to *decode* or interpret the *receiver* as being uninterested in the conversation, disliking the topic of discussion, disliking the sender, and/or communicating incompetently. The *sender's* perceptions can affect her or his *feedback*; now the *sender* will abbreviate the *message* and back away in order to end the conversation. The *receiver* may not be aware of his or her distressing nonverbal behavior and may decode the *sender's* *feedback* as rude or unfriendly. The *receiver* later phones (a *channel*) to discuss the conversation. The *sender* wants to nonverbally communicate to the *receiver* that she or he doesn't want to engage in *encoding* (putting thoughts into words) and slams down the phone or pushes the off button (a nonverbal *message*) when the *sender* hears (a *channel*) the *receiver's* voice. The outcomes of these communication episodes may dissatisfy both the *sender* and the *receiver*. The dissatisfaction is directly caused by the relationships of the model components and how they affect each other.

Chapter Review

Motivation: How has this helped me?

- **The importance of studying interpersonal communication**

It's important to study interpersonal communication because we live in a diverse, technology-oriented, fast-paced society. Knowing that interpersonal communication affects our thoughts, feelings, and interactions with others; enables us to create, maintain, and dissolve relationships; and helps us achieve career success can motivate us to communicate competently.

- **How intrapersonal communication can help us**

We can use intrapersonal communication and goal setting to reduce social anxiety that can rob us of our confidence and motivation to communicate in a competent manner.

Knowledge: What have I learned?

- **How we can define interpersonal communication**

We can define interpersonal communication as communication that involves at least two people who establish a communicative relationship. Interpersonal communication involves partners who have the power to simultaneously affect each other through their behavior, whether it is positive or negative. Interpersonal communication competence is effective and appropriate and is facilitated if we are motivated to communicate, knowledgeable, and skillful. Competent communicators are also civil and ethical.

- **The contexts that influence interpersonal communication**

The perception of interpersonal communication competence is influenced by culture, relationship, gender, and individual contexts.

- **The types of communication that are related to interpersonal communication competence**

Intrapersonal, interpersonal, and relational communication are types of communication related to interpersonal communication competence. Relational communication entails meaning on a content level and on a relationship level that includes perceptions of affection, control, and respect.

- **Principles of communication**

Principles of communication include the ideas that communication is transactional, irreversible, an ongoing process, and inevitable.

- **The components involved in a transactional model of communication**

Transactional communication models illustrate and isolate specific components involved in the communication process and show their relationship to each other and the process itself. The components include the sender who encodes, the receiver who decodes, the message, feedback, the channel, and noise.

Skill: What skills have I developed?

- **Metacommunication**

Metacommunication (communication about communication and/or communication about relationships) checks our understanding of content- and relational-level meanings and can increase our interpersonal communication competence. At the content level, metacommunication can suggest how the actual meaning of a message is to be interpreted. Metacommunication at the relational level can make clear our perceptions of how we and our relationships are perceived in terms of affection, control, and respect.

Study Questions

1. How do diversity, technology, and the fast pace of modern life affect communication?
2. What is interpersonal communication competence? How can we facilitate perceptions of communication competence?

3. How do the culture, relationship, gender, and individual contexts affect interpersonal communication and perceptions of communication competence?
4. Define *interpersonal communication* and explain the difference between impersonal and personal forms of interpersonal communication.
5. Define *intrapersonal communication* and describe two types of intrapersonal communication.
6. What is relational communication, and how does it relate to content and relational messages? What are three meanings that can be communicated at the relational level?
7. Define *metacommunication* and provide examples of metacommunication that relate to the content and relational levels of meaning.
8. What are four principles of communication that can clarify the meaning and functions of communication?
9. What are the components of the communication process that are illustrated in a transactional communication model?

Names to Know

Brian H. Spitzberg and **William R. Cupach,** p. 5—Communication researchers who developed the communication competence model based on motivation, knowledge, and skill. Spitzberg teaches at San Diego State University, and Cupach teaches at Illinois State University at Bloomington-Normal.

Paul Watzlawick, Janet Beavin, and **Dan Jackson,** p. 22—Psychotherapists and members of the Palo Alto Group who in 1967 developed the idea that messages have content and relational meaning. Their classic work *Pragmatics of Human Communication* elucidates and models basic communication patterns.

Julia T. Wood, p. 15—Noted communication scholar who has conducted extensive research in the area of gender communication and relationships. A professor at the University of North Carolina at Chapel Hill, Wood has won numerous national awards for her teaching and scholarship.

Key Terms

CHAPTER 2

Perception and Communication

"Perception is a guess or estimate of what is 'out there' depending on how we read the clues; therefore it can never be absolute and often is unreliable."

Earl Kelley, educator

In this chapter, we will answer the following:

Motivation: How will this help me?

- It is important to study perception and communication because we often communicate on the basis of different perceptions. Additionally, engaging in perspective taking to understand others' perceptions can improve our communication competence.

Knowledge: What will I learn?

- How to characterize perception
- The stages involved in the perception process
- Perceptual biases and how they affect communication
- How contexts influence perception and communication

Skill: Why do I need to develop this skill?

- Describing sense data and perception checking can improve our communication competence.

Illusionist David Copperfield influences his audiences to perceive that he can levitate across the Grand Canyon, escape from Alcatraz Island, and make the Statue of Liberty disappear. What factors affect how we perceive and what we perceive as "real"? Do you or someone you know perceive that "all [fill in the blank with a particular group] are [fill in the blank with an adjective]"? Have you and a partner ever argued about whose perceptions are correct? In reality, perceptual differences don't necessarily mean that one person's version of "truth" is better than another's. Try to recall some instances of perceptual disagreement as you read the material in this chapter regarding perception in general and how our perceptions of others influence our interpersonal communication. In this chapter, we will increase our motivation to communicate competently by learning why it's important to study perception and communication. Engaging in perspective taking can increase our motivation to communicate with others who are different from us. We will also increase our knowledge by learning about the characterization of perception, the stages in the perception process, how our perception of reality is biased, how our perception is influenced by contexts, and the challenges of perception and communication as they relate to stereotyping and prejudice. Finally, we will learn two skills that can improve our interactions with others—how to communicate descriptive rather than inferential statements, and how to engage in the skill of perception checking.

Introduction to Perception

Have you ever misjudged the distance between you and another person or something that is inanimate (and therefore accidentally bumped into someone or walked into a wall)? Have you ever thought that someone "looked" unintelligent but revised your opinion after speaking with her or him? These questions concern perception. Perception is learned; it isn't an innate ability. Perception occurs when sense data—what we see, hear, smell, taste, and/or touch—is transmitted to the brain. The brain almost instantly transforms the sensory messages into conscious perceptions by attaching meaning to the sense data. This process occurs in three stages.

How can we characterize perception?

Perception is the process of selecting, organizing, and interpreting sensory information. "Seeing" is not the same as "perceiving." A man who regained his sight after thirty years of blindness makes clear the difference between sight and perception: "When I could see again, objects literally hurled themselves at me. One of the things a normal person knows from long habit is what *not* to look at. Things that don't matter, or that confuse, are simply shut out of their seeing minds. I had forgotten this, and tried to see everything at once; consequently I saw nothing."[1]

Why It's Important to Study Perception and Communication

The study of perception as it relates to communication deserves merit because the relationship between the two is reciprocal and because we often communicate on the basis of different perceptions. Understanding how perception affects communication can motivate us to communicate competently.

Why is it important to study perception and communication?

Reciprocal Relationship

What would you think if a significant other suggested that you "lose a few pounds"? Would you perceive a message designed to help you, or would you perceive a message designed to criticize you? How would you respond to this message? Whether you say, "I know you're just trying to help" or "You should talk; you don't look so hot yourself!" will depend on how you perceive the message. This is an illustration of how communication influences perception and perception influences communication. Our perception of reality is created, in part, through communication. For example, suppose a trusted friend tells you about a professor who assigns too much work and treats students unfairly. You may avoid enrolling in this professor's classes if you believe your friend's characterization. Although you never personally interact with the professor, you perceive that he or she is unreasonable, and this idea becomes a part of your reality. In fact, you communicate this perception when someone asks what you know about this professor. These examples also illustrate the reciprocal relationship between perception and communication.

Different Realities

Perhaps one semester you are forced to enroll in one of this professor's classes. Surprisingly, you find the professor's assignments reasonable and his or her treatment of students

Perception can be distorted.

Source: © BIZARRO – DAN PIRARO, KING FEATURES SYNDICATE.

fair. Maybe you wonder what caused your trusted friend to have such a "distorted" perception of the professor. As illustrated in the "Bizarro" comic, one person's truth or reality isn't another's. Although people perceive the same things differently, we assume that our perceptions are true reflections of reality, and we communicate on the basis of this assumption. We all have different realities, and even the truths we hold dear may be proven incorrect. This creates the potential for problematic communication situations in which we may find ourselves arguing about the "correct" version of reality.

Recall that our culture(s), relationships, gender, and individual characteristics affect our perceptions of communication competence. Competent communication involves speakers and listeners who communicate freely and openly about their and others' perceptions and what influences their perceptions. Similarly, competent communicators maintain their perspectives yet consider opposing information. Competent conversation partners realize that while their own perspectives may be accurate, they can see the validity in the perspectives of others.

KNOWLEDGE power • Is It a Masterpiece or Something a Child Could Have Painted?

With a partner or in a group, discuss some examples of perceptions that you hold or have held in the past that were at odds with other people's perceptions. For example, perhaps you and a partner disagreed about perceptions regarding a particular movie, a meal at a restaurant, someone's character or personality, or a controversial topic. Did any of the disagreements about whose version of reality was "correct" escalate into an argument? Were you or your conversation partner eventually able to realize some validity in the other's perspectives and/or conclude that your own version of reality was suspect? How did you or your conversation partner communicate this realization?

The Stages in the Perception Process

The perception process involves three distinct stages that occur almost simultaneously: selection, organization, and interpretation. These stages are illustrated in Figure 2.1, "The Perception Process."

Selection

What are the stages involved in the perception process?

Imagine the most recent walk to your communication class. Can you describe all of the people you passed on your way to class? Do you remember the smells you encountered and the sounds you heard? Of course you don't; it's impossible to perceive all of the stimuli in your environment. Therefore, during **selection**, the first stage of the perception process, we select from the environment the stimuli to which we will attend. Two types of stimuli tend to be selected from all the stimuli that bombard our senses and compete for attention: stimuli that are salient and stimuli that are vivid.

Salience **Salience** refers to stimuli that are selected from the environment based on their interest, use, and meaning to us. For example, were you ever in a crowded restaurant or store and were aware of others' conversations but didn't pay attention to what was being said until, suddenly and without warning, someone from across the room mentioned your name? The reason you selected that particular stimulus from the environment is because your name is meaningful to you. You wouldn't pick out someone else's name from the low-level noise of conversation unless that particular name was also meaningful to you.

Vividness **Vividness** refers to stimuli that are selected from the environment because they are noticeable. We tend to pay attention to stimuli that are intense, large, and repetitious and demonstrate movement. The girl who raises her voice, the guy who is 6'10", the student who peppers her speech with too many "y'knows?" and the friend who uses broad gestures and talks with his hands are all likely to be noticed.

Once we have selected material from the environment to attend to, we next organize the material to help us in its interpretation.

Organization

Organization occurs when we categorize the stimuli we have selected from the environment to make sense of it. Researchers have discovered that we tend to organize stimuli in certain ways, particularly on the basis of schemas, figure and ground, proximity, similarity, and closure. These patterns influence how we organize the stimuli we attend to.

> **KNOWLEDGE power • This Offer Won't Last, So Call Now!**
>
> With a partner or in a group, think about television commercials that consistently "grab your attention," whether or not you like them. Describe the commercials, and discuss whether you select them from the environment because they mean something to you or because they are noticeable (e.g., they are intense, large, or repetitious or include lots of movement or action).

Schemas **Schemas** are mental templates that enable us to organize and classify stimuli into manageable groups or categories. Schemas typically are general views of people and their social roles. For example, we may categorize

Figure 2.1: The Perception Process

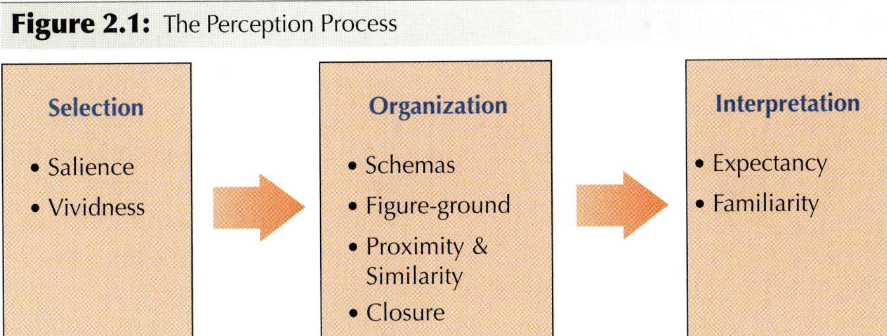

others based on their appearance (pretty, ugly, fat, thin, etc.) and their group membership (Jewish, Republican, Junior League member, etc.). We may also categorize people according to roles, such as parent, student, or doctor. Schemas are used to determine the origin of a memory when we can't recall the source (e.g., we may attribute a comment about a flu epidemic to a particular person only because she or he belongs in the schema of "medical students").[2] The various schemas we use each day help us make sense of the world and

KNOWLEDGE ON THE CUTTING EDGE

"Rights" versus "Right": Are You a Civil Communicator?

"Whatever happened to freedom of speech?" "I can do and say what I want!" How many times have you heard, read, or communicated these or similar sentiments? Do we have a right to wear offensive phrases on our T-shirts? Is it acceptable for people to boom four-letter obscenities from car speakers? These actions may be constitutionally protected rights, but that doesn't mean they are "right." Simply put, although we *can* engage in such behaviors, it doesn't mean that we *should*.

Recall from Chapter 1 that "civility" entails a sacrifice of our individual desires and passions for the overall greater good of the community. However, respect for others and restraining our desires appear to be losing to what has been described as the "rights talk" that is pervasive in modern society. Because we perceive that we have minimal, if any, obligations to others, we easily confuse desires with "rights" and turn to the Constitution to protect offensive speech and behavior. However, the framers of our Constitution most likely imagined the right to engage in heated political discussions that reflected the value of responsibility to the community. Although the Constitution protects a variety of our rights, our norms or rules of conduct should provide us with the discipline to exercise these rights with respect for others and the larger social community we are part of. Unfortunately, too many of us perceive that our right to engage in uncivil and disrespectful communication makes it right to do so.[3]

Fortunately, some individuals and groups perceive that having a right to engage in uncivil communication doesn't mean that it's "right." For example, scholars at the First Amendment Center worked with leaders from the Christian Educators Association International (CEAI) and the Gay, Lesbian, and Straight Educators Network (GLSEN) to write guidelines for educators and parents on issues concerning sexual orientation in public schools. Finn Larsen, executive director of CEAI, asserted, "We need to be sensitive to listen and show respect for individuals with opinions on all sides of this issue even if we don't agree with them."[4] Specifically, schools have been encouraged to form task forces of individuals who hold divergent views about homosexuality. Schools are also asked to agree on ground rules for civil debate. Parents are encouraged to realize that school districts not only have a responsibility to meet their needs but also must provide a safe environment for those who hold different views of sexual orientation. CEAI and GLSEN leaders perceive the push for common ground as a breakthrough and suggest that a lack of basic civility is often what leaves people feeling angry, shut out, and ready to fight.[5]

As we increasingly decry rude and uncivil behavior in modern life, we can hope that people will once again perceive a responsibility to community and work to strengthen the norm of civility. It is indeed possible to perceive that "having a right" doesn't mean that it is "right" to act on that right.

Figure 2.2: Figure-Ground Organization

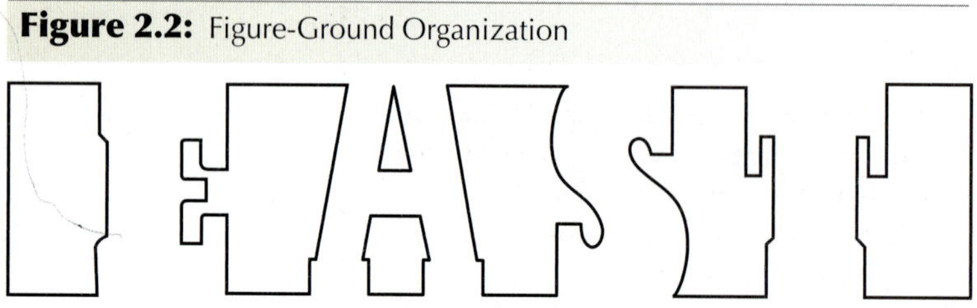

enable us to make generalizations and predictions about others. For example, we may be asked to babysit a friend's five-year-old child. We may therefore use the schema of "young children typically have short attention spans" to predict that the child will need a variety of activities to occupy her or his time. We risk engaging in stereotyping when our generalizations about others based on schemas ignore the possibility of individual differences. Stereotypes are generalizations that lack validity and are discussed later in this chapter in "Overcoming Communication Challenges: Stereotyping and Prejudice."

Figure-Ground Organization **Figure-ground organization** occurs when a portion of the stimuli selected from the environment is the focal point of our attention ("figure") and the rest is placed in the background ("ground"). For example, what do you perceive in Figure 2.2, "Figure-Ground Organization"? It's easy to perceive irregularly shaped geometric figures that aren't quite rectangles in this particular illusion. However, if we place the geometric figures in the background and bring the spaces between them in the forefront, we can see the letters "EAST." The figure and ground organization also applies to communication situations. Have you ever been in a crowded room and paid attention to various conversations? When we begin to focus on one particular conversation and others recede into the background, we are organizing based on the principle of figure-ground.

Proximity and Similarity We also organize stimuli selected from the environment on the basis of proximity and similarity. We organize on the basis of **proximity** when we group stimuli that are physically close to each other. For example, describe what you perceive in Figure 2.3, "Organization Based on Proximity." Do you describe this illusion as four pairs of lines or eight parallel lines? If you perceive four pairs of parallel lines, you are organizing based on the principle of proximity. Organization based on proximity also applies to communication situations. Suppose your professor begins your class by saying that far too many students failed the last exam. Your professor then calls your name and asks to speak with you after class. Because these messages occur in close temporal proximity, you may believe that your professor wants to speak to you about your poor test grade. However, your professor may want to talk to you about a topic totally unrelated to the test.

We also tend to group elements together based on size, color, shape, and other characteristics. When this occurs, we organize on the basis of **similarity**. For example, follow the directions and look at the words listed in the "Memory Test" on the next page.

Figure 2.3: Organization Based on Proximity

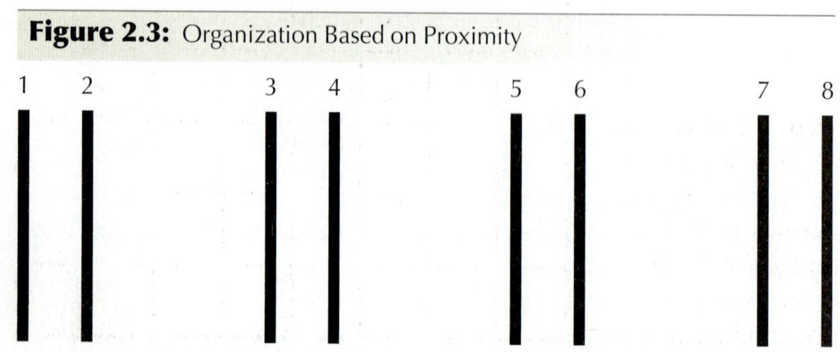

The point of the memory test is not to remember as many words as possible but to uncover the method you use to remember the words. Most likely you grouped the words into categories of items that share something similar. You may have grouped items that related to pets, the solar system, shapes, and fruits. This illustrates the idea that we tend to group similar elements together. Organization based

Memory Test

Directions: Read the following words and prepare to remember as many as possible. Turn the page once you have read the words and write as many words as you can on a piece of scratch paper. Return to the text on the previous page once you are finished writing the words that you remembered.

Cat	Sun	Square	Apple
Lemon	Bird	Planet	Dog
Triangle	Plum	Fish	Moon
Star	Circle	Orange	Rectangle

on similarity also applies to communication situations. Think back to your days in high school. Were your high school classmates organized into various cliques based on similar interests, activities, and communication styles? Did your high school include the jocks who were loud and aggressive, the popular people who were talkative and happy, and the artists who were introverted and quiet? The proverb "birds of a feather flock together" describes organization based on similarity.

Closure Another way we can organize stimuli is through **closure**, that is, filling in the "missing pieces" to form a whole or complete picture. Figure 2.4 illustrates organization based on closure. How would you describe it?

At first glance, Figure 2.4 looks like a solid grid, but none of the lines touch to actually form a grid. Instead of seeing the empty spaces, we fill in the spaces that "hide" the intersections with illusory rectangles or circles. Organization based on closure also applies to communication situations. Have you ever tried to fill in some missing information to make sense of your communication experiences or to understand people? Perhaps you've achieved closure by explaining the actions of an acquaintance who won't leave a cheating partner by surmising that he or she is emotionally needy or too weak to let go. Although our perceptions of the missing information may be false, we all tend to fill in the blanks to create a complete picture.

So far, we have read that sensory information is selected from the environment and organized in various ways to facilitate interpretation. The final stage in the perception process is interpretation.

Figure 2.4: Organization Based on Closure

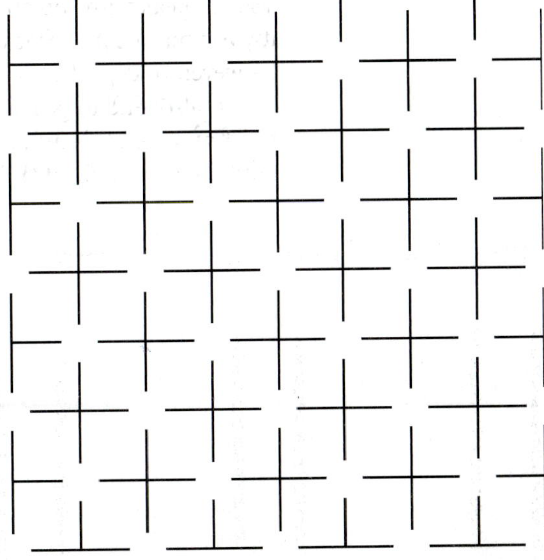

Interpretation

We **interpret** stimuli that we have selected and organized from the environment when we assign meaning to the stimuli. For example, we may select from the environment our roommate standing in the middle of a crowd (selection), focus on the frown on her or his face as being in the foreground (organization), and believe that our roommate is unhappy (interpretation). However, friends standing next to

Figure 2.5: Do You Know These Phrases?

us tell us that they didn't see a frown on our roommate's face. Later that day, we ask our roommate about the sad look and learn that she or he was merely deep in thought. This example illustrates that our interpretations of sense data may be incorrect and that we may select and organize stimuli from the environment (like a frown) that others fail to perceive. We will later learn the skill of perception checking, which will enable us to determine whether our interpretation of stimuli is correct. For now, note that the interpretation of stimuli is influenced by both expectancy and familiarity.

Expectancy Our interpretation of stimuli is influenced by **expectancy**, or what we expect to perceive. In other words, we become accustomed to seeing stimuli in certain ways and therefore often don't perceive the obvious. For example, have you ever written a paper and, even after proofreading it, later discovered that you overlooked some obvious misspellings? Typically, we focus on our meaning and not the written words while we proofread. However, we still may be surprised when our paper is returned to us because we don't expect to find misspelled words after we proofread it.

Familiarity Our interpretation of stimuli is also influenced by **familiarity**, that is, how familiar we are with the stimuli. This idea is evidenced in Figure 2.5, "Do You Know These Phrases?" Sometimes familiarity adds to what we expect to perceive. Read the phrases out loud, very slowly, one word at a time. Do you perceive a second "a" in "light as a a feather?" Do you see a second "the" in "love is in the the air" and a second "a" in "hungry as a a horse?" Familiarity with stimuli can explain why your professors sometimes hand back your assignments with words, clauses, or even sentences circled in red because you have typed them twice. It may be that you are so familiar with what you have written that you fail to perceive anything out of the ordinary.

Expectancy and familiarity also affect communication situations. Have you ever failed to notice a change in a friend's appearance (a form of nonverbal communication)? You may have been so familiar with your friend that you failed to notice any change. Perhaps you once got your braces off, had your ears pierced, or shaved off a moustache. Did any of your friends fail to notice the change in your appearance? If so, your friends didn't perceive the difference in your appearance because they didn't expect to see a change.

What we perceive is considered to be our reality or our truth; however, our reality may not match the reality of others, even if we perceive the same stimuli. Various perceptual errors and biases can result from the fact that we all perceive differently.

Perceptual Biases

Perceptual biases occur because we all perceive differently. These biases can affect how we communicate with others, how we perceive others' communication, and how we interpret and evaluate others' behavior. For example, suppose an employee is tagged for low productivity. A supervisor may perceive the employee's low productivity to be a result of a personal defect or a negative personality characteristic. This perception may influence the

KNOWLEDGE ON THE CUTTING EDGE

Technology Update: Person Perception and Computer-Mediated Communication (CMC)

Do you use email, access personal Web sites, and/or participate in Internet chat rooms? If so, you probably realize that the nonverbal cues that help us form impressions of others are limited in these communication venues in comparison with the cues available in face-to-face communication. Language features tend to be the primary cues for personality perceptions in CMC. One study of CMC-related person perception found that readers can accurately judge the personality characteristics of extroversion and introversion from the text of email messages. Compared to introverts, people who are extroverts tend to use:

- fewer tentative words (e.g., "trying" or "maybe")
- fewer words that communicate negative emotions
- fewer words that indicate inclusion (such as "with" and "include")

The study also illustrated a high degree of agreement among the readers who perceived the personality of the email authors.[6]

Researchers have also studied person perception by comparing personal Web sites with other contexts where personality is expressed, such as bedrooms and offices. "Identity claims" (expressions about our personality that are directed to the self and others) are deliberately manifested in personal Web sites, whereas inadvertent self-expression occurs in physical contexts (e.g., a disorganized CD collection may illustrate a tendency toward clutter, and dirty soccer shoes may indicate a preference for certain athletic activities). Studies have documented that observers can learn at least as much about others by viewing their Web sites as they can from viewing bedrooms and offices. The identity claims on Web sites convey valid information and allow clear and coherent perceptions about an author.[7]

Chat room exchanges are similar to casual interactions with others because of the synchronous nature of real-time communication. People agree more about the personality perceptions of chat room partners in one-on-one chats than in group interactions. The chaotic nature of group chat rooms (in which people tend to type messages simultaneously) may account for this finding, as well as the finding that people in group interactions are perceived less favorably than those in one-on-one interactions.[8]

What are perceptual biases and how do they affect communication?

supervisor to deny the employee a salary increase or consider terminating her or his employment. However, something in the employee's work situation, such as malfunctioning equipment or unreliable team members, may be the cause of the productivity problem.[9] The attribution that a personality flaw is the cause of poor job performance is an example of a perceptual bias that can result in serious consequences. In addition to faulty attributions, selectivity and confusing fact with inference can bias our perceptions and cause errors.

Selectivity

Our perception of sense data can be biased in terms of selective attention and selective perception.

Selective Attention **Selective attention** occurs when we ignore certain parts of a stimulus and attend to others. Perhaps you've heard the story of the teenager who asks his parents for a car. The parents respond by saying, "We'll buy you a car, but there are a few conditions: you must purchase your own insurance, pay for your gas, and help us with errands every now and then." However, the teenager hears only "We'll buy you a car." This is selective attention because the teenager perceives just one part of a message.

Selective Perception **Selective perception** occurs when we see what we want to see, hear what we want to hear, and believe what we want to believe. I'm sure you recognize the

KNOWLEDGE power • Love Is Blind

With a partner or in a group, recall instances when you or someone you know was subject to perception based on selectivity. For example, in terms of selective attention, can you think of a time when you or someone else "heard" some parts of a message and ignored others? Has someone ever perceived only a part of a message that you communicated and missed the rest of it? Have your friends ever perceived some bad qualities in a relational partner that you had not noticed (selective perception)? After you share your examples of selectivity and its influence on perception, discuss ways we can prevent selectivity from biasing our perceptions.

phrase "love is blind," which means that even though others perceive a partner's faults, the other person in the relationship may not see any. A person who has fallen in love perceives only the good qualities, even when others inform her or him about the partner's bad characteristics, and thus demonstrates selective perception.

Confusing Fact with Inference

Another form of perceptual bias is confusing fact with inference. Has anyone ever asked you, "Why are you so crabby today?" This is an example of inference (perception based on interpretation); perhaps you hadn't felt crabby. Were you ever upset by someone who promised to help you with an assignment and then forgot about it? This is also an inference; maybe the person had an emergency. Have you ever thought a good friend was too busy for you because he or she didn't respond to your email? This is an inference; suppose the friend was out of town. The point is that you can't be *sure* that someone is "crabby," forgot about a promise, or was too busy for you. These are all perceptions; they are your interpretations of sense data. An **inference** is an interpretation based on a fact, such as "She wore an *ugly* red dress" or "He left for the airport *a long time ago*." Although everyone you ask may agree that her dress was red or that 7:15 A.M. was the time when he left for the airport, not all would share the inferences that her dress was ugly or that he left a long time ago. On the other hand, a **fact** is independently verifiable by others, such as "She wore a red dress" or "He left for the airport at 7:15 A.M." Facts are often, but not always, based on sense data, such as what we see, hear, taste, smell, and touch. Statements of fact are made after observation and don't go beyond what is observed. There are at least five ways we can distinguish between a fact and an inference:[10]

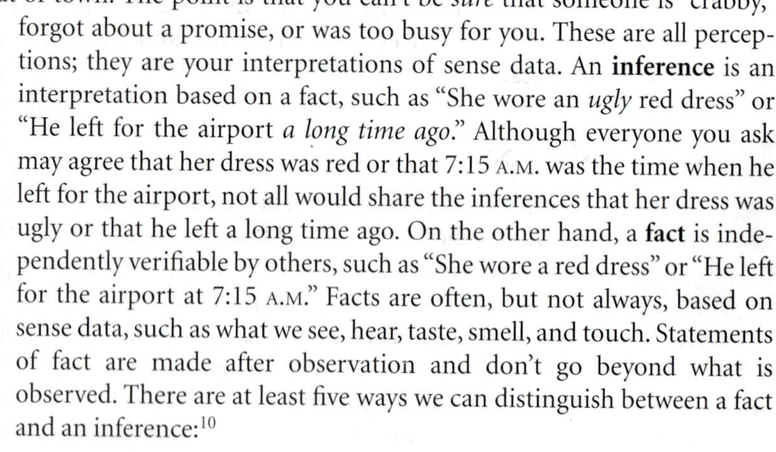

It's a fact that this student is sleeping; it's an inference that he's a "slacker."

- Facts are ascertained only after observation; inferences can be made at any time.
- Facts rest on what is observed; inferences go beyond observation and include information about causality, states of being, and other factors.
- Facts approach certainty; inferences have varying degrees of probability.

KNOWLEDGE power • Truthful Information or Hurtful Gossip

With a partner or in a group, discuss some situations when you or someone you know mistakenly confused a fact with an inference. For example, perhaps you overheard and repeated some gossip or accused someone of a misdeed without having any factual knowledge about the incidents. After sharing your examples, discuss how you might avoid confusing facts with inferences in the future.

- Facts are limited; inferences are unlimited.
- Facts lend themselves to agreement; inferences lend themselves to disagreement.

Consider an additional example of confusion between facts and inferences. As illustrated in the photo on the previous page, have you ever seen a professor become angry when a student falls asleep in class? The professor isn't angry because of the fact or the sense data that "the student is sleeping in class." The professor is angry because of the interpretation of sense data: "This student is bored with the material, this student doesn't appreciate the time and effort needed to create a good lecture, and this student is lazy, rude, and insubordinate." The problem that results from confusing fact with inference is that we believe and act on our inferences as if they are correct, even though they may be wrong. We believe that our statements of interpretation are actually statements of fact, and we often assume that we have fact-based knowledge that we really don't possess. For instance, perhaps the student who falls asleep in class spent the previous night caring for a sick family member. Maybe the student has to work two jobs to pay college tuition bills. The reason the student falls asleep in class may have nothing to do with the professor, the course material, or the student's personality. Confusing facts with inferences can result in perceptual biases and problematic communication.

Attributional Errors

Attributions concern reasons for or causes of behavior. Psychologist **Fritz Heider**, known as the "father of attribution theory," suggested that we make interpretations about someone's personality based on his or her behavior.[11] **Attribution theory** explains exactly how we create explanations or attach meaning to our own or another's behavior. We tend to overemphasize inherent characteristics or personality and underemphasize situational factors when we explain the reasons for others' behavior. This is called the **fundamental attribution error**. For example, have you ever thought that a friend's lack of preparedness and study, laziness, and/or irresponsibility caused him or her to fail a test? You committed the fundamental attribution error if you ignored some situational factors that might have explained the poor grade, such as the friend's illness or need to study for a major test in another class. Besides assigning reasons for others' behavior, we also provide explanations for our own behavior. Specifically, we tend to attribute inherent characteristics or our personality to successful behavior and situational factors to our unsuccessful behavior. This is called the **self-serving bias**. Have you ever done poorly on a test and attributed your results to tricky test questions, questions that covered material that wasn't supposed to be on the test, or a professor who deliberately included difficult questions to fail as many

KNOWLEDGE power • Taking Credit or Assigning Blame

With a partner or in a group, discuss situations involving you or someone you know that illustrate the fundamental attribution error and the self-serving bias. After sharing your experiences, ask your partner or group to identify whether the situations reflect the fundamental attribution error or the self-serving bias. For example, can you remember a time when you or someone else blamed a victim for his or her misfortunes? Have you or has someone you know ever taken credit for an achievement that was at least partially based on luck or on the work of others? Can you recall a situation when you or someone else minimized personal responsibility for a less-than-optimal outcome?

students as possible? Have you ever done well on a test and attributed your grade to preparedness and good study habits? If so, you committed the self-serving bias. Attribution errors such as the fundamental attribution error and the self-serving bias may lead us to incorrectly perceive that someone is personally responsible for her or his misfortunes, take unrealistic credit for what we do well, and minimize personal responsibility for what we do poorly.

COMPETENCE: Motivation / Knowledge / **Skill**

Describing Sense Data and Perception Checking to Prevent Perceptual Bias

How can describing sense data and perception checking improve communication competence?

Recall that perception is inherently a subjective activity and that because of differences in selection, organization, and interpretation, we all perceive different realities. We therefore can set a personal goal to understand others' perceptions and to communicate in a manner that facilitates the understanding of our own perceptions. A variety of studies demonstrate that setting goals motivates us to complete tasks and to achieve high levels of success in occupational, academic, and personal contexts. Setting specific and realistic goals and defining strategies for their implementation have been proven to enhance task performance and skill.[12] Remembering our goals can also cause us to pause before communicating in ways that may be perceived as ineffective and/or inappropriate. We can therefore establish goals to recognize the subjectivity of perception, better understand others' perceptions, and facilitate understanding our own perceptions. For example, realistic goals that can help prevent fact-inference confusion are "I will make it a point to consider whether an observation or an opinion is communicated before I offer a response" and "I will communicate my observations of sense data and what I think they mean instead of assuming my partner's reasons for her or his behavior." One way we can achieve these goals is by using the skill of perception checking.

Perception checking suggests that we recognize that no one has a corner on the truth and that each stage in the perception process is influenced by our own biases. A **perception check** has three elements: a description of sense data, at least one interpretation (perception) of the sense data, and a request for feedback. We can improve our

SKILL practice • Communicating Descriptions Based on Sense Data

Read the following inferences and consider what sense data may prompt someone to make the inferences. With a partner or in a group, communicate the sense data that may be the basis for the inferences:

- "I guess you forgot about changing my work schedule next week."
- (*sarcastically*) "Thanks for not inviting me to the party!"
- "Obviously what I say doesn't matter because you showed up late."
- "That professor doesn't care about what life is like outside the classroom."
- "Boy, are you sensitive!"

perception checking by learning to separate facts from inference. Because the first step of a perception check is a description of what someone says or does, we need to focus on sense data rather than on the inferences we make from sense data. For example, telling someone "I see that you look crabby" is an inference or interpretation based on sense data. We can ask ourselves what causes us to infer that a person is crabby or recall the three stages of the perception process and work backward (i.e., interpretation-organization-selection). A person's frown and failure to respond to our pleasant "hello" are sense data that can cause us to infer that someone is crabby.

As illustrated in Table 2.1, "Perception Checking," a perception check includes a description of what someone says or does (sense data), one or two inferences or interpretations about what the sense data mean, and a request for feedback. We offer our interpretations in a tentative manner to illustrate we realize our perception(s) may be incorrect, and we can follow our interpretation(s) with a question (e.g., "Am I on the right track?" or "Is it one of these?") or a rising inflection to indicate that we desire feedback about our interpretation(s). For example, instead of asking, "Why are you so crabby?" we can use a perception check:

- *"I haven't seen you smile this morning* (sense data). *Is anything wrong?*" (The request for feedback is included in the interpretation that "something may be wrong.")

Instead of sarcastically saying, "Thanks for forgetting to help me with my assignment," we can use a perception check:

- *"When you didn't show up to help me with my assignment* (sense data), *I thought that either you forgot or that something bad happened* (two interpretations). *Am I right?*" (request for feedback).

Similarly, instead of angrily remarking, "I guess you're just too busy to email," we can use a perception check:

- *"I sent you an email three days ago and I haven't received an answer from you* (sense data). *Have you been busy or is something else going on?*" (This perception check communicates that the perception may be incorrect because it's possible that "something else is going on.")

SKILL practice • Perception Checking

With a partner or in a group, practice perception checking by responding to the following situations with sense data, one or two interpretations, and a request for feedback.

Situation One:

You and your relational partner usually surprise each other with small gifts on the monthly anniversary of your first date. Your partner hasn't sent you a note, presented you with a gift, or even mentioned your anniversary this month. You decide to speak with your relational partner and use a perception check.

Situation Two:

You are working on a group project for your communication class. Someone in your group seems to criticize each suggestion you make about the project. You decide to talk to this person and communicate a perception check.

Situation Three:

You are at a coffee bar and are waiting to pay for your drink. Your server appears to glance in your direction yet does not stop when you attempt to make eye contact. When you finally do manage to speak with the server, you decide to use a perception check.

Situation Four:

You ask a classmate to meet you at the library so you can study together for an upcoming test. Your classmate doesn't show up, and you decide to communicate a perception check when you see her or him in class the next day.

Situation Five:

You and a coworker usually meet every Wednesday to have lunch in the corporate cafeteria. However, the coworker has begged off your lunch meetings three times in a row. You decide to perception check to find out why your coworker has "avoided" your get-togethers.

It's important to have a realistic perception of communication guidelines and skills such as perception checking; in other words, they won't always work! One underlying assumption associated with the use of communication skills is that people are rational beings and that rational attempts at competent communication will result in responses that are effective and appropriate. Don't be surprised when this assumption proves false. Although you may engage in effective and appropriate communication that respects your partner and his or her perceptions, your partner may respond in an incompetent manner. For example, consider a perception check such as "I saw you talking to the guy next to you while I made my suggestions during the meeting. Did you disagree with what I suggested,

Table 2.1: Perception Checking

- A description of sense data (e.g., "You slammed the door when you got home.")
- At least one interpretation (perception) of the sense data (e.g., "I'm thinking something bad happened at work or maybe you're mad at me.")
- A request for feedback (e.g., "Am I completely off-base here?")

or were you talking about something else?" Communicating this perception check may prompt the unexpected reply, "Mind your own business!" There may be nothing we can say or do to convince our colleague that our perception check isn't a nosy attempt at obtaining personal information. Remember that flexibility and strategy are integral to competent communication. A responsible judgment in this scenario might be to realize that nothing we can say or do will convince our partner of our true motivation. Perhaps we should learn from such an experience and maintain a hopeful vision of communication at some future time.

Contexts and Perception

The various contexts that affect us and our resultant perceptions validate and reinforce our assumptions about people, behavior, and communication. We become sure that our view of reality is objective and correct, and we tend to forget that it is our contexts that help to create our "reality."[13] The culture, relationship, gender, and individual contexts filter all the stimuli we select, organize, and interpret from our environment and influence how we communicate our perceptions.

Culture Context

How do contexts influence perception and communication?

Members of cultural groups learn and share similar perceptions based on their shared experiences and what their culture teaches them. In general, our perceptions are similar to those of other individuals who belong to the same cultural and co-cultural groups as we do.[14]

Cultural Groups Some researchers suggest that the fundamental attribution error is a U.S. phenomenon that reflects the predominant U.S. cultural belief that the individual and her or his actions are the primary force that shapes life outcomes. People from other cultural backgrounds typically don't make judgments about individuals when they attempt to explain causal relationships or reasons for behavior.[15] For example, people in cultures such as the United States typically believe that we are responsible for our lots in life and may cite individual weakness and poor choices as the reasons for poverty or crime. However, people in cultures such as Africa and the Middle East tend to believe that life is determined by forces outside our control, such as fate or destiny, and typically do not blame an individual and her or his choices and actions for undesirable life outcomes.[16] Similarly, our cultural beliefs can influence our perception of the environment and our communication about it. Recent research suggests that East Asians' emphasis on collectivism and the belief that the group takes precedence over the individual influences them to perceive more information in the environment than Westerners who emphasize individualism. Japanese and U.S. college students viewed animated artwork in which appeared a large and colorful "focal fish" with background images of smaller fish and animals, vegetation, rocks, shells, and snails (see Figure 2.6, "Focal Fish Artwork"). When asked to recall the objects in the focal fish animation, the Japanese students recalled more background information than the U.S. students. The Japanese students also recalled more relationships among the objects in the environment than the Americans.[17] Our cultural beliefs not only influence our perceptions of the world but also affect our communication behavior. Recall from Chapter 1 that in high-context cultures, much of the meaning of

Figure 2.6: Focal Fish Artwork

Source: © Masuda and Nisbett. Masuda, T. and Nisbett, R. E. (2001). "Attending Holistically vs. Analytically: Comparing the Context Sensitivity of Japanese and Americans." *Journal of Personality and Social Psychology* 81 (2001): 922–934.

communication is indirect and implicit and that in low-context cultures, communication is direct and assertive. People will be perceived as credible if they communicate in an outspoken manner in the United States because this low-context culture values open and forceful expression. On the other hand, people will be perceived as shallow if they communicate in a direct and assertive manner in Japan because this high-context culture values indirectness and modesty.[18] The same behavior can be perceived differently by persons who belong to different cultures.

Co-Cultures Members of the same culture may perceive an identical phenomenon differently because of the influence of the co-cultures(s) to which they belong. For example, interpersonal aspects of work relationships are emphasized in the Japanese, Indian, Middle Eastern, and Latin cultures in addition to co-cultures associated with these groups. One study of Mexican Americans and Anglo-Americans illustrated how cultural beliefs can affect a work group's communication and success. When asked what can be done to improve success at work, the Mexican American respondents perceived that a focus on socioemotional aspects of interactions with coworkers (e.g., social harmony, graciousness, and collegiality) is more important than a focus on task-related considerations. However, the Anglo-American respondents perceived that an increased task focus would increase work group success. These findings suggest that Mexican Americans and Anglo-Americans may perceive and evaluate work groups, coworkers, and communication differently, based on the beliefs associated with their cultural groups.[19]

Relationship Context

Perception affects communication and behavior within the family, among friends, and among coworkers. In particular, perceptions of self-disclosure are related to marital satisfaction and attributions for behavior differ in happy and unhappy couples.

Family Attributions for positive and negative behavior affect marital communication. Specifically, if a partner does something negative in a happy marriage, the other partner typically perceives that the negative behavior is situational and fleeting. The attribution in such a case may be a bad mood, excessive stress, and a need for sleep. However, if a partner does something negative in an unhappy marriage, the other partner tends to perceive the negative behavior as stable and internal ("She or he is always rude and selfish; that's just the way she or he is"). Similarly, if a partner does something positive in a happy marriage, the other partner typically perceives that the behavior results from something internal and stable. On the other hand, if one partner does something positive in an unhappy marriage, the behavior tends to be attributed to the situation rather than something internal. In general, happy couples engage in relationship-enhancing attributions, and unhappy couples engage in distress-maintaining attributions. Once such attributions are established, behaviors that confirm the attributions receive attention, and behaviors that should disconfirm the attributions tend to be ignored.[20]

Friends In a similar way, our expectations about friends and friendship can affect our perceptions of others. For example, perhaps you believe that a friend is someone who is reliable and dependable. You may reconsider your perception of a "friend" who is late to drive you to class or completely fails to show up. On the other hand, you may reevaluate your perception of an "acquaintance" who offers to help you with a project, run an errand, or spend time and effort to satisfy your needs.

We also evaluate our friends on the basis of traits we believe they possess. While we tend to form impressions of strangers and acquaintances primarily based on roles or categories to which they belong (e.g., "student, male," etc.), we perceive our friends in terms of personality traits.[21] Our perceptions of friends are additionally influenced by their use of disclaimers. **Disclaimers** are used to prevent others from forming negative judgments about a speaker and to disassociate one's identity from her or his communication and behavior. Recent research illustrates that the use of disclaimers draws more attention to undesired personality traits. Conversation partners will therefore analyze a speaker's communication for evidence of the negative trait. In other words, if a friend says, "I'm not lazy, but . . ." and follows the disclaimer with a statement about "slacking off" and failing to finish a class assignment, we will perceive our friend as possessing the disclaimed trait even *more* because of the use of the disclaimer.[22]

Coworkers Imagine three people who decide to view a film together. One person, a speech pathologist, noticing the actors' accents and how they pronounce their words, decides overall that the film is "realistic." The second person, an aerobics instructor, watches the actors chase the bad guys, jump from buildings, and escape from near-death situations without once catching their breath. The aerobics instructor therefore concludes that the film is "ridiculous." The third person, a computer specialist, notices the advanced software, complicated gadgets, and modern technological devices used in the film. The computer specialist believes that the development of the futuristic technology used in the movie is extremely plausible and therefore perceives the film to be "cutting edge." "Realistic, ridiculous, cutting-edge"; these perceptions of the same phenomenon can be attributed to the observers' occupational roles.

Just as our occupational role can influence our perceptions, our position in an organizational hierarchy can affect our ability to engage in perspective taking. You will soon read that perspective taking allows us to see the world as others perceive it and can improve our motivation to communicate in a competent manner. Research suggests that people who hold powerful positions within an organization, such as supervisors and managers, are less likely to take their subordinates' perspectives. People in management positions may not need to understand how their subordinates perceive the world because they have control over valuable resources and are less dependent on others to accomplish their goals. People in positions of authority may also have increased demands on their attention and it therefore may be difficult for them to engage in perspective taking with their subordinates. Persons who hold powerful positions typically don't make conscious decisions to ignore the perspectives of others. In fact, failing to engage in perspective taking helps managers to be action-oriented, focus on goal attainment, and enables them to adapt to a complex organizational world. When people in powerful positions do engage in perspective taking, they tend to make less accurate estimations of how others think and perceive the world than those in less powerful positions.[23]

Gender Context

Many researchers who study communication and gender contend that women and men are socialized into separate gender cultures whose members share understanding about communication goals, methods to achieve these goals, and how to interpret each other. Families, schools, and experiences in social life teach us how to interact with others. For example, boys are taught that talk is used to achieve instrumental goals such as negotiating power and position on a status hierarchy, to assert identities, to solve problems, and to argue points of view. Conversation is viewed as a way to demonstrate knowledge and superiority and as a method to gain respect. Consider whether you are comfortable asking others for information and directions. If you are not, it may be because you perceive that such communication places you in a low-status position and suggests that others are more knowledgeable and powerful than you are. In general, boys and men tend to perceive communication as a means to an end. On the other hand, girls are taught that communication functions to build and maintain harmonious relationships that take priority over instrumental goals; communication is perceived to foster intimacy and to be the crux of relationships. Once again, consider whether you are comfortable asking others for information and directions. It may be that you perceive asking for help as a way to "connect" with others and to communicate cooperation and support. In general, girls and women tend to perceive communication as an end in and of itself. Of course, not all men perceive communication as a way to achieve instrumental goals, and not all women perceive communication as functioning primarily to establish and maintain relationships. However, such views of communication can influence women and men to perceive the same situation differently.[24]

Women tend to view communication as a way to create and maintain harmonious relationships.

KNOWLEDGE ON THE CUTTING EDGE

Putting It in Context: Communication, Sex, and Perception

Study the "standard" configuration of blocks below. Can you ascertain which circle of "responses" is identical to the standard configuration that appears at the left? (The answer is written upside-down at the end of this box.)

This mental rotation test of spatial ability has been used to study differences in perceptual ability between females and males. Researchers cite sex hormones such as testosterone as the most important factor that contributes to differential perceptual-cognitive abilities between females and males. Males typically perform better than females in perceptual tests in which they are required to imagine rotating or manipulating an object in some way, such as this mental rotation test. Males also tend to outperform females in tests that require navigating through a route and in tests such as guiding or intercepting projectiles. Such differences in perceptual ability are manifested as early as three years of age. For example, studies illustrate that male three- and four-year-olds are better at targeting and mentally rotating figures embedded within clock faces than are girls of the same age. On the other hand, females are better at perceptual tests that entail identifying matching items and performing certain manual tasks that require precision. Females also outperform males in terms of perceiving and recalling landmarks. Researchers conclude that females tend to use landmarks to orient themselves in terms of location more than men do.

Evolutionary psychologists suggest that we must look beyond modern life to understand differences in female-male perceptual ability. Evolutionary history indicates that 50,000 or more years ago, females gathered food, tended the home, and cared for children. Males hunted and scavenged for food, created and used weapons, and defended a group from enemies and predators. Such role specialization could have put different selection pressures on females and males. In other words, the survival of our ancestral mothers was enhanced by their memory of the location of home and family, a legacy that continues today in females' superior ability to perceive landmarks. Similarly, skills in navigating with three-dimensional space could have helped our ancestral fathers track and kill prey, a legacy that lives on in males' superior ability in target-directed motor skills.

Exposure to male hormones during the prenatal period tends to enhance spatial-perceptual abilities. However, sex differences in perception vary from slight to large, and females and males tend to overlap enormously on many perceptual tests. On the other hand, large differences in spatial-perceptual ability between females and males do exist, specifically in males' high ability to engage in visual-spatial targeting.[25]

Standard

Responses

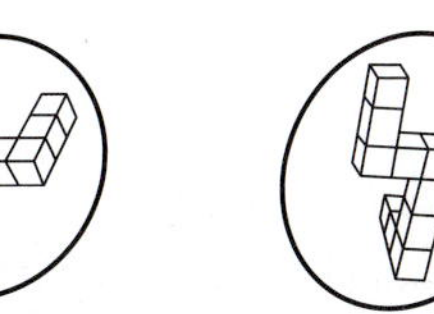

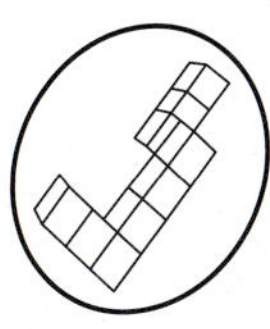

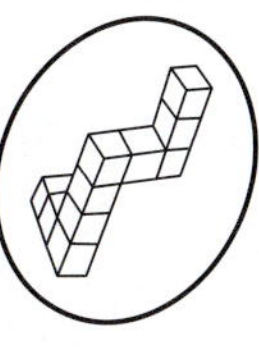

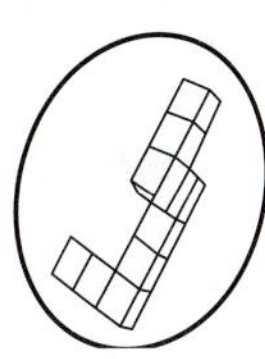

Answer to the mental rotation test: the first and fourth responses are identical to the standard configuration.

Source: Used with permission of Ammons Scientific Ltd. from Mental rotations, a group test of three-dimensional spatial visualization by S. G. Vandenberg and A. R. Kuse. *Perceptual and Motor Skills*, 47, 599–604, 1978.

Individual Context

The context of the self or the individual context also affects perception. Specifically, our physiology and self-concept influence our perception.

Physiology Our physiology, including our senses, health, fatigue, and hunger, influences the perception process. Has a family member ever told you to turn down the volume on your radio, CD player, or TV? Did you respond that the volume was set at just the right level, and it wasn't too loud? Have you ever mentioned that a food was too spicy for you to eat? Did your partner respond that the food wasn't all that spicy? Can you remember a

Perspective taking can help us perceive the world as others perceive it.

time when you had difficulty concentrating on your professor's comments because you had skipped breakfast, were tired, or weren't feeling well? Individual physiological factors such as the senses, health, fatigue, and hunger can affect perception.

Self-Concept In addition to physiology, our self-concept affects how we perceive reality. The self-concept refers to perceptions that we hold about ourselves, a topic that is discussed in depth in Chapter 3. For example, people who perceive themselves as lovable and others as trustworthy perceive others and relationships in positive ways. In contrast, people who perceive themselves and others as unlovable and unloving may perceive relationships as harmful and potentially dangerous.[26] Additionally, persons with high self-esteem tend to have high opinions of others, and those with low self-esteem typically have low opinions of others.[27]

Contexts and Improving Communication Competence

How can engaging in perspective taking improve our communication competence?

One way we can understand how contexts influence others' realities is to engage in perspective taking. **Perspective taking** occurs when we use our imagination to "walk in another's shoes" and perceive the world as others perceive it. Perspective taking can also improve our motivation to communicate competently by understanding how others perceive effective and appropriate communication. For example, suppose we conclude that our parents are overprotective and unreasonable because they won't let us attend an out-of-town party. We can put ourselves in their place and perhaps now perceive that our parents' restriction is motivated by love and concern; they worry about the late hour, alcohol consumption, and impaired driving. Although we may still be angry that our parents deny us the opportunity to attend the party, we now understand where they're coming from. Because we understand the assumptions underlying their restriction, we may be more open to future communication with our parents. The "Non Sequitur" comic also illustrates how perspective taking can help us perceive how others view the world. Danae learns that her horse Lucy perceives that pulling a buggy isn't "fun" when she puts herself in Lucy's place. In general, "the more people understand each other's point of view and inner experience, the better they can accept and adjust to each other."[28] Perspective taking can potentially reduce our social anxiety when we communicate with others who perceive the world differently than we do. Perspective taking can also help us perceive as personally rewarding our interactions with those who hold both similar and different perceptions.

MOTIVATION & mindwork • Walk a Mile in My Shoes

Think about a disagreement you have had with a conversation partner such as a family member, coworker, friend, or classmate. The disagreement need not be of major importance; perhaps you disagreed about a course of action, an opinion about a person or event, or a particular belief. Attempt to take the perspective of your conversation partner; that is, imagine yourself in her or his place within the culture, relationship, gender, and/or individual contexts to temporarily perceive the disagreement from her or his perspective. When you are finished, consider whether perspective taking provided you with a better understanding of why your conversation partner's perceptions differed from your own. How can perspective taking help you deal with any future disagreements you may have with others?

OVERCOMING COMMUNICATION CHALLENGES

Stereotyping and Prejudice

Even someone who is perceived as an extremely competent communicator may find herself or himself in situations in which the interaction may be potentially dysfunctional and distressing. Interestingly, those aspects of communication that are typically perceived to be positive may also have destructive forms and applications. For example, although honesty is considered moral, it can also be destructive and embarrassing. Similarly, although empathic listening is considered to be a competent form of communication, the empathic individual may experience emotional distress when others communicate their problems. Moreover, incompetent communication can result when any behavior is used in the extreme. For example, although compliments are generally viewed as a competent form of communication, they may be perceived as attempts at ingratiation or manipulation if used too often. Reading about communication that is difficult and problematic and learning how to cope with such communication will enable us to understand how people function effectively in everyday conversation.[29]

Stereotyping and holding prejudiced feelings about others may stem from our perceptions and our need to classify and organize the stimuli we attend to. Unfortunately, stereotyping and prejudice may result in dysfunctional, distressing, and potentially destructive consequences. Fortunately, we can learn to minimize the human tendency to engage in stereotypic and prejudicial perceptions.

Stereotyping

Fill in the blanks: "All (include a type of person) _______ are (include an adjective) _______." Can you come up with one or more groups of people and adjectives to fill in the blanks? "All _______ are _______" is an example of a stereotype. **Stereotypes** are generalizations that are often based on only a few perceived characteristics. It doesn't matter if the characteristics are accurate or inaccurate or whether they are positive or negative; stereotyping ignores individual differences and places people in particular groups. Stereotypes occur because we need to quickly organize and remember information that we might need to achieve our goals in our daily lives. But because stereotypes ignore individual differences, they contribute to perceptual inaccuracies.

Competence & Critical Thinking

mycommunicationlab

THE SAGA OF SUSAN AND JUAN AND PERCEPTION

Susan and Juan have just finished Thanksgiving dinner at Susan's home. Juan met Susan's parents for the first time during the dinner. Susan and Juan appear to have different perceptions about her parents' comments and the success of the evening overall.

You can view *The Saga of Susan and Juan* by accessing the "Small Group and Interpersonal Videos" on the "MyCommunicationLab" Web site. Answer the following questions about Susan and Juan's perceptions:

- How do Susan and Juan's perceptions differ regarding her parents' reactions to Juan's employment status?
- How might the various contexts that influence communication affect Susan and Juan's perceptions of her father's comments and the outcome of the evening overall?
- How might perspective taking have helped Susan and Juan during the Thanksgiving dinner and during their conversation afterward?
- Do you think that Susan and Juan communicated in a competent manner as they attempted to resolve the situation? Explain.
- Could perception checking have helped Susan and Juan engage in competent communication? Create a perception check that may have facilitated their interaction.

SUSAN: Oh, I'm so happy with how tonight went. Oh, it was wonderful. If, you know, I was a little nervous going into it, but I think it was beautiful. It was a beautiful Thanksgiving. Wasn't it?

JUAN: I have a headache.

SUSAN: Well, do you think you had too much wine? I mean, when I drink wine I get a headache. But I guess maybe it could have been something in the food? My mother spices the turkey so much. Juan, actually, you know what, don't do any more. Don't help me clean up. No, go sit down, relax, I'll get you some aspirin. I'm sure . . .

JUAN: No, I don't—I don't really need aspirin. I just . . .

SUSAN: You know, you're just like my dad. Go on, go sit, relax a bit, and I'll get you . . .

JUAN: Let me—let me just . . .

SUSAN: Some aspirin. I'm sure he has an aspirin for you.

JUAN: Let me ask you one thing. I mean, what's up with your dad?

SUSAN: What do you mean, what's up with him?

JUAN: I just, you know, I felt like he was asking me so many questions, and—and—and . . .

SUSAN: Well, he's interested in your life.

JUAN: Oh, yeah. That—that—that I . . .

SUSAN: Same as my mom, you know.

JUAN: Yeah. I was just don't understanding his questions about work. I mean, does—did you talk to them about me and my job and my job situation?

SUSAN: Well, I mean, I told him that you were looking for a job, a new job, yeah.

JUAN: Yeah, but it didn't sound like he was concerned about finding me a job, but more about why don't I have a job anymore. I mean, did you tell him I was laid off? I mean . . .

SUSAN: No, I'm sure I didn't tell them that you were out of a job, I just told him that you were looking for a new position.

JUAN: But why? I mean, why would . . .

SUSAN: Because it just comes up in natural conversation. That's what you're spending most of your time doing. I mean, I didn't think it was something that I had to run by you, to tell them that you were looking for a new position. I mean . . .

JUAN: It would be nice. It's the first time I meet your parents, you know? I'm—I'm here visiting, trying to meet the parents of the woman that I'm spending time with. And suddenly I get grilled by your father, just knowing that I don't have a job. That's not a good first impression, trust me. Not in any book.

SUSAN: You made a fine first impression on my parents. I'm sure he was just making conversation. I mean, my father is—is—is sweet. And, I mean, I know he's opinionated, but he's kind, and he liked you. And my mother, oh, my mother loved you. My mother—what? What about my mother?

JUAN: I don't know. I just . . . I—I—I didn't felt quite embraced when I was only asked about my job and my . . .

SUSAN: I mean, that's the most important thing that's happening to you right now, your looking for your job. When I shared that with my family, I didn't share it with them saying that you were out of work. I just shared it that you were looking for a new job, which is great. And you'll find one.

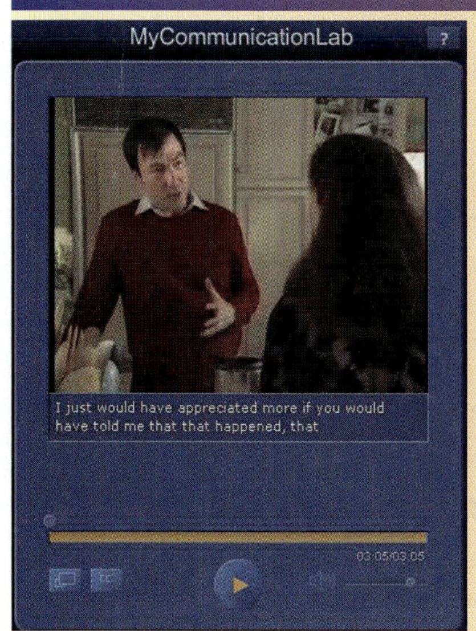

JUAN: I just would have appreciated more if you would have told me that that happened, that that conversation went through, because I just want to know how much do they know about us? I mean, I just—we've been together for two months, and he already knows I don't have a job? I mean . . .

SUSAN: Well, now he doesn't know that you don't have a job, he knows that you're looking for a job. There's a difference. I didn't tell them that you were out of work.

JUAN: I just don't . . .

SUSAN: I mean, I'm sorry. If I—if I had known that that would have put you in a difficult position, I wouldn't have told them. Juan, my family is important to me, but you're . . .

JUAN: I just—I just want to make sure that in order for us to have a healthy relationship, we just need to talk about what's going on with us, just you and me, before we mention anything that's going on with us to anybody else. That's all . . .

SUSAN: All right.

JUAN: . . . I'm asking.

You may be thinking, "I just read that the second step in the perception process is 'organization' and that we can organize on the basis of schemas. Isn't that a form of stereotyping?" The difference between "organizing" and "stereotyping" is that stereotypes are exaggerated generalizations. They may be based on partial truths, but they may also include beliefs that go beyond the facts. For example, the stereotypes "all men are pigs" or "all blondes are dumb" obviously go beyond the facts and leave no room for individual differences. Furthermore, "careful generalizations" (such as the schema example mentioned earlier in this chapter about young children having short attention spans) point out the possibility of individual differences. However, we typically don't consciously consider individual differences when we stereotype.[30] Unfortunately, without our realizing it, stereotyping can blind us to the unique attributes and perceptions of a person and to the diversity and variety of people within a culture.

KNOWLEDGE power • All ______ are ______?

Think about the group(s) to which you belong (e.g., cultural, ethnic, and racial groups; sexual orientation; religion, age, physical characteristics, appearance) and some characteristics that might be stereotypically assigned to your group(s). With a partner or in a group, discuss whether the stereotypes are inaccurate or accurate and whether they apply to you. Would you resent being stereotyped on the basis of the identified characteristics? When you are finished, consider whether you have ever stereotyped others on the basis of their culture, religion, sex, age, physical characteristics, or appearance. Are your stereotypes based on what you have learned from friends and family, from minimal experiences with groups of individuals, and/or from the media? Do you believe that others would resent being stereotyped on the basis of characteristics that you have identified? Could your stereotypes of others be just as inaccurate as the stereotypes of the group(s) you are part of?

Prejudice

Prejudice can be defined as a negative feeling toward and rejection of others who are not members of our group(s). Prejudice is based on stereotyping and is a fairly common phenomenon. Prejudiced perceptions are based on faulty and inflexible generalizations and include irrational feelings of dislike, biased perceptions, and even hatred for members of "out-groups." We tend to hold prejudices because they may lead to social rewards such as being accepted and liked by our own "in-groups." Our prejudice may stem from the need to feel positive about our in-group(s) and to protect our in-group(s) from real or perceived threats. For example, suppose we are not accepted into the college of our choice. It may be easier to blame affirmative action policies for the rejection rather than admit that our scholastic background, extracurricular activities, test scores, and personal essay may be deficient.

Minimizing Stereotypic and Prejudicial Perceptions

Table 2.2, "Techniques for Minimizing Stereotypic and Prejudicial Perceptions," summarizes the ways we can avoid the harmful effects of stereotyping and prejudice. We can set a goal to minimize stereotypic and prejudicial perceptions by revising or discarding them when we discover an "exception to the rule"; we should change the rule instead of declaring an exception.[31] We can also use clarifying terms such as "often," "sometimes," and "generally" when talking about groups of people. In sum, when we become consciously aware that we may be thinking about people based on a stereotype or prejudice, we will be "less likely to put others at a disadvantage based solely on a label that can be attached to them."[32] Another method to reduce the harmful effects of stereotyping and prejudiced perceptions is to engage in "equal-status contact," which refers to individuals of different ethnicities, races, and religions who come together as equals to improve intergroup relations and communication. Research demonstrates that if we learn to communicate with individuals who are different from ourselves, we may realize that our stereotyped and/or prejudiced perceptions are no longer useful. This results when our preexisting categories are challenged continuously and in many different ways.[33] Learning about the contexts that affect others and engaging in perspective taking can also reduce the negative results of stereotyping and prejudiced perceptions. Still, changing our stereotypes and prejudiced perceptions is a lifelong process, and we shouldn't expect change overnight.[34]

Table 2.2: Techniques for Minimizing Stereotypic and Prejudicial Perceptions

- Revise or discard stereotypes when we discover an "exception to the rule."
- Use clarifying terms such as "often," "sometimes," and "generally" when talking about groups of people.
- Engage in "equal-status contact" between individuals of different ethnicities, races, and religions.
- Learn about the contexts that affect others.
- Engage in perspective taking.
- Remember that changing our stereotypes and prejudiced perceptions takes time; we shouldn't expect change overnight.

A CASE STUDY IN ETHICS

The Phantom Blogger

Competent communication includes an ethical dimension of well-based standards of right and wrong. Recall from Chapter 1 that a systematic approach to dealing with everyday ethical behavior involves asking a series of questions: Have I practiced any virtues today (e.g., integrity, trustworthiness, honesty, responsibility)? Have I done more good than harm today? Have I treated people with dignity and respect? Have I been fair and just today? Have I made my community stronger because of my actions? You probably now realize that the answers to these questions depend on your subjective perception of reality, that is, what you perceive to be virtuous, beneficial, and respectful. Read the following and consider whether you perceive the SMU professor to have acted in an ethical manner.

Southern Methodist University students became increasingly concerned when an anonymous blogger wrote about conversations students had with an unidentified professor. The unnamed university resembled SMU, and the characterizations of the professor's students were insulting. Phantomprof .blogspot.com included perceptions about the high incidence of eating disorders on campus and about wealthy students who attended the university to obtain a "Mrs. Degree." The blog also offered statements that students uttered in the professor's office during one-on-one conferences:

- "I'm not spoiled! I only drive the cars my dad gives me."
- "I haven't been to your class for two weeks because my doctor diagnosed me with a disease . . . acid reflux."
- "The company offered me 30K—and with what my father gives me, that's only 60K a year. Who can live on that?"

Eventually, an adjunct professor who taught writing and ethics to communication students was unmasked as the Phantom Blogger. Shortly thereafter, the professor was informed that SMU no longer needed her services; however, the reason given was that the university was attempting to rely less on part-time faculty.

Rita Kirk, SMU's chair of corporate communications and public affairs, said that the Phantom Blogger's comments and perceptions angered parents and students and raised ethical and legal questions. Kirk suggested that students perceive private conversations with professors as confidential. Even though names on the blog had been changed, SMU officials were worried about student statements such as "The girls in my sorority house are all cokeheads" and "Is it date rape if you know the guy?"

The Phantom Blogger defended her site by saying that she never intended to embarrass anyone and that she believed that she was writing funny and odd stories about her experiences as a university instructor. However, SMU students were divided about the Phantom Blogger. One former student characterized the professor as one of her best instructors at SMU. On the other hand, the editor of the student-run newspaper perceived the instructor as a "double agent." Another student asserted that the blog exaggerated and emphasized stereotypes that didn't reflect the entire student body.

Even though the Phantom Blogger offered praise for some of her students, it was the criticism of others that caught the attention of students and administrators. The Phantom Blogger believes that some students who didn't even know her misperceived themselves as the subject of stories about exorbitant budgets for cars and clothes, athletes who could barely read, and students who routinely plagiarized. Stereotypes or not, Kirk contended that such descriptions caused problems in the classroom because students came to her and asked questions such as "Am I being judged because I have good shoes?"

The Phantom Blogger incident started discussions about whether student-professor confidentiality guidelines should be established. Kirk added that she has always been a free speech advocate but that free speech doesn't come without consequences.[35]

Do you perceive one-on-one conferences between professors and their students as confidential? Is it unethical to post on a blog comments made during private student-instructor conferences? Is your perception of the Phantom Blogger's ethics affected by the idea that she could have influenced stereotyped perceptions of SMU students? The Phantom Blogger perceived that she was merely writing "funny and odd" stories about university life. How would you perceive the stories if you thought that you were a student described in a blog post?

Chapter Review

Motivation: How has this helped me?

- **The importance of studying perception and communication**

Perception affects communication and communication affects perception. We communicate on the basis of perceptions and tend to believe that our perceptions are true reflections of reality. Competent communicators realize that although their perceptions may be accurate, they can also see the validity of others' perceptions.

- **Engaging in perspective taking can improve our communication competence**

Engaging in perspective taking to understand how the culture, relationship, gender, and individual contexts influence us to perceive the physical environment, people, and communication can help us perceive the world as others perceive it. Perspective taking can also improve our motivation to communicate competently by understanding how others perceive effective and appropriate communications.

Knowledge: What have I learned?

- **How we characterize perception**

Perception is the process of interpreting sensory information and experiences. Although people perceive the same things differently, we assume that our perceptions are true reflections of reality, and we therefore communicate on the basis of this assumption.

- **The stages involved in the perception process**

The perceptual process includes selecting stimuli from the environment, organizing the stimuli, and interpreting the stimuli. We typically select from the environment stimuli that are salient and vivid, and we organize stimuli on the basis of schemas, figure-ground, proximity, similarity, and closure. The interpretation of stimuli is influenced by both expectancy and familiarity.

- **Perceptual biases, and how they affect communication**

Selectivity, confusing fact with inference, and faulty attributions are examples of perceptual bias. We may ignore parts of a message, perceive what we want to perceive, misinterpret a message, and make incorrect interpretations of someone's personality and behavior when we communicate on the basis of perceptual bias.

- **How contexts influence perception and communication**

Cultural and co-cultural groups teach us beliefs and values that influence how we perceive "reality." The relationship context illustrates that perception is influenced by our friends, family, and occupational roles and power. The gender context illustrates that women and men tend to hold different perceptions of communication and how it functions. The individual context, which includes our physiology and self-concept, also influences our perceptions of reality.

Skill: What skills have I developed?

- **Describing sense data and perception checking can improve our communication competence**

Descriptions based on sense data (i.e., avoiding fact-inference confusion) and perception checking (describing behavior, adding one or two interpretations of the behavior, and requesting feedback about the interpretation[s]) helps us recognize that no one has a corner on the truth and that each stage in the perception process can be influenced by our own biases and perceptual errors.

Study Questions

1. How does perception relate to communication?
2. Describe and explain the three stages in the perception process.

3. Describe and explain the two types of stimuli that tend to be selected from the environment.
4. What are some of the ways we organize stimuli that we have selected from the environment?
5. Describe and explain two factors that influence interpretation.
6. In what ways does "selectivity" bias our perceptions?
7. What does it mean to confuse "fact" with "inference"?
8. What are some attributional errors that can bias perception?
9. What are the steps in a perception check?
10. How do the culture, relationship, gender, and individual contexts affect perception and communication?
11. Describe and explain stereotyping and prejudice and what we can do to minimize stereotypic and prejudicial perceptions.

Names to Know

Fritz Heider, p. 45 (1896–1988)—psychologist known as the "father of attribution theory," Heider explored the nature of human relationships. He believed that people seek explanations for the behavior of others based on their perceptions of specific situations or long-held beliefs.

Key Terms

attribution theory, 45
attributions, 45
closure, 41
disclaimers, 51
expectancy, 42
fact, 44
familiarity, 42
figure-ground organization, 40
fundamental attribution error, 45
inference, 44
interpretation, 41
organization, 38
perception, 36
perception check, 46
perspective taking, 54
prejudice, 58
proximity, 40
salience, 38
schemas, 38
selection, 38
selective attention, 43
selective perception, 43
self-serving bias, 45
similarity, 40
stereotypes, 55
vividness, 38

CHAPTER 3

The Self-Concept and Communication

> "The real Self is not I but We."
>
> Fritz Kunkel, early-20th-century psychoanalyst

In this chapter, we will answer the following:

Motivation: How will this help me?

- It is important to study self-concept because our self-concept influences how we accept praise, defend viewpoints, and communicate our accomplishments.

Knowledge: What will I learn?

- How to characterize the self-concept
- The characteristics and components of the self-concept
- How contexts influence the self-concept

Skill: Why do I need to develop these skills?

- Facework can help save our face and the face of others
- Nondefensive reactions can improve our communication competence

Do you know someone who describes herself or himself in a negative manner? Perhaps you know someone like supermodel Tyra Banks, who maintains a positive body image and self-concept in spite of criticism about her weight. Maybe you or someone else believes the labels that others use to characterize personality, appearance, or overall ability. Do you think that others perceive you in the same manner that you perceive yourself? These related ideas concern our self-concept and how it is formed.

No matter how we perceive ourselves or how others perceive us, our self-concept is inextricably entwined with communication. In this chapter, we will learn that understanding how the self-concept affects communication can motivate us to communicate competently. Creating realistic goal statements and constructing a mental inventory of our strengths and talents can also increase our motivation to communicate in a competent manner. In addition, we will increase our knowledge by learning about characteristics of the self-concept, defensive and nondefensive communication, and the problems associated with inflated self-esteem. Finally, we will learn how to communicate competently by using face-saving and nondefensive messages.

Introduction to the Self-Concept

If you could describe yourself in one word, which word would you choose? Can you select a single dominant personality trait, belief, and/or role to adequately describe how you perceive yourself? Perhaps you believe that it's impossible to characterize who you are with one noun or adjective and that many words are needed to describe who you really are. You may see your self-concept as multidimensional and therefore need to use a variety of descriptors to characterize how you perceive yourself. Think about how you might describe yourself to others as you read the next section about the conceptualization of the self-concept and why it's important to study the self-concept as it relates to communication. Similarly, consider the people in your life who have influenced and continue to influence how you perceive yourself. Focus on their communication about you and ask yourself if your communication may have similarly contributed to how others see themselves.

How can we characterize the self-concept?

Characterization of the Self-Concept

Quite simply, **self-concept** refers to how we perceive ourselves. Communication scholars contend that our self-concept is formed, sustained, and changed by our interactions with others.[1] This means that the self-concept is primarily a social phenomenon that is influenced by our relationships. Consider the people in your life who have shaped the way you perceive yourself: how have their comments affected your self-concept? Of course, just as others affect our self-concept, our communication can significantly influence the self-concept of others. Even a comment not intended to affect a person's sense of self, such as a mild put-down said as a joke, can have an impact on her or his self-concept. However, it may be impossible to say that the formation of the self is entirely social because research suggests that biologically influenced personality traits are a major component of our self-concept.[2] Five general clusters of traits labeled the "Big Five" can influence our self-concept:

1. extroverted vs. introverted
2. agreeable vs. antagonistic
3. open vs. not open
4. neurotic vs. stable
5. conscientious vs. undirected

Included within the clusters are specific personality traits for which people may be "hardwired." These traits include sociability, spontaneity, selflessness, selfishness, independence, curiosity, vulnerability, and carelessness.[3]

The Formation and Development of the Self-Concept

Our culture(s), relationships, our gender, and our own self-talk influence the formation and development of the self-concept. The theory of **symbolic interactionism**, developed by sociologist **George Herbert Mead** in the 1920s, posits that our view of self is shaped by those with whom we communicate. Two processes, the Pygmalion effect and social comparison, strongly influence how we perceive ourselves.

The Pygmalion Effect The **Pygmalion effect** illustrates the way our **significant others** (people who are important to us) influence our self-concept. In the classic study "Pygmalion

KNOWLEDGE ON THE CUTTING EDGE

Communication, Self-Concept, and Civil Discourse: Are You a Civil Communicator?

Some scholars suggest that there may be a connection between uncivil discourse and words used to describe the self. These scholars contend that today's "vocabulary of the self" reflects the overemphasis on individualism as a societal value and is devoid of responsibility and accountability. Words such as *self-expression, self-assertion, self-realization, self-approval,* and *self-acceptance* are favored more than words such as *self-denial, self-discipline, self-control, self-reproach,* and *self-sacrifice.*[4] This vocabulary implies that "the old ethic of self-discipline has given way to a new ethic of self-esteem and self-expression. This has endangered the practice of traditional civility."[5]

Roy F. Baumeister, a leading researcher in the area of self-esteem, recommends a shift in focus from "self-esteem" to "self-control and self-discipline" to truly benefit self and society.[6] This doesn't mean that we must restrict our everyday behaviors or that we must eliminate self-expression. However, it does mean that we should realize that everything we want to express may not be worthy of expression. It also means that "we can choose to express one part of ourselves rather than another. Although it may appear that we give up self-expression when we exercise [civility], in truth, restraint can be as much an expression of our Selves as is unfettered behavior."[7]

The emphasis on "the self" in Western culture has contributed to the increase in uncivil communication.

in the Classroom," psychologists Robert Rosenthal and Lenore Jacobson describe an experiment in which certain teachers had been informed that they had exceptionally intelligent students. In reality, the students who were identified as exceptional were no different than any other student in their grade. At the end of the school year, the students who were described as extremely bright actually did perform at a high level and even improved their IQ scores. The researchers concluded that these children performed well because of their teachers' expectations. The teachers communicated their high expectations to their students by providing them with extra verbal and nonverbal reinforcement. Furthermore, the teachers didn't react negatively when their students answered questions incorrectly. The teachers directly and indirectly communicated to their students that they were high achievers, and the students actually came to believe that they were high achievers. In other words, the expectations of their teachers influenced the students' self-concepts.[8]

Social Comparison Our self-concept is also influenced when we engage in **social comparison** with others. Comparing our athletic ability or relational success to others is an example of social comparison, as is asking classmates about their scores on a test. These examples illustrate that social comparison provides us with knowledge about ourselves in terms of how we measure up to others.[9] Recent research illustrates that social comparison is an important determinant of self-perception in Western cultures. Specifically, we tend to respond negatively when others perform better than we do on a consequential task, even when we receive positive feedback about our above-average performance. We compensate by comparing ourselves with people who perform with average ability and subsequently evaluate ourselves much higher than we evaluate the average performers.[10] For example, we may be dissatisfied when we receive a "B" on an important test because we know that classmates received an "A." However, it's probable that we'll also compare ourselves with classmates who receive a "C" and decide that we really performed much better on the test than those who received the average scores.

Why It's Important to Study Self-Concept

Just as communication affects our self-concept, our self-concept affects how we communicate with others. Our self-concept can be placed on a continuum that ranges from "healthy" or "strong" to "unhealthy" or "poor." Healthy self-concepts can result in a realistic acknowledgment of our strengths and weaknesses, and therefore we may accept praise and defend viewpoints even when opposed by others. Unhealthy self-concepts can result in exaggerated and unrealistic perceptions of our strengths and weaknesses, and therefore we may[11]

Why is it important to study the self-concept?

- downplay our strengths
- exaggerate our accomplishments
- fail to value our successes
- expect others to perceive us negatively

Such individuals may be overly self-critical because it may be easier and less painful to criticize oneself than to hear the criticism of others. People who have an unhealthy self-concept may also boast about their accomplishments to mask feelings of insecurity and inadequacy.[12] In all, knowledge about the relationship between the self-concept and interpersonal communication can motivate us to communicate in a competent manner.[13]

Creating realistic goal statements designed to improve our self-concept can increase our motivation to communicate. It's important to remember that our self-concept isn't formed in an instant, and neither can it change in an instant. Therefore, we must set realistic goals

KNOWLEDGE power • "You're Just Saying That to Make Me Feel Better!"

Although you may think you reply to compliments, defend opinions, and communicate about your accomplishments in a competent manner, it is important to remember that communication competence is an impression based on others' perceptions. To gain insight about how your self-concept may affect your communication, ask a minimum of three trusted friends and/or family members for an honest appraisal of how you communicate in terms of praise, opposing viewpoints, and accomplishments. Ask for specific examples regarding the topic of the interactions and what and how you communicated. You may be surprised at what you learn.

Figure 3.1: Setting Realistic Goal Statements

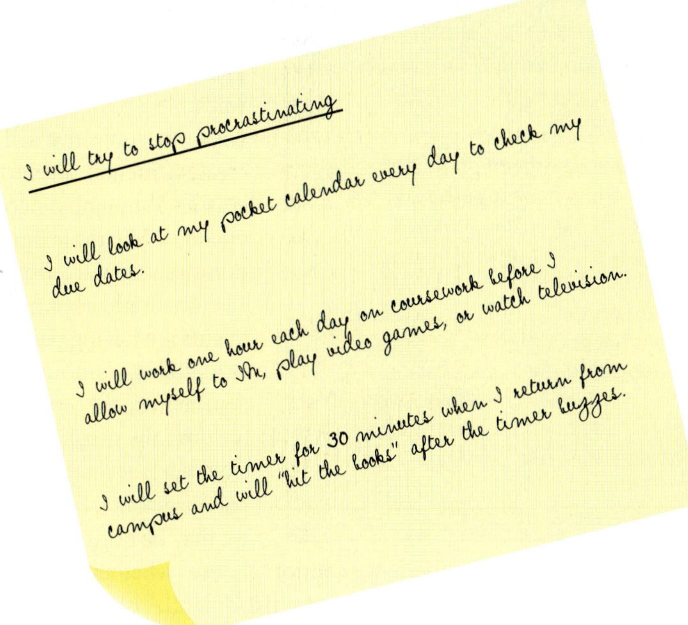

for ourselves and not mentally beat ourselves up if we don't meet them. An example of an unrealistic goal is "I will be a confident communicator in all situations and will never let my nerves get the best of me." A more realistic goal is "I will gain confidence and learn how to manage my anxiety so I can contribute to discussions in my communication class." And if it turns out that we do lack confidence and experience anxiety while engaged in class discussion, we need to give ourselves a break; we will have many more opportunities to work on this specific aspect of our self-concept. Figure 3.1, "Setting Realistic Goal Statements," illustrates additional examples of realistic goal statements.

MOTIVATION & mindwork • I Want to Change . . .

Are there any characteristics associated with your self-concept that you wish to change? Choose one aspect of your self-concept that you would like to alter. Your choices need not be monumental; for example, you may wish to change your perception of yourself as a procrastinator. Write two or three realistic and manageable goal statements regarding the aspect of your self-concept that you desire to change. Examples of "procrastination" goal statements are "I will work on an assignment each day for fifteen minutes until it is complete" and "I will create a 'computer curfew' so I can spend most of the night studying." Discuss your goal statements with your classmates and ask for feedback about their realism and practicality. Remember these goal statements when you find yourself beginning to exhibit the aspect of your self-concept that you want to change. Read your goal statement(s) daily, don't give up, and soon you may find that you have successfully altered for the better a behavior associated with your self-concept.

MOTIVATION & mindwork • I'm Not So Bad After All!

Take a moment or two to think about your talents. In what areas do you excel or believe that you may be naturally gifted? Are you artistic, athletic, musical, or mechanical? Have you always been good at math? Can you easily take objects apart and put them back together? What other talents do you possess? Take a sheet of paper, fold it in half, and create a list of talents on the left-hand side of the page. Similarly, refer to the "Your Personal Strengths" table for a list of twenty-four strengths. Think about your strengths and list them on the right-hand side of the page. You can also learn which strengths are your highest personal strengths or "signature strengths" by accessing the 240-question VIA Signature Strengths Questionnaire at www.authentichappiness.org. Review your talents and strengths when you have a low day or when someone's criticism is especially hurtful. You'll realize that you're not so bad after all!

Another reason why it's important to study our self-concept concerns how we perceive ourselves. We tend to perceive ourselves subjectively and often in a more negative light than is warranted. One method to contend with our subjective self-concept is to create a mental inventory of our talents and strengths. According to psychologist **Martin Seligman**, talents are nonmoral characteristics that are usually innate and automatic. Examples of talents are having perfect pitch or athletic ability. Although talents can be augmented, the improvements made are typically small. Strengths are moral traits such as integrity, valor, kindness, and originality. For example, although we may be born with the talent to recognize musical notes when we hear them, we cannot "choose" whether or not to have perfect pitch. However, we can choose to be courageous, original, or kind. Listed in Table 3.1, "Your Personal Strengths," are the twenty-four strengths identified by Seligman. We can develop these

Table 3.1 Your Personal Strengths

Virtue Cluster	Strengths
Wisdom and Knowledge	Curiosity/Interest in the World; Love of Learning; Judgment/Critical Thinking/Open-Mindedness; Ingenuity/Originality/Practical Intelligence/Street Smarts; Social Intelligence/Personal Intelligence/Emotional Intelligence; Perspective
Courage	Valor and Bravery; Perseverance/Industry/Diligence; Integrity/Genuineness/Honesty
Humanity and Love	Kindness and Generosity; Loving and Allowing Oneself to Be Loved
Justice	Citizenship/Duty/Teamwork/Loyalty; Fairness and Equity; Leadership
Temperance	Self-Control; Prudence/Discretion/Caution; Humility and Modesty
Transcendence	Appreciation of Beauty and Excellence; Gratitude; Hope/Optimism/Future-Mindedness; Spirituality/Sense of Purpose/Faith/Religiousness; Forgiveness and Mercy; Playfulness and Humor; Zest/Passion/Enthusiasm

Source: Martin E. P. Seligman, PhD. Professor of Psychology, University of Pennsylvania. Reprinted with permission.

strengths with practice and dedication; unlike talents, they involve choices about acquisition, usage, and enhancement.[14]

Characteristics and Components of the Self-Concept

Our self-concept is affected by the characteristics we believe we possess and has many components. Characteristics and components associated with the self-concept include self-image and self-esteem, its multidimensional nature, the relationship between self-concept and self-disclosure, and its subjective character.

Self-Image and Self-Esteem

What are the characteristics and components of the self-concept?

Take a look at Figure 3.2, "The Self-Concept." This figure illustrates the idea that aspects of our self-concept can be organized according to our beliefs and evaluations about ourselves and the contexts that influence us. At the beginning of this chapter, *self-concept* was defined as how we perceive ourselves. Our self-concept is affected by the characteristics we believe we possess (e.g., strengths and weaknesses, personality traits) and how we evaluate these characteristics. Our self-concept, located on the top of the hierarchy, is made up of self-image and self-esteem, which are located directly underneath.

Self-Image The **self-image** is a descriptive term; it refers to the characteristics we believe we possess. Our self-image may include the roles we perceive we inhabit, the words we use when we describe ourselves, and how we believe others perceive us. For example, if you describe yourself as a student who does volunteer work and who is looking for a mate, you have communicated several aspects of your self-image (the roles of student, giving citizen, and someone who desires a relationship). Our self-image also involves how others see us. We use other people's comments to check our self-perceptions, and they reinforce or change the perception of what and who we are. For instance, you may perceive yourself as someone who is unselfish and generous. However, this self-perception may change when a

Figure 3.2: The Self-Concept

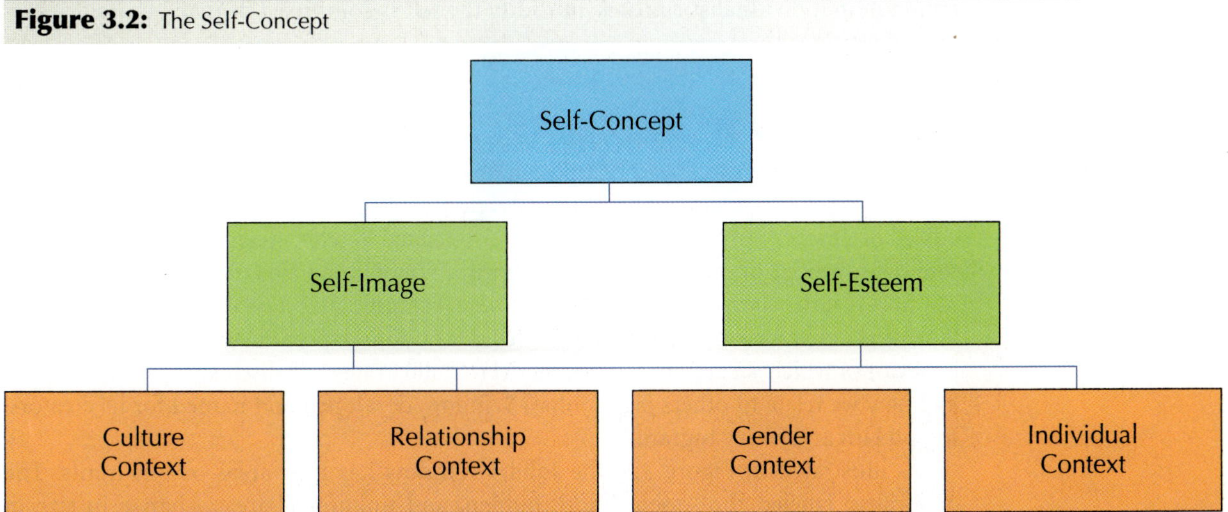

KNOWLEDGE power • Do You Like Yourself?

Do you have a healthy sense of self-worth? You can assess your level of self-esteem by taking the thirty-question revised self-esteem test at www.psychtests.com/tests/personality/self_esteem_r_access.html. After obtaining the results of your assessment, consider whether you may need to revise those aspects of the self you consider to be worthwhile.

coworker mentions the volunteer work he does or the charities to which she donates.

Self-Esteem **Self-esteem,** on the other hand, is evaluative; it depends on what we perceive to be worthwhile and/or valuable. In other words, self-esteem goes beyond our self-image to include the value or importance we place on our perceived characteristics. For example, based on quite a few gutter balls, you may perceive that your bowling ability is poor. However, this belief may be an inconsequential component of your self-concept. It may be that your perceived weakness is not that important to you and doesn't negatively affect your overall self-concept. In addition, you may believe that you are a sensitive and kind person (self-image) and that sensitivity and kindness are valuable and worthwhile characteristics to possess (self-esteem). In this instance, your belief about yourself and your positive evaluation of that belief are likely to contribute to a healthy self-concept.

Perceived as Multidimensional

Even though people tend to view the self in terms of a gestalt or whole, theorists suggest that it has many components. The self-concept can be simultaneously perceived as mental and physical and as private and public.[15] Our mental self may be composed of perceptions of how intelligent we are and what we assume our strengths to be. Our physical self may include perceptions of our body and how physically attractive we think we are. Our private self may include perceptions of self that we do not readily disclose to others; for example, we perceive ourselves to be overly cynical or unemotional. Our public self may include those aspects of the self that we desire others to perceive, such as that we have a nice personality and enjoy having fun. Other components of self include personality characteristics, social roles, and our moral principles. Although the self-concept is multidimensional, some people believe that there is a stable and resilient "true self" that underlies all of our other "selves." Although the idea of a true self or "real self" as a single entity is common in individualist cultures, in reality the self is comprised of many characteristics and perceptions.[16]

Influenced by Self-Disclosure

Self-disclosure refers to the act of willingly sharing information about ourselves to others. Not only is self-disclosure related to the development of interpersonal relationships (discussed in Chapter 10) but self-disclosure is also related to self-perceptions. We may choose to disclose aspects of our self-concept to family members and close friends that we choose not to reveal to others. Their reactions, in turn, can influence how we perceive ourselves. Similarly, conversation partners may inform us about aspects of our self-concept and behavior of which we are unaware. A model that illustrates self-disclosure, self-awareness, and how we relate to others is the Johari Window, developed and named for its creators, Joseph Luft and Harry Ingram.[17]

As illustrated in Figure 3.3, the **Johari Window** has four areas or quadrants. The quadrants, labeled the "open, blind, hidden, and unknown" areas, change in size in terms of what, how much, or how little we disclose about the self and what, how much, or how little we know about the self in relation to others.

Figure 3.3: The Johari Window

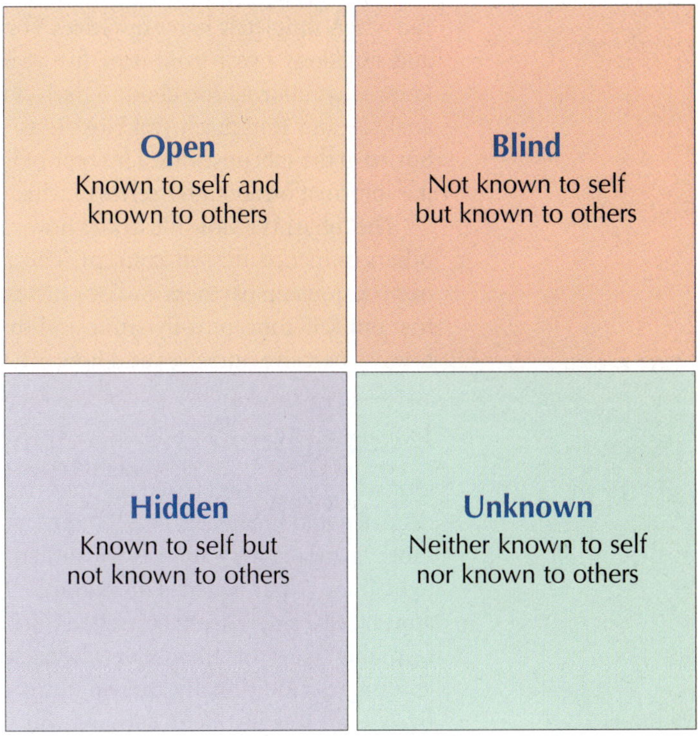

Open Known to self and known to others	**Blind** Not known to self but known to others
Hidden Known to self but not known to others	**Unknown** Neither known to self nor known to others

Source: Luft, J. *Group Processes: An Introduction to Group Dynamics,* 3E © 1984, printed with permission from The McGraw-Hill Companies, Inc.

The Open Quadrant The **open quadrant** includes information about ourselves that we and others know. This information can be anything that we reveal to others, such as how old we are or what we do for a living. If asked to draw our Johari Window as it relates to our best friend, we will probably draw a large open quadrant because we probably self-disclose to our best friend. However, if we are asked to draw a Johari Window as it relates to an acquaintance, the open quadrant will be relatively small.

The Blind Quadrant The **blind quadrant** includes information about ourselves that we don't know but others do. For example, has anyone ever pointed out a habit about which you were unaware? Maybe you were told that you crack your knuckles, bite your lip, or fidget with a pen when you are nervous. Similarly, maybe you are unaware that the self you present to others is perceived as somewhat immature because you pepper your conversations with "y'know," "like," and "uhm." This area also includes information and judgments of our personality about which we are unaware. You are probably familiar with the use of the word *but* in a phrase such as "I hate to tell you this, *but*. . . ." You know that the information following the "but" is not going to be complimentary. If this information is about your personality ("sometimes you think you're funny but you really come off as obnoxious") or behavior ("I think you're too tough on your girlfriend or boyfriend"), it belongs in the blind area, because it is information about yourself that you don't know but others do. The more we become self-aware and learn how others perceive us, the more we can shrink our blind quadrant.

The Hidden Quadrant The **hidden quadrant** includes information about ourselves that we know but that others do not. Can you think of a secret that you haven't told anyone? This secret need not be deep and dark; maybe there's some information about yourself that you haven't shared with others because the need to share hasn't arisen. For example, you may be allergic to orange juice, you may believe that Beethoven composed the best classical music, or you may have punched a sibling when you were a child. Are these disclosures appropriate in your typical, everyday conversations? Probably not. This type of self-information rests in the hidden quadrant, because it is information about yourself of which you are aware but others are not. Once again, if asked to draw our Johari Window as it relates to our best friend, we will probably draw a small hidden quadrant because the two of us most likely engage in self-disclosure. However, if we are asked to draw a Johari Window as it relates to an acquaintance, the hidden quadrant will be fairly big.

The Unknown Quadrant The **unknown quadrant** refers to the "unknown" information about ourselves that neither we nor others know about. This area will always exist because we can never completely know ourselves. For example, we don't know how we will react to events and situations a year from now, five years from now, or a decade from now. We also don't know what information about ourselves is contained in our subconscious. Hypnosis, dream analysis, and Rorschach (inkblot) tests are methods that try to uncover self-information buried in the subconscious. This type of information rests in the unknown quadrant, because it is information about ourselves of which neither we nor others are aware.

The Johari Window illustrates how self-disclosure, self-awareness, and how we relate to others influence our self-concept. The amount and type of our self-disclosure depend on our relationship partners and our life experiences. This knowledge can help us remember that our self-concept is dynamic and that self-disclosure can provide us with insight into how we perceive ourselves and how others perceive us.

Based on Subjective Information

Our self-concept isn't based on objective sense data. It is possible for our self-concept to be distorted and incorrect. The "Luann" comic illustrates that we can perceive ourselves in a more favorable light than is warranted, or we can perceive ourselves in a more negative light than is warranted. For example, can you think of musicians or movie stars who appear self-centered and conceited during interviews? These people may possess an overly favorable view of themselves because they believe the ingratiating praise of their entourages. Additionally, can you think of a time when you perceived yourself more negatively than was justified? Perhaps you received a speeding ticket, got a bad grade on an assignment, or burned a meal. If your self-talk consisted of messages such as "I always mess up!" or "There I go again!" you probably exaggerated the seriousness of the event and the frequency with which you experience these situations. Everyone has down days, but some people continually view themselves in an unrealistically harsh manner, which can influence how they communicate with and interpret the communication of others.

Our self-concept may be distorted and incorrect.

Source: LUANN: © GEC Inc./Dist. By United Feature Syndicates, Inc.

The "Face" We Present to Others

Motivation
Knowledge
Skill
COMPETENCE

Face not only relates to our perceived self-concept but also involves how we want others to perceive us and our worth.[18] Also labeled "impression management" or "identity management," face is additionally concerned with behaviors we enact to influence others to perceive us in certain ways.[19] If we desire to present a "casual" face, we can purposefully wear jeans and sneakers and say "hi ya" when meeting people for the first time. On the other hand, if we desire to present a "professional" face, we can purposefully wear a suit and say "pleased to meet you." Sociologist **Erving Goffman** suggested that the creation of our identity or face is a collaborative process that involves ourselves and our conversation partners. Goffman contended that everyday life is similar to a performance in which we adopt roles in public by putting on a face. He believed that we use conversation to create identity bids (e.g., "I am a polite person" or "I am an intelligent person"), which may or may not be accepted by others.[20] However, face-to-face conversation isn't the only way that our identities are formed, sustained, and/or changed. Face is also related to the image of self that is presented on the Internet. Have you ever typed your name into a search engine and reviewed the results? This may be an important way to manage our public face because part of the modern-day hiring process is a Web search on prospective employees. In addition to studying personal Web sites, corporate recruiters are increasingly investigating job applicants on social networking sites (SNS) such as MySpace, Xanga, and Facebook. The information on networking sites provides employers with information about a job applicant's judgment and often presents recruiters with red flags. For example, comments posted about alcohol consumption and sex can make potential employees look immature and unprofessional and suggest values at odds with those of a corporation.[21] Although people who use SNS are increasingly aware of the danger of posting personal information, recent research suggests that college students are not concerned about future employers who may view their profile. Students are more concerned about being visible and are therefore motivated to reveal personal aspects of their self-concept on SNS.

How can using facework help save our face and the face of others?

What happens when our public image is threatened or proven to be false? Embarrassment and shame may be the result of losing face, which occurs when our desired social identity or self-concept is disconfirmed. Think about a situation in which you felt guilty, embarrassed, or ashamed. Perhaps you perceive yourself to be a trustworthy person and desire this aspect of your self-concept to be perceived by others. If others discover that you have told a secret or cheated on a relational partner, your embarrassment and shame indicate that you have lost face.[22]

KNOWLEDGE power • Matching "faces"?

What aspects of the self do you portray to the public on your Web site or social networking site profile? (If you don't have a Web or networking site, create one on paper.) Consider the informality or formality of the language you use, the drawings and/or photos that you include, and other characteristics (such as likes and dislikes, accomplishments, and beliefs) that reflect who you are. Ask a classmate to analyze the Web site or social networking site profile based on these ideas, and obtain her or his feedback about the "face" you present to others. Does the face you want to present online match the face perceived by your classmate?

KNOWLEDGE ON THE CUTTING EDGE

Technology Update: Self-Concept, Identity, and Computer-Mediated Communication (CMC)

Do your self-perceptions affect how you use CMC and/or how you portray yourself online? A variety of studies have established a relationship between self-perceptions and CMC use. For example, we use the Internet primarily to obtain information rather than seek entertainment or decrease feelings of loneliness when we possess "self-concept clarity" (i.e., we hold consistent, stable, clear, and confident beliefs about ourselves). On the other hand, we may use CMC to explore different facets of the self and to experiment with different selves if we lack self-concept clarity.[23] Research also reveals that compared with persons with high self-esteem, individuals with low self-esteem prefer the use of email rather than face-to-face communication. This preference is a consequence of the anonymous and asynchronous nature of email, which allows us considerable control over our self-presentation. The preference for email communication is particularly noticeable when the risk of rejection is high, such as asking for a date or disclosing personal information. In such cases, persons with low self-esteem may use email not only to control their self-presentation but also to control the pace of interaction and the transmission of cues that indicate nervousness.[24]

Not only does our self-concept affect how we use CMC but CMC also allows us to manipulate personal identities to a greater extent than face-to-face communication or other person-to-person media. Think about the identities or roles you play in real life; your gender, race, accent, age, and other nonverbal factors allow you to adopt a limited number of roles in face-to-face communication. However, we can adopt an unlimited number of computer-mediated online identities. These identities are communicated via personal markers such as writing style, ".sig" (signature attachment), and the way we conduct ourselves with various members of chat rooms and user groups. In all, language use is extremely important in CMC use because we construct our identities through our language.[25] In addition, the way we present ourselves is extremely flexible and easy to transform in virtual environments. Users can create "avatars" or digital representations of themselves in terms of gender, age, race, class, socioeconomic background, and even species, eye color, and foot size. Research reveals that our self-representations in virtual environments influence how we behave in these environments. In particular, users who have attractive avatars tend to exhibit higher self-confidence and tend to be more friendly and extroverted than users who have unattractive avatars. Users with attractive avatars exhibit increased self-disclosure and are willing to approach opposite-gendered strangers. These findings suggest that the appearances of our avatars shape how we perceive ourselves and interact with others in digital environments.[26]

Compared with face-to-face presentation, CMC enables us to self-censor to a greater extent and manage our online identities more strategically, which provides us with a greater opportunity to misrepresent ourselves. However, in terms of an online dating environment, research suggests that CMC discourages deceptive self-presentation because of the possibility of future face-to-face communication. We therefore tend to balance our desire for self-promotion with the need for an accurate self-presentation in online dating environments. The assumption that CMC users frequently, explicitly, and intentionally lie about themselves in such environments has been found to be simplistic and inaccurate.[27]

Fortunately, we can help maintain face by making use of "facework." **Facework** or "face-saving communication" is designed to prevent loss of face and restore face if lost; it is a fundamental aspect of communication competence. In particular, we can help save our face and the face of others by . . .[28]

- overlooking a face-threatening act, such as glossing over a mistake or acting as if face hasn't been threatened, to minimize the extent of embarrassment or annoyance (e.g., "That's OK, I do that all the time too.")
- responding with humor—laughter releases nervous tension and demonstrates that an offense isn't that serious (e.g., "This would make a great scene in a romance/horror/adventure flick!")
- offering an apology to admit blame and seek atonement (e.g., "It was my fault that this happened. I'm sorry.")

There are many techniques we can use to help ourselves and others save face in embarrassing situations.

- communicating an explanation to minimize responsibility or to justify the behavior (e.g., "I didn't mean it" or "It wasn't so bad.")
- engaging in physical remediation (such as adjusting clothing or cleaning a spill)

For example, suppose you or a classmate is greeted with laughter while walking into a classroom. Stuck to a shoe is a long trail of toilet paper. You can save face or help your classmate save face by

- saying, "Oh, it's not that big a deal!" or "Like this has never happened to any of you before!" (overlooking or minimizing the face-threatening act)
- saying, "Don't expect this kind of excitement every day!" (responding with humor)

SKILL practice • Face-Saving Communication

Respond to the following situations with face-saving communication:

- In the middle of a weekly business meeting, you knock over a glass of water on the table, threatening others' papers, including those that belong to the boss. What can you say to save face?
- You attend a party and engage in casual conversation with an acquaintance. You notice that someone named Terry shouts loudly, bumps into people, and appears intoxicated. Disgusted, you describe Terry to your acquaintance as a "pathetic loser." Your acquaintance bristles and asserts, "I'm going out with Terry." What can you say to save face?
- A friend drops by with a gift for your birthday. Both you and your friend notice a gift tag on the bottom of the present, upon which is written your friend's name and "Love, Grandma." What can you say to save your friend's face?
- You attend a formal wedding in a solemn house of worship. You've been dealing with a queasy stomach, and you can't help but emit a loud belch during a brief pause in the ceremony. What can you say to save face?

- saying, "I'm (he's) sorry for the disruption." (offering an apology)
- saying, "My (Her) shoes were probably wet, and I (she) must have walked past the restroom and tracked it in." (offering an explanation)
- putting the toilet paper in the trash (physical remediation)

In summary, our self-concept, which includes both self-image and self-esteem, significantly influences how we communicate with others. This multidimensional concept is influenced by self-disclosure, is subjective, and is the basis of the face we present to others. The self-concept is also affected by our culture; family, friends, and coworkers; gender; and our particular expectations, beliefs, attitudes, and values. In other words, various contexts influence our self-concept.

Contexts and Self-Concept

Recall that perspective taking is an important mental activity that can affect the perception of communication competence. For example, suppose we experience an initial hostile reaction to someone we perceive as a braggart. Putting ourselves in the place of the braggart may reveal that

How do contexts influence the self-concept?

- what we consider bragging is not perceived similarly in other cultures
- the braggart is repeating messages about the self that he or she received from family members
- learned gender expectations may have influenced the braggart to communicate in a particular manner
- the braggart actually perceives himself or herself as inadequate and feels insecure

Understanding the influence of the culture, relationship, gender, and individual contexts on the braggart's self-concept and communication behavior can help us create the most effective and appropriate responses to her or his messages. Perspective taking may also prevent us from allowing our initial hostile reaction to result in incompetent communication.

Culture Context

Do you identify with the politically and economically dominant culture in your country? Perhaps you perceive one or more of your co-cultures to be more significant than the dominant culture in shaping your identity. Who we are and how we see ourselves are influenced not only by the dominant culture in which we live but also by the co-cultures with which we identify.

Dominant Culture We have learned that no culture is exclusively individualist or collectivist but that cultures tend to be more one than the other. In a culture that is primarily collectivist, identity is based on group membership, such as the family or the work organization. Unlike individualist cultures, children are taught to be dependent on others.[29] Americans find it difficult to fully understand that people may not think of themselves as distinct from others within collectivist cultures. In India, for example, the dominant belief is that all selves share an underlying consciousness. The Japanese self-concept derives from networks of people to whom people are obligated and vice versa. In Japan, the self-concept is created in terms of group membership and interaction.[30]

Unlike collectivist cultures, being independent and self-sufficient is highly valued in individualist cultures.[31] Children are taught to be self-reliant in such cultures, and they are encouraged to express their individualism via their room decorations, dress, hairstyles, and school papers. Individual identity can also be reflected in verbal communication behavior, such as the manner in which we respond to others. For example, you may communicate an unpopular opinion among those who disagree with you or go out of your way to demonstrate that you are your own individual. For Americans, "being true to oneself is first and foremost. Thus, Americans continually search for their individual identities and insist on others' recognition of their different interests, styles, and preferences."[32] Moreover, Americans incorrectly assume that people from other cultures embrace individualist values such as individuality, self-reliance, and independence. When asked about their culture, Americans often say that they have no culture, because they think that everyone is an individual who is free from the cultural assumptions that are imposed on them. The belief that each person is a unique biological and psychological being is deeply ingrained and seldom questioned among Americans.[33]

Co-Cultures Co-cultures within a culture, such as our ethnic groups, also influence our self-concept and communication. An ethnic identity is based on common traditions, values, origins, and history. An ethnic identity also includes the knowledge of belonging to a particular group and the shared experiences of its members. For example, the Native American co-culture is more collectivist than the more politically powerful European-American culture. This may result in a Native American employee feeling uncomfortable when singled out and praised by a superior in front of coworkers.[34]

The gay, lesbian, bisexual, and transgender (GLBT) community is also considered by some to be a co-culture. The process of "coming out" includes exploring one's sexual identity and sharing that identity with others. Achieving self-acceptance is a crucial step in coming out, and the process is easier when we are less reliant on others for our self-concept and self-esteem. A healthy level of self-esteem has also been found to be important after the coming out process in that it can mitigate the harmful psychological effects (e.g., depression) of societal oppression.[35]

Relationship Context

Just as the culture context influences the self-concept, so does the context of family, friends, and individuals with whom we work. Many researchers believe that the analysis of the relationship context is critical to understanding the self-concept.[36]

Friends and Family Family members, especially our parents, contribute to our self-image and self-esteem in a variety of ways. Similarly, significant others also contribute to who we think we are and how we evaluate ourselves. Friends, teachers, coaches, and bosses are examples of significant others who influence us with their communication and the labels and names they choose to call us. For example, positive labeling, such as telling a child that he is "bright" and "creative," can enhance the self-concept. On the other hand, constantly telling a child that she is "stupid" or "a monster" will most likely damage the self-concept, even if the labels are incorrect and unrealistic.[37]

Coworkers People with whom we work also affect our self-concept in terms of our perceived **self-efficacy**, the belief in our ability to manage prospective situations.[38] Our self-efficacy perceptions are highly significant in career persistence and success. Role models and persons who can provide us with on-the-job encouragement help us dispel doubts about our self-efficacy perceptions. Our self-efficacy perceptions are also influential in choosing a career, and "the low proportion of women in technical vocations can be traced back to women's low perceived self-efficacy regarding technical problem-solving skills." Therefore, the communication of encouragement from female role models who work in technical fields can significantly influence the self-efficacy perceptions of young women and encourage them to become computer scientists or engineers.[39]

In addition, features of our work affect our self-concept after we have chosen a career. A ten-year longitudinal study of adult socialization and occupations reveals that challenging work experiences that require self-directed thought can positively affect the self-concept, particularly as it relates to personal efficacy and self-perceived competence. The authors of the study suggest that work experiences that involve autonomy, creativity, and individual decision making continually influence the development of adult personality and significantly enhance the self-concept over time.[40] Our self-concept also influences our behavior in organizations and our motivation to engage in work-related activities. For example, we may be motivated to complete on-the-job projects, attend meetings, and turn assignments in prior to deadlines if we perceive ourselves as "conscientious" and desire feedback from coworkers that will enhance our self-perception. Similarly, we may be motivated to work hard for an organization or team because our identity is tied to the outcomes of the group and our coworkers hold us in high regard because of our group membership. In other words, we may work hard to achieve organizational success to publically validate our self-perceptions.[41]

Gender Context

From the moment we are born, our sex influences others' behavior toward us and how we perceive ourselves. Parents often dress male babies in blue clothes and female babies in pink. Little boys are given toy trucks and action figures, while little girls are given toy houses and dolls. Our gender identity becomes a part of our self-concept beginning at age four to seven years, and it is at this point that our self-concept begins to be affected by what we believe about femininity and masculinity.[42]

In the film *Kindergarten Cop*, tough-guy detective John Kimble (Arnold Schwarzenegger) goes undercover in the traditionally "feminine" profession of kindergarten teacher and bonds with his pupils.

Furthermore, the way women and men describe themselves is influenced by gender expectations. Women typically mention characteristics such as generosity, sensitivity, and having care and concern for others when asked to describe themselves. Women also tend to be more concerned about their body image and physical appearance than are men. On the other hand, when men describe themselves, they don't tend to comment about their physiques. Instead, they typically mention characteristics such as ambition, energy, power, and control.[43]

Of course, many men have self-concepts that include care and concern for others, just as many women have self-concepts that include power and control. Similarly, a recent study of gender, self-esteem, and group membership illustrates that both women and men possess an equal sense of self-worth based on their relational group memberships.[44] Therefore, it is best to think of gendered self-concepts as a matter of degree rather than as polar opposites.

Individual Context

Our self-concept is influenced by the expectations we have of ourselves based on our self-fulfilling prophecies and our inner critic.

Self-Fulfilling Prophecies **Self-fulfilling prophecies** concern the expectations we have and the predictions we make for ourselves. Self-fulfilling prophecies are evident when we behave in ways that reinforce our self-perceptions and self-expectations, and they can make a predicted outcome of an event likely to occur. For example, perhaps you perceive yourself as unable to sustain a relationship because of a past experience. You may have experienced relational difficulties previously, and your past experiences cause you to predict that you won't be successful in your social life. Therefore, while on a date, you demonstrate a lack of confidence and communicate beliefs such as "I don't know why you said you'd go out with me." The result of your negative self-reinforcing behavior is that your predicted outcome (your date will not be successful) is now more likely to occur than if you hadn't perceived yourself as socially inept and hadn't predicted a failed social life. Hopefully, your self-fulfilling prophecies that include positive predictions and result in positive outcomes outnumber the self-fulfilling prophecies that include negative predictions and result in negative outcomes. Consider Figure 3.4,

Figure 3.4: The Cyclical Nature of Self-Fulfilling Prophecies

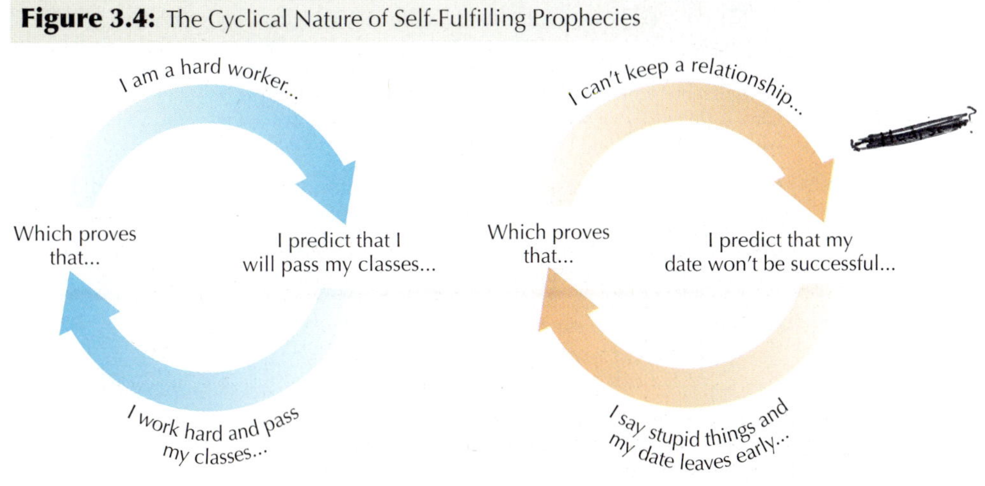

Competence & Critical Thinking

mycommunicationlab

AISHA'S TERM PAPER AND THE SELF-CONCEPT

Aisha is working on a term paper when her friend Debby asks her go to the movies. Aisha says that she can't go and talks about the difficulty she is experiencing trying to write her term paper.

You can view *Aisha's Term Paper* by accessing the "Small Group and Interpersonal Videos" on the MyCommunicationLab Web site. Answer the following questions about Aisha's self-concept and Aisha and Debby's communication:

- Describe Aisha's self-concept and her self-esteem based on the situation depicted in this video.
- How might "social comparison" and the "Pygmalion effect" relate to Aisha's sense of self?
- Is it realistic to believe that Debby can improve Aisha's self-concept?
- Do you think that Aisha is influenced by a self-fulfilling prophecy (why or why not)? Describe the self-fulfilling prophecy and how she might change it if you believe she is affected by one that is negative.

DEBBY: Hey, Aisha. Come on, let's go. The movie starts in, like, half an hour. You're not even dressed yet.

AISHA: Oh, god. I—I totally lost track of the time. Look, I'm not going to be able to go.

DEBBY: Oh, no. Come on. I've been waiting for this for a long time.

AISHA: I know. I'm sorry. I just—I'm not anywhere close to being finished with this paper and it's due tomorrow. I'm really—I'm not going to be able to go.

DEBBY: OK. Do you want some help?

AISHA: You're going to help me?

DEBBY: Yeah, why not?

AISHA: No, I—look, I got it, it's fine.

DEBBY: OK. Are you sure? You seem a little stressed out.

AISHA: It's fine. Just—just got to work on it, OK?

DEBBY: OK. Well, do you want to just have a quick cup of tea or something with me first, or . . .

AISHA: I don't think that's going to help, Debby. Look, I've been—I've been trying to write this paper all weekend, and I can't even get past the first sentence. I've written it probably like a hundred times. But everything I write, nothing sounds right, nothing is right.

DEBBY: OK. No, that's—you're going to be fine. You're going to be totally fine. And you know, it's—it's going to be OK. You just have to sit down and—and just—just take a breath, and we'll go over your notes. I'll help you. I'll totally help you on this one.

AISHA: You finished your paper, now you're going to write mine for me, too.

DEBBY: Oh, come on. You help me—you helped me on lots of things before.

AISHA: Oh, right. 'Cause you really need my help. Come on, Debby. I mean, I'm just, it's like, I'm the stupidest person in this class.

DEBBY: Oh, that's not true. That is not true.

AISHA: It is true. Everyone sits there every day, like asking questions, I have no idea what they're talking about, taking notes and stuff. And I—I just—I don't even understand what's going on. You know, and I look through these notes, and—and I'm trying to write, and I can't even get past the first sentence.

DEBBY: You are being way too hard on yourself. You got—this is a really tough class. A lot of people don't pass this class the first time. And you have been doing great. This is a really tough paper. This is the biggest paper of the whole course. You've just got to give yourself a break on this. This is going to be fine. And it's hard. You know that it's the hardest thing to do is start a paper. And you're a good writer. Come on. You've helped me with a thousand things before. Let me help you with this.

AISHA: What's the point, Debby, really? I mean, I don't belong here. Who am I kidding with this?

DEBBY: That's not true. You know that you belong here. This is exactly what you want to do, and you worked really hard to get here. You're just being hard on yourself because you have high standards. But, you know, I think sometimes you're a little too hard on yourself. You've got to cut yourself a break.

AISHA: But I just, I mean, I thought, you know, if I just—if I just worked harder, I'd be able to get it. But I can't get it. I just . . .

DEBBY: I think if we just take things step by step—hey, look. Let's go through your outline. We'll just go through your outline, and I'll help you break down the topics. We'll just try it that way. It'll be easier that way. I'll be manageable, and I'll help you. I'm a fast typer. If you want to dictate, I can—I can do it, honestly. *(pause)* Look. This is probably going to take all night. So why don't we stop now and, like, just get a cup of coffee. And then we'll sit down and look at the outline.

AISHA: OK.

"The Cyclical Nature of Self-Fulfilling Prophecies"; we can see that self-fulfilling prophecies reinforce the self-concept, affect behavior, and can influence how others perceive us.

Inner Critic Self-fulfilling prophecies are also influenced by what some psychologists call an "inner critic." Our **inner critic** produces intrapersonal communication messages such as "I've failed at this before and I'll fail at this again" and "I'll never reach my goals." Everyone has an inner critic, and we often believe that this inner voice communicates the truth. Our inner critic tends to focus on what isn't finished and ignore what we've accomplished. The demanding and judging inner critic is cited as a reason for the approximately 90% of college students who admit that they feel inferior to others in one way or another.[45]

Defensiveness and Nondefensive Reactions

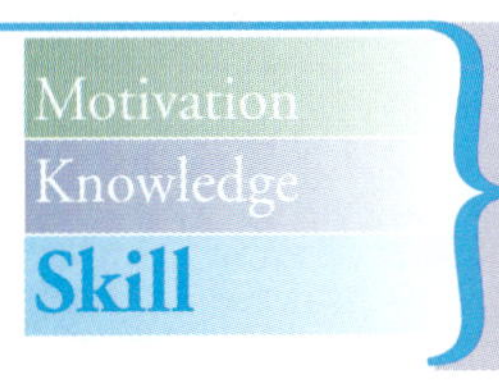

Have you ever felt that your self-concept was under attack, and you responded with attempts to protect your self-concept, even at the expense of others? If so, you experienced the communication of defensiveness. When confronted with face challenges, people often become defensive and communicate defensive reactions. **Defensiveness** refers to a physiological, emotional, and cognitive response that results from the perception that our face is threatened or is under attack. Think back to a recent situation in which a significant other criticized you. It doesn't matter whether the criticism concerned an issue of major

How can communicating nondefensive reactions improve our communication competence?

importance (e.g., "You habitually lie to people") or minor importance (e.g., "You leave the lights on in the computer room when you leave"); if you believed that your self-concept or face was threatened, you probably felt defensive.

Defensive Reactions

What do you typically do to reduce the physical and psychological discomfort when someone communicates a face-threatening act? If you are like most people, you probably respond with a defensive reaction. **Defensive reactions** (sometimes labeled "defense mechanisms") defend your self-concept and public face when you are feeling threatened. Defensive reactions are typically inappropriate and ineffective responses to challenges to our face; they can communicate disrespect and disconfirmation, promote heated arguments, and cause conversation partners to ignore relational problems and potential solutions. The various types of defensive reactions include sarcasm and verbal aggression, excuses, avoidance, and denial.[46]

Sarcasm and Verbal Aggression It's very tempting to strike back at a critic who communicates a face-threatening act. Striking back at the source of the criticism with sarcasm and verbal aggression is one example of a defensive reaction. For example:

OTHER: You're not seriously going to wear that, are you?

YOU: You should talk. I saw what you wore yesterday and you looked ridiculous!

OTHER: I'm only trying to help.

YOU: Thank you sooo much. I'll be sure to send you my "before and after" photos.

Excuses We can attempt to save face when we're the target of face-threatening communication by suggesting that the communication is of little importance or isn't within our control.

OTHER: You promised you'd call yesterday and you didn't.

YOU: Yeah, well, it got real busy at work and no one could fill in for me.

OTHER: Too busy for a phone call or email?

YOU: Well, you know how the boss snoops around to see what we're doing. I didn't want to get in trouble. Besides, you hardly ever check your email.

OTHER: So I guess it's better to blow me off and not even try to call, even after you got off work!

YOU: I got off work late and I was really tired. Besides, I thought you were out and that it was no big deal that I didn't call.

OTHER: It is a big deal! You made a promise and you broke it!

Avoidance We can avoid dealing with face-threatening acts by ignoring the communication, changing the subject, and/or physically leaving the room where our conversation partner is speaking.

KNOWLEDGE power • Shouting, Excusing, Avoiding, or Denying?

Explain the following four types of defensive reactions to someone who knows you well and who has criticized you in the past:

1. Sarcasm and verbal aggression
2. Excuses
3. Avoidance
4. Denial

Ask your conversation partner for specific examples of defensive reactions you communicate when your face is threatened, and determine whether you have a habitual response that can be classified in one of the aforementioned categories. (Be prepared for some defensiveness on your part.) Discuss how you can protect your self-concept in a more effective and appropriate manner in future communication episodes.

OTHER: I am really mad at you!

YOU: (You wear headphones and listen to music as you pretend not to hear.)

OTHER: Did you hear me? I need to talk to you about something important! Take off those headphones!

YOU: (You slowly take off the headphones.) I don't know what the problem is, but why don't we talk about it later. I want to finish listening to this.

OTHER: (growing increasingly frustrated) No! This is important; I want to talk about it now!

YOU: Hey, I just remembered that what's important is finishing my English paper tonight; it's due tomorrow. (You begin to walk out of the room.)

OTHER: Wait a minute! (shouting) I want to talk about this now!

Denial The denial of face-threatening communication undermines the perceptions of others. One interesting note about defensive reactions is that they are often strongest when the criticism directed toward us is true.[47] Even when we secretly agree with the face-threatening communication, we may deny its validity in an attempt to save our desired social identity.

OTHER: I know you want a home entertainment center for our apartment, but there's no way we can afford it.

YOU: Sure there is. If I want something badly enough, I always buy it and things work out in the end.

OTHER: But the payments for a complete system are at least $500 a month. Even if we wanted to just get a plasma HDTV without all the other equipment, we'd have to rob Peter to pay Paul. And we'd also have to get more insurance because we both know that there've been some burglaries in the complex.

YOU: Nah! No one would want to rob our junky little apartment. Trust me; you worry too much.

Nondefensive Reaction Skills

Compared with defensive reactions, nondefensive reactions validate a critic's thoughts and feelings and communicate respect, even if we disagree with the criticism directed toward us. Asking open-ended questions, guessing about specifics, agreeing with the truth, and agreeing to disagree are ways to respond to others in a nondefensive manner.[48] However, before communicating nondefensive reactions, we must learn to recognize that we are feeling defensive. When we sense the onset of a rapid heartbeat, experience shortness of breath, and feel "hot under the collar," we should first take a deep breath and pause before speaking by silently counting to three. This will slow us down and prevent an ineffective and inappropriate response such as a defensive reaction. We can then train ourselves to immediately ask an open-ended question.

Asking Open-Ended Questions Face-threatening and critical communication is sometimes offered in general terms; therefore, asking open-ended questions can help us understand our conversation partner. For example:

OTHER: I don't like your attitude!
YOU: *What have I done?*
OTHER: (laughing) You are such an idiot!
YOU: *Why are you saying this?*
OTHER: You don't pay enough attention to me!
YOU: *When was the last time I ignored you?*

Asking an open-ended question demonstrates that we are trying to understand our conversation partner and enables us to move to additional types of nondefensive responses.

Guessing About Specifics Even after asking an open-ended question, we may still be unsure of the meaning of a face-threatening act or criticism. Our next step may be to guess about specifics. Guessing about specifics enables our conversation partner to communicate an in-depth response and examine her or his assumptions. For example:

OTHER: I don't think you care about me.
YOU: *Why not?* (Open-ended question)
OTHER: You don't treat me right.
YOU: *How do I act when I don't treat you right?* (Open-ended question)
OTHER: You act like you don't care.
YOU: *Is it because we've been staying in on Friday and Saturday nights?* (Guessing about specifics)
OTHER: No.
YOU: *Is it because I didn't hang out with you at Chuck's party?* (Guessing about specifics)
OTHER: Yeah, well, I guess so.

Agreeing with the Truth How many times have you criticized someone and expected a nondefensive response of agreement? Most of us typically prepare and mentally rehearse our responses to a partner's expected defensive reactions. Agreeing with the truth is a nondefensive response that is rarely expected. As illustrated in the "Cathy" comic, this response also has potential for deflecting a conversation that can get out of hand if it includes defense mechanisms. For example:

OTHER: You're just being difficult.

YOU: *You're right; I am.*

OTHER: This is the third time you're late!

YOU: *I'm sorry. I'll really try to be on time from now on.*

OTHER: What you said was so rude.

YOU: *Yeah, I know. I need to be more careful.*

Notice that these responses do not include self-put-downs. We can agree with the truth if we believe that the comments directed to us are accurate or likely. However, sometimes criticism and face-threatening communication are overgeneralizations (e.g., they include the words *always* or *never*) or negatively relate to our overall self-concept. If this is the case, we can agree with the portion of the comments we believe to be true and disagree with the rest.

Agreeing with the truth can deflect a conversation that is getting out of hand.

SKILL practice • Nondefensive Reactions

Respond to the following situations with nondefensive reactions:

- You and a friend go on a vacation together, and you act as the "principal photographer." Upon viewing the printed photographs, your friend tells you that the photos are blurry, you didn't take enough "people shots," and you're an overall lousy photographer. How can you respond nondefensively?
- You are in the beginning stages of a romantic relationship. You and your new significant other tease each other, and the taunts and barbs become increasingly intense. All of a sudden, your significant other declares, "You are definitely not like my ex!" How can you respond nondefensively?
- You work very hard on an assignment for one of your classes. You are disappointed when you learn you received a "C" for the work, and you become angry as you walk to your professor's office to talk about the grade. However, you realize that it's best to communicate nondefensively with your professor. How can you respond nondefensively?
- Your boss calls you into her or his office and says that a coworker has complained about your actions on the job. How can you respond nondefensively?

Agreeing to Disagree When we remain calm and rational during a face-threatening act, we often find there is some truth to what our conversation partner tells us. However, even if we can't find any truth in our partner's comments, we can validate his or her right to have an opinion. For example:

OTHER: If you keep partying the way you do, you're going to flunk.
YOU: *You may be right, but I think I can handle it.*
OTHER: Why do you listen to that stuff? It's awful.
YOU: *I respect your opinion, but I like alternative music.*

Of course, it goes without saying that we must be aware of our nonverbal communication, especially our tone of voice, when we communicate any type of nondefensive response. Sounding angry or sarcastic communicates defensiveness and prevents us from interacting in a competent manner. In general, communicating a nondefensive response in a voice that quivers with emotion is better than striking back in anger or responding with other defensive reactions that neither validate nor attempt to respectfully keep a conversation going.

Remember to be realistic about the guidelines and skills designed to improve self-concept and communication. As mentioned in the previous chapter, guidelines can fall short, and skills don't always work. For example, you can't assume that the competent communication you direct toward a more powerful person will be returned in kind. Consider the nondefensive response of agreeing to disagree. Telling your college professor "I respect that you gave my project a 'D,' but I believe I deserve a better grade" is not likely to result in your desired outcome. Similarly, after receiving criticism at work about arriving late, a response such as "You're correct when you say that I've been late a lot, but I disagree that it's causing problems" will probably result in defensiveness, anger, and the possibility of having to find a new job. The best course of action when communicating with someone more powerful than you may be to remain silent or use other communication tactics designed to save face and reduce defensiveness.

OVERCOMING COMMUNICATION CHALLENGES

Inflated Self-Esteem

Self-esteem was once assumed to influence students' grades, sexual behavior, substance abuse, and relationships with peers. In 2000, the American Psychological Society (APS) created a task force headed by **Roy F. Baumeister** to examine scientific studies that included objective measures of self-esteem. After reviewing more than two hundred studies, the APS task force concluded that low self-esteem predisposes young people to engage in neither sexual behavior nor drug or alcohol abuse. Additionally, although there is a correlation between self-esteem and grades, the task force revealed that achieving high grades leads to higher self-esteem (not the other way around). The APS task force found only two consistent findings concerning the benefits of high self-esteem: people with high self-esteem are significantly happier and more satisfied with their lives than people with low to moderate levels of self-esteem, and people with high self-esteem are persistent and resilient.[49] Surprisingly, the APS task force discovered that inflated self-esteem affects academic performance and interpersonal relations.

Academic Performance

In regard to academic performance, the APS task force found that artificially inflating students' self-esteem can actually decrease grades. One study reviewed by the task force revealed that attempts to bolster self-esteem among struggling college students can backfire. When at-risk students received messages that instructed them to boost their self-esteem (e.g., students were told to think, "I can be proud of myself," "I can do this," and "I am satisfied with myself"), the result was an average failing grade. On the other hand, when at-risk students received messages designed to instill a sense of responsibility for their grades (e.g., students were told to think, "I need to work harder," "I can learn this material if I apply myself," and "I can control what happens to me in this class"), the result was an average passing grade.[50] Similarly, people with inflated self-esteem often become defensive in the face of embarrassment, criticism, and having their authority questioned. In the academic setting, receiving passing grades that don't actually reflect academic performance in K–12 classes can cause college students to become offended, demoralized, or angry when they don't achieve the grades they believe they deserve.[51]

Interpersonal Relations

In addition to affecting academic performance, inflated self-esteem affects interpersonal relations. Some educators believe that children in school programs designed to "enhance positive self-perceptions" actually have learned self-importance and self-gratification. Another unfortunate result of such programs is that children fail to learn respect for others.[52] People with inflated self-esteem also tend to become defensive and seek reassurance when others criticize or correct them. Additionally, adults with inflated self-esteem believe that they get along well with others, communicate support to partners, and manage conflicts well. However, when rated by others, such individuals are labeled antagonistic, rude, unfriendly, and overall less likable than people with less self-esteem. In fact, in ego-threatening situations, people with inflated self-esteem are liked significantly less than people with lower self-esteem.[53]

Overall, self-esteem is now considered to be a multilayered concept, and respondents in self-esteem studies may include individuals who are narcissistic or who pretend to have higher levels of self-esteem than reality suggests. Researchers believe that further studies should focus on the various meanings and components related to self-esteem. Experts also suggest that high self-esteem should develop from achievement (instead of assuming that achievement should result from high self-esteem). Educators are now encouraging "earned self-esteem" that results from meeting standards at home and in schools. Similarly, we can "refine" our self-esteem by focusing on setting goals that mutually benefit self and other. For example, instead of focusing on making a good impression when communicating, we may want to focus on learning new information or better understanding our conversation partners' ideas.[54] Focusing on goals that benefit ourselves and others can stabilize our sense of self-worth and may help us avoid the problems associated with inflated self-esteem.

A CASE STUDY IN ETHICS

"I'm a Loser . . ."

We have learned that competent communication includes an ethical dimension of well-based standards of right and wrong. Asking "Have I practiced any virtues today (e.g., integrity, trustworthiness, honesty, and responsibility)?" "Have I done more good than harm?" "Have I treated people with dignity and respect?" "Have I been fair and just today?" and "Have I made my community stronger because of my actions?" can provide us with a systematic approach to dealing with everyday ethical behavior. Read the following situation and consider whether requiring students to write "I'm a loser" sentences is an ethical way to influence self-concept and behavior.

Think back to your days in middle school. How would you feel if a teacher made you write "I am a loser because . . ." as a result of not completing your homework? Far from a hypothetical situation, Spanish teacher Julie Barrentine had students write "loser sentences" over and over on a piece of paper if they failed to complete their assignments. The idea to use the word *loser* in the sentences, which came from Barrentine's students, was intended to be a humorous way to motivate them to finish their homework. However, parents complained to school officials once they found out about the loser sentences. In addition to stopping the practice, officials sent letters of apology to all of Barrentine's 137 students.

The loser sentences story was exposed in the media, and many people indicated that they thought the teacher crossed the line between "discipline" and "humiliation." Some parents suggested that Barrentine be disciplined so she would be perceived as a "loser." However, others responded that they were happy to see a teacher who held students accountable for completing their assignments. Emails to the *Dallas Morning News* about the incident included the following:

- "God forbid that kids get disciplined because they don't do their homework . . . or for anything else, for that matter."
- "None of the parents or principals addressed the real issue—the students not turning in their work."
- "The teacher was wrong in applying the term 'loser' to any student. While it is fine when one kid says it to another, it takes on an entirely different meaning when coming from a teacher."

One parent in particular suggested that the loser sentences could have a damaging effect on students' self-concept. "People in authority don't realize that little things like this make a big difference in someone's self-esteem. Negativity is destroying our young children," she wrote.[55]

Do you believe the "I'm a loser" sentences reflect well-based standards of right and wrong? Do you believe that writing loser sentences effectively influences self-concept and behavior? Is it acceptable for students to call each other "loser" but not acceptable for teachers to apply this term to their pupils?

Chapter Review

Motivation: How has this helped me?

- **The importance of studying the self-concept**

Our self-concept influences how we accept praise, defend viewpoints, and communicate our accomplishments. Our self-concept also affects how others perceive us. Creating realistic goal statements and not mentally "beating ourselves up" if we don't meet them can improve our self-concept and increase our motivation to communicate.

Knowledge: What have I learned?

- **How we can characterize the self-concept**

The self-concept refers to how we perceive ourselves. Our self-concept is formed, sustained, and changed by our interactions with others.

- **The characteristics and components of the self-concept**

The self-concept is based on characteristics we believe we possess (self-image) and characteristics we believe to be worthwhile or valuable (self-esteem). The self-concept is also multidimensional, is influenced by what we disclose to others and what others disclose to us (as illustrated by the Johari Window), and is subjective.

- **How contexts influence the self-concept**

Our self-concept is influenced by culture, relationship, gender, and individual contexts. Cultures that are primarily individualist suggest that people have unique identities. Similarly, our family, friends, and people with whom we work significantly affect our self-perceptions. Socialization (especially what people learn about masculinity and femininity) also affects how we perceive ourselves. Finally, the self-fulfilling prophecy and our inner critic influence our self-concept.

Skill: What skills have I developed?

- **Facework can help save our face and the face of others**

Facework is designed to prevent loss of face and restore face if lost. We can help save our face and others' by glossing over a mistake or acting as if one's face hasn't been threatened, responding with humor, communicating an apology, offering an explanation to minimize responsibility or to justify behavior, and physical remediation.

- **Communicating nondefensive reactions can improve our communication competence**

Nondefensive reactions such as asking open-ended questions, guessing about specifics, agreeing with the truth and agreeing to disagree when our face is threatened can validate a critic's thoughts and feelings and communicate respect.

Study Questions

1. What is a self-concept? How does the way we perceive ourselves influence how we communicate with others?
2. How do significant others, social comparison, and the Pygmalion effect relate to the self-concept?
3. How do self-image and self-esteem relate to the self-concept?
4. Describe how the self-concept is multidimensional.
5. Describe and explain the four quadrants associated with the Johari Window.
6. Why is the self-concept considered to be subjective?
7. What is "face," and how can we competently manage face-threatening situations?
8. How does the culture context influence our self-concept?

9. In what ways do family, friends, and coworkers affect our self-concept?
10. In what way is the self-concept affected by gender?
11. How do self-fulfilling prophecies affect the self-concept?
12. What is defensiveness? How does defensiveness manifest itself in communication?
13. What are some nondefensive ways we can respond to others?
14. What are some of the negative consequences of having inflated self-esteem?

Names to Know

Roy F. Baumeister, p. 65/87—psychologist at Florida State University who has published extensively in the areas of emotion, interpersonal processes, and identity. Baumeister recommends that researchers should de-emphasize the study of self-esteem and concentrate on self-control and self-discipline to benefit self and society.

George Herbert Mead, p. 64 (1863–1931)—philosopher and psychologist whose major contribution to the field of social psychology was his analysis of how the human self arises in the process of symbolic interaction or communication.

Martin Seligman, p. 68—psychologist and best-selling author who teaches at the University of Pennsylvania. Seligman is known as a founder of positive psychology, a research area that encompasses positive emotions, positive character traits, and positive institutions.

Erving Goffman, p. 73 (1922–1982)—sociologist who was a pioneer theorist in the area of face-to-face interaction and who developed the dramatistic perspective regarding interpersonal communication. Goffman's classic 1959 book, *The Presentation of Self in Everyday Life,* continues to influence modern students of symbolic interaction.

Key Terms

blind quadrant, 71
defensive reactions, 82
defensiveness, 81
face, 73
facework, 74
hidden quadrant, 71
inner critic, 81
Johari Window, 70
open quadrant, 71
Pygmalion effect, 64
self-concept, 64
self-disclosure, 70
self-efficacy, 77
self-esteem, 70
self-fulfilling prophecies, 79
self-image, 69
significant others, 64
social comparison, 65
symbolic interactionism, 64
unknown quadrant, 72

CHAPTER 4

Emotion and Communication

"There can be no knowledge without emotions. To the cognition of the brain must be added the experience of the soul."

Arnold Bennett (1867–1931), British novelist and playwright

In this chapter, we will answer the following:

Motivation: How will this help me?

- It is important to study emotions and communication because emotions are a likely component of every conversation in which we participate and because they affect our motivation to communicate.
- Engaging in mindfulness and rational emotive behavior therapy can help us manage our emotions.

Knowledge: What will I learn?

- How to characterize emotions
- Fast-track circuit and slow-track circuit emotions
- Types of emotions
- How contexts influence emotions and communication

Skill: Why do I need to develop these skills?

- Owning our emotions can improve our communication competence

Halle Berry broke down while accepting her Best Actress Academy Award Oscar in 2002. Have you ever found yourself in a situation in which you cried in public? Have you ever gotten so angry that you practically lost control? Are you the type of person who rarely experiences emotional highs and lows, or are you emotionally variable; that is, do you quickly shift from one emotion to another? Whether we see ourselves as emotionally stable or emotionally variable, it is virtually impossible to experience a day during which we feel no emotion whatsoever. The emotions we experience influence our judgments, priorities, decisions, and behavior. In this chapter, we'll increase our motivation to communicate competently by learning about the relationship between emotion and interpersonal communication and why it's important to study emotion and communication. We'll also increase our motivation by engaging in mindfulness and a technique that can help us replace debilitative emotions (i.e., those that get in the way of effective functioning) with facilitative emotions. We will also increase our knowledge by learning about how emotion relates to communication, how physiology relates to emotions, how we can classify emotions, and how our emotions are influenced by contexts. We will also learn the skill of owning our emotions to increase our chances of being perceived as communicating effectively and appropriately.

Introduction to Emotions

How do you characterize emotion? You may include the word *feelings* in your description but also incorporate the idea that "thoughts" are somehow related to emotions. You may also want to include the physiological experiences that accompany emotions in your depiction. Although it is recognized that communication affects emotion and emotion affects communication, there is little agreement regarding the definition of emotions.

How can we characterize emotions?

Emotions have been defined as simply the experience of energy that moves through our body. This definition implies that emotional energy is neutral and that the sensation of feeling, physiological reactions, and thoughts give emotions their meaning. Other definitions include the idea that emotions involve not only thoughts, psychological states, and biological processes but also behavioral propensities. Still others maintain that emotions are socially constructed and learned.[1] Despite disagreement regarding the influence of cognition, psychology, and behavior, most research suggests that **emotions** are feelings we experience that result from the interaction of physiology, cognitions, and social experience and that they significantly affect how we communicate with others and interpret others' communication.

Why It's Important to Study Emotions and Communication

Knowledge about emotions and communication increases our motivation to communicate competently. Emotions are inherent in just about every communication episode in which we participate. Similarly, emotions affect physical and relational health.

Emotions are also associated with intrapersonal communication. Our feelings affect our readiness to communicate; when, how, and why we communicate; and how we interpret and respond when others communicate with us. Emotions are described as one of the most consequential outcomes of interaction because they influence our interpretation of messages and our perception of self and other. Some researchers suggest that it is impossible to understand communication without acknowledging the impact of emotions.[2]

Why is it important to study emotions and communication?

Not only do emotions affect communication in general but also they influence physical and relational health. For example, people who fail to communicate emotional distress may experience unexplained headaches or stomachaches.[3] Think about what you were feeling the last time you failed to communicate. Did the suppressed emotions show up as physical ailments? Moreover, the way husbands and wives communicate their emotions affects the stability and quality of their marriage. In one longitudinal study of the emotional interaction of married couples, observers predicted with more than 80% accuracy which couples would break up during the following five years. Marriages headed for divorce had husbands who displayed hostile emotions and an absence of empathy, as well as wives who expressed vulnerability and also failed to empathize.[4] Think about your intimate relationships. Do you tend to communicate hostility, sadness, and/or a lack of empathy?

KNOWLEDGE power • Am I Happy, Angry, or Sad?

Do you know how others perceive your expression of emotion? Find a trusted friend, coworker, and/or relational partner and ask:

- What emotion(s) would you use to describe me? Why?
- Do you believe I am emotionally stable or emotionally variable? Explain your answer.
- Do you think I communicate my emotions in a competent manner? If not, how can I improve?

You may find yourself becoming somewhat "emotional" (e.g., defensive) as you listen to your conversation partner(s) describe your expression of emotion. But remember that communication competence is based on others' perceptions. Consider carefully the answers you receive, and decide how you might improve your expression of emotion and thereby improve others' perceptions of your communication competence.

KNOWLEDGE ON THE CUTTING EDGE

Incivility on-the-job: Are You a Civil Communicator?

Think about your experiences as a customer and/or a worker in any type of business or organization. Can you recall instances of "workplace incivility"? Behaviors that are rude, discourteous, and disrespectful and display a lack of regard for others characterize workplace incivility. Workplace incivility differs from workplace violence, aggression, and emotional abuse because it is often unclear whether the uncivil behavior is specifically designed to harm others. For example, knuckle-cracking and belching may be offensive and undignified but is typically not intended to harm a specific individual. Similarly, not crediting the accomplishments of others or failing to return phone calls may suggest a lack of common courtesy and unprofessional behavior, but may not be intended as insults against particular targets. Other examples of workplace incivility include:

- using profanity
- talking loudly and/or talking about personal matters
- cell phones ringing during meetings and speakerphones used in public
- interrupting frequently
- turning one's back and/or working on something else while someone is talking during meetings

Workplace incivility is pervasive and results in harmful consequences to employees and to organizations as a whole. For example, 71% of more than 1,100 respondents in a 2001 survey experienced uncivil behaviors at work during a five-year period. These respondents reported feeling anxious, nervous, moody, sad, and worried and experienced increased minor illnesses.[5] In a 2004 workplace incivility study, emergency medical professionals, law enforcement officers, managers, attorneys, and physicians reported feeling depressed, disappointed, and irritated by uncivil behaviors. One respondent admitted, "I was hurt and angry and a little scared. At first I wanted to get even, but there was too much at stake." Employees affected by workplace incivility may distrust coworkers, reduce their productivity, and eventually leave the organization.[6]

Uncivil workplace behaviors are frequently ignored or tolerated. Often leaders prefer to believe that such behavior will eventually go away rather than take steps to correct it. Uncivil workplace behaviors may also be tolerated because they are demonstrated by persons in positions of authority. One study respondent asserted, "Your higher ups set the tone; how they act toward each other dictates how you treat your colleagues."[7] Some organization leaders are simply unprepared or ill-equipped to deal with uncivil behavior. However, workplace incivility can be diminished if managers become aware of the nature and costs of uncivil behavior and encourage open discussion about it. A corporate culture that promotes awareness and open discussion can encourage employees to reveal occurrences of workplace incivility. Similarly, awareness and accountability can influence employees to engage in self-monitoring to prevent themselves from demonstrating uncivil behavior. Overall, leaders of organizations can successfully reduce workplace incivility through systematic awareness and early intervention.[8]

Emotions and Physiology: Fast-Track and Slow-Track Circuit Emotions

It is important to learn about the role of physiology in the experience of emotions to fully understand emotions and how they can be managed. Both the "fast-track" circuit and the "slow-track" circuit are involved in the experience of emotions.

Emotions and the Fast-Track Circuit

What are fast-track circuit and slow-track circuit emotions?

As illustrated in Figure 4.1, three parts of the brain are involved in the processing of emotions. The brain stem that surrounds the top of the spinal cord controls basic life functions such as breathing and movement. Sometimes called the "reptilian brain," it is shared by all species that have a nervous system. The limbic system rings and borders the brain stem. Sometimes labeled the "emotional brain," this part of the brain is involved in emotions, memory, and learning. The neocortex is the seat of the intellect. Sometimes called the "thinking brain" or the "new brain," the neocortex controls reason and rational decision making. It was long thought that sense data went first to the thinking brain to be analyzed and then to the emotional brain. In other words, psychologists believed that thoughts and perceptions always preceded the experience of emotion. However, neuroscientists have discovered a brain circuit that sends sense data directly to the emotional brain and bypasses the thinking brain. The emotional brain is quicker than the thinking brain, and this **fast-track circuit** is reflected in emotional reactions and brain activity that occur before we have time to rationally analyze a situation. In other words, emotion precedes thought; we react emotionally to a situation and then actually think about it.[9] If you have ever blown up at someone and later believed that you had overreacted, you experienced the fast-track circuit of emotions.

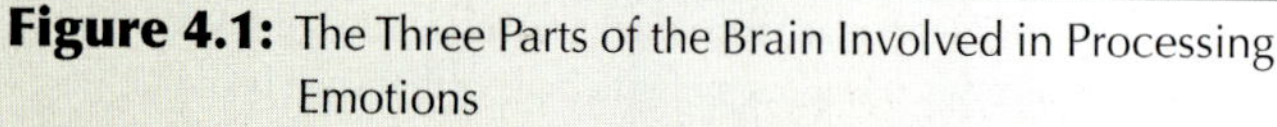
Figure 4.1: The Three Parts of the Brain Involved in Processing Emotions

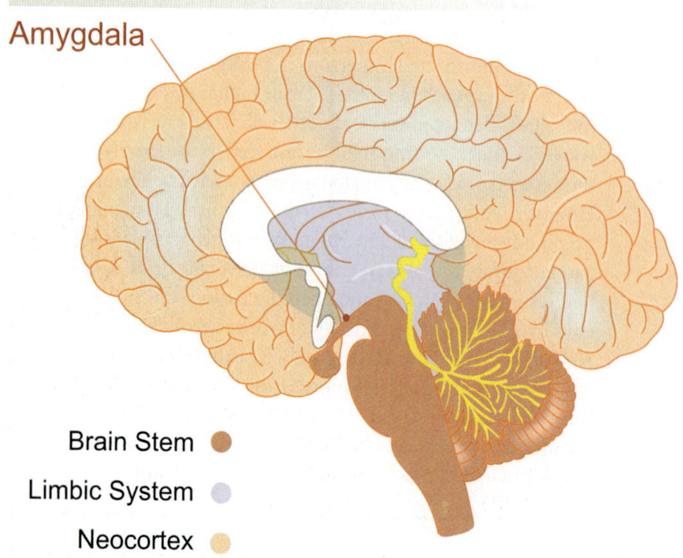

The Amygdala Emotions such as fear, anxiety, and anger are processed in the **amygdala** (ah-MIG-dah-la), an almond-shaped structure that is located in the emotional brain or limbic system (see Figure 4.1). The automatic responses that result from the amygdala are a result of evolution and are "wired" in the nervous system. Evolutionary biologists suggest that at one time, emotional knee-jerk reactions were necessary for survival and the continuation of the species. Although we no longer must make instant decisions about whether a charging prehistoric creature is something to be eaten or is something that will eat us, the amygdala continues to appraise sense data so quickly that it never enters conscious awareness.[10] This is why we sometimes experience an emotion and can't explain it. Have you ever become anxious or frightened while walking alone at night or upon seeing a stranger when the elevator doors open?

Former Red Sox pitcher Pedro Martinez experienced a "knee-jerk" emotional reaction that resulted from his amygdala when former Yankees' bench coach Don Zimmer charged at him during Game 3 of the ALCS.

If so, maybe you tried to talk yourself out of your fear and told yourself that you were feeling "paranoid" or "overreacting." In reality, your fear and anxiety most likely stemmed from the appraisal of the amygdala based on cues that had not been processed by your conscious mind. In such cases it's best not to dismiss our fear; instead, we should find someone with whom to walk or refrain from entering the elevator.[11]

The Fight-or-Flight Syndrome The amygdala not only instantaneously assigns emotional significance to sense data but also sends a crisis message to all parts of the brain. This crisis message is labeled the **fight-or-flight syndrome**. For example, if as small children we experienced fear when we were chased by a dog, the amygdala will match this event to our current situation and influence us to experience fear at the sight of any dog. This fearful reaction occurs before we have time to rationally analyze the current situation, and whether or not we remember ever being chased by a dog. The fight-or-flight syndrome can occur when the perceived threat is physical or when it is social, such as when we receive face-threatening communication in the form of criticism.

Although the physiology behind the fight-or-flight syndrome evolved millions of years ago, the crisis response that originates in the brain continues to operate as it did then. Sensory acuity is heightened, complex thought is stopped, and the amygdala activates the car-diovascular system and signals the secretion of the hormone norepinephrine (which makes the senses more alert). Similarly, resources are shifted from the thinking brain to other sites to facilitate survival. For example, our heart may beat faster and our rate of breathing may increase. These physiological responses occur because the rapid heartbeat brings extra oxygen to our muscles and prepares us to fight or to flee. In addition to our rapid heart rate and shortness of breath, we may break

KNOWLEDGE power • I'm Scared and I Don't Know Why!

With a partner or in a group, discuss a situation in which you felt an emotion such as fear, anxiety, or anger for no apparent reason. How did you know you were feeling your emotion? Can you explain your emotion in retrospect? How can your knowledge of the fast-track circuit of emotions and the role of the amygdala help you make sense of "unexplained" emotions that you may experience in the future?

into a sweat. This physiological response occurs because sweat cools the body in preparation to fight or to flee. Moreover, adrenaline and other hormones are forced into our bloodstream. The extra adrenaline enables blood to clot faster, should we receive an injury. Additionally, glucose pools in our muscles to provide instant strength and energy. Our muscles also receive blood that has been diverted from the digestive system, and this leaves a cold, empty feeling in the pit of our stomach.[12] In a social situation, these physiological changes prepare us to flee (e.g., walk away) or to fight back with angry responses and defensive reactions.

Emotions and the Slow-Track Circuit

When perceptions do affect emotions, it is through a **slow-track circuit** in which the thinking brain rationally analyzes a situation and then communicates with the emotional brain. We are usually aware of the thoughts that lead to emotions in the slow-track circuit. For example, we may evaluate a situation (e.g., "that person is good-looking" or "I deserve a better grade"), and an emotional response may follow (e.g., "anticipation" or "frustration"). Complicated emotions such as embarrassment and apprehension follow the slow-track circuit and take seconds or minutes to process.[13]

Types of Emotions

How often do you find yourself labeling your emotions? Perhaps you label your feelings in terms of polar opposites, such as happy versus sad or excited versus bored. Psychologists categorize emotions to facilitate their study and to help explain how they influence behavior. We can classify emotions in three ways: by placing them in the categories of primary or mixed, by clustering them into emotion families, and by distinguishing them as facilitative or debilitative.

What are the various types of emotions?

Figure 4.2: A Model of the Emotions

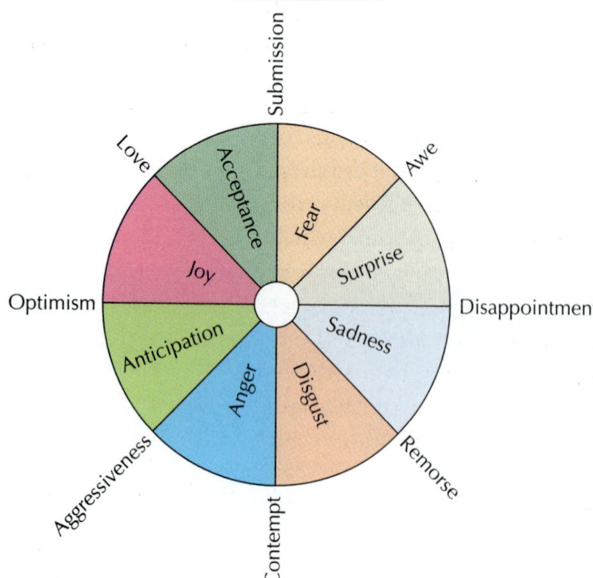

Source: Plutchik, *Emotion: A Psychoevolutionary Synthesis*, © 1979 Individual Dynamics, Inc. Reproduced by permisssion of Pearson Education, Inc.

Primary and Mixed Emotions

One classification system developed by psychologist **Robert Plutchik** suggests that eight **primary emotions** blend to form **mixed emotions**. This classification system moves us beyond primary emotions and labels our complex feelings in terms of various blends of emotion. Plutchik identified the eight primary emotions as anger, anticipation, joy, acceptance, fear, surprise, sadness, and disgust. These primary emotions are also classified in terms of their intensity; they are represented on the wheel in Figure 4.2. The eight primary emotions blend to form mixed emotions; they are represented outside the wheel. For example, two primary emotions, surprise and sadness, blend to form disappointment.[14]

Emotion Families

We can also cluster emotions into **emotion families** that share common characteristics. This classification system enables us to more precisely identify the various

KNOWLEDGE ON THE CUTTING EDGE

Technology Update: Emotion and Computer-Mediated Communication

How do you express your emotions when you use email or engage in instant messaging? You most likely are familiar with and perhaps use "emoticons," which are pictorial representations of feelings that help to communicate a sender's feelings and the intent of her or his written message, such as ☺ and ;-). Emotions are used more in positive communication than in negative communication and are used more among friends than among strangers.[15] Additional ways of communicating emotions online include using all capital letters, using many exclamation points, writing in special fonts and colors, and bolding and italicizing words. Special symbols and words can also communicate feelings, such as "lol" (laugh out loud) or a milder form of amusement, "heh." The recognition of emotion as crucial to computer-mediated communication (CMC) is evidenced in the development of three-dimensional virtual environments. Such virtual environments include 3-D versions of avatars (complete with emotionally expressive faces, bodies, and behaviors) that enable people to see and hear the facial expressions and voices of 3-D others. Second Life is a 3-D virtual environment that is created and owned by its residents, millions of people from around the world (you can access Second Life at http://secondlife.com). The ability to communicate emotion in virtual environments such as Second Life has recently been studied with respect to expression and interpretation of touch. In one study, a networked "force-feedback haptic device" similar to a joystick was used to transmit emotion through a virtual interpersonal handshake. Participants were asked to generate seven different emotions using the device, and others were asked to recognize emotions on the basis of virtual touch. Study results demonstrated that participants in a virtual reality context are able to express emotions by using different touch-related movements and these differences enable others to interpret the various emotions via the haptic device. The researchers concluded that people who engage in virtual communication can transmit and interpret touch-related emotional cues with accuracy above chance and in a manner similar to face-to-face communication.[16]

Even when emoticons or other methods of communicating emotions are not specifically used in CMC, it is possible to discern emotional content by relying on implicit behavior to infer the emotions of others. Although there are fewer nonverbal cues of emotion, CMC users interpret emotional content based on communication style. In particular, emotions can be interpreted by determining who more frequently emails and engages in instant messaging, who responds more often, and who includes more information in messages.[17]

In addition to the expression of emotion in CMC, researchers study how emotions are affected by CMC use. Early studies suggested that large amounts of time online caused or increased user depression and anxiety,[18] but more recent research shows no association between time spent online and depression, anxiety, or social fearfulness. Additionally, chat room users who are socially fearful can use the Internet as a low-risk opportunity to rehearse communication skills that will help them during face-to-face interactions. Current research suggests that CMC helps people manage and reduce depression and provides users with a large social support network.[19]

related emotions we may experience and communicate the full range of our feelings to a conversation partner. Characteristics unique to a family and variations of the characteristics (which result from differences in biology, learning experiences, and specific situations) are included in each family. Emotion families are also described in terms of physical variations. For example, physical variations within the anger family include at least sixty expressions that share muscular patterns and features, such as lowered brows and tightened lips. Additional physical variations include a tightened lower eyelid and tightening of the lip corners. It is hypothesized that these variations result from whether the anger is controlled, simulated, spontaneous, or specific to an event in which anger is provoked. Table 4.1, "Emotion Families," lists the main emotion families and their "family members."[20]

Facilitative and Debilitative Emotions

Another way to look at emotions is to determine whether they are facilitative or debilitative. **Facilitative emotions** contribute to effective functioning; **debilitative emotions**

Table 4.1: Emotion Families

Emotion	Family Members
Anger	fury, outrage, resentment, wrath, exasperation, indignation, vexation, acrimony, animosity, annoyance, irritability, hostility, and, perhaps at the extreme, pathological hatred and violence
Sadness	grief, sorrow, cheerlessness, gloom, melancholy, self-pity, loneliness, dejection, despair, and, when pathological, severe depression
Fear	anxiety, apprehension, nervousness, concern, consternation, misgiving, wariness, qualm, edginess, dread, fright, and terror; as a psychopathology, phobia and panic
Enjoyment	happiness, joy, relief, contentment, bliss, delight, amusement, pride, sensual pleasure, thrill, rapture, satisfaction, euphoria, whimsy, ecstasy, and, at the far edge, mania
Love	acceptance, friendliness, trust, kindness, affinity, devotion, adoration, infatuation, and *agape*
Surprise	shock, astonishment, amazement, wonder
Disgust	contempt, disdain, scorn, abhorrence, aversion, distaste, and revulsion
Shame	guilt, embarrassment, chagrin, remorse, humiliation, regret, mortification, and contrition

Source: See Goleman, D. *Emotional Intelligence.* New York: Bantam Books, 1995.

detract from effective functioning.[21] This classification system enables us to analyze our feelings in terms of intensity and duration and provides the basis of techniques that can help us manage our emotions. Think about which emotions get in the way of your life. Does anger detract from your ability to get along with people? Does jealousy? How about fear? Now think about these three emotions in terms of how they could possibly facilitate meeting your goals and living the life that you want. For example, if you become angry when a friend "jokingly" puts you down in front of others, you may speak up assertively instead of remaining quiet as usual. If you become jealous when someone flirts with your partner, you may increasingly begin to verbalize your appreciation for your partner and how much you care for her or him. If you are afraid that failing your communication class will result in academic suspension, you may work exceedingly hard on your class projects and study intensely for all your tests. The point is that an emotion can either be facilitative or debilitative, depending on its intensity and duration. For example, it's realistic to feel irritated or frustrated if someone has lied about you, but it's not reasonable to rage and scream about the lie for days at a time. Intense emotions that are long-lasting turn facilitative emotions into debilitative emotions.[22]

Once we are able to categorize our emotions as primary or mixed, clustered into families, and distinguished as facilitative or debilitative, we can then learn how to manage and communicate our emotions so that we will be perceived as effective and appropriate.

Managing Our Emotions

Motivation
Knowledge
Skill
COMPETENCE

We can learn to manage our fast-track and slow-track circuit emotions by becoming aware of our physiological reactions as soon as we experience them. We can also learn to manage our emotions by engaging in a technique to make our debilitative emotions facilitative. Learning to manage our emotions can increase our motivation to communicate. For example, we may try to avoid communicating with others if we believe we are incapable of controlling our emotions because we fear we may engage in angry outbursts, or we may experience bouts of social anxiety that make us afraid of communication in general. To counteract these tendencies, we can remind ourselves that emotions can positively affect communication and that it is possible to manage our negative emotions that cause our interactions to be perceived as ineffective and inappropriate. This can reduce our social anxiety and increase our perception of the personal rewards that may result from interacting with others, even when their (or our) emotions are intense and long-lasting.

How can engaging in mindfulness and rational emotive behavior therapy help us manage our emotions?

Managing Fast-Track Circuit Emotions

Recall that rational thought and decision making occur in the thinking brain. When signals from the emotional brain reach the thinking brain, the result can be "neural static." This is why we can't think straight when we are emotionally upset. From solving a complex problem to uttering a simple sentence, our thinking brain is negatively affected by the experience of intense negative emotions,[23] and we need to change the physiological experience of emotions to communicate competently. One way we can change the physiological experience of our emotions is to engage in mindfulness. **Mindfulness** is being aware of not only our thoughts but also the physical sensations of our body as we experience them. The guiding principle is to be present moment to moment but without critique or judgment. This involves a shift in mental activity away from the situation at hand. In other words, we act as an observer who nonjudgmentally perceives the physiological experience of our own emotions.[24] Once we become aware of our physiology, we can pause, take a deep breath or two, and collect our thoughts to prevent an emotional outburst. This is not easy to do, and it takes practice. There will be times when we may not be aware of the specific emotion we are experiencing, but the physiological changes associated with the fast-track circuit will tell us that we are becoming emotionally aroused.

We can make a point to engage in mindfulness and rational emotive behavior therapy during stressful situations.

MOTIVATION & mindwork • Listening to "Body Talk"

Mindfulness

Recall the last time you found yourself in a discussion that turned into an argument. Can you remember the exact point when you began to feel angry? How did your body tell you that you were becoming angry? Did you experience:

- Shortness of breath
- The sensation of being overheated (literally, "hot under the collar")
- Sweaty palms and excessive perspiration
- Rapid heartbeat
- Stomach in knots or butterflies in the stomach
- Weak knees
- Light-headedness

When we begin to feel any of these physiological experiences during emotional arousal, we can take a deep breath, pause, and/or even metacommunicate that we are becoming angry and need a "time out" to regain our composure. Make it a goal to be mindful and to monitor your body the next time you are emotionally aroused.

Managing Slow-Track Circuit Emotions

We can also manage our slow-track circuit emotions to help us communicate in a competent manner. These techniques concern the thoughts that cause us to experience emotions.

Thoughts and Feelings Most people probably believe that people or events actually cause emotions. For example, receiving a "C" on an assignment may "cause" us to feel frustration, or being turned down for a date may "cause" us to feel anger. However, both of these examples are false. In reality, it is our thoughts that cause our emotions; neither events nor people cause us to feel. For example, if we receive a "C" on an assignment and we think that we deserve an "A," we feel frustrated. However, if we receive a "C" on an assignment and we believe that we're lucky to have passed at all, we experience relief. Similarly, if we are turned down for a date and think that we've been treated poorly, we may feel angry. On the other hand, if we are turned down for a date and we believe that it's no big deal, we may feel fine and not experience any type of negative emotion. The idea that our thoughts influence the experience of emotion is represented in Table 4.2, "Thoughts Cause Emotions."

Table 4.2 Thoughts Cause Emotions

People/Event	Thought	Emotion
A significant other tells you that you are "crazy."	"He is being disrespectful!"	anger
	"She doesn't mean it."	calm
Your rent is raised $50.00 a month.	"I already can't afford to pay my bills!"	frustration
	"John's rent was raised $100.00 so I guess I'm lucky."	relief

MOTIVATION & mindwork • Which Thoughts Cause My Emotions?

Think about the last time you experienced an emotion that had a negative impact on your life (e.g., anger, frustration, contempt). Try to remember the thoughts that may have caused your emotions. Then try to remember the last time someone blamed you for causing her or his emotion(s). Consider the thoughts that may have actually caused the other person's experience of emotion. Do you believe that your feelings and others' feelings could have changed in the situations that you recalled if the thoughts that prompted the emotions had been different?

Rational Emotive Behavior Therapy **Rational emotive behavior therapy (REBT)** is a clinical technique that was developed by psychologist **Albert Ellis** to teach people how to reduce the intensity and duration of debilitative emotions. In REBT, we take responsibility for our emotions and realize that we (and not other people or situations) cause our feelings.[25] REBT directs us to identify and dispute our irrational thoughts that distort our emotions and actions. One format of REBT follows the first six letters of the alphabet:[26]

A = **A**ctivating event ("I'm going to dinner with my girlfriend or boyfriend and meeting her or his parents for the first time.")
B = irrational **B**elief ("I must not make any mistakes or else they'll think poorly of me.")
C = emotional **C**onsequences (fear, extreme anxiety)
D = **D**ispute the belief ("How do I know that my girlfriend or boyfriend's parents will think less of me if I don't know what fork to use or say something I shouldn't?")
E = **E**ffective new thinking ("I'll do the best job I can, and her or his parents won't think I'm a loser just because I make a mistake.")
F = new **F**eeling (determination, anticipation, and excitement; a reduction of fear and extreme anxiety)

REBT can be used in a variety of situations when irrational thoughts interfere with effective and appropriate communication. For example, what thoughts come to mind when you have a job interview or discuss a grade with a professor? Perhaps you have thoughts such as "I always say something stupid on job interviews" and "I'll just die if my professor doesn't change my grade." You can dispute these unrealistic thoughts and replace them with beliefs that are reasonable. This will decrease the intensity and duration of debilitative emotions such as fear and anxiety and increase your motivation to communicate in a competent

MOTIVATION & mindwork • Managing My Debilitative Emotions

Think about some situations in which you can use REBT to change the thoughts that cause your debilitative emotions. Such situations may include a first date, asking a boss for a raise, refusing a request, and asking someone to change her or his behavior. With a partner or in a group, practice changing your irrational thoughts to those that are rational using the "A-B-C-D-E-F" approach.

manner. Prior to a job interview, you can tell yourself, "Who says that I *always* say stupid things on job interviews? I've made some mistakes in the past, but I don't have to make mistakes again. I'll try to take a breath before I speak, and I'll do the best job I can." Before a discussion with your professor, you can tell yourself, "Will I really *die* if the professor doesn't change my grade? It will be bad for me if he or she doesn't agree to the grade change, but I'll survive!" Although replacing unrealistic thoughts with those that are realistic may not completely eliminate our debilitative emotions, they will help us manage such emotions and influence the perception of communication competence.

Expressing Our Emotions

- "I was in a good mood until you got me angry!"
- "I don't want to hurt your feelings."
- "Sometimes you make me feel nervous."

Have you ever communicated thoughts like these? Even though we may realize that it's our thoughts that cause our emotions, we still may falter when it comes to expressing our emotions in a competent manner. We need to set realistic goals, improve our emotional intelligence, learn how and when to display our emotions, and accept responsibility for our feelings when we interact with others.

How can owning our emotions improve our communication competence?

Setting Realistic Goals

We have learned how to manage our emotions by becoming mindful of the physiological responses associated with our emotions as we experience them and by replacing irrational thoughts with rational thoughts. We also need to be attuned to the emotional reactions of others, and, at the same time, know how and when to communicate our feelings in an effective and appropriate manner. There are ways we'll learn to skillfully communicate our emotions to others, but we should be realistic about changing the experience and expression of our feelings. Our habitual emotional reactions to people and situations have been formed over the course of a lifetime. Consequently, changing our emotional responses will take effort. Just as realistic goal setting can help us improve our self-concept and motivation to communicate competently, setting goals can also help us sustain our motivation to manage our emotions and communicate our emotions in a competent manner. We can therefore set realistic goals for ourselves and not give up if we have difficulty meeting them. An example of an unrealistic goal is "I will always communicate calmly in a stressful situation." A more realistic goal is "I will try to pause and take a deep breath before I react in a stressful situation." We should also give ourselves another chance if we find ourselves communicating our emotions ineffectively and inappropriately; we will have many opportunities to practice the management and communication of our emotions.

Improving Our Emotional Intelligence

Do you know someone who seems to effectively manage his or her emotions and knows exactly how you're feeling, even when you don't verbalize your emotions? People who can manage their emotions well and who sense and respond to others' feelings have emotional intelligence. Psychologist **Daniel Goleman** defines **emotional** intelligence (EQ) as knowing how to manage our feelings and to read and respond effectively to the emotions of others. EQ includes the ability to persist even when frustrated, to control our impulses and delay gratification, to regulate our mood and prevent distressful emotions from overwhelming our ability to think rationally, and to empathize with others. Studies demonstrate that EQ is unrelated to a person's IQ or to scores on other tests of intelligence. EQ is an influential factor in career advancement, and leaders with high EQs are more effective than those with lower EQs. Emotional intelligence also promotes close and affectionate relationships and greater relational satisfaction.[27]

KNOWLEDGE power • Testing Your EQ

Do you think you are emotionally intelligent? You can get an idea of your EQ by taking the Emotional IQ test at the Psychtests Web site (scroll down to the free Emotional IQ test). This seventy-question test takes approximately thirty-five minutes to complete: www.psychtests.com/test/iq/emotional_iq_r2_access.html. You can access an additional EQ assessment at: http://quiz.ivillage.co.uk/uk_work/tests/eqtest.htm (a twenty-question assessment).

We can improve our EQ by becoming mindful of the emotions that we experience as they occur. Recall that this is a way to manage our fast-track circuit emotions. Even when involved in a heated argument, we can pause, take a breath, and tell ourselves that we are aware that we are feeling anger and excitement. Realizing, for example, that we are experiencing intense anger provides us with a degree of freedom because we can decide whether to communicate our anger or to let go of it. We can also develop our EQ by marshaling positive feelings such as enthusiasm, confidence, and optimism. Focusing on positive emotions can facilitate complex thinking and help us solve problems creatively. For example, a study of 500 first-year students at the University of Pennsylvania revealed that scores on a test of optimism predicted actual first-year grades better than SAT scores or high school grades. A study conducted at Met Life found that new salespeople who were optimists sold 37% more insurance during their first two years than did pessimists.[28] Both hope and optimism are emotions that can be learned, cultivated, sustained, and communicated. In particular, you may want to review the mental inventory of talents and strengths that you created while reading about the self-concept in Chapter 3. You can remind yourself of your talents and strengths to sustain your hope and optimism whenever you experience a down day.

The Communication of Emotions

We can learn how and when to communicate our emotions by following guidelines that include assessing whether we want to communicate our emotions, expanding our emotional vocabulary, and accepting responsibility for our feelings.

Assessing Our Emotions Although we cannot "make" someone feel an emotion, we may hesitate to communicate certain emotions that we believe may be hurtful to others or may exacerbate problems we are experiencing. In addition, we may hesitate to communicate negative emotions because we believe that others will react negatively to us (e.g., they won't like us or consider us incompetent communicators). However, research suggests that the communication of negative emotions is not problematic when they are expressed in a manner appropriate to the situation and when we consider to whom they are communicated. Specifically, our willingness to communicate negative emotions that express a need to a (potentially) close relationship partner may elicit help from a (potential) partner, may influence others to like us, can help us build larger social networks, and can facilitate the establishment of intimacy.[29] We may also realize that we have an unethical motive for communicating our emotions (e.g., to manipulate with guilt or to control with anger). If this is the case, choosing not to communicate our emotions may be constructive. Sometimes we may decide that our physical environment or social role makes it inappropriate for us to communicate our emotions; for example, shedding a few tears alone in the library bathroom may be more appropriate than with our peers at the library study hall. We may also choose to keep our emotions to ourselves for reasons of privacy. After all, it is irrational to think that we are required to tell all of our feelings to everyone or even to our significant others.

If we do decide to communicate our emotions, we should first assess the state of our emotions. If we are feeling extremely strong emotions, we may regret communicating our feelings if we do not wait until the intensity subsides. It's probably beneficial to cool down before communicating intense emotions.

Expanding Our Vocabulary We can improve how we communicate our emotions by expanding our vocabulary of feeling words. We can:

- Use a variety of single words, such as *"I'm angry, frustrated, and relieved!"*
- Describe our physiological and physical symptoms; for example, *"My heart is pounding and my hands are shaking!"*
- Implicitly describe an emotion by mentioning a course of action (that we may or may not follow); for example, *"I want to punch a hole in the wall and then give you a big kiss!"*[30]

Review the families of emotions in the "Emotion Families" table. We need to be sure to choose a variety of words to express our feelings, and we shouldn't rely on the first emotion that we experience, which is usually the strongest and most negative. For example, how would you feel if a friend agreed to stop by your apartment at 7 P.M. to drive you to a party but didn't show up until after 10? Of course, you would feel angry, but wouldn't you also feel relieved and happy that your friend wasn't in an accident? Might you also feel disappointed because your friend didn't even think to call? Communicating only your anger would make it impossible for your friend to understand the full range of your feelings, and he or she would respond to you based on your anger alone. Your friend would probably

We can improve how we communicate our emotions by using a variety of single words.

Source: LUANN: © GEC Inc./Dist. by United Features Syndicate, Inc.

react differently if you communicated more than one emotion, especially if that one emotion is negative.

Owning Feelings We can also improve the communication of our emotions by accepting responsibility for our feelings. It is *our* physiology and *our* beliefs that are responsible for our emotions; no one can *make* us feel anything. Therefore, statements such as "You make me so angry" and "You hurt my feelings" are false. It is more ethical and correct to say "I get angry when you . . ." and "I feel hurt when you . . ." rather than suggest that someone else is responsible for how we feel. A simple way to accept responsibility or "own" feelings is to combine our emotion(s) word(s) with a description of behavior. The behavioral description should involve sense data and be specific and completely nonjudgmental. For example:

Ineffective ownership:	"You make me happy when you say those things."
Effective ownership:	*"I feel happy when you say I'm a good cook."*
Ineffective ownership:	"I was in a good mood until you came home and started arguing with me."
Effective ownership:	*"I get angry when you tell me that I'm 'wrong.'"*
Ineffective ownership:	"You get me all upset when you mess up the apartment."
Effective ownership:	*"I get upset when you leave your dirty clothes in the bathroom, the kitchen, and the den."*

Recent research illustrates that listeners prefer statements that suggest they are actually the cause of *positive* emotions compared with statements in which speakers take responsibility for them. In other words, we tend to react more positively when speakers attribute their positive emotions to us than when speakers own their positive emotions.[31] We become defensive if we are blamed for causing others' negative emotions, however, and overall it's best to own emotions.

These guidelines and skills designed to improve the communication of emotions may not lead to an anticipated result. It's possible that positive outcomes will result when we suggest that others cause our emotions. For example, telling a relational partner "You make me feel totally insecure" can prompt a response such as "You know, I've been told that before by other people in my life. . . . I'm sorry for coming on so strong." There is no guarantee that following the guidelines and skills for the communication of emotions will

SKILL practice • Owning Our Emotions

Reword the following statements to illustrate that you own your emotions. Remember to accept responsibility for your emotions and to communicate the specific behaviors that may trigger the emotions. Be sure to base the specific behaviors on sense data, such as what we see, hear, or touch.

- "You make me angry when you act like such a jerk!"
- "You upset me when you ignore me."
- "It makes me happy when you treat me so well."
- "I was in a bad mood until you started to cheer me up."
- "My professor gets me confused when she or he talks about stuff that I don't understand."

Competence & Critical Thinking

DRIVE ME NUTS AND EMOTIONS

In this clip, Mike and his friends Dave and Steve are looking for a parking spot at their college. Mike is concerned that he will be late for class, but finally follows a student to his car and turns on his blinker to signal that he will take the spot. All of a sudden, a female student cuts in front of Mike and takes the spot he is waiting for.

You can view scene one in *Drive Me Nuts* by accessing the "Small Group and Interpersonal Videos" on the MyCommunicationLab Web site. Answer the following questions about Mike and his emotions:

- Describe Mike's emotions in terms of primary and mixed emotions, emotion families, and facilitative and debilitative emotions.
- What nonverbal behaviors indicate what Mike may be feeling?
- What word does Mike use that expresses an emotion? Should he have used more than one emotion-related word to express his feelings?
- Mike tells the student who took his parking spot that he used his blinker for "common courtesy." Why do you believe she responded uncivilly to his suggestion that he acted in a civil manner?
- Dave tells Mike to "Just let it go." To what is he referring? In terms of emotions, what are some techniques that Mike could use to "let it go"?

MIKE: This is ridiculous, man. Seriously, we'd think with all the expanding they're doing, they'd add parking, too.

DAVE: What, are you kidding me? That would be the logical thing to do.

MIKE: I really hate this school.

DAVE: All right, all right, just don't hit these people.

MIKE: I'm really going to be late for my class. I have five minutes.

DAVE: We all have five minutes to be to class.

STEVE: We'll be so late for this class, we'll be early for the next one. *(the guys laugh)*

MIKE: Yeah, keep cracking jokes.

DAVE: He's a riot today.

STEVE: I'm a riot every day.

DAVE: Just make a left here. *(a car cuts in front of Mike and Mike honks his horn)*

MIKE: Are you serious? Just look at this girl!

DAVE: Go, all right? Move on to the next one.

MIKE: All right, yeah, look at all those people.

DAVE: *(seeing a student walk to his car)* Follow this guy.

MIKE: All right.

DAVE: Where's he going, you think? He's going to his car. Follow him.

MIKE: All right, I'm going, I'm going, I'm going.

STEVE: Get him.

DAVE: Not so close, you're scaring the hell out of him . . . Probably thinks we're stalking him.

STEVE: This isn't Halloween, buddy.

DAVE: Yeah . . . That's good. Slow.

MIKE: Any slower, you're going backwards.

DAVE: You guys are just full of clichés today. *(the guys laugh)*

MIKE: Too bad it's not an English final.

DAVE: Man.

MIKE: All right. There he goes. Going to get in his car. My blinker is on. No one's coming around me . . . *(a student cuts in front of Mike and takes the parking spot he's waiting for)* Oh, are you serious? *(Mike honks his horn)* I don't believe this. Hey, What's the matter with you? You don't see I had my blinker on?

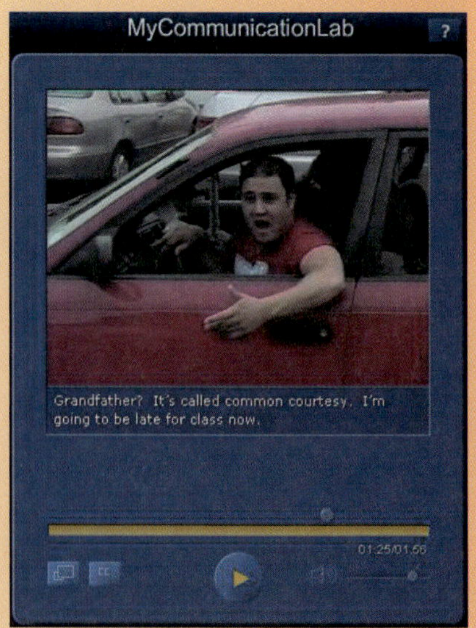

STUDENT: Yeah. But when you drive like my grandfather, you're going to lose a spot.

MIKE: Grandfather? It's called common courtesy. I'm going to be late for class now.

STUDENT: Sorry. In that case, thank you.

MIKE: Ach! Look at this girl!

DAVE: All right. All right.

MIKE: Unbelievable. Now, oh, we'll really be late now. Might as well just skip class.

DAVE: Just let it go.

result in the response we desire. Consider what can happen if we own our emotions when communicating with someone who wants to control us and our relationship. Saying "I felt hurt when you said I was 'uncooperative'" may lead to a response in which our feelings are discounted, such as "You're making a big thing out of nothing!" or (sarcastically) "Well, if that's the way you want to take it, then soorrry." Chapter 9 contains more information about discounting others' perceptions and emotions, a covert form of verbal abuse. The point to remember here is that effective and appropriate communication on our part doesn't guarantee that our conversation partner will use effective and appropriate communication in return. The competent expression of emotions depends not only on the needs and experiences of our conversation partner but also on our situation, goals, and what past behavior has left us feeling better or worse in the long run.[32]

Contexts and Emotions

How do contexts influence emotions and communication?

In addition to our physiology and our cognitions, the culture, relationship, gender, and individual contexts influence how we experience and communicate our emotions. These contexts also affect how we interpret others' emotions. Knowing that the culture, relationship, gender, and individual contexts influence the interpretation of others' emotions will help us refrain from making faulty attributions about the reasons for others' behavior. This knowledge should also help us understand why others communicate or fail to communicate their emotions.

Culture Context

Happiness, sadness, and anger are emotions that people experience and express cross-culturally. However, cultures differ in terms of display rules and decoding rules.

Display and Decoding Rules Culturally influenced **display rules** tell people how and when to display emotions, and culturally influenced **decoding rules** tell people how to interpret emotions when they are displayed. People who live in cultures that are primarily individualist tend to express a wider variety of emotions than do members of cultures that are primarily collectivistic. In collectivist cultures, emotional behaviors that facilitate group cooperation and harmony are emphasized more than in individualist cultures. For example, the more collectivist Korean culture teaches its members to be more emotionally

Each culture has its own display rules that teach us when, where, and how to express our emotions in a competent manner.

reserved than people who live in the United States, and public displays of affection (i.e., kisses and hugs) are not seen in public in Korea as often. Display rules also apply to the verbal expression of emotion. For example, "British English" is less emotionally demonstrative than "American English." It is common for the British to minimize the strength of emotion-laden comments with euphemisms or phrases such as "There's one thing that is somewhat worrisome" or "Perhaps I'm a bit sad." On the other hand, an American may communicate the full intensity of felt emotions with comments such as "This is a terrible problem!" or "I am deeply depressed."[33]

Co-cultures and Emotions Co-cultures within a larger culture influence the interpretation and expression of emotion. For example, the decoding rules associated with various ethnic groups influence the meaning assigned to emotional expression. In one study in which college students were asked to view photographs to identify displays of emotion, African American students perceived the emotions as being more intense than the white, Hispanic, and Asian students, and the Asian students perceived them as being the least intense. The African American students perceived anger expressions more frequently than the other students, and the white students perceived the display of many emotions as being appropriate more than the other students. The Asian students perceived the same emotions evaluated as appropriate by the white students as being least appropriate.[34] The results of this study demonstrate that one component of competent communication is to understand and respect how people different from ourselves interpret and express emotions. In addition, this study illustrates that it is necessary to consider the influence of our own cultural context when judging the emotions of others.

Relationship Context

In addition to the culture context, the relationship context, which includes our family, friends, and persons with whom we work, influences the interpretation and expression of emotion.

Families and Friends Families provide us with expectations for the expression of emotions, and parents teach their children what they should and should not feel. For example, families differ in terms of the expectations they have regarding emotional expressivity and emotional restraint. We may be expected to express our emotions more freely with the members of our family than with strangers, acquaintances, or even friends. On the other hand, we may have been taught to stifle our emotions, especially those that are intense, for the sake of maintaining harmony. Perhaps you once visited a friend at home and were invited to stay for dinner. If you come from a family that emphasizes emotional restraint, you may have become uncomfortable with the emphatic political discussion or the

SHERMAN'S LAGOON By J.P. Toomey

Families and relationship partners have expectations for the expression of emotions.

Source: © SHERMAN'S LAGOON – JIM TOOMEY. KING FEATURES SYNDICATE.

raucous laughter during a supper characterized by joke telling. On the other hand, if you come from a family that emphasizes emotional expressivity, you may have become uncomfortable with a silence so unbearable that all you could hear was the silverware scraping the plates. Some parents additionally teach their children what they should or should not feel.[35] Think about some of the emotion-related messages that you received from your parents. Were you told that you should appreciate your siblings? Were you told that you should feel thankful when you receive a gift? Parents also teach children how emotions should be expressed. For example, perhaps your parents told you that it was OK to feel angry at a sibling but that you shouldn't hit her or him.

Coworkers Emotion in the workplace is complex and multifaceted, and it is studied by researchers in a variety of academic disciplines. In general, five categories of workplace emotion describe the experience and communication of emotion on the job. These categories are not mutually exclusive, and it is possible to experience multiple types of emotion at the same time in the same job:[36]

1. Emotional labor: emotions prescribed by an organization as a part of the job. Flight attendants, servers at restaurants, and workers at tourist attractions are typically told to smile and communicate in a positive manner, no matter what they're feeling.
2. Emotional work: emotions that are authentic and play a central role in working with others. Nurses, social workers, teachers, and ministers engage in emotional work with patients, clients, students, and parishioners.
3. Emotion toward work: emotions such as job satisfaction, stress, and burnout that result from our thoughts and attitudes about work itself.
4. Emotion at work: emotions expressed in the workplace that result from various social roles (e.g., spouses, friends, children). Although we expect workers to suppress private emotions at work, this is not always possible.
5. Emotion with work: emotions that result from interactions with coworkers and supervisors. Our relationships with coworkers influence our emotions more than our on-the-job tasks, and our relationships with supervisors influence the display and communication of emotions. For example, subordinates conceal or distort their

emotions if they believe that a supervisor will use their emotional displays to block their chances of upward mobility or other organization-related goals. Employees may express negative emotions in indirect ways, such as not showing up or being late for meetings and talking about people behind their backs, or manage their negative emotions by denying their existence or by expressing the emotions in a private setting.[37]

Gender Context

Gender influences the processing, interpretation, and communication of emotions as they relate to masculinity and femininity.

Masculinity and Emotions For the most part, masculinity is associated with emotional reserve and control; however, the expression of aggression and anger is considered appropriate.[38] On the other hand, an Oxford University study found that 77% of the men they polled believed that it is acceptable for men to cry. The Oxford study also demonstrated that 63% of the male respondents who were at least fifty years old had never seen their father cry. However, only 44% of male respondents eighteen to twenty-nine years old gave the same response, suggesting there may be a generational shift regarding the characterization of masculinity and how acceptable it is for men to express sensitivity or vulnerability.[39]

Femininity and Emotions In general, women are taught to be "feminine" by being sensitive and caring. Girls and women are also taught to be "nice" and that aggression and anger are the antithesis of "niceness." Both self-report and observational data demonstrate that women communicate both positive and negative emotions in conversation more than men do. Women are also better than men at recognizing nonverbal emotion cues of the face, voice, and body, with the possible exception of anger.[40]

Individual Context

Our personality affects how we experience and communicate emotions. Three of the Big Five personality traits discussed in Chapter 3, extroversion, neuroticism, and agreeableness, have a strong influence on our emotions. People who are extroverted (sociable and outgoing) tend to experience positive emotions more frequently than other people. It is interesting to note that magnetic resonance imaging (MRI) illustrates that extroverts have greater brain activity in response to positive stimuli than to negative stimuli. The increased brain activity associated with positive stimuli may be the basis for the frequent experience of positive emotions over negative ones. People who are highly extroverted also believe they are better able to manage and communicate their emotions than other people. In contrast, people who are neurotic (i.e., tend to think negatively about themselves) typically experience negative emotions more frequently, consider themselves less happy, and see themselves as less skilled in emotional management and communication than others. MRI research also illustrates that people who receive high scores on measures of neuroticism have greater brain activity in relation to negative stimuli than to positive stimuli. And people who are agreeable (friendly and cooperative) believe they are happier and better able to manage and communicate their emotions than those who are not agreeable.[41]

OVERCOMING COMMUNICATION CHALLENGES

Workplace Bullying and Mobbing

- "He yelled at me in front of everyone at the meeting because I was taking notes. Aren't you supposed to take notes at a meeting?"
- "I was told that he was talking about me behind my back to other employees. I was even cautioned to consider legal counsel."
- "He prohibited me from traveling to the workshop, even though my requests for leave time and travel reimbursement were approved by my dean and the vice president. He also told me I was responsible for the plane ticket and the registration fee."[42]

What do these situations have in common? These comments were made by faculty at the same community college about the same person who bullied them—their president. These comments reflect a phenomenon called workplace bullying. **Workplace bullying** is a type of emotional abuse that most often emanates from a powerful person such as a boss. **Mobbing**, another form of bullying that occurs at the workplace, occurs when a person in authority, typically the perpetrator, creates a circle of allies, "the mob," that helps carry out the emotional abuse. Members of the mob bully the victim because they fear losing their jobs or actually enjoy taking advantage of the employee's vulnerability. Labeled the "silent epidemic," emotional abuse is estimated to affect one in six U.S. workers each year. Approximately 25% of U.S. companies report some degree of bullying, and more than 80% of workers report having witnessed one or more incidents of bullying.[43]

Victims of workplace bullying and mobbing report distress, illness, and depression. Employees who are abused also may feel embarrassment, fear, shame, anger, guilt, and disgrace, and the stress that results from workplace bullying may exceed that of excessive workloads and long working hours. The damage that results from repeated emotional assaults is gradual and cumulative, and victims often resign or are ultimately forced out of their place of employment. Workplace bullying robs employees of their professional integrity, their reputation, and their competence.[44]

Unlike workplace incivility (caused by disrespectful behaviors that may or may not be intended to harm an individual), on-the-job emotional abuse specifically targets a victim and is designed to force a person out of the workplace. Intentionally abusive, bullying and mobbing behaviors such as the following are displayed continuously:[45]

- restrictions on expression and contact with others
- constant criticism about work and private life
- gossip, ridicule, and demeaning communication
- being ignored and subject to "the silent treatment"
- verbally aggressive communication delivered one-on-one or in the presence of others

Unfortunately, employees who are bullied do not have the law on their side. Unlike federally protected civil rights, no law restricts emotional abuse on the job. Various "healthy workplace" bills have been introduced in state legislatures since 2003, but none has become law. Nonetheless, workers who are bullied can take steps to deal with emotional abuse. For example, employees can work to regain their emotional strength and make rational decisions about how to respond to bullying behaviors. Although most research suggests that people with less power are typically the victims of bullying, such "victims" can reject the idea that they are helpless by acting to help themselves. To regain emotional strength, they can engage in positive self-talk and make it a point to communicate with persons who value them. They can channel their energies away from their organization toward enjoyable pursuits. Employees can also contact organizations such as the Workplace Bullying and Trauma Institute for advice and research. They can weigh the options of remaining in the hostile work environment or seeking other employment, and they can decide to "blow the whistle" in an attempt to end the silence about workplace bullying if they decide to leave their organization.[46] However, potential whistle-blowers may face disbelief from coworkers, bosses, and human resources personnel, and they may be dismissed as problem employees. The Project for Wellness and Work-Life (PWWL) provides eight guidelines to communicate stories of abuse:[47]

1. Be rational: engage in linear storytelling and provide concrete examples of how the bullying situations unfolded.
2. Express emotions appropriately: communicate the emotionality of the bullying experience while remaining calm and without displaying the emotions described.
3. Provide consistent details: tell and retell consistent and detailed stories so that they will be interpreted as truthful and credible.
4. Offer a plausible story: consider referencing published literature about on-the-job emotional abuse because decision makers may need to be convinced that workplace bullying is a "real" phenomenon.
5. Be relevant: get to the point and avoid discussing how the abuse has caused injury, trauma, and sadness. Focus on the bully's behaviors and reactions.
6. Emphasize your competence: establish the fact that bullying does not result from poor performance or from being perceived as a problem employee. Discuss all proactive efforts to resolve work-related problems and incidents of bullying.
7. Show consideration for others' perspectives: engage in perspective taking and demonstrate your attempts to understand the bully's behavior. Recognize that others may disbelieve stories of workplace bullying and, instead, blame the victim.
8. Be specific: use language that is clear and easily understood; for example, avoid pronouns such as "they" and "she" to refer to various people so that listeners will find it easy to follow the story.

A CASE STUDY IN ETHICS

Gays in the Military—Protest by the Westboro Baptist Church

We have read that competent communication includes an ethical dimension of well-based standards of right and wrong. When deciding whether to communicate our emotions, we can ask ourselves questions that relate to "everyday ethics." For example, we can ask ourselves if the communication of our emotions will reflect a virtue (e.g., integrity, trustworthiness, honesty, or responsibility). We can also ask if the expression of our emotions will result in more good than harm and if the communication of our emotions will entail treating others with dignity and respect, reflect fairness and justice, and make our community stronger. Read about the protests conducted by members of the Westboro Baptist Church and consider whether the protests and efforts to stop them are ethical.

How would you feel if, while attending a funeral, an organized group held signs and chanted, "God hates fags" and "Thank God for dead soldiers"? Would you become outraged, depressed, and/or confused if you heard the protesters shout, "America is doomed" and "Thank God for IEDs" (booby traps)? Fred Phelps and members of his Westboro Baptist Church (WBC) use the funerals of U.S. soldiers who fought in Iraq as an opportunity to protest U.S. policy concerning homosexuality and the military. According to the WBC, the United States is "doomed" because it supports gays, and our involvement in Iraq reflects God's anger at the U.S. "homosexual agenda." The WBC also uses its anti-gay rhetoric to communicate anti-Semitism, racism, and anti-Catholicism.

The WBC protests have inspired the federal "Respect for America's Fallen Heroes Act" and at least seventeen states to create legislation restricting protest activities near funerals. A number of legislators considered the emotions of the deceased's family and friends as a reason for voting for such bills. For example, Wisconsin State Senator Ron Brown stated that such legislation "protects the safety of those who are grieving," and Indiana State Senator Brent Steele asserted that the WBC's "invasion of a family's grief is unconscionable." Moreover, Indiana State Senator Anita Bowser suggested that the type of protest conducted by the WBC during emotionally charged occasions such as funerals may incite violence and is therefore no more protected than yelling "fire" in a crowded theater. Senator Steele agreed with Senator Bowser that the legislation concerns a public safety issue and questioned, "When people are at their most frazzled time emotionally, what little thing would it take for a loved one to tee off and go back there and hurt someone?"[48]

Although most people agree that the WBC tactics are deplorable and depraved, not everyone agrees that the way to stop hate mongering is through legislation. Those who oppose such legislation suggest that our increasingly legalistic nation may eventually find itself debating amendments that ban trash talk at sporting events. They contend that not every word or hateful poster is a threat and that we risk demeaning the public when we believe that the state is responsible for shielding citizens from unpleasant speech.[49]

Do you believe that members of the Westboro Baptist Church act in an ethical manner when they engage in protest at military funerals? Is it ethical to consider constituents' emotions in voting for or against legislation? Is it ethical to use legislation to protect citizens from speech that disparages others?

Is it ethical to engage in protest at military funerals?

Chapter Review

Motivation: How has this helped me?

- **The importance of studying emotions and communication**

Emotions are a likely component of every conversation in which we participate and deserve study because they affect our readiness to communicate; when, how, and why we communicate; and how we interpret and respond when others communicate with us.

- **Engaging in mindfulness and rational emotive behavior therapy**

Engaging in mindfulness allows us to nonjudgmentally perceive the physiological experience of our emotions. Being mindful enables us to manage our fast-track circuit emotions that occur before we have time to rationally analyze a situation. We can also improve our emotional intelligence (the ability to manage our feelings and read and respond effectively to others' emotions) by becoming mindful of the emotions as they occur. We can also manage our slow-track circuit emotions by using rational emotive behavior therapy to change our irrational thoughts to rational thoughts.

Knowledge: What have I learned?

- **How we can characterize emotions**

Emotions are processes that result from the interactions of physiology, cognition, and social experiences, and they have a significant impact on how we communicate with others and interpret others' communication. Emotions also affect our physical and relational health.

- **Fast-track and slow-track circuit emotions**

Fast-track circuit emotions are reflected in emotional reactions and brain activity that occur before we have time to rationally analyze a situation. When perceptions do affect emotions, it is through a slow-track circuit in which the thinking brain rationally analyzes a situation and then communicates with the emotional brain. We are usually aware of the thoughts that lead to emotions in the slow-track circuit.

- **Types of emotions**

Emotions can be classified in a variety of ways. One classification system suggests that eight primary emotions blend to form mixed emotions. Other classification systems posit that emotions can be clustered in "families" that share common characteristics. Emotions are also categorized in terms of being facilitative (those that contribute to effective functioning) or debilitative (those that detract from effective functioning). Intensity and duration distinguish facilitative emotions from debilitative emotions.

- **How contexts influence emotions and communication**

The culture context influences emotions in terms of display and decoding rules. The relationship context indicates that our family and those with whom we work influence emotional restraint. The gender context influences the experience and expression of emotion in expectations associated with femininity and masculinity. The individual context illustrates that our personality affects the experience and communication of emotions.

Skill: What skill have I developed?

- **Owning our emotions can improve our communication competence**

Owning our emotions communicates that we accept responsibility for our feelings. A simple way to own our feelings is to combine our emotion(s) word(s) with a description of behavior based on sense data.

Study Questions

1. What are emotions and why should they be studied in relation to communication?
2. What is the difference between fast-track circuit emotions and slow-track circuit emotions?
3. What is the fight-or-flight syndrome? What causes us to want to flee or fight?
4. Describe mindfulness and how it can be used to manage fast-track circuit emotions.
5. Describe rational emotive behavior therapy and how it can be used to manage slow-track circuit emotions.
6. What are primary and mixed emotions; emotion families; and facilitative and debilitative emotions?
7. How can we express our emotions in an effective and appropriate manner?
8. How do the culture, relationship, gender, and individual contexts affect emotions and communication?
9. What is mobbing? Describe some behaviors that illustrate mobbing and what victims can do to contend with mobbing.

Names to Know

Albert Ellis (1913–2007), p. 103—psychologist who developed rational emotive behavior therapy, in which debilitative emotions can be managed by replacing irrational thoughts with rational thoughts.

Daniel Goleman, p. 104—psychologist and author of *Emotional Intelligence*. Goleman contends that in much of life, self-awareness, self-discipline, persistence, and empathy are of greater consequence than IQ.

Robert Plutchik, p. 98—psychologist who developed a theory showing eight primary human emotions: joy, acceptance, fear, submission, sadness, disgust, anger, and anticipation. Plutchik argued that all human emotions can be derived from these.

Key Terms

amygdala, 96
debilitative emotions, 99
decoding rules, 109
display rules, 109
emotion families, 98
emotional intelligence (EQ), 104
emotions, 94
facilitative emotions, 99
fast-track circuit emotions, 96
fight-or-flight syndrome, 97
mindfulness, 101
mixed emotions, 98
mobbing, 113
primary emotions, 98
rational emotive behavior therapy (REBT), 103
slow-track circuit emotions, 98
workplace bullying, 113

CHAPTER 5 Verbal Communication

"Words are also actions, and actions are a kind of words."

Ralph Waldo Emerson (1803–1882), American poet

In this chapter, we will answer the following:

- It is important to study verbal communication because the symbols used in verbal communication are crucial for the expression of meaning and interaction with others.

Knowledge: What will I learn?

- How to characterize verbal communication
- The relationship between verbal communication and meaning
- How verbal communication influences thought
- How contexts influence verbal communication

Skill: Why do I need to develop these skills?

- Using specific and concrete words, indexing and owning our thoughts, and dating information can improve our communication competence.

Have you ever had an assignment returned upon which your instructor wrote, "a unique approach" or "this is different"? Are these comments meant to praise or meant to criticize? And how might you interpret the following statement: "The internal validity of the Likert-type scale makes the statistical significance of the results highly suspicious." Do you know what "internal validity" refers to? What is a "Likert-type scale" or "statistical significance"? This sentence is difficult to interpret without some knowledge of research methodology. The instructor's comments and the sentence about research illustrate that it may be difficult to understand verbal communication. The verbal communication we use in our conversations influences how others perceive our communication competence. Just as Angelina Jolie travels the world and shares the plight of those in need, we can make a difference with our verbal communication by learning about others and sharing our knowledge. In this chapter, we will learn that understanding why it's important to study verbal communication and knowing about our basic human needs can motivate us to communicate competently with others. We will also increase our knowledge by learning about the characterization of verbal communication, how verbal communication influences thought, characteristics of verbal communication, the influence of contexts on verbal communication, and gender-biased language. We will also learn the skills of using specific and concrete words, owning our thoughts and indexing, and dating information to increase the chances that others will perceive us as effective and appropriate communicators.

Introduction to Verbal Communication

Verbal communication concerns the use of words to create and convey meaning. Can you recall a time when you were unable to communicate verbally with others? Perhaps you had your tonsils removed, experienced a bad sore throat, or were hoarse from too much shouting. If you are not fluent in ASL (a signed language made up of symbols and a grammar for their use) or grew tired of using paper and pen to communicate, you probably found it difficult to convey your thoughts and feelings. Perhaps you appreciated what you once took for granted—the ability to use words to engage in verbal interaction. The words used in verbal communication enable us to define and classify; express our beliefs, attitudes, thoughts, and feelings; organize our perceptions; and talk about hypothetical events, events that occurred in the past, and events that may occur in the future.

How can we characterize verbal communication?

Characterization of Verbal Communication

We communicate verbally with **symbols** or words that stand for something else. However, misunderstandings based on verbal communication occur because the relationship between words and what they stand for is arbitrary. This means that there is no inherent or logical relationship between words and the things they represent. For example, suppose a being from outer space beams down to planet Earth and somehow winds up in your bedroom. Looking around your environment, the space creature stares fixated at an object never seen before: a clock. The being does not know what the object is, what the object is used for, or how to label the object. The uninvited extraterrestrial guest cannot even guess the name of the object because there's no apparent connection between what something is called (the symbol) and what something is (the referent).

The idea that words are symbolic and representative of something else is illustrated in Figure 5.1, "The Triangle of Meaning." Originally developed by linguists **C. K. Ogden** and **I. A. Richards**, the triangle of meaning shows that the relationship between words and what they stand for is arbitrary.[1] The line that connects the symbol (word) and thought illustrates that we have our own meaning for a word, which may or may not be the same meaning understood by someone else. The line that connects the referent (thing) and thought shows that we create mental images of the things we actually encounter. The broken line between the symbol and referent illustrates that there is an arbitrary relationship between a

Figure 5.1: The Triangle of Meaning

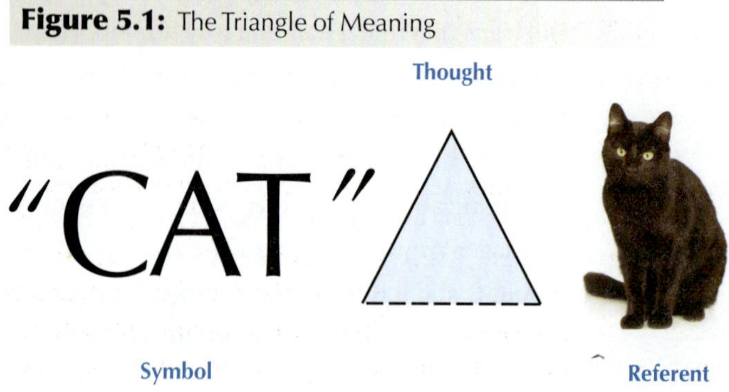

KNOWLEDGE power • □☆○☾▭△

With a partner or in a group, create a code to communicate information to others. For example, you can make up symbols to communicate directions to a specific location, instructions associated with a recipe, or a description of a particular TV show or movie. Devise a symbol key (that is, what each word or symbol means) and create a short paragraph written in your code. Provide the key and paragraph to your classmates so they can decode your new language. When you are finished, discuss how this activity relates to the relationship between words and what they stand for.

symbol and what it represents. There is no connection between the symbol and referent except the one we make with our thoughts.

Why It's Important to Study Verbal Communication

Motivation
Knowledge
Skill
COMPETENCE

Have you ever struggled to find just the right word to express what you are thinking? Have you ever regretted your choice of words or used words incorrectly? If you are familiar with such experiences, you have firsthand knowledge that effective verbal communication is difficult without the words needed to express our meanings. Therefore, understanding that the symbols used in verbal communication are crucial for the expression of meaning can motivate us to become competent communicators. Maybe you once told your parents that you "love" them, told your roommate that you "love" your car, and told a friend that you "love" pepperoni pizza. Obviously the word *love* has many meanings and may not be the best word to use in all situations to describe positive feelings toward someone or something. Suppose we can't find a different word to describe our feelings other than "love." Our communication may be ineffective because we fail to get our precise meaning across to a conversation partner. Overall, verbal communication enables us to interact with others—an important reason why verbal communication deserves study.

Why is it important to study verbal communication?

Interpersonal Communication Motives and Verbal Communication

Knowing the needs and motives that drive us to interact with others can also motivate us to communicate competently. Think about all of your communication during the past twenty-four hours. What functions did your communication serve? Perhaps you interacted with others to maintain your self-concept, express support, and/or meet a need. Research concerning why people interact reveals that persuasion and the expression of emotion are two general motives for verbal communication. We also communicate with others to solve problems, develop relationships, and engage in impression management,[2] and we are motivated to communicate with others to fulfill basic human needs. In fact, some researchers contend that it is difficult to separate "motives" from

People who experience communication apprehension interact to be included with others rather than for pleasure or relaxation.

"needs" and "communication" because needs are manifested in motives and communication; that is, a need produces a motive, which in turn generates communication behavior.[3]

Communication scholar **Rebecca B. Rubin** and her colleagues developed and validated the Interpersonal Communication Motives (ICM) scale based on the belief that people use interpersonal communication to express needs for affection, inclusion, and control. Rubin also identified six prominent motives for interpersonal communication:

1. Pleasure—"fun"
2. Affection—"caring"
3. Inclusion—"sharing feelings"
4. Escape—"filling time to avoid other behaviors"
5. Relaxation—"unwinding"
6. Control—"power"

These communication motives have been studied in relation to communication apprehension and communication satisfaction. Studies demonstrate that people who are typically apprehensive about engaging in interpersonal communication are less likely to communicate for pleasure, to control others, or to express affection. Instead, people who tend to be apprehensive about communication do so primarily for inclusion. This means that anxious individuals need to feel included despite their apprehension and that communication is a plea for acceptance rather than a source of pleasure or relaxation. Furthermore, verbally communicating for pleasure, relaxation, and inclusion are related to high levels of communication satisfaction. In terms of working in groups, perceptions of satisfaction result from the affection motive. Group members tend to be happiest when they engage in social rituals and when members express concern for each other.[4]

Once again, think about all of your communication during the past twenty-four hours. You were most likely to be satisfied with the outcomes of your interactions if they fulfilled your motives for pleasure, affection, inclusion, and relaxation.

Verbal Communication and Meaning

What is the relationship between verbal communication and meaning?

Can you recall the last time you engaged in conversation and were misunderstood? Did the misunderstanding arise from different ideas about the meaning of a word? Perhaps the misunderstanding related to the purpose of your comments (e.g., your mock put-down, "Hey, loser!" was interpreted as an overt insult). The misunderstanding that you and your conversation partner(s) experienced may have resulted from differing denotative or connotative meanings and/or a problem associated with the rules involved in coordinating and managing meaning.

KNOWLEDGE ON THE CUTTING EDGE

Profanity and Curse Words: Are You a Civil Communicator?

Do you curse in front of others? Approximately a third of the respondents in a 2002 Public Agenda poll admitted they use foul language in public.[5] A 2006 Associated Press-Ipsos poll found that 74% of respondents frequently or occasionally hear profanity in public, two thirds believe people curse more today than twenty years ago, and 64% admit to using the "F-word." Additionally, 74% of women and 60% of the men questioned said they are bothered by profanity.[6] Nonetheless, swearing occurs in schools and at sporting events, is overheard in shopping malls, is flaunted by radio "shock jocks," is found on TV and in the movies, is emblazoned on clothing, and is used in public by politicians.

Some researchers believe that cursing can be beneficial. Swearing sometimes helps to diffuse stress and anger in certain contexts. In particular, cursing with a group of friends may imply that we are relaxed and feel free to let off steam. Swearing can also be an effective way to vent aggression and forestall physical violence. But even though swearing can help us feel good every now and then, it can become habit-forming, and we may begin to pepper our speech with curse words no matter what the occasion. In addition, far from venting aggression in an effective manner, we may displace our anger by swearing at an innocent victim if we are the target of curse words. And swearing may actually lead to physical violence; arguments that escalate into physical assaults almost always involve cursing. Overall, cursing reflects uncivil behavior. Civil behavior involves self-restraint for the sake of others. This means that swearing is uncivil because it entails expressing ourselves without concern for our community. Cursing is recognized as uncivil by cities that have ordinances that ban swearing in public (e.g., Raritan, New Jersey, and Fostoria, Ohio). Restaurant and shop owners also recognize the uncivil nature of cursing and can ask customers to leave if they use language that other patrons find offensive.[7]

One way we can curb our use of curse words is to find inoffensive substitutes. We can make up our own cuss words (e.g., "You are such a *Skeezicks*!") or replace curse words with words that reflect alliteration or assonance (e.g., "Everything I touch turns to *trash*"). However, breaking the habit of cursing may be difficult. Realistic goals can motivate us to keep curse words out of our vocabulary. For example, we may initially set a goal to drop a couple of curse words every few days before working our way up to our desired state. Reining in our impulses, including the impulse to curse and use hurtful words, recognizes that free speech should be tempered by the norm of civility.[8]

Denotative and Connotative Meanings

Do you experience a strong emotional reaction when you read the word *jihad*? In 2002, Harvard senior Zayed Yasin sought to deliver a commencement address he titled "My American Jihad." Yasin asserted that his use of the word *jihad* referred to what the Qur'an defines as an "internal struggle," such as the struggle to do right even at a personal cost. He also said that he wanted to reclaim the word from its incorrect interpretation as a "holy war." However, Harvard students began two online petitions in which they suggested that his use of the word was offensive and insensitive. One petition demanded that Yasin include an explicit condemnation of violent jihad in his speech, and the other insisted that a more appropriate graduation speaker be chosen to present the commencement address. In the end, Yasin agreed to Harvard's suggestion to change the title of his speech to "Of Faith and Citizenship," and he presented the speech without incident.[9] The meaning we have for the word *jihad* illustrates denotative and connotative meaning.

Figure 5.2 illustrates that the words that make up a language can be placed on a continuum that ranges from highly denotative to highly connotative. **Denotative** meaning is accepted as "correct," and this type of meaning is found in dictionaries.

Words with primarily denotative meanings tend to change very slowly, if at all. For example, when we look up the meaning for the word *girl* in the dictionary, we find a definition similar to "a young female." This definition is general and probably hasn't changed over the centuries. Similarly, the denotative meaning for the word *jihad* is "internal

Figure 5.2: The Denotative-Connotative Continuum

DENOTATIVE MEANING	CONNOTATIVE MEANING
The Dictionary Definition	The Personal, Emotional, Subjective Definition
The word *girl* means:	The word *girl* means;
• "A female child"	• Positive connotation: "A youthful-looking, pretty woman" • Negative connotation: "An immature, childlike woman"

struggle." On the other hand, **connotative** meaning is emotional and personal and may engender disagreement. Connotative meanings are typically not found in dictionaries, and words with connotative meanings change very quickly. To return to the example of *girl,* this word has a highly negative connotative meaning if we associate *girl* with insults that suggest immaturity. However, our connotative meaning for a word can change rapidly, depending on the context in which meaning occurs. Although we may generally feel insulted if, as an adult, we are referred to as a girl, we may feel complimented if we are called a "girl" after the words *beautiful* or *intelligent.* Furthermore, our connotative meaning for the word *jihad* will vary according to our experiences, beliefs, and attitudes. Whether or not we agree with Yasin's meaning or with the meanings held by the Harvard petitioners, the point is that connotative meanings can produce strong emotional reactions.

Advertisers, speechwriters, editors, and others engaged in "word craft" realize that connotative meanings can produce highly negative reactions. As a result, **euphemisms** replace words associated with unpleasant and negative connotations with those associated with pleasant or neutral connotations. Many euphemisms in the English language concern natural body functions and taboo topics such as death and sex. For example, although the words *death* and *die* are associated with unpleasant connotations, less bothersome connotations arise from "passed away," "deceased," and "gone to a better place."

In reality, most words have both connotative and denotative meanings and don't produce automatic, emotional reactions. A word such as *girl* may not produce any type of emotional meaning and may be used and understood as a way to get someone's attention. However, imagine that your friends use words such as *patriotism, liberal, money,* and *love* in a particular conversation. Will you and your friends implicitly share the same definitions for these words? Probably not. The use of these words can lead to misinterpretations, demonstrating that even words that are not associated with highly negative connotative meanings can contribute to misunderstandings and miscommunication.

KNOWLEDGE power • Do We Really "Rest" in the Restroom?

With a partner or in a group, brainstorm a list of euphemisms designed to make something unpleasant or negative appear pleasant or positive. (One way to begin is by thinking about the euphemistic language used in television commercials for various products and services.) Compare your list of euphemisms with your classmates'; what similar categories of people, places, or things are labeled with euphemisms? What can euphemisms tell us about what is considered positive or negative in American culture?

The Coordinated Management of Meaning

Even though it may be difficult to assign meaning to our verbal communication, we attempt to coordinate meaning through the application of various communication rules. Communication theorists **W. Barnett Pierce** and **Vernon Cronen** developed the **coordinated management of meaning** (CMM) to explain how people agree on the meaning of verbal communication. According to this theory, the application of syntactic, semantic, and pragmatic rules enable conversation partners to experience meaning based on coherence, coordination, and mystery.[10]

Syntactic, Semantic, and Pragmatic Rules Syntactic rules refer to how symbols are arranged, and **semantic rules** refer to what symbols mean. **Pragmatic rules** help us interpret verbal communication within a given context. Pragmatic rules also enable us to determine how to respond or behave within that context. As illustrated in Figure 5.3, "Syntactic, Semantic, and Pragmatic Rules," all three types of rules work together to help us understand verbal communication. For example, suppose someone says to you, "I just got back from a great vacation!" What does this sentence mean? Would you understand the statement in the following format: "From vacation just I back got a great." Probably not. Because speakers of a language follow the same syntactic rules, we have a better understanding of the meaning of utterances. However, we may still struggle to communicate exactly what we mean and to understand others' comments because verbal communication is symbolic. What do you think of when you hear "great vacation"? Although our shared semantic rules tell us that *great* means something "positive" and that *vacation* means something "out of the ordinary," our own specific meanings for "great vacation" will vary. For example, do you think a great vacation means basking in the sun on a deserted beach? Do you think of camping, hiking, and climbing mountains as activities that occur during a great vacation? Maybe you think a great vacation includes dancing till dawn at popular nightclubs in exciting cities. Pragmatic rules can help us understand meaning when meanings are unclear. If you and a conversation partner are talking about the world's best beaches, it's likely (but not definite) that the statement, "I just got back from a great vacation!" refers to the topic of discussion—beaches. Our pragmatic rules tell us that meaning is situational. This means that if your conversation focused on great cities in Europe, a "great vacation" comment would possibly concern London or Paris.

Coherence, Coordination, and Mystery According to CMM, participants in conversations experience meaning through coherence, coordination, and mystery. **Coherence** refers to "making meaning" and is **coordinated** by the rules we use to manage talk and create our social realities. **Mystery** refers to the idea that coherence and coordination are arbitrary and are created by language. Mystery also suggests that the words we use not only create and name things in our experience of reality but also limit them and can make them invisible. If we realize that words limit our experience of reality, we can understand that there may be something more to reality than what is communicated by words.

Figure 5.3: Syntactic, Semantic, and Pragmatic Rules

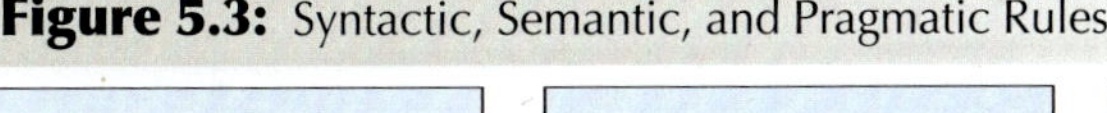

Syntactic Rules How symbols are arranged	Semantic Rules What symbols mean	Pragmatic Rules What symbols mean in a given context

Although what is "more" is unknown and mysterious, this knowledge can help us transcend the power of words to limit our perceptions of the world.[11] For example, suppose you are feeling anxious about an upcoming job interview. You can attempt to alleviate your fears by knowing that you and your interviewer will probably share syntactic and semantic rules that will help you experience coherence and coordinate meaning. Pragmatic rules will help you predict that most, if not all, interview questions will concern job-related topics. Similarly, pragmatic rules will help you predict that your answers will be interpreted in terms of how well you meet the job requirements and whether you appear to be a good "fit" within the company. However, you may realize that there's more to reality than words can communicate and that getting the job may be based on something that is invisible and "mysterious."

Skills For Improving Verbal Communication

- "Engineering students are 'nerds.'"
- "I know what you really mean."
- "Liz has lots of energy."

How can using specific and concrete words, indexing and owning our thoughts, and dating information improve our communication competence?

Can you recognize how these sentences may cause misinterpretations if we use them in conversations with others? These sentences illustrate three categories of problematic verbal communication: abstraction, indiscrimination and allness, and static evaluation. We can reduce the misinterpretations caused by these types of problematic talk when we communicate with specific and concrete words, engage in indexing and own our thoughts, and date information.

Abstraction

Abstraction refers to levels of specificity in language. In general, highly connotative words also tend to be highly abstract. On the one hand, abstract language helps people avoid the necessity of constantly "overexplaining" what they mean. For example, if we tell a good friend that we think she or he is "smart," we have eliminated the need for a wordy overexplanation. We need not overexplain by saying, "You get 'A's and 'B's in most of your classes" (meaning that our friend is knowledgeable about academics), "You read the daily newspaper and discuss world politics" (meaning that our friend is knowledgeable about current events), or "You often can predict when someone will ask to go out with you" (meaning your friend is knowledgeable about the nuances associated with budding relationships). However, which meaning—"academic smarts," "current event smarts," or "relationship smarts"—will our friend apply to our compliment about being smart? Our friend might possibly have her or his own interpretation of what we mean by "smart." The following two examples show that abstract language is problematic and can lead to serious consequences:

- On January 25, 1990, seventy-three people were killed as a result of a Boeing 707 that crashed in New York. The National Transportation Safety Board asserted that miscommunication between the air traffic controllers and the flight crew was involved in the crash. Although the airline pilots used the words "running out of fuel" when communicating with the controllers, they failed to use specific language that would have resulted in an immediate clearance for landing. "FAA rules call for pilots to declare 'minimum fuel status' when they need to land without undue delay and 'a fuel emergency' when they should be given first priority for landing."[12]

- In a week of televised reruns of the World Trade Center attacks on September 11, 2001, Eunice Stone called the police from a roadside diner in Georgia. She had listened to what she had thought were terrorist-sounding plans discussed by three men who looked like they were from the Middle East. Stone overheard the men use sentences such as "Do you think we have enough to bring it down?" and "If we don't have enough, I have contacts. We can get enough to bring it down." But what did the abstract language in the phrase "bring it down" actually refer to? Were the men talking about "bringing down" a building like the World Trade Center? Were the men talking about "bringing down" an airplane? In reality, the three men, all medical students in clinical training at Larkin Hospital in Florida, were talking about bringing a car to Miami, yet they were the subject of a two-state, nationally televised search. They were subsequently asked to leave Larkin Hospital because their presence would be "too disruptive."[13]

You may think that these examples are atypical and that you will never experience such abstraction-related problems when you talk to others. Although the consequences of your abstract language use may not be as dire, they may cause problems in your interpersonal communication and relationships. The idea that language can move from highly abstract to highly specific and concrete is illustrated in Figure 5.4, "The Ladder of Abstraction." For example, have you ever called someone a "jerk" (or worse)? Near the top of the ladder of abstraction, where language is the most abstract, is the sentence "You're a jerk." *Jerk* is a word that is so abstract that it can mean just about anything negative. Moving down the ladder of abstraction is the sentence "You're lazy." This sentence is more specific than "You're a jerk" (it implies something to do with physical activity), but it still is open to a myriad of meanings. The sentence near the middle of the ladder, "You don't help around the house," is even more specific than the previous sentence, but what is the meaning of the word *help*? Does "help" mean doing our fair share of dusting, vacuuming, and washing, or does it mean that we lift our legs while someone else vacuums underneath them? Moving on, perhaps you once communicated at the next level of specificity when you told a roommate or partner, "You don't clean up after yourself around the house." Maybe you thought that you clearly communicated your meaning and were surprised when you discovered articles of clothing scattered across the floor. Because "clean up after yourself" is an abstract phrase, your roommate or partner could have interpreted it to mean putting the dishes in the dishwasher after a meal. The lowest level of the ladder of abstraction includes the most specific and behaviorally oriented language with **concrete words** based on sense data, such as "You leave your shoes, socks, and books near the door instead of taking them to your room." This sentence is so specific that there is no doubt as to its meaning.

Figure 5.4: The Ladder of Abstraction

SKILL practice • Using Specific and Concrete Words

Reword the following statements to make them more specific. Use words located at the bottom of the ladder of abstraction, that is, sense data, concrete words (those that appeal to the senses), examples, and precise words such as names and titles.

- "I like going to concerts."
- "You should be more careful next time."
- "He's a reckless driver."
- "She's always late."
- "Why can't we talk about anything interesting?"

Indiscrimination and Allness

Indiscrimination and allness refer to the failure to recognize the unique and unknown qualities of a person, place, or thing. Specifically, **indiscrimination** occurs when we fail to make distinctions among similar but different persons, places, or things. In indiscriminate verbal communication, we focus on categories or groups instead of uniqueness and individuality. "All women are too emotional" and "Men only think of themselves" are examples of indiscrimination. We verbalize a stereotype when we use indiscriminate language. **Allness** refers to the incorrect idea that it is possible to know everything about a person, place, or thing, and allness occurs when we draw conclusions based on evidence that is insufficient and biased. Not only is it impossible to know everything and perceive all things, but our perceptions are also influenced by culture, relationship, gender, and individual contexts that can cause us to selectively perceive data, misperceive data, or completely fail to perceive data. For example, someone from a Western culture may believe that all persons from Eastern cultures engage in ineffective methods of conflict resolution such as avoiding a conflict or accommodating ("giving in"). There are two problems associated with this belief: not *all* Easterners avoid or give in during conflict, and avoidance and accommodation are typically considered beneficial conflict management styles in Eastern cultures because they reflect interdependence and collectivism.[14]

Indexing and Owning Our Thoughts

Indexing acknowledges differences in thought and opinion and can prevent us from engaging in indiscriminant verbal communication. Indexing-related words and phrases include "maybe," "it could be," and "perhaps." For example, instead of saying, "He failed his classes because he partied too much," we can say, "*Maybe he failed his classes because he partied too much.*" Instead of saying, "Your parents trust you but don't trust your friends," we can say, "*It could be that your parents trust you but don't trust your friends.*" **Owning our thoughts** is one method of acknowledging the power of words to influence others. Accepting responsibility for our thoughts and attitudes suggests that we realize that we don't know "everything" and that our perceptions are influenced by culture, relationship, gender, and individual contexts. Owning our thoughts also suggests that we realize that others may think differently than we do, acknowledges the validity of other viewpoints, and implies that we may be willing to change our opinions. One way we can own our thoughts and opinions is by using the pronouns *I* and *my* with words such as *think, believe, feel, perceive, thoughts, beliefs,* and *perception*. Instead of saying, "The death penalty is immoral," we can say, "*I believe the death penalty is immoral.*" Similarly, instead of

SKILL practice • Indexing and Owning Thoughts

Reword the following statements to acknowledge the probability of differences in thought and opinion when communicating generalizations. Indexing-related words and phrases include "maybe," "it could be," and "perhaps." In addition, illustrate that you accept responsibility for your thoughts. You can use the pronouns *I* and *my* with words such as *think, believe, perceive, thoughts, beliefs,* and *perception.*

- "The dinners at your favorite restaurant cost too much."
- "You should always support the president."
- "The best movies have car chases and explosions."
- "You need to have a better opinion of yourself."
- "That professor doesn't do a good job of lecturing to the class."

saying, "She broke up with him because she got tired of him," we can say, *"My perception is that she broke up with him because she got tired of him."*

Static Evaluation

Are you the same person you were one year ago? Have you ever returned to a favorite location and noticed a few changes? The point is that people, places, and things change as time progresses, yet our verbal communication doesn't always reflect such changes. We engage in **static evaluation** when we use verbal communication that ignores the idea that persons, places, and things change. Static evaluation occurs when we use the word *is,* such as "Ethan is dependable" or "Ariana is considerate." Realistically, Ethan is *usually* dependable, and *in general,* Ariana is considerate. Failing to use such qualifying language indicates that Ethan and Ariana never change from one situation to the next.

Dating Information

Dating information, which entails specifying a time that something was known to be true, can add precision to our comments. For example, "I enjoyed my vacation in San Francisco" doesn't communicate as much meaning and specificity as *"I enjoyed my vacation in San Francisco ten years ago,"* and "I talked with Loren and he was feeling good" doesn't communicate as much meaning and specificity as *"I talked with Loren two weeks ago and he was feeling good."* Dating information implies that we recognize that our beliefs, attitudes, and emotions may be subject to change under different temporal circumstances.

We need to be realistic about the guidelines and skills designed to improve our verbal communication. We have read that indexing and owning our thoughts with qualifiers such as "perhaps," "maybe," and "in my opinion" imply that we accept responsibility for our opinions and that we acknowledge the power of words to influence perception. However, we may be perceived as being uncertain of our opinions or insecure when we use indexing as a verbal communication skill. Similarly, our conversations may appear endless if we always communicate with specific and concrete words from the bottom of the ladder of abstraction. Remember that competent communication is strategic and that we should consider our goals, our conversation partner(s), the topic, and the situation when we decide to use skills designed to improve verbal communication.

Competence & Critical Thinking

mycommunicationlab

WORDS THAT WOUND AND VERBAL COMMUNICATION

Lindsay has asked his girlfriend Clara to critique the presentation on sexual harassment that he'll be presenting to a campus group.

You can view *Words That Wound* by accessing the "Small Group and Interpersonal Videos" on the MyCommunicationLab Web site. Answer the following questions about the verbal communication used by Lindsay and Clara:

- What may be Lindsay's connotative meanings for the names "Joe Stud" and "Diane Sex Kitten?"
- What may be Clara's connotative meanings for the names "Joe Stud" and "Diane Sex Kitten?"
- Do Lindsay and/or Clara use abstract words in this video? (Describe.) What skill could they have used to avoid the problems associated with abstract language? What could they have said in place of the abstract words?
- Do Lindsay and/or Clara illustrate "allness" in this video? (Describe.) Do they make use of indexing-related words? Do they own their thoughts?
- Do Lindsay and/or Clara illustrate "static evaluation" in this video? (Describe.) What skill could they have used and what could they have said to avoid the problems associated with static evaluation?

LINDSAY: Hey, honey.

CLARA: Hey, what's going on?

LINDSAY: Nothing, how are you?

CLARA: You know, hanging out.

LINDSAY: It's good to see you.

CLARA: Good to see you.

LINDSAY: Hey.

CLARA: So what's going on? What you been doing all day?

LINDSAY: Uh, I finally finished that speech that I've been working on.

CLARA: Oh.

LINDSAY: Yes.

CLARA: You want to try it out on me?

LINDSAY: Yeah, yeah, I'd love to. Oh, um, I haven't really done it in front of anybody, so . . .

CLARA: That's OK.

LINDSAY: You know it's for the sexual harassment board, you know this.

CLARA: Right.

LINDSAY: All right. So it's going to start out, and I've got Joe Stud and Diane Sex Kitten, and they're going to eat lunch together at the cafeteria. And Joe Stud is walking by Diane, and he rubbed Diane, and he rubs up against her, you know, he's trying to, uh . . .

CLARA: I'm sorry. Will you go back—just a second.

LINDSAY: Yeah.

CLARA: "Joe Stud" and what's her name?

LINDSAY: "Diane Sex Kitten." It's a joke. It's, yeah, I mean . . .

CLARA: Joke?

LINDSAY: It's just supposed to show that—that Joe is a good-looking guy, and Diane is a good-looking woman, but I want to do it, you know, in kind of a humorous way so people, you know, so it's not too serious.

CLARA: You're going to make a joke out of all of this?

LINDSAY: Well, they're just—they're just the names, is all I'm saying.

CLARA: But they're offensive names.

LINDSAY: How are they offensive?

CLARA: Well, I mean, "Joe Stud" and "Diane Sex Kitten"? You're making it sound like, I don't know, 'cause they're good-looking people they're, you know, like oversexed, like . . .

LINDSAY: No. No, no, no, no, no, no. I'm not doing that at all. All I'm showing is that they're good-looking people, and that they can be victims of sexual harassment, or they can be sexual harassers. That's it, you've got to listen to my whole speech. You're getting hung up on the name. So what—what's going to happen "is" . . .

CLARA: Yeah, but the name automatically makes me think that, you know, you're, like, advocating the sexual harassment, that you're claiming that because somebody is good-looking, they're automatically some kind of sexually promiscuous person.

LINDSAY: Well, I'm not saying at all that they're sexually promiscuous.

CLARA: It doesn't matter if that's what you're trying to say. That's what it sounds like.

LINDSAY: No, I think you're being too sensitive, all right? I think these—you don't realize that they're just names.

CLARA: I'm being too sensitive? You're going to get up and do this in front of a whole group of people tomorrow? And you think I'm being sensitive.

LINDSAY: Yeah, I don't think everyone's going to find these names as offensive as you do. I mean, do you not see the greater point of the speech, it's actually against sexual harassment. I'm not . . .

CLARA: It doesn't sound like it's against sexual harassment.

LINDSAY: Well, because you're not listening to the whole thing because . . .

CLARA: I'm listening to what you're calling them, and it's completely offensive.

LINDSAY: It's not offensive to most people. I think you have to realize not everyone shares your worldview about the proper names for what you can call men and women. And anyway . . .

CLARA: And you think it's OK to call a woman a "sex kitten"?

LINDSAY: In the context of this speech, to get across a simple point in a . . .

CLARA: A simple point, that's against sexual harassment. But what you're saying is completely inappropriate.

LINDSAY: You're being way too serious about this, way too serious. It's–it's a heavy topic, right? I was trying to make it a little bit lighter by showing . . .

CLARA: Yeah, it's a heavy topic. You shouldn't be joking about it.

LINDSAY: So there can't be any humor in it. It's got to be all serious, all the time.

CLARA: You know who you sound like? You sound just like Tim.

LINDSAY: Like Tim. What are you talking about? I don't sound anything like Tim.

CLARA: This type of thing is exactly the sort of thing that would come out of his mouth.

LINDSAY: No, Tim is—Tim is offensive. I am nothing like Tim.

CLARA: This is offensive.

LINDSAY: No, Tim is really offensive. Tim yells degrading things to women out of car windows, and he says really disgusting things about people's sisters. Tim has problems, all right? I am nothing like Tim.

CLARA: But you're going to get up onstage tomorrow, and you're going to say degrading things about women to an entire group of people. I don't really see the difference in that.

LINDSAY: That—that's not what I'm doing.

CLARA: And I don't really know . . . Yeah, but this doesn't sound like you. I can't even believe that this would come out of your mouth.

LINDSAY: You really think I'm like that. You think that all of a sudden it . . .

CLARA: I didn't think you were like that.

LINDSAY: Oh, but now because of this one thing you've changed your entire opinion of me.

CLARA: It doesn't sound like something that would come out of your mouth. And I can't believe that you can't see how offensive that is.

LINDSAY: I can't believe that you can't see that not everybody finds that offensive.

CLARA: It doesn't matter if everybody doesn't find it . . .

LINDSAY: You, you're getting . . .

CLARA: If one person in the audience finds that offensive, you've ruined the whole thing. It's a serious topic, and you have to be so careful about what you're saying.

SKILL practice • Dating Information

Reword the following statements by using the skill of dating information. Specifying a time that something was known to be true can add precision to your comments.

- "I was impressed with her when I met her."
- "I phoned him and he sounded angry."
- "You seemed in a hurry the last time we got together."
- "I felt like a loser."
- "You should have returned that present earlier than you did."

Verbal Communication's Influence On Thought

How does verbal communication influence thought?

The symbols used in verbal communication influence our perceptions of the world. For example, an Oxford University study had respondents smell a cheesy aroma while one of two labels simultaneously flashed on a screen. Respondents who read the "cheddar cheese" label rated the aroma as "pleasant," but respondents who read the "body odor" label did not.[15] Words are often carefully chosen to affect people's attitudes and are consciously used to influence thoughts. The words used in verbal communication can also influence us subtly in a manner we are unaware of. How we react to others' communication and how others react to our communication are significantly based on the words that are expressed during verbal communication.

Carefully Chosen Words Affect Thought and Action

Words are often specifically used to influence thought and action. For example, note the following analogy and pay particular attention to the italicized words: "An *undeveloped fertilized egg* doesn't describe a baby any more than a seed describes a rose bush."[16] What did you envision when you read "undeveloped fertilized egg"? How might the overall terminology used in this analogy influence your thoughts? Whether you agree or disagree with the analogy, you can see that words have the power to influence beliefs and behavior in our conversations with others. Suppose you find yourself in a discussion about abortion. Would you use the label "pro-life" or "pro-choice"? How might you react to hearing the word *murder* versus *prevention*? Would you use labels such as "fetus" or "zygote," or would you use labels such as "baby" or "pre-born child?" Even if you've never engaged in a discussion about abortion, you can probably understand how the phrases "eliminating a product of conception" and "fighting for the rights of the unborn" can influence thought.

The powerful influence of words on thought is recognized by governments that have "information ministries" and political candidates who have "media advisors."[17] In fact, the government, military, and big business have been accused of deliberately using language that conceals the truth and/or shifts responsibility to influence people's perceptions. For example, in 2006 the U.S. Department of Agriculture used the phrase "low food security" to describe persons with moderate incomes who can't afford to buy food and go hungry.[18]

The National Council of Teachers of English (NCTE) presents an annual Doublespeak Award to speakers who use language that is grossly deceptive, evasive, and/or confusing. The 2005 Doublespeak Award went to Philip A. Cooney, the former chief of staff for the White House Council on Environmental Quality, who deliberately included the adjectives "significant" and "fundamental" before the word "uncertainties" to create doubt about the link between the greenhouse effect and global warming.[19]

KNOWLEDGE power • Language Screens

Language has been described as a screen through which we filter truth. In other words, language colors facts rather than reports them, and "truth" results from the words we choose when we communicate with others. Access "Dennis Rodman and the Art of the (Metaphoric) Screen" to read two versions of an infamous basketball incident and to recognize the words that influence our perception of the event: www.americanrhetoric.com/rodmanphase1.htm.

Words Subtly Affect Thought

We may believe that we are aware of how words are used to influence our perceptions; however, many words we hear, read, and use to describe people, things, and events can subtly influence our perceptions in ways we're unaware of. For example, have you ever read that Christopher Columbus "discovered" America? Reflect on this idea for a moment. How might the word *discovered* subtly influence thought? This terminology suggests that Native Americans were invisible or insignificant until a European recognized their existence.[20] Another example of the ability of words to subtly influence thought concerns how we label co-cultures or racial or ethnic groups. For example, do you label people of color "nonwhite"? The label "nonwhite" implies that "whiteness" is the standard and norm; consider why white people aren't labeled "people of noncolor." Have you ever heard people of color labeled "minority group"? How does the label "minority group" subtly affect our thoughts? Some people believe that "minority group" suggests insignificance or something that is negligible.[21] Will U.S. citizens of European ancestry accept the label "minority group" when "nonwhites" outnumber "whites" in the year 2050?[22] The words used to describe people, places, and things can, unbeknownst to us, affect our thoughts.

Contexts and Verbal Communication

Our culture, relationship, gender, and individual contexts affect our use of verbal communication and how we interpret others' verbal communication. For example, consider "*She looks like a million dollars; she had some aesthetic enhancements and is wearing a lot of bling.*" Think about the influence of the culture, relationship, gender, and individual contexts in the preceding sentence as you read the following information about the influence of contexts on our verbal communication.

Culture Context

How do contexts influence verbal communication?

The relationship between culture and language is reciprocal. Changes in our language affect culture, and changes in our culture affect language.[23] Culture influences our language (and therefore how we perceive the world), and the language we speak reflects cultural values.

Culture Influences Language Linguists **Edward Sapir** and **Benjamin Lee Whorf** hypothesized that culture significantly affects how people think and communicate. The **Sapir-Whorf hypothesis** posits that culture influences language and that language influences cultural differences in thought. The original version of their hypothesis, sometimes labeled the "deterministic" or "firm" version, suggested that language is like a prison because we are trapped by our language and cannot escape its influence on how we perceive the world. The deterministic position holds that we cannot perceive something unless we have the words to describe it. The "relativistic" or "softer" version of the Sapir-Whorf hypothesis, which is more widely accepted than the deterministic position, suggests that language reflects what we need to know to cope within our culture and reinforces our culturally influenced patterns of thought, beliefs, attitudes, values, and rules for behavior. The relativistic version also posits that the language we use influences us to perceive and label certain things in our environment.[24]

Sapir and Whorf explained their hypothesis with a hypothetical story of a guard who walks into a warehouse that contains gasoline barrels labeled "empty." The guard decides to light a cigarette and the result is an explosion. Sapir and Whorf explained that the guard thought it was safe to light a cigarette because the English language has no word for "empty-of-original-gas-content-but-incendiary-fumes-may-remain." Does this story sound unrealistic? Unfortunately, Sapir and Whorf's hypothetical example became all too real for the passengers aboard ValuJet flight 592 in 1996. Although potentially flammable oxygen generators aboard the jet had been labeled "Oxygen canisters—empty," they were suspected as the source of a fire and subsequent crash. While the canisters were empty of their original contents, they contained a trace of a chemical considered to be "hazardous waste" that requires special handling.[25] However, the English language is based on a cultural assumption of linear cause-effect thinking typical of individualist cultures. Consequently, English influences speakers to think and speak according to polar opposites or dichotomies.[26] It is therefore much easier to think and speak in English in terms of the polar opposites of "full" and "empty" instead of words that can more accurately reflect the true nature of the situation; that is, words that describe a middle ground between two extremes.

Language and Cultural Values Think about the influence of your culture on your verbal communication. As illustrated in the "Sherman's Lagoon" comic, much of what a culture values or devalues is evident in the language of its members. In general, individualist cultures place a high degree of importance on the spoken word, and verbal communication is often used to express individualism.[27] For example, English is the only language in which the "I" is capitalized in writing. In addition, the English language has one word for the first-person singular as it relates to others, and speakers of English say, "*I* have three siblings," "*I* work with my supervisor," and "*I* enjoy spending time with my friends." This cultural-linguistic distinction may influence members of individualist cultures to think of themselves as entities that exist apart from others. By contrast, in terms of how the first-person singular relates to others, there are more than ten words for "I" in Chinese, more than twelve words for "I" in Vietnamese, and more than a hundred words for "I" in Japanese. These languages reflect the underlying assumptions of collectivist cultures, and their words for "I" demonstrate the relationship between the speaker, other persons, and the type of event being spoken about.[28] Similarly, the dominant U.S. culture is thought to be a relatively informal culture that downplays linguistic expressions of status. English has only one word for singular "you," whereas Spanish (*tu* and *usted*) and German (*du* and *Sie*) have two. This cultural-linguistic distinction may influence English speakers to think

KNOWLEDGE ON THE CUTTING EDGE

Words without English Equivalents

You most likely know that languages differ in terms of symbols (words) and syntax (grammar). What you may not realize is that languages also differ in regard to the availability and variety of words that communicate meaning. Some words in other languages do not have English equivalents. For example, what English word would you use to describe an object, such as a teacup, that is museum-quality but has a crack running down its side? The crack is considered to be an aesthetic flaw that represents the spirit of the moment in which the teacup is created. You probably cannot think of a word because there is no word in English that encompasses all of these characteristics. However, the Japanese word *wabi* (which rhymes with "bobby") describes such a treasured cultural object. Have you ever attempted to describe your feelings about someone you once loved but now do not? Maybe you used the word *like* to describe your feelings but realized that while you "like" your roommate, the "like" you feel for your ex-lover is something quite different. Perhaps you tried to describe your current feelings by using the phrase "but we're still friends." Once again, your "friends" are people with whom you socialize and whose company you enjoy; however, you may no longer meet with your former lover. There is no word in English that describes the feeling a person has for someone once loved. However, the Russian language includes such a word, *razbliuto* (pronounced ros-blee-OO-tow). Other words that have no English equivalents include *Farpotshket* and *Bilita mpatshi*. *Farpotshket* (Yiddish; pronounced "far-POTCH-ket") refers to a bad situation that becomes worse after someone tries to fix it. For example, if water flows from the faucet in a heavy stream after you try to repair a slight drip, you can say your faucet is "farpotshket." *Bilita mpatshi* (Bantu; pronounced bee-LEE-tah mm-POT-she) refers to blissful dreams. Although the English language includes a word for terrible dreams, "nightmares," English lacks a word for dreams that are glorious, legendary, and blissful.[29]

of formality and status differently than do speakers of Spanish and German. People who visit the United States often comment about the informality of Americans in a wide variety of contexts.[30]

Relationship Context

Do you and members of your family have names for people or things that are not known or understood by persons outside your family? Do you and your friends or colleagues make use of idiosyncratic words that others are unaware of or don't understand? Our families, friends, and coworkers affect our verbal communication in terms of personal idioms and jargon.

Much of what a culture values or devalues is evident in the language of its members.

Source: © SHERMAN'S LAGOON – JIM TOOMEY. KING FEATURES SYNDICATE.

> **KNOWLEDGE power • Do You Have the "Clicker"?**
>
> Can you think of personal idioms created and shared by you and a close friend, intimate partner, and/or your family? What do they describe? With a partner or in a group, share your personal idioms and analyze whether your idioms are more similar or different than your partner's or group members' idioms.

Family and Friends Our families and friends develop unique communication codes based on personal **idioms**, words or phrases that are used with a specific meaning in a particular language. Personal idioms are typically created as relationships become more intimate. Within a family, idioms can be based on the experiences of individual members and/or an entire family. Because those on the "outside" of a relationship or family neither use nor understand personal idioms, they become a part of the unique communication codes shared by our friends and those to whom we are related. For example, "frobbled" is a personal idiom that refers to what happens when our mouth is so cold after eating ice cream that we can't talk properly, and "dinka" is a personal idiom that means "turn here" (from the sound a turn signal makes).[31] Only the relational partners or family members who created this idiom are aware of its meaning.

Friends and romantic partners tend to use idioms that describe each other (e.g., nicknames) and people outside a relationship.[32] Family members, friends, and intimate partners also create personal idioms for food, pets, transportation, work, and even the indescribable "stuff" under the couch. Some idioms are passed down from generation to generation, and many family words are created by children and subsequently used by all family members.[33]

Coworkers **Jargon** is a specialized vocabulary shared and understood by members of particular occupational groups. Jargon often functions as a shorthand code or quick method for sharing meaning.[34] Perhaps you've watched a television medical show in which an emergency room doctor shouts instructions that end with "stat!" "Stat" is much easier and quicker than saying, "This patient may die if you don't immediately do what I say!"

Medical professionals and persons in other occupations make use of specialized terminology or jargon.

KNOWLEDGE ON THE CUTTING EDGE

Technology Update: CMC and Verbal Communication

Technology has dramatically changed our vocabulary, and the more technology evolves, the more our language changes. Some researchers suggest that the Internet allows language users to be inventive and adaptive because it is a new medium that blends speaking and writing. Internet-mediated language is different from writing because of its immediacy and changeability, and it's different from speech because of the absence of nonverbal cues such as pitch, rhythm, and loudness. "Net lingo" blends aspects of speech and writing and yet is not completely either. The same is true of communication produced by cell phone-based messaging. Users regard this form of textual communication as something other than writing. Cell phone lingo is described as a hybrid of speech and writing in which people try to speak with their fingers. People interrupted while text-messaging don't say, "Hold on, I'm writing." Instead, they say, "Hold on, I'm talking to someone."[35]

In addition, the Internet has added a wide variety of acronyms and new words to verbal communication. Acronyms include "RUOK" ("Are you OK?") and "CUL8R" ("See you later"). Shorthand terms used by cell phone users such as BBLR ("Be back later"), GR8 ("great"), and HAND ("Have a nice day") have been included in the *Oxford English Dictionary*. New words or words with new meanings include:

- Worm—a type of virus
- Sneakernet—sharing data files with others the old-fashioned way, by walking them over to their desks
- Intranet—a private network contained within a business or organization
- Spam—the modern version of junk mail
- Flamebait—a posting on a public forum designed to elicit extremely strong responses

NetLingo.com includes thousands of words and definitions of Internet terms to enlighten those who aren't familiar with new acronyms and words spawned by technology. We can turn to NetLingo.com if we don't know the meanings of the following words:

- Byte
- Cookie
- Eyeballs
- Spaghetti code
- Uninstalled

Read the following examples of jargon and guess which occupations they refer to. Then try to guess the meaning of the jargon:

- Behavior adjustment unit
- Flotation support system
- Manually operated humus excavator
- Therapeutic misadventures

"Behavior adjustment unit" is jargon used by prison officials for "solitary confinement." "Flotation support system" is used by furniture salespersons to mean "waterbed." "Manually operated humus excavator" is jargon used by government officials and means "shovel." Doctors use "therapeutic misadventures" to refer to "malpractice cases."

Gender Context

The effect of the gender context on our verbal communication reflects learned gender expectations . . . to a point. In general, both men and women tend to talk about work, movies, and television, and both talk about sex and sexuality with members of the same sex. Female friends tend to talk about people, feelings, problems, relationships, family, food, fashion, and men. Male friends tend to talk about music, sports, work, hobbies, and women.[36] In one study in which respondents were asked to describe dramatic or interesting life experiences, women made more reference to emotions, motivations, and themselves, and men made more references to destructive actions, time, and space.[37] Moreover, men often begin a meeting by establishing who is best informed about movies, books, current events, or other topics, perhaps because men tend to view communication primarily in terms of status and hierarchy. Talking about such topics at the beginning of a meeting enables men to size up the competition and negotiate where they stand in relation to each other. Interestingly enough, both men and women talk about people and the details of everyday life. Although the term **gossip** has negative connotations, this word also refers to talking about people (rather than talking against them). Both men and women gossip; however, they gossip about different topics. Men's interest in the details of politics, news, and sports is parallel to women's interest in the details of the personal lives of others and their relationships.[38]

A few caveats are in order when it comes to the relationship between gender and verbal communication. Many researchers suggest that there are more similarities than there are differences in gender communication, and that the overemphasis on differences doesn't paint a realistic picture of gender and communication.[39] In addition, research on gender communication typically fails to account for the relationship between the communicators, the topic under discussion, and the overall context. For example, one study found that women use "feminine language" (characterized by questions, intensive adverbs such as *very* and *so,* and personal pronouns) when talking to their husbands or other men. However, men use "masculine language" (characterized by interruptions and directives) when talking to women, but change their styles when speaking with their wives.[40] It must be remembered that our language patterns don't typically follow one particular gender style to the exclusion of the other. We can choose whether to verbally communicate in a manner that reflects a masculine style, a feminine style, or a style that reflects aspects of both.

Individual Context

- Bling
- Homey
- Thirsty

KNOWLEDGE ON THE CUTTING EDGE

Putting It in Context: Sex and Verbal Communication

Research has demonstrated that compared with males, females produce more words in a given time period, use more words correctly, produce longer sentences, and use better grammar and pronunciation. Women tested in such diverse countries as Japan, England, the Czech Republic, Nepal, and the United States excel at verbal communication.[41] These findings are based on studies that illustrate that certain regions of the prefrontal brain area are activated differently during language tasks in females and males. One study demonstrated that the prefrontal area is activated in both the left and right hemispheres in women, but only the left hemisphere activation is evidenced in men. This suggests that it is easier for women to articulate words.[42] Similarly, compared with men, women are less likely to develop language difficulties when they experience left-hemisphere damage due to strokes. This may result from right-hemisphere language areas taking over some of the language functions in the left-hemisphere language areas.[43] Neuroscientists believe that although the corpus callosum (the bundle of nerves that links the right and left hemispheres of the brain) takes a cylindrical shape in men, it bulges in one or more places toward the rear in women. MRI brain scans support the idea that this "brain architecture" causes women to be more efficient with their words.[44]

Although slang can establish commonality among its users, it changes very quickly.

Source: © SALLY FORTH–KING FEATURES SYNDICATE.

Can you define these words according to their slang meanings? **Slang** is a specialized vocabulary shared by people with similar experiences and interests. Slang functions to establish a sense of belonging and commonality among its users, which include members of groups such as young people, people who enjoy hip-hop and rap music, and even the devoted fans of the *Star Trek* movies and television shows. Youth, oppression, sports, and vice most often are the basis for slang. Young people are the most powerful stimulus for creation and use of slang. For example, young people use slang to define status, establish bonds with peers, and to confound adults. Although adults who use slang may be perceived negatively by young people (as suggested in the "Sally Forth" comic), research reveals that teachers who strategically use slang words such as "cool, sweet" and "awesome" positively influence student motivation, affective learning, and classroom climate.[45] As of this writing, current slang words include "bling" (anything that's new or shiny, such as jewelry), "homey" (friend), and "thirsty" (to really want something). As you may have guessed, slang changes very quickly and often "dies" from disuse or becomes a part of the common language. Lexicographers (people who compile dictionaries) suggest that the majority of new words included in dictionaries come from new inventions and from slang.[46] However, slang changes so rapidly that the words compiled for a printed dictionary could possibly be out-of-date by the time the dictionary goes to press.

To review, let's return to the sentence, "*She looks like a million dollars; she had some aesthetic enhancements and is wearing a lot of bling.*" The culture context is represented when

KNOWLEDGE power • What's a "Blow-Off" Class?

Do you use slang words with people who share your interests and activities? For example, what college-oriented slang do you use in your discussions about academic life? Do you use slang related to any of your hobbies and abilities (e.g., stamp or coin collecting, scrapbooking, music, sports)? Are your slang words related to your age and/or generation? With a partner or in a group, list the slang words you use, and discuss how you might be perceived if you used slang with people who do not share your interests or age group. How might you perceive "outsiders" who use slang words related to your interests and age group?

she is described as looking like "a million dollars." Cultural values are expressed in language, and these values influence the words we use when we compliment others, in this case, a sum of money. However, not all cultures view an association between a person and a sum of money as complimentary. For example, the French believe that equating someone with money is an insult because it communicates a sexual connotation.[47] The relationship context is represented in terms of the jargon "aesthetic enhancements" (cosmetic surgery). This comment can also be characterized as gossip (the gender context), and the individual context is represented by the use of slang ("bling"). This sentence illustrates the various ways in which contexts can affect verbal communication.

OVERCOMING COMMUNICATION CHALLENGES

Gender-Biased Language

"Scientist: Man in Americas earlier than thought." This headline describes a November 2004 CNN.com article about archaeologists who believe that humans may have settled in North America over 50,000 years ago.[48] Do you think that the title of the article is an example of biased language? Before you can properly answer this question, consider the characterizations of biased language and inclusive language.

Gender-Biased Language

Biased language fails to acknowledge and validate others. Some forms of language, such as racial slurs, are extremely biased and can be characterized as hate speech. However, subtle forms of biased language are pervasive, transmit society's prejudices, and influence thought.[49]

One form of biased language perpetuates gender stereotypes. Specifically, the English language more often reflects and values "masculinity" over "femininity." One reason that English devalues women is because (white) men have controlled the creation of language and set its standards. This has occurred throughout history as men have predominantly held political, economic, and social power. Therefore, men have "provided themselves with more positive words to describe themselves, and given themselves more opportunities to use those words."[50]

There are numerous examples of gender bias in the English language. For example, "he" is often used to represent both men and women. However, studies concerning the use of "he" as a generic have revealed that the word produces male images more than images of both sexes. In fact, when female college students were asked to interpret the generic "he," 87% assumed that the word referred exclusively to men.[51] Another study concluded that the generic "he" does not accomplish the purpose for which it was intended. Instead, the generic "he" communicates that females occupy an inferior position in our culture and that the male is the standard or norm.[52] Man-linked words, such as *freshman, chairman, mailman,* and *fireman,* also communicate the inferior status of females. A study of female high school seniors revealed that they believed that jobs described by man-linked words were not appropriate for women.[53] However, as more women occupy these and other roles and professions, more gender-neutral words are being created to describe them (e.g., *first-year-student, chairperson, mail carrier,* and *firefighter*).[54] On the other hand, some roles occupied by women continue to reflect and perpetuate their limited status in society by the addition of the diminutive "-ette" or "-ess." The diminutive ending also can change the meaning of a word and create sexual connotations. For instance, a "major" suggests the masculine characteristics of strength and leadership, but a "majorette" suggests the feminine characteristic of attractiveness (in particular, a young woman in a skimpy outfit who tosses a baton during halftime). The word *master* embodies the masculine characteristic of power (such as a "master of ceremonies" who presides over the entertainment), but the word *mistress* changes the meaning of the word to one that suggests a sexual liaison. A "host" implies someone who embodies the masculine idea of self-reliance (e.g., someone who interviews guests on a television talk show), but a "hostess" embodies the feminine idea of caring for others (e.g., someone who makes sure that everyone has food and drink at a party).[55]

The diminutive -ess and -ette endings (e.g., hostess), which imply that the feminine gender is a substandard version of the masculine, can be replaced with gender-neutral words that describe both men and women (e.g., TV personality).

Gender-Inclusive Language

We can avoid biased language by making use of language that is inclusive. **Gender-inclusive language** that communicates respect for others may be a first step in changing the way our culture negatively stereotypes and devalues women through verbal communication.[56] For example, the generic pronoun "he" can be avoided in a number of ways. One way is to pluralize, and another is to leave out the pronoun. We can also use a double pronoun.[57] For example, instead of saying, "Every student is expected to complete his assignment on time," say:

- *"All students are expected to complete* ***their*** *assignments on time."* (pluralizing)
- *"Every student is expected to complete* ***the*** *assignment on time."* (eliminating the pronoun)
- *"Every student is expected to complete* ***her*** *or* ***his*** *assignment on time."* (using a double pronoun)

Occupations and roles can also be made gender-neutral by avoiding man-linked words. For example:

- Instead of saying "chairman," say *"chair," "head,"* or *"chairperson"*
- Instead of saying "fisherman," say *"fisher"* or *"angler"*
- Instead of saying "foreman," say *"supervisor"* or *"superintendent"*

Furthermore, the diminutive -ette and -ess endings, which imply that the feminine gender is a substandard variation of the masculine, can be replaced with gender-neutral words that can describe both men and women. For example:

- Instead of saying "majorette," say *"major"* or *"drum major"*
- Instead of saying "mistress," say *"speaker"* or *"leader"*
- Instead of saying "hostess," say *"host"* or *"organizer"*

What do you think about gender bias in language? Some people think that advocating the use of inclusive language smacks of "political correctness" run amok. Although some people associate negative connotations such as "oversensitivity" and "thought police" with "political correctness," the phrase can also mean "respect" and "inclusion."[58] The latter connotations suggest that "politically correct" inclusive language doesn't restrict freedom of expression. Additionally, there are a number of reasons why we may want to consider avoiding gender-biased language. We know that language can influence one's self-concept. We also know that language can subtly influence thoughts. Competent communicators reject language that is disrespectful or devalues and excludes others; they understand that language not only reflects but also can perpetuate cultural attitudes.

"Scientist: Man in Americas earlier than thought." Did you picture prehistoric women when you read the title of this article? What do you now believe about this title, biased language, and the influence of language on thought?

A CASE STUDY IN ETHICS

Offensive Verbal Communication?

Competent communication involves an ethical dimension of well-based standards of right and wrong. We can ask ourselves questions that relate to "everyday ethics" when deciding on the language we use in our verbal communication and how to respond to the language use of others. For example, we can ask ourselves if our language use reflects virtues such as integrity, trustworthiness, honesty, and responsibility. We can also ask if the endorsement of others' verbal communication will result in more good than harm. We can ask if our language use and our responses to others will entail treating others with dignity and respect, reflect fairness and justice, and make our community stronger. You can gain insight about your ideas concerning ethical verbal communication by reading "A Case Study in Ethics: Offensive Verbal Communication?"

Southwest Airlines passenger Lorrie Heasley found herself as the cause of several complaints after fellow passengers took offense to her T-shirt. Under pictures of President George W. Bush, Vice President Dick Cheney, and Secretary of State Condoleezza Rice was a phrase similar to the popular film title *Meet the Fockers.* No one made an issue of her T-shirt as she waited two hours near the gate at the airport, and neither the pilot nor the crew members commented on her shirt when she boarded the plane. However, passengers began to complain about the T-shirt after Heasley and her husband moved to the front of the aircraft. After conversing with the flight attendant, Heasly agreed to hide the words by covering her shirt with a sweatshirt. However, the sweatshirt slipped while she was trying to sleep, and she was subsequently told to wear the shirt inside out or to leave the plane at the next stop. Heasly and her husband chose to leave the plane.

Heasley intends to press a civil rights case against Southwest Airlines. FAA rules allow airlines to deny boarding to customers whose clothing is "lewd, obscene, or patently offensive." ACLU lawyer Allen Lichtenstein asserts that the real issue is that Southwest allowed Heasley to wear the shirt onboard and then ordered her to cover up or deplane only when people said they were offended. In other words, "They changed rules in the middle of a flight simply because someone didn't like it and it might be problematic." Moreover, Lichtenstein contends that Heasley's T-shirt is "protected" political speech under the Constitution. However, a spokesperson for US Airways asserted: "At any point when a passenger has a complaint against another and it becomes an issue that could disrupt the flight, our attendants have the discretion to take the appropriate action."

Heasley said she thought that the T-shirt was hilarious and that she wore it as a gag to make her parents, both Democrats, laugh when they picked her up at the airport. She also thought she had a right to wear the T-shirt and said, "I have cousins in Iraq and other relatives going to war. Here we are trying to free another country and I have to get off an airplane in mid-flight over a T-shirt. That's not freedom." Heasley asserted, "I have always flown Southwest everywhere I go. I will never fly with them again. They can disrespect somebody else."[59]

If you perceive that "offensive language" is indeed present in this incident, whose language is offensive (passenger Heasley or the flight crew that operated under the guise of "appropriate action")? Do you believe Heasley and/or Southwest Airlines engaged in ethical behavior regarding communication that may be considered "offensive"? What role does freedom of speech play in this scenario?

Chapter Review

Motivation: How has this helped me?

- **The importance of studying verbal communication**

It's important to study verbal communication because the symbols used in verbal communication are crucial for the expression of meaning and interaction with others. In addition, our motives to communicate with others fulfill basic human needs. We are typically satisfied with the outcomes of our verbal communication if they fulfill our motives for pleasure, affection, inclusion, and relaxation.

Knowledge: What have I learned?

- **How we can characterize verbal communication**

Verbal communication concerns the use of words to create and convey meaning. Verbal communication may be problematic because words are symbolic, which means that there is no inherent relationship between words and what they stand for.

- **The relationship between verbal communication and meaning**

Most words have denotative (universal or "correct") meanings and connotative meanings that are subjective, emotional, and easily changed. Syntactic, semantic, and pragmatic rules help us interpret the meaning of verbal communication. Moreover, the theory of the coordinated management of meaning suggests that such rules can help us ascertain meaning in terms of coherence, coordination, and mystery.

- **How verbal communication influences thought**

Words are often carefully chosen to affect people's attitudes and are consciously used to influence thoughts and behavior. The words used in verbal communication can also influence us subtly in a manner of which we are unaware. How we react to the communication of others and how others react to our communication are significantly based on the words that are expressed during verbal communication.

- **How contexts influence verbal communication**

Verbal communication is influenced by the culture, relationship, gender, and individual contexts. For example, the relationship between culture and language is considered to be inseparable. The Sapir-Whorf hypothesis suggests that culture influences how we think and communicate. Similarly, the social context influences our verbal communication in that our family, friends, and coworkers may develop unique communication codes based on personal idioms and jargon. The gender context influences verbal communication in terms of expectations regarding the topic of talk. Depending on their age and how they see themselves in society, individuals create and use special types of verbal communication such as slang.

Skill: What skills have I developed?

- **Using specific and concrete words, indexing and owning our thoughts, and dating information can improve our communication competence**

Using specific and concrete words based on sense data, indexing and owning our thoughts by using qualifiers such as "maybe" and "it could be," and dating information can help minimize the problem caused by abstraction (unspecific language), indiscrimination and allness (a verbalized stereotype and the failure to make distinctions), and static evaluation (verbal communication that fails to note change).

Study Questions

1. Describe the triangle of meaning, that is, the relationship between symbols, thoughts, and what symbols stand for.
2. Explain denotative and connotative meanings and how the coordinated management of meaning enables us to interpret communication.
3. What is abstraction, and what consequences can result from communicating in an abstract manner? How can we avoid the problems associated with abstract language?

4. Describe indiscrimination, allness, and static evaluation. What communication skills can we use in place of these problematic forms of verbal communication?
5. How does verbal communication influence thought? Provide examples of the words people choose to discuss controversial topics.
6. What is the relationship between the culture, gender, relationship, and individual contexts and verbal communication?
7. What is gender-biased language and why is it harmful? How can we avoid the use of gender-biased language?

Names to Know

C. K. Ogden (1889–1957) and **I. A. Richards** (1893–1979), p. 120—linguists who developed the "triangle of meaning," a model that illustrates the relationship between symbols and what they stand for. Ogden and Richards's classic text, *The Meaning of Meaning* (1923), is grounded in psychological theory.

W. Barnett Pierce and **Vernon Cronen**, p. 125—communication theorists from the Fielding Institute at the University of Massachusetts who created the coordinated management of meaning (CMM) to explain how people agree on the meaning of verbal communication.

Rebecca B. Rubin, p. 122—communication scholar who developed the Interpersonal Communication Motives (ICM) scale and identified six prominent motives for interpersonal communication: pleasure, affection, inclusion, escape, relaxation, and control. Rubin teaches at Kent State University.

Edward Sapir (1884–1936) and **Benjamin Lee Whorf** (1897–1941), p. 134—linguists who developed the Sapir-Whorf hypothesis, which posits that culture influences language and language influences cultural differences in thought.

Key Terms

abstraction, 126
allness, 128
biased language, 140
coherence, 125
concrete words, 127
connotative, 124
coordinated management of meaning, 125
coordination, 125
dating information, 129
denotative, 123
euphemisms, 124
gender-inclusive language, 141
gossip, 138
idioms, 136
indexing, 128
indiscrimination, 128
jargon, 136
mystery, 125
owning thoughts, 128
pragmatic rules, 125
Sapir-Whorf hypothesis, 134
semantic rules, 125
slang, 139
static evaluation, 129
symbols, 120
syntactic rules, 125

CHAPTER 6 Nonverbal Communication

"The most important thing in communication is hearing what isn't said."

PETER F. DRUCKER (1909–2005), WRITER, MANAGEMENT CONSULTANT, AND UNIVERSITY PROFESSOR

In this chapter, we will answer the following:

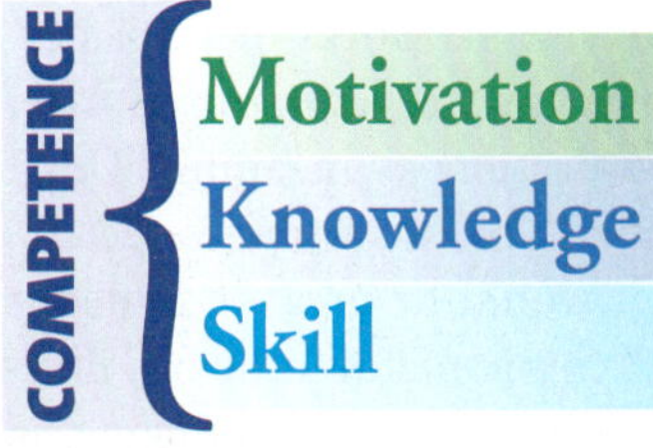

Motivation: How will this help me?

- It is important to study nonverbal communication because the majority of a message's meaning comes from nonverbal behavior. In addition, most relational messages arise from nonverbal communication.

Knowledge: What will I learn?

- How to characterize nonverbal communication
- The functions of nonverbal communication
- The types of nonverbal communication
- How contexts influence nonverbal communication

Skill: Why do I need to develop these skills?

- The use of nonverbal immediacy skills increases the likelihood that we will be perceived as competent communicators

Despite assurances that their marriage was strong, the nonverbal communication of Prince Charles of England and the late Princess Diana suggested otherwise. Have you ever disbelieved someone's comments but didn't understand why? For example, perhaps you told a friend a story that you thought was interesting and funny. You noticed that your friend looked down and didn't smile at you when you finished. When you asked your friend what she or he thought of the story, your friend responded in a barely audible voice, "Yeah, it was an interesting story. I liked it." Nonverbal behavior can influence us to disbelieve someone's spoken words.

In this chapter, we will learn that we can increase our motivation to communicate competently by understanding why it's important to study nonverbal communication. We will also increase our knowledge by learning about the conceptualization of nonverbal communication, some functions and types of nonverbal communication, and how nonverbal communication is influenced by contexts. We will also learn how to skillfully perform nonverbal immediacy behaviors.

Introduction to Nonverbal Communication

Imagine you and a friend are attending a party. Your friend notices an extremely attractive person and wants to strike up a conversation. However, your friend notices that this person is looking down at the floor and sitting with her or his arms and legs crossed. Your friend interprets the attractive person's nonverbal communication as meaning "Don't bother me. I want to be left alone!" A short time later, you walk by the attractive person and hear her or him mutter, "I don't know anyone here; it would be great if someone would talk to me." This example, along with the "Garfield" comic pictured below, illustrates that nonverbal communication is ambiguous (i.e., can have many meanings) and powerful (e.g., can influence our behavior). Specifically, the attractive person's downcast eyes and crossed arms and legs may have various meanings or mean nothing at all. Similarly, your friend formed an impression based on nonverbal communication that influenced his or her behavior (that is, not speaking to the attractive person).

How can we characterize nonverbal communication?

Nonverbal communication refers to all forms of communication other than words themselves. This form of communication occurs via gestures, body orientation and posture, touch, facial expression and eye contact, vocal qualities and accents, body shape, clothing and artifacts (such as jewelry and tattoos), the environment in which both verbal and nonverbal communication takes place, and how close or far away we sit or stand from others. Even time is a form of nonverbal communication. Nonverbal behavior is an integral part of the overall study of communication because it is a significant channel for creating and sharing meaning.

Even though nonverbal communication is an important channel of meaning, the interpretation of nonverbal behavior isn't always straightforward because nonverbal communication is ambiguous. One reason that accounts for such ambiguity is that nonverbal behaviors can have various meanings. Consider the various meanings associated with a pat on the back. It can be interpreted as an expression of sympathy ("I'm so sorry"), encouragement ("Way to go!"), or merely an attempt to engage our attention ("Hey!"). The influence of contexts also affects how we interpret nonverbal communication. For example, Navajo children are typically taught that it is impolite to make prolonged eye contact with others. However, lack of eye contact is considered disrespectful in the

Nonverbal communication can have many meanings and can influence our behavior.

Source:

KNOWLEDGE ON THE CUTTING EDGE

Communication, Nonverbal Behavior, and Civility: Are You a Civil Communicator?

According to an Associated Press-Ipsos poll, rudeness is increasing in our culture because of our high-tech, fast-paced existence. The poll revealed that the most commonly cited example of incivility was aggressive or reckless driving, with 91% of the respondents citing road rage as the most frequent complaint.[1]

Some researchers view road rage as symbolic interpersonal communication. The symbolic behavior associated with road rage varies from silently swearing under our breath as we drive (which the researchers label "human communication") to using our vehicles to nonverbally express our anger (which the researchers label "vehicular communication"). The most common form of vehicular communication is cutting off other drivers, followed by speeding, not allowing drivers to merge, and tailgating. Researchers have found that vehicular communication is used much more often than human communication in episodes of road rage. Persons who instigate road rage incidents tend to blame the other driver. These individuals typically believe that other drivers' internal characteristics contribute to road rage incidents and are unable to see that their own behaviors influence road rage. This self-serving bias is exacerbated by deindividuation, in which drivers relate to others on the road as "cars" instead of "people." Deindividuation subsequently causes them to aggress even more and feel that their actions are justified.

The fact that our attributions strongly influence incidents of road rage suggests that intervention programs that focus on perceptions could reduce this form of uncivil nonverbal behavior. For example, research conducted at SUNY Albany studied the effect of cognitive-behavioral interventions on aggressive drivers who volunteered for an intervention program and on drivers who were mandated to the program through the court system. Drivers were educated about the ramifications of aggressive driving, motivational techniques, progressive muscle relaxation training, alternative coping strategies, and strategies for dealing with problematic perceptions. Such strategies included targeting faulty assumptions and challenging distorted and maladaptive thoughts. Many of the drivers in the study didn't perceive the extent of their problem; therefore, they were taught to perceive themselves as "aggressive drivers," which was a difficult attribution change for some respondents. Study results indicated that as a group, the respondents averaged 64% improvement in aggressive driving behaviors. Although these results are preliminary, it appears that cognitive-behavioral interventions can significantly decrease road rage, this dangerous and potentially fatal form of uncivil nonverbal communication.[2]

Road rage is the most commonly cited example of uncivil behavior.

dominant U.S. culture.[3] Nonverbal communication can also be ambiguous because nonverbal behavior may be intentional or unintentional. For example, although we may not consciously and intentionally end our sentences with a rising inflection (sometimes labeled "up-talk"), we may be perceived as insecure or immature on the basis of this nonverbal behavior. Because nonverbal communication is ambiguous, it's best to interpret nonverbal behavior in conjunction with verbal communication.

Why It's Important to Study Nonverbal Communication

Although nonverbal messages are ambiguous, nonverbal communication is nonetheless worthy of study because it is powerful. The majority of a message's meaning comes from nonverbal communication, and most relational messages arise from nonverbal behavior.

Meaning

Why is it important to study nonverbal communication?

Research demonstrates that between 65% and 93% of the meaning of messages comes from nonverbal communication.[4] For example, suppose you are arguing with a younger sibling, relative, or child. The child screams and stomps her or his feet, and you demand an apology for the inappropriate behavior. The child puts her or his hands on the hips, sticks out her or his tongue, and shouts, "I'm sorry!" Do you think the child is truly sorry for the behavior? You probably answered "no" to this question because the nonverbal communication caused you to believe that the child wasn't truly sorry, although the verbal communication suggested otherwise. Other studies have found that nonverbal communication is twelve to thirteen times more powerful than the verbal messages it accompanies.[5] Overall, when nonverbal messages contradict verbal messages, we tend to believe the nonverbal communication.

Relational Messages

Nonverbal behavior is worthy of study because it communicates relational-level meanings more than verbal communication.[6] Recall from Chapter 1 that the relational level of meaning most often entails the implicit communication about the relationship between conversation partners. A smile or touch can communicate liking or connection, a closed fist and loud tone of voice can communicate control, and a lack of eye contact or a sarcastic snarl can communicate that one relationship partner disrespects the other. Some communication scholars label nonverbal communication as "the relationship language."[7]

KNOWLEDGE power • Your Words Say, "No" but Your Eyes Say, "Yes!"

With a partner or in a group, recall a time when someone said something to you that contradicted her or his nonverbal behavior. Specifically describe the nonverbal behavior and why it suggested that the words you heard didn't ring true. Similarly, recall a time when someone doubted the sincerity of your words. Do you think your nonverbal behavior communicated the opposite of what your speech conveyed? Specifically describe the forms of nonverbal behavior that suggested your true meaning(s).

Functions of Nonverbal Communication

Motivation
Knowledge
Skill
COMPETENCE

Can you recall a time when you held your hand in front of you with your fingers pointing upward as you shouted, "Stop"? Perhaps you held your hand out, and others knew you wanted them to stop even though you didn't say a word. Can you remember the last time you pounded your fist on a table or when your breathing became audible when you were angry? Maybe you can recall a conversation during which someone tried to interrupt you and you responded by raising your voice and increasing your rate of speech. The previous questions and examples suggest one way we can study nonverbal communication, that is, organize various behaviors into categories that describe how nonverbal communication functions. Nonverbal communication functions to repeat, substitute for, accent, complement, and regulate verbal communication.

What are the functions of nonverbal communication?

Repeating

One function of nonverbal communication is merely **repeating** what is communicated verbally. For example, we might point our index finger at something as we say, "It's over there," and lift our hand in the air with the palm facing down as we say, "She's about this high." We may also shrug our shoulders as we say, "I don't know" when answering a question. Consider how your nonverbal communication might repeat the statement, "It stinks!" You most likely would wrinkle your nose and perhaps purse your lips while conveying this message. Nonverbal behavior that repeats what is stated verbally can often stand alone and convey the verbal meaning without the necessity of accompanying words.

Substituting

Additionally, nonverbal communication can function as a **substitute** for verbal communication. For example, what nonverbal behaviors might express the following?

- "A-OK"
- "I don't know"
- "Borrrrrring!"

Notice that touching our thumb with our index finger (or lifting our thumb in the air and curling our fingers), shrugging our shoulders, and yawning are nonverbal behaviors that can take the place of verbal communication.

Emblems are a category of nonverbal behaviors that often function to substitute for verbal communication. As Figure 6.1 shows, **Emblems** are nonverbal behaviors that can be translated directly in a word or two of verbal communication. We are usually very conscious of our use of emblems, but it's important to note that emblems are culturally specific; that is, a particular emblem in one culture will not have the same meaning in another. For example, the "A-OK" emblem of the index finger touching the thumb refers to "money" in Japan, means "you're worth zero" in France and Belgium, and is a vulgar sexual reference in Greece and Turkey. Americans shake their head back and forth as the emblem for "no," but this particular emblem means "I don't understand" in Turkey.[8] Can you imagine what may ensue if an American shakes her or his head back and forth after being approached by a vendor in a Turkish market?

Culturally dependent emblematic meanings have been problematic for some of our national leaders. For example, Vice President Richard Nixon flashed the "OK" sign when he arrived in Latin America in the mid-1950s. Unfortunately, that gesture was decoded as an

Figure 6.1: Nonverbal Emblems

Thumbs-Up Gesture
United States: "good, positive, or OK"
Mid East: obscene gesture

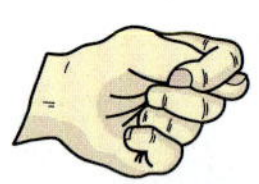

Fig Gesture (thumb inserted between index and 3rd finger)
United States: unknown (gesture isn't emblematic)
Germany, Holland, Denmark: an invitation to have sex
Portugal and Brazil: a wish for good luck or protection

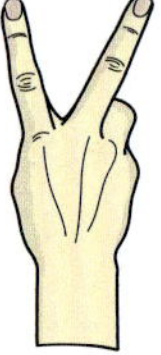

"V" Sign
United States: "peace" or "victory"
Great Britain: insult if palm faces inward toward body (e.g., "up yours")

Vertical Horn
United States: University of Texas "Hook 'em Horns" salute
Portugal, Spain, Italy: "cuckold"

insult directed toward the Latin American people. Similarly, President George H. W. Bush insulted thousands of Australians during a 1991 visit in which he thought he flashed the "V" for "Victory" sign. Unfortunately, President Bush's palm faced inward toward his body as he made the sign, which changed the meaning of his emblem from "victory" to "up yours." President George W. Bush and his family flashed the "Hook 'em Horns" sign at the University of Texas marching band at his 2005 inaugural parade. Shocked Norwegians translated this emblem according to their own culturally specific meaning: a salute to Satan. Norway's largest newspaper, *Verdens Gang*, subsequently explained to its readers that this emblem, popular with heavy metal groups, is a salute to the Texas Longhorn band.[9]

Accenting

In addition to repeating what is said verbally and substituting for verbal communication, nonverbal communication also functions to **accent** or emphasize the spoken word. We can accent the spoken word by pounding our fist on a table, thrusting an index finger close to someone's face, and changing the volume of certain words as we speak them (e.g., "I said that I'd THINK about it!"). Sometimes illustrators are used to accent the spoken word. **Illustrators** are typically gestures that are directly tied to speech. For example, pointing movements can help identify a specific person, place, or thing. Illustrators can also depict spatial relationships and can accent or organize important parts of an utterance. These gestures may be in the form of rhythmic chopping gestures (e.g., "We must first do this [gesture], then this [gesture], and then this" [gesture]). However, illustrators need not always be gestures. For example, the momentary widening of our eyes often occurs along with spoken adjectives and is used to accent or emphasize verbal communication.[10]

Complementing

In addition to accenting, nonverbal communication functions to **complement** verbal communication. Like nonverbal behaviors that accent the spoken word, complementing nonverbal communication adds meaning to verbal communication. Examples of complementing nonverbal behaviors include weeping while telling a sad story and blushing when communicating embarrassment. Sometimes it's difficult to distinguish nonverbal behaviors that accent verbal communication and nonverbal behaviors that complement the spoken word. However, we usually have less control of complementing nonverbal behaviors than we have of accenting nonverbal behaviors.

Regulating

Nonverbal communication also functions to **regulate** the flow of verbal behavior. Why is it that people who engage in face-to-face conversation need not say "over" or "I'm finished talking now; it's your turn" when switching the roles of verbal sender and receiver? It's because subtle shifts in nonverbal behavior signal that a speaker is finished with her or his turn and/or a listener desires a turn to speak. We tend to increase our eye contact with a conversation partner to signal that we are finished speaking. We also tend to decrease eye contact and raise our volume if our partner tries to speak and we're not ready to give up a turn. To signal that we're ready to speak, we may straighten our posture, raise our index finger, and perhaps take an audible inhalation of breath.

Types of Nonverbal Communication

What are the types of nonverbal communication?

We have read that nonverbal communication functions to repeat, substitute for, accent, complement, and regulate the spoken word. Four general categories of nonverbal communication are used to carry out these functions: kinesics (gestures, body orientation and posture, touch, facial expression and eye behavior), paralanguage (vocal qualities and accents), physical characteristics (attractiveness, body shape, and artifacts), and the environment (the physical environment, time, territoriality, and proxemics). Note that these classifications have a practical

KNOWLEDGE ON THE CUTTING EDGE

Technology Update: Computer-Mediated Communication and Nonverbal Communication

With the exception of computer-based innovations such as Skype software, webcams, and virtual reality environments, computer-mediated communication (CMC) is primarily textual and limits the exchange of nonverbal information. Early research about CMC reflects this assumption and is based on a **cues-filtered-out approach** that characterizes CMC as primarily verbal and without the benefit of nonverbal cues. The cues-filtered-out approach posits that the functions served by nonverbal communication in face-to-face (ftf) interaction are not met because nonverbal cues are absent in CMC. This means that CMC is impersonal because the social meaning expressed by nonverbal communication is nonexistent. The absence of nonverbal cues also affects the degree of **social presence**, or the perception of a receiver's involvement in an interaction. A conversation partner is deindividuated as the perception of social presence decreases, and this can result in antisocial behavior in CMC. For example, one empirical CMC study of the cues-filtered-out approach found that the expression of bad news resulted in less polite and face-saving messages than the ftf communication of bad news.[11]

In contrast to the cues-filtered-out approach, recent CMC research tends to reflect a **hyperpersonal approach** that assumes that the filtering of nonverbal cues is advantageous for communicators. The hyperpersonal approach posits that CMC users strategically manipulate their identity and plan and edit their communication to achieve relational goals. The hyperpersonal approach can facilitate relational development because of visual anonymity; that is, CMC users don't have cues that demonstrate the physical attractiveness of their conversation partners. Similarly, the asynchronous nature of much CMC allows us to construct and fine-tune messages to portray ourselves in the best possible light. Recent research illustrates that, compared with voicemail, email messages tend to be more face-saving because of the ability to construct more polite messages. Consistent with the assumptions that underlie the hyperpersonal approach, the reduced nonverbal cues associated with email messages and the ability to plan, edit, and control "performance" result in the creation of more socially desirable messages.[12]

Whether or not CMC is ultimately found to be impersonal or hyperpersonal compared with ftf communication, it is our perception of the experience of communication that matters. As in the ftf context, it is individual perception, not the qualities of a medium or channel, that determines the evaluation of a communication experience.[13]

KNOWLEDGE power • Mind Reading

Can you recognize emotion from facial expression and tone of voice? Simon Baron-Cohen, director of the Autism Research Centre at the University of Cambridge, England, has developed the Mind Reading program to help people on the autistic spectrum learn about nonverbal behaviors and emotions. Increase your knowledge by linking to a demonstration of mind reading at www.spectronicsinoz.com/product.asp?product=14473.

purpose. Most of us learn effective and appropriate nonverbal behaviors, seemingly without effort, by imitating others and by adapting our behavior based on their responses. However, some individuals with neurological disorders may be inexpressive or inadvertently send hostile nonverbal messages rather than friendly ones. In these cases, "social skills training" based on role playing, practice, and feedback can teach people to effectively use nonverbal cues to function in society. The classifications of nonverbal behaviors are also used to train individuals from one culture to decode and encode the nonverbal communication of people from another culture. Even individuals in specific professions can be taught to better encode and decode nonverbal communication. For example, nurses have been taught to identify "microexpressions" or extremely brief facial expressions.[14] Although the various types of nonverbal behaviors make interesting and entertaining reading, they also serve an important practical purpose—helping others improve their communication and relationships with others.

Kinesics

Kinesics, or the category of body movement and position, includes gestures, body orientation and posture, touch, and facial expressions and eye behavior.

Gestures **Gestures** are movements of the body used to communicate thoughts, feelings, and/or intentions. Gestures appear to naturally accompany speech, and people need not learn hand gestures by watching and modeling others' behavior. Researchers have discovered that children and adolescents who are blind from birth gesture as often and in the

Research demonstrates that we have difficulty finding words when we can't gesture freely.

KNOWLEDGE power • "My Hands Are Tied."

Do you gesture when you speak primarily to complement your verbal communication or to help you retrieve language while labeling objects and while referring to words with spatial connotations? Engage in a conversation with others in which you firmly clasp your hands in front of you or behind your back. Communicate for at least five minutes without allowing yourself to gesture. Did you find it difficult to communicate without gesturing? Why or why not?

same manner as sighted people. Therefore, people don't need to see gestures prior to gesturing on their own.

Recent research suggests that people not only gesture to communicate information to others and to acknowledge interaction partners but also to help retrieve language. For example, stroke patients gesture more when they attempt to name or label objects, and people who don't even realize they gesture in fact do so when asked to come up with words that match particular definitions. In general, people gesture more when they refer to words and concepts with spatial connotations such as "under" and "adjacent" than when they refer to abstract concepts such as "thought" or "evil." One interesting study demonstrated that people have difficulty finding words when they can't gesture freely. Gestures precede spoken words by as much as three seconds, and it may be that gestures aid in accessing words. Just as memories are retrieved when the senses are activated, words may be retrieved with gestures.[15]

Body Orientation and Posture In addition to gestures, **body orientation and posture** can communicate meaning. Body orientation involves the extent to which we face or lean toward or away from others. Both body orientation and posture can indicate whether we are open to interaction. For example, the positioning of the arms and legs while standing can indicate that we are available to talk with some people but not others, and the positioning of the arms, legs, and torso while seated can inhibit other people from entering into our conversations.

Posture and body orientation can also indicate status and power. More relaxed and expansive postures are typically associated with high status and dominant individuals. Although most studies of responses to emotional situations focus on facial expressions, recent research demonstrates that posture can communicate fear. Fear contagion, or the rapid spread of fright that occurs in crowds, often occurs when people view others who adopt fearful postures.[16] Body orientation and posture can also help us retrieve certain memories. One theory of memory suggests that activating a "sensory fragment"

How we position our bodies can indicate whether we want to communicate to others.

such as a sight, sound, odor, or body position can facilitate memory retrieval. For example, we will more easily recall an event that happened while we were golfing if we stand as if we are holding a golf club.[17]

Haptics **Haptics**, or touch, is related to the development of emotional and mental adjustment. Touch provides infants with comfort and protection and helps young children develop their identities. Adults also need touching and may turn to licensed touchers such as massage therapists to fulfill the need for touch. The meanings that are associated with touching behavior depend on what body part is touched, the intensity of the touch, the duration of the touch, the method of the touch (such as closed or open fist), and the frequency of the touch. The meaning of touch is also dependent on the physical context (such as the home, the university setting, an airport) and the age, sex, and relationship between the person who is touched and the person who does the touching.

Facial Expression and Eye Behavior **Facial expression and eye behavior** are difficult to describe and measure because there are so many configurations and types of face and eye behavior. However, the face and eyes are an extremely potent source of nonverbal communication in that they are involved in opening, closing, and regulating the channels of interaction, and they function as the prime communicator of emotion.

In the 1970s, **Paul Ekman**, a leading researcher in the area of facial expression, began to systematically analyze and measure facial expressions and what they communicate. Ekman and his colleagues developed the Facial Action Coding System (FACS) as a method to recognize and interpret facial expressions. FACS describes forty-three "action units," or movements that facial muscles can perform, and it illustrates all of the combinations of action units, which results in more than 10,000 possible facial expressions. FACS teaches people which muscles are associated with particular facial expressions and what specific movements the face can perform.[18]

Facial expression and eye behavior are related to **interaction management**, or the regulation of communication. For example, we open our mouths and simultaneously inhale as a sign of our readiness to speak. Making eye contact with someone also indicates that communication channels are open, whereas avoiding eye contact suggests that communication channels are closed. Eye contact also regulates the flow of communication with turn-taking signals. Glancing at grammatical breaks and the end of thought units enables us to obtain feedback about how we are being received, to see if our conversation partner will allow us to continue, and to signal to our partner that we are ready to switch to the role of the listener. When the speaking and listening roles change, the speaker will gaze at the listener as the utterance comes to a close. The listener will maintain the gaze until he or she assumes the speaking role, at which time the new speaker will look away.

In addition to regulating interaction, the face is the clearest indicator of what someone is feeling. As illustrated in the "Unmasking the Face" photographs, Paul Ekman's research has established that seven emotions have a universal facial expression: sadness, surprise, disgust, happiness, anger, fear, and contempt. Can you recognize these emotions in the facial expressions in the "Unmasking the Face" photographs?

KNOWLEDGE power • The Facial Action Coding Scheme

The Facial Action Coding Scheme (FACS) was developed to recognize and interpret facial expressions. How might FACS benefit behavioral scientists and computer graphics animators? Can you recognize the FACS action units that comprise a facial expression? You can access a demonstration of how the FACS coding works at http://face-and-emotion.com/dataface/faq/scored.html.

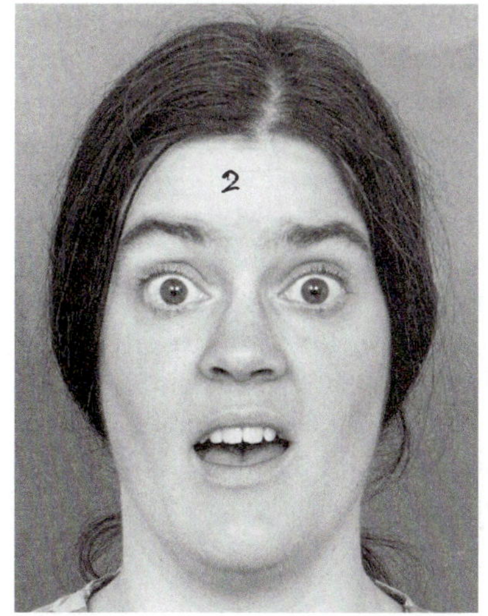

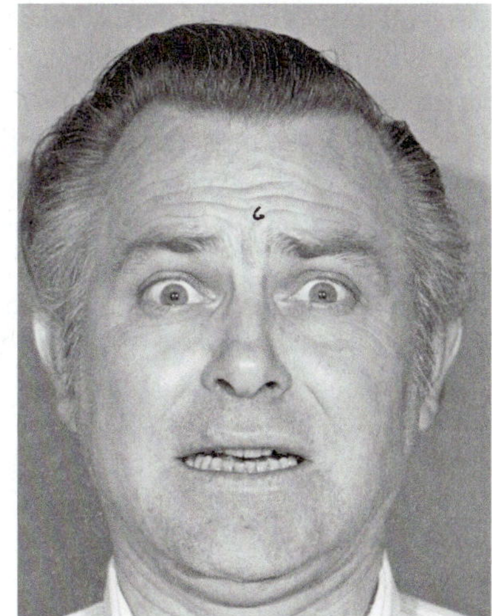

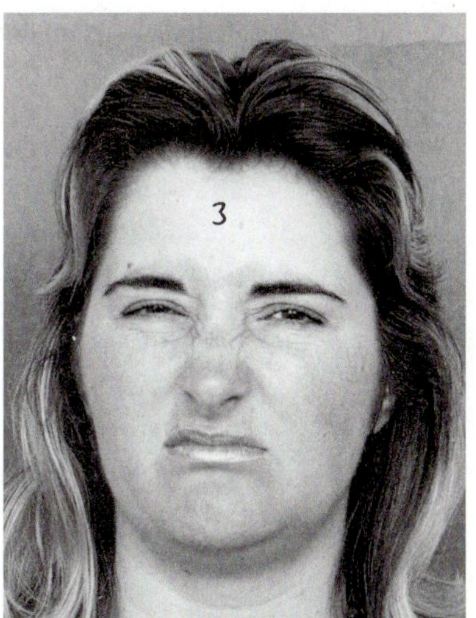

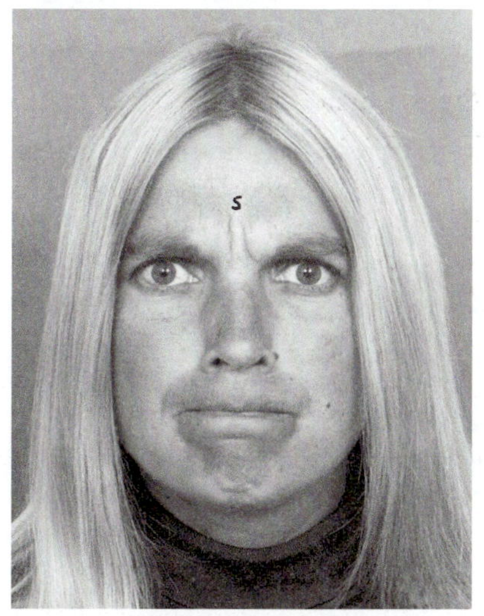

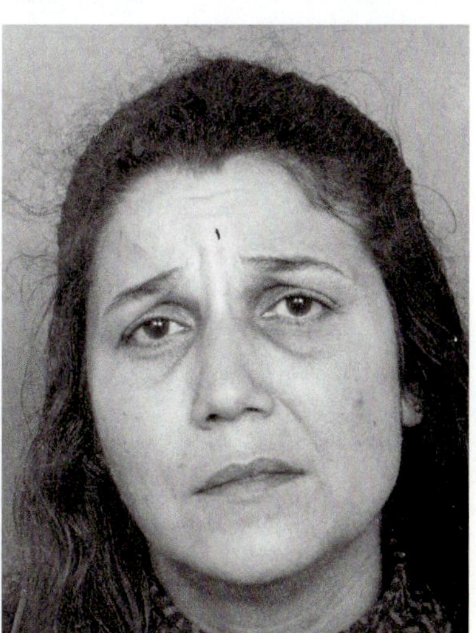

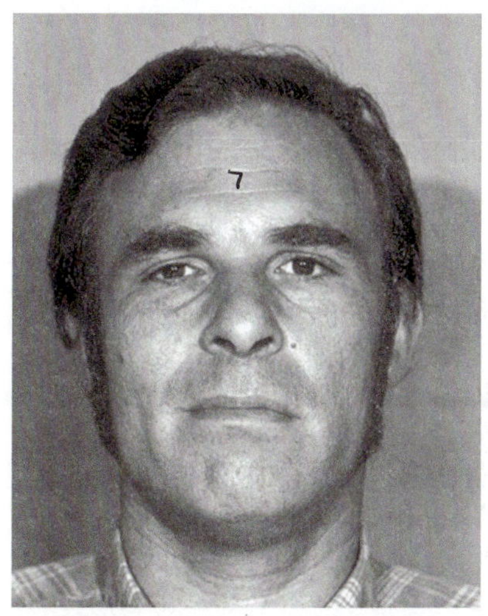

Ekman's "Unmasking the Face" Photographs.

 (Top row, L to R: surprise, fear, disgust; Middle row, L to R: anger, happiness, sadness; Bottom row: contempt)

Ekman has also researched how the face illustrates multiple emotions all at once. These **affect blends** may be one emotion evidenced in one facial area and another emotion shown in a different area, two different emotions illustrated in one part of the face, or a facial display that results from muscle action that is associated with two emotions. For example, we can raise our eyebrows in surprise and, at the same time, lift the corners of our mouth to smile with happiness. We can also show anger and surprise when we raise one eyebrow and lower the other toward the eye.[19] **Microexpressions**, which are extremely fast facial movements that last less than a fifth of a second, also can reveal emotions, especially those we are trying to conceal.[20] Imagine someone who eagerly anticipates a holiday present such as a gift card, iPod, or PDA (personal digital assistant). After opening the box expected to contain the desired gift, the recipient instead finds a pair of socks. Although she or he may attempt to hide the emotion felt on seeing the socks, others may perceive a brief and fleeting expression of disappointment. The microexpression of disappointment may give the people near the recipient some insight about what he or she truly feels.

Ekman's research has been used to teach police officers and judges how to read clues in facial expressions, and it has also been used by airport security officers, the FBI, and CIA agents to size up potential terrorists. The Department of Defense is using Eckman's research to develop computer technology that will scan and analyze videotaped facial movements. Ekman is also researching whether specific expressions of anger made of subtle facial movements can signal a forthcoming attack. The results of these investigations will not be publicized and instead will be made available only to law enforcement and security agents.[21]

Paralanguage

The second category of nonverbal communication is **paralanguage**, or "**vocalics**." This category includes vocal qualities (such as volume, pitch, inflection, speed, and silence) and accents. Paralanguage concerns *how* we say something rather than *what* we say.

Vocal Qualities Vocal qualities include:

- volume (loudness or softness)
- pitch (highness or lowness)
- inflection (vocal emphasis)
- speed (rate)
- silence

Our vocal qualities affect how others perceive us and interpret our messages. We can choose to alter our vocal qualities to sound assertive, sympathetic, or sarcastic. Say the following italicized sentence out loud, and see if you can alter your voice to express assertion, sympathy, and sarcasm: "*I'm so sorry.*"

In general, attractive voices are resonant, not too nasal, not too monotonous, and midrange in terms of pitch. We also associate personality characteristics with vocal qualities. For example, a low pitch, especially in males, is perceived to be sophisticated, sexy, appealing, and masculine. Vocal qualities can communicate emotions and elicit corresponding emotional feelings in listeners. University of Southern California researchers have developed software that recognizes "irritation" from vocal cues. The software is designed for commercial use and can read increasing levels of frustration in the voices of people using telephones to communicate with others. Depending on the level of frustration detected, callers are offered a soothing computerized response or are immediately routed to a human operator.[22]

Silence is a vocal quality that can communicate many meanings. Giving someone "the silent treatment" can communicate our displeasure. Silence can also communicate uneasiness, such as when we cannot find the words to express ourselves. It can also communicate contentment and the pleasure we feel in the company of someone we care for.

KNOWLEDGE power • "I Don't Have an Accent but They Do!"

Can you guess where a speaker comes from when you listen to her or his accent? Access www.pbs.org/speak/seatosea/americanvarieties/map/map.html to listen to twelve audio speech samples and match them to various regions in the United States.

Accents Another component of paralanguage is **accents**, the particular way that words are pronounced. Accents vary according to ethnicity, age, and geographical location. There is no universal standard regarding the correct ways to pronounce words in "American English." Some people believe that the way Midwesterners pronounce words is accentless and therefore "standard," but even people in the Midwest communicate with an accent. In general, we tend to stereotype others on the basis of their accents. One common stereotype is that Southerners sound friendly but are not as intelligent as Northerners. Another common stereotype is that New York and New Jersey accents sound "rude" and "unpleasant" and that New Yorkers pronounce words "incorrectly." However, linguists assert that pronunciation isn't associated with intelligence or personality. What is considered "standard" pronunciation is based on nothing more than social processes; that is, those groups with status and power impose their standards on others, and their standards include what is considered to be the proper and improper pronunciation of words.[23]

KNOWLEDGE ON THE CUTTING EDGE

Linguistic Profiling

Research suggests that Americans can make a positive identification of a caller's ethnic background 80% of the time based on the single word *hello*. We all have perceptions about the person with whom we share a telephone exchange; however, it is illegal to discriminate on the basis of someone's perceived ethnic or racial background. When members of particular racial or ethnic groups experience discrimination based on language, grammar, speech patterns, and accent, it is called "linguistic profiling."[24]

A number of studies have revealed that linguistic profiling occurs when members of African American, Hispanic American, and European American co-cultures attempt to rent apartments. Stanford linguist John Baugh conducted a study in which he used an African American communication style, a Hispanic American communication style, and a European American communication style when phoning San Francisco Bay area apartment managers about renting a unit. Baugh received far more appointments to view apartments in white areas when he made use of a European American communication style than when using the other two communication styles.[25] Audio samples of Baugh using of the three communication styles can be found at www.stanford.edu/~jbaugh/baugh.fft.

Baugh believes that awareness of linguistic profiling can help members of co-cultures who may be victims of discrimination. Baugh contends that when he began his studies of linguistic profiling, he didn't expect to find "that linguistic profiling affects the deaf, and it extends to sexual orientation as well."[26]

Can you recognize the cultural background of individuals based on their communication style? You can assess your ability by taking the Web-based quiz that accompanied a 2001 *ABC World News Tonight* story about linguistic profiling: www.uiowa.edu/~c103112/profile.html.

Physical Characteristics

The nonverbal category of physical characteristics includes general attractiveness (height, weight, hair, skin color), body shape, and artifacts such as clothing, jewelry, and other accessories and personal objects.

General Attractiveness and Body Shape What is the first question often asked when we learn that a friend is attracted to someone? We probably ask, "What does she or he look like?" In general, we use appearance, such as **general attractiveness** and **body shape**, to judge others' backgrounds, characters, personalities, talents, and potential future behavior. Studies demonstrate that physical attractiveness can help people obtain employment and receive high salaries. In addition, judges and juries are less likely to perceive attractive defendants as guilty, and such defendants receive shorter sentences than unattractive defendants.[27]

Recent changes in clothing mannequins and fashion dolls suggest that the characterization of physical attractiveness is undergoing transformation, at least as it relates to women. The Goddess clothing mannequin, which reflects various faces, skin tones, and body proportions and sizes, is a response to the time and culture in which we live. The Goddess mannequins illustrate people of various ethnic backgrounds and recognize different body types and standards of beauty. Even the idealized blond-haired, blue-eyed fashion doll is becoming obsolete. The Bratz line of fashion dolls not only illustrates cutting-edge fashion trends but also comes in a variety of skin tones and hair colors and textures. The Bratz dolls were introduced in 2001 and have become extremely popular worldwide because of their multicultural appeal.[28]

Artifacts **Artifacts**, including clothing, jewelry, accessories, and personal objects such as briefcases and backpacks, also communicate about the person who wears them. Clothes are an important aspect of first impressions, and we infer personal attributes such as age, nationality, socioeconomic status, group identification, occupation, personality, and interests from clothing.[29] Badges, tattoos, and jewelry also have communicative value. A ring with a single diamond worn on the fourth finger of a woman's left hand communicates that she is engaged; a man's forearm tattoo may communicate love for a specific person or affiliation with a particular group.

Physical characteristics and artifacts also have political and cultural meanings. For example, North Korean communist leader Kim Jong Il informed the male population that they should conform to a "socialist style" of hair that is no longer than two inches. Because the North Korean government was growing increasingly wary of outside influences, the short-hair campaign was launched on state-run television as a way to dictate cultural tastes. Similarly, barbers in southern Baghdad have risked their lives to shave men's beards or cut their hair in a Western style. It was reported in early 2005 that at least twelve barbers had been killed by gangs of militant Islamicists in an effort to enforce strict religious rules about hair. Moreover, although the headscarf or *hijab* is a symbol of piety for millions of Muslim women, several European nations have banned the wearing of headscarves based on the belief that they symbolize a particular political ideology or radical activism.[30]

Environment

The final category of nonverbal communication concerns the environment, which includes features such as architectural style, lighting, color, temperature, and time. The environment also includes the territory that we claim as our own and proxemics, or the distance between interactants.

Physical Environment The physical environment in which we communicate influences the quality of our interactions. We tend to perceive our environments in particular ways and to include such perceptions in the messages we develop and encode. Perceptions of formality based on furniture, decorations, color, and other factors can influence communication behavior. Perceptions of extreme formality typically result in communication that is less relaxed, more hesitant, and more stylized. Perceptions of privacy, based on how enclosed an environment may be (i.e., the number of people the environment can accommodate), can also influence communication behavior. Perceptions of privacy can result in close speaking distances and messages designed for a particular person instead of a general group.[31]

Time Time, or **chronemics**, is another environmental factor that influences nonverbal behavior. **Monochronic time** refers to time perceived as a commodity. Individuals who have a sense of urgency, believe that time shouldn't be wasted, and feel that people should do things one at a time adhere to a monochromic time system. **Polychronic time** refers to time perceived as limitless and not quantifiable. Individuals who believe that time should be adjusted to people's needs, that it's acceptable to change schedules and deadlines, and that people can do several things simultaneously adhere to a polychronic time system.

One way that time influences nonverbal communication is in terms of standing in line. Do you and your friends stand in line while waiting for a bus or taxi, or do you gather in a disorganized group? Standing in line is a characteristic of individuals and cultures, such as Scandinavia and the United States, that are primarily monochromic time-oriented. Gathering in a group without standing in line is a characteristic of individuals and cultures, such as Latin American and Mediterranean cultures, that are primarily polychronic time-oriented. People who adhere to a monochromic time orientation expect to be waited on one at a time; people who adhere to a polychronic time orientation expect to be waited on en masse.[32]

Territoriality **Territoriality** refers to a stationary area or fixed geographical location to which we lay claim and protect from invasion by others. Our territory may include our room, our bathroom, our car, and even our particular seat at the dinner table. Interestingly, we also claim places to which we have no legal ownership rights. Do you "own" chairs in which you habitually sit during classes? Are you surprised or perturbed when someone sits in "your" seat? Parking spots, library desks, and even places in line are staked out as our territories. Additionally, we prevent territorial invasion in a number of ways. We place nameplates on the outside of our domiciles and office doors, and we hope that others will recognize that we "own" a parking spot or seat in a classroom if we use it long enough or often enough. Sometimes we use markers such as books, coats, and notebooks to communicate the ownership of territory such as a table in the library.

Territory is often related to status and power. High-status individuals in the workplace often have offices with windows and larger offices than low-status individuals. High-status workers also may have more barriers, such as outer offices and secretaries, to prevent territorial invasion. On the other hand, low-status workers may often be victims of "prairie-dogging," a type of territorial invasion that occurs when coworkers pop over cubicle partitions to begin or barge in on conversations.[33]

Proxemics Unlike the physical environment or our territory, **proxemics** refers to how people use space and distance. Also labeled "personal space," proxemics can reveal how we

What does your physical environment or territory communicate to others?

feel about ourselves and how we feel about others. Anthropologist **Edward T. Hall** has identified the four distances of personal space used by most people in Western cultures. These distances also imply the relationship between the interactants and the kind of interaction in which they may be involved:[34]

- **Intimate Distance:** contact to 18 inches—This distance is sometimes called our "personal space bubble" and is used for touching and intimacy, as well as physical aggression and threat. People who communicate within the range of intimate distance may have close relationships and may communicate confidential information. On the other hand, intimate distance may be used by enemies to threaten each other and "get in each other's face." Sometimes we are forced to endure personal space invasion and share intimate distances with people we do not know. Have you ever squeezed into a crowded elevator, bus, or subway? If so, you probably felt discomfort and tried to cope by avoiding eye contact, backing away (if possible), and/or changing your body orientation. Interestingly, "Asians, Pakistanis, Native Americans, North Americans and Northern Europeans prefer greater distances when talking than do Southern Europeans, Arabs, and South Americans."[35] How might a North American feel and what might she or he think if a South American invaded her or his personal space bubble? How might a South American interpret the North American's response to the space invasion?
- **Personal Distance:** 18 inches to 4 feet—This distance is preferred for informal conversation and to keep people "at arm's length." Most Americans prefer personal distance when interacting with others.
- **Social Distance:** 4 to 12 feet—This distance is appropriate for business discussions and conversations that are neither personal nor private. The inner range (4 to 7 feet) is appropriate for people who work together and for conversations that involve conducting business. Because we typically stand or sit at farther distances the more formal our interaction becomes, the outer range (7 to 12 feet) is appropriate for communicating respect and the recognition of status.
- **Public Distance:** 12 feet and beyond—This distance is used by instructors in their classrooms and for other public speaking situations. This distance is also sometimes used to communicate with strangers.

Not only can nonverbal communication be clustered into four categories concerning kinesics, vocal behavior, physical characteristics, and the environment, but it also can be classified in terms of what is perceived as attractive by others and tends to promote interaction. These types of nonverbal communication are called "immediacy behaviors."

KNOWLEDGE power • "Get Outta My Face!"

Invading Another's Space

You probably can easily imagine how you might feel if a stranger or acquaintance invaded your personal space bubble. But have you ever thought about how you might feel if you were the person who committed the invasion? Attempt to get within the intimate distance zone by slowly and subtly inching closer to an acquaintance or friend while conversing. Your conversation partner is likely to back away or exhibit other negative sanctions to inform you that you have broken a nonverbal rule of appropriateness. Reflect on your feelings while participating in this activity. Do you feel powerful and excited, or do you feel apprehensive and guilty? How can you ethically use differences in personal space to enhance your communication in various situations?

Nonverbal Immediacy Behaviors

Immediacy refers to physical or psychological closeness between people involved in interaction. Nonverbal immediacy behaviors have primarily been studied in college classrooms. Research suggests that immediacy behaviors are associated with more positive evaluations of instructors by their students and increased perceptions of learning.[36] Nonverbal immediacy behaviors and increased perceptions of learning have also been related to students' willingness to talk during class discussions and in out-of-class communication.[37] Overall, studies illustrate that the more we make use of immediacy behaviors, the more others will tend to like us, evaluate us highly, and prefer communicating with us. Conversely, the less we make use of immediacy behaviors, the more others will tend to dislike us, evaluate us negatively, and avoid communicating with us. We can read about specific immediacy behaviors in Table 6.1, the "Immediacy-Nonimmediacy Behavior Chart."

How can the use of nonverbal immediacy behaviors improve our communication competence?

A number of positive communication-related outcomes result from the use of immediacy behaviors. Immediacy behaviors contribute to perceptions of approachability, responsiveness, and understanding; are associated with decreased anxiety on the part of a conversation partner; and enhance the perception of communication competence. On the

SKILL practice • Nonverbal Immediacy Behaviors

Choose a partner with whom you will engage in a discussion about a controversial topic. Have members of the class observe your interaction and rate your use of the immediacy behaviors listed in Table 6.1, "Immediacy-Nonimmediacy Behavior Chart." (If possible, videotape your interaction.) Choose a controversial topic about which you and your partner disagree and about which you feel passionate. Don't focus on your nonverbal communication as you discuss the topic; try to be as natural and real as possible. When you are finished with the conversation, ask your classmates to evaluate your use of immediacy behaviors (and watch your nonverbal communication on the video if possible). Consider what you may want to change to make your nonverbal communication more immediate.

Table 6.1: Immediacy-Nonimmediacy Behavior Chart

Category	Immediacy Behaviors	Nonimmediacy Behaviors
Verbal Immediacy	Use of pronouns such as *we* and *us*. Talk with others. Statements that infer liking: *I like your dress. I really like that. You are right.*	Use of *you, you and I*. Talk to or at others. Guarded statements of liking *(Your dress is OK)*. *That's dumb. That's a stupid idea.*
Appearance	Attractive. Clean, neat. Informal clothing but not sloppy. Appropriate hairstyle.	Unattractive. Dirty, unkempt. Formal clothing. Inappropriate or unusual hairstyle.
Gesture and Body Movement	Leaning toward another. Open body position. More gestures. More positive-affect displays. Relaxed body position. Calm movements. Positive head movements.	Leaning away from another. Closed body position. Fewer gestures. More negative-affect displays. Tense body position. Nervous movements. Negative head movements.
Face and Eye	Eye contact and mutual gaze. Facial expressions that show pleasure. Smiles a lot.	Limited eye contact. Averted eye gaze. Facial expressions that show displeasure. Frowns a lot.
Voice	Short pauses. Few silences. Positive vocal inflections. Vocal variety. Relaxed tones (calm). Sound confident. Dynamic, animated, interested. Friendly vocal cues.	Lengthy pauses and silences. Sarcasm. Monotonous, dull, irritated tones. Nasal. Harsh sounding. Sneering sounds. Bored, unfriendly vocal cues.
Space	Moves closer to a person. Stands closer to a person. Sits closer. Orients more directly. Leans forward while seated.	Leans away from a person. Sits farther away. Leans away or back while seated. Stands farther away. Indirect body orientation.
Touch	Touch on hand, forearm, shoulder. Pat. Friendly handshake. Frequent touch. Hugging.	Avoids or withdraws from touch. Clammy or distant handshake. Seldom touches. Slapping, hitting, striking another.
Environment	Warm, secure, pleasant environments. Soft colors. Movable chairs. Moderate to soft illumination.	Cold, distant, ugly environments. Bright illumination. Fixed seating. Ugly rooms. Ugly colors.
Scent	Pleasant, inoffensive scents. Familiar scents. Scents of one's own culture.	Unpleasant, offensive scents. Unfamiliar scents. Scents from other cultures.
Time	Short latency of response. Promptness. Spending more time with another. Spending time with another when they choose.	Long latency of response. Delinquent about being on time. Spending little time with another. Often glances at watch or clock.

Source: From V. Richmond and J. McCroskey, *Nonverbal Behavior in Interpersonal Relationships*, 5e. Published by Allyn and Bacon, Boston, MA. Copyright © 2000 by Pearson Education. Reprinted by permission of the publisher.

other hand, immediacy behaviors are associated with some disadvantages. Specifically, some people mistake immediacy behaviors for cues that communicate a desire for intimacy. Immediacy behaviors also promote communication between people, which isn't always rewarding! However, the advantages of using of immediacy behaviors outnumber and outweigh the disadvantages.[38]

In terms of nonverbal communication, it's important to be realistic about improving encoding and decoding ability. It is difficult to change habitual patterns of behavior, and learning to be more nonverbally immediate may entail a great deal of time and effort. Additionally, trying to improve our nonverbal communication by altering our behaviors may not result in the interpretations that we desire. For example, a woman who attempts to communicate power and status by adopting a husky voice may be perceived as having romantic inclinations.

Remember that competent communicators are flexible and that competent communication takes into account our goals, our conversation partner(s), the topic under discussion, and the situation.

Contexts and Nonverbal Communication

Suppose you witness a male job candidate meeting his prospective female boss for the first time. The female smiles and touches the man on his shoulder; the man doesn't smile and appears to fidget as he engages in small talk. How might you interpret these nonverbal behaviors? The culture, relationship, gender, and individual contexts influence the interpretation of nonverbal communication.

Culture Context

How do contexts influence nonverbal communication?

Nonverbal display rules and the interpretation of nonverbal communication are dependent on the culture in which they're enacted. Furthermore, perceptions of communication competence as it relates to nonverbal behavior vary across cultures and among co-cultures within the United States.

Nonverbal Display Rules Cultural belief systems have an impact on repertoires of nonverbal communication and the rules that guide their display. **Display rules** govern when and under which circumstances nonverbal behaviors are considered appropriate. People from Mediterranean cultures are likely to believe that intense displays of emotion are appropriate, whereas Americans of northern European background tend to believe that people should display neutral or calm emotions in public. Furthermore, cultures differ in terms of meanings that are attributed to nonverbal communication. Specifically, interpretations of nonverbal communication are based on whether the behavior is considered to be random (i.e., it has no meaning whatsoever), idiosyncratic (i.e., when only partners understand the relational meaning), or shared (i.e., when people collectively understand that a shrug of the shoulders means "I don't understand").[39] Interestingly, cultural rules regarding the appropriateness of nonverbal communication influence the behavior of avatars in virtual environments such as Second Life. For example, study results suggest that avatars communicate with other avatars within the range of personal distance. An avatar that is positioned within another avatar's intimate distance is perceived as committing a personal space invasion. Additionally, similar to face-to-face communication, avatars positioned closely together adhere to the nonverbal communication rule of exhibiting limited mutual eye gaze (so as not to stare) compared to avatars that are positioned far apart.[40]

KNOWLEDGE power • "They Are So Rude!"

Have you traveled or lived abroad, or are you an immigrant in the culture in which you presently live? Discuss your perceptions of persons from the current culture and cultures with which you are familiar. Pay particular attention to how you characterize such individuals and reflect on the basis for your characterizations (e.g., nonverbal communication). How might your knowledge of cultural display rules and the interpretation of nonverbal communication influence your future assessments of others who are culturally different from you?

Nonverbal Communication Competence Because repertoires, display rules, and interpretations of nonverbal communication differ cross-culturally, misperceptions about the effectiveness and appropriateness of such behavior are common. Nonverbal display rules are usually learned via cultural observation and experience and remain out of our awareness unless our expectations have been violated. This means that members of a specific culture typically use their own display rules to judge the appropriateness of nonverbal behavior associated with other cultures. Negative judgments of others' personalities, attitudes, and intelligence often result when members of one culture use their own rules or norms to interpret and evaluate the nonverbal communication of persons of other cultures.[41] In other words, viewing another's nonverbal behavior from our own cultural context leads to misinterpretations of communication competence.

U.S. Co-Cultures Behaviors understood as "competent" for Americans vary in terms of the various co-cultures that exist within the United States. For example, Latinos may avoid direct eye contact with others as a sign of respect or perceive touch to be normal and appropriate during conversation. However, other people may perceive indirect eye contact as an indication of inattentiveness and touching behavior as a violation of personal space. Similarly, Native Americans typically use silence as a sign of respect, thoughtfulness, and/or uncertainty, and other people may perceive this behavior as an indication of boredom, disagreement, or a refusal to provide feedback. African Americans generally perceive that speaking with intensity is appropriate when disagreeing with others, but other people may perceive this behavior to be a precursor to violence.[42] Of course, not all Latinos avoid direct eye contact, not all Native Americans use silence to communicate respect, and not all African Americans speak with intensity while disagreeing with others. Remember that cultures and co-cultures are fluid and influenced by immigration patterns, by other cultural values disseminated through the media and technology, and by factors such as class, socioeconomic status, and gender.

Relationship Context

Just as the culture context influences the encoding and decoding of nonverbal communication, so does the context that involves family, friends, and coworkers. Nonverbal communication is associated with family rules and rituals and is an integral part of gang "families." Nonverbal behavior is also involved in the perceptions of our workplace supervisors.

Family and Friends It may be considered appropriate and funny in some families and with some friends to burp out loud after dinner; other families and friends may be horrified. Families may also regulate who can kiss whom and the age at which a child stops sitting on a parent's lap or climbing into a parent's bed. In addition to family rules, families develop verbal and **nonverbal rituals**. Because the rituals are repetitive in nature, they help to preserve and maintain a particular family's identity. Family rituals include private codes such as gestures and facial expressions whose meaning is known only to the family members, patterns or habits such as where family members sit at the kitchen or dining room table, and symbolic rituals, such as presenting particular types of gifts that have specific meaning for the family members involved.[43]

An interesting area of nonverbal study associated with "family" communication involves how gang members nonverbally communicate. People join gangs because they represent families. Often unlike their biological or normative families, gangs provide caring and recognition for their members. Gang signs or emblems are used by members to communicate solidarity with their particular gang or to taunt other gangs. Some express attitudes (such as "power" or "number one"); others are used to identify the gang to which a member belongs.[44] (See Figure 6.2.)

Gangs also use clothing to identify themselves and to communicate meaning. The way clothing is worn and the color of the clothing vary with each gang. For example, some gangs wear their shirts buttoned only at the collar while others wear their shirts open. Some gang members may wear hats turned toward the left of their bodies and the left leg of their pants rolled up, while rival gang members wear the same type of clothes but favor the right side of their bodies. Professional and college sports team apparel is used also to represent individual gangs. The uniform of the British Knights is used by the Crips to stand for "Blood Killers," and the uniform of the Los Angeles Dodgers is used by the Gangster Disciples with the initial "D" standing for "Disciples." Even certain colors are associated with gangs. The colors black and blue are associated with the Gangster Disciples, and the color orange is associated with the Future Stones.[45]

Coworkers Research reveals that supervisors who exhibit nonverbal immediacy behaviors can signal liking, positive evaluation, and positive affect for their subordinates. Supervisors who are perceived as immediate are also seen as credible and interpersonally attractive by their subordinates. Subordinates who perceive their supervisors as immediate express positive attitudes about their supervisors and positive attitudes about communication with their supervisors, and they reciprocate their supervisors' immediacy behaviors. Supervisor immediacy is positively related to motivation and job satisfaction. Employees who are highly motivated and satisfied are typically more productive than those who are not and are less likely to leave their jobs. These findings are particularly relevant to modern organizations because of the high cost of training new workers in today's technologically oriented economy.[46] Nonverbal immediacy is also associated with perceived supervisor Machiavellianism. Machiavellian supervisors often attempt to achieve interpersonal goals in terms of manipulation, strategic self-presentation, and ingratiation tactics. Subordinates' perceptions of supervisor Machiavellianism are strongly associated with a lack of nonverbal immediacy, and employees tend to hold negative attitudes about such supervisors, as well as low levels of motivation and job satisfaction.[47]

Figure 6.2: Two Gang Identification Signs

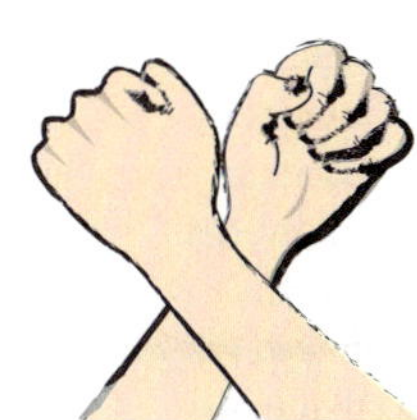

Black Gangster Disciples

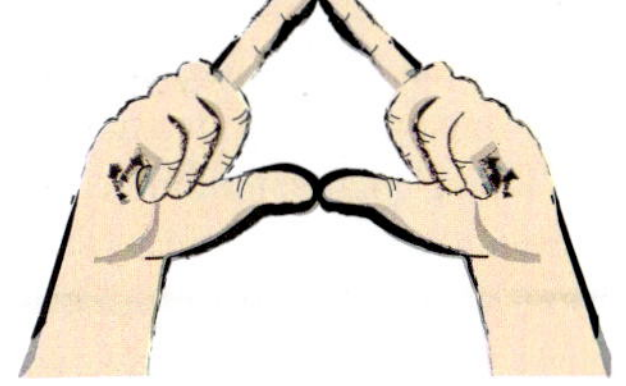

Imperial Gangsters

Source: Used with permission of Taylor and Francis from *Kids Killing Kids: Managing Violence and Gangs in Schools*, by T. K. Capozzoli, 1999.

Gender Context

Our nonverbal communication is often based on the stereotypes and expectations that we think are appropriate for our gender. Gender also influences the interpretation and expression of nonverbal communication.

Gender Stereotypes and Expectations Adhering to gender stereotypes is generally more comfortable for most people than deviating from the norm. Girls and women may learn to use softer and higher voices to communicate a positive gender message of femininity. Boys and men may learn to use a loud volume while speaking in order to communicate authority and power. Gender expectations about vocal qualities have even found their way into the realm of technology. Because of gender stereotypes and expectations, German drivers of BMWs reacted negatively to female-sounding artificial voices that communicated directions. Even though the drivers knew they were listening to a computer-based voice in their cars, BMW responded to their discomfort and switched to a male-sounding synthetic voice. Similarly, although the evidence regarding touching behavior is mixed, the meaning of touch can be linked to power and dominance. Studies have revealed that men respond negatively to women of equal status who engage in touching, but women do not respond negatively to men of greater, equal, or lesser status who touch them. It may be that masculine expectations teach men to find touch acceptable only by someone of higher status. Furthermore, men tend to expand their personal space while receiving messages as a means of expressing status and control. Women tend to hold their limbs nearer their bodies than do men and often appear to use a small amount of personal space. Women's use of space may derive from instructions about femininity. It is rare to see women lean back in chairs, clasp their hands behind their heads, and rest their feet upon their desks; this is considered masculine nonverbal behavior. Research has also discovered that with the exception of anger, women's faces are more emotionally expressive in both artificial and natural settings.[49]

Interpretations of Nonverbal Communication Differences in male-female nonverbal communication can contribute to misinterpretations across gender lines. For example,

KNOWLEDGE ON THE CUTTING EDGE

Putting It in Context: Communication, Sex, and Nonverbal Communication

In truth, there is no consensus regarding why women are more nonverbally skilled than men. One explanation suggests nonverbal differences are learned and that they reflect differences in gender. However, one summary of studies concerning gender communication found that masculinity and femininity scores (regardless of biological sex) do not predict and are unrelated to nonverbal sensitivity. Another possible explanation for differences in male-female nonverbal ability concerns power and social stratification. However, various studies demonstrate that oppression is not linked to nonverbal sensitivity. Increasing evidence suggests that male-female differences in nonverbal sensitivity are related to biology. Researchers at SUNY Buffalo found that girls and boys ages eight to eleven use different parts of their brains to recognize faces and expressions. Girls use more of their left brain than boys in recognizing facial expressions, and they are better at discriminating nonverbal meaning in particular parts of the face, such as the mouth or eyes. Similarly, in a study in which respondents were asked to judge happy and sad male and female faces, men were correct only 70% of the time when judging sad expressions on women's faces, but women were correct 90% of the time when judging sad expressions on men's faces. Positron emission tomography (PET) scans revealed that women's limbic systems or "emotional brains" were less active than the limbic systems of men who scored worse in the study. In other words, men's brains worked harder than women's when judging facial expressions, but the extra effort failed to increase their scores.[48]

KNOWLEDGE power • You Sit Like a (Wo)Man!

Have you ever tried to use the nonverbal behaviors associated with the opposite gender? In a mixed-sex group, enact the following gender-related nonverbal behaviors while conversing, and answer the following questions at the end of the activity. If you are male:

- Keep your knees pressed tightly together while conversing. Either cross your legs at the ankles or cross your legs at the knees. Clasp your hands in your lap or rest your hands close to your body on top of a desk.
- Smile frequently, use more direct eye contact than usual, and increase your use of "prompts" to indicate you are listening (e.g., "uh-huh," head nods).
- Speak in a soft tone of voice, and end some of your declarative sentences with a rising intonation.

If you are female:

- Spread your legs apart, rest your right ankle on your left knee, or thrust your legs straight out in front of you. Clasp your hands behind your neck or keep your arms outstretched on top of a desk.
- Don't smile, reduce your facial animation, and look away often in the role of the speaker and listener.
- Use a lower pitch with reduced inflections, and speak louder than usual.

Answer the following questions when you have finished the activity:

- Did you feel uncomfortable enacting the learned nonverbal behaviors associated with the opposite gender? Why or why not?
- Would you stereotype or have a negative reaction if you saw someone enacting opposite-gender learned nonverbal behaviors?
- Can you imagine any benefits resulting from adopting the learned nonverbal behavior of the opposite gender?

research shows that women smile more than men as a way to be polite and to promote pleasant conversations. However, men may misinterpret women's smiles as a signal that indicates sexual interest. Similarly, when women display dominance gestures to men, they are rated higher on sexuality and lower in dominance than are men who use the same gestures when speaking with women.[50] It is probably best for both genders to recognize the various meanings associated with nonverbal behaviors and to engage in perspective taking before making stereotyped gender assumptions associated with such behaviors.

Overall, women are more skilled than men in interpreting nonverbal behaviors. A wide variety of cross-cultural studies reveal that women are more sensitive to nonverbal cues, as well as more nonverbally engaged than men. A review of seventy-five studies regarding the ability to ascertain others' feelings from facial and vocal expressiveness resulted in the finding that women possess better decoding skills. Women may be more nonverbally sensitive than men because they are perceived to have a less dominant role in society (and therefore must be better able to read nonverbal cues of the dominant group to enhance survival). Women may also be more nonverbally sensitive because they are more attuned to the nonverbal rules that guide communication and are expected to be more nonverbally sensitive, and because women have more opportunities to practice nonverbal sensitivity in occupations that are stereotypically perceived as "feminine" (e.g., teachers, nurses).[51]

Individual Context

Do you know how to spot a liar? What nonverbal cues tell you that someone is trying to deceive you or hide something? When scientists asked such questions to more than 2,000 people from nearly sixty countries, the most frequent answer centered on eye contact. Most people believe that liars avert their gaze. Additional nonverbal **deception cues** or behaviors that people typically associate with lying include fidgeting behaviors and throat-clearing. However, there is no general telltale sign of a lie. Past research on deception detection has traditionally taken place in laboratories under highly controlled conditions. Conversely, recent research has been conducted in naturalistic settings (e.g., hospitals and police stations) and focused on whether the deception cues in the controlled studies mirror those outside the lab.

Lab Studies Lab studies suggest a number of general behaviors are exhibited by people engaged in deception. Liars tend to:

- move their arms, hand, and fingers less than truth tellers
- blink less than people telling the truth
- communicate with high-pitched or tense voices
- fill their speech with more pauses than truth tellers

However, researchers caution that not all liars exhibit these behaviors and that they may be natural behaviors for certain individuals.[52]

Naturalistic Studies Current studies that take place outside the lab suggest that deception cues associated with lying do not result from actually telling lies but from the experience of emotion, content complexity, and impression management. A liar may speak with a higher-pitched voice, which may be the result of feeling guilty, excited, or afraid while lying. A liar may include few details in an explanation because of the complex content of the lie. A liar may also exhibit few illustrators while lying because of her or his attempt to control the situation and to engage in impression management. Researchers who study deception in natural settings not only suggest that there is no single nonverbal behavior that is associated with lying but also propose that typical lab studies do not take individual differences into account. For example, researchers have coded the deception cues of videotaped suspects speaking to police in interrogation rooms and have studied their nonverbal behavior in relation to forensic evidence, witness accounts, and actual suspect confessions. In contrast to results found in some lab studies, the crime suspects didn't fill their speech with disturbances (e.g., stuttering and false starts and stops), and there was no decrease in the use of illustrators. The researchers further concluded that the differences between lying and truth telling depended on each individual. Some suspects increased their eye contact when lying; others averted their gaze. In fact, stressed truth tellers may exhibit the same nonverbal behaviors as liars because of the intense conditions of police interrogations. The only differences found between liars and truth tellers in this real-life situation was that liars paused longer and blinked less frequently than those suspects who told the truth.[53]

Let's return to the example of the male job candidate and his prospective female boss. The culture context may influence our interpretation of the nonverbal behavior. Specifically, our culture may teach us the display rule that it's appropriate to smile when we meet someone. Therefore, we may interpret the job candidate's failure to smile as an illustration of rude behavior. However, not all cultures (e.g., the French) teach its members that it's appropriate to smile when meeting others; consequently, the job candidate may merely be adhering to his culture's display rules about smiling.[54] We may also view the boss as interpersonally attractive and credible because of her use of immediacy behaviors and because she is more powerful than the applicant (and is therefore justified in engaging in touch behaviors). However, it's possible that we may view the woman's touching as inappropriate because it can evoke a sexual connotation. In addition, we may interpret the job candidate's fidgeting behavior as a deception cue (we correctly or incorrectly believe that he has something to hide about his employment history). It's important to remember that

KNOWLEDGE power • "I Can See L-I-E Written All Over Your Face!"

What deception cues do you display when lying, trying to hide an emotion felt while speaking, or otherwise not telling the complete truth? Engage in a competitive card game (e.g., poker, bridge, cribbage) with others and ask a nonparticipant or observer to watch you as you play. Attempt to control your nonverbal behaviors when you realize that you have a good hand or that you may win the game. When the game ends, compare your perception of your deception cues with the deception cues witnessed by the observer. Discover if the observer's perceptions are similar to your own.

nonverbal communication is ambiguous, can have various meanings, and is best interpreted in conjunction with verbal communication. It's also important to remember that our interpretations of nonverbal communication are significantly influenced by the culture, relationship, gender, and individual contexts.

OVERCOMING COMMUNICATION CHALLENGES

Stalking

Stalking has been defined as "a harmful course of conduct involving unwanted communications and intrusions repeatedly inflicted by one individual on another."[55] Knowing the characteristics associated with stalking behaviors can help us contend with a stalker and with verbal and nonverbal stalking-oriented communication.

Characteristics

There are five basic characteristics associated with stalking behaviors:

1. persistence
2. they are directed toward a particular individual
3. intrusiveness
4. they are unwelcome
5. they provoke concern and/or fear in the victim

Approximately 10 to 23% of the general population believe they are or have been victims of stalking. However, research indicates that men and women differ when it comes to perceptions of stalking and stalking behaviors. Females appear more afraid and threatened by stalking behaviors than are males, and males tend to associate such behaviors as a routine or natural part of courtship. All told, it is difficult to pinpoint when behaviors associated with courtship or relational pursuit become "persistent." After all, behaviors such as following, visiting, and gathering information about a specific individual can be interpreted as romantic and friendship building. Therefore, it is the cumulative impact of such behaviors (which individually may appear harmless) that influences the perception of stalking. Nonverbal behaviors related to stalking include leaving pictures and/or notes on windshields or doorsteps; moving away from public, social, and personal distance to intimate distance; "appearing" at work or school or "lying in wait" at these locations; and surveillance, which includes a variety of covert efforts to observe the victim from a distance.[56]

Competence & Critical Thinking

mycommunicationlab

THE REUNION AND NONVERBAL COMMUNICATION

Rick and his cousins Dominic and Suzette are trying to plan a family reunion. Suzette informs her cousins that she has made arrangements for the reunion to take place at a fancy restaurant, but Rick wants the reunion to occur at a bar and Dominic wants the reunion to take place at a barn in the country.

You can view *The Reunion* by accessing the "Small Group and Interpersonal Videos" on the MyCommunicationLab Web site. Answer the following questions about the nonverbal communication included in the video:

- Do you perceive nonverbal behavior that repeats, substitutes for, accents, complements, and/or regulates the spoken word?
- Identify the types of nonverbal communication that are illustrated in the video (e.g., kinesic behavior, paralanguage, physical characteristics, and nonverbal communication associated with the environment).
- What types of nonverbal immediacy and nonimmediacy behaviors are illustrated in the video?
- How might the culture, relationship, gender, and individual contexts influence Rick, Dominic, and Suzette's nonverbal communication?

RICK: I don't think Saturday's going to be a good day. 'Cause I don't think a lot of people are going to be able to come on a Satur—I know I can't come on a Saturday.

SUZETTE: Oh, you have plenty of advance notice.

DOMINIC: OK . . . but that's schedule, that's timing. What I'd like to decide is where.

SUZETTE: Mm-hmm.

RICK: Yeah.

SUZETTE: I totally agree. I totally agree.

DOMINIC: OK, first, and then—'cause everybody's going to have input about when.

SUZETTE: Well, let's just keep it short, then, because "the where" I have taken care of. I've contacted a place that's just phenomenal. And I love it there, Maison Henri. I've spoken to Henri himself, and he is very willing to put forth an effort, a special effort for this event, and just introduce to our family some of his most select items on the menu. I think that we'll all be very pleased. And look no further, is what I say.

RICK: Isn't that a country club? Isn't there the yacht place?

SUZETTE: The yacht club is right next door. That's another thing that's in its favor. People could, okay, there's a yacht race, there's a . . .

DOMINIC: I think what—I think what Rick's kind of bringing up is that it's too formal.

SUZETTE: Is that true? Is that what you're bringing up?

RICK: It's going—it's going to be, yeah, it's going to be really formal. I mean, it's going to be too formal. I mean, it's a get-together. We're not—it's—no one's getting married. No one's dying.

DOMINIC: Can you see Audrey walking in there with her slippers that she never takes off?

RICK: No.

DOMINIC: They're not going to let her in there.

RICK: No, they wouldn't.

DOMINIC: So . . .

RICK: Well . . . I mean, how many kids are going to come?

SUZETTE: I don't know if Audrey's, you know, really . . .

DOMINIC: No, don't suggest that Audrey shouldn't come. I mean . . .

SUZETTE: I don't think she's quite fit enough.

RICK: Audrey . . .

DOMINIC: I don't think that we can—we can't . . . my mother's sister. We've got to invite her.

RICK: We can't not, not invite people.

SUZETTE: But we can't make other people uncomfortable because there's a few wearing their bedroom slippers.

RICK: Well, I mean, if it's only going to be this family . . .

DOMINIC: Come on. I mean, she's—she's flavor . . .

RICK: . . . and it's going to be closed . . .

DOMINIC: . . . in this family.

RICK: That's true. She is flavor. I mean, but we can't . . .

SUZETTE: Yes, I remember—I remember a wedding about five years ago, and she was quite "flavored."

RICK: That was the first time we'd all seen each other in a long time. So, you know, I don't think that having a place, having a place, having a catered, you know, get-together as—as formal as Henri's place . . .

SUZETTE: I don't think you've ever been inside Maison Henri. I don't think you've ever stepped foot. How can you make such a judgment?

DOMINIC: I mean, what–what–what—did you have an idea where?

RICK: Because it's three generations, we have three, almost four now, four generations, a friend of mine—a friend of mine manages this bar, but it's not a bar. It's not like a—it's not like a–a dusty little bar. It's a huge place. It's really nice.

SUZETTE: No.

RICK: It's beautiful.

SUZETTE: No, absolutely not.

RICK: How can you say . . .

SUZETTE: Because the very reason.

RICK: . . . "no"?

SUZETTE: Four generations. Children, toddlers, babies in a barroom?

RICK: We're going to be able to have the entire place . . .

SUZETTE: Smoke-filled bar, yes, but the residual smoke from the night before . . .

RICK: No, no, no. You cannot smoke in bars anymore. You know that. You haven't been able to for a year.

SUZETTE: I think it sends the wrong message, no.

RICK: . . . pool. There's got—they've got darts. They've got a foosball table. There's a little arcade.

SUZETTE: Dangerous. Those are dangerous. Darts with little children running around?

DOMINIC: It's the opposite end of the spectrum here. I mean . . .

RICK: There's only ten children.

DOMINIC: Can you see Uncle Bob walking into a bar and listening to that music? He'll be out within one minute.

RICK: We have total rein of—we would have total rein of everything there. They have a kitchen. We—we would be able to—to order and eat anything we would want. All we would have to do is rent it for an afternoon.

SUZETTE: Order and eat everything we want. What do they have, buffalo wings and popcorn? I don't think so.

RICK: Of course they have buffalo wings and popcorn. But they have sandwiches, they have entrees. If you want, if you would want to make up a menu to be like, these are the kind of things we would want . . .

SUZETTE: Well, that's what I've done. I've met already with Maison Henri and we have prepared a menu that I think would be very pleasing.

RICK: Well, then, why are we here if you are already, I mean, that doesn't make any sense. You can't go and say, well, "This is where we're going to . . ."

DOMINIC: I just want to . . .

RICK: ". . . come here, this is the menu that we're going to have . . ."

SUZETTE: Ricky, I would think . . .

DOMINIC: Rick. Suzette.

SUZETTE: . . . that you would be . . .

DOMINIC: Suzette.

SUZETTE: . . . grateful for my energy and time.

DOMINIC: Suzette. We are grate—we are grateful, we are grateful, that's why you're here. I mean, just the fact that you showed up shows that, you know, you want to contribute, and you—you both are interested. I just wanted to remind you why we're here in the first place. I mean, when we were kids, do you remember the annual summer picnic my mother used to throw?

RICK: At the lake, yeah.

DOMINIC: Yeah. We got, I mean, the adults were inside having their cocktails. We kids were outside running around with balloons, water balloons, throwing at each other, having a great time. It extended from the morning to the day. People came during the morn—during the morning or afternoon, whenever they could.

SUZETTE: Dominic.

DOMINIC: So it wasn't so formal. It wasn't so informal, either. And so any—I—I have an idea that I want to throw out to you. There's this barn in New Hampshire. It's a restored barn. My wife's family, every other Christmas they rent this place.

SUZETTE: A barn? A barn?

DOMINIC: It's not a barn with animals. It's a barn that's been restored. It's antiques in it. It's fabulous. You'll love it. It has, like, ten rooms in it. Each room has . . .

SUZETTE: Out in the country?

DOMINIC: It's like a half-hour out of Nashua, something like that. It's not another country.

SUZETTE: No, sir. There are mosquitoes. There are insects.

DOMINIC: So stay in the car, Suzette. I mean, each place, each—each room has its own entrance. There's a great family room. We could have a—a family dinner together. If you want to do a formal affair, you could contact one of the restaurants. I mean, it's a tourist area. They're going to have a great restaurant there.

SUZETTE: Dominic, it sounds run of the mill. It just sounds . . .

DOMINIC: Then you could do that. People who want to do that could go do that. Then the—the ones like Rick, he could go out, there's a place called Doyle's, I think, downtown, something like that. It's an Irish pub. You know? People could do that. But at some point—

SUZETTE: So where do we reunion? If some people are at the bar . . .

Contending with Stalking Behaviors

The best way to contend with stalking is to prevent it from occurring in the first place and by managing the stalker and stalking behaviors. Regrettably, little research exists that informs victims how to effectively manage stalking.

Verbal Communication Strategies Competent communication is apparently inapplicable to stalking situations. For example, competent communicators may be reluctant to end a potentially harmful relationship for fear of causing a partner to lose face. Competent communicators may also engage in perspective taking with a relational partner and fail to reject the partner because of feelings of guilt and concern. Although competent communicators may attempt verbal limit setting and gentle relationship de-escalation tactics, these techniques are ineffective when applied to stalkers. Trying to rationally negotiate the end of a relationship and set boundaries on the stalker's behavior only reinforces the behavior. Therefore, persons being stalked should end all contact and not respond to contact attempts made by a stalker. Persons being stalked are advised to seek advice and guidance from counselors, religious advisors, law enforcement officials, victims' advocates, friends or family, and/or threat-management professionals.[57]

Nonverbal Communication Strategies Behaviors that are likely to erode a stalker's interest in her or his victim tend to be effective. Persons who are being stalked are advised to make use of security systems, to shred documents, and to alter routines. Other nonverbal communication strategies include avoiding contact with a stalker (e.g., not showing up at a place where the stalker is likely to be), screening calls or changing telephone numbers, altering everyday routines, changing careers, and moving.[58]

A CASE STUDY IN ETHICS

"Does It Take a Village (and Corporal Punishment) to Raise a Child?"

We have learned that competent communication includes an ethical dimension of well-based standards of right and wrong. We can ask ourselves questions that relate to everyday ethics when we decide to encode and decode nonverbal communication. For example, we can ask if our nonverbal communication will reflect a virtue such as integrity, trustworthiness, honesty, and responsibility. We can ask ourselves if our communication and our interpretation of others' nonverbal communication reflects dignity, respect, and fairness. We can also ask ourselves if the expression of our nonverbal behaviors and the interpretation of the nonverbal behaviors of others will result in more good than harm, and even whether they have the potential to strengthen our community. We can gain insight into our ideas about ethical nonverbal communication by reading this case study.

In 1995, four African American youths were beaten by members of the Nation of Islam for attempting to steal a cash register in a Dallas, Texas, mall. The young men and Nation of Islam members knew each other from a previous mall incident. At that time, the Nation of Islam members offered the youths some volunteer work. However, the young men rejected the offer.

Many members of the African American community supported the beatings meted out by the Nation of Islam members. Much of the support for the beatings stemmed from the idea that America has "spared the rod and spoiled the child." Furthermore, the Nation of Islam teaches self-reliance, and the actions against the youths were supported by those who believe in taking care of one's own. When asked about the beatings, the Nation of Islam and its supporters cited the African proverb that it takes a village to raise a child.

On the other hand, detractors asserted that the Nation of Islam "villagers" took the law into their own hands. Those who opposed the actions of the Nation of Islam suggested that the villagers believed that violence within the African American community was an acceptable means of punishment and was more important than the physical well-being of the youths. Some maintained that true adherents of the African proverb would have called the youths' parents and asked them to take care of the situation. Security guards and shop owners could call the police if the parents did nothing. The detractors asserted that just as the youths attempted to break the law, so did the members of the Nation of Islam by assaulting the young men.[59]

Do you think that corporal punishment is an ethical form of nonverbal behavior? Do you believe that cultural belief systems influence whether we perceive corporal punishment as ethical? Do you think that parents in Western cultures spoil their children because they "spare the rod"? Were the actions of the Nation of Islam members an ethical expression of how a village should raise a child? Does the fact that the youths rejected the Nation of Islam's earlier offer to undertake volunteer work affect your opinion?

Chapter Review

Motivation: How has this helped me?

- **The importance of studying nonverbal communication**

It's important to study nonverbal communication because the majority of a message's meaning comes from nonverbal communication and most relational messages arise from nonverbal behavior. In addition, we tend to believe nonverbal communication when nonverbal messages contradict verbal messages.

Knowledge: What have I learned?

- **How we can characterize nonverbal communication**

Nonverbal communication refers to all forms of communication other than words.

- **The functions of nonverbal communication**

Nonverbal communication can repeat, substitute for, accent, complement, and regulate verbal communication. The interpretation of nonverbal behavior is risky because it can be ambiguous.

- **The types of nonverbal communication**

There are various categories of nonverbal communication that convey meaning to others. These categories include kinesics (gestures, body orientation, posture, touch, facial expression, and eye behavior), paralanguage (vocal qualities and accents), physical characteristics (body shape and general attractiveness, clothing, and artifacts), and the environment (architectural style, lighting and color, temperature, noise, time, territoriality, and proxemics).

- **How contexts influence nonverbal communication**

Nonverbal communication is influenced by the culture, relationship, gender, and individual contexts. For example, perceptions of nonverbal communication competence vary across cultures and among co-cultures within the United States. In addition, every family develops its own nonverbal rules and rituals, and gang "families" make use of emblems, colors, and clothing to communicate solidarity and to taunt other gangs. Similarly, nonverbal immediacy behaviors affect employee motivation, job satisfaction, and perceptions of supervisors. The gender context also influences the expression and interpretation of nonverbal communication in terms of stereotypes and expectations. Researchers in the area of deception cues contend that typical lab studies don't take individual differences into account and that there is no general telltale sign of a lie.

Skill: What skills have I developed?

- **How nonverbal communication improves communication competence**

Using nonverbal immediacy behaviors (e.g., leaning toward a conversation partner, exhibiting head nods and smiles, making eye contact) increases the likelihood that we will be perceived as competent communicators.

Study Questions

1. Why is it difficult to interpret nonverbal communication? Include some specific examples in your answer.
2. Why is it important to study nonverbal communication?
3. Describe and explain the functions of nonverbal communication.
4. Describe various types of nonverbal behavior associated with body movement and position, paralanguage, physical characteristics, and the environment.
5. What are some nonverbal immediacy behaviors, and how do they affect interpersonal communication?

6. How do the culture, relationship, gender, and individual contexts affect the perception and communication of nonverbal behaviors?
7. What are some examples of stalking behaviors, and how can we verbally and nonverbally contend with stalkers and stalking behavior?

Names to Know

Paul Ekman, p. 156—a leading psychologist and researcher in the area of facial expression, Ekman and his colleagues developed the Facial Action Coding System (FACS) as a method to recognize and interpret facial expressions. Ekman's interests include the physiology and expression of emotions and interpersonal deception.

Edward T. Hall, p. 162—renowned anthropologist who has identified four distances of personal space used by most members of Western cultures. Hall taught at many universities including Harvard and Northwestern and developed the concept of "high-context" and "low-context" cultures while teaching intercultural communication for the U.S. State Department in the 1950s.

Key Terms

accenting, 152
accents, 159
affect blends, 158
artifacts, 160
body orientation and posture, 155
body shape, 160
chronemics, 161
complementing, 152
cues-filtered-out approach, 153
deception cues, 169
display rules, 165
emblems, 151
facial expression and eye behavior, 156
general attractiveness 160
gestures, 154
haptics, 156
hyperpersonal approach, 153
illustrators, 152
immediacy, 163
interaction management, 156
intimate distance, 162
kinesics, 154
microexpressions, 158
monochronic time, 161
nonverbal communication, 148
nonverbal ritual, 167
paralanguage, 158
personal distance, 162
polychronic time, 161
proxemics, 161
public distance, 162
regulating, 153
repeating, 151
social distance, 162
social presence, 153
stalking, 171
substituting, 151
territoriality, 161
vocalics, 158

CHAPTER 7

Conversation and Communication Style

"The real art of conversation is not only to say the right thing in the right place, but to leave unsaid the wrong thing at the tempting moment."

LADY DOROTHY NEVILL (1825–1915), BRITISH AUTHOR

In this chapter, we will answer the following:

Motivation: How will this help me?

- It is important to study conversation to improve our informal conversations and our interaction in formal contexts.
- Our knowledge of how conversation functions can help us manage our communication apprehension and facilitate our ability to interact competently.

Knowledge: What will I learn?

- How to characterize conversation
- How conversation functions
- How contexts influence conversation and communication style

Skill: Why do I need to develop these skills?

- Competent conversation skills enable us to effectively and appropriately begin, sustain, and conclude conversations.

In early 2003, news investigator and reporter Geraldo Rivera discussed an upcoming military operation during a broadcast from Iraq. Military officials denounced Rivera, said that he put the operation at risk, and strongly suggested that he leave the country. Rivera obviously said "the wrong thing at the wrong time." Perhaps you know someone who also commits communication blunders; maybe she or he discloses too much, interrupts too often, or takes too much time to answer a question. Maybe *you* are described as someone who exhibits these communication patterns while conversing with others! What do such communication patterns mean? What can we do to facilitate the perception of communication competence when we converse with others? These questions will be answered in the upcoming pages. Specifically, this chapter covers understanding why it's important to study conversation and how knowing the dynamics involved in conversation can increase our motivation to communicate competently. We will also increase our motivation to communicate by understanding the relationship between conversation, communication apprehension, and motivation. Reading about various characteristics associated with conversations and communication style will increase our knowledge, and we will improve our interactions with others by learning skills associated with competent conversationalists.

Introduction to Conversation and Communication Style

How often in any given day do you engage in conversation with others? A better question would ask if you can recall a day when you conversed with no one. Most people want and need contact with others, and contact is most often established through conversation.

How can we characterize conversation?

It is probably incorrect to consider any act of conversation "simple"; even small talk or chitchat is a highly coordinated accomplishment between people who may or may not know each other well. The complexity of conversations is evidenced in the definition; that is, **conversations** are locally managed and interactive sequential interchanges.[1] "Locally managed" means that the participants determine the topic, who gets to speak, for how long, and in what order. This differs from communication in more formal contexts such as interviews, in which the topic is predetermined and participants occupy the roles of questioner and responder. *Interactive* means that at least two people must participate in a conversation, and *sequential* refers to the idea that participants take turns exchanging messages. Sequential also relates to organization in that conversations have beginnings, middles, and endings. Those who study conversations focus on all sorts of talk, from conversations about serious issues such as medicine and the law to routine topics family members discuss at a dinner table. Researchers who study conversations engage in what is called **conversation analysis**. Conversation analysts study the order, the organization, and the orderliness of everyday interaction.[2] Conversation analysts also study what communication "does." Before reading about speech acts and what conversation does, it is important to understand why the study of conversation has merit.

> **KNOWLEDGE power • What Conversation "Does"**
>
> Charles Antaki of Loughborough University in Great Britain has created an interactive Web site that enables users to transcribe and analyze portions of conversations. The site includes audio and video clips, a section that demonstrates various levels of specificity in transcriptions, and a section that demonstrates the interactive consequences of everyday talk. To reach the Web site, go to "An Introductory Tutorial in Conversation Analysis" at www-staff.lboro.ac.uk/~ssca1/sitemenu.htm.

Why It's Important to Study Conversation

Understanding the structure of everyday talk and how it operates can improve how we communicate in conversations and how we communicate in more formal contexts, as well as help to make society function as it should.

Why is it important to study conversation?

Have you ever been in a conversation in which you couldn't express your views because others talked over you or interrupted you? In a different conversation, perhaps an awkward silence compelled you to say something you wouldn't normally say. What makes some conversations successful and others unsuccessful? Learning about the dynamics and technical details of how conversation works may improve our ability to effectively and appropriately participate in conversations.

Another reason to study everyday conversation is because the features involved in conversation are the basis of more formal interactions, such as interviews and court testimony. We tend to adapt what we know about everyday talk to more controlled and task-oriented situations. Therefore, knowing about some components of conversation and performing actions based on these components will enable us to communicate competently in formal contexts.

Everyday conversation also helps to enable society to function as it should. The economy, the law, religion, courtship, socialization, and education all depend on effective and appropriate conversation. These institutions provide structure and order for society, and they rely on everyday talk to carry out their functions.

Conversation, Communication Apprehension, and Motivation

Understanding the dynamics of conversation can motivate us to interact competently with others. However, we may want to avoid conversations with others because we believe that they won't want to listen to what we have to say. We may also become nervous prior to and during conversations because we believe we'll say something stupid. We may therefore clam up and force ourselves to endure long periods of uncomfortable silence. Communication scholar **James C. McCroskey** and his colleagues have conducted extensive research in **communication apprehension (CA)**, an individual's level of fear or anxiety associated with either real or anticipated communication-related outcomes. Traitlike CA is the most problematic form of CA because it is harder to avoid; it can occur over a wide range of communication contexts. Context-based CA, on the other hand, occurs only in specific situations (e.g., public speaking contexts). Receiver-based CA depends on the person with whom we speak; for instance, we might experience CA only around one particular person at work. Situational CA depends on the environment in which a conversation takes place; for instance, we might experience CA only when we find ourselves in an unfamiliar situation. McCroskey and others maintain that people who experience a high degree of CA typically avoid conversations and find conversing with others to be an unpleasant experience. A high degree of CA reduces our motivation to communicate in a competent manner.[3] McCroskey and his colleagues contend that "reduced willingness to communicate results in an individual being less effective in communication and generating negative

How can our knowledge of conversation functions help manage our communication apprehension?

MOTIVATION & mindwork • Does CA Affect Your Motivation to Communicate?

James C. McCroskey's Personal Report of Communication Apprehension scale, or PRCA-24, is the standard method used to determine levels of CA. Scores range from 24 to 120, and the average level of CA for North American populations is 72. In general, our motivation to communicate competently may be negatively affected if we score higher than 80. You can access the PRCA-24 at www.jamescmccroskey.com/measures/prca24.htm.

KNOWLEDGE ON THE CUTTING EDGE

Conversations, Cell Phones, and Civility: Are You a Civil Communicator?

According to a 2002 Public Agenda survey, approximately six in ten Americans favor banning cell phone use in restaurants, movies, museums, and other public places.[5] The worldwide phenomenon of cell phone incivility prompted officials in Campinas, Brazil, to pass a law that fines ringing cell phone owners up to $135 and allows officials to escort them from libraries, movie theaters, and classrooms. In New York City, a number of restaurants have sections that restrict cell phone use, and other restaurants post signs that request courteous cell phone conversations. However, pleas for cell phone courtesy have not been entirely successful. For example, actor Kevin Spacey stopped his Broadway performance and demanded, "Tell them you're busy!" when an audience member answered a cell phone during a show. Some equate the "secondhand intimacy" of listening to loud cell phone conversations with secondhand smoke and suggest that, like the laws against smoking in public, there should be laws that limit cell phone use in public places.[6]

Cell phone users and their conversations are considered exceptionally uncivil for a variety of reasons. Some researchers suggest that cell phone use can be ego-enhancing at the expense of others; cell phone users are "telling people around them, 'You don't matter, and I must be very important.'"[7] Another reason why cell phone conversations are often viewed as uncivil is because users feel insulated from people around them. People who use cell phones in public often speak loudly about intimate topics that are normally discussed in private because others can hear only one side of the conversation. Also, studies demonstrate that people judge cell phone conversations as more intrusive and annoying than face-to-face conversations, even when the volume and content of both channels of conversation are controlled. Researchers suggest that hearing only one side of a conversation is the primary cause of listeners' discomfort. You will soon read about the "cooperative principle," which states that conversations are based on an underlying commitment to share meaning. It has been hypothesized that this commitment to cooperate and share understanding is automatically triggered yet thwarted when listening to only one side of a conversation. Researchers similarly report that listener ratings of incivility are equivalent to hearing only one side of cell phone conversations when only one person is audible in face-to-face conversations.[8] In other words, "people pay more attention when they hear only half a conversation. It's apparently easier to tune out the continuous drone of a complete conversation, in which two people take turns speaking, than it is to ignore a person speaking and falling silent in turns."[9]

Courteous cell phone use includes the following:[10]

- Speak softly. Most mobile phones are more sound-sensitive than regular phones, and shouting isn't needed to make ourselves heard.
- Respect others' personal space. If possible, move to a private space when using a cell phone, and refrain from use where people can't escape our conversation.
- Don't interrupt a face-to-face conversation when the cell phone rings. Having a conversation in front of someone who is physically present tells the person that the phone is more important than she or he is.
- Don't speak about private matters on a cell phone. Remember that this information not only is annoying to others but also can be used against us (e.g., we may leak company confidential information while talking in public).
- Turn off the cell phone at most public places, including restaurants and physician waiting rooms.

Are you a courteous cell phone user? You can take an online "cell phone etiquette" quiz at http://reviews.cnet.com/4520-10779_7-5843439-1.html to find out.

People who talk loudly on cell phones often feel insulated from others around them.

perceptions of himself or herself in the minds of others involved in communication."[4] Fortunately, we can manage communication apprehension. For example, we can engage in rational emotive behavior therapy (REBT), a technique discussed in Chapter 4 that replaces irrational thoughts with rational thoughts to reduce debilitative emotions such as anxiety. We can also remind ourselves that knowledge and skills related to how conversation functions can increase our motivation and facilitate our ability to interact competently with conversation partners. Reminding ourselves of our conversational knowledge and skills can increase our perception of positive outcomes that may result from interacting with others and enhance perceptions of our communication competence.

How Conversation Functions

- "Hey, did you hear what happened at work yesterday?"
- "No; tell me about it."
- "I don't know what happened; I want you to tell me!"

Have you ever found yourself in a similar conversation? Perhaps you once thought you were asking someone for information, but your conversation partner thought you were creating a dramatic preface to an upcoming story. We can prevent or minimize such misinterpretations by understanding and studying the meaning and structure of everyday talk, that is, by focusing on how conversation works.

How does conversation function?

Speech Acts

Participants in conversation design their talk to convey social action, accomplish goals, and do "communicative work." In other words, not only do conversationalists *say* something to each other when they talk, they also *do* something at the same time. This "doing" is sometimes called "conversational action" but is more typically labeled "speech acts." **Speech acts** include greetings, criticism, invitations, congratulations, insults, promises, requests, and warnings. The interpretation of a speech act occurs as a result of a problem-solving process in which participants use commonsense reasoning to interpret the action during the talk.[11] For example, if you know that someone in class wants to ask you out, you will interpret her or his questions about upcoming events as "probes," a conversational action used to discover what you like to do. Speech acts are also interpreted on the basis of rules and assumptions that are created by social agreement and shared by people in the same linguistic group. To illustrate this point, imagine yourself in a situation in which someone asks, "Do you know the time?" What might the questioner think if you merely answer, "yes" and then go about your business? Speech act theory enables you to immediately understand the question as a request for you to look at your watch and state the time to the person who asks the question. Knowledge of speech acts will most likely prevent you from inferring that the questioner is asking you a yes-or-no question concerning your knowledge of time.

Although speech act theory reveals the assumptions and expectations that are prevalent in everyday talk, it cannot explain all conversations. Consider the following:

TEENAGE SON (GRABBING THE CAR KEYS): *I'm off.*

MOM (SMILING): *You sure are, but we've known that for a long time!*

In this conversational fragment, the "doing" or speech act associated with the words "I'm off" is considered to be leave-taking behavior. However, "I'm off" can also be interpreted

KNOWLEDGE power • Is It a Question or Statement?

Speech act theory is not only used to analyze interpretations of conversation but also to help individuals learn a second language. The University of Minnesota's Center for Advanced Research and Language Acquisition (CARLA) includes the study of speech acts as a method to improve foreign language teaching and learning effectiveness.

To learn about descriptions of speech acts revealed through empirical research, access www.carla.umn.edu/speechacts/descriptions.html.

as an idiom that refers to a mentally unbalanced state. The "doing" or speech act associated with the words "You sure are, but we've known that for a long time!" can be labeled an "assertive" that describes the son's state of mind. This example reveals that speech act theory can't explain how conversation effectively functions when the "doing" can have more than one interpretation or when people (purposefully) misinterpret what a portion of talk is supposed to do (such as suggest leave taking or describe a mental state). Therefore, speech act theory should be used in conjunction with a speaker's nonverbal behavior, the characteristics of a situation, and the conversational context (i.e., where a portion of talk is located in a particular conversational sequence) to interpret a message.[12]

The Cooperative Principle

Speech acts will be most effective if individuals engaged in conversation follow the "cooperative principle" developed by British philosopher **Herbert Paul Grice**. The **cooperative principle** suggests that conversation partners use their talk to facilitate understanding.[13] A cooperative conversation results if participants follow the four maxims or rules associated with the cooperative principle that are illustrated in Figure 7.1, "The Cooperative Principle and Conversation Maxims." For example:

1. The **quality maxim** states that we should provide information that is truthful. We should refrain from lies, distortions, and misrepresentations.
2. The **quantity maxim** states that we should offer information that is sufficient to keep a conversation going. We should refrain from offering too little or too much information in relation to our conversation partner(s).
3. The **relevancy maxim** states that we should provide information that pertains to the topic under discussion. Going off on a tangent and engaging in an abrupt topic change are uncooperative actions.
4. The **manner maxim** states that we should be organized and specific when we speak. We cooperate with our conversation partners when we choose language and use it in a manner that is easy to understand.

People usually adhere to the cooperative principle and follow the maxims because they provide underlying assumptions that aid in the interpretation of a speaker's comments. In other words, a speaker's talk will be generally assumed to be truthful, sufficient, relevant, and clear.[14] If we are confused about what a portion of talk is supposed to "do," we can assume that a speaker is adhering to the cooperative principle and look for situational clues to interpret her

KNOWLEDGE power • Abbott and Costello's "Who's on First?"

Bud Abbott and Lou Costello were a popular comic duo during the mid-twentieth century. Their "Who's on First?" is an excellent example of the limitations of speech act theory. The confusion about whether "Who's on First" is a "question" speech act or whether it's a declaration or an "assertive" speech act ("Who" being the name of a baseball player) begins a series of humorous misunderstandings based on additional misinterpretations of speech acts.

By yourself or with a group, analyze "Who's on First?" in terms of speech acts and their misinterpretations. A transcript and audiovisual files of "Who's on First?" are available at www.americanrhetoric.com/speeches/abbott&costellowhosonfirst.htm (audio file and written transcript) and www.youtube.com/watch?v=IEaKjRyPjVY&search=who's%20on%20first (audiovisual file).

or his message. For instance, in the previous example of the teenage son and his mom, the son can infer that his mother really knows that his speech act is one of leave taking (she can see from the situation that he has the car keys in hand). He can also see from the situation that his mom is smiling when she says, "You sure are, but we've known that for a long time!" This information, along with the assumptions and expectations associated with the cooperative principle and its maxims, will help the son interpret his mother's comments as being playful or teasing. This interpretation cannot be adequately explained by speech act theory alone.

Figure 7.1: The Cooperative Principle and Conversation Maxims

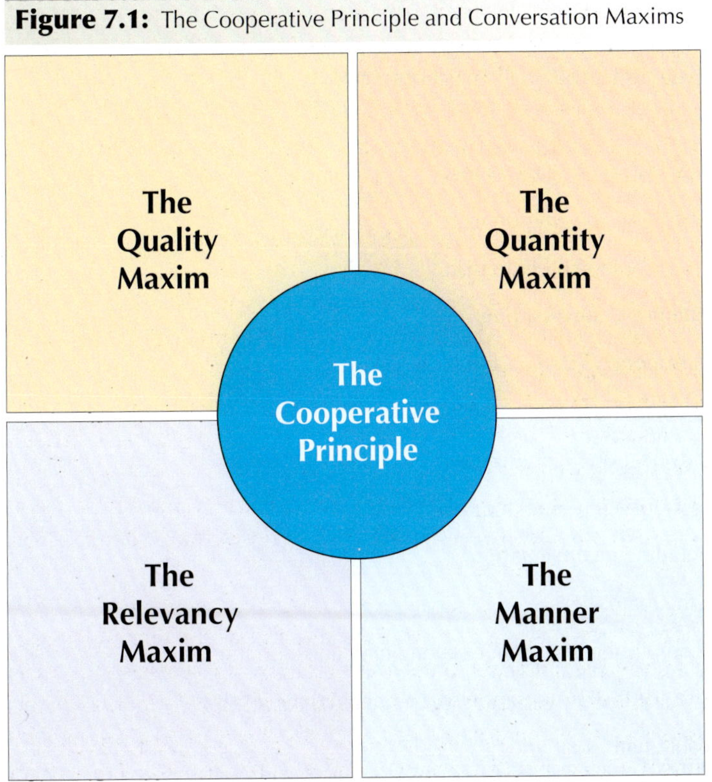

Skills of Competent Conversationalists

What skills are used by competent conversationalists?

Even though most of our interactions are likely to be successful, there will be times when we find ourselves in difficult or challenging conversations. We can more appropriately and effectively manage our interactions and even our success in life if we know and can perform skills associated with competent conversations. A study that tracked Stanford University MBAs ten years after they graduated found that grade-point averages had no bearing on the graduates' success but their ability to converse with others did. Unfortunately, a Roper poll commissioned by the National Communication Association found that although most Americans prefer face-to-face communication and believe they are fairly good communicators, nearly one in five Americans admits to feeling uncomfortable making small talk in a social situation such as a party.[15]

What seems to come naturally or easily to some (such as the ability to converse with ease) may not come easily to others. Perhaps you can think back to your elementary, middle, or high school years and recall a child who didn't fit in. Perhaps this person constantly interrupted others or made irrelevant comments that were unrelated to the topic of conversation. Adults may also have problems engaging in conversation with others, and they similarly may be regarded as "strange" and suffer from social ostracism. The good news is that such individuals can be taught the skills that will enable them to competently converse with others. A number of these skills are summarized in Table 7.1, "Skills of Competent Conversationalists."

Beginning a Conversation

Conversations have identifiable beginning sections, middle sections, and concluding sections. It isn't necessary to begin a conversation with a clever or "perfect" opener; ordinary

Table 7.1: Skills of Competent Conversationalists

Skills for beginning a conversation:

- Ask questions that will engage others
- Ask questions about the environment
- Ask questions about the other person

Skills for sustaining a conversation

- Provide and respond to free information
- Credit the source of ideas
- Maintain conversational coherence
- Engage in appropriate turn taking

Skills for concluding a conversation

- Summarize the main ideas
- End with a compliment or positive statement (if appropriate)
- Make plans to see the conversation partner again (if necessary)
- Indicate closure with "exit lines"

KNOWLEDGE power • Are You a Competent Conversationalist?

There are a number of conversation self-tests available to assess conversational proficiency. Loren Ekroth, author and founder of "Conversation Matters," created the Conversation Mastery Test, which has twenty-five items related to various aspects of conversational competence. You can access the Conversation Mastery Test at www.conversation-matters.com/mastery.html.

comments or questions work well. One skill associated with competent conversation is to begin by asking questions that will engage others. Our major goal at the beginning of a conversation is to show interest in and involve another person in talk; therefore, we can try to ask questions about topics that a potential conversation partner will want to talk about. We can involve someone in conversation by asking questions about the physical setting and by asking questions about the other person.

Asking Questions About the Environment One of the easiest ways to come up with questions that will engage others is to consider the environment in which we and our potential partner are located. Examples of opening questions that are likely to engage others include:[18]

- In a college classroom—*What do you know about the professor? I was absent yesterday; what did we talk about? What do you think will be on the next exam?*
- In line for a movie—*What movie are you going to see? What have you heard about the movie? Do you like comedies/action movies/romances?*

KNOWLEDGE ON THE CUTTING EDGE

Asperger's Syndrome

If you have ever met someone who speaks a little too loudly, stands a little too close, speaks at length about minutiae unrelated to the topic of discussion, and makes socially inappropriate comments, you may have encountered an individual with Asperger's syndrome (AS). AS is a neurological impairment that is shared by approximately 2.5 million Americans and affects approximately one in every three hundred people. Interestingly, most persons with AS are male. People with AS can communicate for practical purposes, but they experience problems with the "social aspects" of communication. For example, individuals with AS may have difficulty understanding nonverbal communication and making eye contact with others, engage in repetitive speech and experience nervous tics, experience problems with figurative meanings and double meanings, miss the purpose of social rituals and may be characterized as rude, talk incessantly about a favorite subject without ever getting to the point, and offend others with their communication and behavior because they don't follow shared communication rules. Persons with AS experience difficulty with people and in situations that typically don't pose problems for others, such as on the playground, at work, with friends, and in intimate relationships. It is in situations that are unpredictable and unstructured, and "where relationships, social sensitivity, and reciprocity matter, that people with AS suffer."[16] Fortunately, research has shown that people with AS can be taught how to express their feelings, interpret nonverbal communication, and engage in conversational turn-taking behavior.[17] We may want to remember the social consequences related to Asperger's syndrome and remind ourselves to be tolerant the next time we converse with someone who speaks a little too loudly, stands a little too close, and/or makes socially inappropriate comments.

- In a club—*What types of bands usually play here? What do you think is the best thing to eat and drink here? Do you know any more places like this where you can listen to live music and meet people?*

We should try to communicate opening questions and comments that are positive. Negative opening questions can discourage others from engaging in conversation and may cast us in a negative light. For example, in the club environment, asking a negative question such as "Don't you think this music is terrible?" may prompt a response such as "Well, why don't you just leave?"[19] If possible, we should also ask questions that are open-ended so that we can obtain information we can use to sustain a conversation. **Open-ended questions** such as "What did you think about the chapter we just read?" encourage meaningful and thorough answers. The open-ended question illustrated in the Luann comic ("How was your summer vacation?") may result in a one-word answer ("Fine"); however, responses to open-ended questions tend to be descriptive and provide us with insight into what a conversation partner thinks and feels. In contrast, **closed-ended questions** such as "Did you like the chapter?" often evoke one-word responses and may not provide us with additional information we can use to keep a conversation going.

Asking Questions About the Other Person Another category of questions that can be used as conversation openers involve those about a potential partner. These questions will be relatively easy to create if we have prior knowledge about the other person. For example, we can ask a potential conversation partner:

- About the other's family—*How are your mom and dad feeling? How is your spouse/partner/girlfriend/boyfriend doing?*
- About the other's recent activities—*How was your last fishing trip? What projects have you been working on lately?*
- About the other in general—*What's new? What's going on in your life?*

Creating questions directed to strangers is more difficult than creating those directed to people we already know, especially if we wish to communicate our interest in getting to know the other person. Commenting on or asking questions about a person's physical appearance and/or clothing can be risky (e.g., one response to, "Hey, you look good. Where

Beginning an interaction with an open-ended question doesn't guarantee an effective and appropriate conversation.

SKILL practice • Asking Questions That Will Engage Others in Conversation

We may sometimes want to converse with someone but can't think of anything to say. One way to engage others in conversation is to ask questions about our surroundings. This isn't always as easy as it seems! Creating sample questions before actually finding ourselves in such a situation can help us become motivated to initiate conversations with others.

Develop at least two conversation-opening questions related to the following environments:

- grocery store
- sporting event
- party
- laundromat/apartment laundry room/dorm laundry room
- weight room/exercise club/fitness center

When you are finished, read your questions to a group of classmates and have them evaluate your questions in terms of their potential effectiveness and appropriateness.

did you get those shoes/that jacket/that tattoo?" might be "None of your business!" . . . or even worse). And there is always the potential for such comments and questions to be stereotyped as pickup lines. We will learn more about how to communicate our interest in and desire to know another person in Chapter 10 about relationships.

Sustaining a Conversation

Imagine yourself in a situation in which you engage someone in conversation with effective and appropriate questions. How can you keep the conversation going? To competently sustain a conversation, we can respond to and provide free information, maintain conversational coherence, engage in appropriate turn taking, and credit the source of our ideas.

Responding to and Providing Free Information One of the benefits of asking conversation-opening questions is that they can provide us with information that we can use to sustain a conversation. **Free information** is "data beyond that which you requested or expected."[20] The use of free information relates to the quantity maxim in that it enables us to offer information that is sufficient to keep a conversation going. We can continue a conversation by asking additional questions about the free information and/or using the free information to switch to other topics. We can also continue a conversation by providing free information that can be used by a responder to further an interaction. For example, suppose we begin a conversation in a classroom environment with "What do you know about this professor?" The responder might answer, "Not a lot, but some of my friends last semester said that I should sign up for her class." The responder's answer to our question has given us at least two pieces of free information: he or she has friends who know something about the professor, and he or she took classes last semester. We can use this free information to ask additional questions and make additional comments: "Did your friends actually enroll in this class?" "Why did your friends suggest that you take this professor?" "Which classes did you enroll in last semester?" "Which class did you like the best?"

Maintaining Conversational Coherence **Conversational coherence** refers to how talk is organized. Comments made by one person should directly relate to the comments made by others.[21] This skill of competent conversation reflects the relevancy maxim because it entails providing information that pertains to the topic under discussion. Conversational coherence also refers to clarity in conversation.[22] This idea relates to the manner maxim because conversational coherence directs us to be organized when we speak. It is natural and expected that a conversation may cover a variety of topics; however, abrupt topic changes violate the relevancy maxim. Going off on tangents disrupts the organization of a conversation and violates the manner maxim. To switch topics in conversation, we can use transitional comments that link one topic to another and use metacommunication (communication about communication). Comments such as "That reminds me of . . ." and "The next thing I want to mention . . ." allow us to effectively and appropriately transition from one idea to the next.

Engaging in Appropriate Turn Taking Researchers suggest that we evaluate others based on how turns are allocated and how smoothly the turn exchanges are accomplished. "Effective turn-taking may elicit the perception that you and your partner really 'hit it off well' or that your partner is a very competent communicator; ineffective turn-taking may prompt evaluations of 'rude' (too many interruptions), 'dominating' (not enough turn-yielding), or 'frustrating' (unable to make an important point)."[23] In general, competent conversationalists:

- Take an appropriate number of turns (individuals in a conversation should have approximately the same number of turns)
- Speak for an appropriate length of time per turn (we shouldn't hog the stage or participate with only one- or two-word responses)
- Recognize and adhere to turn-exchanging and directing cues, such as a glance at the end of a thought unit or a change in pitch
- Refrain from interrupting except to clarify utterances or agree with what a speaker is saying[24]

SKILL practice • Sustaining a Conversation

In groups of four, practice the skills involved in sustaining a conversation. In the first part of this activity, two participants should engage in conversation, and two participants should evaluate the conversationalists in terms of their use of free information, their ability to maintain conversational coherence, whether they engage in appropriate turn taking, and whether they credit the source of ideas. Evaluators should take notes and orally critique the conversation participants after five to ten minutes. (The actual length of the conversation will be determined by your instructor.) The second part of this activity is exactly like the first except that the evaluators switch roles and become conversation partners (and vice versa). The conversations can begin with participants asking questions about the surroundings and/or the conversation partner.

Crediting the Source of Ideas **Crediting sources** is similar to including footnotes or references in a written paper. Crediting a source results in a number of benefits. One benefit is that listeners can ascertain whether the source is biased, unbiased, and/or knowledgeable enough to comment about the topic at hand. Crediting a source is also a reflection of our ability to adhere to the quality maxim because we don't misrepresent ourselves as the source of an idea. Furthermore, verbally acknowledging sources we know (e.g., friends and acquaintances) will prevent them from becoming angry with us, should they discover we're using their thoughts as our own. Our friends and acquaintances will appreciate the credit when we acknowledge them in our conversations.

Concluding a Conversation

A conversation typically comes to a close when a topic has been "talked out" and/or when a participant has to leave. There are a number of techniques that can be used to communicate that it's time for a conversation to end. In particular, we can:

- Summarize the main ideas that have been expressed by a conversation partner. This not only signals that the conversation is about to end but also signals that we have been listening and understand what our conversation partner has been saying.
- End with a compliment or positive statement such as "I enjoyed talking with you" or "I appreciate the info."
- Make plans to see a conversation partner sometime in the future. Merely saying, "Let's get together again sometime" or "I'll call you later" may give the impression that we are giving our conversation partner the brush-off. Instead, be specific in terms of time and place, such as "Let's meet at the library at 1 P.M. on Tuesday."
- Come up with **exit lines** in case the previous techniques are ignored or not perceived as closing signals by a conversation partner. Exit lines often focus on situations outside the conversation that may cause us to conclude that a conversation is nearing its end. For example, we might say, "I haven't eaten lunch so I really need to run to the snack bar before my next class." Another example of an exit line that can be used at a gathering is "I haven't seen 'so-and-so' for a long time; let me catch her or him now while I can."

Nonverbal behaviors that communicate leave-taking cues include decreasing eye gaze and positioning one's body toward an exit. Additional leave-taking behaviors include offering one's hand for a handshake, glancing at a watch or clock, gathering one's possessions, and placing both hands on top of the thighs if seated (this allows leverage for standing up).

Remember to be realistic about the effective and appropriate use of guidelines and skills associated with conversations. Beginning a conversation by using questions to engage someone may not always work. Furthermore, attempting to extricate ourselves from a conversation with exit lines may backfire (e.g., a conversation partner may respond, "You haven't eaten yet? Me either! Let's go to the cafeteria together!"). Recall that communication competence is based on the perceptions of a conversation partner, not on our perceptions of our effectiveness and appropriateness. In other words, we may think that we're a competent conversationalist, but we may not have many conversations if others disagree with our perception.

Competence & Critical Thinking

mycommunicationlab

TALK, TALK, TALK AND CONVERSATION

Alberto is sitting by himself in a small room at a company party. Clarence, a coworker he's never met before, enters the room and begins a conversation.

You can view *Talk, Talk, Talk* by accessing the "Small Group and Interpersonal Videos" on the MyCommunicationLab Web site. Answer the following questions about the nonverbal communication included in the video:

- Analyze this video in terms of the maxims associated with the cooperative principle. Do Clarence and Alberto follow the quality, quantity, relevancy, and manner maxims?
- Do you think Alberto experiences communication apprehension? Explain why or why not.
- Overall, does Clarence illustrate the skills associated with competent conversationalists? Does Alberto?
- What skill of competent conversationalists does Clarence use to end the conversation?
- What advice would you give Alberto to improve his ability to converse with others?

CLARENCE: Hello. Anyone sitting here?

ALBERTO: No.

CLARENCE: May I? Thanks. I notice you're new at the company, right?

ALBERTO: Yes, I am.

CLARENCE: I'm Clarence Aiken.

ALBERTO: Alberto.

CLARENCE: Alberto. Welcome, welcome.

ALBERTO: Thank you.

CLARENCE: You're with—is it R&D?

ALBERTO: Yes.

CLARENCE: Wonderful. Well, how are you enjoying it?

ALBERTO: Oh, it's—it's good.

CLARENCE: Good. How long have you been with the company?

ALBERTO: Oh, about five weeks.

CLARENCE: Brand new.

ALBERTO: Yeah.

CLARENCE: Well, I hope you're finding it challenging.

ALBERTO: Ah, it is.

CLARENCE: Motivating?

ALBERTO: Yes. Definitely.

CLARENCE: Good. So where are you from?

ALBERTO: Uh, New York.

CLARENCE: Alberto from New York.

ALBERTO: Yeah.

CLARENCE: I spent many years in New York.

ALBERTO: Uh-huh.

CLARENCE: Are you from there originally?

ALBERTO: No, no.

CLARENCE: How long were you in New York?

ALBERTO: Four years.

CLARENCE: Four years?

ALBERTO: Yeah.

CLARENCE: That's a pretty long time.

ALBERTO: Yeah.

CLARENCE: Did you enjoy it?

ALBERTO: It was, uh, OK.

CLARENCE: Just OK. New York, one of the most cosmopolitan cities in the world. Thank you. Just OK, huh?

ALBERTO: Yeah, it's, uh, noisy.

CLARENCE: That it is.

ALBERTO: Yeah.

CLARENCE: That it is. Very vibrant city, however.

ALBERTO: Yes. Umm . . .

CLARENCE: Well, did you come up specifically for this job?

ALBERTO: Yes, I did relocate.

CLARENCE: I'm sure you're an excellent addition to R&D.

ALBERTO: Thank you.

CLARENCE: Well, I, uh, I think I see a coworker of mine. (*Alberto mumbles*) I'm sorry?

ALBERTO: No, nothing, I—yeah.

CLARENCE: If you'll excuse me, I'll say hello to Peter.

ALBERTO: OK.

CLARENCE: Well, good luck to you.

ALBERTO: Mm-hmm. Thank you.

CLARENCE: Wish you much luck in my company. Take care now.

Contexts, Conversation, and Communication Style

The culture, relationship, gender, and individual contexts affect our ability to converse with others and our perceptions of competent conversations. Specifically, contexts influence **communication style**, or how people verbally and nonverbally communicate, the preferred amount of talk and silence, and the degree of familiarity with which conversation partners speak.[25] Communication style describes general tendencies, however, and there are exceptions and individual differences.

How do contexts influence conversation and communication style?

Culture Context

Communication researchers have studied cultural differences in communication style in terms of topic management and rules for turn taking. For example, research suggests that the structure of conversation differs in Asia and in the West. In Asia, a main topic is introduced later in a conversation, after the initial introduction of incidental topics and minor points, and the main point is often followed by a final period of small talk. Conversations in Western cultures typically begin with a main point that is followed by some form of support for the point and/or small talk. Conversations in Western cultures tend to conclude with a restatement of the main point and/or a concluding point. Additionally, turn taking is influenced by status and hierarchy in Japanese conversations. High-status individuals often take the last turn; this is the point in a conversation where it is least likely for someone to lose face. The length of turns in Japanese conversations also tends to be longer than the length of turns in American conversations because the Japanese include many details in their talk. Americans tend to distribute turns unevenly, and the person who initiates a topic may take the most turns when discussing that topic.[26]

Co-cultures within the United States influence communication style, and this line of research can help us recognize potential sources of misinterpretation. However, scholars disagree about the merit of research concerning co-cultures and communication style. Some scholars contend that such research divides and separates "us" from "them"; others maintain that the research can further our understanding of diverse cultures and communication. Communication researcher **Donal Carbaugh** suggests we consider both viewpoints when we read about co-cultures and communication style. Carbaugh explains that both dynamics can connect us to a "common humanity" that is evident in such research but can also enlighten us about features of communication that can distinguish one culture from another.[27] Be cautious when reading about the various communication styles associated with co-cultures. One problem associated with this research is that the European American communication style is often considered the standard against which all others are compared. (In fact, the information in this chapter about how conversation functions and skills of competent conversationalists reflect European American conversation rules.) All communication styles have merit, and the European American style is considered the standard because those who hold the economic and political power in the American culture typically use this style. Other problems associated with this line of research include the failure to take into consideration the great diversity that exists within co-cultures and to realize that communication style is affected by context (e.g., whether we're speaking with close friends or people we've met for the first time). Moreover, many Americans are members of and identify with more than one co-culture, and their communication style illustrates features associated with a number of co-cultures. Also, members of co-cultures don't exhibit all of the features associated with a particular communication style all of the time. Therefore, it's crucial that we reject the idea that illustrations of communication style are rigid descriptions of how people communicate in all situations.

African American Communication Style African Americans typically encourage and respect language artistry and an expressive communication style. The verbal creativity of

KNOWLEDGE ON THE CUTTING EDGE

Technology Update: Conversing with Computers

Researchers are currently dealing with how to make synthesized speech closer to human speech by modulating tone and expression. IBM is developing the Natural Expressive Speech (NAXPRES) Synthesizer, which is based on recordings of human speakers and can respond in real time. Synthetic speech is typically produced by linking words or pieces of words of recorded human speech, but this type of synthesized speech sounds mechanical and unnatural. To combat this problem, the NAXPRES researchers record phonemes (the smallest units of sound) and then arrange sequences of recorded phonemes to create words. The recorded phonemes are analyzed according to pitch, timing, and loudness and are catalogued in the NAXPRES searchable database. The NAXPRES Synthesizer contains approximately 10,000 recorded samples of each of the roughly forty phonemes in the English language. NAXPRES is therefore able to assemble the best phoneme recordings in a row and make pitch adjustments if necessary for the spoken speech to sound natural. Because this processing occurs in a millisecond, people can converse with the computer in real time.[28]

You can learn more about NAXPRES and listen to the synthesized speech at IBM's interactive Web site: www.research.ibm.com/tts.

African American speech may also exhibit a rhythmic quality similar to African languages in that some syllables are accented more strongly, accented differently, and held longer than the speech of communication styles associated with other co-cultures. African Americans from all economic, educational, and social strata often include proverbs, rhymes, and popular phrases in everyday conversation. African Americans and European Americans may also employ different rules for turn taking. European Americans typically take turns that last as long as the number of points requires. This requires conversation partners to wait their turns until all the points have been made. On the other hand, African Americans may take a turn whenever it's possible to do so, such as after at least one point is made to establish the value or truth of each point before new points can be discussed.[29]

Asian American Communication Style Asian Americans tend to be sensitive to others' feelings and may be unwilling to directly challenge someone in public. Instead, Asian Americans typically employ indirect communication and interact in a tactful manner that often recognizes status. For example, in an effort to save face and prevent disharmony, Asian Americans may say "yes" to mean "I heard you" instead of "no." "Asian-Americans may prefer silence to spoken language in situations where interpersonal disagreement is evident."[30] The communication style associated with Asian Americans tends to be restrained, indirect, and respectful.

Deaf Communication Style Members of the Deaf culture communicate in a direct manner. Deaf culture members often talk about topics that may be considered "personal" in other co-cultures. Topics that range from intimate medical details to others' physical appearance are often freely discussed. Similarly, positive and negative gossip and talking behind someone's back are expected because sharing information is the norm in Deaf culture and "talking behind someone's back" does not carry a negative connotation as it does in other co-cultures. The Deaf culture communication style is differentiated from other communication styles in terms of additional features. For example, to signal a desire to converse with a member of Deaf culture, it is acceptable to wave in the direction of the person, tap the person on the shoulder, stomp on the floor or bang on a table (the vibrations will signal that someone wants to communicate), and flash the lights in a room.[31]

KNOWLEDGE ON THE CUTTING EDGE

Code Switching

Because the rules for talk and expectations for conversation are culturally learned (and are rarely violated by members within a co-culture), they appear to be normal and/or natural to members of particular co-cultures. This can lead to negative evaluations of individuals from other co-cultures who follow their own "normal" or "natural" rules for talk. In an effort to avoid negative evaluations and maintain cultural identity or identities, members of co-cultures may engage in code switching, or the alternating use of languages or communication styles, often within a single phrase or sentence. Members of co-cultures may choose to make use of features typically associated with communication styles associated with other co-cultures based on the social situation, age of the conversation partner(s), relationship intimacy, and conversation topic. For example, some African Americans may use a style of speech that members of other co-cultures may describe as extremely emotional, assertive, and even confrontational. Therefore, African Americans may code-switch by changing their language and style when conversing with European Americans. But code switching is not a process limited to the African American co-culture. For example, European Americans (especially suburban teenagers) may adopt the conversational style associated with the African American hip-hop community to communicate their affiliation with this particular co-culture.[32]

European American Communication Style The European American communication style tends to be direct and explicit. European Americans typically assume that the spoken word is of primary importance and that nonverbal communication is secondary and serves to modify the meaning of words. They also tend to be informal and address everyone in the same way (such as using first names easily and early in relationships). European Americans typically dislike people who "talk too much" and prefer a form of interaction in which speakers take frequent turns after only a few sentences are spoken.[33] In fact, the European American style of turn taking has been likened to a game of table tennis during which "your head goes back and forth and back and forth so fast it almost makes your neck hurt."[34] European Americans tend to be uncomfortable with silence and may fill a conversational pause that lasts for more than a few seconds.[35]

Gay Communication Style Recall from Chapter 1 that communication scholars disagree as to whether a gay co-culture is a reality. On the one hand, some researchers contend that there is no consensus regarding what constitutes a gay co-culture because of the diverse individuals who consider themselves homosexual, bisexual, or transgendered. On the other hand, other researchers assert that the gay co-culture indeed exists and that its members make use of an extensive system of communication. Some studies reveal that the use of humor and puns are pervasive in the language of the gay co-culture and that a sharp wit and verbal facility are highly prized. Verbal ambiguity is also a part of the gay communication style, so that a message can be denied if a conversation partner takes offense.[36]

Latina/o American Communication Style Latina/os tend to exhibit an expressive communication style and value eloquent speech. The communication style of Latina/os may be judged by other co-cultures, especially those that value a succinct communication style, as flowery or overly dramatic. Latina/os tend to be courteous and agreeable and enjoy socializing with others, often to the frustration of individuals who want to get down to business. Latina/os also value respect and will refrain from arguing or disagreeing in public. Like other co-cultures, Latina/os may use English and Spanish to engage in code switching to communicate their identities and cultures.[37]

Native American Communication Style Native Americans tend to be more implicit than explicit in their communication style. The use of silence is an important feature in this communication style, especially as a response to ambiguity. Meeting people for the first time, dealing with an angry person, and consoling someone who is grieving are social situations in which silence is appropriate. Native American communication is typically restrained and agreeable. Saving face is important in the Native American communication style, and Native Americans tend to be polite and to avoid being singled out in public.[38]

Relationship Context

Think about your family, friends, and coworkers. How have they influenced your communication style? Families and couples tend to follow unspoken rules about conversations as relationships mature, conversation tends to differ in same-sex and mixed-sex friendships, and coworkers exchange important information in informal conversations that travel along the organizational grapevine.

Families Most U.S. families believe that it's important to put thoughts into words to understand family members and to coordinate behavior. Still, families may fluctuate between periods of more conversation and less conversation over time. Although there may be a large amount of explicit talk during courtship and early marriage, unspoken understandings may be the rule as a marital relationship matures. Research has found that families and couples make use of an implicit style of communication as they become increasingly stable and homogeneous. For example, if spouses agree about their marital roles, there may be less need for talk used to coordinate behavior. However, periods of explicit talk are expected if a relationship or family becomes unstable and/or undergoes redefinition. Marriage partners tend to replace culturally determined conversation rules with their own personally negotiated rules to determine effective and appropriate conversations. Research illustrates that wives and husbands are similar in their communication styles when it comes to maintaining conversations. Moreover, husbands and wives do not differ significantly in the amount of talk per conversation; they take an approximately equal number of turns talking for similar amounts of time, and neither partner interrupts more than the other. All told, wives and husbands engage in "similar kinds and amounts of conversational maintenance behaviors."[39]

Friends Men in same-sex friendships engage in conversations during which they self-disclose and discuss feelings, but they do so less often than women in same-sex friendships. Closeness is primarily achieved by sharing activities and exchanging favors in friendships among males. On the other hand, conversation is often considered the primary component of friendships among women. In terms of cross-sex friendships, research that focuses on communication style reveals that men talk more than women, receive positive evaluations of their communication by both women and men, and are perceived to have greater influence over their female friends than their females friends have over them. In addition, many women and men communicate according to gender stereotypes in cross-sex friendships. Women typically initiate more topics in cross-sex friendship conversations, which reinforces perceptions of female expressivity and facilitation. Men tend to decide which topics will be discussed at length in cross-sex friendship conversations, which reinforces perceptions of male power and control. Although male domination and female subordination is typically reflected in cross-sex friendship conversations, status and power differences between men and women are changing, and expressivity, facilitation, power, and control in cross-sex friends' conversations may now depend more on negotiation than on stereotyped gender expectations.[40]

Coworkers **Formal communication** within an organization flows along official paths or networks that are prescribed by the organization. A subordinate may be required to communicate with her or his immediate supervisor and then be referred to a high-ranking manager prior to meeting with a company vice president. However, not all messages follow prescribed paths within an organization. **Informal communication** that flows via the grapevine typically relates to gossip or topics of personal interest but may also include rumors about an organization if a formal communication channel is ineffective in providing company-related information. Research suggests that informal communication is 75 to 95% accurate. Additionally, workers tend to be more satisfied with their jobs when they use the grapevine for conversations with coworkers, and managers who pay attention to informal communication may find it a helpful source of information about employee problems and concerns.[41]

Gender Context

Scientific research has found that the communication styles of women and men are more similar than different. Furthermore, gender alone cannot predict communication style because of the influence of additional characteristics and contexts that affect how people converse. One study that reviews gender communication research conducted since the 1980s reveals that the communication style of women and men is so similar that native English speakers reading transcribed audio conversations cannot guess which conversational examples are produced by women or men. Specifically, women and men both make use of

KNOWLEDGE ON THE CUTTING EDGE

Putting It in Context: Communication, Sex, and Conversation

We learned in Chapter 5 that the female brain facilitates language use. Women have smaller brains and more gray matter than men, which has been linked to superior verbal facility. Additionally, estrogen plays a role in a female's ability to easily engage in conversation. Estrogen increases the linguistic "highways" in the brain and enhances a variety of verbal skills. Studies demonstrate that estrogen not only affects a woman's ability to pronounce words but also heightens verbal memory and the ability to find "the right words." Neuroscientists have also discovered that women's brains don't rest in the same way that men's brains rest. There is more neural activity in the female brain and 15% more blood flow than in the male brain. Women's brains are constantly working and don't take "mental naps" as often as male brains; for example, males may "zone out" in front of a TV without actually being involved in a program. Engaging in conversation is hard work for a male because he has a smaller hippocampus (the memory center), fewer neural pathways from sensory centers to the hippocampus, and less verbal memory. A way to relax for women may be the very activity that overstimulates a male brain—engaging in conversation.[42]

stylistic features such as interruptions, directives (i.e., telling others what to do in a direct manner), questions, and intensive adverbs (such as "really") with similar frequencies. However, women and men are evaluated differently when they make use of other stylistic features. For example:

- Both women and men make use of **tag questions**, which are added to the end of declarative sentences. A tag question changes a sentence to a question, as in "That was a delicious dinner, *don't you think?*" The frequency with which women and men use tag questions is unclear, and studies result in inconsistent findings about the gender-linked use of tag questions. Research suggests that women and men are judged differently when they use tag questions in conversation. In general, women are judged as less knowledgeable and less intelligent than men when they make use of tag questions in conversations, but men are not.[43]
- Speaking longer, louder, and more directly are stereotypically assumed to fit with a masculine model of communication style. These features also stereotypically reflect power and authority. Therefore, a man can enhance both his masculinity and authority by adopting these features of communication style. On the other hand, although women who speak loudly, for a long time, and in a direct manner may command more attention and respect, they may be evaluated negatively for compromising their femininity by acting "pushy, aggressive and unfeminine."[44]
- Although women are often considered to be more indirect in their conversational style than men, both men and women tend to be indirect in different circumstances. An **indirect communication style** includes meanings that don't arise directly from the actual words used in communication. For example, saying "It sure is hot in here" can be interpreted as an indirect request to turn on the air conditioner or open a window. Women tend to be indirect when asking others to do things, whereas men tend to be indirect when expressing weakness, errors, problems, and emotions other than anger. Indirectness can function to avoid conflict and can be a satisfying way to communicate when unstated meanings are shared, such as in irony, sarcasm, and figures of speech.[45]

In terms of communication style, there are "no generic forms that clearly and unerringly point to the gender of the speaker."[46] In addition, research concerning gender and communication style is typically based on samples of middle-class European Americans and ignores the idea that patterns of interactions are affected by age, race, ethnicity, social class, and sexual orientation. In addition, differences may not be large or substantial, even in studies in which gender differences are found to be "statistically significant." Studies regarding communication style and gender differences reveal inconsistent results, in part because such differences aren't apparent in all situational contexts. Although knowledge of general patterns of gender-linked communication styles can help prevent misunderstandings, these differences are minimal and shouldn't be used to stereotype the communication of women and men.

Individual Context

Do you know someone who seems to talk too much? Have you been told and/or do you think you talk too much? Research on **talkaholics,** or people who know they consistently and compulsively communicate, was introduced into the scientific literature in the early 1990s. About one in twenty people are estimated to be talkaholics.

One line of research concerning talkaholics questions whether it is possible to talk "too much" in Western culture. These studies suggest that people label someone a talkaholic if they don't like what the person talks about and that this same person will not be described as a talkaholic if she or he talks about positive qualities associated with her or his listeners. In addition, being labeled a talkaholic may be a function of a person's communication competence. "There may be communicatively competent individuals who are talkaholics and are highly successful communicators who are not thought of as talking too much, and communicatively incompetent talkaholics (and non-talkaholics) who are highly unsuccessful communicators, at least some of whom may be described as 'talks too much' in response to their communication incompetence."[47] Another line of research concerning talkaholics suggests that such individuals talk nonstop and that others perceive their behavior as a serious problem. Persons engaged in a conversation with talkaholics become irritated, disgusted, and impatient. Talkaholics tend to accurately perceive their behavior yet fail in their attempts to change it.

Being perceived as a talkaholic may cause others to become irritated, disgusted, and impatient.

OVERCOMING COMMUNICATION CHALLENGES

Conversational Dilemmas

As noted earlier in this chapter, there will be times when our conversations are difficult and challenging, even though most of our conversations are likely to be successful. Occasionally we may experience conversations during which we feel that we can't say anything right; whatever we say creates a problem or some sort of undesirable outcome. Such types of difficult communication encounters are called **conversational dilemmas**. Conversational dilemmas need not accompany or result from rule violations, yet as illustrated in the "Baby Blues" comic, they foster negative feelings such as embarrassment and defensiveness when we realize that we may be trapped in one. Examples of conversational dilemmas include:

- being caught in a lie
- saying something we shouldn't

Conversational dilemmas occur when we perceive that we can't say anything right.

- being judged as not saying anything right
- feeling torn between telling the truth (even if it is hurtful) and lying to be tactful

Suppose a friend wants to marry someone you don't particularly like. How will you respond if your friend asks whether he or she should marry the future bride or groom? Even though people caught in conversational dilemmas can use various strategies to cope with such situations, conversational dilemmas are difficult to resolve. There are six categories of responses to conversational dilemmas:[48]

1. Direct responses—this category includes blunt talk (e.g., "I'd never marry someone like the person you want to marry") or honest but tactful communication (e.g., "I'll probably look for someone with a different sort of personality when I want to get married.")
2. Indirect responses—included in this category are strategic ambiguity, vagueness, or subtlety to avoid directly stating the truth, as well as sarcasm, hints, humor, and nonverbal cues (e.g., "Hah! You're asking me about who to marry? I'll never get married so don't ask me 'marriage questions'!")
3. Deception—this category involves a direct misrepresentation of the truth (e.g., "I think the person you're engaged to will make a good spouse.")
4. Impression management—this category includes apologies, excuses, explanations, and reassurances (e.g., "I'm sorry but I can't answer your question; I'm not a good judge of character. However, everything I've seen tells me that your future spouse will make a good one.")
5. Pleasing the other—included in this category are compromises and giving in to avoid conflict or additional awkwardness (e.g., "OK, OK, I'll answer your question, but don't blame me if you get married and you regret your decision or don't get married and regret your decision.")
6. Soliciting the other's help—asking for more information and/or asking the other's cooperation to resolve the dilemma (e.g., "Well, first tell me why you want to marry this person. It's difficult to answer such a question when I don't know what you're looking for in a spouse.")

Researchers have discovered that communicatively competent individuals are able to extricate themselves from conversational dilemmas in a manner that saves face for self and the other. Such individuals tend to choose more sophisticated and effective responses than people who aren't communicatively competent. However, we cannot label certain tactics as

KNOWLEDGE power • "I Can't Win!"

Review the four types of conversational dilemmas and six categories of responses to conversational dilemmas. Think about a past conversation when you felt trapped. To which type of conversational dilemma does your example relate? To which response to a conversational dilemma does your example correspond? With a partner or in a group, share your conversational dilemma, and tell your partner or group how you attempted to resolve the dilemma. Ask your partner or the group to assess your effectiveness and appropriateness and (if warranted) to suggest other tactics for dealing with the dilemma.

more beneficial than others. "What determines optimality is a complex issue that demands consideration of such things as the others involved in the exchange, the context within which the exchange occurs, and the goals of each interactant. With some people one response is preferred over another; in some settings one response is more appropriate than another; and sometimes it is important to a person to be sophisticated, and sometimes it is not."[49]

A CASE STUDY IN ETHICS

Cell Phone Subterfuge

Competent communication includes an ethical dimension of well-based standards of right and wrong. To help us make decisions and select communication strategies that are effective and appropriate, we can ask ourselves a series of questions: Have I practiced any virtues today (e.g., have I demonstrated integrity, trustworthiness, honesty, and responsibility)? Have I done more good than harm (e.g., have I shown appreciation and gratitude to others)? Have I treated people with dignity and respect? Have I been fair and just? Have I made my community stronger because of my actions? Read the following case study about cell phone subterfuge and consider whether staged phone calls, alibi clubs, and fake noises are ethical ways to engage in conversations with others.

James E. Katz, professor of communication at Rutgers University, suggests that some people use cell phones to indirectly communicate with people who surround them. For example, some people stage fake phone calls as explanations for their behavior, such as scolding a pretend child for invading a wallet when they find themselves without cash in a checkout line. Others pretend to be talking on their cell phone when they are actually trying to get a good angle to take a photo on it. Still others create fake phone calls for reasons of safety. Loudly saying, "I'll meet you in a few minutes!" may be helpful when we think we're being followed.

In addition to using cell phones to stage fake phone calls, some people, with the help of other cell phone users, use their cell phones to lie. "Cell phone alibi clubs" are flourishing in many parts of the globe as a way to help callers make excuses and hide their whereabouts. People pay a fee to join a club and are subsequently linked to thousands of members to whom they can send text messages en masse that ask for help. When a potential collaborator indicates her or his willingness to phone a "victim," the caller and collaborator create a lie, and the collaborator phones with the excuse. Similar to alibi clubs, companies offer audio recordings that can be played in the background of such phone calls. Sounds such as honking horns, a dentist's drill, and ambulance sirens can be used to make a phone call sound realistic.

Although fake cell phone calls, cell phone alibi clubs, and background audio recordings may reflect questionable ethics, some individuals find nothing wrong with their use. Harry Kargman, founder of a company that sells audio background sounds, says that using background sounds is "not necessarily malicious or nefarious." Michelle Logan, founder of an alibi club based in San Diego, suggests that such clubs spare others' feelings with "white lies."[50]

Do you think it's ethical to stage fake phone calls? Is it ethical to use alibi clubs and/or background audio recordings? Do you agree with Michelle Logan that alibi clubs spare others' feelings?

Chapter Review

Motivation: How has this helped me?

- **The importance of studying conversation**

It's important to study conversation because knowing the structure and dynamics of everyday talk can improve our conversations in general, improve how we communicate in more formal contexts, and help society function as it should.

- **The relationship between conversation, communication apprehension, and motivation**

Communication apprehension can cause us to avoid conversing with others and reduce our motivation to engage in competent communication. Knowing that we can manage communication apprehension by engaging in REBT and reminding ourselves that knowledge and skills related to how conversation functions can facilitate our ability to interact competently.

Knowledge: What have I learned?

- **How to characterize conversation**

Conversations are locally managed and interactive sequential interchanges. Conversations are a complex and highly coordinated accomplishment between people who may or may not know each other well.

- **How conversation functions**

Conversation functions according to speech acts and the cooperative principle. Speech acts and the cooperative principle reveal the assumptions and expectations that are prevalent in everyday talk and help us understand what talk "does."

- **How contexts influence conversation and communication style**

Our communication style and how we interpret others' communication style are influenced by various contexts. The culture, relationship, and gender contexts provide us with habitual ways of conversing that are typically shared by group members. Additionally, the individual context can influence us when we judge others to be compulsive talkers. Although it is common to deny the effectiveness and appropriateness of communication styles that differ from our own, it's important to remember that all communication styles have merit.

Skill: What skills have I developed?

- **Skills used by competent conversationalists**

To begin a conversation, we can ask questions that will engage others, such as questions about the environment and questions about the other person. To sustain a conversation, we can provide and respond to free information, credit the source of ideas, maintain conversational coherence, and engage in appropriate turn taking. To conclude a conversation, we can summarize the main ideas, end with a compliment or positive statement, (if appropriate) make plans to see a conversation partner again, and (if necessary) indicate closure with exit lines.

Study Questions

1. What is the definition of conversation, and what does that definition mean?
2. Why is it important to study conversations and engage in conversation analysis?
3. What are speech acts, and how does speech act theory apply to the study of conversations?
4. What is the cooperative principle? Describe the four maxims associated with the principle and how they relate to conversation.
5. What types of questions can we use to begin a conversation? Provide examples in your answer.
6. What are some skills we can use to sustain a conversation? Provide examples in your answer.
7. What is communication style, and how does it relate to the culture context?
8. How do the relationship, gender, and individual contexts relate to conversations and/or communication style?
9. What are conversational dilemmas? How can we extricate ourselves from such dilemmas?

Names to Know

Donal Carbaugh, p. 194—communication researcher who publishes in the area of intercultural communication. He teaches at the University of Massachusetts, and his book *Cultures in Conversation* received the International and Intercultural Division of the National Communication Association's 2006 Outstanding Book of the Year Award.

Herbert Paul Grice (1913–1988), p.184—British philosopher who postulated the existence of the cooperative principle in conversation and associated maxims of conversation that are derived from the cooperative principle.

James C. McCroskey, p. 181—communication scholar who conducts extensive research in the areas of nonverbal immediacy and communication apprehension. He is a professor in the Department of Communication Studies at West Virginia University and an author of more than two hundred articles and book chapters and more than thirty books.

Key Terms

closed-ended questions, 188
communication apprehension (CA), 181
communication style, 193
conversation analysis, 180
conversational coherence, 190
conversational dilemmas, 199
conversations, 180
cooperative principle, 184
crediting sources, 191
exit lines, 191
formal communication, 197
free information, 189
indirect communication style, 198
informal communication, 197
manner maxim, 184
open-ended questions, 188
quality maxim, 184
quantity maxim, 184
relevancy maxim, 184
speech acts, 183
tag questions, 198
talkaholic, 199

CHAPTER 8

Listening and Confirming Responses

"We are all regular people seeking the same thing: the guy on the street, the woman in the classroom, the Israeli, the Afghani, the Zuni, the Apache, the Irish, the Protestant, the Catholic, the gay, the straight, you, me—we all just want to know that we matter. We want validation."

Oprah Winfrey, media mogul, motivational speaker, and philanthropist

In this chapter, we will answer the following:

Motivation: How will this help me?

- It is important to study listening and confirming responses because speakers feel validated when we listen and respond with care and attention.

Knowledge: What will I learn?

- How to characterize listening and confirming responses
- The stages in the listening process
- How contexts influence listening and confirming responses

Skill: Why do I need to develop these skills?

- Listening and confirming communication—such as prompting, questioning, reassuring, analyzing, offering advice, and giving constructive criticism—can increase the chances that we will be perceived as competent communicators.

Oprah Winfrey's ability to listen and empathize with her guests encourages them to reveal their feelings and honestly discuss their problems. Do you know someone who listens well to others and confirms their beliefs and emotions? Do people feel comfortable discussing their problems with you because of the way you listen and respond? Listening and responding to others communicates that we **validate** or acknowledge and respect them and their thoughts and feelings. In this chapter, we will learn how to validate others by improving our ability to listen and respond in a competent manner. Specifically, we will increase our motivation to listen and respond competently by understanding why it's important to study listening and confirming communication and by improving our ability to receive and interpret verbal and nonverbal messages. We will increase our knowledge by reading about stages in the listening process and types of confirming responses. We will also learn to perform skills that will validate and confirm others.

Introduction to Listening and Confirming Responses

Think back to your days in elementary school. Did your teachers provide you with instruction in reading, writing, and speaking? You probably had many childhood storybooks, practiced handwriting, and learned vocabulary words and how to pronounce them. However, did your teachers ever instruct you about listening? We engage in listening more than we read, write, and speak, yet rarely are we taught how to listen well to others.

How can we characterize listening and confirming responses?

Listening has been defined as a complex activity that involves the process of receiving, constructing meaning from, and responding to spoken and/or nonverbal messages.[1] As illustrated in Figure 8.1, compared with reading, writing, and speaking, we spend approximately 60% of our "communication time" engaged in listening.[2] In particular, we engage in:

- **Comprehensive listening**—when we want to learn, understand, and recall information. Listening to an instructor give a lecture is an example of comprehensive listening.
- **Evaluative listening**—when we want to judge the soundness of a message. Critical thinking, discussed later in this chapter, can help us analyze and evaluate the messages we listen to.
- **Appreciative listening**—when we want to enjoy and appreciate the messages we listen to. For example, we may make it a point to focus on a conversation partner's nonverbal communication as she or he acts out a story while speaking.
- **Empathic listening**—when we want to understand and experience the feelings of a conversation partner. Engaging in empathic listening by using a feelings paraphrase is discussed later in this chapter.

Unfortunately, most of us are poor listeners. Interpersonally, we tend to remember after only two days about 25% of the information we listen to. College students listen effectively to approximately 50% of a professor's lecture and remember approximately 25% of what was listened to only two days later.[3] In terms of career success, numerous studies illustrate that listening is one of the top five skills expected of employees and that mistakes and loss of sales result when employees listen in an ineffective manner.[4] Many of us engage in **disconfirming listening**, that is, listening that does not acknowledge and

Figure 8.1: Approximately 60% of Our "Communication Time" is Used to Listen

We "listen" to one book a day.
We "speak" a book a week.
We "read" a book a month.
We "write" a book a month.

respect a speaker's verbal and nonverbal messages. Disconfirming forms of listening include:

- **Defensive listening**—we interpret messages as criticism and personal attacks.
- **Pseudolistening**—we pretend to listen even though we focus on our own thoughts and miss the speaker's message.
- **Confrontational listening**—we listen carefully for flaws in a message to refute them or attack the speaker in response.
- **Literal listening**—we listen to messages on the content level and ignore messages on the relationship level (i.e., messages that characterize our relationship with the speaker in terms of affection, respect, and control). Literal listening also occurs when we overlook nonverbal communication and the emotional tone of a message. For example, when we happily reply, "Good to hear it!" after someone sighs and hesitantly says, "I feel OK," we respond on the basis of literal listening.

Many of us are poor listeners because we haven't been taught about the listening process and don't know that we have the ability to improve how we listen. We also may not have been taught how to respond to others after listening to them speak. Before we specifically discuss the listening process and how we can improve our listening and responding ability, we will first review why it's important to study listening and confirming responses.

Why It's Important to Study Listening and Confirming Responses

What can we do to help people cope with their problems? Is there a way we can communicate with others that will facilitate their recovery from disease? How can we contribute to a stable marriage and relational satisfaction? The answer to these questions is the same: listening and confirming responses can help others and enhance our relationships. Learning about the positive outcomes that result from listening and responding with confirmation can increase our motivation to communicate in a competent manner.

Why is it important to study listening and confirming responses?

Speakers feel acknowledged, honored, and validated when we listen with care and attention. This happens when we are fully emotionally present with others, withhold judgment, and avoid distractions.[5] Similarly, confirming responses help others cope more successfully with problems, manage upset feelings, and maintain both a positive sense of self and a positive outlook on life.[6] Confirming responses have also been correlated with and, in some cases, found to directly result in improved resistance to and recovery from disease and infection, enhanced psychological adjustment, and reduced mortality.[7]

Researchers have discovered that husbands who listen to their wives tend to have happy and stable marriages, whereas husbands who fail to listen to their wives may find themselves headed for divorce. Conflicts that involve various family members can also be resolved with effective listening.[8] In addition, confirming responses are related to relational satisfaction.[9] In all, listening and confirming responses are relationally significant because they signal commitment, compassion, interest, and even love.

KNOWLEDGE ON THE CUTTING EDGE

Listening, Confirming Responses, and Civility: Are You a Civil Communicator?

Do you "listen with your mouth rather than with your ears"? That is, do you listen only for flaws in an opponent's argument so that you can refute them? Sometimes we listen without respect for others because we are certain they are wrong. This type of listening, "confrontational listening," is uncivil.

Confrontational listening communicates that others are not worthy of our respect. On the other hand, civil listening requires that we keep an open mind and that we treat others as equals even if we dislike their opinions. Civil listening isn't easy because we must acknowledge the possibility that others may be right and that we may be wrong. However, if we expect others to listen civilly to us and give us an opportunity to persuade them to our way of thinking, we must first listen civilly to them and give them an opportunity to convert us to their way of thinking. Civil listening is also time-consuming. Recall from Chapter 1 that the rapid pace of modern life contributes to rampant incivility in our society. It may be that people who already think they are too busy won't spare the time to engage in civil listening. However, we may find that others will patiently listen to us in return if we attempt the difficult process of listening civilly to others.[10]

We can improve our ability to engage in civil listening by:[11]

- Planning our listening—we can make a conscious effort to make listening our goal instead of refutation.
- Demonstrating that we are listening—we can take the task of listening seriously by engaging in nonverbal immediacy behaviors, such as providing eye contact and nodding, and verbal behaviors such as "prompting" ("uh-huh," "go on," "I see").
- Becoming fully involved with a speaker—we can engage in active listening and respond with confirmation.

Stages in the Listening Process

"You're not hearing me!" How often have you been the target of this accusation? People often say this to communicate the perception that their conversation partner is not listening to them. Hearing is involved in the receiving stage of the listening process when we attend to auditory stimuli in our environment. However, hearing is not the same thing as listening because listening includes the interpretation of stimuli, the second stage in the listening process. Listening also includes responding, the third stage in the listening process. These stages are illustrated in Figure 8.2, "Stages in the Listening Process."

What are the stages in the listening process?

Stage One: Receiving Verbal and/or Nonverbal Messages

Receiving involves selecting verbal or nonverbal stimuli from the environment and attending to the stimuli. Sometimes receiving messages involves hearing; at other times, we receive

Figure 8.2: Stages in the Listening Process

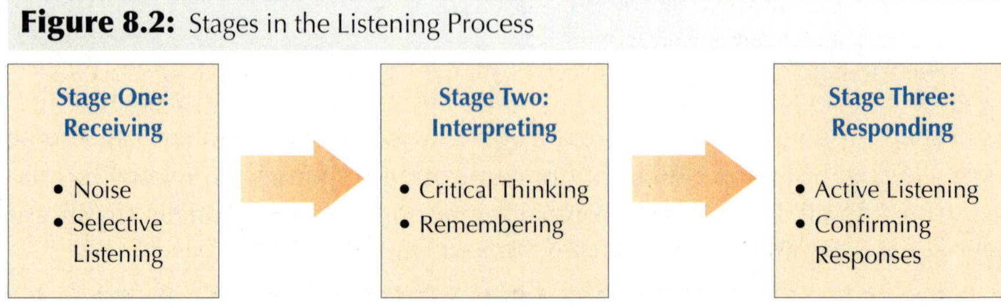

messages through the visual channel. Various obstacles can make it difficult to receive stimuli from the environment and listen to others. These obstacles include:

- Message overload—the overwhelming number of messages we encounter each day makes it difficult to engage in effective listening all of the time.
- Preoccupation—we're often too wrapped up in our own thoughts to receive messages and listen effectively.
- Message complexity—messages that are complicated (e.g., include jargon, foreign words, slang, and technical data) often make it difficult to listen, and we may tune out as a result.

Additional obstacles to effective listening include noise and selectivity.

Noise Recall from Chapter 1 that noise is anything that can interfere with the listening process. For example, if we are attempting to listen to a significant other while watching our favorite television program, the physical noise of the program will interfere with our ability to be fully attentive to the speaker (and we will probably miss portions of the television show). In addition, semantic noise might interfere with our ability to listen. If a stranger walks up to us and says, "Yo, dude!" or "Hey, girl!" as a conversation starter, we may focus on our intrapersonal communication (e.g., "What a jerk!") if we dislike such forms of address. Psychological noise such as feeling tired, hungry, or preoccupied with another matter can also interfere with the listening process. Moreover, our very physiology creates noise that interferes with the listening process. People can understand extremely rapid speech, up to 600 words per minute. Because most people speak at about 100 to 150 words per minute,[12] however, we can concentrate on our own thoughts while someone is speaking. Our attention wanders, and we may stop listening to what someone says.

Selective Listening Another problem related to receiving verbal and nonverbal stimuli is **selective listening**, which occurs when we attend to some parts of a message and ignore others. It's not possible to select and attend to all stimuli from the environment;

KNOWLEDGE ON THE CUTTING EDGE

Do Deaf People Listen?

N.B.: Deaf with a capital "D" indicates membership in Deaf culture

Deaf people do listen—with their eyes! As much as a hearing person listens to spoken language, a Deaf person's eyes listen to a visual language. American Sign Language or ASL is a visual-spatial language that uses non-manual markers (or NMMs): facial features that convey meaning and grammatical information. Facial grammar is not the same as facial expression. Facial expressions convey emotional affect, while non-manual markers convey specific and restricted grammatical information. For example, the mouth area and various mouth movements convey adjectival and adverbial information while the eyebrows, eyes, and head convey information about the type of sentence (e.g., declarative, interrogative, etc.). All of the nuance of sound, pitch, timbre, volume, affect, emotion and more can be conveyed with ASL and/or any other visual language on the planet. ASL is not a universal gestural language; it is not mime, gestures, or the game of charades that you may have played as a child. ASL is the rich, complex language of Deaf Culture that uses neutral space, a 3-dimensional area in front of the body, to establish and refer back to subjects. ASL conversations take place within the confines of this signing space and it is in this space that Deaf people listen.

© 2007 by Helene Cohen-Gilbert. Helene Cohen-Gilbert is a native ASL signer who holds RID CSC certification and a Texas BEI Level V certification and is court certified in the state of Texas. Gilbert is also the founder of Hand-in-Hand, an ASL interpreter education consulting firm (http://handinhandtexas.com/index.html). This essay is printed with permission from the author.

KNOWLEDGE power • "Where's That Noise Coming From?"

Pause for a moment and assess the noise around you that you must contend with. What auditory or visual stimuli in your environment can interfere with your ability to listen? What physiological sensations or internal messages may be hindering your ability to listen? Think about what you can do to reduce the influence of noise on your ability to listen effectively.

our fast-paced and technologically oriented society causes us to be bombarded with information. Therefore, as illustrated in the "Cathy" comic, we sometimes fail to perceive parts of messages that don't interest us, make us uncomfortable, or conflict with our opinions. We may also isolate parts of messages that are of interest to us, that make us happy, or with which we agree. For example, do you know someone who was told, "Let's still be friends" while at the receiving end of a breakup message? Perhaps this friend, still in love with a relational partner, sublimated the "I don't think we should see each other anymore" part of the message and happily concluded that the relationship had a chance of survival because the partner wanted to stay friends.

Improving Our Ability to Receive Verbal and/or Nonverbal Messages

We can improve our ability to receive messages by reducing or eliminating distractions, refraining from making judgments before hearing someone out, and recognizing our propensity to engage in selective listening. For example, we can mentally prepare ourselves to listen by blocking distracting thoughts that might interfere with the listening process. We may want to engage in self-talk to tell ourselves that we must give the speaker our full attention (we can return to our thoughts once the conversation ends). We can also catch ourselves thinking, "I know what she or he's going to say" or "What a stupid comment!"

Selective listening occurs when we attend to some parts of a message—such as those that make us happy and are of interest to us—and ignore the rest.

Even if we consider ourselves to be experts about a topic, there is always the possibility that we will learn something new when someone speaks. We can acknowledge as well that we may often miss parts of a message. We can counteract the tendency to selectively listen by planning to respond with a paraphrase of what we believe the speaker means, as discussed in the section on messages that reflect confirming responses.

Stage Two: Interpreting Verbal and/or Nonverbal Messages

Interpreting verbal and/or nonverbal messages concerns attaching meaning to the messages we listen to. Our ability to interpret messages is influenced by our ability to engage in critical thinking and by how well we can remember messages.

Critical Thinking **Critical thinking** refers to activities involved in analyzing and evaluating messages. To successfully analyze a message, we must suspend or at least delay judgment before we form an opinion. Recall the last time you listened to some negative gossip. Did you immediately believe that the message was truthful? Did you attempt to separate fact from inference, assess the source(s) of the information, and/or focus on the form of reasoning to evaluate the story? We should critically analyze the messages we listen to before we accept their validity.

Remembering Research illustrates that there are various types of memory and that we use memory in different ways when we listen. Short-term listening is more closely associated with interpersonal skills in a variety of contexts, such as making positive impressions in job interviews. Specifically, respondents with good short-term memory ask more questions during an interview than those with poor short-term memory, and they tend to be perceived as having excellent listening skills.[13]

Improving Our Ability to Interpret Verbal and/or Nonverbal Messages

We can engage in critical thinking skills and use techniques to improve our short-term memory in order to enhance our ability to interpret the messages we listen to. Specifically, we can use our critical thinking skills to separate fact from inference, assess evidence in terms of sources, and focus on the form of reasoning. Suppose a classmate says, "My big brother took our professor's class, and he said that our prof dates students. I saw our instructor leave a restaurant with a good-looking student just the other day! But I guess all instructors try to date their students." Instead of immediately accepting the validity of this information, we should:

- Separate fact from inference. Recall from Chapter 2 that a fact is independently verifiable and an inference is an interpretation and/or evaluation of a fact. We can identify as a fact that a professor left a restaurant with someone but can't say with certainty that the other person is a student, even if the person carried a backpack and/or wore a sweatshirt sporting the name of a university. More important, even if a professor and student leave a restaurant together, it doesn't mean they're involved in a romantic relationship.
- Assess the source(s) of the information. The classmate contends that her or his brother knows that the professor has relationships with students. We have no reason to believe that the brother is a credible source.

- Focus on the form of reasoning. The classmate suggests that all instructors date their students based on the unproven assertion that one professor dates students. This is an error in induction, that is, making a general conclusion based on a limited number of specific instances (in this case, a single instance that fails to separate fact from inference).

In addition to engaging in critical thinking, we can also use a memory improvement technique that lasts a mere five seconds and can help us remember people's names. Have you ever attended a party, met someone new, and realized once your conversation ended that you had forgotten her or his name? This often occurs because we're too busy thinking about what we're going to say next and/or what others may be thinking about us. However, remembering names validates our conversational partner(s). The five-second strategy for remembering names involves five steps:[14]

1. (00:01) Focusing on the moment of introduction—refrain from rehearsing what we plan to say or worrying about the impression we'll make.
2. (00:02) Listening for the name—listen for every letter in the person's name, especially the first initial.
3. (00:03) Repeating the name aloud and visualizing the name—repeat the name to make sure we get it right, and then imagine the first initial etched on the person's forehead. A visual image can help us remember someone's name.
4. (00:04) Thinking of someone we know with the same name—this once again creates a visual image to help us remember the person's name.
5. (00:05) Using the name during and at the end of the conversation—this will personalize the conversation and reinforce our memory.

Stage Three: Responding to Verbal and/or Nonverbal Messages

Active listening involves verbal and nonverbal responses to others that let them know we are paying attention and taking responsibility for understanding their meanings. At its most basic, active listening requires us to be attentive to others and to expend mental and emotional energy to understand and respond in an effective and appropriate

MOTIVATION & mindwork • "I'm Sorry; What Was Your Name Again?"

Look around the room before class begins and approach five people you do not know. Individually tell these students that you are practicing your ability to remember names by using the technique in your textbook. As an alternative, you can form a small group of students you haven't met and use five to ten minutes of class time to practice your ability to remember others' names. Engage in a brief conversation with each person, and mentally use the five-second strategy to remember their names. Try to locate the five individuals after class ends, and attempt to remember their names. Assess whether the five-second strategy helped you remember the names of others.

KNOWLEDGE power • Your Daily Listening Habits

Do you typically rate yourself as an effective, average, or ineffective listener? Choose three situations in which you played the role of listener during the past twenty-four hours. Did you allow noise or selectivity to hamper your ability to receive messages? Did you engage in critical thinking and attempt to remember the communication from others as you interpreted messages? Did you engage in active listening when you responded? After deciding on your typical listening habits and rating yourself as effective, average, or ineffective, talk to the individuals involved in your three listening situations to obtain their feedback about your listening ability. You may be surprised at what you "hear"!

manner. Many people don't realize that effective active listening requires time and effort. On the other hand, **passive listening** is practiced by those who believe that it's a speaker's responsibility to ensure that the listener understands. Passive listeners tend to equate hearing with listening and assume all they must do is, like sponges, soak up communication directed toward them. Because passive listeners merely absorb information, they believe that any misunderstanding is the fault of the speaker. Clearly, this is far from the truth.

Improving Our Ability to Respond to Verbal and/or Nonverbal Messages with Active Listening

We can improve our ability to engage in active listening by learning about and communicating confirming responses. **Confirming responses** can be defined as verbal and nonverbal behaviors that validate others with expressions of affection, respect, and concern. Increasing our repertoire of confirming responses enables us to strategically choose the most effective and appropriate comments as they relate to the other person, the other person's communication, ourselves, and the situation. **Brant R. Burleson**, a communication scholar who has conducted extensive research in the area of support and confirming messages, has discovered that people who make use of a variety of response styles are perceived as sensitive, concerned, and involved.[15]

Types of Confirming Responses

Consider a situation in which a speaker discloses a problem and a listener fails to respond. It's not that the listener doesn't want to respond; the problem is that she or he doesn't know how to react. Perhaps you've been in a similar situation. As a speaker, how might you feel when you don't receive a response from the person who is listening to you? As a listener, how might you feel when you can't think of something to say? Responding, the last component of the listening process, communicates our attention and interest in a speaker and our own reactions to what we listen to. We can respond to others with various types of confirming responses, specifically, prompting and questioning, reassuring and expressing concern, analyzing and advising, judging (criticizing constructively), and paraphrasing thoughts and feelings. These responses communicate our attentiveness and interest. In

How can the use of confirming responses improve our communication competence?

addition, we can respond with **supportive communication**, a type of confirming response that is recognized within a culture as intending to convey assistance.[16]

Prompting and Questioning

"Go on." "I'm listening." "What happened next?" These comments are examples of prompting and questioning, skills that invite conversation partners to continue speaking and offer additional information. These skills reflect active listening because they let others know we are paying attention and taking responsibility for understanding their meanings.

Prompting **Prompts** include silence, sounds, or words that let a speaker know that we not only are listening but also desire the speaker to continue. Prompts can be placed on a continuum that ranges from complete silence to vocalizations such as "Mmm" and "uh-huh" to words ("yeah") and complete sentences ("I see" and "Go on"). One problem with prompting is that prompts may be communicated in an insincere manner and can mask the fact that a listener isn't paying attention. For example, maybe you've been involved in a phone conversation during which you hear your listener respond with "Mmm" and "uh-huh" but you also hear the clicking and clacking of a computer keyboard in use. Defensiveness is a common result of such an experience because the listener disconfirms us by suggesting that what we have to say is not as important as using the computer. Therefore, it is best to give a speaker our full attention and to use prompts in conjunction with other types of confirming responses.

Questioning Asking questions enables us to obtain additional information and/or guide a speaker to a certain conclusion that we have in mind. Chapter 7 showed that open-ended questions encourage others to respond at length and include detail and that closed-ended questions usually point to a yes or no answer. Both types of questions can communicate confirmation because they illustrate that we are involved in a conversation and are interested in what a person has to say.

There are a number of suggestions and caveats to consider in questioning others. We should probably avoid asking too many questions at one time, which can send a speaker on a wild goose chase; both the speaker and listener can lose sight of the real topic. Too many questions may also lead a speaker to believe that she or he is being given the "third degree." We should also avoid questions that communicate criticism and/or reflect a hidden agenda or underlying motive. Leading and loaded questions are especially problematic. A **leading question** is a type of closed-ended question that suggests the "correct" answer and/or attempts to guide a respondent's answer. Leading questions also communicate judgment and criticism. "You mean you *finally* broke up with her or him?" is an example of a leading question. Rather than seeking to clarify or support, this question suggests that the breakup should have occurred long ago. A **loaded question** is a type of closed-ended question that typically provides only two alternatives and presupposes something that has not been proven or accepted. For example, "Do you want to go out with that person or me?" is a loaded question because there may be other alternatives (you may want to go out with someone else or no one at all). This question also presupposes that you want to go out with either person when this actually may not be true. Leading and loaded questions may be unethical and can result in a defensive conversation partner who believes she or he is the target of manipulation.

KNOWLEDGE ON THE CUTTING EDGE

Technology Update: The Internet and Supportive Communication

Do you sometimes go online to seek and express support? If so, what do you communicate? The two most common types of communication in online support groups are statements of empathic understanding and statements of self-disclosure in which users share their experiences about a condition and/or a problem. People are attracted to online support groups because of anonymity; we tend to disclose more about our problems online than face-to face (ftf) because we may believe that we aren't as readily judged. Online support seekers also use the Internet to find others who share their problems and concerns and perceive these support networks as valuable. The attraction of online support is particularly significant for people who contend with uncommon problems and may not be able to locate and associate with any ftf support groups in their vicinity.

Computer-mediated comfort and support is additionally expressed via email messages, social networking sites, and online memorials. Unlike the anonymity in online support groups, most people use email to maintain ties with friends and family. One study that researched college students' authentic supportive emails (rather than self-reported descriptions of email messages) found that messages are primarily sent by family members, friends, and romantic partners. The problems addressed in emails include deaths of loved ones, loneliness, romantic difficulties, physical illness, problems with friends and roommates, and academic challenges. Both women and men send email messages that include advice and concern for a recipient's emotional state. However, women tend to be more satisfied with the use of email as a medium for social support than are men.

Social networking and online memorial sites also provide us with an opportunity to share condolences and support those in mourning. For example, college students turned to social networking sites for solace in the aftermath of the 2007 tragedy at Virginia Tech in which thirty-three people were killed by a lone gunman. The "Hokies Nation" Virginia Tech site on MySpace was inundated with condolences and virtual sympathy cards, and more than 500 groups were created by people from around the world on the Facebook social networking site. One group, "A Tribute to Those Who Passed at the Virginia Tech Shooting," included more than 87,000 members less than one day after the tragedy and was created for those who wanted to pay respect to the victims and others who were affected by the killings.[17] Sites devoted to online memorials, such as www.911digitalarchive.org, www.aidsquilt.org, and www.legacy.com, also allow strangers and friends alike to offer their support and share the loss of those who have died. John Bikus, the head of marketing at Legacy.com, says his site contributes to community building by enabling people to communicate with families of the deceased.[18] "Online memorials thus have the potential to function both as a monument, albeit an electronic one rather than one of granite or marble, and as a wake, a gathering to commemorate and to comfort through acts of communication."[19]

Reassuring and Expressing Concern

"I'm worried about you but I'm sure you'll be OK." "I've been in a similar situation so I know what you're going through." These comments are expressions of concern and reassurance. Reassurance and responses that express concern communicate that we care about our conversation partner, sympathize with a speaker, and/or empathize with her or his feelings. We can express our concern by suggesting that we understand a conversation partner's thoughts and feelings because we have been in a similar situation. This type of response is called **relational feedback.** It is a brief description of a situation that parallels the speaker's and points to a connection between the speaker's experience and our own.[20] We can also express concern and reassurance by empathizing with a speaker. **Empathy** occurs when we not only attempt to understand the thoughts and feelings of others but also vicariously experience the emotions of others.[21] Empathy isn't the same as sympathy. **Sympathy** refers to feeling sorrow *for* another person rather than feeling *with* that person. For example, suppose a friend tearfully tells us that a beloved pet has been put to sleep. We can attempt to empathize with our friend by imagining ourselves dealing with the death of our own four-legged companion. We can also imagine that we are the friend who is contending with the loss of a particular beloved animal. Engaging in perspective taking can help us empathize with others. We can also improve our ability to empathize by observing a speaker's nonverbal behavior for insight into how the speaker may be feeling.

Unfortunately, our messages may not be perceived as helpful, even if we communicate concern and reassurance in a manner that confirms others. For example, steering a conversation away from a speaker's problems to a lengthy description of our own experience in a similar situation will not be perceived as helpful. For this reason our comments about our personal experience should be brief when we engage in relational feedback. Additional problems associated with the expression of concern and reassurance include the perception of a lack of interest or understanding on the part of a listener. Perhaps you've expressed a problem and felt the listener was not truly interested when she or he responded with "I know you can handle this" or "Oh, you'll be all right." Similarly, overusing reassurance may mistakenly communicate that we believe that a speaker should not feel as she or he does. Expressions of concern and reassurance are best used in conjunction with other types of confirming responses.

Analyzing and Advising

"I think the real reason you're angry is because you waited until the last minute to begin your research paper. You may want to get started right away when you receive your next assignment." These sentences illustrate analyzing and advising. Analyzing and advising are confirming responses that should be communicated with caution. Our analysis of a problem may be incorrect, and our advice may worsen a situation. Therefore, it's important to consider some guidelines for their use.

Analyzing **Analyzing** is another term for "interpreting" or "reframing." When analyzing another's comments, we may attempt to inform a speaker about how she or he may really feel about a situation, share a different perspective of what a problem means, and/or communicate a psychological insight. For example, suppose a friend meets a good-looking stranger at a party and gives this person her or his phone number. After three days without a call, the despondent friend suggests that the person "was just being polite" and "isn't really interested." We can analyze the situation by putting a new spin on it; specifically, we can suggest that the good-looking someone really wants to call but is too shy, lost the friend's phone number, has been exceptionally busy, or wants to play hard to get. Problems associated with analyzing another's situation include being perceived as a know-it-all, especially if we preface our analysis with comments such as "I know what your real problem is . . ." or "The reason you are upset is . . ." It's not unusual to have a negative reaction when someone suggests that she or he knows more about us than we do. With this in mind, suggestions for offering analysis include:

- asking the speaker if she or he is willing to listen to some alternative explanations about a problematic situation
- suggesting our explanations in a tentative manner (we can use the skill of "indexing" from Chapter 5)
- making sure that our explanations are plausible

Advising Giving **advice** to others means suggesting a solution. Offering advice is probably our most common response when someone comes to us with a problem. However, too many people are in a rush to tell others how to solve their troubles without attempting to first truly understand them.[22] Unwanted consequences associated with offering advice include the possibility that a problem-holder may become defensive because the advice-giver is perceived to be in a "one-up" position and the advice may threaten a problem-holder's face. Another drawback is that advice can backfire. Can you think of any situations in which you were offered advice, you followed the advice, and the situation was made worse? Have you ever given advice and then were blamed when the result was not what was expected? To counteract these potential problems, we may want to consider the following suggestions for offering advice:

- Let the speaker ask for advice before we offer it. If we believe strongly in our solution yet the speaker doesn't request advice, we should ask if the speaker is willing to listen to our suggestions.
- Provide ourselves with an out if the advice doesn't work as expected. We can accomplish this by offering the advice in a tentative manner (which will also reduce the possibility of defensiveness because it communicates that we don't have a corner on the truth). We can preface our advice with "This worked for me, but there's no guarantee that it will work for you" or "I'm not saying that this solution will always work, but it's something you might want to think about."
- Be willing to read between the lines if our advice is rejected. If we find our partner saying, "Yes, but . . ." to each of our suggestions, we should try not to take these responses as a personal rejection of our ability to help solve a problem. Instead, consider that although our conversation partner asked for or accepted our invitation to listen to advice, she or he may be better helped by listening to our statements of concern and reassurance.

Judging (Criticizing Constructively)

"Thanks for putting all the dishes in the dishwasher; you did a great job of fitting everything in. However, you didn't scrape off the plates, and this can create a problem because the food may stick even after the wash. Next time, how about scraping the food off the dishes before loading them?" These sentences illustrate the communication of an evaluation in the form of constructive criticism. We communicate an evaluation when we judge behaviors or others; that is, we suggest that something is good or bad, favorable or unfavorable, or right or wrong. Another name for judgment that is designed to confirm others is **constructive criticism**. "Criticism" is such a tainted word that even the thought of receiving constructive criticism can cause defensiveness. However, constructive criticism can call attention to problems, encourage growth, and promote learning.[23] One method for the communication of constructive criticism involves four steps:

1. Describe the other person's behavior with specific and detailed examples. For example, suppose we agree to teach a teenager how to drive. On one of our outings, we notice that the teen slows down and coasts through a number of stop signs. We can begin our constructive criticism message by saying, "I've noticed that you haven't come to a complete stop at the last three stop signs." Because this is a description based on observation, the driver is not likely to become defensive.
2. Preface a "negative" with a "positive" whenever possible. Be sure that the praise is realistic and not seen as a superficial technique for softening the blow. Before offering an evaluation in the case of the teenage driver, we can say, "You're doing a great job driving, and you're really making progress."
3. We can own our thoughts and feelings to communicate that it is our evaluation that we are expressing and not the "absolute truth." We can also suggest our evaluation in

a tentative manner by indexing our comments and using qualifiers. For example, we can tell the teenage driver, "I think coasting through a stop sign is a bad move because you can get a ticket and, even worse, hit another car."

4. Because constructive criticism focuses on behavior instead of attacking a person, it is appropriate to suggest a behavioral change. We can consequently tell the teenage driver, "Be sure you come to a complete stop the next time you come to a stop sign."

Even though our constructive criticism may be designed to confirm another person, our conversation partner may become defensive as we begin to describe our viewpoints or behaviors that we believe should be altered. Therefore, we may want to let the speaker ask for constructive criticism or ask the speaker if he or she is willing to listen to our evaluation. We should also refrain from saying, "I told you so!" or "I'm only saying this for your own good!" because these comments put us in a one-up position that can result in defensiveness.

Paraphrasing Thoughts and Feelings

"It seems to me that you may be reacting to more than just one situation and you're feeling confused. Am I right?" These sentences illustrate a paraphrase. A **paraphrase** rewords a speaker's message in terms of our understanding of its meaning. Paraphrasing does not entail parroting back a speaker's entire message but instead requires us to interpret the meaning of a speaker's message and to communicate that meaning in our own words. Because we can never be certain of what a speaker means or how a speaker feels, paraphrasing is a way to check whether we have correctly understood a speaker's message. Even if a speaker informs us that our paraphrase is incorrect, she or he has learned that we are listening attentively and will feel validated because we are sincerely trying to understand

SKILL practice • Communicating Constructive Criticism

Imagine yourself in the following situations, and with a partner or in a small group, engage in constructive criticism. Ask your partner or a member of the group to give you an oral critique about the effectiveness and appropriateness of your constructive criticism.

- You believe that your significant other has been taking you for granted. She or he rarely compliments you, forgets to phone, and has stopped asking you for your opinion. Constructively criticize your significant other.
- Your coworker has just finished writing a project report and is prepared to give it to the boss. The coworker appears to be very proud of the report and implies that she or he may be promoted because of it. She or he asks you for your opinion before giving it to the boss. You think the report is terrible! Constructively criticize your coworker.
- Your best friend comes over and, once again, tells you about her or his troubled love life. You have secretly always thought that your friend goes after the wrong type of people, even though she or he knows better. Constructively criticize your friend.
- You asked your roommate to clean up the apartment, and she or he agreed. When you return from work, your roommate meets you at the door with a smile on his or her face, obviously proud of the work she or he's done. Upon closer inspection, you realize that the apartment is still filthy. Constructively criticize your roommate.

her or his thoughts and/or feelings. Moreover, responding with a paraphrase eliminates the need for us to immediately offer advice after listening to a problem-holder, and it respects others' ability to solve their own problems. All told, paraphrasing includes:

- Rephrasing a speaker's comments to communicate our understanding of what the speaker means
- Communicating the paraphrase in a tentative manner so we don't appear to have a corner on the truth or that we know what a speaker means or feels better than she or he does
- Asking for feedback or ending a paraphrase with a rising inflection to obtain speaker feedback about the clarity of our understanding
- Delivering the paraphrase in a nonjudgmental manner, meaning we avoid words that are evaluative (e.g., *good, bad, right, wrong*) and nonverbal behaviors that communicate that we disapprove of the speaker and/or speaker's comments (e.g., shaking our head back and forth, rolling our eyes)

In general, there are two types of paraphrases: one that focuses on the literal content and one that focuses on a speaker's feelings, even if the feelings aren't expressed verbally. It is likely that we'll use both types of paraphrasing in attempting to understand another's thoughts and feelings.

Paraphrasing for Content A **content paraphrase** can be used when we have listened to a lot of information, we have been given complex directions and/or instructions, and when the information is technical and laden with unfamiliar jargon. Content paraphrases can additionally be used to ascertain the relational level of meaning, to comprehend other meanings that may not be communicated in an overt manner, and to buy time to allow ourselves to calm down in a heated discussion or argument. For example, suppose we are listening to someone tell us a story about trying to get into a class that had already reached the maximum enrollment. The speaker describes how the uncooperative advisor insisted that she or he take a night class that had not yet filled. We can respond to the speaker by focusing on the relational level of meaning by saying something like "It sounds like the advisor was trying to control you" or "I hear you saying that the advisor didn't respect you or what you wanted." We can also suggest a meaning that the speaker had not communicated in an overt manner, such as "It seems to me that the advisor wasn't fair; is that what you're thinking?" We can also use a content paraphrase during a heated discussion. Paraphrasing can slow down a conversation because it forces us to think about how to respond before we actually do so. Specifically, paraphrasing will validate a conversation partner because we tentatively summarize the meaning of her or his communication in our own words and check to see if our interpretation is correct *before* we respond with our own viewpoints.

Paraphrasing respects the ability of others to solve their own problems.

Paraphrasing for Feelings **Feelings paraphrasing** requires us to monitor a speaker's nonverbal communication for clues about what the speaker may be feeling. If we were to use a feeling paraphrase to respond to the speaker who wasn't allowed to enroll in a class, we could say, "You sound real frustrated and upset, am I right?" It may be tempting to react to this example of a paraphrase with the idea

SKILL practice • Paraphrasing Thoughts and Feelings

Practice your ability to paraphrase thoughts and feelings by responding to the following statements:

- "My girlfriend/boyfriend promises to call and then doesn't. I become so angry, but then I get so many apologies and excuses that I give her or him another chance. This has been going on for at least a month, and it's pretty confusing."
- "My boss gave me three reports to read and edit over the next five days. Three reports in five days! Have you ever been so busy with work that you had to read reports while going to the bathroom?"
- "He played his music so loud that my walls reverberated every night. Finally I called him at 3 A.M. and gave him a piece of my mind. Then he made it worse by blasting opera all morning. I think I got around three hours of sleep last night."
- "My mom and I got into this really big fight the last time I went home. I think she still sees me as a baby and someone she can boss around. I told her that I can make my own decisions, but she wouldn't shut up. Finally I told her to mind her own business, and I stormed out of the house. I want to tell her I'm sorry, but she needs to apologize too."

that it overstates the obvious. However, paraphrasing for feelings communicates that we validate another person's emotions. Paraphrasing for feelings works especially well when emotions run high. Recall from Chapter 4 that people can't think rationally when they experience intense emotions. Once people are allowed to express intense emotions and feel that their emotions are acknowledged, respected, and understood, they are able to calm down and respond in a rational manner. In conjunction with other types of confirming communication, paraphrasing for feelings is a powerful way to demonstrate that we validate others, their thoughts, and their feelings.

It's important to be realistic about the effective and appropriate use of skills and guidelines associated with listening and confirming responses. Remember that engaging in a content paraphrase with a more powerful or irrational conversation partner may not lead to a desired result. For example, "Don't put words in my mouth!" might be the angry response to our communication of a content paraphrase. Silence may be best in situations such as these because nothing we can say or do will convince an irrational partner of our confirming motivation. Remember that flexibility and strategy are integral to competent communication. Knowing that communication skills won't always "work" can help us plan for and anticipate situations that would otherwise be unexpected.

Contexts, Listening, and Confirming Responses

How do contexts influence listening and confirming responses?

Is confirming communication perceived similarly across cultures? Are listening and confirming responses just as important among coworkers as they are among family and friends? Do women and men listen and offer support in a similar manner? How can we best ask for support? These questions will be answered in terms of the contexts that affect listening and confirming communication, that is, culture, relationship, gender, and individual contexts.

Competence & Critical Thinking

mycommunicationlab

JUGGLING ACT (UNABRIDGED) AND LISTENING AND CONFIRMING RESPONSES

Vicky is a new mom, an employee, and a college student. She calls some friends to see if they can babysit so she can go to work. Vicky arrives at her apartment and finds her friend Val tidying her kitchen. Much to Vicky's relief, Val can babysit, but Vicky is feeling overwhelmed and she tells Val about her problems.

You can view *Juggling Act* (unabridged) by accessing the "Small Group and Interpersonal Videos" on the MyCommunicationLab Web site. Answer the following questions about the confirming responses included in the video *(you can click on the maximize icon to eliminate the material in the "notes" section and enlarge the picture)*:

- What types of confirming responses are illustrated in the video?
- Are the confirming responses communicated in an effective and appropriate manner?
- Could Val have used other types of confirming responses in this conversation? Explain.

VICKY: *(Vicky calls some friends on her cell phone)* Hey, Christina, it's Vicky. I'm in a jam. I need a babysitter for tonight. My babysitter can't stay. I have to go to work. And I need somebody to watch D.J. Could you please give me a call back on my cell phone or at work? Thanks, bye. . . . Hey, Tony. It's Vicky. I'm in a jam. I need a babysitter for tonight. I have to go work, and I need somebody to watch D.J. Please give me a phone call back, either on my cell phone or at work, it really doesn't matter. Thanks, bye. *(Vicky arrives at her apartment)* Hey, Val.

VAL: Hi.

VICKY: Thanks for coming by.

VAL: Not a problem.

VICKY: I know it's just moving on; to cancel all your plans.

VAL: Oh, not a big deal.

VICKY: You don't have to do that.

VAL: You know how impulsive I am, OK?

VICKY: Mack was OK with you canceling on him?

VAL: Mack is fine, and I will see him tomorrow. *(Vicky crouches down and rubs her eyes)* Vicky, are you okay?

VICKY: No. I just—I can't do this anymore. It's—I go from the baby in the morning to class, and then back to work, and then back here. I just—I can't do it anymore. It's too much.

VAL: Vicky, I know it's hard, OK? But work, as far as that, it's all under control, OK? The position opened up at the office, and my boss is expecting to hear from you. I've mentioned you, and he's woman-friendly, OK, and the hours are so flexible because you'd be working from home. And, let's see, you have the Internet, and you have your laptop. OK? You can spend more time with the baby that way. So promise me you'll call him in the morning.

VICKY: All right, but what about school? I'm three weeks behind on my classes.

VAL: Right, school. I mean, did you talk to the counselor?

VICKY: I don't have time to go there.

VAL: Vicky, you have to make time for the counselor, OK? If anybody could help you right now, it's her. I mean, she's so understanding. For me?

VICKY: Oh, maybe I can go tomorrow and after class.

VAL: Look, Vicky, you are so amazing, OK? I have so much faith in you. I know you can do it, all right? And look, if you need me, I'm right here, all right?

VICKY: Thanks, Val.

VAL: You're welcome. *(they hug)*

Culture Context

The perception of appropriate and effective listening and confirming responses is affected by the culture(s) and co-culture(s) to which we belong.

Cultures The United States is said to be a low-context culture that values direct expression of thoughts and feelings. It follows that U.S. communication scholars have concentrated their research on speaking rather than listening.[24] The limited research concerning differences in cross-cultural listening suggests that cultural values influence listening and responding with confirming communication. Some research suggests that knowledge of cross-cultural listening differences can affect the ability to conduct international business. Richard Lewis, author of *When Cultures Collide: Managing across Cultures,* writes that listening is not uniform across cultures. Specifically, the French tend to listen for information, Germans typically listen for information and technical details, and people in many Arab countries tend to listen for know-how. Therefore, tailoring managerial communication in terms of the presentation of information or the presentation of procedural knowledge can facilitate business negotiations in these cultures.[25] Knowledge of such cross-cultural listening styles can enable us to adapt our communication for the most effective reception of our messages.

Co-Cultures The limited research available suggests that confirming communication is extremely important in close relationships across various co-cultures.[26] One study of Chinese American and European American college students found that members of both co-cultures rate friends' emotional support skills more highly than their friends' other communication skills.[27] A similar study discovered that Chinese American and European American married couples view emotionally supportive messages as the most important type of confirming communication in their marriages.[28]

Relationship Context

Listening and confirming communication are expected in our familial relationships and in our relationships with friends. Listening and confirming responses are also associated with organizational success.

Research suggests that gay couples receive more confirming communication from friends than from family members.

Family and Friends Attending to the informational and emotional meanings of messages, listening attentively, and communicating support are ranked among the top five features of family functioning.[29] Family members expect emotional support from each other and to share in both joys and sorrows. However, because members of extended families are increasingly inaccessible, family members create informal support systems of neighbors and friends to turn to when support is needed.[30] Communication of confirming responses and perceptions of emotional supportiveness are crucial for the development and maintenance of friendships.[31] In addition, the types of relationships in which we are involved (i.e., married relationships, heterosexual cohabiting relationships, and homosexual relationships) influence a family's willingness and ability to listen and to offer confirming responses. Research suggests that married heterosexual individuals receive more familial support than individuals in gay and lesbian relationships. Gays and lesbians perceive more confirming communication from friends than from family members. Gays and lesbians may not rely on family support in the same way as heterosexuals, who expect the family to provide support unconditionally.[32]

Coworkers Listening is critical for organizational success. Listening to customers enables organizations to receive information about their products or services and information about the competition, and it can increase sales and customer satisfaction. Managers who listen to employees demonstrate support and contribute to employee satisfaction and productivity. Listening also enhances upward mobility. In particular, the ability to listen and empathize with others is related to an employee's chances of promotion within an organization.[33] Confirming communication at work also affects job satisfaction and performance. Confirming communication, such as encouragement, reassurance, and advice, assists employees in their careers and contributes to the development of intimate relationships with coworkers that are as close as familial relationships.[34]

Gender Context

The gender context influences the listening behavior of women and men and affects how we respond when others communicate about their problems.

Listening and Communication Style Women tend to be dissatisfied with the way that men typically listen. In a study of approximately 4,500 women, 77% of the respondents reported that they weren't satisfied with their male partners' amount and kind of listening. In the same study, 69% of the respondents said that men don't listen to or ask questions about their partner's opinions or activities, and 41% of the respondents thought that men exhibit nonverbal cues that indicate they don't listen when women speak.[35] Women's dissatisfaction with how men listen may be due to differences in communication style. For example, women tend to ask more questions than men overall, and women typically communicate more prompts than men. Furthermore, women use "yeah" to indicate that they are paying attention and to encourage a speaker to continue, but men tend to use "yeah" when they agree with what a speaker says. The result is that women perceive that men don't listen to them when they speak.[36]

Troubles Talk According to sociolinguist **Deborah Tannen**, ethnographic research involving case studies suggests that when women talk about their problems, their underlying

KNOWLEDGE ON THE CUTTING EDGE

Putting It in Context: Communication, Sex, and Listening and Confirming Responses

Differences in listening behaviors and the communication of empathy have been linked to neurological differences between women and men. Researchers have found that males tend to listen with one side of the brain, whereas females listen with both sides. MRI scans demonstrate differences in the brains' temporal lobe, which is located on the side of the head between the ears and the eyes. When engaged in a listening task, the temporal lobe on the left side of males' brains is more active than the right side. However, both the left and right temporal lobes are active when females are engaged in a listening task. In addition, females have better-developed corpus callosa than men. The corpus callosum is the bundle of nerves that connects the two brain lobes, and women may be more able to cross from the right to left hemisphere because of their better-developed corpus callosa. This means that a female listener may be more distracted by competing details being processed by both sides of her brain, whereas a male listener can more easily focus and tune out distractions because he is processing information on one side of the brain. On the other hand, a female listener may be better able to juggle more than one conversation at once, and a male listener may not be able to process more than one conversation at a time.[37]

KNOWLEDGE power • "Do This" or "The Same Thing Happened to Me"?

Recall a time in the recent past when you went to a relational partner with a problem or mentioned an issue or situation that was troublesome. Consider the listening and communication style of your partner. If you are a woman in a heterosexual relationship, try to remember whether your male partner made minimal use of prompts to communicate that he was listening to you. If you are a male in a heterosexual relationship, try to remember whether your female partner asked lots of questions and said "yeah" to indicate she was listening to you. Reflect on the confirming responses you received. If you are a female, recall whether your male partner advised you how to solve your problem or troublesome situation. If you are male, recall whether your female partner described a similar difficult situation or problem with which she was once involved. If you are in a same-sex relationship, consider whether your partner's listening style best reflects the style associated with the male gender or female gender or reflects both. Overall, do you believe that your listening responses are more similar to or different from your partner's? Finally, consider whether the conclusions based on ethnographic methodology (e.g., case studies) or empirical methodology (which involves tests for statistical significance) best match your conclusions based on personal observation and reflection.

relational message requests acknowledgment and validation. Therefore, women engage in "troubles talk," or relational feedback, as a way to connect with others and to demonstrate empathy, connection, and relational concern. Tannen suggests that women become frustrated when men respond to their problems with advice and instructions. Similarly, men may become angry when women attempt to comfort them with a similar disclosure of their own. Men may perceive that women attempt to put themselves in a one-up position by minimizing the problem when women communicate a similar problem that they have experienced.[38]

Not all researchers agree with the idea that learned gender expectations significantly influence how men and women communicate confirmation and support. Empirical evidence demonstrates that gender differences in the communication of support are small in magnitude, and most gender-related studies of social behavior use research designs that assess differences but ignore similarities.[39] Overall, empirical research about the influence of gender on communication fails to support the conclusion that men and women differ significantly in their communication of and reactions to confirming messages.

Individual Context

Supportive and confirming communication has been researched mostly at the individual level of analysis. Studies have found relationships between an individual's use of comforting strategies and personality variables such as empathy, prosocial orientation, and communication apprehension.[40] However, most of the research on the individual level concerns the ability to communicate support to others, and very little has been conducted on how problem-holders can best communicate their need for support.[41]

Have you ever found yourself in a situation in which a conversation partner complained about the same problem for days, weeks, or months? If so, perhaps you became

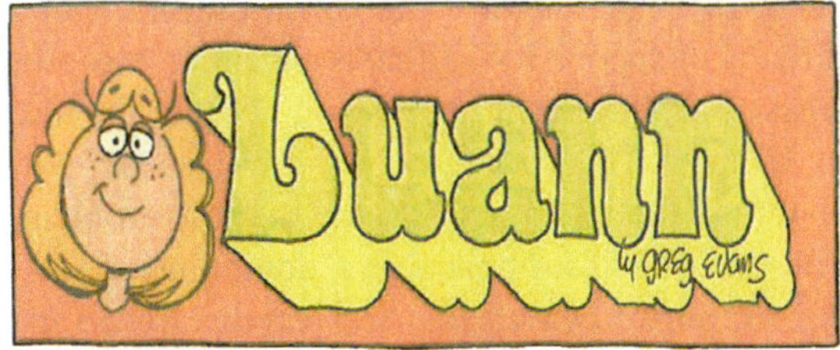

Sometimes problem-holders experience difficulty receiving the support they need.

Source: LUANN: © GEC Inc/Dist. By United Feature Syndicate, Inc.

annoyed because you perceived that little or nothing was done to solve the problem. Your conversation partner may also have become annoyed because she or he didn't receive the desired support. The way your conversation partner communicated about her or his problem and asked for support may have resulted in your failure to offer a supportive response. Sometimes problem-holders experience difficulty receiving the support they need because potential support providers feel helpless, vulnerable, uncomfortable, and confused about what to say. Problem-holders face a dilemma in that communicating their need for support can drive away potential support givers, but they won't receive the support they need if they fail to communicate their distress. In general, support seekers can communicate their distress to others in four ways:[42]

Using Positive Coping Strategies These strategies involve the disclosure of a problem and how the problem-holder is effectively coping with the problem. Saying, "I failed the test but I'm studying hard for the next one" is an example of a positive coping strategy statement. This strategy may fail to signal the need for support if a potential support giver assumes the problem-holder is coping well.

Using Poor Coping Strategies These strategies entail the expression of distress without the disclosure of attempts to cope with the problem. Saying, "I failed the test and I don't know what to do!" is an example of a poor coping strategy statement. This strategy may result in negative feelings and rejection from a potential support-giver.

Providing No Information This strategy is used when a problem-holder does not explicitly communicate her or his need for support. Support givers may be reluctant to offer assistance in the absence of information because they believe their support will be perceived as intrusive and subsequently rejected.

Using balanced coping strategies can increase the possibility that a problem-holder will receive the support he or she needs.

Using Balanced Coping Strategies These strategies involve the communication of a problem and clear messages that suggest that a distressed individual is engaging in coping efforts. Saying, "I failed the test and I'm real upset, but now I'm studying hard for the next one" is an example of a balanced coping strategy. This strategy can minimize a support provider's feelings of helplessness and therefore increase the possibility that the problem-holder will receive the support she or he needs. In all, if support givers "do not have to take full responsibility for a victim's well-being, support providers may feel less threatened and hence may be able to provide more effective assistance."[43]

OVERCOMING COMMUNICATION CHALLENGES

Face-Threatening Acts

Regardless of the intentions of a speaker, a message isn't perceived as confirming unless a listener perceives it as such. Some messages designed to communicate confirmation and support do just the opposite because they are perceived as disconfirming the listener. Such messages often are described as face-threatening acts.

Chapter 3 defined "face" as a person's desired public image. Positive face refers to an individual's need for acceptance and approval from others; negative face refers to an individual's desire for freedom and autonomy. **Face-threatening acts (FTAs)** occur when messages are perceived as challenging someone's face needs. For example, advice may challenge our face needs if we perceive it as a threat to our ability to take care of ourselves and our problems. Fortunately, "facework," or politeness strategies, can buffer the face threats that are associated with supportive messages. Supportive messages can be communicated with **positive politeness,** or strategies that boost or protect someone's esteem or self-image, and/or **negative politeness,** or strategies that confirm or protect someone's sense of independence or personal control. For example, suppose we are in a position to offer advice to a friend. We can choose to use one or more of the following five strategies that can more or less protect our friend's face:[44]

1. Making use of the "bald on record" strategy. This occurs when we offer advice to others regardless of potential face threats.
2. Offering advice but adding comments that affirm positive face needs. Before offering advice, a support giver can say, "I think you've been doing a great job handling your problem so far" as a way to address positive face needs.
3. Offering advice but adding comments that affirm negative face needs. For example, before offering advice, a support giver can attempt to soften the extent to which the advice tells a problem-holder what to do or the degree to which an individual may feel obligated to follow the advice. A support giver might say, "I don't mean to tell you what to do" or "You may want to try something like this; I can't guarantee that it will work" as ways to redress threats to negative face.
4. Committing the face-threatening act "off the record." This occurs when we share a similar experience without explicitly suggesting that a listener solve her or his problem in the same manner. This is an indirect strategy aimed at saving an advice recipient's face; however, a drawback associated with this strategy is that the problem-holder may not perceive the way we solved our similar problem as constituting advice.
5. Failing to communicate the advice. This strategy will avoid all threats to an individual's face.

Studies demonstrate that both college-age and older adults tend to perceive direct offers of assistance from support givers as being the most face-sensitive and most helpful. Advice and expressions of concern are typically perceived as somewhat more face-threatening and less helpful. Attempts to protect or bolster a problem-holder's positive face are perceived as more helpful and sensitive than messages that threaten positive face and messages that honor or threaten negative face.[45] Overall, research is mixed concerning which specific politeness strategy to use with which particular type of problem, person, and situation. However, "it is clear that regard for face, and particularly regard for positive face, is associated with the perceived helpfulness, appropriateness, and sensitivity of advice for a distressed other."[46]

A CASE STUDY IN ETHICS

Cochlear Implants

Competent communication includes an ethical dimension of well-based standards of right and wrong. We can ask ourselves a series of questions to help us choose communication strategies that are effective and appropriate as they relate to listening and confirming responses. Specifically, we can ask: Have I practiced any virtues today (e.g., have I demonstrated integrity, trustworthiness, honesty, and responsibility)? Have I done more good than harm (e.g., have I shown appreciation and gratitude to others)? Have I treated people with dignity and respect? Have I been fair and just? Have I made my community stronger because of my actions? Read this case study and consider whether implanting a deaf child with a cochlear device is an ethical way to improve her or his listening ability. (Note that "Deaf" indicates membership in Deaf culture and "deaf" indicates an auditory condition.)

Peter and Nita Artinian, both Deaf, have a young deaf daughter, Heather. Peter's hearing brother, Chris, and his hearing wife, Mari, have a deaf son. Within the extended family of both Deaf and hearing individuals, a battle rages regarding whether to surgically implant the children with a cochlear device. A cochlear implant can help deaf or hard-of-hearing individuals perceive sounds. Success cannot be guaranteed after the device is implanted underneath the skin behind the ear, and long periods of adjustment and therapy are expected after implantation. Effective recognition of sound and use of intelligible speech are not guaranteed, and a hearing aid will be ineffective because of the nerve damage that results from implantation. However, many hearing parents and doctors perceive the cochlear implant to be a modern miracle and a cure for deafness. Both sides of the cochlear debate have been argued within the Artinian family.

Peter fears that the implants will destroy Deaf culture and obliterate his culture's language, American Sign Language (ASL). His concern has been echoed by various Deaf advocates who compare the more powerful hearing culture and its support of implantation with other powerful groups that have engaged in cultural genocide and attempted to eradicate cultures by suppressing their language. Peter's mother has argued that Heather will suffer as an outsider in a hearing world, but Peter has countered that implanting Heather will cause her to miss out on the Deaf life that he embraces. Peter's argument is similar to those of other Deaf culture advocates who believe that they are not afflicted with a disability. Members of Deaf culture contend that the idea of "curing" a Deaf individual is similar to "curing" a black person by changing her or him into someone who is white. Peter has also reminded his mother that Heather changed her mind about the implant and signed, "I'm not ready to have a cochlear implant yet. I'm too afraid." However, his mother has lectured Peter that he should "forget Deaf" and that first he is a father who should do what's right for his child. Furthermore, she has asserted that the decision to implant should not be Heather's but her parents'.

Peter's hearing brother, Chris, and his hearing wife, Mari, implanted their deaf son when he was one year old. Their child can speak and has been mainstreamed into a public school. Mari's Deaf mother has described the type of hearing that implanted people experience as "robotic hearing at best." She has argued against implantation and laments that her grandson has only a rudimentary knowledge of ASL. Mari's mother is afraid that she and her husband, who is also Deaf, will lose the ability to communicate with their grandson.[47]

Is it ethical to make use of cochlear implants if the devices have the potential to eliminate a culture's language and eventually the culture itself? Is it ethical for a dominant culture to prescribe what is considered a "disability" and to "fix" persons who are considered disabled? Is it ethical to implant a child with a cochlear device against her or his wishes?

Chapter Review

Motivation: How has this helped me?

- **The importance of studying listening and confirming responses**

It's important to study listening and confirming communication because listening and responding with confirmation helps others and speakers feel acknowledged, honored, and validated when we listen with care and attention. Listening and responding with confirmation also communicates commitment, compassion, and interest.

Knowledge: What have I learned?

- **Characterizing listening and confirming responses**

Listening has been defined as a complex activity that involves the process of receiving, constructing meaning from, and responding to spoken and/or nonverbal messages. Confirming responses can be defined as verbal and nonverbal behaviors that validate others with expressions of affection, respect, and concern.

- **The stages in the listening process**

The listening process occurs in three stages: receiving, interpreting, and responding to a verbal and/or nonverbal message. Noise and selective attention can make it difficult to receive messages, critical thinking and remembering influence how we interpret messages, and active listening responses communicate that we pay attention and take responsibility for understanding the meanings of others.

- **How contexts influence listening and confirming responses**

The limited research concerning differences in cross-cultural listening suggests that cultural values and communication patterns affect listening and responding with confirming communication. The relationship context concerns the members of our social networks (friends, family, and persons with whom we work) we may turn to in times of need. In addition, ethnographic research suggests that listening styles and preferences regarding supportive communication differ because of learned gender expectations. However, empirical research fails to support this conclusion. Research at the individual level illustrates that balanced coping strategies minimize support providers' feelings of helplessness and are most likely to result in support from others.

Skill: What skills have I developed?

- **Confirming responses can improve our communication competence**

Prompting (responding with silence, sounds, or words) lets a speaker know that we are listening and desire the speaker to continue. Asking open-ended and closed-ended questions, reassuring others, and responding with concern, empathy, and relational feedback communicate that we support them and sympathize. Analyzing or interpreting another's comments (paraphrasing) communicates that we are sincerely trying to understand her or his thoughts and/or feelings. Tentatively giving advice to suggest a solution to some difficulty or problem, and offering constructive criticism about others' enables us to evalute others thoughts, feelings, and behaviors in a constructive manner.

Study Questions

1. Describe the characterization of listening and confirming responses and why their study is warranted.
2. How can noise and selective listening interfere with how we receive messages?
3. How do critical thinking and remembering influence the ability to interpret messages?
4. What is active listening?

5. What are some examples of confirming responses? Explain the various responses, provide examples, and present guidelines for their use.
6. How do the culture, relationship, gender, and individual contexts affect listening and confirming responses?
7. What are face-threatening acts, and how do they relate to confirming responses?
8. What strategies can we use to protect others' face when we offer advice?

Names to Know

Brant R. Burleson, p. 213—communication researcher who teaches at Purdue University. He studies social support and well-being; emotional support processes such as comforting, communication and emotion; and social interaction skills and their effects on personal and social outcomes.

Deborah Tannen, p. 223—well-known sociolinguist who teaches at Georgetown University and studies conversation and communication style. She has published twenty books, including the best seller *You Just Don't Understand: Men and Women in Conversation.*

Key Terms

active listening, 212
advice, 216
analyzing, 216
appreciative listening, 206
comprehensive listening, 206
confirming responses, 213
confrontational listening, 207
constructive criticism, 217
content paraphrase, 219
critical thinking, 211
defensive listening, 207
disconfirming listening, 206
empathic listening, 206
empathy, 215
evaluative listening, 206
face-threatening acts (FTAs), 226
feelings paraphrase, 219
leading questions, 214
listening, 206
literal listening, 207
loaded questions, 214
negative politeness, 206
paraphrase, 218
passive listening, 213
positive politeness, 226
prompts, 214
pseudolistening, 207
receiving, 208
relational feedback, 215
selective listening, 209
supportive communication, 214
sympathy, 215
validating communication, 205

CHAPTER 9

Disconfirming Communication and Setting Boundaries

"Nobody can make you feel inferior without your consent."

ELEANOR ROOSEVELT (1884–1962), FIRST LADY, AUTHOR, AND SOCIAL ACTIVIST

In this chapter, we will answer the following:

- It is important to study disconfirming communication and setting boundaries to avoid relational dissatisfaction and to set and maintain emotional, relational, sexual, and spiritual limits regarding what we believe is safe and appropriate.

Knowledge: What will I learn?

- How to characterize disconfirming communication and boundaries
- The difference among assertive, aggressive, and submissive communication
- How contexts influence disconfirming messages and boundary setting

Skill: Why do I need to develop these skills?

- Empathic assertion, "the broken record," and assertive metacommunication are skills we can use to establish boundaries and improve our communication competence.

Although Eleanor Roosevelt was born into a family of wealth and status, she championed the poor and disenfranchised throughout her life. While First Lady and after her husband's death, she was ridiculed in the press and criticized for her beliefs and behavior. Roosevelt responded to her detractors by stating that she'd continue to engage in social activism that reflected her beliefs. Roosevelt also suggested that she'd attract criticism no matter her endeavors but would continue to "be herself." Perhaps you know people who attract criticism yet set personal boundaries with messages that prevent or stop insults, ridicule, and/or other types of disconfirming communication. In this chapter, we will learn how to increase our motivation to interact competently with others, even when they communicate disconfirming messages. We will increase our knowledge by learning about communication climate, disconfirming communication, and boundaries; aggressive, submissive, and assertive communication; different types of disconfirming messages; and covert verbal abuse. We will also learn how to skillfully establish boundaries with assertive messages.

Introduction to Disconfirming Communication and Setting Boundaries

If you could use weather metaphors to describe your interpersonal relationships, which metaphors would you use? Would you describe one relationship as "stormy," another as "warm," and perhaps one as "calm"? These weather metaphors relate to the emotional tone of a relationship, often referred to as the **communication climate**.

How can we characterize disconfirming communication and boundaries?

Disconfirming Communication

Communication climates can be charted on a continuum from positive and confirming to negative and disconfirming, depending on the messages that characterize a relationship. **Disconfirming communication** fails to validate others and creates negative communication climates. We communicate disconfirmation when we ignore people, do not acknowledge their thoughts and feelings, and refuse to accept their opinions and emotions. Most relationships can be characterized by a mix of confirming and disconfirming communication; however, relationships characterized by conflict, hurtful messages, and defensiveness can be described as having a negative or disconfirming communication climate. Note that disconfirmation is not the same thing as disagreement. We can still validate others, even though we may not agree with their thoughts and feelings. Saying, "I disagree with your opinion, but I understand your reasons for thinking the way you do" validates a conversation partner. However, saying, "You're wrong!" or "That's a stupid thing to say" is invalidating and disconfirming. We can also disagree with yet validate others by setting a boundary that communicates our limits.

Boundaries

A **boundary** is an edge or limit that defines us as being separate from others. Emotional, relational, sexual, and spiritual boundaries let others know that we have limits to what we believe is safe and appropriate; these are pictured in Figure 9.1, "Boundaries." Specifically, emotional boundaries can prevent or stop people from insulting us. Relational boundaries refer to the roles we play that define and limit appropriate interaction. Sexual boundaries place limits on what we believe is safe and appropriate sexual behavior. Spiritual boundaries inform others that they cannot tell us that their religious beliefs are the only truth and that we can choose the correct spiritual path for ourselves. In general, a boundary is a limit that separates self from other and promotes integrity.[1]

Figure 9.1: Boundaries

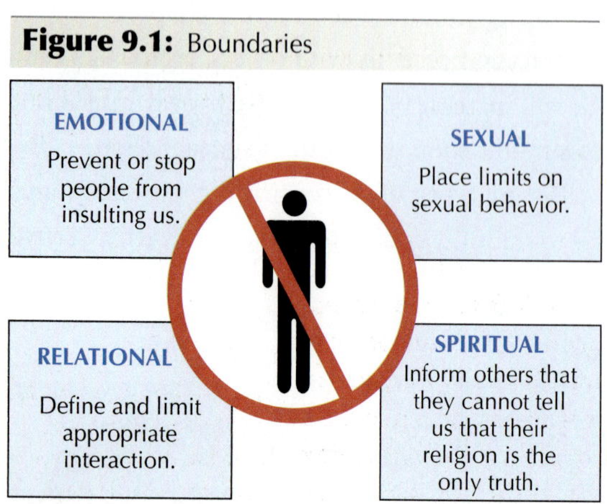

Boundaries can be flexible, and they can vary from person to person. For example, we may decide after the fact that we are uncomfortable with someone's words or actions and subsequently create a new boundary with revised standards about what constitutes acceptable communication and behavior. We may accept healthy and safe expressions of anger from people we are close to but refuse to tolerate acquaintances who displace their anger on us. Boundaries enable us to limit the actions of people who intend to hurt us yet can include people we believe to be trustworthy.[2]

Personal questions are an example of boundary violations.

Source: © BABY BLUES – BABY BLUES PARTNERSHIP, KING FEATURES SYNDICATE.

Boundary violations occur when others knowingly or unknowingly cross our emotional, relational, sexual, and spiritual limits. Such violations may be committed on the basis of malice, ignorance, or thoughtlessness, or even with the intention of kindness. Boundary violations can be illustrated in disconfirming messages such as personal questions, inappropriate touching, and communication that attempts to control how we should think and feel. We can also weaken and violate our own boundaries when we:

- Pretend to agree when we disagree
- Conceal our true feelings
- Engage in an activity that we really don't want to do (and we fail to make our opinion known or to state our preference)
- Decline to join an activity we really want to do
- Do too much for others
- Ignore our needs

Because boundary violations are potentially harmful, it is up to us to immediately protect and restore a boundary if it is violated.

Why It's Important to Study Disconfirming Communication and Setting Boundaries

Understanding why it's important to study disconfirming communication and setting boundaries can motivate us to become competent communicators. Research reveals that satisfying relationships result when partners repeatedly use confirming communication and create positive communication climates. On the other hand, negative communication climates and relational dissatisfaction result when partners repeatedly use disconfirming communication.[3] Sometimes we fail to recognize that communication directed toward us

Why is it important to study disconfirming communication and setting boundaries?

KNOWLEDGE ON THE CUTTING EDGE

Are You a Civil Communicator? Why Manners Matter

"Please." "Excuse me." "Thank you." How often do you communicate these and similar messages? A nationwide Associated Press poll suggests that the use of words and phrases associated with good manners is declining: 70% of those questioned in the poll said that people are ruder today than they were twenty years ago, and 74% of people who live in urban areas reported their own use of bad manners. Respondents also cited causes for rude behavior, such as parents who fail to teach manners to their children, the fast pace of modern life, the perception that polite behavior is "weak" and that courtesy is the same as snobbery, and the view that manners and etiquette are unreal, dishonest, and restrictive.[4] Some suggested that the decline in manners results from the extreme form of individualism that is a cultural norm in the United States. Americans' respect for rules of conduct has been overpowered by talk about "rights" and the belief that we don't have obligations to others. In an attempt to reverse the decline in civility caused by bad manners, the Louisiana State Senate unanimously passed good manners legislation that requires students to address all school employees in a courteous fashion. The "Yes Sir, No Sir" bill suggests incivility in our schools is so severe that good manners must be legislated.[5]

"Please." "Excuse me." "Thank you." Can such words really make a difference? Good manners reinforce membership in a community and connect us to others. Good manners have been described as "part of the glue that holds a civilized society together," and small courtesies can lead to more civil behavior in a variety of contexts. Good manners also suggest that we respect others and that we honor their boundaries. In all, "good manners really do make a difference in both personal and professional life. They will never go out of style."[6]

is disconfirming. We may experience confusion or hurt and not know why, or we may even feel insulted in response to communication that appears "nice" on the surface.[7] Therefore, knowing about disconfirming messages and how to respond competently to them can motivate us to change negative communication climates to those that are positive. This knowledge can also provide us with insight about our negative reactions to communication that superficially appears confirming. And learning how to communicate in an assertive manner will help us set and maintain our boundaries and enable us to withstand others' attempts to violate them.

Assertive, Aggressive, and Submissive Communication

One way we can create and maintain our boundaries is through assertive communication. **Assertive communication** entails standing up for our needs, rights, and wants while respecting the needs, rights, and wants of others. Assertiveness is not the same thing as **aggressive communication**, which involves standing up for our needs, rights, and wants at the expense of others. It also differs from **submissive communication**, which entails failing to stand up for our needs, rights, and wants. Figure 9.2, "Aggression,

What is the difference among assertive, aggressive, and submissive communication?

Figure 9.2: Aggression, Assertion, and Submission

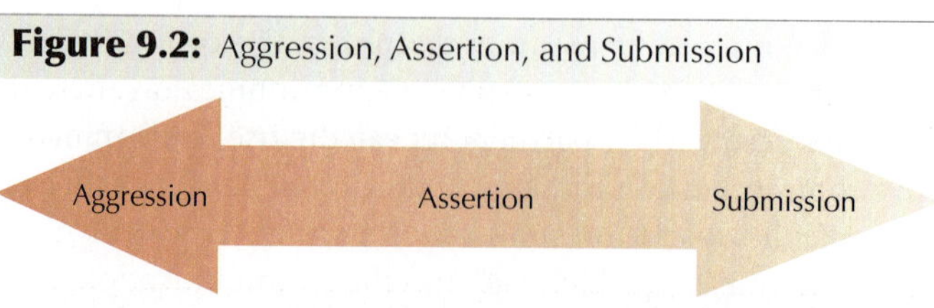

Assertion, and Submission," illustrates aggressiveness, assertiveness, and submissiveness on a continuum.

Our conversation partners and the specific situations in which we find ourselves influence where we might place our typical style of talk on the aggression-assertion-submission continuum. However, we tend to rely on one style of communication behavior more than others. For example, a "situationally aggressive" person may typically communicate in an aggressive manner yet may make use of assertion or submission at times, depending on the situation and the people involved. On the other hand, a "generally submissive" or "generally aggressive" person tends to rely on one particular style, no matter the situation or the persons involved.[8] Aggressive, submissive, and assertive verbal and nonverbal behaviors are illustrated in Table 9.1.

Aggression

We engage in aggressive communication when we stand up for our beliefs, rights, and needs and ignore the beliefs, rights, and needs of others. Aggressive communication also threatens the face of others. Benefits associated with an aggressive style of communication include the ability to protect ourselves in a society characterized by competition and hostility. People who communicate aggressively also are able to exert control over their lives and the lives of others. Examples of aggressive behavior include:

- comments that attack one's character (e.g., "You're so stupid; what do you know?")
- negative comments about one's appearance (e.g., "You look ugly no matter what you wear.")
- teasing, threats, use of profanity, and ridicule (e.g., "What the hell's the matter, crybaby? The truth hurts, doesn't it?")

Nonverbally, aggression is communicated by staring at others, invading personal space, yelling or using a sarcastic tone of voice, and pointing a finger in someone's face and/or raising a fist.

Although people who communicate in an aggressive manner may have their needs met more often than those who communicate in a submissive manner, their communication style

Table 9.1: Aggressive, Submissive, and Assertive Communication

Aggressive Verbal Communication: attacks on one's character and appearance; teasing; threats, profanity; ridicule	**Example** "You are so rude! Mind your own business and stop asking me questions about my private life!"	**Aggressive Nonverbal Communication:** staring; personal space violations; yelling and sarcastic tone of voice; pointing a finger and making a fist
Submissive Verbal Communication: denial; joking; changing a topic; disclaimers; qualifiers; apologies	**Example** "Well, uh, I guess it's all right to tell you. I really shouldn't but OK, here goes . . ."	**Submissive Nonverbal Communication:** lack of or minimal eye contact; hesitant tone of voice; giggling; adaptors; slouched posture
Assertive Verbal Communication: owning thoughts and feelings; metacommunication	**Example** "I appreciate your interest, but I want to keep that information to myself."	**Assertive Nonverbal Communication:** consistent eye contact; strong tone of voice; straight posture; minimal adaptors

KNOWLEDGE ON THE CUTTING EDGE

Technology Update: Disconfirming Communication and Flaming

Do you think JuggHed's comment in the following exchange is a compliment or a put-down?

ARCHEE: I think that the client really appreciates my contribution.

JUGGHED: ALL the clients at Riverdale appreciate you.

ARCHEE: What's THAT supposed to mean?!?!

It's difficult to interpret JuggHed's comment, but ArchEE's reply suggests that he perceives JuggHed's message as a hostile attack, or "flame."[9]

Flaming is characterized by intense and/or negative language, swearing, and communication that is intended and perceived as disconfirming. Early studies suggested that flaming is a computer-mediated communication (CMC) phenomenon that results from the reduced availability of nonverbal cues and the "computer subculture" (e.g., hackers and computer enthusiasts who reject established values and norms of civility). However, the results of early studies are suspect because:

- The studies use different definitions of flaming and measure different behaviors.
- Observed and self-reported instances of flaming tend to be exaggerated.
- The specific task-completion experiments used in the studies produced increased stress and instances of more flaming in CMC groups than in face-to-face (ftf) groups.[10]

Flaming is no longer considered a universal CMC phenomenon and is not as widely prevalent as once thought. The reduced cues explanation cannot account for flaming because it is not found universally across every newsgroup, bulletin board, and network. Recent research suggests that group norms and social contexts contribute to levels of flaming. In other words, flaming occurs if it is considered among the social norms of the group in which it happens. One study of four university-related Usenet social newsgroups found that behavioral norms, cultural identification, and views about religion and national conflicts influenced the type and amount of flaming. Messages among the four newsgroups illustrated a significant difference in levels of flaming, and more than 76% of the flames occurred when the interaction concerned political, religious, or cultural topics. This research suggests that the history of interaction among group members and the cultural, religious, and political background of CMC users affect the level of flaming in newsgroups. Another recent study found that flaming varies according to newsgroups concerned with health-related topics. A newsgroup that focused on a life-threatening illness and one that focused on an emotional disorder varied significantly in the tendency to flame. The group brought together by a shared interest in a serious physical health issue avoided flames almost entirely, whereas the group that discussed the emotional disorder chose flaming as an accepted group norm.[11]

Flaming is also related to CMC users' individual motives and gender. People flame to satisfy needs or to achieve personal goals. Specifically, users flame to pass time, to escape, and to have control and dominance over others. High levels of assertiveness and sensation-seeking predict flaming, and males engage in flaming more than females.[12]

Returning to the example of ArchEE and JuggHed, ArchEE may not know whether he's been flamed because he's not familiar with the norms and social context of his newsgroup and with JuggHed's motives and personality. This example illustrates that "computer-mediated communication is looking more and more like any other medium of communication where the tone and emotional content is affected by social and interaction context, rather than the medium itself."[13]

may prove harmful to both themselves and their targets. In particular, a person who exhibits aggressive behaviors is likely to be viewed as an incompetent communicator and may find that others avoid engaging her or him in conversation. People subjected to aggressive communication may experience depression, inadequacy, and humiliation and subsequently function ineffectively in their relationships, occupations, and families.[14] Sometimes people communicate aggressively because they believe it's the only way to get their thoughts and feelings across to others. These people haven't learned the assertive skills that enable them to stand up for their beliefs and communicate wants in a way that doesn't violate others' boundaries.

Submission

Submissive communication is also called nonassertion, passivity, or deference. No matter what the label, it is the reluctance or inability to express our beliefs, rights, and needs. Submissive communication allows people to avoid conflict, eschew responsibility, and even control others (think of a person who whines, cries, or plays the martyr until getting her or his own way). Some people use **passive aggression** to control others. Passive-aggressive responses appear to be submissive (i.e., they suggest we ignore our needs and rights) but actually ignore the needs and rights of others. Consider the example of someone who asks a roommate to empty the trash. The roommate, who would rather not take out the trash, grudgingly agrees to the request (a submissive response), but one hour later, the trash is still in the apartment. The roommate is asked two more times to take out the trash and agrees to do so but fails to accomplish the task. Agreeing to a request and failing to comply is an example of passive aggression because the needs and rights of the person who makes the request are ignored.

Most research-based conclusions about submissive communication reflect a Western assumption that it is best to be assertive. Submissive people are characterized as having lives directed by others and as suppressing feelings of anger that can erupt at unexpected times and over insignificant events. People who usually make use of a submissive style of communication are described as often feeling guilty about their successful attempts at manipulating others.[15] This may lead to feelings of pity, irritation, or disgust from a submissive person's relational partner. However, some people may be happy as submissive partners in a **complementary relationship** in which one partner has more power and control than the other. Similarly, "although assertiveness is generally linked to healthy personality adjustment in Western psychology, there is a danger in assuming that nonassertiveness is maladaptive."[16] Cultures that are primarily collectivist typically encourage interdependent relationships in which people are expected to defer to authority and are discouraged from asserting themselves as individuals.[17]

People can demonstrate submissive communication in a variety of ways. Denying the existence of a problem, joking, changing the topic, and avoiding a situation and/or person are forms of nonassertive behaviors. People who communicate in a submissive manner may allow others to intimidate them and violate their boundaries. Sometimes we act submissively because we don't know or lack the confidence to communicate in an assertive manner. At other times, we may act submissively because we're afraid that we might "make" another person feel angry or sad. No matter what the reason, submissive communication may include:

- disclaimers (e.g., "I understand if you say 'no,' but I was wondering . . ." or "It doesn't really matter to me . . .")
- qualifiers such as "I guess" and "I may be wrong"
- overuse of apologies (e.g., "I'm sorry to bother you . . .")

Nonverbally, submissive behaviors include a lack of or minimal eye contact, a hesitant tone of voice, excessive giggling, overuse of adaptors, and slouched posture.

Assertion

Assertive communication entails standing up for our beliefs, rights, and needs while respecting the beliefs, rights, and needs of others. Assertive communication allows us to develop caring, honest, and accepting relationships; maintain our boundaries; and respect the boundaries of others. Assertive communication also fosters fulfilling

KNOWLEDGE power • How Assertive Are You?

You can assess your tendency to use assertive communication by accessing the Assertiveness Test–abridged in the "Free Tests for Everyone" section of the Psychtest Web site: http://www.sychtests.com/tests/alltests.html. When you have completed the test, analyze your results and consider whether you may want to communicate in a more or less assertive manner.

relationships, reduces fear in anxiety-provoking situations, and enables us to live our own lives without being controlled by others. Be aware, however, that assertive communication is not a panacea; people who typically make use of an assertive style of communication may risk conflict and rejection (e.g., they may be fired from their place of employment).[18] Verbal communication associated with assertion includes owning thoughts and feelings by saying, "I want," "I don't like," and "I need." Assertive communication also entails the use of metacommunication (communication about communication), such as the comments listed in Table 9.2. Nonverbally, assertive communication involves consistent eye contact without staring, a strong tone of voice, straight posture, and minimal use of adaptors.

It may appear that assertive communication is the best method to use when maintaining and enforcing our boundaries, yet remember that communication competence involves flexibility and strategy. For example, people are sometimes taught that it's best to remain courteous when someone else is rude because we shouldn't stoop to someone else's level. However, some people disregard a polite message and may need something stronger, such as "I'll scream if you touch me again" or "I'll embarrass you in front of everybody if you continue to tell them about my past." Similarly, it may be best to accept criticism from your seventy-year-old grandma who is never satisfied with your correspondence. She may complain that she doesn't like emails, you don't write often enough, your letters aren't long enough, and she wants only hand-written letters. She will not be pleased no matter what you do, but you may make things worse if you assertively say that you correspond the best way you know how and that you don't want to listen to her complaints (would you want to see your seventy-year-old-grandma cry?). In the end, consider your goals, the other person, and the situation before deciding whether aggressive communication, submissive communication, or assertive communication will be the most effective and appropriate response. If you believe that assertive communication is likely to work best, there are a number of techniques that you can use to communicate about your rights and needs and, at the same time, respect the rights and needs of others.

Table 9.2: Assertive Metacommunication

- "Why are you asking?" or "Why is this a concern of yours?"
- "I don't want to answer that question or talk about this subject."
- "That's private information."
- "I don't feel comfortable talking about this."
- "I don't know you well enough for me to talk about this or answer this question."

Setting Boundaries with Assertive Communication

Perhaps you've been in a situation in which someone was angry at someone else but took it out on you. Maybe you've been in a situation in which someone repeatedly asked you to do something despite your refusals. Perhaps you've listened to someone denigrate an ethnic or racial group. The communication in these situations reflects displacement messages, many request messages that ignore our refusals, and messages that communicate prejudice. These types of messages are examples of disconfirming communication that can violate our boundaries. However, we can respond with communication skills that will set and reinforce our boundaries.

How can we establish boundaries and improve our communication competence with assertive messages?

Displacement Messages and Empathic Assertion

Have you ever been yelled at by someone only because you were the closest target available? If so, you experienced a type of disconfirming communication called displacement.

Displacement Messages **Displacement messages** occur when we are the target of emotions such as anger and frustration that result from situations and experiences in which we are not involved. Suppose your roommate sleeps in and misses the first half hour of a class. Although your roommate slinks into class, the professor makes a snide remark about latecomers, to which your roommate takes offense. In her or his next class, your roommate receives a grade on a term paper that will determine the final grade in the course, and it's a "D." Your roommate then rushes off to work and is promptly chastised by the boss for not closing properly the previous night. By this time, your roommate is ready to explode. Upon coming in the door, your roommate hears you casually remind her or him to do the dishes. Your roommate screams, "What do you think I am, a @#$%! moron who can't remember anything!" and slams the door of her or his room. Stunned, you try to gather your wits about you. You have a number of choices. You can act aggressively by flinging open your roommate's door and giving her or him a piece of your mind. This reaction is apt to cause a defensive spiral built on anger and hurt feelings. You can also choose to act submissively by not saying anything and letting the incident slide. You may realize that your roommate has had a bad day and has taken it out on you without really meaning to; therefore, you remain silent. Although this response reflects empathy and avoids creation of a defensive spiral, it teaches your roommate that she or he can violate your boundaries and use you as a target when things don't go as planned. A final choice is to respond assertively with a response that communicates your ability to engage in empathy and perspective taking yet, at the same time, sets your boundaries.

Setting Boundaries with Empathic Assertion **Empathic assertion** is a type of communication that "involves making a statement that conveys recognition of the other person's situation or feelings and is followed by another statement which stands up for the speaker's rights."[19] In the roommate situation, we can respond with an empathic assertion by knocking on the door and saying, "*I know you too well to think you're really this angry about a reminder to do the dishes. You must have had a bad day at school and work. How about we start over; do you want to talk about it?*" Notice how the empathic assertion recognizes the situation and gives the angry roommate a chance to start over. This implies that we do not want to be the target of disconfirming communication. This response can be made even more assertive with the inclusion of additional boundary-setting metacommunication by replacing *"How about we start over; do you want to talk about it?"* with *"Stop yelling at me and let me know what happened today to make you so angry."*

Effective and appropriate empathic assertion takes practice. As noted previously, the portion of our brain known as the amygdala is constantly on guard against attacks, whether they are physical or verbal. Recall from Chapter 4 that when the amygdala recognizes a verbal attack, it shunts blood away from our "rational or thinking brain" and into the "emotional brain," and we become defensive and react in ways designed to protect our self-image. It is easy to become defensive when we are the victim of displacement; therefore, it's best to take a deep breath (to reoxygenate the thinking brain), silently count to three (to help us prepare our message), and then reply with a response that reflects empathic assertion. It also goes without saying that our nonverbal behavior should be congruent with the intent of our message. If we invade our roommate's personal space and thrust a fist in her or his face, we are communicating in an aggressive rather than assertive manner.

Many Request Messages and the "Broken Record"

Can you recall a time when you said "no" to a request but the person making the request continued to bombard you with reasons why you should say "yes"? If so, you were on the receiving end of another type of disconfirming communication, one known as "many request messages." The broken record technique may help you respond to many request messages.

Many Request Messages The people in our lives, family, friends, and even strangers, may make many requests about the same subject and try to get us to do things even though we refuse. They may give us lots of attractive reasons why we should comply or attempt to make us feel guilty if we don't comply. They may also believe that we will eventually give in as long as they don't give up. Therefore, **many request messages** violate our boundaries, and the people who use them refuse to take "no" for an answer.

The Broken Record We can use the broken record technique to maintain our boundaries in response to someone who continues to ask us to do something in spite of the numerous times we decline. The **broken record** is an assertive skill that entails repeating the same words over and over again. There are up to three steps associated with the broken record:

1. Ask for details (if you don't understand the other person).
2. Agree with the truth and/or that person's right to an opinion.
3. Refuse to comply with the request and add reasons if necessary.

We can use the broken record the first time we suspect someone is not respecting our boundaries and pushing us to comply with a request we have just refused. If the other person persists with the request, we can continue to agree with whatever she or he says and use the same words over and over again that say we will not do it.[20] For example, suppose a friend asks you to watch her or his kids:

FRIEND: Could you do me a favor? Do you think you could watch the kids for me tonight?

YOU: I normally would, but I've had a horrible week and need time to be alone for a while. Maybe some other time. *(Refusal to comply with the request and reasons why)*

FRIEND: That's too bad. I asked the kids who they wanted to stay with, and they all said you. You're really good with them, and they'll be so disappointed when I tell them you don't want to babysit them.

YOU: It's not that I don't want to babysit them, and it's good to hear that they like staying with me, but I want to be alone for a while. Maybe some other time. *(refusal/broken record)*

FRIEND: Look, I really could use your help. I hate calling around to try and find a sitter.

YOU: I know that you dislike looking for a babysitter, but I want to be alone for a while. Maybe next time. *(Agreeing with the truth and refusal/broken record)*

FRIEND: Maybe you need company to get you in a good mood! Sometimes my energy kicks in when I'm with my kids because they're so much fun. I bet you'll begin to feel better if you spend a couple of hours with them.

YOU: You may be right, but I want to be alone for a while. Maybe next time. *(Agreeing with person's right to an opinion and refusal/broken record)*

After hearing a broken record repeated again and again, someone who tries to manipulate us with many request messages will finally give up. The broken record should be used in conjunction with nonverbal behaviors such as standing up straight, looking the other person in the eyes, and speaking firmly and clearly. This will say that we can communicate our needs and rights while, at the same time, respect the needs and rights of the other person.

Hate Speech and Boundary-Setting Responses to the Communication of Prejudice

Have you ever been in a conversation during which someone made a disparaging remark about a particular gender, racial or ethnic group, religion, or sexual orientation? If so, you were talking with someone who made use of hate speech, a third type of disconfirming communication.

SKILL practice • The Broken Record

Prepare five different persuasive messages to one or more of the following situations. Each message should include a reason why the target should comply with your request:

- Ask a friend who is on a diet to try your home-baked cookies.
- Ask a student who has to study for an important exam to accompany you on a weekend trip.
- Ask a coworker to take your Friday night shift so you can attend a social event.
- Ask a friend to lend you some money so you can pay off this month's credit card bill.
- Ask a colleague to buy some candy/wrapping paper/candles/cookie dough for your child's school fund-raiser.

Have a partner practice the broken record as you attempt to persuade her or him to grant your request in one of the situations. Switch places so that you can practice the broken record in response to your partner's persuasive attempts.

Hate Speech Recall from Chapter 2 that "prejudice" can be defined as a negative feeling toward and rejection of out-group members based on faulty and inflexible generalizations. **Hate speech** is based on prejudice and can be defined as "that which offends, threatens, or insults groups based on race, color, religion, national origin, gender, sexual orientation, disability, or a number of other traits."[21] Every year, more than half a million college students are targets of hate speech, and every minute "a college student somewhere sees or hears racist, sexist, homophobic or otherwise biased words or images."[22] Examples of hate speech messages that communicate prejudice include sexist language, communication that reflects able-ism, racist remarks, heterosexist language, and messages that reflect ageism:

- **Sexism** refers to language that disparages women or men.
- **Able-ism** is reflected in messages that denigrate people on the basis of their physical or mental ability.
- **Racism** places certain groups in inferior positions because of skin color, religious background, and/or ethnic background.

"I'm Not a Racist"

Few people admit racism. When accused of racist comments or activities, some will say:

- "It was all in fun."
- "You're overreacting."
- "We never meant that."
- "I'm not a racist."

Some campus bias incidents leave lingering tension and confusion, with one side seeing racism and another seeing oversensitivity on the part of those who have lodged a complaint. Saying, "I didn't mean to hurt anyone" doesn't remove the hurt. Don't ask, "Can't they take a joke?" Instead ask, "Why didn't I realize this 'joke' was offensive?"

Rise up. The world won't change if people don't change it.

We can do our part to fight hate on campus by attempting to understand what people find offensive.

Source: Willoughby, B. *10 Ways to Fight Hate on Campus.* Atlanta, GA: Southern Poverty Law Center, 2002.

- **Heterosexism** includes derogatory terms used for lesbians, gays, bisexuals, and people who are transgendered.
- **Ageism** disparages people based on their age.

Recall from Chapter 5 that the Sapir-Whorf hypothesis posits that language not only reflects a culture's beliefs, attitudes, and values but also perpetuates beliefs, attitudes, and values. Language also influences our perceptions of others and how we communicate about them. This means that hate speech can perpetuate prejudice, influence us to disconfirm certain groups of people, and influence us to perceive such groups in terms of unproven stereotypes. It's not difficult to see that messages that communicate prejudice demonstrate lack of respect and fail to validate others. In addition, research demonstrates that hate speech strips people of their dignity, causes everyday anxiety and distress, and creates intense psychological and emotional pain.[23]

Boundary-Setting Responses to the Communication of Prejudice Individuals who are targets of hate speech typically respond with one or more behaviors: a passive-withdrawal response (silence), an assertive reply (one that is direct, appropriate, and concerns a person's thoughts and feelings), an attempt to use humor to deflect the incident (such as turning a hateful comment into a joke), and an aggressive reply (one that is retaliatory and/or disconfirming). People who remain silent believe that this is one way to take "the moral high ground," but research suggests that a passive response may be perceived as weakness. In regard to bystanders, experts contend that those who don't speak up unwittingly encourage more hate speech and other forms of abuse. However, when peers challenge the language of others, the number of degrading messages tends to decrease, and perceptions and stereotypes may be challenged. Failing to set boundaries in response to hate speech can "escalate tensions" and "brew discontent and fear,"[24] but setting boundaries has the potential to moderate intolerance and the pain inflicted on others.

We can motivate ourselves to speak up against hate speech by expecting to find ourselves in a hate speech situation sometime in the future. We can imagine ourselves speaking up and prepare something to say before an incident occurs. One way to respond to hate speech is to ask questions. "Do you know any [woman/man/African American/etc.] who doesn't act the way you think they 'all' do?" "Do you know any [Muslim/individual who uses a wheelchair/homosexual] personally?" "Are you saying that you don't know [an octogenarian/Chinese person/transgendered person], and yet you 'know' what they think and how they act?" Asking questions such as these cannot make someone sensitive, but they have the potential to promote introspection and sensitivity. Because bigotry is not

KNOWLEDGE power • Can You "Speak Up"?

In 2005, the Southern Poverty Law Center published *Speak Up! Responses to Everyday Bigotry* as a way to combat comments that cause us to laugh uncomfortably, become frustrated and angry, and later wish we had said something. *Speak Up!* is a compendium of stories about everyday bigotry collected from people across the United States, and it includes suggested responses to situations involving family members, friends and neighbors, coworkers and supervisors, classmates and instructors, and strangers in public places. You can access *Speak Up!* at www.tolerance.org/speakup.

We can nonverbally respond to offensive jokes by remaining silent and exhibiting a disapproving frown.

based on logic, logical attempts to show a bigot the error of her or his ways are likely to fail. Therefore, we can respond with "Thanks for explaining" and then move on after a bigot answers our questions. In addition, rather than responding with disconfirming communication that may result in anger and defensiveness, we should set boundaries by explaining what is and isn't acceptable. We can set boundaries with statements such as "I won't listen to that kind of talk or those kinds of jokes," "I'm going to have to change the way I think about you," and/or "I've decided I'm not going to spend time with you anymore." Notice that these statements don't attack and don't accuse others of being wrong. Instead, they let people know our boundaries and communicate that we can assertively stand up for our beliefs. We can also indicate displeasure by remaining silent and exhibiting a disapproving frown in a situation in which laughter is an expected response, such as after a joke that is racist or sexist in nature. If we are asked, teased, or criticized about our nonverbal response, we can then inform the joke teller and others that we find the joke offensive, demeaning, and prejudicial.[25]

Remember to be realistic about the effective and appropriate use of skills and guidelines associated with disconfirming communication and setting boundaries. For example, using assertive communication with a more powerful person may not result in our desired

KNOWLEDGE power • "I Wish I Would Have Said . . ."

With a partner or in a group, recall a time when you were the target and/or a bystander in a hate speech episode. Discuss the situation with your partner or group, and describe how you and others responded to the hate speech. Decide whether the responses to the hate speech were competent and whether alternative responses would have been more effective and appropriate. Next, imagine yourself in the situation(s) again and engage in out-loud practice of your boundary-setting message(s).

Competence & Critical Thinking

mycommunicationlab

THE NAME GAME AND DISCONFIRMING MESSAGES AND SETTING BOUNDARIES

Kathy is talking to her friends, Ethan, Ryan, and Maria, about her choice to take her husband's name upon their marriage. Maria tries to convince her to keep her maiden name, even though Kathy is committed to the name change.

You can view *The Name Game* by accessing the "Small Group and Interpersonal Videos" on the MyCommunicationLab Web site. Answer the following questions about the disconfirming responses included in the video:

- What types of disconfirming messages are illustrated in the video?
- Does Kathy respond to her friends' comments with aggressive, submissive, or assertive communication. Explain.
- Do you think that Kathy set her boundaries in a competent manner? Why or why not?

MyCommunicationLab

I am. I can't wait to just get the wedding over with and start our lives together.

MARIA: Oh, Kathy, it's so beautiful. You must be so excited.

KATHY: I am. I can't wait to just get the wedding over with and start our lives together.

RYAN: So are you going to be Kathy Rabino, or are you going to be Kathy Fudd?

KATHY: I'm going to change my name.

MARIA: Kathy. This isn't like the '50s, when people got married right out of high school. You've accomplished a lot as Kathy Rabino. Aren't you proud of that? Doesn't that mean anything to you?

ETHAN: I just don't see you anyone would want to change their name to Fudd. You going to name the kid Elmer?

RYAN: You could still accomplish goals as Kathy Rabino and take on your husband's name and still accomplish other goals. It's not like you're changing. You're still the same person.

MARIA: Are you really sure about that?

KATHY: Excuse me, but this happens to mean a lot to me. You know, I respect tradition. And from work to kids to bills, you and your partner are the only constants in a relationship. And call me crazy, but somehow taking his name really reinforces the strength of the marriage for me.

MARIA: All I meant was that so many women lose themselves in marriage. And call me crazy, but I think that changing your name is the first step to losing who you are.

KATHY: Look. That may be true in some cases. But Tom loves me because I know who I am, and I have confidence in myself, and I'm too strong to ever lose sight of what I want.

RYAN: Kathy, you know what you want in your life and your marriage. Taking on your husband's name is a symbolic gesture. It just reinforces your feelings about the relationship.

ETHAN: Yeah, but Fudd?

RYAN: I definitely respect your decision, Kathy. There are valid arguments on both sides. But it basically comes down to doing what's right for you. Say he was a successful journalist or an attorney, you might not want to change your name. It could be a professional suicide.

MARIA: Absolutely. I mean, don't you see, Kathy, there's a lot on the line here.

KATHY: Relax. In case you haven't noticed, I am not Katie Couric. I'll graduate in May, and I'll begin my career in education. You know, you're right. Maybe if it were a different time in my life I would make a different decision. For now, this is what I want. It's what I want to do.

outcome. Similarly, telling our boss not to make ethnic jokes in our presence may be less effective than remaining silent when coworkers laugh (and explaining our reaction later when asked about it). In sum, competent communicators are strategic, flexible, and prepared for the inevitable occasions when their normally effective and appropriate communication skills don't work as planned.

Contexts and Their Influence on Disconfirming Communication and Setting Boundaries

Are messages that are considered confirming in one culture considered disconfirming in another? How do our family, friends, and persons with whom we work affect the communication of disconfirming messages? Does gender influence the tendency to engage in aggressive, submissive, or assertive behavior? Is assertiveness considered to be a stable personality trait? The culture, relationship, gender, and individual contexts influence disconfirming messages and boundary-setting messages.

How do contexts influence disconfirming messages and boundary setting?

Culture Context

In Chapter 6 we learned that members of Middle Eastern cultures tend to stand closer to others than members of Western cultures. This means that someone from a Western culture may perceive a boundary violation when someone from a Middle Eastern culture "invades" the intimate space distance of eighteen inches or less. This example illustrates that cultural belief systems and rules for behavior influence perceptions of which messages are disconfirming and aggressive and which are not.

Disconfirming Messages We have read in previous chapters that the possibility of communicating disconfirming verbal and nonverbal messages is great in intercultural communication. Americans may inadvertently violate others' boundaries and create negative communication climates when following American communication rules while interacting with people from other cultures. For example, "an open-faced American rushing in with extended hand and first names violates a culture prizing formal ritual in initial contacts with strangers."[26] Boundaries, to some extent, are influenced by the culture in which we live; therefore, we should remember that people may unwittingly cross a boundary not from malice but from ignorance.

Assertive Communication Just as various cultures have different perceptions of what is considered confirming and disconfirming, cultures have different ideas about the effectiveness and appropriateness of communicating in an assertive manner. Because the United States is a low-context culture that favors communication that is direct and to the point, it follows that in the United States, people who are assertive are perceived as competent communicators. This is not the case in high-context cultures. The assertive manner in which Americans talk about themselves during employment interviews is negatively perceived by Dutch employers, who tend to believe that Americans "oversell" themselves when they assertively mention their outstanding qualities. On the other hand, American employers tend to believe that Dutch job applicants "undersell" themselves.

Dutch applicants expect an interviewer to ask them about their accomplishments and are careful not to brag.[27]

Co-Cultures Research about U.S. co-cultures suggests that members of the dominant culture may unwittingly express disconfirmation and that members of various co-cultures have different ideas about the value of assertive communication. Communication scholar **Gust A. Yep** suggests that heteronormativity maintains fear, hostility, and hatred toward human sexual difference. **Heteronormativity** refers to the belief that everyone should be heterosexual and assumes that heterosexual experience is synonymous with human experience. Heteronormativity teaches us that homosexuality is a shameful "condition," that it is deviant, and that something is wrong if we are anything other than heterosexual. Yep maintains that heteronormativity in the United States causes deliberate disconfirming messages that attempt to change the identity of lesbian, gay, bisexual, and transgendered (LGBT) persons and disconfirming messages that can be classified as examples of hate speech. Heteronormativity even makes it acceptable for gay-affirmative individuals to ask members of the LGBT community disconfirming questions that are rarely considered appropriate among heterosexual couples (e.g., "Who is the 'man' in your relationship?" or "What do you do in bed?"). Awareness of heteronormativity may enlighten us about oppressive beliefs that consider one form of sexual identity as normal and/or better than all others and contribute to the acceptance of different forms of human sexual expression.[28]

The value of assertive communication also varies in terms of co-cultures. Children who speak in an assertive manner are generally regarded positively by mothers of European ancestry. However, Navajo mothers typically believe that children who communicate assertively are undisciplined, discourteous, self-centered, and mischievous.[29] Asian Americans may be "situationally assertive"; that is, they may be assertive in some situations (e.g., with friends, in informal settings, with other Asians) and submissive in others (e.g., with authority figures, in a classroom, and in counseling situations).[30]

Relationship Context

One common myth about U.S. families is that there once was a "golden age" of families. In truth, family life has been and continues to be characterized by conflict, disconfirming communication, and a failure to use the confirming communication skills discussed in previous chapters. Friends and persons with whom we work also communicate disconfirming messages.

Family Communication Disconfirming messages are evident in parent-child communication and affect perceptions of marital satisfaction. Although parents may believe that their children learn rude and disrespectful communication from their friends, these disconfirming behaviors are taught to children at home without their parents' realization. Parents don't recognize that interrupting and talking over their children's messages communicate disrespect and that children model their disrespectful behavior.[31] Children are also invalidated when they're on the receiving end of messages that indirectly disrespect them, such as being ignored.[32]

Disconfirming messages also affect perceptions of marital satisfaction. Research demonstrates that feeling validated by one's spouse results in marital satisfaction and a positive perception of the marital relationship. However, disconfirming marital communication decreases the extent to which a spouse feels understood and validated by her or his partner.[33] Sociologist **John M. Gottman** has identified four types of

Parents often don't realize that they use disconfirming messages when communicating with their children.

Source: Jumpstart: © United Feature Syndicate, Inc.

disconfirming messages that not only contribute to marital dissatisfaction but also predict divorce:[34]

1. **Criticism**—Whereas **complaints** are aimed at specific actions and behaviors, criticism involves negative words about a partner's personality or character. Criticism is common in most relationships but can usher in the other three types of disconfirming messages if pervasive.
2. **Contempt**—Contempt is based on long-simmering negative thoughts about a partner and is evident in sarcasm, name-calling, hostile humor, and mockery. Nonverbally, contempt is communicated by eye rolling, sneering, and "tsking." Contempt is described as the most poisonous disconfirming message because it communicates disgust with a partner.
3. **Defensiveness**—Defensiveness occurs when we believe that our self-concept is under attack. Communicating defensively is a way to blame a partner (e.g., "You're the problem, not me!") and typically escalates a conflict.
4. **Stonewalling**—Also labeled "withdrawal," stonewalling occurs when a partner physically and/or mentally disengages from a situation. A stonewaller fails to give verbal and nonverbal feedback during a conversation and may act as if she or he doesn't care what a partner has to say. Stonewalling typically occurs when the other three disconfirming responses become overwhelming and it is perceived as a way out.

Gottman has found that the use of these four disconfirming messages, along with how a couple recalls their relational history and the amount of their physiological stress, can predict the occurrence of future divorce with 94% accuracy.

Friends Friends also communicate disconfirming messages that may be intended to provide emotional support. **Anti-comforting messages** are often so incompetent that they

KNOWLEDGE power • "Don't Take It So Hard!"

Recall some of the anti-comforting messages that you have received or communicated to others. With a partner or in a group, analyze why these messages are anti-comforting and in what way they disconfirm the recipient. Discuss the confirming messages you could have received or communicated in place of those that were anti-comforting. If you cannot think of anti-comforting messages, you can access the examples compiled by Dale Hample, professor of communication at Western Illinois University, at www.wiu.edu/users/mfdjh/Anti-Comforting.doc.

make a situation worse and disconfirm a person's desired face. Examples of anti-comforting messages about relational breakups include:

- "Don't take it so hard."
- "I think she was a slut."
- "That's OK. You don't need him anyway."
- "That's too bad. Wanna go out on Friday?"
- "Aww, that's nothing. You know how I got dumped?"

These messages are disconfirming for many reasons. "Don't take it so hard" devalues the upset person's feelings. "I think she was a slut" implies that the upset person was incompetent or wrong for having been in the relationship. "You don't need him anyway" suggests that the upset person should be pleased instead of having negative feelings. "Wanna go out on Friday?" is disconfirming because it minimizes the upset person's emotions by tangentially moving to another topic (wanting to go out). Finally, "Aww, that's nothing. You know how I got dumped?" is disconfirming because it changes the focus of the conversation away from the upset person. These and other anti-comforting messages are disconfirming because they discount, disregard, and/or diminish others' feelings.[35]

Coworkers Some researchers believe that CMC is diminishing the "human moment" at work. The **human moment** refers to an encounter that happens only when people share their emotional and cognitive attention and the same physical space. Human moments in an organizational setting are diminishing because they require energy and because email and other mediated forms of communication are taking the place of face-to-face (ftf) contact. In particular, we tend to perceive that it's much easier to write a quick email than to meet a colleague ftf, even if the colleague is in close physical proximity. The consequences of overreliance on CMC in work settings include self-doubt, oversensitivity, and disconfirming messages. In addition, coworkers can slowly lose their sense of cohesiveness, and an organization's communication climate may be reflected in distrust, disrespect, and dissatisfaction. Some corporations have embraced the philosophy of "high tech requires high touch" to counteract the effects of the diminishing human moment. For example, one real estate developer instituted the practice of providing employees a free pizza lunch each week in the office. A consulting firm assembled "performance groups" with competing companies to build trust and share ideas. Note that CMC and ftf communication in an organization can augment and support what is written in emails and what occurs in meetings. However, the strategic use of the human moment can reduce the disconnection among colleagues that may result from excessive CMC use in the workplace.[36]

Gender Context

Gender expectations affect the communication of assertive, submissive, and aggressive messages. Both men and women tend to make use of aggressive forms of communication.

Assertive and Submissive Communication It is widely accepted that gender expectations influence the tendency to communicate in an assertive, aggressive, or submissive manner. American women of European ancestry have traditionally been taught to behave submissively in order to communicate femininity. On the other hand, American men of European ancestry have been taught that it is appropriate for them to behave aggressively to communicate strength and dominance. These internalized gender expectations create a double bind for women. Women who work in professional contexts may have to choose between being perceived as submissive and therefore weak or being perceived as assertive and therefore unfeminine. The dilemma that many women face is manifested in comments such as "He's strong and confident" but "She's harsh and bossy." Women in professional contexts often feel they must choose between being effective women or effective professionals, but they cannot be both simultaneously.[37] However, a woman's use of an assertive communication style may become more acceptable as women

Gender expectations influence our perception of competent, assertive communication.

KNOWLEDGE ON THE CUTTING EDGE

Putting It in Context: Communication, Sex, and Aggressive Behavior

PET scans of male and female brains demonstrate that males have more neural activity in the limbic system, the region of the brain that is associated with reactions to emotional situations. In general, this neural activity results in males typically expressing emotions through physical action and attacking if angered.[38] Although the amygdala regulates many of our emotions and aggressive impulses, the amygdala is usually smaller in the male brain and may lead to increased aggression. There is also less of a link from the amygdala to the frontal lobe in the neocortex, which provides us with impulse control and plays a role in moral decision making.[39]

Brain chemicals and hormones also play a role in aggressive behavior. Male brains have less serotonin, a brain chemical that calms us down. This may result in a male reacting to a perceived threat with physical responses instead of talking about the situation. Males also have less of the bonding chemical oxytocin in the brain. Oxytocin contributes to feelings of empathy, and the "higher oxytocin levels in a brain, the less aggressive the person is likely to be."[40] Testosterone, found in greater quantities in male brains, is also related to aggressive behavior. Testosterone levels increase during episodes of competition, such as athletic contests and arguments. Testosterone has been blamed for excessive risk taking and violent behavior; however, some psychologists suggest that males with high testosterone levels typically learn to manage their aggression in socially acceptable ways, such as channeling their aggression into sports and social assertiveness. Males with high levels of testosterone may respond more aggressively when provoked than males with low levels of testosterone, but aggressive impulses don't characteristically rule their nature.[41]

continue to inhabit important roles in society. In fact, women's self-reported assertiveness levels have increased to the point that recent studies demonstrate no gender differences in assertiveness.[42]

Aggressive Communication Gender differences in the communication of aggression are influenced by the sex of an instigator, the sex of a target, the nature of a provocation, and whether an aggressor empathizes with a target. Gender stereotypes would have us believe that men communicate more aggressively than women, but a study of more than 5,000 married couples found that men and women tend to engage in approximately equal amounts of verbal aggression when communicating with partners. This may result from the fact that powerful individuals (typically male) need not use aggressive communication to demonstrate their power. Therefore, men may be less aggressive than the gender stereotype suggests, and women may engage in more aggressive behavior than is generally expected.[43] Furthermore, men and women demonstrate similar levels of indirect aggression by the time they reach young adulthood. **Indirect aggression** is a communication strategy that is used when the costs of direct aggression are too high. This strategy makes use of social exclusion and seeks to harm the social status of a target by manipulating her or his reputation. For example, failing to invite "one of the guys" to a ballgame and talking negatively about him behind his back illustrates indirect aggression. Because the costs of direct aggression are greater for women than for men, it has been argued that women typically make use of indirect strategies to exert their power. Although adolescent girls tend to use indirect aggression more than adolescent boys, studies of adults have found little or no difference in women and men's use of indirect aggression.[44]

Individual Context

Personality theorists tend to view assertiveness as a stable underlying characteristic that reflects fundamental individual differences. One study that supports the idea of assertiveness as a stable personality trait occurred across thirty to forty years. A pattern of lifetime stability was found for assertiveness, whereas a pattern of lifetime change was found for the personality traits of self-confidence, cognitive commitment, outgoingness, and dependability.[45] Assertiveness is also included in the five factor theory, a widely accepted view of individual personality differences discussed in Chapter 3. One factor in the five factor theory is extroversion, which includes characteristics such as being "adventurous, sociable, talkative, and assertive." Although talkativeness and assertiveness are both correlated with extroversion, it is possible for an assertive person to be relatively quiet (e.g., the "strong, silent type"). However, many studies suggest that most people who are assertive are also talkative and vice versa; thus, these characteristics are combined under the extroversion factor.[46]

OVERCOMING COMMUNICATION CHALLENGES

Covert Verbal Abuse

Name-calling. Threats. Putdowns. These are examples of blatant types of aggressive communication that may come to mind when we read the words "verbal abuse." **Verbal abuse** has been characterized as verbal or nonverbal communication intended to and/or perceived as intending to cause psychological pain to another person.[47] Such verbal abuse may take the form of public or private humiliation, name-calling, threats, criticism, insults, blame, and accusations. A subtler form of verbal abuse is sometimes unrecognizable to the persons at whom it is aimed. This type of abuse is insidious and covert.

Covert Verbal Abuse

Day-to-day **covert verbal abuse** may be more harmful than overt forms of verbal abuse because of its subtle nature and its resulting harmful consequences.[48] This type of verbal abuse may consist of:[49]

- hurtful remarks that are delivered in a caring and sincere manner (e.g., "I'm only telling you this for your own good, but you look ridiculous in those clothes.")
- messages that judge or deny the validity of a partner's thoughts, perceptions, or feelings (e.g., "You don't know what you're talking about!" or "You twist things all around.")
- jokes that criticize or put down a partner (which an abuser can defend by saying that the partner "can't take a joke, is too sensitive, and overreacts")
- verbal messages that are incongruent with nonverbal behaviors (such as saying, "I'm listening" while watching TV or constantly interrupting with topic changes)
- messages that trivialize a partner and/or a partner's accomplishments (e.g., "Yes, I'm happy that you received an 'A' on your term paper. The professor must have really liked the designer notebook that you used to turn in your report.")

Covert verbal abuse can be unexpected, irrational, and unpredictable. The target of such abuse may get the feeling that something is not right and/or that she or he has just been put down but can't pinpoint the cause of this feeling. People who are victims of covert verbal abuse may feel confused, disoriented, and off balance because their perceptions of reality are constantly challenged. They may also feel helpless, depressed, and emotionally drained. In addition to emotional and psychological effects, "a prolonged state of emotional stress—especially if you feel out of control, overwhelmed, and helpless—literally undermines and breaks down your tissues and body systems."[50] In all, an abuser's ability to undermine a partner's sense of self creates the emotional and physical toll that results from covert verbal abuse.[51]

We can enforce limits and reestablish or confirm boundaries in response to covert abuse.

Contending with Covert Verbal Abuse

The first step in dealing with covert abuse is to recognize it for what it is: abuse. A covert verbal abuser aims to confuse and weaken a partner to make her or him easy to control. The process is insidious and difficult to recognize. Once recognized, however, steps can be taken to minimize or eliminate the effects of the abuse. One technique is to use rational emotive behavior therapy (REBT), as discussed in Chapter 4, to learn effective ways to intrapersonally react to an abuser's comments. Even if a partner is confused and unsure about the validity of a covert verbal abuser's comments, REBT can teach a victim unconditional self-acceptance. Another technique to counteract covert verbal abuse is to create and maintain boundaries with assertive communication. It's natural to believe that differences can be talked out in a reasonable and loving manner, but this assumption holds true for partners who are rational and psychologically healthy. However, defending, explaining, compromising, apologizing, and negotiating are ineffective ways to deal with covert verbal abuse because they assume a rational partner. Instead, an appropriate response to covert verbal abuse should enforce limits and reestablish or confirm boundaries. Comments such as "I will not allow your criticism to influence my feelings" and "I refuse to listen to your comments any longer" communicate our boundaries. Similarly, we can set limits by saying, "I don't accept that" or "I'm going to end this conversation and leave if you don't stop trivializing my accomplishments" (and then do it). Remember that appropriate boundary-setting messages may not be effective against a covert verbal abuser because such abusers tend to be irrational. Moreover, if a covert verbal abuser reacts to boundary-setting messages with extreme anger and threats of bodily harm, a partner should not deal with such abusive behavior alone and should question the health of remaining in the relationship.[52]

A CASE STUDY IN ETHICS

Jap Road

Recall that competent communication includes an ethical dimension of well-based standards of right and wrong. We can ask ourselves a series of questions to help us choose communication strategies that are effective and appropriate as they relate to disconfirming communication. Specifically, we can ask: Have I practiced any virtues today (e.g., have I demonstrated integrity, trustworthiness, honesty, and responsibility)? Have I done more good than harm (e.g., have I shown appreciation and gratitude to others)? Have I treated people with dignity and respect? Have I been fair and just? Have I made my community stronger because of my actions? You can gain insight into your ideas about ethical communication by reading the following case study about "Jap Road."

How would you feel if a street name included a disparaging word about an ethnic group? This is the question that Sandra Tanamachi answered when she fought to change the name of Jap Road in rural Fannett, Texas. Tanamachi maintained that the street name was derogatory and demeaning to Japanese Americans. However, Earl Callahan, who has lived on Jap Road most of his life, said that he feels like a part of his heritage is being destroyed. Callahan asserted that he and his neighbors who live on Jap Road are against the use of racial and ethnic slurs. He also maintains that there's a difference between calling a road "Jap" and calling a person a "Jap."

The word *Jap* became a slur during and after World War II when it was used to demean Japanese and Japanese American people. On 28 July 1986, Congressional Resolution 290 was passed, which states that the word *Jap* is racially offensive and prohibits the word for use on any federally owned building or land. But Callahan and others don't perceive Jap Road as being racially offensive. Local historians point out that the Yoshio Mayumi family, who owned a farm in the area, named the road. Callahan's family bought the Mayumi farm in 1924, and the street sign has evoked fond memories of the Mayumi family for him. He suggested that the word *Jap* isn't a problem and the true issue is the feelings behind the word. "If we lived in a society where everyone and everything is equal, and where there is an atmosphere of forgiveness, then words can't hurt you," he maintained. Other citizens of Fannett have said that the blame rests on the overblown need to be politically correct and that it will be impossible to make the "J-word" disappear.

Although Jap Road at one time may have been used to honor a Japanese family, the Japanese Americans who fought to rename the road suggested that it holds a much different meaning for people who live outside of Fannett. Tanamachi said that if the name of the road doesn't change, it will remind her grandchildren of a time when Japanese Americans were hated in the United States. Callahan countered that he and others were only trying to preserve the Japanese heritage in the area and that now there's a possibility that it will be eradicated with a name change with no ties to the Mayumi family. "Years from now, my grandchildren may not even know that there was once a Japanese family who lived there," he said.[53]

Do you believe that Jap Road is an example of disconfirming communication? Do you agree with the need to change the name of Jap Road, or should the name remain to teach people about the historical use of disrespectful language? Is it ethical to keep a street name that may disparage a group of people, even if the motivation is to educate others?

Chapter Review

Motivation: How has this helped me?

- **The importance of studying disconfirming communication and setting boundaries**

It's important to study disconfirming messages and setting boundaries because relational dissatisfaction results when partners repeatedly use disconfirming communication. In addition, learning how to communicate in an assertive manner will help us set and maintain our boundaries and enable us to withstand others' attempts to violate them.

Knowledge: What have I learned?

- **How to characterize disconfirming communication and boundaries**

Disconfirming communication fails to validate others and creates negative communication climates. We communicate disconfirmation when we ignore people, fail to acknowledge their thoughts and feelings, and refuse to accept their opinions and emotions. A boundary is a limit or edge that defines us as being separate from others. Emotional, relational, sexual, and spiritual boundaries let others know that we have limits to what we believe is safe and appropriate.

- **The difference among assertive, aggressive, and submissive communication**

One way we can create and maintain our boundaries is through assertive communication. Submissive communication allows others to take advantage of us, and aggressive communication leads others to become guarded and withdraw from us, but assertive communication entails standing up for our beliefs, rights, and needs while respecting others' beliefs, rights, and needs.

- **How contexts influence disconfirming messages and boundary setting**

Disconfirming and assertive communication are influenced by various contexts. The culture context affects what is considered to be disconfirming and whether assertive communication is judged to be effective and appropriate; the relationship context demonstrates that disconfirming messages may be communicated by family, friends, and coworkers; the gender context illustrates more similarities than differences between women and men in the communication of assertive and aggressive messages; and the individual context suggests that assertiveness may be a stable personality characteristic.

Skill: What skills have I developed?

- **How to set boundaries and improve our communication competence with assertive messages**

Empathic assertion includes making a statement that conveys recognition of another person's situation or feelings and is followed by another statement that stands up for the speaker's rights. We can use empathic assertion in response to displacement messages that target us as the recipient of anger and frustration (even though we aren't involved in the situations that caused the anger and frustration).

The broken record is an assertive response that entails repeating the same words over and over again. We can use the broken record in response to "many request messages," which attempt to persuade us to do things even though we refuse.

In response to hate speech, we can question a speaker's beliefs and use assertive metacommunication to set boundaries by explaining what is and isn't acceptable.

Study Questions

1. What is disconfirming communication?
2. What are boundaries, and how do they relate to communication? What are boundary violations?
3. Describe aggressive, submissive, and assertive messages in terms of verbal and nonverbal communication.

4. What are three types of disconfirming communication, and how can we respond with specific types of assertive metacommunication?
5. How do the culture, relationship, gender, and individual contexts affect communication climate, disconfirming communication, and assertive communication?
6. What is covert verbal abuse, and how can we competently respond to it?

Names to Know

John M. Gottman, p. 247—world-renowned psychologist who researches marital stability and divorce prediction in terms of emotions, physiology, and communication. Gottman is an emeritus professor of psychology at the University of Washington, the author of best-selling books and of academic articles, and the cofounder of the Gottman Institute.

Gust A. Yep, p. 247—communication researcher and professor of communication studies and human sexuality studies at San Francisco State University. Yep's scholarly research focuses on communication at the intersections of race, class, gender, sexuality, and nationality.

Key Terms

able-ism, 242
ageism, 243
aggressive communication, 234
anti-comforting messages, 248
assertive communication, 234
boundary, 232
boundary violations, 233
broken record, 240
communication climate, 232
complaints, 248
complementary relationship, 237
contempt, 248
covert verbal abuse, 252
criticism, 248
defensiveness, 248
disconfirming communication, 232
displacement messages, 239
empathic assertion, 239
flaming, 236
hate speech, 242
heteronormativity, 247
heterosexism, 243
human moment, 249
indirect aggression, 251
many request messages, 240
passive aggression, 237
racism, 242
sexism, 242
stonewalling, 248
submissive communication, 234
verbal abuse, 251

CHAPTER 10

Interpersonal Relationships

"Like navigation, relationships have a constant balance of forces whose management creates the ultimate direction of progress. . . . Communication researchers have taken the lead in showing that the manner of steering between these forces, rocks, or storms is the key to ultimate happy landing or shipwreck."

STEVE DUCK, DANIEL AND AMY STARCH DISTINGUISHED RESEARCH PROFESSOR IN COMMUNICATION STUDIES, UNIVERSITY OF IOWA

In this chapter, we will answer the following:

Motivation: How will this help me?

- It is important to study interpersonal relationships because relationships can affect our physical and psychological health, provide us with social support, affect our self-concept, and have an impact on our future success and happiness.

Knowledge: What will I learn?

- How to characterize personal and romantic relationships
- Theories that explain interpersonal relationships and self-disclosure
- Models of relational development
- How contexts influence interpersonal relationships

Skill: Why do I need to develop these skills?

- Skills related to initiating and bonding, maintaining, repairing, terminating, and reconciling relationships can improve our communication competence.

Pop singer Britney Spears and rapper Kevin Federline filed for divorce in October 2004 after two years and one month of marriage. Citing "irreconcilable differences," the couple had rarely been seen together in public in the months prior to the divorce announcement. Have you been involved in a relationship that began well but eventually terminated? Have you attempted to terminate a relationship, but your partner wouldn't let go? Perhaps you tried to reconcile with an ex-partner, but the reconciliation attempts failed.

Interpersonal communication is integral to initiating, strengthening, maintaining, terminating, or attempting to repair a relationship. In this chapter, we will learn how to increase our motivation to communicate competently by understanding why it's important to study interpersonal relationships. We'll learn about relationships in terms of what motivates us to communicate in a competent manner in organizational and educational contexts. We will also increase our knowledge by learning theories about why we form relationships, models of relational development, and about relational transgressions. We will learn skills that relate to relational initiation, bonding, maintenance, repair, termination, reconciliation, and healing a relationship after a transgression is committed.

Introduction to Interpersonal Relationships

Think about a relationship you have with a family member, friend, instructor, coworker, and acquaintance. What communication characteristics of these relationships distinguish one from another? Just as we learned in Chapter 1 that communication can be viewed on a continuum from personal to impersonal, our relationships can also be viewed on a continuum that ranges from personal to impersonal.

How can we characterize personal and romantic relationships?

Characteristics of Personal Relationships

In impersonal relationships, we communicate with others based on their social or occupational roles (e.g., nurturer, server, disciplinarian, cashier). By contrast, personal relationships are distinguished by three important characteristics: explanatory ability; predictive ability; and uniqueness.

Explanatory Ability Do you tell yourself to lay low for a while because you know that a partner's emotional outburst will eventually subside? Perhaps you were once asked about a friend, family member, or intimate partner's behavior. You may have responded, "She (or he) gets this way sometimes when she's (or he's) really upset." These examples illustrate that the more we know about a relational partner, the better we can explain that person's behavior.

Predictive Ability Perhaps you know to put your arms around a particular family member when she or he gets upset, yet with another family member you know that a brief talk about toughing it out will help to calm her or him. Returning to the previous

KNOWLEDGE power • Not Close, Closer, Closest

Think about three relationships in which you are involved: one that you would categorize as impersonal, one that you would define as somewhat personal, and one that you would classify as personal. Analyze these relationships in terms of your ability to explain and predict the behavior of your relational partners and in regard to the uniqueness of the relationships. Ask yourself:

- Can I explain why my partners will react in the manner that they do in the midst of conflict or while attempting to show affection and/or gratitude?
- Can I predict how my partners will react during stressful situations, in the midst of conflict, or while attempting to show affection and/or gratitude?
- Do my partners and I make use of idiosyncratic words, speak to each other as unique human beings, and follow rules that we have developed and applied to our specific relationships?

With a partner or in a group, discuss your ability to explain and predict relational behavior in addition to the unique aspects associated with your three relationships. Do you find that your explanatory and predictive power increases as your relationships become more personal? Do characteristics of your relationships become more unique as they become more personal?

KNOWLEDGE ON THE CUTTING EDGE

What Is the Role of the Family? : Are You a Civil Communicator?

According to a 2005 Associated Press-Ipsos poll, 70% of those questioned believe that Americans are ruder today than they were twenty or thirty years ago, and 69% of the respondents blamed celebrities, athletes, and public figures who behave rudely and are poor role models for the increase in rudeness. Similarly, 73% of those questioned pointed to TV shows and movies that include rude behavior as the cause for the increase in incivility. However, 93% of the respondents placed the blame on parents who fail to teach civility to their children.[1] Additionally, parents model rude and uncivil behavior that is mimicked by their children. Specifically, children watch their parents shout obscenities at drivers whose skills aren't up to par, engage in sideline rage during athletic activities, and bicker and fight whether or not the children are present.

Stephen L. Carter, the William Nelson Cromwell Professor of Law at Yale University, contends that children should learn within the family to respect others and communicate in a respectful manner. One way that parents can teach their children civil behavior is by sacrificing their own interests for "the larger good." For example, parents who openly bicker in front of their children teach the lesson of thinking only of themselves, whereas postponing an argument until the children are no longer in earshot (and resolving it in a civil manner) is a sacrifice made for the sake of civility. Parents should make a conscious effort to disagree with an attitude of mutual respect so children can learn that adults *can* demonstrate respect and love even when they aren't in agreement. And teaching respectful behavior means that parents must be civil when they contend with rude shopkeepers, lousy drivers, and intrusive telephone salespersons. Parents should also teach their children about civil communication by not saying behind people's backs what they wouldn't say face-to-face. Children who see their parents set aside their own concerns for the larger good are more likely to do the same when they reach adulthood.[2]

Children may mimic the rude and uncivil behaviors modeled by their parents.

example of someone who asks about a relational partner's behavior, you may respond, "She (or he) will calm down in a few minutes." These examples illustrate the idea that the more we know about a relational partner, the better we can predict that person's behavior.

Uniqueness Recall from Chapter 5 that individuals in relationships tend to develop idiosyncratic words that outsiders don't understand. Individuals involved in personal relationships also communicate with each other as unique human beings instead of as people who merely inhabit roles. Personal relationships further differ from impersonal

Figure 10.1: The Triangle of Love

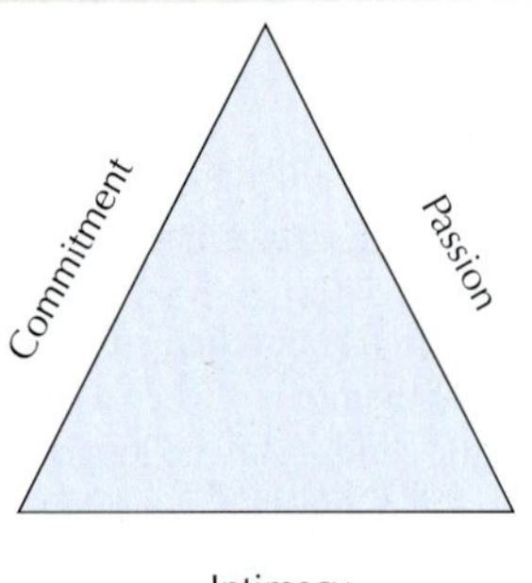

Source: From R. J. Sternberg and M. L. Barnes, *The Psychology of Love.* Copyright 1988 by Yale University Press. Reprinted by permission.

relationships in that communication rules change from those imposed by culture to those that are established by the relational members themselves. For example, there may be rules in your particular family about what specific topics can be talked about, who can talk about them, and when and where the topics can be talked about.

Characteristics of Romantic Relationships

Although interpersonal relationships can take a variety of forms, we will focus on four types: romantic relationships (and in the Contexts part of this chapter), family relationships, relationships between friends, and relationships in the workplace.

Like friendships, romantic relationships in Western culture are voluntary, but romantic relationships differ from friendships in that they are centered on the love-based characteristics of intimacy, passion, and commitment.[3] These characteristics are illustrated in Figure 10.1, "The Triangle of Love."

Intimacy **Intimacy** involves feelings of tenderness, connection, and closeness. It also includes warm feelings and affection for a romantic partner. Intimacy typically remains stable over the course of a relationship and accounts for the comfort that romantic partners feel in each other's company.

Passion **Passion** is most important during the early stages of relationship development. Passion typically refers to the fireworks or sparks between people who are attracted to each other. In addition to sexual feelings, passion can entail an ardent desire for another based on emotional, intellectual, or spiritual attraction.

Commitment **Commitment** refers to the decision to maintain and sustain a relationship based on love. Commitment tends to be the strongest predictor of relational satisfaction and is the most stable characteristic in the triangle of love. Commitment is the intention to stay together, despite the difficult times that are an inevitable part of any romantic relationship.

KNOWLEDGE power • Intimacy, Passion, or Commitment?

Two scientifically valid tests are available online to assess your "love type" and attachment style. The forty-nine-item Love Type Test, based on the triangle of love, can be found at www.personalityonline.com/tests/tests.html. The Close Relationships Questionnaire, which measures attachment style, is based on psychologist Martin Seligman's theory of authentic happiness. The thirty-eight-item assessment can be accessed at www.authentichappiness.org.

Why It's Important to Study Interpersonal Relationships

Motivation
Knowledge
Skill
COMPETENCE

Why is it important to study interpersonal relationships?

Studying interpersonal relationships is important because relationships can affect our physical and psychological health, provide us with social support, affect our self-concept, and have an impact on our future success and happiness. Social isolation tends to increase the risk of death, whether the cause is cancer, heart disease, stroke, accident, or suicide. Relational problems have been related to depression, failed marriages, family violence,

KNOWLEDGE ON THE CUTTING EDGE

Motivation to Communicate: At Work and in Class

Think about your place of employment. What motivates you to perform well and communicate competently on the job? Numerous studies suggest that organizational and interpersonal effectiveness can be enhanced when employees feel empowered; that is, they perceive:

- their jobs as meaningful
- themselves as competent employees
- that they have choices
- that their job-related behavior makes a difference

Disempowerment, although not the opposite of empowerment, occurs when a work event is perceived as an affront to an employee's dignity and as a disrespectful and inconsiderate violation of appropriate communication. Disempowered employees experience a decline in task motivation and the motivation to communicate in a competent manner. For example, "impaired interpersonal interactions" occur when employees are recipients of rude, verbally abusive, disrespectful, and dishonest communication. Negative attitudes and behaviors that result from employee disempowerment can spread vicariously to others in an organization and create a negative communicate climate. Employee behavior that reflects interpersonal and motivational effectiveness occurs when employees are recipients of considerate, honest, sincere, courteous, and respectful messages. Consequently, communication-related interventions are often suggested to reduce the harmful outcomes from perceptions of disempowerment. However, persuading employees and managers to engage in effective and appropriate communication within an organization is extremely difficult because it requires a fundamental change in habitual behavior and organizational culture.[4]

Now consider your communication class. What motivates you to communicate competently with your instructor? Interpersonal behavior in the classroom also affects students' motivation to communicate in a competent manner. Research reveals that college students typically report five motives that prompt communication with their instructors:

1. relational motives—to develop interpersonal relationships with instructors
2. functional motives—to learn more about course requirements, needed materials, and the like
3. participatory motives—to demonstrate understanding of course material
4. excuse-making motives—to explain why assignments are incomplete
5. sycophantic motives—to make a favorable impression on an instructor

The way students perceive instructor communication affects their motivation to communicate competently. Chapter 6 explained that nonverbal immediacy behaviors can motivate students to communicate. Both verbal and nonverbal instructor communication that is confirming and supportive is associated with the student relational motive, whereas antisocial instructor communication that is disconfirming and defensive is associated with student excuse making and sycophantic motives. Moreover, students who perceive an in-group relationship with their instructors (i.e., a relationship in which instructors can joke and tease students, communicate about their performance, and listen to students who communicate about personal problems) report using the relational, functional, participatory, and sycophantic motives at a higher rate than students who perceive out-group relationships with their instructors. Students in in-group relationships with their instructors perceive themselves as playing a support role in the classroom in which their input is welcomed and needed. Students to whom instructors respond positively may also communicate to fulfill the relational, functional, participatory, and sycophantic motives to create an in-group relationship.[5]

and job dissatisfaction. Interpersonal relationships have also been found to be just as significant as alcohol consumption, smoking, and diet in affecting physical and psychological health. In fact, more than one hundred scientific studies demonstrate that interpersonal relationships with family, friends, and members of our community contribute to happiness, health, and longer lives. Because those with whom we share relationships provide us with social support, our intimate partners, friends, family, and even associates at work can help us cope with the stress of modern life. Moreover, relationships affect our self-concept. In Chapter 3 we learned that comments from significant others affect how we perceive ourselves. We also compare ourselves with our relational partners and use their reactions to alter our behavior and self-concept. Young adults increasingly realize the central role that relationships play in their lives. One study of "the millennial generation" (young adults born since the early 1980s) suggests that marriage, time with children, relationships with coworkers, and friendships are central to their thinking about the future.[6]

Theoretical Perspectives About Interpersonal Relationships and Self-Disclosure

Perhaps among your circle of friends, you've heard the question, "Why does she (he) stay with him (her)?" Maybe you've been asked what attracted you to your relational partner. Just as we seek to find the underlying reasons for the formation, maintenance, and termination of our own relationships, social scientists develop theories to explain the larger question of human relationship development. Two widely accepted theories are social exchange theory and social penetration theory.

What are some theories that can explain interpersonal relationships and self-disclosure?

Social Exchange Theory

The oft-quoted response to a marital partner who asks whether he or she should leave his or her spouse is "Are you better off with her (him) or without her (him)?" This question describes the heart of **social exchange theory**, developed by psychologists **John Thibaut** and **Harold H. Kelley**, in which perceived rewards and costs determine whether people develop, maintain, or terminate their relationships.[7] As illustrated in Figure 10.2, "Social Exchange Theory," **rewards** refer to features of a relationship that are considered positive, and **costs** relate to features of a relationship that are considered negative. Relationship rewards can take the form of good feelings, need fulfillment, economic stability, and social status. Relationship costs can take the form of anxiety, insecurity, and the investment of too much time and too much energy. Although the preferred ratio between rewards and costs varies from person to person and from time to time, social exchange theorists contend that people conduct a cost-benefit analysis when determining whether they should invest in a relationship, given what they get out of it. Therefore, in contemplating a relational breakup, we may actually list reasons why we should stay (rewards) and why we should leave (costs). Social exchange theorists also maintain that we enter relationships with an idea about rewards and costs

Figure 10.2: Social Exchange Theory

based on our experiences in past relationships and on relationships we have observed among our friends, family, and the media. These expectations are called the **comparison level (CL)**. In addition, social exchange theorists suggest that we decide whether to form, sustain, or dissolve relationships based on what else is "out there." In other words, we use our **comparison level of alternatives (CLalt)** to compare the rewards we are receiving with those we may receive in alternative relationships.

Social Penetration Theory

Social Penetration Theory Social **penetration theory** developed by psychologists **Irwin Altman** and **Dalmas Taylor**, states that relationships develop and change in terms of the type and depth of the self-disclosure between relational partners.

Self-Disclosure and Social Penetration Theory **Self-disclosure** refers to the act of willingly sharing information about ourselves with others. The information we choose to share may range from what can be considered insignificant (e.g., "I like Coke better than Pepsi") to information that can be considered extremely significant (e.g., "I've decided to move to attend an out-of-state university"). Social penetration occurs when our self-disclosure moves from superficial topics, such as our favorite breed of dog or where we spent our last vacation, to topics that are more intimate, such as our worldview or fears. However, the intimacy of our relationships is characterized not only by the depth of topics about which we self-disclose but also by the breadth or variety of topics about which we self-disclose.[8]

As illustrated in Figure 10.3, "Social Penetration Theory," social penetration theory compares developing relationships with an onion that is cut in wedges and peeled. Specifically, the theory suggests that we have various layers of information about ourselves. Our onion cut into wedges illustrates the breadth or variety of topics about which we and our relational partners can converse. When our onion is peeled away, it reveals layers that illustrate the depths at which we self-disclose intimate information. We develop intimate relationships with others when we self-disclose a wide breadth of topics in an in-depth manner. In other words, we allow others to penetrate through the outside onion layers of superficial topics (e.g., "Have you seen any good movies lately?"), to middle layers of topics that are not readily known to others (e.g., "Who did you vote for in the last presidential election?"), and finally to the onion's core of deeply personal topics (e.g., "Do you believe in God?").

Self-Disclosure and Relational Success Engaging in self-disclosure doesn't guarantee relational success. Disclosing a disturbing secret to an intimate partner may even contribute to the demise of the relationship. Although self-disclosure can contribute to the development, maintenance, and enhancement of relationships, it can also cause problems for us, our partner, and our relationship. Because of the risk, we should ask ourselves the following questions before deciding to engage in self-disclosure:

- Am I planning to disclose an appropriate amount of information (we don't want to overwhelm a potential partner with a wide breadth of material)?
- Am I planning to disclose an appropriate type of information (we don't want to frighten off a potential partner with intimate and in-depth details of our personal life)?

Figure 10.3: Social Penetration Theory

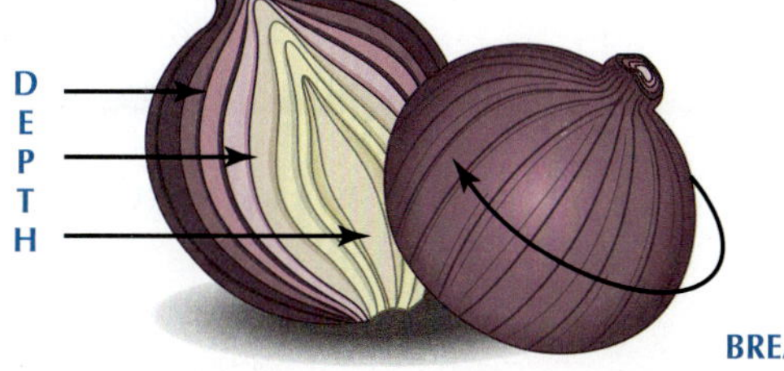

- Will I be embarrassed if my disclosure is communicated to others (we should make sure that the risks associated with disclosing to an untrustworthy partner are those we can live with)?
- Can I effectively and appropriately deal with my disclosure if it's not reciprocated (we should realize that although disclosure usually begets disclosure, this isn't always the case)?
- Will my disclosure place an unfair burden on my partner (we don't want to unfairly ask a partner to keep a secret or self-disclose only to relieve ourselves of guilty feelings)?

Models of Relational Development

Theories such as social exchange and social penetration explain and predict why relationships are created, maintained, and dissolved. We also study relationships by looking at models that describe and illustrate the process of relational development. Stage models, which classify relationships in terms of distinct developmental phases; process models, which describe relationships in terms of partners' needs and attributions; and combination models, which address the perspectives of both stage and process models, are used to study the life cycle of relationships.

What are some models of relational development?

Stage Models

A common type of model is the **stage model**, which suggests that relationships follow a trajectory and can be classified in terms of particular stages of integration, maintenance, or termination. A well-known stage model is **Mark Knapp** and **Anita Vangelisti**'s "ten-stage model" or "staircase model" of relationship development.[9] Knapp and Vangelisti's model of relationship development characterizes the nature of a relationship at specific moments during its evolution. Ten stages describe the broad phases of coming together and coming apart. As illustrated in Figure 10.4, "Knapp and Vangelisti's Stage Model of Relationship Development," the stages of coming together are:

1. initiating (casual interaction with the goal of establishing a relationship)
2. experimenting (small talk about a variety of subjects to discover whether the relationship is worth pursuing)
3. intensifying (an increase in the breadth and depth of self-disclosure)
4. integrating (relational partners and others view them as a couple)
5. bonding (characterized by a public ritual that formalizes the exclusive nature of the relationship)

The stages of coming apart are:

1. differentiating (relationship partners attempt to regain their unique identities)
2. circumscribing (constriction of the breadth and depth of self-disclosure)
3. stagnating (relationship partners close themselves off from each other)
4. avoiding (partners physically distance themselves from each other)
5. terminating (the relationships ends)

The staircase model can describe relationships among close friends, business partners, and romantic relationships. It also can describe relationships that end after only a few

Figure 10.4: Knapp and Vangelisti's Stage Model of Relationship Development

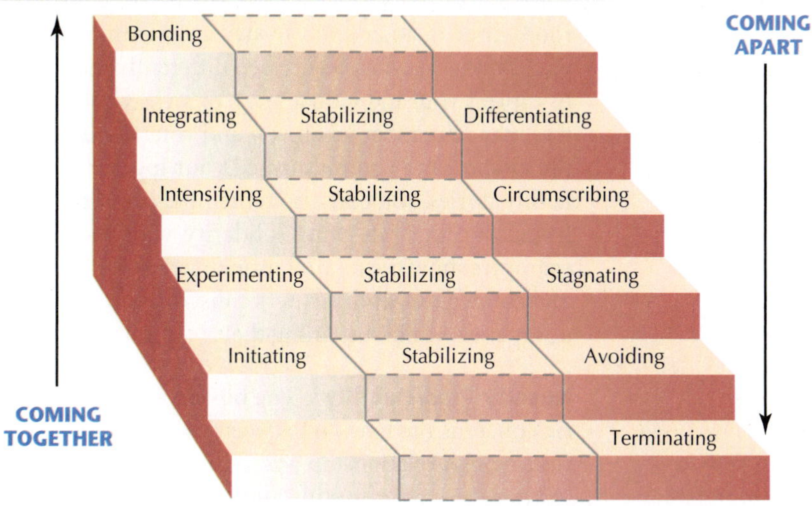

Source: From M. L. Knapp and L. Vangelisti, *Interpersonal Communication and Human Relationships,* 5e. Published by Allyn and Bacon, Boston, MA. Copyright © 2005 by Pearson Education. Reprinted by permission of the publisher.

stages and relationships that never move beyond the early stages. However, there are drawbacks associated with the staircase model and other stage models of relationship development. One criticism is that stage models treat relationship development as an invariant succession of stages and that the earlier stages are necessary before reaching later stages. However, not all relationships develop and deteriorate in a step-by-step manner; for example, some partners marry during the intensifying and integrating stages, and other partners may leave a relationship during the stages related to relationship maintenance. The model also doesn't illustrate the idea that one partner may believe the relationship reflects a particular stage (e.g., "differentiating"), while the other partner believes that the relationship reflects another (e.g., "avoiding"). Additionally, stage models don't include the opposing forces or tensions that occur in all relationships, no matter what the stage. However, these opposing forces are reflected in the process model of dialectical tensions.

The Dialectical Tension Process Model

Process models reflect the idea that relationships are ongoing and that relational meaning ebbs and flows, based on partners' attributions. Communication scholar **Leslie Baxter** has developed a process model of **dialectical tensions** showing that relationships oscillate between opposing ends of a continuum. Dialectical tensions suggest that relationships evolve and change over time because partners constantly reassess and redefine their needs. Similarly, the dialectical tensions model allows partners to experience a decline in their relationship without automatically moving to disintegration. As shown in Figure 10.5, "Dialectical Tensions," at least three dialectics function as examples of the normal push-pull in relational life: autonomy/connection, novelty/predictability, and openness/closedness.[10]

Autonomy-Connection The **autonomy-connection dialectic** reflects the tension between wanting to be independent and wanting to feel connected. Sometimes we desire to spend time with friends, partners, family members, and coworkers; at other times, we

Figure 10.5: Dialectical Tensions

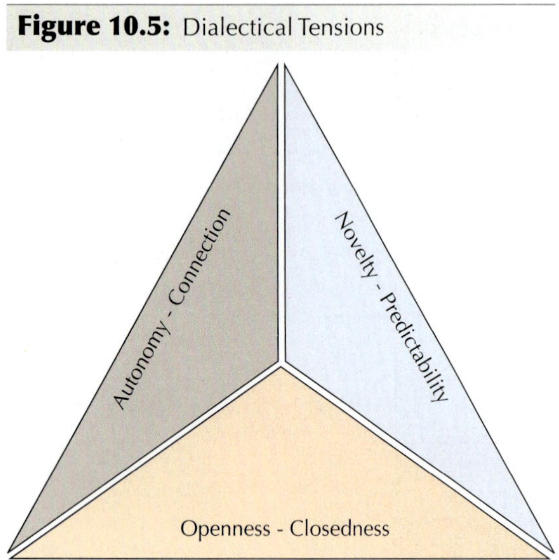

want to be alone and prefer to emphasize our individuality. Perhaps you remember a time when you closed your bedroom door in an attempt to stay away from the closeness of your family. Maybe you dressed differently than your friends to express your individual sense of style. On the other hand, you may remember when you and your family assembled in the kitchen and communicated your togetherness by telling family stories. You may also remember dressing just like your friends to illustrate your solidarity with the group. These examples show the natural human needs for both autonomy and connection, and partners constantly attempt to preserve uniqueness while sustaining their relational bond.

Novelty-Predictability The **novelty-predictability dialectic** concerns the tension between wanting predictability and routine in a relationship and desiring novelty and newness. At times we prefer routine and stability in our relationships. We take comfort in knowing that we can count on our friends to meet us at our usual gathering spot. We don't have to worry about our romantic partner not showing up for a regularly planned evening out, and we enjoy the routine nature of communicating with coworkers on a day-to-day basis. However, too much predictability in our relationships can cause boredom, and we seek to infuse our relationships with novelty. For example, we may ask to meet our friends at a new restaurant. We may also enjoy the combination of excitement and anxiety brought by a new relational partner who may or may not show up for a last-minute outing. We may feel invigorated and enthused with our established relationships at work when a new employee with innovative ideas is hired. These scenarios illustrate our need for relational security and stability, and our need for relational spontaneity and unpredictability.

Openness/Closedness The **openness/closedness dialectic** reflects the tension between wanting to self-disclose and engage in open communication and desiring privacy. Sometimes we feel the need to share our innermost thoughts and feelings with others; at other

The autonomy-connection dialectic reflects the tension between wanting to be independent and wanting to feel connected.

Source: © ZITS–ZITS PARTNERSHIP, KING FEATURES SYNDICATE.

KNOWLEDGE power • Managing Your Dialectical Tensions

Think about a meaningful relationship in which you're involved. With a partner or in a group, describe which dialectical tensions underlie communication with your relationship partner. (Be prepared to give examples of discussions that illustrate the tension between autonomy and connection, novelty and predictability, and openness and closedness.) Relate how you and your partner manage the dialectical tension(s) by neutralization, selection, separation, or reframing. Brainstorm additional methods that can facilitate the management of dialectical tensions in your relationship.

times we feel the need to be reserved. At times we want to become close to others by revealing our emotions; at other times we want to protect ourselves by withholding information that can leave us vulnerable. For example, how might you respond if a good friend asks for your opinion about a potential romantic relationship that you secretly feel will be detrimental to your friend? Do you tell your friend that you think the future romantic partner is a loser? If you do, will your comments come back to haunt you when your friend becomes engaged to that person? Do you tell your friend nothing because you want to keep your true thoughts to yourself? If you do, will you regret not being open about your true feelings when your friend comes to you for support after she or he is rejected? These examples illustrate the need to express ourselves (openness) and the opposing need to refrain from expression (closedness).

Dialectics are a natural part of all healthy relationships, and relational partners have at least four ways to deal with the tension caused by conflicting needs:[11]

1. **Neutralization**—giving up some of what relational partners want so their desires can be partially met, that is, negotiating between the two extremes of a dialectic continuum. For example, although college students who live on campus or in an apartment may want to be autonomous from their parents, they may realize that, however bothersome, one or two calls per week from Mom and Dad can be tolerated. From the opposite perspective, although parents of college students may want to know every detail about their offspring's life, they may realize that an email every now or then is sufficient to remain connected with their child. In this example, neither the college students nor their parents are completely meeting their needs for autonomy or connection, but they have compromised so that their needs are partially met.
2. **Selection**—placing emphasis on one dialectic need and ignoring or neglecting the opposite dialectic need for a certain period of time. For example, we may deliberately ignore the need for autonomy during a 24/7 weeklong family reunion, and we may just as deliberately ignore the need for connection and concentrate on some "alone time" for a few days after the reunion ends.
3. **Separation**—giving priority to a specific dialectic need in certain circumstances and placing emphasis on the opposing dialectic need in others. For example, we may desire a day-to-day routine that affords stability and a sense of security in our lives (predictability), but during an overseas trip, we may engage in spur-of-the-moment adventures, such as waking up without a plan for the day, taking walks without a map, and hopping a train to a last-minute destination (novelty).
4. **Reframing**—engaging in perspective taking to redefine opposing dialectics as no longer threatening a relationship. For example, suppose a female believes that her male partner rejects her when he comes home from work and stares at the TV or goes into the computer room and shuts the door. She wants to talk to him about his day and share her experiences; he wants to relax without the need to communicate. The female partner may

believe that his lack of communication and need to be alone is a quest for autonomy in the face of her attempts at connection. However, suppose she reads about the influence of gender and brain differences on communication. She learns that males tend to perceive communication as a means to an end rather than an end in itself. She reads that communication isn't typically as pleasurable for men as it is for women and that men often perceive communication as work. The female partner also learns that communication entails more brain power for men than for women because women's brains are hardwired to facilitate communication. Armed with this knowledge, she engages in perspective taking and reinterprets her partner's behavior. Because she now redefines the dialectic, she realizes that her partner isn't rejecting her by not talking after a long day at the office; his silence is an attempt to relax and rejuvenate in his home, a place where he isn't forced to "work" (that is, talk). The dialectic of autonomy (e.g., the male partner's lack of communication and need to be alone) will continue to be present in the relationship but will no longer be seen in *opposition to* or in *conflict with* the need for connection.

So far, we have discussed stage models that describe linear movement between relationship phases and process models that view change and redefinition as a natural part of the relational life cycle, no matter the stage of a relationship. Both of these perspectives are addressed in the combination model of relationship development.

Combination Models

The "communication in the relational life cycle" model is a combination model that includes dialectical tensions and focuses on communication strategies associated with relationship phases. In Figure 10.6, "Communication in the Relationship Life Cycle," the block arrows that point from the dialectical tensions to the relationship strategies show that these opposing forces can influence communication and the relationship itself during any given phase. Moreover, although sequenced into a series of phases, the doubled-ended stick arrows illustrate that with the exception of the initiation and reconciliation phases, movement can occur forward and backward between the phases as a relationship changes and relational stability ebbs and flows. For example, a relational partner may realize that she or he wants to change a platonic friendship that has been maintained for some time to one that is more romantic. She or he may use communication strategies associated with bonding (those that relate to the identification of the individuals as a couple) to move the relationship to a new dimension of intimacy. Similarly, after engaging in reconciliation strategies following a breakup, a couple may strengthen the new meaning of their relationship by using bonding strategies (without the necessity of engaging in strategies related to initiation). Note that the arrow travels in one direction from the reconciliation phase to the bonding phase. This is because a relationship is reconciled only *after* a breakup, even though bonding, repair, and reconciliation strategies can alter the meaning of a relationship. Sometimes a specific feeling, event, or discussion will change the intensity or definition of a relationship. Such **turning points** help to explain the uniqueness of all relationships based on a variety of experiences and different responses to those experiences. Studies of both college-age and older adult samples reveal that turning points such as a first date, meeting the family, a routine-breaking event (e.g., going camping together), physical separation, reunion after a physical separation, the expression of passion (e.g., the first kiss, the first expression of "I love you"), external competition from either a rival or competing demands, helping a relational partner through a crisis situation, and changing one's attitude about the relationship are turning points that can significantly change the meaning of a relationship.[12] The stick arrows that

Figure 10.6: Communication in the Relationship Life Cycle

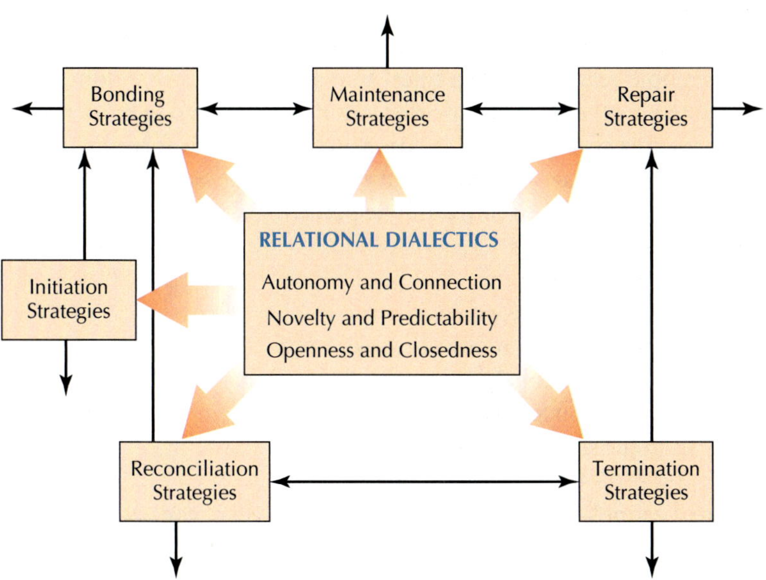

point outward from each phase indicate that termination can occur at any time without the necessity of moving through particular stages. For example, you may know someone who was on the receiving end of a totally unexpected "sudden death" breakup.

To summarize, the communication in the relationship life cycle combination model includes a description of relationship stages (similar to the staircase stage model) and illustrates that relational meaning changes based on partners' attributions (similar to the dialectical tensions process model). We will use the phases in this model to discuss strategies and skills related to relational development.

Skills in the Life Cycle of a Relationship

Motivation
Knowledge
Skill
COMPETENCE

There are a number of strategies or clusters of skills that characterize communication associated with each phase of a relationship. We will begin with initiation strategies.

Initiation Strategies

How can skills related to initiating and bonding, maintaining, repairing, terminating, and reconciling relationships improve our communication competence?

The **initiation phase** of a relationship relates to the first words we utter to a potential relationship partner to whom we are attracted. **Attraction theory** predicts that we are drawn to and may initiate relationships with people who we believe are physically attractive, who are in physical proximity to us, and who are similar to us. But exactly *how* can we approach a nice-looking person who lives close by and appears to share similar attitudes?

In Chapter 7 we learned some techniques for approaching others and initiating conversations. These skills include asking questions that will engage others, such as those that focus on the environment and the people with whom we speak. However, these techniques may prove unsuccessful in trying to communicate interest in initiating a relationship. Communicating about the environment, the other person's family, or recent activities may be excellent ways to start a conversation, but they may fail to indicate that we are looking for more than a conversation partner. To compensate for this problem, some people rely on "pickup lines" that suggest a desire to initiate a relationship. A **pickup line** is a rehearsed question or comment designed to make the communicator appear attractive to a potential relationship partner. Unfortunately, there is no guarantee that a potential partner will perceive a pickup line as creative or humorous; in fact, a pickup line can actually backfire and be perceived as rude or offensive. Examples of pickup lines include:

- Excuse me; I think it's time we meet.
- Do you have a friend who can introduce us?
- If I could rearrange the alphabet, I'd put "u" and "i" together.
- Did it hurt . . . when you fell from heaven?
- Of all the fish in the sea, you're the one I'm hooked on.

Pickup lines are a gamble—did you giggle or groan when you read these examples? Although they may elicit a chuckle and be perceived as a creative way to meet someone, there is no guarantee that they will be successful. Experts warn that "canned come-ons" should be the last resort for attempting to initiate a relationship because they may communicate insincerity and can be used to attract anyone. Pickup lines fail to communicate a potential partner's uniqueness and what special individual features a communicator finds attractive.

Pickup lines can be the cause of a relationship that never gets off the ground, and a direct approach may have a better chance of success in initiating a relationship. A direct approach is sincere, honest, and gets straight to the point. An example of a direct approach to initiating a relationship is "Hi, my name is ____ and I've seen you at ____. I'd like to get to know you better." Another direct approach entails a sincere compliment about a person's smile or clothing. Even approaching a stranger and saying, "Hi, how are you?" may be more effective than resorting to a pickup line.[13] However, as mentioned in Chapter 7, a direct approach to relationship initiation can be interpreted as a pickup line or be the cause of an unexpected response.

SKILL practice • Relationship Initiation Strategies

With a partner or in a small group, share the pickup lines that you've communicated, heard about, or had directed toward you. Discuss whether the lines were successful. Similarly, discuss whether a direct approach is preferred among members of the group, and list examples of initiation strategies that reflect a direct approach. Finally, practice out loud with your partner or a group member with either a pickup line or a direct approach that you think may have the best chance of initiating a relationship. You and your partner or group can also present your discussion findings to your class by creating two skits that illustrate successful and unsuccessful initiation strategies.

Bonding Strategies

Bonding is the phase that follows the initiation strategies. Perhaps you have successfully initiated a relationship with a pickup line or a direct approach. What did you do to get to know your partner better and establish yourselves as a couple? Using **bonding strategies** such as asking questions about a potential or new relational partner and identifying yourselves as a couple can strengthen and potentially change the meaning of a relationship.

Asking Questions We may ask questions to get to know our potential relational partner better and, in turn, answer questions she or he directs toward us. This process may last days, weeks, and even months as we become more familiar with our relational partner. Initial questions that focus on a partner's values and personality rather than questions that concern income and relational or sexual history tend to be successful. Examples of such questions include:

- What do you look for in a friend?
- Do you like to socialize in groups?
- How to you like to spend your time or what are your interests?
- How would you define your personality?
- What matters to you in life?

Identification as a Couple Once a relationship has been initiated and we learn more about a potential relational partner, additional skills associated with bonding identify the

KNOWLEDGE ON THE CUTTING EDGE

Technology Update: Initiating and Bonding Online

The process of relational initiation and bonding that begins online is similar to relationships that begin in face-to-face settings. Early theories of computer-mediated communication suggested that initiating interpersonal relationships in cyberspace would be more difficult than face-to-face communication because the channel is less personal and filters out nonverbal communication. However, recent research has discovered that Internet communication can be described as **hyperpersonal**, or more sociable, personal, and intimate than what is found in face-to-face interaction. Although little research exists about online relationships that eventually move to off-line settings, extant studies demonstrate that it is easy to start relationships online. Although attraction theory predicts that we focus on others who are physically pleasing, live in close proximity, and have something in common, Internet users aren't biased by physical appearance or constricted by geographic limitations. People encounter others' messages in newsgroups and chat rooms and initiate interaction based on the knowledge that they have something in common. Relationships that initiate and bond online tend to begin in places people regularly visit, such as particular Web sites or blogs. Users may focus on communication from a specific person and respond with a request to exchange email addresses. What typically follow are telephone conversations and the suggestion to meet off-line. Taking the relationship to a face-to-face setting can be considered a turning point that transforms the relationship; at this stage, both users already know each other well, and physical appearance isn't as influential in affecting the overall relationship. Because of these reasons, both friendship and romantic cyberspace relationships often survive the transition to an off-line setting. Moreover, meeting people and starting online relationships is advantageous for a number of reasons: it can protect our identity; we can learn about a potential partner prior to exchanging personal information (e.g., by "Googling" the partner's name, securing an online profile, and reading her or his blog comments or contributions to a newsgroup); and we can exchange email and have phone conversations without revealing our personal identity. Currently, 74% of the 10 million Internet users who are single and actively looking for romantic partners have looked for romance online. Overall, online technology has the capacity to positively influence communication and relationships with others.[14]

Competence & Critical Thinking

mycommunicationlab

DO YOU COME HERE OFTEN? AND INTERPERSONAL RELATIONSHIPS

Bill is relaxing over a drink in a bar when he is approached by Kathleen. A conversation ensues.

You can view *Do You Come Here Often?* by accessing the "Small Group and Interpersonal Videos" on the MyCommunicationLab Web site. Answer the following questions about their self-disclosure and relational initiation:

- Explain Bill and Kathleen's self-disclosure in terms of Altman and Taylor's Social Penetration theory.
- Do Bill and Kathleen self-disclose in an effective and appropriate manner? Do you believe they considered the questions/guidelines for self-disclosure included in your text?
- What verbal communication strategies does Kathleen use to initiate a relationship with Bill? Does she use the verbal communication strategies in a competent manner?
- What nonverbal communication strategies does Kathleen use to initiate a relationship with Bill? Does she use the nonverbal communication strategies in a competent manner?
- How does Bill verbally and nonverbally communicate to Kathleen that he is not interested in initiating a relationship?

KATHLEEN: Martini, please. Hi.

BILL: Hi.

KATHLEEN: Kathleen.

BILL: Bill.

KATHLEEN: Nice to meet you.

BILL: Glad to meet you.

KATHLEEN: How you doing?

BILL: Good. How are you?

KATHLEEN: I'm all right.

BILL: Great.

KATHLEEN: You in town on business?

BILL: Mm-hmm.

KATHLEEN: Yeah, me too.

BILL: Yeah, what do you do?

KATHLEEN: Oh, finance. How about you?

BILL: Oh, I'm a recruiter. Dealing with a recruiting firm. Health insurance, managed care, that type. Industry. Here on business.

KATHLEEN: Yeah. *(to the bartender as she receives her drink)* Oh, thank you. *(to Bill)* So you here with anyone?

BILL: No, not—not for a couple of days at least. One of the guys from the office might come down, but just here I'm solo. How about yourself?

KATHLEEN: Free as a bird. It's just me. I do a lot of consulting, so I'm used to it.

BILL: Yeah, yeah; me too.

KATHLEEN: Gets a little lonely though, sometimes.

BILL: You know, I—I get used to it and keep myself busy and work and hobbies, and I, you know, relax.

KATHLEEN: How about back home? You married?

BILL: Oh. Excuse me. No, no, not married. Was married. Not anymore.

KATHLEEN: Oh. I'm sorry to hear that.

BILL: It happens.

KATHLEEN: Yeah.

BILL: A lot.

KATHLEEN: Hmm.

BILL: You're married, are you?

KATHLEEN: Hmm. Not anymore. How about kids? Got any kids?

BILL. Mm-hmm. Boy and girl, nine and twelve, about to be ten and thirteen.

KATHLEEN: Hmm. It's a fun age.

BILL: Yeah, yeah. They're a handful, but I enjoy them. They stay with their mother.

KATHLEEN: And so what do you do in your free time?

BILL: Um, I've got hobbies, you know, things I like to do, games, all—all kinds of games. I'm a games kind of guy, chess, big—big chess enthusiast.

KATHLEEN: Chess, really.

BILL: Yeah, you like chess?

KATHLEEN: Well, I have always wanted to learn.

BILL: Oh, okay.

KATHLEEN: Do you think maybe you could teach me a few things?

BILL: Well, it's not quite like that. You know, it takes time. It's been nearly twenty-five, almost thirty years, really, that I've been playing. I'm actually—tournament or two away from obtaining my master's rating. So I enjoy it.

KATHLEEN: Wow, that's great.

BILL: Yeah.

KATHLEEN: I am very impressed.

BILL: I like it. I like it a lot.

KATHLEEN: So come on. I know you could teach me something.

BILL: Oh, no, I, you know, I . . .

KATHLEEN: Yeah.

BILL: Do you know how the pieces move?

KATHLEEN: Yup, that much I know.

BILL: Okay. Well, I would recommend getting a beginner's book on it . . .

KATHLEEN: Oh, no.

BILL: . . . details opening and things.

KATHLEEN: Books are really boring.

BILL: Oh, yeah. Well, it's happening where I am with my—my chess ability.

KATHLEEN: Well, listen. You know, I would really just much rather learn it from you. Do you think that we could—we could go back to my room and . . .

BILL: I have such a long day tomorrow. I've got to prepare.

KATHLEEN: It's pretty early now.

BILL: I've got a really . . .

KATHLEEN: Yeah.

BILL: . . . big meeting. And it's . . .

KATHLEEN: Uh-huh.

BILL: . . . it's got to happen a certain way. So maybe another time, run into you or something. Did I get something on my jacket?

KATHLEEN: No, you didn't.

BILL: Yeah. So what do you do again? What was it that you said?

two individuals as a couple. Bonding tactics strengthen the idea of separate individuals perceiving themselves (and being perceived by others) as united. Bonding skills include:

- use of nicknames and the development and use of slang and/or jargon understood only by the couple and/or others in their social milieu
- use of the words *we* and *us*
- communication that relates to the nature of the relationship, such as "I think you're a good friend and I really like you" and "We really have something special"

The successful use of bonding skills and the perception of two individuals as a couple may transition to the next phase of relational development in which the relationship is maintained.

Expressing appreciation for a relational partner can help maintain the relationship.

Maintenance Strategies

The next phase in the relationship life cycle concerns maintenance strategies. What do you do to sustain your relationships and not take your partners for granted? It may help to think of relationships as gardens in which trees and flowers are maintained with care and attention. Just like the contents of a garden, a relationship will deteriorate and perhaps die if we don't take actions to prolong its health. **Maintenance skills** sustain the meaning of the relationship held by the relational partners. Maintenance behaviors have been conceptualized as both nonstrategic and strategic actions that prevent relational deterioration. We use nonstrategic maintenance behaviors in everyday talk that is ordinary, mundane, and perhaps trivial. However, everyday talk is important because it provides relational partners with an image of their relationship and an idea of its future. When we tell jokes, suggest a restaurant for dinner, and talk about other people's relationships, clothing, or personality characteristics, we communicate as a couple about our shared worldview, attitudes, and understanding of our relationship. Relationships are sustained by the realization that partners share priorities and values.[15]

Strategic behaviors also contribute to relationship maintenance. Five strategies that we can use to maintain our relationships are:[16]

1. **Positivity**—we can attempt to make interactions pleasant by being cheerful, doing favors, and avoiding criticism of our partner. We can also engage in prosocial behaviors such as expressing appreciation for a partner.
2. **Openness**—we can engage in direct discussions about our relationship, give and seek advice, and demonstrate empathy.
3. **Assurances**—we can support, comfort, and communicate feelings for our relationship partner.
4. **Social networks**—we can rely on and accept our relationship partner's friends and family.
5. **Sharing Tasks**—we can help equally with chores and other tasks that must be done.

Relational maintenance research has been extended to include additional strategies and skills used among friends and family members, gay and lesbian couples, and persons of color. For example, positivity, openness, and assurances are used less in friendships and more in romantic relationships. Similarly, assurances, sharing tasks, and sending cards or phoning the other are used more among family members and less in friendships. Homosexual couples engage in the same maintenance behaviors as heterosexual couples, with the inclusion of the additional maintenance behavior of "being in a gay-lesbian supportive environment," and African American married couples and European American couples use the same relational maintenance strategies.[17]

One way to communicate the maintenance strategy of positivity is by expressing appreciation for our relationship partners. **Appreciation** communicates that we feel grateful and that we are thankful for our relational partner and the relationship itself. Most people desire to be genuinely appreciated, yet we tend to more often comment about negative aspects of our relationship and relationship partner. We typically believe that our partner "already knows" that we appreciate her or him, and we take it for granted when others behave in ways that somehow benefit us. Think about partners in intimate, friendship, familial, and work relationships. Can you recall the last time you expressed your appreciation for them? We can communicate appreciation for a relational partner by using a simple three-step method:[18]

1. Describe the specific actions that we believe contribute to our well-being.
2. Describe the particular need(s) that the partner fulfills.
3. Describe how we feel when our needs are fulfilled (we can actually say the words, "I appreciate . . .").

These three steps do not have to occur in any particular sequence. For example, we can express our appreciation to a coworker by saying:

> "*You knew I needed to leave early yesterday* (describe the need)
> *and you finished up the report even though I didn't ask you to.* (describe the specific action)
> *I appreciate your going the extra mile for me.*" (describe how you feel)

We can also express our appreciation to a partner in a friendship, familial, or romantic relationship by saying:

> "*I appreciate* (describe how you feel)
> *you for listening to me talk about my trouble.* (describe the specific action)
> *I really needed to talk to someone.*" (describe the need)

Sometimes we can express our appreciation about behaviors of others that are mundane or routine. A simple "*I appreciate you for . . .*" or "*Thank you for . . .*" (express what the relational partner has said or done) will suffice. For example:

> "*I appreciate you for doing the laundry.*"
> "*Thank you for taking care of the pets.*"
> "*I appreciate you for taking phone messages for me.*"

One benefit associated with the expression of appreciation is that we may be perceived as sympathetic, understanding, and attractive. An additional benefit of this and other positivity skills is reciprocation: our relational partner is likely to communicate cheerfulness,

SKILL practice • Expressing Appreciation

Identify three or four relationships in which you are involved (e.g., relationships with a friend, family member, romantic partner, or coworker). Try to recall a time when your relationship partners met a particular need or merely carried out their part of the bargain to keep your relationship going. With a partner or in a group, practice expressing appreciation to your partners by using the three-step method or by beginning your comments with, "I appreciate . . ." Actually communicate these statements of appreciation to your partners when you next see them, and challenge yourself to continue expressing statements of appreciation every few days.

carry out favors, avoid criticism, and express appreciation for us. Positivity has also been related to satisfaction with a relational partner and the relationship itself. Using a strategy of positivity and the skill of expressing appreciation to maintain a relationship is rewarding to both partners.[19]

Repair Strategies

Have you or people you know become dissatisfied with a relationship? Did this cause relational decline or even lead to cheating? According to the communication in the relationship life cycle model, people can feel dissatisfied with their partner and the relationship as a whole even if both partners engage in relationship maintenance strategies. To improve relationships that appear to be in decline, we can use **repair strategies**. These strategies are not limited to a particular phase in the relationship life cycle. Recall that the dialectical tensions between autonomy and connection, novelty and predictability, and openness and closedness can contribute to perceptions of relational decay regardless of whether a relationship moves toward termination. Repair strategies—namely, neutralization, selection, separation, and reframing—can be used to manage dialectical tensions. These strategies can also be used to repair the results of relational transgressions, which contribute to the deterioration of relationships. **Relational transgressions** violate relational expectations or rules. Serious relational transgressions, such as infidelity and unfaithfulness, and lesser transgressions, such as breaking the relational rule of not talking about past romantic partners, may require repair strategies.

Unfortunately, not a lot of research has contributed to the formulation of typologies of relational repair strategies. In one study of both maintenance and repair behaviors, strategies such as sharing activities, engaging in prosocial behavior, and making use of metacommunication and relational talk (which were used most when both partners desired to repair their relationship) were found to help preserve a relationship. Changing problematic behavior, accepting or forgiving a transgression, and reassessing the relationship have also been related to relational rejuvenation.[20] In a study of deception detection, married partners included communication about their relationship most often in the repair process. Friends also tended to mention their relationship, but coworkers were least likely to do so.[21] In general, when trying to repair a relationship, we should:

- Identify the problem(s) affecting our relationship. We can use metacommunication and confirming responses (see Chapter 8) to discover if our partner perceives the relationship and relational problems as we do.

- Decide which overall strategies and specific skills to use to repair the relationship. We should also consider what changes in behavior we are willing to make to repair the relationship.

Overall, the research concerning repair strategies suggests that engaging in prosocial behaviors and direct metacommunication can positively affect our relationships. However, there is no guarantee that dialectical tensions will be managed well, that the everyday irritants associated with relationships will be handled effectively, or that a relationship can deal with and move beyond a relational transgression. A relational partner may feel the need to use communication strategies designed to terminate the relationship.

Termination Strategies

Have you ever been on the receiving end of a termination message? Has a partner looked you in the eyes and communicated directly that she or he wanted to end the relationship, or did your partner drop hints and otherwise communicate the intention to break up in an indirect manner? According to the communication in the relationship life cycle model, repair strategies may be unsuccessful, and we may find ourselves using **termination strategies**. Although both partners need to experience honesty and clarity at the end of a relationship, communicating termination strategies in a direct and forthright manner is easier said than done. Most termination talk is indirect and communicated in general terms. Partners often believe that it's kinder to allow a relationship to drift apart than to be direct. Sometimes we even act unethically by provoking a partner into initiating a breakup![22] One of the most painful cognitive and emotional outcomes of a breakup is the doubt and confusion it creates; therefore, relational partners need explanations about a termination. In reality, we don't truly spare our partner's feelings by avoiding contact and refusing to tell her or him in a direct manner that the relationship is over and why it should end.[23] Typically we use manipulation strategies or withdrawal/avoidance strategies, and only sometimes do we use positive tone strategies:[24]

- **Manipulation**—Manipulation tactics are unethical and entail intentionally provoking a relational partner to initiate a breakup. We may purposefully leave an email on our computer screen that demonstrates an intimate relationship with someone else, or we may fail to keep our promises and commitments by not showing up at prearranged times or intentionally "forgetting" to attend important

KNOWLEDGE power • Bye-Bye, Love

Think about a relationship that ended successfully or unsuccessfully. If you were the partner who made use of termination strategies, identify which strategies you employed and why you believe they were competent. If you were the partner on the receiving end of termination strategies, identify which strategies your partner used and whether you believe they were used competently. Write a script using competent communication that you believe would have resulted in a more effective and appropriate termination of the relationship. With a partner or in a group, read your script aloud and discuss whether your script is realistic, honest, clear, and positive.

events. Manipulation occurs when we fail to take responsibility for our desire to terminate a relationship and intentionally act in a dishonest manner to get our partner to take action. We should therefore avoid this termination strategy.

- **Withdrawal/Avoidance**—The withdrawal/avoidance strategy uses indirect tactics, such as reducing the frequency and/or intimacy of contact with a partner, to achieve relationship termination. Telling a partner that we're too busy doing other things to spend time together and failing to return phone calls are two tactics associated with the withdrawal/ avoidance strategy. This strategy may not be clearly unethical, but it lacks the directness and clarity of positive tone strategies.
- **Positive Tone**—The positive tone strategy uses direct communication that indicates a desire for termination yet demonstrates respect for and saves the face of a relational partner. Skills associated with the positive tone strategy include owning our thoughts and feelings, using descriptive language, and using metacommunication. Positive tone tactics honor what was once a meaningful and intimate partnership with another individual and communicate the desire to end on a positive note. An example of a positive tone termination message is *"I've thought about this for a long time and I've made a difficult decision. We had a lot of good experiences together and I'll always remember the fun times. However, I am at a point where I want us to see each other exclusively, but you've repeatedly told me that you want to go out with others. I no longer want to experience hurt and disappointment each time I hear you tell me how much I mean to you, knowing that you continue to date other people. In the long run, it will be better for me if we stop seeing each other."*

Reconciliation Strategies

Relational termination isn't always successful (sometimes thankfully so). Perhaps you or people you know once experienced a breakup but later renewed the relationship with **reconciliation strategies**. The research concerning communication and reconciliation is almost nonexistent, but one study discovered that reconciliation strategies are more diverse than maintenance and repair strategies.[25] For example:

"Vulnerable appeal" relationship reconciliation strategies are direct and request that a couple get back together after a breakup.

- Spontaneous development strategies can help couples spend more time and do more activities together.
- With a third-party mediation strategy, outsiders encourage a partner to initiate the reconciliation.
- High-affect/ultimatum strategies include comments about rival suitors and statements such as "It's now or never."
- Tacit/persistence strategies involve asking a former partner to do something without intending to reconcile.
- Mutual interaction strategies entail communication about why a relationship has been terminated and how the relationship can be improved (e.g., "We were afraid to talk about our problems, but we can start over and be more honest with each other").
- Avoidance strategies appear to be intentional efforts to evade the issues associated with the breakup during an attempted reconciliation.
- Vulnerable appeal strategies are direct requests for reconciliation ("I think we should get back together").

We need to be realistic about the guidelines and skills designed to enhance relationships and to acknowledge that they may not achieve our desired result. For example, if our communication skills aimed at bonding are directed toward someone more powerful than we are, they may be perceived as insincere attempts at ingratiation. Similarly, although experts suggest that the best termination strategy is direct and to the point, the result of such a strategy may be rage, tears, or other inappropriate and ineffective responses. And there is no guarantee that reconciliation strategies will bring ex-partners back together after a breakup. Be prepared for unexpected responses, and consider you, your partner, and the nature of a relationship before deciding to use a particular communication skill.

Contexts and Interpersonal Relationships

Not only do communication strategies and skills affect relational development but also the culture, relationship, gender, and individual contexts influence our communication and the development of our various interpersonal relationships.

Culture Context

Research demonstrates that perceptions of friendship differ from culture to culture and among co-cultures in the United States.

How do contexts influence interpersonal relationships?

Culture Unlike family and work relationships, friendships are perceived as mostly voluntary and spontaneous in individualist cultures. However, people in collectivist cultures perceive friendships to be less spontaneous and to involve more long-term commitment and obligation. Specifically, people in the Chinese culture typically make few short-term acquaintances, and friendships are based on *quanxi,* or social connections. Although connections are important in the United States and are typically made through networking in one's area of employment, connections in China underlie the purposeful cultivation of friendships. Family relationships can also differ from culture

Our cultures and co-cultures affect our relationships with others.

Source: BALDO © 2004 Baldo Partnership. Dist. by UNIVERSIAL PRESS SYNDICATE. Reprinted with permission.

to culture. Decision making in collectivist cultures such as Japan, Korea, and China is highly dependent on family members. Families typically decide on their children's university, profession, and marital partner. In terms of romantic relationships, Americans tend to emphasize passion and intimacy, but more collectivist cultures perceive that acceptance by family members takes precedence over passion and intimacy and that commitment is more important than romantic love. Dating is also perceived differently in diverse cultures. For example, dating a person more than twice in Spanish culture may mean that an engagement and marriage will ensue. In India, marriages tend to be arranged by parents, and in Algeria, the selection of a spouse may require the acceptance of the entire extended family.[26]

American Co-Cultures There are also differences among ethnic groups within the United States in terms of relationships. Latina/os tend to believe that support is most important in their relationships, and Asian Americans emphasize positive and caring exchanges or ideas. African Americans typically believe that respect and acceptance is most important in their relationships, and European Americans perceive recognizing individual needs as an important relational characteristic.[27] Despite the many similarities between homosexual and heterosexual relationships, close friends may be more important for gays than for straights because of strained relationships with their families. Regarding romantic relationships, perceptions of success and competence may be different for gays and lesbians than for heterosexuals. For example, gays and lesbians typically measure success in terms of equality, happiness, and satisfaction, and heterosexuals measure success in terms of commitment, marriage, and endurance.[28]

Relationship Context

Our relationships with family members, friends, and coworkers affect our communication and the formation of relationships with others.

Families Whom do you consider to be members of your family? Perhaps you include a biological, adoptive, and/or step (grand)mother and/or (grand)father; assorted aunts, uncles, and cousins; the person with whom you or a parent has chosen to cohabit; and maybe your pets. Recent statistics support the idea that there's more than one definition of "family." Approximately 4 million unmarried cohabiting couples reside in the United States, as do about 12 million single-parent families. There are between 1.5 and 2 million gay fathers and lesbian mothers in the United States, as well as 5 million children who have a gay father or lesbian mother.[29] Because families come in all shapes and sizes, modern definitions tend to focus less on typical family roles (e.g., mother and father) and more on how a family functions. Here we define **family** as a "network of people who share their lives over long periods of time bound by ties of marriage, blood, or commitment, legal or otherwise, who consider themselves as family and who share a significant history and anticipated future of functioning in a family relationship."[30]

The family in which we are raised strongly influences our relationships throughout our lifetime. Early patterns of attachment with our parents affect the attachments we form as adults. Children who are allowed to be both affectionate and independent with their mothers are likely to be comfortable with intimacy and trust in adulthood.[31] Adults also experience the influence of their family of origin in their perceptions of the quality and stability of their romantic relationships. Research illustrates that love, satisfaction, and commitment in a relationship increase or decrease over time as perceptions of support from one's social network (e.g., friends and family) increase or decrease. Similarly, initial levels of network support actually predict subsequent levels of love, satisfaction, and commitment approximately a year and a half after the initial levels are identified.[32]

Friends Think about those individuals you consider your friends. Why do you believe these people are your "friends" as opposed to "acquaintances"? You may be thinking that your friends like the same things you do (e.g., sports, music), share the same values, and are there for you when you need them. These qualities characterize relationships among friends. In fact, we choose our friends on the basis of similarity, need fulfillment, and support:

- Similarity—we tend to be attracted to people who validate who we are and what we believe. Of course, it's possible to have friends with personalities that differ from ours. This most often occurs when the differences fulfill our needs.
- Need fulfillment—a timid person may choose a friend who is extremely extroverted because they complement each other. On the other hand, a sports enthusiast may choose a fellow sports enthusiast as a friend because they "fit" together; that is, both provide something that the other person needs, someone to listen to and enjoy stories about sports.

KNOWLEDGE power • "You Gotta Have Friends"

Identify three people you consider friends. Do you and your friends have similar social interests, personalities, values, and cultural backgrounds? If not, do the differences between you and your friends help to fulfill a need? What, if any, other needs do your friends fulfill? Do your friends support you during difficult times? Did you ever end a friendship because a friend "changed"; that is, you no longer shared similarities or she or he failed to fulfill a need and/or wasn't available when you needed support? After analyzing your friendships, do you believe that "similarity, need fulfillment, and support" fully capture the essence of friendship?

We choose our friends on the basis of similarity, need fulfillment, and support.

- Support—we expect our friends to be there for us. We count on friends to accept us even with our flaws and to accept us as we change over time.[33]

In all, friends are people we like who like us. Recent research suggests that adults tend to have only two friends who can be described as "close." Moreover, one in four Americans report that they have nobody with whom they can discuss important issues. Fifty percent more people today than twenty years ago report that their spouse is the only person in whom they can confide. Sociologists suggest that while our overall ties are growing (due, in part, to the Internet), Americans are more socially isolated today than they were two decades ago because we don't typically discuss matters that are personally important with "Internet friends."[34]

Persons with Whom We Work Americans are spending 10% more time on the job than forty years ago, and workplace relationships can contribute to job satisfaction or dissatisfaction.[35] Formal relationships include those that subordinates have with superiors and superiors have with subordinates. Coworkers, or individuals at the same level in the organizational hierarchy, also have relationships with each other, and informal relationships occur in the workplace. However, obstacles exist regarding the formation of cross-sex friendships on-the-job. Professionals tend to be apprehensive about establishing cross-sex friendships because friendly comments (e.g., "That shirt looks good on you") may be misinterpreted as sexual harassment, because coworkers may perceive the friendship as an office romance, and because the coworker targeted for friendship may misinterpret friendly overtures as evidence of sexual or romantic interest.[36] It's interesting to note that research suggests that up to 80% of U.S. employees have experienced a romantic workplace relationship.[37] Benefits of workplace romances include greater work satisfaction, but there are many drawbacks. A failed workplace romance can be extremely difficult for the partners because they may be forced to continue to work together, even when hard feelings remain about the breakup. Because workplace romances can be detrimental to relational partners as well as to many others in an organization, some businesses have explicit rules that prohibit such relationships.[38]

KNOWLEDGE ON THE CUTTING EDGE

Putting It in Context: Communication, Sex, and Interpersonal Relationships

One biological difference between males and females concerns the brain chemical oxytocin. Oxytocin, the bonding chemical, is found in larger quantities in the brains of females, which suggests that females are more biochemically focused on bonding with a partner and in strengthening those bonds than are males. In addition, brain imaging research reveals that intense romantic love is evidenced in dopamine-rich brain regions associated with reward and motivation. Elevated levels of the brain chemical dopamine produce core feelings of romantic love: energy, elation, focused attention on novel stimuli, sexual arousal, and the motivation to win a "reward." Women typically show more activity in particular brain areas associated with reward, attention, and emotion, and men tend to show more activity in visual processing areas of the brain, including one tied to sexual arousal. Testosterone levels also alter when people fall in love. Testosterone, a male sex hormone linked to aggression and sex drive, rises in men and falls in women. However, testosterone returns to normal levels once the passionate early stages of love subside.[39]

Gender Context

Communication scholar Julia Wood asserts that women and men differ in how they approach relationships. In terms of friendship, both women and men value close same-sex friends and the ideals on which friendships are built: acceptance, trust, and intimacy. However, how these ideals are expressed tend to differ in male and female same-sex friendships. Specifically, self-disclosure and intimate communication create closeness in friendships between women. Communication in female same-sex friendships tends to be supportive, caring, and therapeutic in nature. Communication between women friends often centers around their relationship because the friendship itself is considered important, interesting, and worthy of discussion. By contrast, male same-sex friends communicate closeness and intimacy in the form of activity rather than talk. Men typically create and experience friendships while engaging in actions that cultivate a sense of camaraderie and companionship, such as watching or playing sports or working on handicrafts or fix-it projects. Because masculine socialization discourages the communication of emotion, men perceive that doing things with and for others is a primary method to express affection. Men are also more likely to help each other with their problems by creating distractions rather than by communicating about difficulties in an explicit manner. Furthermore, male same-sex friends communicate intimacy in an indirect, nonverbal manner by engaging in friendly competition and affectionate punches and backslapping. Unlike female same-sex friends, men typically refrain from directly discussing their friendship.

Recent research suggests that while men express closeness in ways that may differ from women, intimacy that grows from engaging in activities is just as valid as intimacy that grows from self-disclosure and relationship talk. Diversionary tactics to relieve men's stress and enhance feelings of closeness are indeed more effective for a man than talking about a problem. However, we have been socialized to perceive friendships and intimate relationships on the basis of a feminine standard that misrepresents and devalues how men typically express intimacy. Regrettably, this standard may be the source of various misunderstandings that can plague heterosexual relationships.[40]

Individual Context

Scholars contend that how well we accept ourselves is linked to how well we accept others. Marriage and family therapists suggest that our relationships will merely become attempts to discover who we are if we try to find intimacy without achieving an identity on our own. Without a sense of who we are, we tend to believe that we need a relational partner to feel complete. We also may believe that we'll be complete if a relational partner needs us. Both of these beliefs do nothing but sabotage our relationships. Moreover, a self characterized by low self-esteem can limit the frequency of intimate communication. Chapter 3 described the self-fulfilling prophecy, an expectation that makes an anticipated outcome likely to happen. The self-fulfilling prophecy occurs when we tell ourselves that we are unromantic or unlovable and we consequently find that we experience difficulty in initiating and maintaining relationships. On the other hand, an inflated sense of self is also associated with relational difficulties. People who are preoccupied with their own satisfaction may experience superficial and unsatisfying relationships. Focusing solely on our own needs can lead to loneliness and depression; therefore, we should recognize the importance of relationships in our lives. In other words, we should emphasize a commitment to others *and* maintain a strong sense of self.[41]

OVERCOMING COMMUNICATION CHALLENGES

Relational Transgressions

Cheating. Lying. Keeping secrets. These behaviors are examples of relational transgressions that violate relational expectations or rules. Although most of the research about relational transgressions focuses on romantic heterosexual partners, transgressions can occur between gay or straight friends, in families, and among coworkers. These transgressions include engaging in extrarelational affairs, keeping secrets, failing to keep commitments, behaving in a manner that disregards the relationship (e.g., choosing to spend time with another person and/or comparing a current partner with previous partners), engaging in ineffective conflict management, and failing to reciprocate affection. Transgressions vary in terms of their detrimental effect on a relationship. Forgetting a partner's birthday or the anniversary of a relationship may be considered a grievous violation of a relational rule for one couple but insignificant for another.[42]

Apologies and Accounts No matter what the transgression, an offended partner typically confronts the transgressor with an accusation, reproach, or hint about the behavior. The transgressor then has to choose from a variety of responses to communicate about the transgression. For example, a transgressor can deny the behavior ("That's not what I told her!"), offer an excuse ("I didn't want to tell you because I knew you'd get angry"), or communicate statements designed to repair a threatened image (e.g., acting angry as if the transgressor is being unjustly accused). The most effective responses after being challenged about a transgression are apologies and accounts. **Apologies** accept responsibility for the behavior and recognize its undesirability. Apologies can also help save the offended partner's face, appease the partner, and restore relational harmony. Combined with nonverbal behaviors that indicate guilt and shame, apologies tend to increase the likelihood that relational stability will be restored after a transgression. Apologies and how they function in conflict situations are discussed more in Chapter 11. Although apologies can successfully manage the initial trauma of a transgression, they fail to provide an explanation for the behavior or what the transgression means to the relationship. Excuses focus on extenuating circumstances (e.g., "She or he came on to me and practically forced me to do it"), but **accounts** typically claim responsibility for behavior but minimize its undesirability or seriousness (e.g., "I knew I shouldn't have lied but I thought it wasn't a big deal"). In terms of infidelity, accounts involving justification have been more effective than excuses in restoring a relationship.

Managing Relational Transgressions The management of relational transgressions isn't easy. The offended partner probably feels anger and pain, and the transgressor may feel guilt, humiliation, and shame. Therefore, emotional damage that results from the transgression must be addressed before it overwhelms the partners and prevents relational repair. Moreover, relational repair is predicated on the analysis of the particular transgression and the rule(s) it violated. Clarifying what rule(s) has been broken helps to manage emotional responses and steers the communication to the source of the problem. It may be that the rule on which a transgression is based needs to be explicitly discussed in terms of what constitutes "rule-following behavior." For example, flirting with a coworker may not violate a relational exclusivity rule, but asking a coworker to lunch may. Similarly, a particular relational rule may need to be renegotiated. Other behaviors that can help to restore a relationship after a transgression include "appeasement and positivity tactics," such as being attentive and spending more time with the wounded partner, saying "I love you" more often, and making concessions (e.g., "I admit that you're right and I'm wrong"). Additionally, relationship talk, such as talking about the transgression's effect on the relationship and expressing beliefs about the relationship (e.g., "Our relationship is strong; we can survive this") can help to restore a relationship. Depending on the nature of the relationship and the transgressor's accounts, the offended partner will ultimately decide to either forgive the transgressor or end the relationship.[43]

A CASE STUDY IN ETHICS

The Secret Lover Collection

Recall that competent communication includes an ethical dimension of well-based standards of right and wrong. We can ask ourselves a series of questions to help us choose communication strategies that are effective and appropriate regarding our relationships. Specifically, we can ask: Have I practiced any virtues today (e.g., have I demonstrated integrity, trustworthiness, honesty, and responsibility)? Have I done more good than harm (e.g., have I shown appreciation and gratitude to others)? Have I treated people with dignity and respect? Have I been fair and just? Have I made my community stronger because of my actions? Read the following case study and consider whether the Secret Lover Collection reflects ethical behavior.

Try to remember the last time you scanned the mind-boggling variety of missives that line the greeting card shelves in your local store. There are cards for every holiday, cards for special occasions, and cards that express sentiments for no particular reason. But have you noticed cards especially designed for persons involved in an extrarelational affair? The "Secret Lover Collection" includes twenty-four different cards with illustrations of hearts, flowers, and star-crossed lovers. The collection includes sentiments such as "I just love breathing you in," "I never expected to fall in love with you," "The holidays won't feel right without you by my side," and "I can't go on like this anymore."

Cathy Gallagher, a former advertising executive and the cards' creator, is tired of listening to people express outrage over the Secret Lover Collection. "The conservatives and the talk shows are just going crazy, like nobody ever had affairs before my cards were out there," she notes. "Well, they did. People make choices. I want to do this without judgment." Gallagher hints that disdain for her cards smacks of hypocrisy. She asks if hotels check couples for a marriage license when they rent a room. Do florists and jewelers ask about the relationship between the recipient and the individual making the purchase? If greeting cards are supposed to be available for all purposes, then why not for an affair?

"A lot of people don't set out to have affairs, but it kind of happens," she maintains. "There are generic cards that say 'I love you' but nothing that explains the emotions specific to their relationship." Gallagher is also somewhat surprised at all the finger wagging. "Affairs have been going on since the beginning of time. This is just facilitating communication between lovers. This isn't for one-night stands. There's an emotional intensity that I'm helping them express."[44]

Is it ethical to help lovers in emotionally intense affairs "facilitate communication"? Do you agree with Gallagher that greeting cards are supposed to help people express feelings, no matter what the situation? Is it hypocritical to judge a greeting card designer for "encouraging" extramarital affairs without judging hotel clerks, florists, and jewelers who fail to "discourage" such affairs?

Chapter Review

Motivation: How has this helped me?

- **The importance of studying interpersonal relationships**

It's important to study interpersonal relationships because relationships can affect our physical and psychological health, provide us with social support, affect our self-concept, and have an impact on our future success and happiness.

Knowledge: What have I learned?

- **How to characterize personal and romantic relationships**

Personal relationships are distinguished from impersonal relationships by three important characteristics: explanatory ability; predictive ability; and uniqueness. Romantic relationships are based on the love-based characteristics of intimacy, passion, and commitment.

- **Theories that explain interpersonal relationships and self-disclosures**

Two theories that can explain why we form relationships are social exchange theory and social penetration theory. Social exchange theory posits that rewards and costs determine whether people develop, maintain, or terminate their relationships. Social penetration theory illustrates how relationships develop and change in terms of the self-disclosure that occurs between relational partners. Although self-disclosure can contribute to the development, maintenance, and enhancement of relationships, it can also cause problems for us, our partner, and our relationship.

- **Models of relational development**

Stage models, process models, and combination models are used to reflect the life cycle of relationships. Stage models suggest that relationships follow a trajectory and can be classified in terms of particular stages that illustrate initiation, maintenance, or termination. Process models reflect the idea that relationships are ongoing and that relational meaning ebbs and flows, based on partners' attributions. The dialectical tensions process model illustrates that relationships oscillate between autonomy and connection, novelty and predictability, and openness and closedness. Combination models describe relationships in terms of movement between relationship phases and dialectical tensions that affect relational stability and change.

- **How contexts influence interpersonal relationships**

The culture context demonstrates that perceptions of friendship and romantic relationships differ from culture to culture. The relationship context illustrates that all varieties of families can strongly influence our relationships throughout our lifetime; friendships are typically based on similarity, need fulfillment, and support; and workplace relationships can contribute job satisfaction or dissatisfaction. The gender context suggests that women and men differ in the way that they approach relationships, and the individual context demonstrates that partners bring unique experiences and personalities to their relationships.

Skill: What skills have I developed?

- **How skills related to initiating and bonding, maintaining, repairing, terminating, and reconciling relationships improve our communication competence**

Initiation skills include communicating pickup lines, using a direct approach to indicate interest in forming a relationship, and asking questions that focus on a partner's values and personality. Bonding skills include the use of nicknames and idiosyncratic slang, the words *we* and *us*, and communication that relates to the nature of the relationship. The expression of appreciation for our relationship partners is a skill that can communicate the maintenance strategy of positivity. Shared activities, prosocial behavior, and metacommunication and relational talk are skills that can help repair a relationship. A positive tone termination strategy is direct and demonstrates respect for and saves the face of a relational partner. Skills associated with the positive tone strategy include owning our thoughts and feelings, using descriptive language, and using metacommunication. Relational reconciliation can be accomplished via third-party mediation, making comments about rival suitors and statements such as "It's now or never," asking a former partner to do something without intending to reconcile, communicating why a relationship has been terminated and how the relationship can be improved, intentional efforts to evade the issues associated with the breakup during an attempted reconciliation, and making direct requests for reconciliation.

Study Questions

1. What distinguishes personal relationships from impersonal relationships?
2. What is the "triangle of love," and how does it relate to romantic relationships?
3. Explain why people form relationships in terms of social exchange theory and social penetration theory.
4. Why is self-disclosure risky? What questions should we ask ourselves before deciding to self-disclose?
5. What are some advantages and disadvantages associated with stage models of relational development?
6. What are dialectical tensions, and how do they affect relationships?
7. What are some communication skills that can indicate to others that we may be interested in initiating a relationship?
8. What are five strategies that romantic partners use to maintain their relationships?
9. Describe some skills that can be used to repair a relationship that is deteriorating.
10. What are three strategies typically used to terminate a relationship?
11. What are some strategies that ex-partners use when they try to reconcile a relationship?
12. How do the culture, gender, and individual contexts affect relationships and relational communication?
13. Why do modern definitions of "family" focus less on typical family roles and more on how a family functions?
14. Upon what bases do we choose our friends?
15. What are some advantages and disadvantages of workplace romances?
16. What are relational transgressions, and how can we repair a relationship after a transgression is committed?

Names to Know

Irwin Altman and **Dalmas Taylor** (1934–1998), p. 263—Psychologists who developed social penetration theory, which explains that self-disclosure moves communication and relationships from relatively shallow, nonintimate levels to deeper ones. Altman is distinguished professor of psychology at the University of Utah.

Leslie Baxter, p. 265—Communication scholar who developed a process model of dialectical tensions that illustrates that relationships oscillate between opposing ends of a continuum. Baxter is the F. Wendell Miller Distinguished Professor at the University of Iowa.

Mark Knapp and **Anita Vangelisti**, p. 264—Communication scholars who developed the well-known staircase model of relational development stages. Knapp and Vangelisti are professors at the University of Texas at Austin and have been honored with numerous awards for their teaching and scholarship.

John Thibaut (1917–1986) and **Harold H. Kelley** (1921–2003), p. 262—Psychologists who developed social exchange theory, which explains human behavior in terms of rewards and costs.

Key Terms

accounts, 284
apologies, 284
appreciation, 275
assurances, 274
attraction theory, 269
autonomy-connection dialectic, 265
bonding strategies, 271
commitment, 260
comparison level (CL), 263
comparison level of alternatives (CLalt), 263
costs, 262
dialectical tensions, 265
family, 280
hyperpersonal communication, 271
initiation phase, 269
intimacy, 260
maintenance skills, 274
manipulation, 277
neutralization, 267
novelty-predictability dialectic, 266
openness, 274
openness-closedness dialectic, 266
passion, 260
pickup line, 270
positive tone, 278
positivity, 274
process models, 265
reconciliation strategies, 278
reframing, 267
relational transgression, 276
repair strategies, 276
rewards, 262
selection, 267
self-disclosure, 263
separation, 267
sharing tasks, 274
social exchange theory, 262
social networks, 274
social penetration theory, 263
stage models, 264
termination strategies, 277
turning points, 268
withdrawal-avoidance, 278

CHAPTER 11 Interpersonal Conflict

"Peace is not the absence of conflict but the presence of creative alternatives for responding to conflict."

Dorothy Thompson (1893–1961), American journalist

In this chapter, we will answer the following:

- It is important to study interpersonal conflict to learn that conflict is natural, and that competent conflict management can promote satisfying relationships

Knowledge: What will I learn?

- How to characterize interpersonal conflict
- Types of interpersonal conflict
- Personal conflict styles
- How contexts influence interpersonal conflict

Skill: Why do I need to develop these skills?

- Using a collaborative conflict resolution method and communicating apologies and forgiveness can improve your communication competence

Bobby Knight, the former head basketball coach at Indiana and Texas Tech universities, has won more NCAA Division I men's basketball games than any other head coach. Knight is also known for his behavior during episodes of conflict, such as throwing a chair across a basketball court and berating members of the press. Do you know someone who acts in an aggressive or violent manner during conflict situations? Perhaps this person believes that "winning at all costs" justifies her or his behavior. Maybe you've found yourself in the middle of an argument and realized there was no way you could win. Do you know that an "I win, you lose" perspective is just one of many ways of thinking about conflict? Do you know that a collaborative conflict resolution strategy can help you and your conflict partner reach your goals? This chapter explains that understanding why it's important to study interpersonal conflict, assuming that the collaborative win-win conflict management method will be rewarding to self and others, and knowing how to REACH for forgiveness can increase our motivation to communicate competently. We will increase our knowledge by learning about types of interpersonal conflict and personal conflict styles. We will learn skills associated with win-win collaborative conflict management, the communication of apologies, and the expression of forgiveness.

Introduction to Interpersonal Conflict

Think of the last time you were involved in an argument. Did your communication and behavior affect your conversation partner's communication and behavior, and vice versa? Did you believe that your partner blocked your ability to fulfill a need or achieve a particular goal? If so, you were engaged in a conflict situation.

How can we characterize interpersonal conflict?

Conflict can be defined as "the interaction of interdependent people who perceive incompatible goals and interference from each other in achieving those goals."[1] This definition of conflict applies to all phases and all types of relationships, including friendships, work-related relationships, romantic relationships, and family relationships. Individuals involved in conflict are mutually dependent on each other. After all, there's no need to resolve differences between people who don't somehow affect each other. Conflict also entails a perception of incompatible goals, whether this perception is accurate and/or overtly expressed. We may fail to realize that people involved in conflict can meet their goals with collaborative conflict resolution skills. Consider a situation in which you want to move to a larger house but your partner insists on staying put. This chapter describes a win-win collaborative conflict management strategy that can help both parties reach their goals.

COMPETENCE
Motivation
Knowledge
Skill

Why It's Important to Study Interpersonal Conflict

Communication scholars William R. Cupach and **Daniel J. Canary** have conducted extensive research in interpersonal conflict. They found that interpersonal conflict is worthy of study for at least four reasons: to improve our competence in conflict management, to learn that conflict is natural, to realize that people develop individually through conflict, and to accomplish satisfying relationships.[2] These reasons are illustrated in Figure 11.1, "Reasons to Study Interpersonal Conflict."

Why is it important to study interpersonal conflict?

Have you ever hidden the remote to thwart a partner's attempt to change the channel on the one working TV in your house? Maybe you once threatened to end a communication episode if you didn't get your way. It may be tempting to achieve our goals by communicating

KNOWLEDGE power • Analyze Your Conflicts

Think about some recent arguments you've been involved in. Analyze these arguments in terms of interpersonal conflict. Were you and your partner(s) interdependent? Did you believe that your partner(s) blocked your ability to fulfill a need or achieve a particular goal? Did your arguments occur across a variety of relationships and at various stages of relational development? Do you think that you and/or your partners could have managed the conflict more effectively and appropriately? Apply what you read here about interpersonal conflict to these situations, and imagine how your knowledge of conflict concepts and use of conflict-related skills could have altered the outcomes.

Figure 11.1: Reasons to Study Interpersonal Conflict

personal attacks, sarcasm, and threats, but learning about various types of conflict, orientations to conflict, and ways to manage conflict can help us resist the impulse to win at all costs and enable us to improve our competence in conflict management.

Conflict is a natural feature in every interpersonal relationship. Conflict occurs between parents and their young children, their adolescents, and their adult offspring. Conflict also occurs in romantic relationships, work relationships, and friendship relationships. For example:

- You and a parent may disagree about how much time you spend studying.
- You and a romantic partner may find yourselves in opposition about the depth of intimacy in your relationship.
- You and a coworker may experience conflict over the number of assigned work hours.
- You and a friend may disagree about how to spend an afternoon together.
- You and your child may disagree about an appropriate bedtime.

A conflict-free relationship is impossible because we all have different needs, wants, and goals. Instead of assuming that people never experience conflict in "perfect relationships," we should more realistically learn how to manage the conflicts in our relationships.

Personal growth occurs when we learn how to manage interpersonal conflict. Conflict gives us experience in identifying others' thoughts and feelings and in detecting and understanding our own. For example, have you ever empathized easily with a friend who told you about a conflict situation because you were once involved in a similar conflict? Conflict helps build empathy because we can understand and actually feel the emotions experienced by others who contend with conflicts like ours. In addition, conflict can facilitate personal development by causing us to think about others' attitudes and opinions, which in turn may influence us to change our own.

KNOWLEDGE ON THE CUTTING EDGE

Communication, Conflict, and Civility: Are You a Civil Communicator?

Sociolinguist Deborah Tannen suggests that the United States can be described in terms of a warlike atmosphere of unrelenting contention; in other words, as an "argument culture." Our argument culture teaches us to approach the world and the people in it as adversaries and influences us to believe that opposition is the best way to meet our needs. Although conflict and opposition are necessary in a democratic society, Tannen believes that this "I win, you lose" approach overshadows our attempts at cooperation and agreement and obscures the middle ground. For example, we may label people we know as for or against foreign intervention, abortion, or the death penalty, whereas in reality, they may have various ideas and mixed emotions about these topics. Additionally, our country has become so politically polarized that candidates risk having their campaign signs defaced, burned, or stolen.[3] The need to win at all costs teaches us to focus on weaknesses in logic and to make a conflict partner look bad instead of trying to understand what leads the partner to believe as she or he does. This influences us to resort to uncivil communication such as verbal aggression and personal attacks instead of listening to someone we disagree with.

The need to win is illustrated in many areas of contemporary society, including education, the media, and politics. For example, you may have been encouraged in classes to engage in what often is labeled "critical thinking." In reality, you may have been required to read an academic work and then rip it to shreds. Criticism is just one form of critical thinking; other forms entail integrating ideas from other fields and examining the historical and philosophical contexts that may have influenced an academic work. In addition, the media promote uncivil forms of conflict over reasoned discourse because television and radio must be entertaining. Our culture urges us to believe that watching people fight is fun, and therefore we contend with talking heads who interrupt and argue loudly about important problems and with reality shows in which uncivil behavior and personal attacks are celebrated. Moreover, our "I win, you lose" mentality influences our politicians to seek information about opponents that can be crafted into uncivil attack ads. Overall, Tannen suggests that uncivil and contentious conflict as public discourse becomes a model for behavior and affects how we experience our interpersonal relationships and how we communicate with others.

It is possible to move beyond a "win-lose" mentality by recognizing that debate, criticism, and aggressive conflict are not the only paths to knowledge and understanding. Although thinking in terms of winning and losing may be effective in some situations, we should instead think in terms of compatibility and collaboration in others. Some conflict-related rules of engagement can remind us to be civil members of the shared community:

- Don't demonize those with whom we disagree.
- Don't affront the deepest moral convictions of others.
- Talk less of rights, which are nonnegotiable, and more of needs, wants, and interests.
- Leave some issues out.

And in the long term, we can foster a belief among the young that being fair and cooperative is just as important as winning. As stated by P. M. Forni, cofounder of the Johns Hopkins Civility Project, "This is civility: the ability to internalize the notion that how you play the game is more important than the final score."[4]

Conflict does not reflect an unhealthy relationship or one that is in trouble. Instead, close, personal relationships are powerfully affected by the way we *manage* conflict. Research reveals that particular patterns of conflict interaction can separate satisfied from dissatisfied couples. Can you think of a situation in which a partner complained about you for messing up the house, not feeding the dog, or forgetting to put gas in the car? Were these complaints often repeated, and did you feel the need to defend yourself each time you were the target of such complaints? Dissatisfied couples often engage in a pattern in which one person complains and the other person defends. However, satisfied couples don't engage in the "complain-defend" pattern and instead use conflict sequences of confirming communication. Learning how to manage conflict can also help us realize that we can resolve our problems without relying on verbal or physical abuse.

KNOWLEDGE ON THE CUTTING EDGE

Technology Update: Interpersonal Conflict and Computer-Mediated Communication

Have you ever engaged in an online conflict? If so, the conflict may have included sarcastic and overtly hostile messages ("flaming"), but it may have included logical and descriptive statements that focused on a problem rather than the online partners. Overall, do you experience more or less conflict online than off-line? Although increasing numbers of individuals are using computer-mediated communication (CMC) to solve problems and interact with others, little attention has been paid to the expression of conflict in CMC. Extant studies of conflict have resulted in inconsistent findings; that is, some studies have found that people express more conflict online than in face-to-face (ftf) groups, and others have found similar levels of conflict in both contexts.

Early studies of conflict and CMC were based on the cues-filtered-out approach, which assumes that CMC provides users with only very limited nonverbal cues. The limited nonverbal cues were thought to reduce the rules for appropriate online behavior and therefore increase conflict communication. However, the inconsistent findings produced by early studies led some researchers to develop an alternative theory of information processing. **Social information processing (SIP) theory** suggests that CMC groups can develop social rules similar to ftf groups if given enough time for an equal amount of message exchange. Similarly, SIP theory posits that CMC and ftf groups may exhibit similar levels of conflict behavior if CMC groups are given time to exchange the same amount of interpersonal communication.

In one study of task conflict regarding goals and choices, relationship conflict about personal issues, and process conflict concerning how tasks should be accomplished, researchers provided additional time to CMC groups to convey messages compared with ftf groups. Results illustrated that the CMC groups initially experienced more relationship and process conflict than the ftf groups, but the differences were not apparent in later stages. Additionally, both the CMC and ftf groups exhibited similar amounts of task conflict during the initial and later stages of message exchange. The researchers concluded that the study results support SIP theory and that with enough time for equivalent message exchange, ftf and CMC groups will develop in a similar manner.[5]

Additional research concerning CMC and ftf conflict has studied whether positive or negative conflict management is higher or lower in the CMC context. Positive conflict management occurs when we express logical statements, share information and alternatives, and challenge early agreement by exploring underlying beliefs. Negative conflict management occurs when we state preferences without a logical argument, suppress differences of opinion, and encourage early agreement without exploring underlying beliefs. Think about the online and off-line conflicts in which you've engaged. Are positive conflicts more prevalent in the online or off-line context? Study results indicate that ftf communication produces higher levels of positive conflict management when communicators contend with "intellective tasks" that require cooperation and convergence. However, there are no significant differences in positive conflict management when CMC and ftf groups deal with idea-generation tasks.[6]

Now that you know about SIP theory and positive and negative conflict management, consider what you can do to make your online conflicts more effective and appropriate.

Types of Interpersonal Conflict

Some types of conflicts are easier to resolve than others; therefore, knowing the type of conflict in which we are engaged can help us decide on the most appropriate and effective conflict management strategy. In order of easiest to most difficult to manage, Figure 11.2, "Types of Conflicts," shows pseudoconflicts, content conflicts, value conflicts, and ego conflicts. In addition, Table 11.1, "Types of Conflicts," describes examples of these interpersonal conflicts and how they can be managed.

Pseudoconflict

What are some types of interpersonal conflict?

A **pseudoconflict** occurs when we falsely believe that a relationship partner has incompatible goals or is interfering with our attainment of our own goals. This type of conflict

Figure 11.2: Types of Conflicts

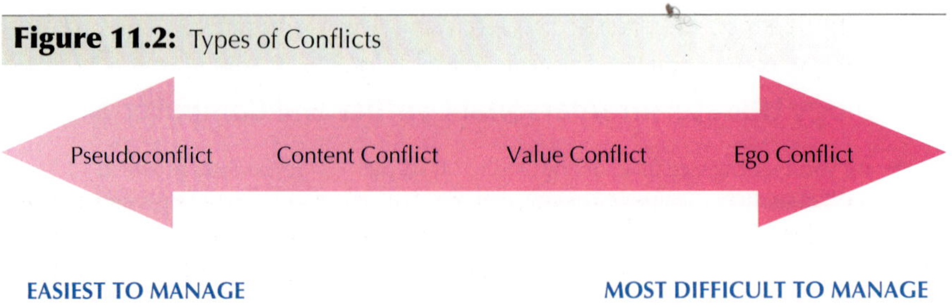

can be resolved when we realize that we are truly not in conflict. One type of pseudoconflict is a consequence of teasing or mocking. For example, suppose during a party and in front of others, a friend imitates the way you walk and talk. You may become upset because you believe this person's goal is to embarrass you while your goal is to maintain face and to act cool in front of the partygoers. When you later explain that you were embarrassed and upset, your friend apologizes and promises to never mock you again. You realize that your friend's goal was not to cause you to lose face in front of your friends; instead, it was to "keep the party going" and have a good-natured laugh. Another type of pseudoconflict occurs when people have simple misunderstandings without realizing their goals are not in opposition. Have you ever been in a situation in which a VCR, DVR, or TiVo has saved the day in a conflict about TV shows scheduled to air at the same time? If so, you eventually realized that your goals and your partner's goals could both be met and that you may have engaged in a pseudoconflict. Pseudoconflicts can involve issues of minor importance, such as what a couple should have for dinner (both partners can cook their preferences), or issues of major importance, such as the example mentioned earlier of one partner who wants to move to a new house and the other partner

Table 11.1: Types of Conflicts

Type	Characterization	Example	Management
Pseudoconflict	We perceive that our partner has goals that are incompatible with ours.	"No, I do not want to go out to see a movie tonight! I want to stay home."	Attempt to find a way to meet both needs (e.g., rent some DVDs).
Content conflict	We dispute factual information.	"Ferrari doesn't make the most expensive car; Porsche does."	Check the facts before the conflict escalates to an ego conflict.
Value conflict	We have differing opinions on issues that relate to personal value systems and issues of right and wrong.	"The United States was wrong to invade Iraq and start a war."	Emphasize areas of agreement or realize that we may have to agree to disagree.
Ego conflict	We believe we must win the conflict to save face.	"You don't know what you're talking about!"	Use communication techniques such as owning thoughts and face-saving skills to move the conflict to a value or content level.

who does not. Pseudoconflicts can be resolved with the use of the win-win conflict management strategy that we'll discuss later in this chapter.

Content Conflict

Content conflict occurs when we disagree about information. These types of conflicts are sometimes labeled "simple" because we can turn to sources to verify the facts in dispute. For example, you may believe that computers were invented in the 1950s, and your conversation partner insists that computers were invented in the 1960s. You may think that Boston Red Sox player Ted Williams was the last person in major league baseball to hit over .400, but your conversation partner says that it actually was Cincinnati Reds player Pete Rose. Content conflicts can also involve information of a personal nature, such as how old Uncle Harry really is and the complete name of Aunt Sally's first husband. Content conflicts can be resolved by finding a credible source with the information, such as a newspaper, magazine or journal, book, Web site, or person. One way to resolve a content conflict is to agree to disagree until a source can be found that can verify the fact(s) under question. We can decide on guidelines for selecting a source to resolve the content conflict (e.g., only sources that have undergone an extensive review process) if many sources are available that both contradict and affirm the fact(s) in dispute.

Value Conflict

Value conflict results when people have differing opinions on issues that relate to their personal value systems and issues of right and wrong. Although pseudoconflicts and content conflicts have the potential to be resolved quickly and easily, value conflicts may remain unresolved. Disagreements about controversial topics such as capital punishment and gun control may center on our ideas of what is moral, just, or worthwhile. Sometimes we can manage a value conflict by agreeing to disagree with a relational partner and focusing on the areas where we agree. For example, we may be intensely opposed to deer hunting and believe that it is an immoral activity that slaughters helpless animals. However, our good friend may be a keen hunter who believes it is a humane way to control the deer population. After countless discussions and attempts to persuade each other that only one position is correct, we may decide to agree to disagree because the conflict about deer hunting is not important enough to destroy a friendship in which both parties enjoy each other's company. On the other hand, a value conflict may be of such importance that the individuals involved cannot agree to disagree, and they dissolve their relationship. For example, we may be of one faith and our mate may be of another. Instead of exposing any future children to both religions and allowing them to choose for themselves, we may strongly believe that our offspring should be raised according to our own religion. If our partner disagrees and insists that future children be raised believing in her or his faith, we may have to dissolve the relationship because we find that there isn't any way to resolve this value conflict.

Ego Conflict

Ego conflict results when individuals believe that they must win at all costs to save face. Because of the face-threatening nature of such a conflict, the issue under discussion becomes secondary to the effort to maintain the perception of credibility or worth. Ego conflicts can develop when a discussion of facts or values is sabotaged by judgmental statements and personal attacks. We may spend the majority of a conflict engaging in defensive reactions and emotional outbursts that have little or nothing to do with the issue

KNOWLEDGE power • Types of Interpersonal Conflicts

Try to recall the most intense and/or destructive conflict you have been involved in or witnessed. Was the conflict about facts, or did it concern values? Did the conflict morph into an ego conflict in which the parties involved believed that they must win at all cost to save face? With a partner or in a group, describe this conflict and discuss how it could have been more effectively and appropriately managed and/or resolved.

at hand once we believe that our face is threatened. Perhaps you can recall a pseudo-, content, or value conflict during which a conversation partner said, "Don't be such a baby" or "Why do you ask such stupid questions?" If so, your reactions were probably related to the personal attacks rather than the topic at hand. Compared with pseudoconflicts, content conflicts, and value conflicts, ego conflicts have the most potential to destroy a relationship. It's probably best to make use of the communication skills included in this book to bring an ego conflict back down to a value or content level.

Personal Conflict Styles

There are three general approaches to interpersonal conflict: win-lose (or lose-win), lose-lose, and win-win. These approaches are reflected in **personal conflict styles**, preferred ways of dealing with conflict situations. We manifest our conflict style in terms of particular behaviors, and these behaviors will change if we switch from one style to another as a conflict plays out. Researchers **Ralph H. Kilmann** and **Kenneth W. Thomas** have identified five basic conflict styles that indicate how much concern we have for the relationship with our conversation partner and how much concern we have for attaining our personal goals: avoiding, accommodating, competing, compromising, and collaborating.[7] These conflict styles are summarized in Table 11.2, "Personal Conflict Styles."

What are some personal conflict styles?

Avoiding

A common way to deal with conflict is withdrawing from or **avoiding** a conflict. We avoid conflict physically when we remove ourselves from the conflict, and we avoid conflict psychologically when we refuse to discuss the issue. Avoidance tactics include withholding complaints, making irrelevant comments to divert attention away from the issue under dispute (as illustrated in "The Duplex" comic); and denying the existence of the conflict.[8] This type of conflict style has been labeled "lose-lose" because the individuals involved in the conflict situation don't accomplish their goals. Two additional harmful consequences may result when we repeatedly avoid conflict. One consequence is that couples who continually avoid conflict may find that tension increases in their relationship. The issue causing the conflict situation repeatedly resurfaces, and relationship partners may experience even more difficulty in resolving their dispute. Moreover, avoiding a conflict can cause us to mull over or think about a real or perceived problem to the extent that we believe the conflict is more severe than it really is. Avoiding a conflict has the potential to make it more difficult to contend with overall.[9] However, avoiding a conflict may be useful when the issue under

Table 11.2: Personal Conflict Styles

Style	Approach	Example	Advantages	Disadvantages
Avoiding	Lose-Lose	"Just leave me alone!"	Can reduce intense emotions; can be effective when used with unimportant issues	Increased relational tension and difficulty solving a dispute; may influence us to perceive a conflict as more serious than warranted
Accommodating	Lose-Win	"Whatever you say."	Can be effective when used with unimportant issues and when we give in for "social credit"	May lead to poor decision making; possibility of being taken advantage of
Competing	Win-Lose	"It's my way or the highway!"	Can be effective in emergency situations and if an issue is critical to our own or our partner's well-being	Damage to a relationship
Compromising	Lose-Lose	"I'll do some of this if you'll do some of that."	Can be effective when we don't have the time to engage in a collaborative conflict style or when the use of other conflict styles aren't successful	Lose a portion of what we desire; may accept a less effective solution to bring about the compromise; feeling dissatisfied with the solution
Collaborating	Win-Win	"Let's work on finding the best solution for both of us."	Goals of both self and other are achieved	Takes time and knowledge of win-win conflict resolution methods

dispute isn't important or when we need some time to calm our intense emotions. In such an instance, we can use metacommunication to tell a partner that we need time to cool off and that we'll return to the discussion when we can effectively deal with our emotions.

Accommodating

Accommodating in a conflict situation entails satisfying our partner's needs at the expense of our own. Accommodators tend to smooth over conflicts and not make waves in order to preserve relational harmony. Although this personal conflict style can preserve our relationship, we can fail to reach our goals. This style has been labeled "lose-win" because the accommodator chooses to lose while a partner meets her or his needs. Habitual accommodation may lead to poor decision making because we fail to voice our knowledge about an issue. The repeated use of accommodation can also result in one person taking advantage of another. On the other hand, accommodating may be an effective conflict style when the

THE DUPLEX By Glenn McCoy

We avoid conflict psychologically when we refuse to discuss an issue.

issue under dispute isn't important and when we decide to give in during this conflict so we aren't pressured to give in during the next (in other words, we "pick our battles").

Competing

When we make use of the personal conflict style of **competing**, we attempt to meet our needs without concern for our partner's needs. We may use any type of tactic to achieve our needs, whether or not the tactic is considered appropriate. If we manipulate the facts, engage in outright lies, communicate verbal attacks, or threaten a partner, we are using the competing personal conflict style. This style is labeled "win-lose" because we believe we must meet our goals no matter the costs, even though the costs typically include relational damage. However, the competing style is beneficial in an emergency situation if an issue is critical to our or our partner's well-being. Suppose our child or younger sibling refuses to wear a seatbelt because it restricts movement. If we refuse to drive unless the child wears the seatbelt, we are using the competing personal conflict style.

Compromising

In **compromising**, the parties in conflict give up part of what they want in order to achieve partial satisfaction in meeting their goals. This conflict style has been labeled "lose-lose" because even though we win some of what we want, we lose the rest. A decision about the issue under dispute may be less than optimal because we decide to give up a highly effective solution to bring about the compromise. In other words, compromisers are interested in creating a workable solution instead of "the best" solution. Moreover, we may walk away from a conflict situation feeling dissatisfied if we settle for making concessions and exchanging offers. However, compromising works well when we don't have the time to engage in a collaborative conflict style or when other conflict styles aren't successful. Suppose you and some friends decide to get together after work to unwind and have fun. Your partner calls at 4:50 P.M. and informs you that you must be home to watch the kids because she or he has been told to return to work to participate in a last-minute client meeting at 6:00. Because there's not a lot of time to engage in collaborative conflict resolution, you and partner compromise; you both decide that you can relax with your friends from 5:00 to 5:30 and then return home so that your partner can return to work only ten to fifteen minutes after the client meeting begins. Although you "lose" because you don't get to spend

KNOWLEDGE power • I'll Give Up Something If You Give Up Something

With a partner or in a group, recall a conflict that was resolved through the personal conflict style of compromising. Discuss whether you and your conflict partner reached the best solution to the dispute and whether you and your partner were satisfied with how the conflict was resolved. What other solutions could have resulted with the use of accommodating or competing conflict styles? Would both you and your partner be satisfied with the conflict resolution if these styles were used instead of compromising?

much time with your friends and your partner "loses" because she or he will arrive late to the meeting, you both "win" because you each receive a portion of what you want.

Collaborating

The **collaborating** personal conflict style is used when we attempt to satisfy both our needs and our partner's needs. This style is labeled "win-win" because the goals of both self and the other are attained. People who make use of the collaborating style realize that conflict is natural and can potentially strengthen a relationship. Collaborators exhibit effective and appropriate communication as they openly discuss differences of opinion and refuse to engage in personal attacks. The collaborating conflict style takes time and may not be the best style to use when a decision is urgent. In addition, the collaborating style includes many of the communication skills we have previously read about and practiced, and it may seem like an overly idealistic way to resolve conflict. However, we can model communication skills for our partner and teach her or him the collaborative win-win conflict resolution method discussed in this chapter.

Collaborative Conflict Resolution

Collaborative conflict resolution can change a dispute originally perceived as win-lose to one that is perceived as win-win. Before discussing a specific collaborative conflict resolution method that we can use in various conflict situations, we'll review collaborative conflict resolution as it relates to communication competence.

Collaboration and Communication Competence

How can using a collaborative conflict resolution method improve our communication competence?

Collaboration requires the motivation to engage in this somewhat difficult win-win approach to conflict, knowledge about collaboration, and communication skills that are used in an effective and appropriate manner. Our motivation to engage in collaborative win-win conflict resolution rests on the assumption that its use will be rewarding for ourselves and our partners. Our knowledge of collaboration involves understanding that differences in beliefs, attitudes, and preferences may not necessarily be in conflict. In other words, collaboration assumes that perceived polar opposites may be compatible. As previously mentioned, collaborative win-win conflict resolution requires using many of the communication skills in this book. Table 11.3, "Collaborative Conflict Resolution Skills," shows these skills and their use in collaborative win-win conflict resolution.

Table 11.3: Collaborative Conflict Resolution Skills

Skill	Characterization	Example
Metacommunication	Communication about communication (content level of meaning) and relationships (relational level of meaning)	"Let's brainstorm possible ways to meet both your goals and my goals without evaluating the suggestions at this point."
Perception checking	A description of sense data, an interpretation (perception) of the sense data, and a request for feedback	"I see that you're not smiling and not talking much. Maybe you don't believe this collaborative approach will work, or maybe you find it hard to generate options. Is it one of these?"
Face-saving skills	Overlooking a face-threatening act; using humor; offering an apology; communicating an explanation; engaging in physical remediation	"I'm sorry I yelled a while back; I shouldn't have lost my temper."
Nondefensive responses to criticism	Validate a critic's thoughts and feelings even if we disagree with the criticism (e.g., asking open-ended questions; guessing about specifics; agreeing with the truth; agreeing to disagree)	"I see how you might think that I only want to win this argument; however, that's not the case. I just want my needs taken seriously."
Expressing emotions	Accept responsibility and own feelings by combining emotion words with a description of sense data	"I get angry when you tell me that I'm 'wrong.'"
Language clarity skills	Owning thoughts, indexing, and dating information	"In my opinion, we can achieve your goals without having to move."
Nonverbal immediacy skills	Function to enhance liking, closeness, approachability, and positive evaluations (e.g., smiling, nodding, making eye contact, forward leaning and direct body orientation, variety in pitch, patting a shoulder, immediate conversational responses)	Individuals in conflict will refrain from engaging in the following behaviors: frowning, avoiding eye contact, using adaptors, leaning backward, sounding aggressive or submissive, applying force when touching, and using silence in conversation.
Skills of effective conversationalists	Asking questions, responding to and providing free information, crediting sources, maintaining conversational coherence, engaging in appropriate turn taking, summarizing the main ideas	"Your comment just reminded me of something that may help us resolve this conflict. Have you finished what you want to say? I'd like to tell about my thoughts."
Active listening and confirming responses	Prompting and questioning, reassuring and expressing concern, analyzing and advising, judging (offering constructive criticism), paraphrasing thoughts and feelings	"Let me see if I understand you correctly: you feel frustrated because you want to eliminate clutter in the house but don't want get rid of any possessions. Am I right?"
Assertiveness skills	Standing up for our beliefs, rights, and needs while respecting the beliefs, rights, and needs of others (e.g., owning thoughts and feelings; using metacommunication; expressing empathic assertion; using the broken record; and boundary-setting responses to the communication of prejudice)	"I know that you've had a rough day and that you're tired and angry, but I don't want you to take it out on me. I'll talk to you when you stop yelling at me."
Relationship maintenance skills	For example, positivity (being cheerful, avoiding criticism, expressing appreciation)	"I think we can solve this problem together. I appreciate you for working with me."

A Collaborative Conflict Resolution Method

The following collaborative conflict resolution method has four steps that concern people, interests, options, and criteria. Specifically, the four steps entail separating people from the problem ("people"), focusing on interests, not positions ("interests"), generating a variety of possibilities before deciding what to do ("options"), and insisting that the results be based on some objective standard ("criteria").[10]

Separate the People from the Problem (People) It is important to "attack a problem" rather than "attack a person" in collaborative conflict resolution. We should perceive a conflict as an opportunity for joint decision making and problem solving and strive to protect our relationship with our partner. To remind ourselves of our collaborative orientation and to reassure our partner that we don't view her or him as "the enemy," we can tell our partner:

- "Working together will allow us to solve this problem in the best way possible."
- "We can work this out even though we've never had to deal with this problem before."
- "I'm sure that we can cooperate and eventually develop a solution that will benefit both of us."

Focus on Interests, not Positions (Interests) "Positions" are conclusions that we believe we need to defend and are specific solutions to interests. "Interests" are reasons that underlie positions and are varied and diffuse. One way to view positions and interests is to assume that a position is "just one solution" and interests are "the reasons why we have come to a specific solution." Arguing about positions or specific solutions can endanger relationships because individuals engaged in conflict may find themselves in a contest of wills. On the other hand, focusing on the interests or the reasons that underlie solutions can result in creative options that enable both parties in conflict to achieve their goals. For example, when we return to the conflict situation about moving to a new house, we can see that wanting to move to a larger home is a position, or "just one solution." We may therefore feel compelled to defend our one position or solution. Similarly, our partner may believe that she or he must defend the position of wanting to stay put. However, if partners focus on interests, or the reasons why they have come to a specific solution, they may find that they both can reach their goals.

In this stage of the collaborative conflict resolution method, we can ask our partner:

- "Why do you want to . . . (*buy a new car*); believe that . . . (*we should punish our child*); hope that . . . (*we'll get married soon*)?"
- What is it that you are trying to achieve by wanting to . . . (*change schools*); believing that . . . (*we should break up*); hoping that . . . (*I'll sell some stock*)?"
- "Why do you feel so strongly about this?"
- "What exact problems are we trying to solve?"

The answers to these questions are the interests or the reasons why we have come to a specific solution. In the case of the partner who wants to move to a larger house, we may discover that she or he has run out of closet space and feels penned in. The partner may feel overwhelmed with all the possessions that have accumulated in the house yet not want to part with them. Wanting more room but not wanting to get rid of possessions is the interest or reason why the partner arrived at a specific solution. The partner who wants to stay put may not want to leave friends in the neighborhood and force the kids to attend different schools. After obtaining the reasons that underlie the specific positions, the partners can then focus on points of agreement and work toward a mutually satisfying solution.

Generate a Variety of Possibilities Before Deciding What to Do (Options) This step entails trying to develop as many options as possible that can meet both parties' interests. For example, we can say:

- "Can you think of at least two other ways of getting what you want?"
- "What might be the perfect situation?"
- "Can we focus on new solutions that would make you feel better?"
- "Let's explore all the options that are available to us."

The key to this step in the collaboration process is to **brainstorm**, that is, generate as many solutions as possible that can meet each partner's needs. Solutions are not judged during the brainstorming phase of collaborative conflict management. Our aim at this point is quantity, not quality; we evaluate the possibilities in the next stage of the collaboration process. The possibilities available to the partners engaged in conflict about space include installing a closet in the garage, building a storage shed in the backyard, asking friends to temporarily store some of the possessions, and paying to store some of the possessions in a self-storage facility. Other possibilities include moving to a larger house down the block or in the same neighborhood so that friends remain in close proximity and the children remain in their schools.

Insist that the Results Be Based on Some Objective Standard (Criteria) A principle of fairness or some objective standard should be used to justify a mutually satisfying solution in collaborative conflict resolution. Fair standards can be based on costs, scientific judgment, what a court might decide, ease of compliance, moral or professional standards, equal treatment, and efficiency. For example, we can say:

- "What do you think is the most important criterion or standard to guide our thinking about which solution is best?"
- "Would you be most satisfied with a solution that is least expensive?"
- "Would you agree to a solution that we can put into place in the least amount of time?"

Any of these questions can apply to the partners who need more space yet desire to stay close to friends and the children's schools.

Collaborative conflict resolution involves making use of a variety of communication skills to help partners reach their goals.

SKILL practice • Engaging in Collaborative Conflict Resolution

Role-play the following situations with a partner, and have other members of the class evaluate you and your partner's ability to engage in win-win collaborative conflict resolution. You will need to create interests or reasons that underlie your positions or solutions to the following conflict situations:

- A friend wants to go bowling while another friend wants to see a movie.
- A parent wants her or his teenager to engage in more study time while the teenager wants to get a part-time job.
- A husband wants to go on an ocean cruise while the wife wants to fix up the house.
- A partner wants lots of pets while the other partner doesn't want even one.
- An employee wants a raise while the boss wants to cut back on her or his work hours.

Remember to be realistic about the guidelines and skills related to conflict communication. There is no guarantee that engaging in collaborative conflict management will meet the needs of all parties in a dispute. Similarly, someone more powerful than you may make use of a win-lose, competing approach to conflict management and reject your request to engage in collaboration, and people who are irrational may not respond appropriately and effectively to your attempts at conflict management. Instead of making use of the collaborative or compromising personal conflict styles, you may need to withdraw or accommodate a relational partner who is extremely angry and aggressive. Even if you initially use conflict management skills in an effective and appropriate manner, feelings may be hurt and angry words may be expressed. Apologies and forgiveness may therefore be competent responses to conflict communication that is ineffective and inappropriate.

Communicating Apologies and Forgiveness

Motivation
Knowledge
Skill
COMPETENCE

The communication of apologies and forgiveness can sooth hurt feelings, restore a relationship, and pave the way for a return to effective and appropriate communication.

Apologies

How can communicating apologies and forgiveness improve our communication competence?

Compared with excuses and justifications, apologies have been found to be the most effective type of account or explanation in resolving interpersonal conflict and argument.[11] Suppose you and a partner agree to meet at a restaurant at 7 P.M. You rarely get to spend quiet time together, and when you do, you find that your time is often rushed. In addition, your partner has a tendency to arrive after your scheduled meeting times. You tell your partner how much you are looking forward to a relaxed and stress-free evening, but on

Apologies have been found to be the most effective type of account or explanation in resolving interpersonal conflict or argument.

this occasion you find yourself sitting alone for at least an hour. In this instance, your partner can offer an excuse that denies responsibility for the offense (e.g., "I know you asked me to meet you at 7, but the traffic was worse than I thought and that's why I'm late"). Your partner can also offer a justification that acknowledges responsibility but doesn't characterize the act as wrong (e.g., "I know I'm late, but we still have enough time to enjoy dinner together"). These two types of accounts differ from apologies in that **apologies** include acceptance of responsibility for an act and acknowledgment that the act is wrong. A complete apology includes:

1. Acknowledging the severity of an offense
2. Taking responsibility for the offense
3. Disparaging the "bad self" who committed the act
4. Offering penitence or restitution
5. Promising appropriate future behavior

Suppose you greet the partner who is late for the restaurant date with the statement "You are irresponsible and selfish; I should have known that you'd be late again. You're never on time!" A content conflict concerning the number of times the partner has been late may be followed by an ego conflict that includes angry insults and put-downs. However, you both eventually realize that the conflict is ruining what's left of the evening and therefore decide to apologize. The latecomer can say, *"I'm sorry I'm late. I know how much you were looking forward to a leisurely dinner with me, and it's my fault that I didn't keep my eye on the time. I promise I'll try harder to be on time in the future."* In addition, you can say, *"I'm sorry I called you 'irresponsible and selfish.' I know that you're a responsible person who*

SKILL practice • Communicating Apologies

With a partner or in a group, practice the communication of apologies by using the five steps that demonstrate that you accept responsibility and acknowledge wrongdoing in the following situations:

- You promise a friend that you will help her or him move to a new apartment but forget about your promise and fail to show up as planned.
- You borrow a sibling's possession without asking, and your sibling confronts you about not asking permission to borrow the item.
- You characterize a coworker's proposal as "weak" and "unworkable" at a meeting your coworker attends. You later learn that your coworker is embarrassed, hurt, and angry.
- You and your romantic partner celebrate your anniversary at a restaurant. You see an old friend and ask her or him to join you for dinner. Your partner later tells you that the anniversary dinner was ruined.
- Think of a recent conflict situation during which you apologized. Did you apologize in an effective and appropriate manner? Reword your apology according to the five steps that indicate your responsibility for the infraction and your acknowledgment of the wrongdoing.

really does think about my needs. I allowed my frustration and anger to get in the way, and I'll try to calm down before I speak from now on." There may be times when all five steps in a complete apology are not necessary to communicate that we accept responsibility for wrongdoing and acknowledge that an act is wrong. In such instances, we can say, *"I know that* [description of problematic behavior] *was wrong and I am sorry for what I did."* Overall, apologies focus more on the person who commits an offense and less on the reasons for or causes of the offending behavior. Apologies seek to persuade someone that whatever the inappropriate behavior, it is not a true representation of our character.[12]

Forgiveness

The necessity of an apology as a prerequisite to forgiveness has been documented in a variety of studies.[13] **Forgiveness** has been defined as the process (rather than the product) of overcoming resentment toward persons who have committed a transgression.[14] Forgiveness occurs when we are motivated to approach a partner and repair a relationship rather than motivated to seek retaliation and/or avoid a partner.[15] It is not the same thing as forgetting, excusing, or denying. In all, forgiveness is a freely chosen move toward reconciliation.[16] Although there are many paths to forgiveness, one method that can help us forgive others is called REACH:[17]

- "R" stands for "recall the hurt" in an objective manner. We should not think of the person who hurt us as evil or wallow in self-pity, but instead use factual language to describe the event and our emotions.
- "E" stands for "empathize." In this step we try to see the world as the transgressor might and attempt to understand why this person hurt us. We can make up a realistic story that the transgressor might tell if forced to explain.
- "A" stands for giving the "altruistic gift" of forgiveness. In this step, we need to recall a time when we transgressed, felt guilty, or were "in the wrong" and were subsequently

MOTIVATION & mindwork • REACH for Forgiveness

Think of someone who said or did something that hurt you. It need not be a major transgression; for example, you can focus on someone who forgot to call, email, or show up at a certain location as promised. Use the REACH technique to attempt to forgive the person and the hurtful action:

- Recall the hurt in an objective manner and use factual language to describe the event and your emotions ("R").
- Empathize with the person who hurt you. Attempt to see the world as she or he does, and make up a story that the person might tell if she or he were forced to explain ("E").
- Recall a time when you transgressed, felt guilty, or were "in the wrong" and were subsequently forgiven. This step will help you give the altruistic gift of forgiveness ("A").
- Create a "forgiveness contract" by imagining yourself writing a letter or journal entry about forgiving the person. You may actually want to write the letter or entry after this exercise ("C").
- Imagine yourself getting angry with the person at some later time yet "holding on to your forgiveness." Remind yourself that even if you react negatively to your memories, it doesn't mean you haven't forgiven the person ("H").

KNOWLEDGE power • How Willing Are You to Forgive?

Can you readily forgive a relationship partner's affront or transgression? To assess your willingness to forgive, take the twelve-item Transgression Motivations Questionnaire at www.authentichappiness.org. For more information about forgiveness in general, access www.forgivenessweb.com.

forgiven. We attempt to perceive forgiveness as a gift for which a transgressor is grateful and which usually helps the forgiving person feel better.

- "C" stands for "committing ourselves to forgive." In addition to communicating our forgiveness to a wrongdoer, we can write a letter of forgiveness to the transgressor, write about forgiving her or him in a journal or diary, or tell a friend that we have forgiven the transgressor. These actions can be perceived as "contracts" of forgiveness that lead to the final step.
- "H" stands for "holding on to forgiveness." This is difficult to do because memories of the event are bound to recur. But forgiveness is not the same as erasing a wrongdoing, and recurring memories don't mean that we have failed in our attempts to forgive. We can therefore attempt not to dwell on the memories. We can remind ourselves that we have indeed forgiven and recall what we have previously written and/or told a friend. Even if we find ourselves reacting negatively to a wrongdoer, it doesn't mean we haven't forgiven her or him.

We can communicate our forgiveness by making use of three general strategies: direct, indirect, and with conditions:[18]

1. A direct strategy includes talking about the issue with the offender. Tactics associated with this strategy include telling the transgressor that we understand, directly saying "I forgive you," and using a third party to mediate between the two of you.
2. An indirect strategy can include tactics such as humor to diminish the impact of the wrongdoing and saying "It's no big deal," using nonverbal behavior such as touching and hugging, changes in vocal patterns and other nonverbal displays, and "returning to normal" as a way of demonstrating that all is forgiven without actually saying something.
3. The strategy of forgiveness with conditions entails offering forgiveness only if the offender adheres to certain stipulations. "I'll forgive you for yelling at me only if you promise not to do it again" illustrates the forgiveness with conditions strategy.

How do contexts influence interpersonal conflicts?

Contexts and Interpersonal Conflict

Perhaps you once engaged in conflict with someone from a different culture; a family member, friend, or coworker; an individual whose gender is different than yours; or someone who exhibited "argumentative skill deficiency." The culture, relationship, gender, and individual contexts influence the types of conflict in which we find ourselves, our topics of conflict, personal conflict styles, and conflict management strategies.

Culture Context

The experience of conflict is highly influenced by culture. Not only do individualist and collectivist cultures teach their members how to effectively and appropriately manage conflict but also co-cultures teach their members about competent conflict management.

Individualist and Collectivist Cultures Individualist cultures teach their members that expressing strong personal opinions and emotions during a conflict episode is appropriate. Members of individualist cultures are expected to manage conflicts by asserting individual interests and by moving quickly toward tangible outcomes or goals. Effective conflict resolution involves dealing openly with a problem and working conjointly on possible solutions. In contrast, collectivist cultures teach members to reflect collective ideas and opinions and to restrain emotions during conflict. In addition, the management of face concerns is emphasized before moving to outcomes or goals in collectivist cultures. Effective conflict resolution requires the subtle negotiation of face-related issues such as pride, honor, dignity, and shame before addressing possible solutions.[19] Furthermore, while individualist cultures prefer direct styles of dealing with conflict, such as collaborating and compromising, collectivist cultures prefer indirect styles that enable everyone involved to save face, such as accommodating and avoiding. For example, members of the Chinese culture tend to be less direct and confrontational than Americans, and Americans use direct solution-oriented styles more than members of the Taiwanese culture do. Dutch and Canadians (both individualist cultures) are taught that it's appropriate to openly confront and accuse others during conflict, but Spaniards and Japanese (both collectivist cultures) are not. Similarly, Arabs and Mexicans tend to use the avoiding style more than Americans, and Americans typically use the competing style more than people in Arab and Mexican cultures.[20] Note that the avoiding conflict style is considered a lose-lose orientation to conflict in individualist cultures (and is described as such in this book). Viewing the avoiding style as involving a low concern for self and others reflects an individualist bias in that this style can effectively and appropriately address the overriding concern of maintaining face for self and others in collectivist cultures.[21]

Co-Cultures In addition to differences in conflict styles among cultures, there are differences in conflict behaviors among various co-cultures within the United States. Members of collectivist ethnic groups such as Asian Americans, African Americans, and Latina/o Americans tend to use more cooperative conflict styles than Americans of European background. European Americans typically use the competing conflict style in romantic relationships, whereas Asian Americans use avoiding, accommodating, compromising, and collaborating in romantic relationships. Research comparing gay, lesbian, and heterosexual couples reveals that heterosexual couples experience more frequent conflict about social issues such as politics, personal values, and parental issues than gay and lesbian couples. Gay and lesbian couples experience more frequent conflict about issues of distrust, such as previous lovers and lying. Social issues may be more contentious topics for heterosexual couples than for gay and lesbian couples because, as members of a socially stigmatized group, gays and lesbians may have similar viewpoints about controversial issues such as civil rights. Additionally, relationships with parents may be more conflictual for heterosexual couples than for gay and lesbian couples because parents tend to be more salient sources of support for heterosexual couples.[22]

Relationship Context

Conflicts among family members and between intimate partners are two areas of study that have received much attention in the conflict literature.

Family Family members overall tend to engage in **conflict rituals,** which are patterns that reinforce specific ways to manage conflict. Your family may have taught you that conflict is bad and should be avoided at all costs, whereas other families teach its members that communicating about any issue in dispute is acceptable. Your family may have taught you that appropriate conflict behavior includes actions that other families may consider unacceptable, such as screaming and slamming doors. For example, the "Sally Forth" comic suggests a conflict ritual that includes reasoned discourse about differences of opinion. How families manage conflict has been found to be more important than the number of conflicts experienced among family members. Conflict management behaviors such as supportive responses, reasoning, and rational discussion positively influence the perception of family conflict and the parent-child relationship.[23]

Friends Like the relationships we have with members of our family, managing conflict in our relationships with friends often depends on our knowledge of what topics or issues seem to trigger conflict. You may have a friend with whom you avoid talking about politics because such conversations routinely become heated and conflictual. On the other hand, you may enjoy talking about politics with a different friend—but know to avoid talking about her or his ex-partner because you hold differing opinions about the ex and the reason for the breakup. Our knowledge of which topics tend to promote conflict episodes with our friends can help us create friendship rules that prescribe effective and appropriate communication in our relationships. Typical friendship rules concern:[24]

- respecting privacy (a conflict may follow if we push our friend to disregard a personal boundary and share information considered to be personal)
- keeping confidences (a conflict may arise if we betray a friend's trust by sharing a secret)
- avoiding public criticism (a conflict may occur and our friend may lose face if we criticize our friend in front of others)

KNOWLEDGE power • Emotional Outbursts or Calm Discussions?

What conflict rituals were taught in your family? Were family members:

- Encouraged to engage in open conflict or taught to suppress disagreements?
- Influenced to express conflict in terms of verbal aggression and/or emotional outbursts or made aware that calm, reasoned discourse was the only acceptable mode of conflict communication?
- Taught that only one person in the family had the ultimate authority to make undisputed decisions or urged to question and disagree with any decisions that affected family members?

Consider the impact of your family rituals on your adult conflict behavior. Is your current ritual-based conflict communication appropriate and effective? If not, how can you revise your conflict rituals to help you deal competently with conflict situations?

Family members establish conflict rituals that reinforce specific ways to manage conflict.

Source: © SALLY FORTH–KING FEATURES SYNDICATE.

- sustaining equity (a conflict may develop if we fail to "give and take" in equal proportions, especially concerning debts and favors)

People with Whom We Work Conflicts are considered a natural part of organizational life and can result in creative problem solving, increased job commitment, and organizational change.[25] However, when workplace conflict becomes destructive, the consequence may be distorted communication patterns and increased stress. Sources of interpersonal conflict in an organization include:[26]

- unequal power distribution (such as when one coworker is promoted and another is not)
- unclear role expectations (such as who is responsible for what)
- insufficient information to make good decisions or understand why something happened
- differences in beliefs, attitudes, values, and rules for behavior

Interpersonal conflict in the workplace is primarily studied between superiors and subordinates and between coworkers. In general, superiors tend to use forcing or competitive strategies based on their power in conflicts with subordinates. Subordinates tend to avoid, compromise, or smooth over problems in conflict communication with their superiors. Among coworkers, research tends to focus on how perceptual issues and organizational environments or climates influence conflict communication. For example, an organization that promotes a "conflict management culture" influences its employees to perceive conflict in terms of problem solving and to make use of communication behaviors such as asking questions and integrating information.[27]

Gender Context

Many researchers contend that women and men engage in different types of conflict behavior because of socialization; in particular, that socialization teaches women to be more sensitive to and aware of existing problems in a relationship. Feminine socialization

KNOWLEDGE ON THE CUTTING EDGE

Putting It in Context: Sex, Communication, and Conflict

Recall the last time you were involved in an intense conflict situation. How long did it take you to calm down once the conflict ended? Psychologist John Gottman and his colleagues have demonstrated what has been described as "impressive information" about the physiological responses women and men experience during conflict. Both experience the fight-or-flight syndrome when faced with stressful situations such as conflict. This instinctive response includes a pounding heart, increased sweating, and an overall increase in energy and alertness. It usually takes a few minutes to return to a normal state once we are aroused. However, more than one point of arousal is common in interpersonal conflicts, and the negative messages exchanged in conflict situations typically prevent physiological recovery. This results in levels of physiological arousal that appear to be an overreaction to an initial cause of conflict. The chaotic thought processes and discomfort caused by physiological arousal is a condition that Gottman calls "flooding."

Can you recall a conflict in which you or your conversation partner experienced flooding? Is the person who experienced flooding male or female? Gottman suggests that males experience flooding more than females and that this difference can be seen even in childhood, as young boys have more and longer-lasting tantrums than young girls. Adult males also tend to have "shorter fuses" and engage in longer-lasting outbursts than women. Similarly, Gottman's studies reveal that a man's blood pressure and heart rate rise higher and stay elevated longer than a woman's in conflict situations. A male's autonomic nervous system, which controls the stress response in the body, may be more sensitive than a female's and take longer to recover from upsetting arguments. This could explain why men more than women tend to withdraw and use the avoiding response in conflict. Because males are more biologically reactive to stress, they may need to withdraw to protect themselves from the discomfort it causes. Gottman contends that this accounts for his findings that in more than twenty different studies of over 2,000 couples, about 85% of the males used an avoidance strategy as a coping mechanism.[28]

Research demonstrates that people characterized by argumentative skill deficiency resort to extreme verbal aggression and sometimes physical violence because they lack the verbal skills to constructively deal with conflict.

teaches women to respond to conflicts by talking about the topic under dispute and attempting to resolve it. Because masculine socialization places little emphasis on how to talk about problems, men may communicate that an issue is unimportant or simply not respond when conflict eventually erupts. Men may also exit a conflict situation if they feel they can't control it and will ultimately "suffer defeat." However, these views are not supported by empirical and observational studies. In fact, one study revealed that the behaviors of women and men actually run contrary to gender-based assumptions of conflict behavior. Specifically, women self-reported that they engage in "distributive strategies" (e.g., making threats, using criticism, shouting) significantly more than their male partners. Men self-reported that they engage in slightly more "integrative strategies" (e.g., showing concern, using reasoning, expressing trust) and avoidance strategies than their female partners. Another analysis of conflict-related gender research revealed that approximately 1% of conflict behavior differences can be explained by gender; this means that women and men act similarly in conflict situations about 99% of the time. Although women and men may exhibit some differences in conflict communication, these differences are found inconsistently because of the influence of the situation, the individuals involved in the conflict, and factors that relate to the relationship between the couple in conflict. Furthermore, the level or type of conflict and relational satisfaction affect whatever sex differences may exist in conflict behavior. Other studies illustrate that conflict communication is influenced more by a partner's behavior than by one's own gender. Moreover, the small differences in gender-related conflict behaviors diminish with age.[29] Overall, women and men are more similar than different in conflict situations.

Individual Context

A number of studies have linked personality characteristics to styles of conflict management. For example, individuals who can be described as manifesting "achievement motivation, dogmatism, and Machiavellianism" have been found to make use of collaborative or competing styles of conflict management. People described as manifesting personality characteristics such as "affiliation" and "nurturance" tend to demonstrate an accommodating style of conflict management.[30] In addition, argumentative skill deficiency is a personality characteristic that has a significant impact on a conflict situation. The words *argumentativeness* and *argument* have negative connotations and imply something that may be potentially destructive. However, "argumentation" in the case of argumentative skill deficiency concerns presenting and defending positions during a conflict. Communication scholar **Dominic A. Infante** and his colleagues suggest that **argumentative skill deficiency** refers to individuals who use verbal aggression to manage their conflicts because they lack the verbal skills to deal constructively with conflict. Persons who are low in "trait argumentativeness" typically are perceived as less skilled in conflict situations, less willing to argue, low in credibility, and less competent communicators. Research additionally demonstrates that the potential for a conflict to escalate into extreme verbal aggression and even violence is heightened when people lack the verbal skills to constructively deal with conflict. Studies suggest that persons who aren't skilled at argumentation tend to provoke others to use verbal aggression, which in turn increases the level of negative arousal in the conflict situation. It has also been found that partners in violent relationships not only are less skilled in managing social conflict but also measure lower in assertiveness and lower in problem-solving skills. Although argumentative

Competence & Critical Thinking

mycommunicationlab

JIM AND JACK JOUST AND INTERPERSONAL CONFLICT

In the very early morning, Jim returns to the apartment that he shares with his roommate, Jack. At 4:30 A.M., Jim plays his CD loud enough to wake Jack, and the roommates discuss the situation.

You can view *Jim and Jack Joust* by accessing the "Small Group and Interpersonal Videos" on the MyCommunicationLab Web site. Answer the following questions about their interpersonal conflict:

- Which type(s) of conflict(s) are evidenced in the video (pseudo-, content, value, ego)?
- Which type(s) of personal conflict styles are illustrated in the video (avoiding, accommodating, competing, compromising, collaborating)?
- Do you think Jim and/or Jack lack the verbal skills to constructively deal with conflict? Would you describe Jim and/or Jack as illustrating argumentative skill deficiency?
- Which communication skills included in the text (and listed in Table 11-3, "Collaborative Conflict Resolution Skills") could be used to better manage Jim and Jack's conflict?

JACK: What are you doing? You know what time it is right now?

JIM: Hey, what's up, Jack?

JACK: What's up? It is 4:30 in the morning.

JIM: Hey, hey, hey. I know it' 4:30 in the morning. I just got out of work.

JACK: Yeah, well, you know, I'm trying to sleep, man. What are you doing? You can't just come home and blast the music whenever you get home. You have to understand that I'm trying to sleep.

JIM: Well, well, you know what, we—you know, you know what, you need to relax a little bit, OK?

JACK: I don't—I don't need to relax. You need to try to—you need to understand you're not the only one who lives there, and that you can't just do whatever you want whenever you want.

JIM: You know I come home, and you know I listen to music.

JACK: Yeah, I realize that. And by the same token, you know I'm sleeping when you're listening to this music. So if you don't mind turning it down, it—I don't think it's unreasonable. It's 4:30 in the morning. I'm not asking you never to listen to music. I'm just saying, when it's this late, if you could keep it quiet.

JIM: You know I get out of work at quarter of 4. And I'm going to come home, and sometimes it's early, and sometimes it's later. And I'm going to come home, and I'm going to sit down, and I'm going to relax in my apartment and listen to my music on my stereo.

JACK: You can listen to it. But can't you keep it quieter? It has to be this loud all the time?

JIM: I don't understand why the time of day matters how loud it is or it isn't.

JACK: But are you—are you joking?

JIM: No, I'm not joking.

JACK: It doesn't—you're not the only one who lives here, man. I'm—I'm in bed, all right? I have class at 9 tomorrow, and you wake me up. And this happens all the time. This can't keep happening anymore. We've got to solve this.

JIM: Wait, wait, wait, wait, wait. Hold—hold on.

JACK: No . . .

JIM: *(referring to the music)* Dude, that's awesome! Come on. Did you hear that? That's great. Wait, hold . . .

JACK: You're not going to turn that up. You can't.

JIM: Why?

JACK: You have no respect, all right? You have no respect.

JIM: I have no respect.

JACK: Yeah, you have no respect.

JIM: What about when I get woken up in the morning from all the phone calls that you get during the day?

JACK: I can't control when people call. You can control when you listen to music and how loud you listen to music. Yeah? Yeah? You understand this is a problem?

JIM: That it's a problem that our schedules are completely different?

JACK: No, that it's a problem that you can't make a simple—you can't make a simple change.

JIM: What are you talking about, a simple change? You know, I know I don't spend a lot of time here, but the time that I do spend here, I want to spend it the way that I want to spend it, that—what I pay for when I am here. I mean, you understood this when we first moved in together. I mean, I don't understand what the big deal is. I mean, what time did you go to sleep? You usually go to sleep at, what, 9? What do you need, twelve hours of sleep?

JACK: You know, you're right. Yeah, this is my fault.

JIM: I'm not saying . . .

JACK: No, you're right.

JIM: No. I'm not saying that this is your fault. You know, it is—so are you saying that it's unreasonable for me to, when I come home, to listen to my music? And I always have to tiptoe around you. It was a tough night at work. What do you want?

JACK: Why can't you use the headphones? What is the difference?

JIM: Doesn't sound the same.

JACK: Well, it doesn't sound the same?

JIM: No, it doesn't.

JACK: Do you think you're being unreasonable? Am I the only one who sees this?

JIM: I don't know. All of my friends do the exact same thing that I do.

JACK: Do you live with them? No, you live with me, all right? And whether we like it or not, this is who we live with.

skill deficiency has been researched as a personality trait, studies indicate that this characteristic can be modified when individuals engage in cognitive restructuring techniques (such as those described in Chapter 4 about emotions) and who participate in argumentative skills training.[31]

OVERCOMING COMMUNICATION CHALLENGES

Couple Violence

"Abuse" occurs in an ongoing and repetitive pattern, and "aggression" implies intent to do harm. Unlike abuse and aggression, **couple violence** may include physical pain inflicted because of an impulsive desire to express a state of heightened arousal. Although this type of violence is typically isolated, approximately 50% of couples in the United States may experience violence in the form of pushing and shoving when a conflict gets out of hand. Many researchers suggest that violence results from attempts to demonstrate power in conflict situations; however, other researchers contend that common couple violence is expressive and may accompany relatively uncontrollable verbal outbursts. This implies that although violence may be a form of power, not all displays of violence result from a motivation to exert power over others.

Couple violence occurs most often during conflict situations. Couples who experience high levels of conflict are more likely to be involved in violent episodes than couples who experience less conflict. We have already read that argumentative skill deficiency can cause people to verbally attack others and that such aggression may lead to interpersonal violence. Conflicts characterized by violence often occur because couples lack the communication skills to defuse a dispute. Contrasting perceptions of conflict interaction also contribute to the enactment of physical violence. Specifically, couple violence can occur when:

- A partner perceives a transgression or an affront that stimulates arousal and possibly anger.
- The partner demands an account, and if the account is not accepted, the conflict mostly likely escalates.
- While one partner perceives her or his behavior as appropriate, the other does not, and vice versa. These perceptions influence the individuals involved in conflict to feel justified in their use of aggressive conflict behavior, including personal attacks.
- Violence may subsequently occur and may be met with violence.

To decrease the incidence of couple violence and to break the cycle of escalation, partners can diffuse a conflict situation by shifting to less emotional talk or to an explicit discussion of the rules for engaging in conflict. Using metacommunication to draw the topic of conflict away from a specific affront and toward the pattern of interaction can reduce the emotional intensity of the situation and reaffirm the parameters established for the conflict. If partners feel compelled to exchange complaints, they should be expressed calmly and in clear and specific terms. Conflict can also be mitigated by listening to a partner's side of the story, sharing feelings, and showing fairness. Accepting some of the blame and demonstrating remorse can de-escalate conflict situations and avoid violent outbursts.[32]

A CASE STUDY IN ETHICS

Parents, Pixels, and Political Parties

Recall that competent communication includes an ethical dimension of well-based standards of right and wrong. We can ask ourselves a series of questions to help us choose communication strategies that are effective and appropriate as they relate to interpersonal conflict. Specifically, we can ask: Have I practiced any virtues today (e.g., have I demonstrated integrity, trustworthiness, honesty, and responsibility)? Have I done more good than harm (e.g., have I shown appreciation and gratitude to others)? Have I treated people with dignity and respect? Have I been fair and just? Have I made my community stronger because of my actions? Read the following case study and consider whether Ted and Teddy Gambordella are engaging in ethical means of conflict management.

Ted Gambordella, a Republican, is incensed that his only son, Teddy, a junior in high school, is a Democrat. Ted is so exasperated with his son's choice of political party that he refuses to fund Teddy's college education unless he becomes a Republican. Teddy accepts his father's refusal to help him through college and maintains that he won't switch parties just to get his father's money. Instead, Teddy started a Web site, www.onemillionreasonswhy.com, to raise college funds. He hopes that supporters will purchase pixels, the dots on computer screens, as advertising space. The pixels cost $1.00 each, and buyers are required to purchase a minimum of 100 pixels. Teddy has sold 10,200 pixels but must sell many more to pay for his college education. However, Teddy says that it's not just about money for college. "It's about spreading knowledge . . . and proving my dad wrong. It's more of a principle thing," he contends.

Teddy says that it will be easier to persuade his dad to change his mind about Republican politics than to change his own party affiliation. Although new to politics, Teddy attends Dallas Young Democrats meetings and says that it's "cool" to talk to people who see the world as he does. "They aren't crazy like my dad tries to make me believe," he says. Jeff Barrows, the sponsor of the Young Democrats club, says that Teddy is the type of person who will work toward a solution if one lies within reach, as evidenced by his online entrepreneurial spirit.

Teddy's mother, Debra, also a Republican, doesn't want to get involved in the father-son conflict and says that she supports both her son and her husband. Debra asserts that Teddy is rebelling by becoming a Democrat, which is better than drinking or doing drugs. Ted echoes similar sentiments and suggests that he's proud of Teddy's initiative, even though he disagrees with his son's political affiliation. Ted asserts that he was liberal in college but now listens to Rush Limbaugh and donates money to the Republican Party. "Democrats are too extreme. I wish they had some moderate voices," Ted contends, but he hopes that Teddy's site promotes some intelligent political discussions.

Teddy admits that he'd like to be a moderate voice of Democrats, but his father shakes his head, chuckles, and says, "He'll grow out of it."

Do you believe that Ted Gambordella is engaging in ethical conflict management? Is Teddy Gambordella responding to his father's conflict behavior in an ethical manner? Is it ethical for Debra Gambordella to stay out of the conflict? Do you think this conflict is being handled in an effective and appropriate manner? What might you do differently if you were involved in such a conflict?[33]

Chapter Review

Motivation: How has this helped me?

- **The importance of studying interpersonal conflict**

It's important to study interpersonal conflict to improve our competence in conflict management, to learn that conflict is natural, to realize that people develop individually through conflict, and to experience satisfying relationships. Forgiveness occurs when we are motivated to approach a partner and repair a relationship rather than motivated to seek retaliation and/or avoid a partner. We can motivate ourselves to forgive others and their hurtful actions when we make use of the REACH technique.

Knowledge: What have I learned?

- **How to characterize interpersonal conflict**

Conflict is the perception of incompatible goals and interference from another in achieving those goals. Conflict is manageable and natural, can lead to individual growth, and can contribute to satisfying relationships.

- **Types of interpersonal conflict**

A pseudoconflict occurs when we perceive that our partner has goals that are incompatible with ours. This type of conflict can be resolved when we realize that we are truly not in conflict. Content conflict occurs when we disagree about information. This type of conflict can be resolved when we turn to outside sources to verify the facts in dispute. Value conflict results when people have differing opinions about issues that relate to their personal value systems. It may not be possible to resolve this type of conflict. Ego conflict occurs when we believe we must win a conflict to save face. Ego conflict can be managed by owning thoughts and using face-saving communication skills.

- **Personal conflict styles**

Personal conflict styles are preferred ways of dealing with conflict situations. The avoiding style includes physically removing ourselves from a conflict or refusing to discuss the topic of conflict. The accommodating style entails satisfying our partner's needs at the expense of our own. The competing style is illustrated when we attempt to meet our needs without concern for our partner's needs. The compromising style includes the parties in conflict giving up part of what they want in order to achieve partial satisfaction in meeting their goals. The collaborating style is used when we attempt to satisfy both our needs and our partner's needs.

- **How using a collaborative conflict resolution method can improve our communication competence**

Collaborative conflict resolution can change a dispute originally perceived as win-lose to one that is perceived as win-win.

- **How contexts influence interpersonal conflict**

Individualist and collectivist cultures and co-cultures teach their members about competent conflict management. Family members tend to engage in conflict rituals; conflict with friends is influenced by the knowledge of what topics trigger conflict; and conflict with coworkers is a natural part of organizational life. Although gender socialization may cause women and men to engage in different types of conflict behavior, research suggests that women and men tend to communicate similarly in conflict situations. Argumentative skill deficiency is a personality characteristic that is characterized by people who use verbal aggression because they lack the verbal skills to deal constructively with conflict.

- **How communicating apologies and forgiveness can improve your communication competence**

The communication of apologies and forgiveness can sooth hurt feelings, restore a relationship, and pave the way for a return to effective and appropriate communication. Apologies include the acceptance of responsibility for an act and an acknowledgement that the act is wrong. Forgiveness, the process of overcoming resentment toward persons who have committed a transgression, can be communicated directly, indirectly, and with conditions.

Skill: What skills have I developed?

- **Using a collaborative conflict resolution method and communicating apologies and forgiveness can improve your communication competence.**

One collaborative conflict resolution method includes separating the people from the problem, focusing on interests (reasons), brainstorming options, and choosing an objective standard to justify a mutually satisfying solution. Communicating apologies that acknowledge our responsibility and wrongdoing, and engaging in forgiveness can sooth hurt feelings, restore a relationship, and promote competent communication.

Study Questions

1. Why is it important to study conflict communication?
2. Explain and describe four types of conflict.
3. What personal styles are used in the management of interpersonal conflict?
4. Describe a collaborative conflict resolution technique.
5. What are the components of a complete apology?
6. How can we communicate that we forgive someone for an affront?
7. How do the culture, relationship, gender, and individual contexts affect the perception of conflict and conflict behaviors?
8. Describe couple violence and how the use of communication can mitigate such violence.

Names to Know

Daniel J. Canary, p. 292—Communication researcher who teaches at the Hugh Downs School of Human Communication at Arizona State University. Canary's research interests include communication and relationship maintenance, conflict communication, and sex and gender similarities and differences in communication.

Dominic A. Infante, p. 313—Communication scholar who developed the argumentative skill deficiency model and who is professor emeritus of communication studies at Kent State University. His research interests include argumentativeness, verbal aggressiveness, personality and communication, family violence, and spousal abuse.

Ralph H. Kilmann and **Kenneth W. Thomas**, p. 298—Researchers who identified five styles of conflict management. Kilmann is president of Organizational Design Consultants, and Thomas is professor emeritus at the Naval Postgraduate School in Monterey, California.

Key Terms

accommodating, 299
apologies, 306
argumentative skill deficiency, 313
avoiding, 298
brainstorming, 304
collaborating, 301
competing, 300
compromising, 300
conflict, 292
conflict rituals, 310
content conflict, 297
couple violence, 315
ego conflict, 297
forgiveness, 307
personal conflict styles, 298
pseudoconflict, 295
social information processing (SIP) theory, 295
value conflict, 297

Endnotes

Chapter I

1. Chen, G.-M., and W. J. Starosta. "Intercultural Communication Competence." In *Communication Yearbook 19*. Ed. B. R. Burleson. Thousand Oaks, CA: Sage, 1996, 353–358.
2. Samovar, L. A., and R. E. Porter. *Communication between Cultures,* 5th ed. Belmont, CA: Wadsworth, 2004. See also "Population and Migration." In U.S. Department of State, Bureau of Population, Refugees, and Migration. 2005. Retrieved 10 November 2006 from www.state.gov/g/prm/mig/.
3. *Trends 2005: A Look at Changes in American Life.* Pew Internet and American Life Project. Washington, DC: Pew Research Center, 2005. See also Madden, M. *Internet Penetration and Impact—April 2006.* Pew Internet and American Life Project. Washington, DC: Pew Research Center, 2006; and Lenhart, A., and S. Fox, *Bloggers: A Portrait of the Internet's New Storytellers.* Pew Internet and American Life Project Washington, DC: Pew Research Center, 2006.
4. White, J. "Wireless Technology Changing Work and Play." *CNN.com,* 17 October 2005. Retrieved 18 October 2005 from www.cnn.com/2005/TECH/10/17wireless.overview.index.html.
5. Rechtschaffen, S. *Time-Shifting: Creating More Time to Enjoy Your Life.* New York: Doubleday, 1996.
6. "New Salary.com Survey Finds Growing Number of Workers Value Personal Time over Money." *Forbes.com,* 12 January 2005. Retrieved 21 February 2005 from www.forbes.com/businesswire/feeds/businesswire/2005/0l/12/businesswire20050111005139.2.html.
7. Gross, M. "Got a Minute? Survey Finds a Nation in a Hurry." *AP/Ipsos Poll,* 31 May 2006. Retrieved 7 June 2006 from www.ipsos-na.com/news/pressrelease.cfm?id=3096. See also "Fed Up? We're Not Gonna Wait." *Dallas Morning News,* 29 May 2006, 7A.
8. Ornish, D. *Love and Survival.* New York: HarperPerennial, 1998.
9. "Schmoozing Is Good for the Brain, U-M Study Suggests." *EurekAlert!* 22 October 2002. Retrieved 2 August 2003 from www.eurekalert.org/pub_releases/2002-10/uomsig102202.php; and Ybarra, O., E. Burnstein, P. Winkielman, M. C. Keller, M. Manis, E. Chan, and J. Rodriguez. "Mental Exercising Through Simple Socializing: Social Interaction Promotes General Cognitive Functioning." *Personality and Social Psychology Bulletin* 34 (2008): 248–259.
10. Spitzberg, B. H., and W. R. Cupach. "Interpersonal Skills." In *Handbook of Interpersonal Communication,* 3rd ed. Ed. M. L. Knapp and J. A. Daly. Thousand Oaks, CA: Sage, 2002, 564–611.
11. Spitzberg, B. H., and W. R. Cupach. *Interpersonal Communication Competence.* Thousand Oaks, CA: Sage, 1984.
12. Ibid.
13. Shiminoff, S. B. *Communication Rules: Theory and Research.* Thousand Oaks, CA: Sage, 1980.
14. "Rudeness Survey Stirs Up Public Debate about the Decline of Civility in the U.S." *Public Agenda* Summer (2002): 1, 5. See also Gross, M. "AP/Ipsos Poll: The Decline of American Civilization, or at Least Its Manners." *Ipsos,* 14 October 2005. Retrieved 4 October 2005 from www.ipsos-na.com/news/pressrelease.cfm?id=2827; and "The Decline of Manners in the U.S." *CNN.com,* 14 October 2005. Retrieved 14 October 2005 from www.cnn.com/2005/US/10/14/poll.rude.ap/index.html.
15. "Ugly Americans." Editorial. *San Francisco Chronicle,* SFGate.com, 5 April 2002. Retrieved 24 May 2007 from http://sfgate.com/cgi-bin/article.cgi?f=/c/a/2002/04/05/ED141479.DTL&hw=Public+Agenda+rudeness+survey&sn=002&sc=979.
16. Cupach, W. R., and D. J. Canary. *Competence in Interpersonal Conflict.* Long Grove, IL: Waveland Press, 1997. See also Lane, S. D. "Dialogic Civility: A Narrative to Live by." *Texas Speech Communication Journal* 29 (2005): 174–183.
17. Carter, S. L. *Civility: Manners, Morals, and the Etiquette of Democracy.* New York: HarperPerennial, 1998. See also Carter, S. L. "Just Be Nice." *Yale Alumni Magazine.* Stephen Carter on Civility, May 1998. Retrieved 14 May 2005 from www.yalealumnimagazine.com/issues/98_05/Stephen_Carter.html; and Forni, P. M. *Choosing Civility.* New York: St. Martins Griffin, 2002.
18. Shanks, T. "Everyday Ethics." *Issues in Ethics* 8, 1 (1997). Retrieved 22 August 2003 from www.scu.edu/ethics/publications/iie/v8bl.everydayethics.html.
19. "NCA Credo for Ethical Communication." In *Ethical Communication.* National Communication Association, 17 July 2004.
20. Spitzberg and Cupach, "Interpersonal Skills."
21. Shanks.

22. Ibid.
23. Spitzberg and Cupach, "Interpersonal Communication Competence."
24. Ibid.
25. Georgoudi, E., and R. L. Rousnow. "Notes toward a Contextualist Understanding of Social Psychology." *Personality and Social Psychology Bulletin* 11 (1985): 76–88.
26. Spitzberg, B. H. "Interpersonal Communication Competence." In *Essays on Human Communication.* Ed. H. T. Hurt and B. H. Spitzberg. Boston: Ginn, 1984, 31–39.
27. Ibid.
28. Storti, C. *Figuring Foreigners Out: A Practical Guide.* Boston: Intercultural Press, 1999, p. 5.
29. Lustig, M. W., and J. Koester. *Intercultural Competence: Interpersonal Communication across Cultures,* 4th ed. Boston: Allyn & Bacon, 2003.
30. Ibid.
31. Ibid.
32. Althen, G. (with A. R. Doran and S. J. Szmania). *American Ways,* 2nd ed. Boston: Intercultural Press, 2002.
33. Lustig and Koester.
34. Yep, G. A. "The Violence of Heteronormativity in Communication Studies: Notes on Injury, Healing, and Queer World-Making." In *Queer Theory and Communication: From Disciplining Queers to Queering the Discipline(s).* Ed. G. A. Yep, K. E. Lovaas, and J. P. Elia. New York: Harrington Park Press, 2003, 11–59.
35. Ibid. See also Mindess, A. *Reading between the Signs: Intercultural Communication for Sign Language Interpreters.* Boston: Intercultural Press, 1999; and Siple, L. A. "Cultural Patterns of Deaf People." In *Intercultural Communication: A Reader,* 9th ed. Belmont, CA: Wadsworth, 2000, 146–157.
36. Yep, G. A. "Encounters with the 'Other': Personal Notes for a Reconceptualization of Intercultural Communication Competence." *The CATESOL Journal* 12 (2000): 117–144.
37. Galvin, K. M., and P. J. Cooper. "Family." In *Making Connections: Readings in Relational Communication,* 4th ed. Ed. K. M. Galvin, and P. J. Cooper. New York: Oxford University Press, 2006, 291–292.
38. Lerner, H. *The Dance of Anger.* New York: Quill, 2001.
39. Galvin, K. M., and P. J. Cooper. "Friends." In *Making Connections: Readings in Relational Communication,* 4th ed. Ed. K. M. Galvin and P. J. Cooper. New York: Oxford University Press, 2006, 327–328.
40. Satir, V. "The Rules You Live By." In *Making Connections: Readings in Relational Communication,* 3rd ed. Ed. K. M. Galvin, and P. J. Cooper. New York: Oxford University Press, 199–205.
41. Stone, E. "Family Ground Rules." In *Making Connections: Readings in Relational Communication,* 4th ed. Ed. K. M. Galvin and P. J. Cooper. New York: Oxford University Press, 2006, 293–301.
42. Duck, S. W. *Meaningful Relationships.* Thousand Oaks, CA: Sage, 1994. See also Nardi, P. M., and D. Sherrod. "Friendship in the Lives of Gay Men and Lesbians." *Journal of Social and Personal Relationships* 11 (1994): 185–199.
43. Galvin and Cooper.
44. Watters, E. "Urban Tribes." In *Making Connections: Readings in Relational Communication,* 4th ed. Ed. K. M. Galvin and P. J. Cooper. New York: Oxford University Press, 2006, 333–336.
45. Eisenberg, E. M., and H. L. Goodall Jr. *Organizational Communication: Balancing Creativity and Constraint,* 4th ed. New York: Bedford/St. Martins, 2004.
46. "Frequently Asked Questions." National Association of Colleges and Employers (NACE) Job Outlook 2006. *NACEWeb.* Retrieved 10 November 2006 from www.jobweb.com/joboutlook/2006/2.htm.
47. Adler, R. B., L. B. Rosenfeld, and R. F. Proctor. *Interplay: The Process of Interpersonal Communication,* 10th ed. New York: Oxford University Press, 2007; and Chambers, H. E. *Effective Communication Skills for Scientific and Technical Professionals.* Cambridge, MA: Perseus, 2001.
48. Klaus, P. *The Hard Truth about Soft Skills: Workplace Lessons Smart People Wish They'd Learned Sooner.* New York: HarperCollins, 2008.
49. Reeder, H. M. "A Critical Look at Gender Differences in Communication Research." In *Making Connections: Readings in Relational Communication,* 2nd ed. Ed. K. M. Galvin and P. J. Cooper. New York: Oxford University Press, 2000, 69–76.
50. Wood, J. T. "Growing Up Masculine; Growing Up Feminine." In *Making Connections: Readings in Relational Communication,* 4th ed. Ed. K. M. Galvin and P. J. Cooper. New York: Oxford University Press, 2006, 108–115.
51. Cahill, L. "His Brain, Her Brain." *Scientific American,* May (2005): 40–47. See also Andersen, P. A. "The Evolution of Biological Sex Differences in Communication." In *Sex Differences and Similarities in Communication,* 2nd ed. Ed. D. J. Canary and K. Dindia. Mahwah, NJ: Lawrence Erlbaum, 2006, 117–135; Society for Women's Health Research. "Sex Differences in the Brain." *Health and Science Facts,* 6 August 2004. Retrieved 2 February 2005 from www.womenshealthresearch.org/site/PageServer?pagename=hs_facts_brain&printer_friendly=1; and Tannen, D. "The Feminine Technique: Men Attack Problems. Maybe Women Understand That There's a Better Way." *Los Angeles Times.* 13 March 2005, 11A.
52. Tannen, D. *You Just Don't Understand: Women and Men in Conversation.* New York: Random House, 2001.
53. Andersen. See also Barnett, R. C., and C. Rivers. "Men Are from Earth, and So Are Women. It's Faulty Research That Sets Them Apart." *Chronicle of Higher Education,* 3 September 2004. Retrieved 3 September 2004 from

www.chronicle.com/temp/email.php?id=1zrfbz21sjena5 pzcqfs356kckhi0wgh; and MacGeorge, E. L., A. R. Graves, B. Feng, S. J. Gillihan, and B. R. Burleson. "The Myth of Gender Cultures: Similarities Outweigh Differences in Men's and Women's Provision of and Responses to Supportive Communication. *Sex Roles* 50 (2004): 143–175.

54. Watzlawick, P., J. Beavin, and D. Jackson. *Pragmatics of Human Communication: A Study of Interpersonal Patterns, Pathologies, and Paradoxes.* New York: Norton, 1967.
55. Tannen.
56. Ibid.

Chapter 2

1. Muenzinger, K. F. *The Psychology of Behavior.* New York: Harper, 1942.
2. Carter, S. L. *Civility: Manners, Morals, and the Etiquette of Democracy.* New York: HarperPerennial, 1998. See also Pitts, L. "Our Coarseness Undercuts the Social Covenant." *Dallas Morning News,* 8 May 2002, 21A.
3. Atkinson, J. "First Consensus Guidelines for Public Schools Regarding Issues of Sexual Orientation." GLSEN: Gay, Lesbian, Straight Education Network. *GLSEN,* 7 March 2006. Retrieved 8 July 2006 from www.glsen.org/cgi-bin/iowa/all/library/record/1912.html.
4. "Public Schools and Sexual Orientation: A First Amendment Framework for Finding Common Ground." *First Amendment Center,* March 2006. Retrieved 8 July 2006 from www.firstamendmentcenter.org.
5. Marsh, R. L., G. I. Cook, and J. L. Hicks. "Gender and Orientation Stereotypes Bias Source-Monitoring Attributions." *Memory* 14 (2006): 148–160.
6. Gill, A. J., and J. Oberlander. "Perception of E-Mail Personality at Zero-Acquaintance: Extraversion Takes Care of Itself; Neuroticism Is a Worry." Boston: Cognitive Science Society, 2003.
7. Vazire, S., and S. D. Gosling. "e-Perceptions: Personality Impressions Based on Personal Websites." *Journal of Personality and Social Psychology* 87 (2004): 123–132.
8. Markey, P. M., and S. M. Wells. "Interpersonal Perception in Internet Chat Rooms." *Journal of Research in Personality* 36 (2002): 134–146.
9. Bradford, D. L., and A. R. Cohen. *Managing for Excellence: The Guide to Developing High Performance in Contemporary Organizations.* New York: Wiley, 1984.
10. Birman, S. I. "Opening the Closed Mind: Making Assumptions, Jumping to Conclusions." *ETC: A Review of General Semantics* (2001/2002): 429–439.
11. Shaver, K. G. *An Introduction to Attribution Processes.* Mahwah, NJ: Lawrence Erlbaum, 1983.
12. Myers, D. G. *Psychology,* 7th ed. New York: Worth, 2004. See also George, M. T. "Planning for Success—Setting Goals." *Officer Review Magazine* 45 (2006): 22; Zimmerman, B. J., A. Bandura, and M. Martinez-Pons. "Self-Motivation for Academic Attainment: The Role of Self-Efficacy Beliefs and Personal Goal Setting." *American Educational Research Journal* 29 (1992): 663, 676; and Bachel, B. K. "Grab Your Goals and Go!" *Career World* 34 (2005): 10–12.
13. Ellinor, L., and G. Gerard. *Dialogue: Rediscover the Transforming Power of Conversation.* New York: Wiley, 1998.
14. Martin, J. N., and T. K. Nakayama. *Experiencing Intercultural Communication: An Introduction,* 2nd ed. New York: McGraw-Hill, 2005.
15. Kollock, P., and P. J. O'Brien. "A Perspective for Understanding Self and Social Interaction." In *The Production of Reality: Essays and Readings on Social Interaction,* 3rd ed. Ed. P. J. O'Brien and P. Kollock. Thousand Oaks, CA: Pine Forge Press/Sage, 2001, 35–59.
16. Storti, C. *Figuring Foreigners Out: A Practical Guide.* Boston: Intercultural Press, 1999.
17. Masuda, T., and R. E. Nisbett. "Attending Holistically versus Analytically: Comparing the Context Sensitivity of Japanese and Americans." *Journal of Personality and Social Psychology* 81 (2001): 922–934.
18. Samovar, L. A., and R. E. Porter. *Communication between Cultures,* 5th ed. Belmont, CA: Wadsworth, 2004.
19. Burks, J. S., R. E. Nisbett, and O. Ybarra. "Cultural Styles, Relational Schemas, and Prejudice against Out-Groups." *Journal of Personality and Social Psychology* 79 (2000): 174–189.
20. Gottman, J. M. *What Predicts Divorce? The Relationship between Marital Processes and Marital Outcomes.* Mahwah, NJ: Lawrence Erlbaum, 1994.
21. Brewer, M. B. and A. S. H. Feinstein. "Dual Processes in the Cognitive Representation of Persons and Social Categories." In *Dual-Process Theories in Social Psychology.* Eds. S. Chaiken and Y. Trope. New York: Guilford, 1999, 255–270.
22. EL-Alayli, A., C. J. Myers, T. K. Petersen, and A. L. Lystad. "'I Don't Mean to Sound Arrogant, But . . .' The Effects of Using Disclaimers on Person Perception." *Personality and Social Psychology Bulletin* 34 (2008): 130–143.
23. Galinsky, A. D., J. C. Magee, M. E. Inesi, and D. H. Greenfeld. "Power and Perspectives not Taken." *Psychological Science* 17 (2006): 1068–1074.
24. Wood, J. T. "She Says/He Says: Communication, Caring, and Conflict in Heterosexual Relationships." In *Gendered Relationships.* Ed. J. T. Wood. New York: Mayfield, 1996, 149–162. See also Tannen, D. *You Just Don't Understand: Women and Men in Conversation.* New York: Ballantine, 1990.
25. Kimura, D. "Sex Differences in the Brain." *Scientific American.com.* 13 May 2002. Retrieved 10 November 2005 from www.sciam.com. See also Kimura, D. "Sex, Sexual Orientation and Sex Hormones Influence Human Cognitive Function." *Current Opinion in Neurobiology* 6 (1996): 259–263; and Myers.

26. Bartholomew, K., and L. M. Horowitz. "Attachment Styles among Young Adults: A Test of a Four-Category Model." *Journal of Personality and Social Psychology* 61 (1991): 226–244.
27. Baron, P. "Self-Esteem, Ingratiation, and Evaluation of Unknown Others." *Journal of Personality and Social Psychology* 1 (1974): 104–109.
28. Tucker-Ladd, C. "Checking Out Our Interpersonal Hunches." 2004. *Psychological Self-Help.* Retrieved 3 December 2004 from http://mentalhelp.net/psyhelp/chap13/chap13k.htm.
29. Spitzberg, B. H. "A Struggle in the Dark." In *Making Connections: Readings in Relational Communication,* 4th ed. Ed. K. M. Galvin and P. J. Cooper. New York: Oxford University Press, 2006, 240–246. See also Cupach, W. R., and B. H. Spitzberg. "Preface." In *The Dark Side of Interpersonal Communication.* Ed. W. R. Cupach and B. H. Spitzberg. Mahwah, NJ: Lawrence Erlbaum, 1994, vii–ix; and Spitzberg, B. H. "The Dark Side of (In)competence." In *The Dark Side of Interpersonal Communication.* Ed. W. R. Cupach and B. H. Spitzberg. Mahwah, NJ: Lawrence Erlbaum, 1994, 25–49.
30. Brislin, R. *Understanding Culture's Influence on Behavior.* Fort Worth, TX: Harcourt Brace, 1993.
31. Summerfield, E. *Survival Kit for Multicultural Living.* Boston: Intercultural Press, 1997.
32. Brislin.
33. Ibid.
34. Summerfield.
35. Nelson, C. M. "Unmasked Blogger Left SMU Smarting." *Dallas Morning News,* 15 May 2005, 1A, 2A.

Chapter 3

1. Adler, R. B., and G. Rodman. "Perceiving the Self." In *Making Connections: Readings in Relational Communication,* 4th ed. Ed. K. M. Galvin and P. J. Cooper. New York: Oxford University Press, 2006, 75–79.
2. Cissna, K. N., and R. Anderson. "Communication and the Ground of Dialogue." In *The Reach of Dialogue: Confirmation, Voice, and Community.* Ed. R. Anderson, K. N. Cissna, and R. C. Arnett. Cresskill, NJ: Hampton Press, 1994, 9–30.
3. McCrae, R. R., and P. T. Costa. "Validation of the Five-Factor Model of Personality across Instruments and Observers." *Journal of Personality and Social Psychology* 52 (1987): 81–90.
4. Ruggiero, V. R. "Bad Attitude: Confronting Views That Hinder Students' Learning." *American Educator* 21 (Summer 2000): 1–10.
5. Forni, P. M. *Choosing Civility.* New York: St. Martin's Griffin, 2002, 168.
6. Baumeister, R. F. "The Lowdown on High-Esteem: Thinking You're Hot Stuff Isn't the Promised Cure-All." *Los Angeles Times,* 25 January 2005. Retrieved 6 February 2005 from www.latimes.com/news/opinion/commentary/la-oe-baumeister25jan,0,1298447.story?coll=la-news-comment.opinions.
7. Forni, 24.
8. Rosenthal, R., and L. Jacobson. "Pygmalion in the Classroom." In *The Production of Reality: Essays and Readings on Social Interaction,* 3rd ed. Ed. J. A. O'Brien and P. Kollock. Thousand Oaks, CA: Pine Forge Press/Sage, 2001, 35–60.
9. Hamachek, D. "Dynamics of Self-Understanding and Self-Knowledge: Acquisition, Advantages, and Relation to Emotional Intelligence." *Journal of Humanistic Counseling, Education, and Development* 38 (2000): 230–243.
10. Seta, J. J., C. E. Seta, and T. McElroy. "Better Than Better-Than-Average (or Not): Elevated and Depressed Self-Evaluations Following Unfavorable Social Comparisons." *Self and Identity* 5 (2006): 51–72.
11. Campbell, J. D. "Self-Esteem and Clarity of the Self-Concept." *Journal of Personality and Social Psychology* 59 (1990): 538.
12. "Symptoms of Low Self-Esteem." *JobBank USA,* 2004. Retrieved 4 December 2004 from www.jobbankusa.com/lowse.html.
13. Galvin, K. M., and P. J. Cooper. "Perception and Self-Concept." In *Making Connections: Readings in Relational Communication,* 4th ed. Ed. K. M. Galvin, and P. J. Cooper. New York: Oxford University Press, 2006, 73–74.
14. Seligman, M. E. P. *Authentic Happiness: Using the New Positive Psychology to Realize Your Potential for Lasting Fulfillment.* New York: Free Press, 2002.
15. Neisser, U. "Five Kinds of Self-Knowledge." *Philosophical Psychology* 1 (1988): 35–59.
16. Kollock, P., and J. O'Brien. "A Perspective for Understanding Self and Social Interaction." In *The Production of Reality: Essays and Readings in Social Psychology,* 3rd ed. Ed. J. O'Brien and P. Kollock. Thousand Oaks, CA: Pine Forge Press/Sage, 2001, 35–60.
17. Luft, J. *Group Processes: An Introduction to Group Dynamics,* 3rd ed. Palo Alto, CA: Mayfield, 1984.
18. Lustig, M., and J. Koester. *Intercultural Competence: Interpersonal Communication across Cultures,* 4th ed. Boston: Allyn & Bacon, 2003.
19. Metts, S., and E. Grohskopf. "Impression Management: Goals, Strategies, and Skills." In *Handbook of Communication and Social Interaction Skills.* Ed. J. O. Greene and B. R. Burleson. Mahwah, NJ: Lawrence Erlbaum, 2003, 357–399.
20. Goffman, E. *The Presentation of Self in Everyday Life.* New York: Doubleday, 1959. See also Goffman, E., *Relations in Public.* New York: Bantam Books, 1971.
21. Contrada, J. D. "UB Communication Professor Calls 'Self-Googling' Shrewd Form of Personal Brand Management." *University of Buffalo Reporter,* 8 April 2004. Retrieved 19 April 2004 from www.buffalo.edu/reporter/vol35/vol25n29/articles/Halavais.htm. See also Maurstad, T. "Take a Look at Your Image in the Internet Mirror."

Dallas Morning News, 17 April 2004, 14E; and "Personal Doesn't Mean Private Online." CNN, 1 January 2007. Retrieved 1 January 2007 from www.cnn.com/2007/TECH/internet/01/01/self.editingonline.sp/index.htm; and Tufekci, Z. "Can You See Me Now? Audience and Disclosure Regulation in Online Social Network Sites." *Bulletin of Science, Technology, & Society* 28 (2008): 20–36.

22. Matsuba, M. K. "Searching for Self and Relationships Online." *CyberPsychology and Behavior* 9 (2006): 275–284.
23. Johnson, A. N. "Self-Esteem, Interpersonal Risk, and Preference for E-Mail to Face-to-Face Communication." *CyberPsychology and Behavior* 7 (2004): 472–478.
24. Wood, A. F., and M. F. Smith. *Online Communication: Linking Technology, Identity, and Culture,* 2nd ed. Mahwah, NJ: Lawrence Erlbaum, 2005.
25. Ellison, N., R. Heino, and J. Gibbs. "Managing Impressions Online: Self-Presentation Processes in the Online Dating Environment." *Journal of Computer-Mediated Communication* (2006): article 2. Retrieved 31 March 2007 from http://jcmc.indiana.edu/vol 11 /issue2/ellison.html.
26. Yee, N., and J. Bailenson. "The Proteus Effect: The Effect of Transformed Self-Representation on Behavior." *Human Communication Research* 33 (2007): 271–290.
27. Cupach, W. R., and S. Metts. "Face Management in Interpersonal Communication." *Making Connections: Readings in Relational Communication,* 4th ed. Ed. K. M Galvin and P. J. Cooper. Los Angeles: Roxbury, 2006, 164–171.
28. Cupach, W., and T. Imahori. "Identity Management Theory: Communication Competence in Intercultural Episodes and Relationships." *Intercultural Communication Competence.* Ed. R. L. Wiseman and J. Koester. Thousand Oaks, CA: Sage, 1993, 112–131.
29. Storti, C. *Figuring Foreigners Out: A Practical Guide.* Boston: Intercultural Press, 1999.
30. Stewart, E. D., and M. J. Bennett. *American Cultural Patterns: A Cross-Cultural Perspective,* rev. ed. Bostonv Intercultural Press, 1991.
31. Storti.
32. Kim, E. Y. *The Yin and Yang of American Culture.* Boston: Intercultural Press, 2001, p. 30.
33. Althen, G. (with A. R. Doran and S.J. Szmania). *American Ways.* Boston: Intercultural Press, 2003. See also Stewart and Bennett.
34. Martin, J. N., and T. K. Nakayama. *Experiencing Intercultural Communication: An Introduction,* 2nd ed. New York: McGraw-Hill, 2005. See also Griggs, L. B. "Interpersonal Effectiveness." In *The Potential Is Yours.* CD-ROM, Griggs Productions, San Francisco, 2002.
35. "Coming Out." Self-help brochures. Counseling Center, University of Illinois. 2006. Retrieved 26 June 2006 from www.couns.uiuc.edu/Brochures/comout.htm. See also Skinner, T. W. F. "The Prevalence of Victimization and Its Effect on Mental Well-Being among Lesbian and Gay People." *Journal of Homosexuality* 30 (1996): 93–121.
36. DeGenova, M. K., and F. P. Rice. "Why Examine Family Background?" In *Making Connections: Readings in Relational Communication,* 4th ed. Ed. K. M. Galvin and P. J. Cooper. New York: Oxford University Press, 2006, 104–107.
37. Yerby, J., N. Buerkel-Rothfuss, and A. P. Bochner. *Understanding Family Communication,* 2nd ed. Boston: Allyn & Bacon, 1990.
38. Bandura, A. *Self-Efficacy: The Exercise of Control.* New York: Freeman, 1997.
39. Wender, I. "Relation of Technology, Science, Self-Concept, Interest, and Gender." *Journal of Technology Studies* 30 (2004): 43–51, 45.
40. Mortimer, J. T. and J. Lorence. "Occupational Experience and the Self-Concept: A Longitudinal Study." *Social Psychology Quarterly* 42 (1979): 307–323.
41. Leonard, N. H., L. L. Beauvias, and R. W. Scholl. "Work Motivation: The Incorporation of Self-Concept-Based Processes." *Human Relations* 52 (1999): 969–998.
42. Bate, B., and J. Bowker. *Communication and the Sexes,* 2nd ed. Long Grove, IL: Waveland Press, 1997. See also Grieve, N. "Beyond Sexual Stereotypes. Androgyny: A Model or an Ideal?" In *Australian Women: Femininst Perspectives.* Ed. N. Grieve and P. Grimshaw. Victoria, Australia: Oxford University Press, 1980, 247–257.
43. Spence, J. T., and R. L. Helmreich. *Masculinity and Femininity: Their Psychological Dimension and Antecedents.* Austin: University of Texas Press, 1978.
44. Foels, R., and T. J. Tomcho. "Gender, Interdependent Self-Construals, and Collective Self-Esteem: Women and Men Are Mostly the Same" *Self and Identity* 4 (2005): 213–225.
45. Cornell, A. W. *The Power of Focusing: A Practical Guide to Emotional Self-Healing.* Oakland, CA: New Harbinger Publishers, 1996.
46. Garner, A. *Conversationally Speaking: Tested New Ways to Increase Your Personal and Social Effectiveness,* 3rd ed. Los Angeles: Lowell House, 1997.
47. Stamp, G., A. L. Vangelisti, and J. A. Daly. "The Creation of Defensiveness in Social Interaction." *Communication Quarterly* 40 (1992): 177–190.
48. Garner.
49. Baumeister, R. E, J. D. Campbell, J. I. Krueger, and K. D. Vohs. "Does High Self-Esteem Cause Better Performance, Interpersonal Success, Happiness, or Healthier Lifestyles?" *Psychological Science in the Public Interest* 4 (2003): 1–44.
50. Baumeister et al. See also Forsyth, D. R., and J. H. MacMillan. "Practical Proposals for Motivating Students." In *College Teaching: From Theory to Practice.* Ed. R. J. Menges and M. D. Svinicki. Hoboken, NJ: Jossey-Bass, 1991.
51. Baumeister et al.
52. McMillan, J. H., J. Singh, and L. G. Simonetta. "The Tyranny of Self-Oriented Self-Esteem." *Educational*

Horizons (Winter 2001): 92–95; and Twenge, J. M. *Generation Me: Why Today's Young Americans Are More Confident, Assertive, Entitled—and More Miserable Than Even Before.* New York: Free Press, 2006.

53. Vohs, K. D., and T. F. Heatherton. "Self-Esteem and Threats to Self: Implications for Self-Construals and Interpersonal Perceptions." *Journal of Personality and Social Psychology* 81 (2001): 1103–1118.
54. Baumeister et al. See also Lerner, B. "Self-Esteem and Excellence: The Choice and the Paradox." *American Educator* 9 (Winter 1985): 10–16.
55. Parks, S. "Work Together and No One Loses." *Dallas Morning News,* 12 May 2003, 2B, 13B.

Chapter 4

1. Childre, D., and H. Martin (with D. Beech). *The HeartMath Solution.* San Francisco: HarperSanFrancisco, 1999. See also Childre, D., and D. Rozman. *Transforming Anger.* Oakland, CA: New Harbinger, 2003; and Goleman, D. *Emotional Intelligence.* New York: Bantam Books, 1995; Reisenzein, R. "What is a Definition of Emotion? And Are Emotions Mental-Behavioral Processes?" *Social Science Information* 46 (2007): 424–428.
2. Metts, S., and J. W. Bowers. "Emotion in Interpersonal Communication." In *Handbook of Interpersonal Communication,* 2nd ed. Ed. M. L. Knapp and G. R. Miller. Thousand Oaks, CA: Sage, 1994, 508–541. See also Dizen, M., H. Berenbaum, and J. K. Kerns. "Emotional Awareness and Psychological Needs." *Cognition and Emotion* 19 (2005): 1140–1157.
3. Karren, K. J., B. Q. Hafen, K. J. Friendsen, and L. Smith. *Mind/Body Health: The Effects of Attitudes, Emotions, and Relationships,* 3rd ed. New York: Benjamin Cummings, 2006. See also Gallo, L. C., and K. A. Matthews. "Understanding the Association between Socio-Economic Status and Physical Health: Do Negative Emotions Play a Role?" *Psychological Bulletin* 129 (2003): 10–15; Butler, E. "Emotional Conversations: Can Hiding Your Feelings Make You and Your Partner Sick?" *Stanford Research Communication.* Revised May 2003. Retrieved 4 November 2006 from www.Stanford.edu/group/i-rite/statements/2001/butler.html; Contrada, R. J., and R. D. Ashmore. "Self and Social Identity: Key to Understanding Social and Behavioral Aspects of Physical Health and Disease." In *Self, Social Identity, and Physical Health.* Ed. R. J. Contrada and R. D. Ashmore. New York: Oxford University Press, 1999; and Finkenauer, C., and B. Rimé. "Keeping Emotional Memories Secret: Health and Subjective Well-Being When Emotions Are Not Shared." *Journal of Health Psychology* 3 (1998): 47–58.
4. Cortina, L. M., V. Magley, J. Williams, and R. Langhout. "Incivility in the Workplace: Incidence and Impact." *Journal of Occupational Health Psychology* 6 (2001): 64–80.
5. Pearson, C. M, L. M. Andersson, and J. W. Wegner. "When Workers Flout Convention: A Study of Workplace Incivility." *Human Relations* 54 (2001): 1387–1419.
6. Ibid.
7. Ibid.
8. Waldinger, R. J., M. S. Schulz, S. T. Hauser, J. P. Allen, and J. A. Crowell. "Reading Others' Emotions: The Role of Intuitive Judgments in Predicting Marital Satisfaction, Quality, and Stability." *Journal of Family Psychology* 18 (2004): 58–71.
9. Goleman. See also Childre, D., H. Martin, and D. Beech. *The Inside Story: Understanding the Power of Feelings.* Boulder Creek, CA: Institute of HeartMath, 2004; LeDoux, J. E. "Emotional Memory Systems in the Brain." *Behavioral Brain Research* 58 (1993): 309–341; and Childre, Martin, and Beech, *The Inside Story.*
10. Goleman. See also Ekman, P. "An Argument for Basic Emotions." *Cognition and Emotion* 6 (1992): 169–200.
11. De Becker, G. *The Gift of Fear: Survival Signals That Protect Us from Violence.* New York: Little, Brown, 1997.
12. LeDoux. See also Goleman, D. *Working with Emotional Intelligence.* New York: Bantam Books, 1998; Key, S., and M. Marble. "Brain Centers Linked to Reactions and Responses." *Gene Therapy Weekly* (13 November 1995): 14–16; and Nesse, R. M. "What Good Is Feeling Good: The Evolutionary Benefits of Psychic Pain." *The Sciences* (November–December 1991): 30–37.
13. Goleman, *Working with Emotional Intelligence.*
14. Derks, D., A. E. R. Bos, and J. V. Grumbkow. "Emoticons in Computer-mediated Communication: Social Motives and Social Contact." *CyberPsychology and Behavior* 11 (2008): 99–101.
15. Bailenson, J. N., N. Yee, S. Brave, D. Merget, and D. Koslow. "Virtual Interpersonal Touch: Expressing and Recognizing Emotions Through Haptic Devices." *Human-Computer Interaction* 22 (2007): 325–353.
16. Baker, A. J. *Double Click: Romance and Commitment among Online Couples.* Cresskill, NJ: Hampton Press, 2005. See also Louderback, J. "On-line Chats Today, 3-D Hangouts Tomorrow." *USA Weekend,* 28 February–2 March 2003: 4; and Chenault, B. G. "Developing Personal and Emotional Relationships via Computer-Mediated Communication." *CMC Magazine,* May 1998. Retrieved 15 August 2005 from www.december.com/cmc/mag/1998/may/chenault.html.
17. Kraut, R., V. Lundmark, T. Mukopadhyay, M. Patterson, and W. Scherlis. "Internet Paradox: A Social Technology That Reduces Social Involvement and Psychological Well-Being?" *American Psychologist* 53 (1998): 1017–1031. See also Turkle, S. *Life on the Screen: Identity in the Age of the Internet.* New York: Simon & Schuster, 1997; and

Rierdan, J. "Internet-Depression Link?" *American Psychologist* 54 (1999): 781–782.

18. Campbell, A. J., S. R. Cumming, and I. Hughes. "Internet Use by the Socially Fearful: Addiction or Therapy?" *CyberPsychology & Behavior* 9 (2006): 69–81. See also Houston, T. K., L. A. Cooper, and D. E. Ford. "Internet Support Groups for Depression: A 1-Year Prospective Cohort Study." *American Journal of Psychiatry* 159 (2002): 2062–2068; and Shaw, L. H., and L. M. Gant. "In Defense of the Internet: The Relationship between Internet Communication and Depression, Loneliness, Self-Esteem, and Perceived Social Support." *CyberPsychology & Behavior* 5 (2002): 157–171.
19. Goleman, *Emotional Intelligence.* See also Plutchik, R. *Emotion: A Psychoevolutionary Synthesis.* New York: Random House, 1980.
20. Goleman, *Emotional Intelligence.* See also Ekman.
21. Tucker-Ladd, C. "Challenging Irrational Ideas." 2000. *Psychological Self-Help.* 2004. Retrieved 24 February 2004 from http://mentalhelp.net/psyhelp/chapt14/chap14g.htm.
22. Ibid.
23. Goleman, 1995.
24. Bohm, D. (edited by L. Nichol). *On Dialogue.* New York: Routledge, 1996. See also Kalb, C. "Buddha Lessons." *Newsweek* 144 (2004): 48–51.
25. Edelstein, M. R. "REBT Therapy." *Three Minute Therapy* 2004. Retrieved 21 February 2004 from www.threeminutetherapy.com/rebt.html.
26. Edelstein, M. R. "Ending Your Self-Inflicted Pain." *Three Minute Therapy.* 2004. Retrieved 21 February 2004 www.threeminutetherapy.com/chapter1.html.
27. Goleman, 1995. See also Goleman, 1998; Goleman, D., R. Boyatzis, and A. McKee. *Primal Leadership: Realizing the Power of Emotional Intelligence.* Boston: Harvard Business School Press, 2002; and Schutte, N. S., J. M. Malouf, C. Bobik, T. Coston, C. Greeson, C. Jedlicka, E. Rhodes, and G. Wendorf. "Emotional Intelligence and Interpersonal Relations." *The Journal of Social Psychology* 141 (2001): 523–536.
28. Goleman, 1995. See also Cherniss, C. *Emotional Intelligence: What It Is and Why It Matters.* Paper presented at the Annual Meeting of the Society of Industrial and Organizational Psychology, New Orleans, LA. 2000.
29. Graham, S. M., J. Y. Huang, M. S. Clark, and V. S. Helgeson. "The Positives of Negative Emotions: Willingness to Express Negative Emotions Promotes Relationships." *Personality and Social Psychology Bulletin* 34 (2008): 394–406.
30. Fussell, S. R. *The Verbal Communication of Emotions.* Mahwah, NJ: Lawrence Erlbaum, 2002.
31. Bippus, A. M., and S. L. Young. "Owning Your Emotions: Reactions to Expressions of Self versus Other-Attributed Positive and Negative Emotions." *Journal of Applied Communication Research* 33 (2005): 26–45.
32. Evans, P. *The Verbally Abusive Relationship: How to Recognize It and How to Respond.* Avon, MA: Bob Adams, 1996. See also Lerner, H. *The Dance of Anger.* New York: Harper-Collins, 1997.
33. Gudykunst, W. B., and Y. Y. Kim. *Communicating with Strangers: An Approach to Interpersonal Communication,* 4th ed. New York: McGraw-Hill, 2003. See also Samovar, L. A., and R. E. Porter. *Communication between Cultures,* 5th ed. Belmont, CA: Wadsworth, 2004.
34. Matsumoto, D. "Ethnic Differences in Affect Intensity, Emotion Judgments, Display Rule Attitudes, and Self-Reported Emotional Expression in an American Sample." *Motivation and Emotion* 17 (1993): 107–123.
35. Sillars, A. L. "Communication and Family Culture." In *Explaining Family Interactions.* Ed. M. A. Fitzpatrick and A. L. Vangelisti. Thousand Oaks, CA: Sage, 1995, 375–399. See also Pearson, J. C. *Communication in the Family,* 2nd ed. Boston: Allyn & Bacon, 1993; and Hochschild, A. "Emotion Work, Feeling Rules, and Social Structure." *American Journal of Sociology* 85 (1979): 551–575.
36. Miller, K. I., J. Considine, and J. Garner. "'Let Me Tell You about My Job': Exploring the Terrain of Emotion in the Workplace." *Management Communication Quarterly* 20 (2007):231–260; Miller, K. I., and J. Koesten. "Financial Feeling: An Investigation of Emotion and Communication in the Workplace." *Journal of Applied Communication Research* 36 (2008): 8–32.
37. Ibid. See also Beck, C. E., and E. A. Beck. "The Manager's Open Door and the Communication Climate." In *Making Connections: Readings in Relational Communication,* 2nd ed. Ed. K. M. Galvin and P. J. Cooper. New York: Oxford University Press, 2000, 295–299; Dougherty, D. S., and K. Drumheller. "Sensemaking and Emotions in Organizations: Accounting for Emotions in a Rational(ized) Context." *Communication Studies* 57 (2006): 215–238; Daw, J. "Road Rage, Air Rage, and Now Desk Rage." *Monitor on Psychology.* American Psychological Association. July–August 2001. Retrieved 5 November 2006 from www.apa.org/monitor/julaug01/deskrage.html.
38. Wood, J. T. "Growing Up Masculine, Growing Up Feminine." In *Making Connections: Readings in Relational Communication,* 4th ed. Ed. K. M. Galvin and P. J. Cooper. New York: Oxford University Press, 2006, 108–115.
39. Asim, J. "Go Ahead, We'll Dry Your Tears." *Dallas Morning News,* 29 September 2004, 23A.
40. Wood. See also Simmons, R. *Odd Girl Out: The Hidden Culture of Aggression in Girls.* New York: Harcourt Brace, 2002; Brody, L. R., and J. A. Hall. "Gender, Emotion, and Expression." In *Handbook of Emotions,* 2nd ed. Ed. M. Lewis and J. M. Haviland-Jones. New York: Guilford Press, 2000, 338–349.

41. McCroskey, J. C., V. P. Richmond, A. D. Heisel, and J. L. Hayhurst. "Eysenck's Big Three and Communication Traits: Communication Traits as Manifestations of Temperament." *Communication Research Reports* 21 (2004): 404–410. See also Lopes, P. N., P. Salovey, S. Cote, and M. Beers. "Emotion Regulations Abilities and the Quality of Social Interaction." *Emotion* 5 (2005): 113–118; Canli, T., Z. Zhao, J. E. Desmond, E. Kang, J. Gross, and D. E. Gabrielli. "An MRI Study of Personality Influences on Brain Reactivity to Emotional Stimuli." *Behavioral Neuroscience* 115 (2001): 33–42.
42. Lane, S. D. Personal Communication. 2 June 2006.
43. Davenport, N., R. D. Schwartz, and G. P. Elliott. *Mobbing: Emotional Abuse in the American Workplace.* Ames, IA: Civil Society Publishing, 1999. See also Lutgen-Sandvik, P. "Take This Job and . . . : Quitting and Other Forms of Resistance to Workplace Bullying." *Communication Monographs* 73 (2006): 406–433.
44. Davenport, Schwartz, and Elliott. See also Peyton, P. R. *Dignity at Work: Eliminate Bullying and Create a Positive Working Environment.* New York: Hove, 2003; Duffy, M., and L. Sperry. "Workplace Mobbing: Individual and Family Health Consequences." *The Family Journal: Counseling and Therapy for Couples and Families* 15 (2007): 398–404.
45. Lutgen-Sandvik.
46. Davenport, Schwartz, and Elliott. See also Hodson, R., V. J. Roscigno, and S. H. Lopez. "Chaos and the Abuse of Power: Workplace Bullying in Organizational and Interactional Context." *Work and Occupations* 33 (2006): 382–416; "WBTI: Workplace Bullying Research." *The Workplace Bullying and Trauma Institute (WBTI).* 2003. Retrieved 25 April 2006 from www.bullyinginstitute.org; Namie, R., and G. Namie. "Bullybusters!" 2005. Retrieved 27 April 2006 from www.bullybusters.org.
47. Tracy, S. J., J. K. Alberts, and K. D. Rivera. "How to Bust the Office Bully: Eight Tactics for Explaining Workplace Abuse to Decision-Makers." *The Project for Wellness and Work-Life.* Report #0701.31 January 2007. © 2007 Arizona Board of Regents.
48. Barillas, M. "Westboro Baptist Church Protests Soldier's Funeral." *SperoNews,* 16 March 2006. Retrieved 9 April 2006 from www.speroforum.com. See also Anti-Defamation League. "Fred Phelps and the Westboro Baptist Church: In Their Own Words." September 2000. Retrieved 2 March 2006 from www.adl.org/special_reports/wbc/default.asp; "Wisconsin Legislators Send Funeral-Protest Bill to Governor." *The First Amendment Center,* 2 March 2006. Retrieved 2 March 2006 from www.firstamendmentcenter.org; Forster, S. "Funeral Protest Measure Advances." *Milwaukee Journal Sentinel.* 1 February 2006; Schneider, M. B. "Protests at Funerals Targeted." *Indianapolis Star,* 20 January 2006; Jackson, C. "New Law Won't Curb Hate." Tolerance in the News. Tolerance.org. 2 June 2006. Retrieved 14 June 2006 from www.tolerance.org/news/article_print.jsp?id=1376.
49. Cottle, M. "Stupid, Mean, Hateful, Ugly—and Perfectly Legal." *Dallas Morning News,* 1 March 2006, 17A.

Chapter 5

1. Ogden, C. K., and I. A. Richards. *The Meaning of Meaning.* New York: Harcourt Brace, 1923.
2. Bochner, A. P. "The Functions of Human Communication in Interpersonal Bonding." In *Handbook of Rhetorical and Communication Theory.* Ed. C. C. Arnold and J. W. Bowers. Boston: Allyn & Bacon, 1984, 544–621. See also Clark, R. A., and J. Delia. "Topoi and Rhetorical Competence." *Quarterly Journal of Speech* 65 (1979): 187–206.
3. Rubin, A. M., and S. Windahl. "The Uses and Dependency Model of Mass Communication." *Critical Studies in Mass Communication* 3 (1986): 184–199.
4. Rubin, R. B., E. M. Perse, and C. A. Barbato. "Conceptualization and Measurement of Interpersonal Communication Motives." *Human Communication Research* 14 (1988): 602–628. See also Anderson, C. M., and M. M. Martin. "The Effects of Communication Motives, Interaction Involvement, and Loneliness on Satisfaction: A Model of Small Groups." *Small Group Research* 26 (1995): 118–137.
5. "Rudeness Survey Stirs Up Public Debate about the Decline of Civility in the U.S." *The Public Agenda: The Inside Source for Public Opinion and Policy Analysis.* Summer (2002): 1, 5.
6. Gross, M. "Watch Your Mouth! Americans See Profanity Getting Worse." *AP/Ipsos Poll* 28 March 2006. Retrieved 29 March 2006 from www.ipsos-na.com/news/pressrelease.cfm?id=3031. See also "Who Gives a @#$% about Profanity? Poll says 75% of Women and 60% of Men Don't Like Swearwords." *CNN.com,* 28 March 2006. Retrieved 29 March 2006 from www.cnn.com/2006/US/03/28/profanity.ap/index.html.
7. Angier, N. "Almost Before We Spoke, We Swore." *New York Times,* 20 September 2005.
8. O'Connor, J. V. *Cuss Control: The Complete Book on How to Curb your Cursing.* New York: Three Rivers Press, 2000; and Carter, S. L. *Civility: Manners, Morals, and the Etiquette of Democracy.* New York: HarperPerennial, 1998.
9. Kahn, A. "Muslim Student Delivers 'Jihad' Speech at Harvard Graduation." *IslamOnline.net,* 7 June 2002. Retrieved 4 March 2003 from www.islamonline.net/english/News/2002-06/07/articlel8.shtml. See also Navarette, R. "Students Need a Free Speech Lesson: Calls to Censor Commencement Speaker Are Disquieting."

DallasNews.com, 7 June 2002. Retrieved 15 June 2002 from www.dallasnews.com/opinion/columnists/navarrette/stories/060702dnedinavarrette.le4al .html.

10. Pearce, W. B. "A Coordinated Management of Meaning: A Rules-Based Theory of Interpersonal Communication." In *Explorations in Human Communication.* Ed. G. Miller. Thousand Oaks, CA: Sage, 1976, 17–36. See also Pearce, W. B., and V. E. Cronen. *Communication, Action, and Meaning: The Creation of Social Realities.* New York: Praeger, 1980.
11. Pearce and Cronen. See also Pearce, W. B., and K. A. Pearce. "Taking a Communication Perspective on Dialogue." In *Dialogue: Theorizing Difference in Communication Studies.* Ed. R. Anderson, L. A. Baxter, and K. M. Cissna. Thousand Oaks, CA: Sage, 2003, 39–56.
12. "Clear Wording Urged to Avoid Airline Crashes." *Dallas Morning News,* 22 February 1990, 3A.
13. Page, C. "Sept. 11 Paranoia Claims Victims, Too." *Community Times Online,* 29 September 2002. Westminster, MD.
14. Kim, M. *Non-Western Perspectives on Human Communication: Implications for Theory and Practice.* Thousand Oaks, CA: Sage, 2002.
15. Stone, A. "Finding the Right Word Odor." *Discover,* September 2005. Retrieved 17 August 2005 from www.discover.com/issues/sep-05/rd/finding-the-right-word-odor/.
16. Bliss, W. W. Dear Abby letter. *Dallas Morning News,* 4 January 1992, 10C.
17. Young, M. E. "Fighting Words: The Other Battle." *Dallas Morning News,* 7 April 2003, 1A, 10A.
18. "Food Security in the United States." Briefing Room. *USDA Economic Research Service.* U.S. Department of Agriculture, 15 November 2006. Retrieved 20 November 2006 from www.ers.usda.gov/briefing/FoodSecurity/.
19. Lutz, W. "The World of Doublespeak." In *Language Awareness: Readings for College Writers,* 8th ed. Ed. P. Eschholz, A. Rosa, and V. Clark. New York: Bedford/St. Martin's, 2000, 498–508. See also "NCTE Doublespeak Award." *National Council of Teachers of English,* 2005. Retrieved 16 June 2006 from www.ncte.org/about/awards/council/jml/106868.htm and "Bush Official Altered Scientific Reports on Global Warming." *Yahoo.com,* 8 June 2005. Retrieved 16 June 2006 from www.yahoo.com/s/afp/20050608/sc_afp/usenvironmentclimate.html.
20. Moore, R. B. "Racist Stereotyping in the English Language." In *Voices: A Selection of Multicultural Readings.* Belmont, CA: Wadsworth, 1995, 9–17.
21. Butler, P. "A Mix of Colors: Country's Swirling Demographics Put New Twist on Meaning of 'Minority'." *Dallas Morning News,* 3 June 2001, 1J, 6J.
22. Pringle, P. "California Looks to Find Identity in Changing Face." *Dallas Morning News,* 24 December 2000, 1A.
23. Samovar, L. A., and R. E. Porter. *Communication between Cultures,* 5th ed. Belmont, CA: Wadsworth, 2004. See also Gudykunst, W. B., and Y. Y. Kim. *Communicating with Strangers,* 4th ed. New York: McGraw-Hill, 2003.
24. Fong, M. "The Crossroads of Language and Culture." In *Intercultural Communication: A Reader,* 9th ed. Ed. L. A. Samovar and R. E. Porter. Belmont, CA: Wadsworth, 2000, 211–216.
25. Lunsford, J. L. "ValuJet Unauthorized as Hazardous Carrier." *Dallas Morning News,* 16 May 1996, 1A.
26. Stewart, E. C., and M. J. Bennett. *American Cultural Patterns: A Cross-Cultural Perspective,* rev. ed. Boston: Intercultural Press, 1991.
27. Rheingold, H. *They Have a Word for It. A Lighthearted Lexicon of Untranslatable Words and Phrases.* Louisville, KY: Sarabande Books, 2002.
28. Gudykunst and Kim.
29. Lustig, M. W., and J. Koester. *Intercultural Competence,* 4th ed. Boston: Allyn & Bacon, 2003.
30. Martin, J. N., and T. K. Nakayama. *Experiencing Intercultural Communication,* 2nd ed. New York: McGraw-Hill, 2005.
31. Galvin, K. M., C. B. Bylund, and B. J. Brommel. *Family Communication: Cohesion and Change,* 6th ed. Boston: Pearson Education, 2004. See also Wilmot, W. W. "The Relational Perspective." In *Making Connections: Readings in Relational Communication,* 4th ed. Ed. K. M. Galvin and P. J. Cooper. New York: Oxford University Press, 2006, 11–19; and Sanz, C. "Revlacormia and Other Family Words." *Dallas Morning News,* 30 October 1988, Fl.
32. Wilmot, 16.
33. Dickson, P. *Family Words: The Dictionary for People Who Don't Know a Frone from a Brinkle.* Washington, DC: Broadcast Interview Source, 1988. See also Sanz.
34. Lustig and Koester.
35. Crystal, D. *Language and the Internet.* Cambridge: Cambridge University Press, 2002. See also Randall, N. "Lingo Online: The Language of the Keyboard Generation." *msn.ca,* 11 June 2002. Retrieved 20 November 2006 from www.arts.uwaterloo.ca/~nrandall/LingoOnline-finalreport.pdf.
36. Fehr, B. *Friendship Processes.* Thousand Oaks, CA: Sage, 1996.
37. Fitzpatrick, M. A., and A. Mulac. "Relating to Spouse and Stranger: Gender-Preferential Language Use." *Gender, Power, and Communication.* Ed. P. J. Kalbfleisch and M. J. Cody. Mahwah, NJ: Lawrence Erlbaum, 1997, 213–231.
38. Tannen, D. *You Just Don't Understand: Women and Men in Conversation.* New York: Ballantine Books, 1990.
39. Barnett, R. C., and C. Rivers. "Men Are from Earth, and So Are Women. It's Faulty Research That Sets Them Apart." *Chronicle of Higher Education,* Volume 51, Issue 2, 2004: B11.

40. Fitzpatrick and Mulac.
41. Fisher, H. *The First Sex: The Natural Talents of Women and How They Are Changing the World.* New York: Ballantine Books, 2000.
42. Baron-Cohen, S. *The Essential Difference: The Truth about the Male and Female Brain.* New York: Perseus, 2003.
43. Ibid.
44. Fisher.
45. Mazer, J. P. and S. K. Hunt. "The Effects of Instructor Use of Positive and Negative Slang on Student Motivation, Affective Learning, and Classroom Climate." *Communication Research Reports* 25 (2008): 44–55.
46. Dalzell, T. "The Power of Slang. Do You Speak American? Words That Shouldn't Be? Sez Who?" 2005. Retrieved 5 January 2005 from www.pbs.org/speak/words/sezwho/slang/. See also Mack, K. "Dictionary Editors Tackle the Tough Word Questions." *Dallas Morning News,* 22 July 2000, 4C.
47. Platt, P. *French or Foe?* 3rd ed. Skokie, IL: Distribooks, 2003.
48. Walton, M., and M. Coren. "Scientist: Man in Americas Earlier Than Thought." *CNN.com,* 17 November 2004. Retrieved 19 November 2004 from http://www.cnn.com/2004/TECH/science/11/17/carolina.dig/.
49. Bosmajian, H. *The Language of Oppression.* New York: University Press of America, 1983.
50. Stewart, L. P., P. J. Cooper, A. D. Stewart, and S. A. Friedley. *Communication and Gender,* 4th ed. Boston: Allyn & Bacon, 2003.
51. Pearson, J. C, R. L. West, and L. Turner. *Gender and Communication,* 3rd ed. Madison, WI: Brown & Benchmark, 1995.
52. Bosmajian.
53. Voyles, S. "Woman Bounced from Southwest Flight for T-shirt." *Reno Gazette-Journal,* 6 October 2005. Retrieved 8 October 2005 from www.usatoday.com/travel/news/2005-10-06-swa-tshirt_x.htm.

Chapter 6

1. Gross, M. "AP/Ipsos Poll: The Decline of American Civilization, or at Least Its Manners." *Ipsos,* 14 October 2005. Retrieved 14 October 2005 from www.ipsos-na.com/news/pressrelease.cfm?id=2827. See also "The Decline of Manners in the U.S." *CNN.com,* 14 October 2005. Retrieved 14 October 2005 from www.cnn.com/2005/US/10/14/poll.rude.ap/indeex.html.
2. Canary, D. J., and M. A. Tafoya. *Road Rage as a Communicative Event.* Presented at the National Communication Association conference, Boston, 2005; and Galovksi, T. E., and E. D. Blanchard. "Road Rage: A Domain for Psychological Intervention?" *Aggression and Violent Behavior* 9 (2004): 105–127.
3. Holmes, S. M. "When Cultural Conflicts Move to the Classroom." *Dallas Morning News,* 7 October 1986, 8C.
4. Burgoon, J. K., and G. D. Hoobler. "Nonverbal Signals." In *Handbook of Interpersonal Communication,* 3rd ed. Ed. M. L. Knapp and G. R. Miller. Thousand Oaks, CA: Sage, 2002, 240–299.
5. Burgoon, J. K., D. B. Buller, J. L. Hale, and M. A. Turck. "Relational Messages Associated with Nonverbal Behaviors." *Human Communication Research* 10 (1984): 351–378.
6. Bower, B. "Past Impressions: Prior Relationships Cast a Long Shadow Over our Social Lives." *Science News Online.* Vol. 171. 9 June 2007. Retrieved 9 June 2007 from www.sciencenews.org/articles/20070609/bob10.asp. See also Andersen, S. M., I. Reznik, and L. M. Manzella. "Eliciting Facial Affect, Motivation, and Expectancies in Transference: Significant-Other Representations in Social Relations." *Journal of Personality and Social Personality* 71 (1996): 1108–1129.
7. McAdams, D. P., J. R. Jackson, and C. Kirshnit. "Looking, Laughing, and Smiling in Dyads as a Function of Intimacy Motivation and Reciprocity." *Journal of Personality* 52 (1984): 261–273.
8. Knapp, M. L., and J. A. Hall. *Nonverbal Behavior in Human Interaction,* 5th ed. Belmont, CA: Wadsworth, 2002. See also Brosnahan, T. *Turkey,* 10th ed. Footscray, Australia: Lonely Planet, 2007.
9. Burgoon, Buller, Hale, and Turck. See also Gomelsky, V. "Fickle Fingers of Fate." *Utne: A Different Read on Life.* November 1999. Retrieved 9 March 2005 from www.utne.com/web_special/web_specials_archives/articles/937-1.html; and "Longhorn Sign Was Bedeviling." *Dallas Morning News,* 22 January 2005, 18A.
10. Bull, P., and G. Connelly. "Body Movements and Emphasis in Speech." *Journal of Nonverbal Behavior* 9 (1986): 169–187.
11. Walther, J. B., and M. Parks. "Cues Filtered Out, Cues Filtered In: CMC and Relationships." *Handbook of Interpersonal Communication.* Ed. M. Knapp and J. Daly. Thousand Oaks, CA: Sage, 2002, 529–563. See also Sussman, S., and L. Sproull. "Straight Talk: Delivering Bad News through Electronic Communication." *Information Systems Research* 10 (1999): 150–167.
12. Wood, A. F., and M. J. Smith. *Online Communication: Linking Technology, Identity, and Culture,* 2nd ed. Mahwah, NJ: Lawrence Erlbaum, 2005. See also Duthler, K. W. "The Politeness of Requests Made via Email and Voicemail: Support for the Hyperpersonal Model." *Journal of Computer-Mediated Communication* 11 (2006): article 6. Retrieved 30 May 2007 from http:\\jcmc.indiana.edu/vol11/issue2/duthler.html.
13. Wood and Smith.
14. Knapp and Hall. See also Argyle, M. *The Psychology of Interpersonal Behavior,* 4th ed. London: Penguin Books, 1983.

15. Rauscher, F. H., R. M. Krauss, and Y. Chen. "Gesture, Speech, and Lexical Access: The Role of Lexical Movements in Speech Production." *Psychological Science* 4 (1996): 226–231. See also Krauss, R. M., and U. Hadar. "The Role of Speech-Related Arm/Hand Gestures in Word Retrieval." In *Gesture, Speech, and Sign*. Ed. L. S. Messing and R. Campbell. Oxford: Oxford University Press, 1999, 94–116; and Begley, S. "Living Hand to Mouth: New Research Shows that Gestures Often Help Speakers Access Words from Their Memory Banks." *Newsweek*, 2 November 1998: 69.
16. Knapp and Hall. See also "Study: Human Posture Can Communicate Fear." *CNN.com*, 19 October 2004. Retrieved 22 October 2004 from www.cnn.com/2004/TECH/science/11/19/med.us.fearcontagi.ap/index/html.
17. Dijkstra, K., M. P. Kaschak, and R. A. Zwann. "Body Posture Facilitates Retrieval of Autobiographical Memories." *Cognition* 102 (2007): 139–149.
18. Conniff, R. "Reading Faces." *Smithsonian Magazine*, January 2004: 44–50. See also Hager, J. C. "Description of Facial Action Coding System (FACS)." *DataFace*, 2003. Retrieved 20 February 2005 from www.face-and-emotion.com/dataface/facs/description.jsp.
19. Richmond, V. P., and J. C. McCroskey. *Nonverbal Behavior in Interpersonal Relations*, 5th ed. Boston: Allyn & Bacon, 2004.
20. Levinson, M. "How to Be a Mind Reader." *CIO Magazine*, December 2004. Retrieved 4 March 2005 from http:\\209.85.165.104/search?q=cache:q1YM6I5yZ3cJ:www.cio.com/archive/120104/communications.html%3Fprintversion%3Dyes+CIO%2Bmagazine%2Bmind%2Breader%2BLevinson&hl=en&ct=clnk&cd=1&gl=us. See also Ekman, P. *Emotions Revealed*. New York: Times Books, 2003.
21. Duenwald, M. "The Physiology of . . . Facial Expressions." *Discover*, January 2005. Retrieved 8 March 2005 from http:\\209.85.165.104/search?q=cache:2VOxYamRQpoJ:discovermagazine.com/2005/jan/physiology-of-facial-expressions+Duenwald%2BPhysiology%2Bfacial%2Bexpressions%2BDiscover&hl=en&ct=clnk&cd=1&gl=us
22. Neumann, R., and F. Strack. "'Mood Contagion': The Automatic Transfer of Mood between Persons." *Journal of Personality and Social Psychology* 79 (2000): 211–223. See also "Irate Caller ID: For Empathy, Press 4." *USC Trojan Family Magazine*. Autumn 2004: 21.
23. Preston, D. R. "Language Prejudice: Language Myth #17." *Do You Speak American?* 2005. *PBS.org*. Retrieved 25 February 2005 from http:\\209.85.165.104/search?q=cache:qgs6Rdol-HgJ:www.pbs.org/speak/speech/prejudice/attitudes/+Speak%2BAmerican%2BLanguage%2BMyth%2B17&hl=en&ct=clnk&cd=1&gl=us.
24. Baker, J. "ABC News Thinks Voice Based Bias 'Sounds' Like a Good Story." *NFHA News*, March 2002. Retrieved 30 June 2005 from www.nationalfairhousing.org/html/Updatearchive/2002/marupdate.Page1.htm. See also Cullen, T. "Linguistic Profiling: Discrimination Based on a Person's Voice." *Wisconsin Real Estate Magazine: Online Edition*, April 2005. Retrieved 30 June 2005 from www.news.wra.org/2005/April/Legal/Legal_0405Story.asp.
25. Purnell, T., W. Idsardi, and J. Baugh. "Perceptual and Phonetic Experiments on American English Dialects Identification." *Journal of Social Psychology* 18 (1999): 10–30.
26. Erard, M. "Can You Be Discriminated Against Because of the Way You Speak?" In *What's Language Got to Do with It?* Ed. K. Walters and M. Brody. New York: W. W. Norton, 2005, 294–299.
27. Knapp and Hall. See also Hamermesh, D. S., and J. E. Biddle. "Beauty and the Labor Market," *American Economic Review* 84 (1994): 1174–1194; and Thomas, K. M. "Court Appearance: A Defendant's Grooming, Clothes, and Behavior Can Help Win or Lose a Case." *Dallas Morning News*, 10 December 1996, 1C, 4C.
28. Navarro, M. "Hip Huggers." *Dallas Morning News*, 30 December 2004, 5E. See also Williams, D. "Move Over Barbie: The Changing Face of Dolls." *Tolerance in the News*, 19 May 2004. Retrieved 9 June 2004 from www.tolerance.org/news/article_tol.jsp?id+996.
29. Reid, A., V. Lancuba, and B. Morrow. "Clothing Style and Formation of First Impressions." *Perceptual and Motor Skills* 84 (1997): 237–238.
30. Choe, S. H. "Kim Not Wild about Hairy Heads." *Dallas Morning News*, 2 February 2005, 19A. See also Worth, R. F. "Iraqi Barbers' Lives at Stake." *Dallas Morning News*, 27 March 2005, 21A; and Robberson, T. "What a Headscarf Means: A Symbol of Piety, a Terroristic Threat, or a Call to Arms?" *Dallas Morning News*, 20 June 2004, 1H, 6H.
31. Knapp and Hall.
32. Storti, C. *Figuring Foreigners Out: A Practical Guide*. Boston: Intercultural Press, 1999.
33. Marvel, B. "The Distance. Communication Is Not All about Words: How We Position Ourselves Speaks Volumes." *Dallas Morning News*, 7 August 2004, 1E, 3E; and Fraine, G., S. G. Smith, L. Zinkiewicz, R. Chapman, and M. Sheehan. "At Home on the Road? Can Drivers' Relationships with their Cars be Associated with Territoriality?" *Journal of Environmental Psychology* 27 (2007): 204–214.
34. Hall, E. T. *The Hidden Dimension*. New York: Doubleday, 1969.
35. Richmond and McCrosky, 304.
36. Christophel, D. M. "The Relationships among Teacher Immediacy Behaviors, Student Motivation, and Learning." *Communication Education* 39 (1990): 323–340. See also McCroskey, J. C., A. Sallinen, J. M. Fayer, V. P. Richmond, and R. A. Barraclough. "Nonverbal Immediacy and Cognitive Learning: A Cross-Cultural Investigation." *Communication Education* 45 (1996): 200–211;

McCroskey, J. C., V. P. Richmond, A. Sallinen, J. M. Fayer, and R. A. Barraclough. "A Cross-Cultural and Multi-Behavioral Analysis of the Relationship between Nonverbal Immediacy and Teacher Evaluation." *Communication Education* 44 (1995): 281–291; and McCroskey, J. C., and V. P. Richmond. "Increasing Teacher Influence through Immediacy." In *Power in the Classroom: Communication, Control, and Concern*. Ed. V. P. Richmond and J. C. McCroskey. Mahwah, NJ: Lawrence Erlbaum, 1992, 101–119.

37. Cooper, P. J., and C. J. Simonds. *Communication for the Classroom Teacher,* 8th ed. Boston: Allyn & Bacon, 2006. See also Jaasma, M. A., and R. J. Koper. "The Relationship of Student-Faculty Out-of-Class Communication to Instructor Immediacy and Trust and to Student Motivation." *Communication Education* 48 (1999): 41–47.
38. Richmond and McCrosky.
39. Lustig, M. W., and J. Koester. *Intercultural Competence: Interpersonal Communication across Cultures,* 4th ed. Boston: Allyn & Bacon, 2003.
40. Antonijevic, S. "From Text to Gesture Online: A Microethnographic Analysis of Nonverbal Communication in the Second Life Virtual Environment." *Information, Communication, and Society* 11 (2008): 221–238. See also Yee, N., J. M. Bailenson, M. Urbanek, F. Chang, and D. Merget. "The Unbearable Likeness of Being Digital: The Persistence of Nonverbal Social Norms in Online Virtual Environments." *Cyber Psychology and Behavior* 10 (2007): 115–121.
41. Hodgins, H. S., and R. Koestner. "The Origins of Nonverbal Sensitivity." *Personality and Social Psychology Bulletin* 19 (1993): 466–473. See also Dew, A. M., and C. Ward. "The Effects of Ethnicity and Culturally Congruent and Incongruent Nonverbal Behaviors on Interpersonal Attraction." *Journal of Applied Social Psychology* 23 (1993): 1376–1389.
42. Orbe, M. P., and T. M. Harris. *Interracial Communication: Theory into Practice*. Belmont, CA: Wadsworth, 2001.
43. Bruess, C. J., and J. C. Pearson. "Interpersonal Rituals in Marriage and Adult Friendship." *Communication Monographs* 64 (1996): 614–626.
44. Lingren, H. J. "Gangs: The New Family." *NebGuide,* 2004. Cooperative Extension. Institute of Agricultural and Natural Resources. University of Nebraska–Lincoln. See also "Gang Signs." *Enhancement Courses for the Teaching Professional*. 2004. Loyola Marymount University. Retrieved 22 December 2004 from www.enhancementcourses.edu/gangs/gang_signs.htm.
45. Walker, V. "Gang Signs and Symbols." *PageWise,* 2002. Retrieved 22 December 2004 from http://209.85.165.104/search?q=cache:0iiY-txH2dQJ:www.nationalconcerned officers.com/gang_signs_%26_symbols.htm+gang%2B signs%2Bsymbols%2BPageWise&hl=en&ct=clnk&cd=2&gl=us. See also Capozzoli, T. K., and R. S. McVey. *Kids Killing Kids: Managing Violence and Gangs in Schools*. Boca Raton, FL: St. Lucie Press, 1999.
46. Richmond, V. P., and J. C. McCroskey. "The Impact of Supervisor and Subordinate Immediacy on Relational and Organizational Outcomes." *Communication Monographs* 67 (2000): 85–95; and Teven, J. J. "Effects of Supervisor Social Influence, Nonverbal Immediacy, and Biological Sex on Subordinates' Perceptions of Job Satisfaction, Liking, and Supervisor Credibility." *Communication Quarterly* 55 (2007): 155–177.
47. Teven, J. J., J. C. McCroskey, and V. P. Richmond. "Communication Correlates of Perceived Machiavellianism of Supervisors: Communication Orientations and Outcomes." *Communication Quarterly* 54 (2006): 127–142.
48. Andersen, P. A. "The Evolution of Biological Sex Differences in Communication." In *Sex Differences and Similarities in Communication,* 2nd ed. Ed. D. J. Canary and K. Dindia. Mahwah, NJ: Lawrence Erlbaum, 2006, 117–135. See also Hall, J. A. "Gender Effects in Encoding Nonverbal Cues." *Psychological Bulletin* 85 (1978): 845–857; and Stewart, L. P., P. J. Cooper, and A. D. Stewart (with S. A. Friedley). *Communication and Gender,* 4th ed. Boston: Allyn & Bacon, 2003.
49. Bate, B., and J. Bowker. *Communication and the Sexes,* 2nd ed. Long Grove, IL: Waveland Press, 1997. See also Nass, C. "Machine Voices." *Do You Speak American? PBS.org,* 2005. Retrieved 5 January 2005 from www.pbs.org/speak/ahead/technology/voiceinterface/; and Brody, L. R., and J. A. Hall. "Gender, Emotion, and Expression." In *Handbook of Emotions*. Ed. M. Lewis and J. M. Haviland-Jones. New York: Guilford, 2000, 338–349.
50. Berryman-Fink, C. "Preventing Sexual Harassment through Male-Female Communication Training." In *Sexual Harassment: Communication Implications*. Ed. G. L. Kreps. Cresskill, NJ: Hampton Press, 1993, 267–280. See also Henley, N. M., and S. Harmon. "The Nonverbal Semantics of Power and Gender: A Perceptual Study." In *Power, Dominace, and Nonverbal Behavior*. Ed. S. L. Ellyson, and J. F. Dovidio. London: Springer-Verlag, 1985, 151–164; and Henley, N., and J. Freeman. "The Sexual Politics of Interpersonal Behavior." In *Women: A Feminist Perspective*. Ed. J. Freeman. New York: McGraw-Hill, 1994, 78–90.
51. Hall, J. A. "How Big Are Nonverbal Sex Differences: The Case of Smiling and Sensitivity to Nonverbal Cues." In *Sex Differences and Similarities in Communication,* 2nd ed. Ed. D. J. Canary and K. Dindia. Mahwah, NJ: Lawrence Erlbaum, 2006, 59–82. See also Begley, S. "Gray Matters." *Newsweek,* 27 March 1995: 48–54; Hall, J. A. "Gender, Gender Roles, and Nonverbal Communication Skills." In *Skill in Nonverbal Communication*. Ed. R. Rosenthal. Cambridge, MA: Oelgeschlager, Gunn, & Hain,

1979, 31–67; Anderson, J. R., D. E. Everhart, J. L. Shucard, T. Quatrin, and D. W. Shucard. "Sex-Related Differences in Event-Related Potentials, Face Recognition, and Facial Affect Processing in Prepubertal Children." *Neuropsychology* 15 (2001): 329–341.

52. Lock, C. "Deception Detection: Psychologists Try to Learn How to Spot a Liar." *Science News Online,* 31 July 2004. Retrieved 24 December 2004 from www.sciencenews.org/articles/20040731/bob8.asp. See also Levine, T. R., and S. A. McCornack. "Behavioral Adaptation, Confidence, and Heuristic-Based Explanations of the Probing Effect." *Human Communication Research* 27 (2001): 471–502.
53. Vrij, A. "Why Professionals Fail to Catch Liars and How They Can Improve." *Legal and Criminological Psychology* 9 (2004): 159–181. See also Mann, S., A. Vrij, and R. Bull. "Suspects, Lies, and Videotape: An Analysis of Authentic High-Stakes Liars." *Law and Human Behavior* 26 (2002): 137–149; and Vrij, A., K. Edward, and R. Bull. "People's Insight into Their Own Behaviour and Speech Content while Lying." *British Journal of Psychology* 92 (2001): 373–389.
54. Platt, P. *French or Foe?* 3rd ed. Skokie, IL: Distribooks, 2003.
55. Cupach, W. R., and B. H. Spitzberg. *The Dark Side of Relationship Pursuit: From Attraction to Obsession to Stalking.* Mahwah, NJ: Lawrence Erlbaum, 2004.
56. Ibid.
57. Ibid.
58. Ibid.
59. James, J. "Islamic Justice? Alleged Beating of Teens at Mall Is Unjustifiable." *Dallas Morning News,* 23 June 1995, 29A.

Chapter 7

1. Svennevig, J. *Getting Acquainted in Conversation: A Study of Initial Interactions.* Philadelphia: John Benjamins, 1999.
2. ten Have, P. *Doing Conversational Analysis: A Practical Guide.* Thousand Oaks, CA: Sage, 1999.
3. "Rudeness Survey Stirs Up Public Debate about the Decline of Civility in the U.S." Public Agenda. Summer 2002, 1, 5; Cox, A. "Where Are Your High-Tech Manners?" *CNN.com,* 1 July 2007. Retrieved 18 July 2007 from www.cnn.com/2007/TECH/ptech/07/01/la.tech.manners/index.html.
4. Batista, E. "Hush-Hush Hooray, Says NYC." *Wired News,* 17 August 2002. Retrieved 9 July 2005 from www.wired.com/techbiz/media/news/2002/08/54608 See also Wu, A. "Cell Phones: All the Rage." *Wired News,* 4 January 2000. Retrieved 9 July 2005 from www.wired.com/culture/lifestyle/news/2000/01/33291, and Callahan, S. "Turn Off That Cell Phone! Bare Your Soul in Private." *Commonweal,* 16 June 2000. Retrieved 9 July 2005 from www.findarticles.com/p/articles/mi_m1252/is_12_77/ai_63912678.
5. Wu.
6. Monk, A., J. Carroll, S. Parker, and M. Blythe. "Why Are Mobile Phones Annoying?" *Behaviour and Information Technology* 23 (January–February 2004): 33–41. See also Monk, A., E. Fellas, and E. Ley. "Hearing Only One Side of Normal and Mobile Phone Conversations." *Behaviour and Information Technology* 23 (September–October 2004): 301–305.
7. Neilsen, J. "Why Mobile Phones Are Annoying." *Jakob Nielsen's Alertbox,* 12 April 2004. Retrieved 2 April 2005 from www.useit.com/alertbox/20040412.html.
8. McKenzie, J. "Mobile Etiquette." *Phoneybusiness.com,* 2006. Retrieved 25 June 2006 from http://phoneybusiness.com/etiquette.html. See also "Etiquette: It Is Very Simple, Just Follow It!" *Phone Manners and Etiquette,* 2004. Retrieved 10 April 2006 from www.nophones.com/manners/etiquette.html.
9. McCroskey, J. C., and V. P. Richmond. "Willingness to Communicate." In *Personality and Interpersonal Communication.* Ed. J. C. McCroskey and J. A. Daly. Thousand Oaks, CA: Sage, 1987, 129–156. See also McCroskey, J. C. "The Communication Apprehension Perspective." In *Avoiding Communication: Shyness, Reticence, and Communication Apprehension.* Ed. J. A. Daly and J. C. McCroskey. Thousand Oaks, CA: Sage, 1984, 13–38; and Lederman, L. C. "High Communication Apprehensives Talk about Communication Apprehension and Its Affect on Their Behavior." *Communication Quarterly* 31 (1983): 233–237.
10. McCroskey and Richmond.
11. Nofsinger, R. E. *Everyday Conversation.* Long Grove, IL: Waveland Press, 1999.
12. Grice, H. P. "Logic and Conversation." In *Speech Acts: Volume 3.* Ed. P. Cole and J. L. Morgan. New York: Academic Press, 1975, 41–58.
13. Ibid.
14. Holtgraves, T. *Language as Social Action: Social Psychology and Language Use.* Mahwah, NJ: Lawrence Erlbaum, 2002.
15. Fine, D. "12 Tips for Making Small Talk." *CNN.com,* 3 March 2005. Retrieved 5 March 2005 from http://cnn.com/2005/US/Careers/03/03/small.talk/index.html. See also "How Americans Communicate." Roper Starch Worldwide. *National Communication Association.* 1998. Retrieved 4 April 2005 from www.natcom.org/research/Roper/how_americans_communicate.htm.
16. Baron-Cohen, S. *The Essential Difference: The Truth about the Male and Female Brain.* New York: Basic Books, 2003, 140.
17. Cohen, J. "Please Understand My Son." *USA Weekend,* 16–18 July 1999, 16. See also Jacobson, S. "A Scouting Manual." *Dallas Morning News,* 9 April 2004, 10E; Carter, R. *Mapping the Mind,* Berkeley: University of California

Press, 1999; and Shaw, S. "Diagnostic Criteria." *AS-IF (Asperger Information),* 2005. Retrieved 1 March 2005 from www.aspergerinformation.net/.

18. Garner, A. *Conversationally Speaking,* 3rd ed. Los Angeles: Lowell House, 1997.
19. Ibid.
20. Ibid., 51.
21. McLaughlin, M. L. *Conversation: How Talk Is Organized.* Thousand Oaks, CA: Sage, 1984.
22. Littlejohn, S. W. *Theories of Human Communication,* 7th ed. Belmont, CA: Wadsworth, 2003.
23. Knapp, M. L., and J. A. Hall. *Nonverbal Behavior in Human Interaction,* 5th ed. Belmont, CA: Wadsworth, 2002.
24. Kennedy, D. W., and C. T. Camden. "A New Look at Interruptions." *Western Journal of Speech Communication* 47 (1983): 45–58.
25. Brislin, R. *Understanding Culture's Influence on Behavior.* Orlando, FL: Harcourt Brace, 2003.
26. Scollon, R., and S. Wong-Scollon. "Face Parameters in East-West Discourse." In *The Challenge of Facework.* Ed. S. Ting-Toomey. Albany: State University of New York Press, 1994, 133–157. See also Watanabe, S. "Cultural Differences in Framing: American and Japanese Group Discussions." In *Framing in Discourse.* Ed. D. Tannen. New York: Oxford University Press, 1993, 176–209; and Gudykunst, W. B., and Y. Y. Kim. *Communicating with Strangers: An Approach to Intercultural Communication,* 4th ed. New York: McGraw-Hill, 2003.
27. Carbaugh, D. *Cultures in Conversation.* Mahwah, NJ: Lawrence Erlbaum, 2005.
28. Aaron, A., E. Eide, and J. F. Pitrelli. "Conversational Computers." *Scientific American,* June 2005, 64–69.
29. Weber, S. N. "The Need to Be: The Socio-Cultural Significance of Black Language." In *Voices: A Selection of Multicultural Readings.* Ed. K. S. Verderber. Belmont, CA: Wadsworth, 1995, 30–36. See also Kochman, T. *Black and White Styles in Conflict.* Chicago: University of Chicago Press, 1981.
30. Ting-Toomey, S. "Intercultural Conflict Styles: A Face-Negotiation Theory." In *Theories of Intercultural Communication.* Ed. Y. Y. Kim and W. B. Gudykunst. Thousand Oaks, CA: Sage, 1988, 213–235. See also Carr-Ruffino, N. *Managing Diversity: People Skills for a Multicultural Workplace.* Austin, TX: ITP, 1996; and Johnson, F. L. *Speaking Culturally: Language Diversity in the United States.* Thousand Oaks, CA: Sage, 2000, 239.
31. Siple, L. A "Cultural Patterns of Deaf People." *Intercultural Communication: A Reader,* 9th ed. Ed. L. A. Samovar and R. E. Porter. Belmont, CA: Wadsworth, 2000, 146–157. See also Mindess, A. *Reading between the Signs: Intercultural Communication for Sign Language Interpreters.* Boston: Intercultural Press, 1999.
32. Houston, M. "When Black Women Talk with White Women." In *Making Connections: Readings in Relational Communication,* 3rd ed. Ed. K. M. Galvin and P. J. Cooper. New York: Oxford University Press, 2003, 103–110. See also Fought, C. "What Speech Do We Like Best? Watch Your Language." *Do You Speak American?* 2005. Retrieved 5 January 2005 from www.pbs.org/speak/speech/reveal; Ribeau, S. A., J. R. Baldwin, and M. L. Hecht. "An African American Communication Perspective." In *Intercultural Communication: A Reader,* 9th ed. Ed. L. A. Samovar and R. E. Porter. Belmont, CA: Wadsworth, 2000, 128–136; and Cutler, C. "What Speech Do We Like Best? Language as Prestige: Crossing Over." *Do You Speak American?* 2005. Retrieved 5 January 2005 from www.pbs.org/speak/speech/prestige/crossing/.
33. Stewart, E. D., and M. J. Bennett. *American Cultural Patterns: A Cross-Cultural Perspective,* rev. ed. Boston: Intercultural Press, 1991. See also Althen, G. (with A. R. Doran and S. J. Szmania). *American Ways: A Guide for Foreigners in the United States.* Boston: Intercultural Press, 2003.
34. Althen, 37.
35. Lanier, A. R. (revised by C. W. Gay), *Living in the U.S.A.,* 5th ed. Boston: Intercultural Press, 1996.
36. Barrett, R. "The 'Homo-genius' Speech Community." In *Queerly Phrased: Language, Gender, and Sexuality.* Ed. A. Livia and K. Hall. New York: Oxford University Press, 1997, 181–201. See also Goodwin, J. P. "Communication and Identification in the Gay Subculture." In *Intercultural Communication: A Reader,* 9th ed. Ed. L. A. Samovar and R. E. Porter. Belmont, CA; Wadsworth, 2000, 158–170.
37. Klopf, D. W. *Intercultural Encounters: The Fundamentals of Intercultural Communication,* 2nd ed. Englewood, CO: Morton, 1991. See also Johnson.
38. Brislin. See also Dutton, B. P. *American Indians of the Southwest.* Albuquerque: University of New Mexico Press, 1983.
39. Sillars, A. R. "Communication and Family Culture." In *Explaining Family Interactions.* Ed. M. A. Fitzpatrick and A. L. Vangelisti. Thousand Oaks, CA: Sage, 1995, 375–399. See also Sillars, A. L., and W. W. Wilmot. "Marital Communication across the Life-Span." In *Life-Span Communication: Normative Processes.* Ed. J. R. Nussbaum. Mahwah, NJ: Lawrence Erlbaum, 1989, 225–294; Surgraff, C. S., and A. L. Sillars. "A Critical Examination of Sex Differences in Marital Communication." *Communication Monographs* 54 (1987): 176–194; and Robey, E. G., D. J. Canary, and C. S. Burggraf. "Conversational Maintenance Behaviors of Husbands and Wives: An Observational Analysis." In *Sex Differences and Similarities in Communication.* Ed. D. J. Canary and K. Dindia. Mahwah, NJ: Lawrence Erlbaum, 1998, 373–392.
40. Wood, J. T., and C. C. Inman. "In a Different Mode: Masculine Styles of Communicating Closeness." *Journal of*

Applied Communication Research 21 (1993): 279–295. See also Braithwaite, D., and J. K. Killan. "Shopping for and with Friends: Everyday Communication at the Shopping Mall." In *Composing Relationships: Communication in Everyday Life*. Ed. J. T. Wood and S. Duck. Belmont, CA: Wadsworth, 2006, 86–95; and Stewart, L. P., P. J. Cooper, A. Stewart, and S. Friedley. "Communication in Cross-Gender Friendships." In *Making Connections: Readings in Relational Communication,* 4th ed. Ed. K. M. Galvin and P. J. Cooper. New York: Oxford University Press, 2006, 337–344.

41. Conrad, C., and M. S. Poole. *Strategic Organizational Communication: Into the Twenty-First Century,* 5th ed. Orlando, FL: Harcourt Brace, 2002. See also Caudron, S. "They Hear It through the Grapevine." *Workforce* 11 (1998): 25–27; and Hamilton, C. *Communicating for Results: A Guide for Business and the Professions,* 7th ed. Belmont, CA: Wadsworth, 2005.
42. Gur, R. C., B. I. Turetsky, M. Matsui, M. Yan, W. Biler, F. Hughett, and R. E. Gur. "Sex Differences in Brain Gray and White Matter in Healthy Young Adults: Correlations with Cognitive Performance." *Journal of Neuroscience* 19 (1999): 4065–4072. See also Fisher, H. *The First Sex: The Natural Talents of Women and How They Are Changing the World*. New York: Ballantine Books, 1999; and Gurian, M. *What Could He Be Thinking? How a Man's Mind Really Works*. New York: St. Martin's Press, 2003.
43. Mulac, A. "The Gender-Linked Language Effect: Do Language Differences Really Make a Difference?" In *Sex Differences and Similarities in Communication*. Ed. D. J. Canary and K. Dindia. Mahwah, NJ: Lawrence Erlbaum, 1998. See also Bate, B., and J. Bowker. *Communication and the Sexes,* 2nd ed. Long Grove, IL: Waveland Press, 1997; and Bradley, P. H. "The Folk-Linguistics of Women's Speech: An Empirical Examination." *Communication Monographs* 48 (1981): 73–90.
44. Tannen, D. *You Just Don't Understand: Women and Men in Conversation*. New York: Ballantine Books, 1990.
45. Tannen, D. *Talking 9 to 5: How Women's and Men's Conversational Styles Affect Who Gets Heard, Who Gets Credit, and What Gets Done at Work*. New York: William Morrow, 1994. See also Tannen, D. *That's Not What I Meant: How Conversational Style Makes or Breaks Relationships*. New York: Ballantine Books, 1986.
46. Mulac.
47. McCroskey, J. C., and V. P. Richmond. "Correlates of Compulsive Communication: Quantitative and Qualitative Characteristics." *Communication Quarterly* 43 (1995): 39–52. See also McCroskey, J. C., and V. P. Richmond. "Identifying Compulsive Communicators: The Talkaholic Scale." *Communication Research Reports* 10 (1993): 107–114.
48. Daly, J. A., C. A. Diesel, and D. Weber. "Conversational Dilemmas." In *The Dark Side of Interpersonal Communication*. Ed. W. R. Cupach and B. H. Spitzberg. Mahwah, NJ: Lawrence Erlbaum, 1994, 127–158.
49. Ibid., 144
50. Richtel, M. "Using Their Cellphones to Dial Up Deception: Through Networks, Liars Find Strangers to Support Their Ruses." *Dallas Morning News,* 26 June 2004, 15A.

Chapter 8

1. Brownell, J. *Listening: Attitudes, Principles, and Skills,* 2nd ed. Boston: Allyn & Bacon, 2002. See also "Listen and Make the Connection." *International Listening Association,* 4 July 2006. Retrieved 31 July 2006 from www.listen.org/Templates/try_new.htm.
2. Steil, L. K. "Listening Training: The Key to Success in Today's Organizations." In *Listening in Everyday Life*. Ed. D. Borisoff and M. Purdy. Lanham, MD: University Press of America, 1991, 205–227.
3. Wolvin, A. S. and C. G. Coakley. *Listening,* 5th ed. Dubuque, IA: William C. Brown Publishers, 1996. See also Steil, L. K., L. L. Barker, and K. W. Watson. *Effective Listening*. Boston: Addison-Wesley, 1983.
4. Breining, B. "Are You Listening Your Way to the Top Spot?" *Dallas Morning News,* 28 May 2002, 2C.
5. Lerner, H. G. "How to Be a Good Listener." In *Making Connections: Readings in Relational Communication,* 3rd ed. Ed. K. M. Galvin and P. J. Cooper. New York: Oxford University Press, 2003, 130–131.
6. Burleson, B. R. "Comforting Messages: Features, Functions, and Outcomes." In *Strategic Interpersonal Communication*. Ed. J. A. Daly and M. Wiemann. Thousand Oaks, CA: Sage, 1994.
7. Albrecht, T. L., B. R. Burleson, and D. Goldsmith. "Supportive Communication." In *Handbook of Interpersonal Communication,* 2nd ed. Thousand Oaks, CA: Sage, 2002, 419–449.
8. Gottman, J. M., J. Coan, S. Carrere, and C. Swanson. "Predicting Marital Happiness and Stability from Newlywed Interactions." *Journal of Marriage and the Family* 60 (1998): 5–22. See also Gottman, J. M. *Why Marriages Succeed or Fail*. New York: Simon & Schuster, 1994.
9. Albrecht, Burleson, and Goldsmith. See also Samter, W. "Unsupportive Relationships: Deficiencies in the Support-Giving Skills of the Lonely Person's Friends." In *The Communication of Social Support: Messages, Interactions, Relationships, and Community*. Ed. B. R. Burleson, T. L. Albrecht, and I. G. Sarason. Thousand Oaks, CA: Sage, 1994, 195–214.
10. Carter, S. L. *Civility: Manners, Morals, and the Etiquette of Democracy*. New York: HarperPerennial, 1998.
11. Forni, P. M. *Choosing Civility*. New York: St. Martin's Griffin, 2002.
12. Wolvin and Coakley.

13. Bostrom, R. N. "The Process of Listening." In *Handbook of Communication Skills,* 2nd ed. Ed. O. D. W. Hargie. New York: Routledge, 1997, 236–258. See also Alexander, E. R., L. E. Penley, and I. E. Jernigan. "The Relationship of Basic Decoding Skills to Managerial Effectiveness." *Management Communication Quarterly* 6 (1992): 58–73.
14. Gabor, D. *How to Start a Conversation and Make Friends.* New York: Fireside, 2001.
15. Samter, W., B. R. Burleson, and L. B. Murphy. "Comforting Conversations: The Effects of Strategy Type on Evaluations of Messages and Message Producers." *Southern Speech Communication Journal* 52 (1987): 263–284.
16. Goldsmith, D. J. "The Role of Facework in Supportive Communication." In *Communication of Social Support: Messages, Interactions, Relationships, and Community.* Ed. B. R. Burleson, T. L. Albrecht, and I. G. Sarason. Thousand Oaks, CA: Sage, 1994, 29–49.
17. Keefe, B. "Virginia Tech Tragedy: Networking Site Provide Outlet for Tribute, Tears." *Atlanta Journal-Constitution,* 18 April 2007. Retrieved 21 April 2007 from http://ajc.com/living/content/printediton/2007/04/18lvvtweb0418a.html. See also Krugel, L. "Social Networking Site Facebook Flooded with Prayers, Rage over U.S. Shooting." *The Canadian Press,* 17 April 2007. Retrieved 21 April 2007 from www.canada.com/topics/news/world/story.html?id=4e7f4f3b-029a-4cdb-8c16-6cf06795f894&k=61428.
18. Wood, A. F., and M. J. Smith. *Online Communication: Linking Technology, Identity, and Culture,* 2nd ed. Mahwah, NJ: Lawrence Erlbaum, 2005. See also Ledbetter, A. M. *Sex Similarities and Differences in E-Mail Social Support: Competing Perspectives.* National Communication Association, San Antonio, TX, 2006; and Young, M. E. "Pouring Their Grief Out on the Internet." *Dallas Morning News,* 7 November 2005, 1A; 2A.
19. Wood and Smith, 113.
20. Ratliff, S. A., and D. D. Hudson. *Skill Building for Interpersonal Competence.* Austin, TX: Holt, Rinehart, & Winston, 1988.
21. Lane, S. D., and S. M. Lane. "Empathic Communication between Medical Personnel and Patients." *Journal of the American Podiatry Association* 72 (1982): 333–336.
22. Covey, S. R. *The 7 Habits of Highly Effective People.* New York: Simon & Schuster, 1989.
23. Heldmann, M. L. *When Words Hurt: How to Keep Criticism from Undermining Your Self-Esteem.* New York: Ballantine Books, 1989.
24. Thomlison, T. D. "Intercultural Listening." In *Listening in Everyday Life: A Personal and Professional Approach.* Ed. D. Borisoff and M. Purdy. Lanham, MD: University Press of America, 1991, 87–137.
25. Lewis, R. D. *When Cultures Collide: Managing Successfully across Cultures.* Boston: Intercultural Press, 1999.
26. Burleson, B. R. "Emotional Support Skill." In *Handbook of Communication and Social Interaction Skills.* Ed. J. O. Greene and B. R. Burleson. Mahwah, NJ: Lawrence Erlbaum, 2003, 551–594.
27. Ibid.
28. Xu, Y., and B. R. Burleson. "Effects of Sex, Culture, and Support Type on Perceptions of Spousal Social Support: An Assessment of the 'Support Gap' Hypothesis in Early Marriage." *Human Communication Research* 27 (2002): 535–566.
29. Fisher, B. L., P. R. Giblin, and M. H. Hoopes. "Healthy Family Functioning: What Therapists Say and What Families Want." *Journal of Marital and Family Therapy* 8 (1982): 273–284.
30. Arliss, L. P. *Contemporary Family Communication: Meanings and Messages.* New York: St. Martin's Press, 1993. See also Galvin, K. M., C. L. Bylund, and B. J. Brommel. *Family Communication: Cohesion and Change.* Boston: Pearson Education, 2004.
31. Burleson, B. R., A. W. Kunkel, and J. D. Birch "Thought about Talk in Romantic Relationships: Similarity Makes for Attraction (and Happiness Too)." *Communication Quarterly* 42 (1994): 259–273. See also Cunningham, M. R., and A. P. Barbee. "Social Support." In *Close Relationships: A Sourcebook.* Ed. C. Hendrick and S. S. Hendrick. Thousand Oaks, CA: Sage, 2000.
32. Kurdek, L. A., and J. P. Schmitt. "Perceived Emotional Support from Family and Friends in Members of Homosexual, Married, and Heterosexual Cohabiting Couples." *Journal of Homosexuality* 14 (1987): 57–68. See also Arliss.
33. Hamilton, C. *Communicating for Results: A Guide for Business and the Professions,* 7th ed. Belmont, CA: Wadsworth, 2005. See also Conrad, C., and M. S. Poole. *Strategic Organizational Communication: Into the Twenty-First Century,* 5th ed. Orlando, FL: Harcourt Brace, 2002; and Sypher, B. D., and T. E. Zorn. "Communication-Related Abilities and Upward Mobility: A Longitudinal Investigation." *Human Communication Research* 12 (1986): 420–431.
34. McGuire, G. M. "Intimate Work: A Typology of the Social Support That Workers Provide to Their Network Members." *Work and Occupations* 34 (2007): 125–147.
35. Borisoff, D., and L. Merrill. "Gender Issues and Listening." *Listening in Everyday Life: A Personal and Professional Approach.* Ed. D. Borisoff and M. Purdy. Lanham, MD: University Press of America, 1991, 59–85.
36. Maltz, D. N., and R. B. Borker. "A Cultural Approach to Male-Female Miscommunication." In *Language and Social Identity.* Ed. J. Gumperz. New York: Cambridge University Press, 1982, 196–216.
37. Tannen, D. *You Just Don't Understand: Women and Men in Conversation.* New York: William Morrow, 1990.

38. Susman, E. "Men Listen, but with Only Half a Brain." *MSN.com,* 28 November 2000. Retrieved 29 November 2002 from http://content.health.msn.com/content/article/1728.65169. See also Wood, J. "Gender, Communication, and Culture." In *Intercultural Communication: A Reader,* 9th ed. Ed. L. A. Samovar and R. E. Porter. Belmont, CA: Wadsworth, 2000, 170–179; Pearson, J. C. *Gender and Communication.* Dubuque, IA: Brown Publishers, 1985; and Cariati, S. "Mars, Venus: Communications Clashes Have Biologic Basis." *Society for Women's Health Research,* 15 November 2001. Retrieved 14 August 2005 from www.womenshealthresearch.org/site/News2?page=NewsArticle&id=5405&news_iv_ctrl=0&abbr=press_&JServSessionIdr010=b0rl4u0hz2.app6b.
39. Goldsmith, D. J., and P. A. Fulfs. "You Just Don't Have the Evidence: An Analysis of Claims and Evidence in Deborah Tannen's 'You Just Don't Understand.'" In *Communication Yearbook 22.* Ed. M. E. Roloff. Thousand Oaks, CA: Sage, 1999, 1–49.
40. Samter, Burleson, and Murphy.
41. Goldsmith, D., and M. R. Parks. "Communicative Strategies for Managing the Risks of Seeking Social Support." In *Personal Relationships and Social Support.* Ed. S. Duck. Thousand Oaks, CA: Sage, 1990, 104–121.
42. Silver, R. C., C. B. Wortman, and D. Crofton. "The Role of Coping in Support Provision: The Self-Presentational Dilemma of Victims of Life Crises." In *Social Support: An Interactional View.* Ed. B. R. Sarason, I. G. Sarason, and G. R. Pierce. New York: John Wiley, 1990, 397–426.
43. Silver, Wortman, and Crofton, 418–419.
44. Brown, P., and S. D. Levinson. *Politeness: Some Universals in Language Use.* New York: Cambridge University Press, 1987.
45. Caplan, S. E., and W. Samter. "The Role of Facework in Younger and Older Adults' Evaluations of Social Support Messages." *Communication Quarterly* 47 (1999): 245–264.
46. Goldsmith, D. J., and E. L. MacGeorge. "The Impact of Politeness and Relationship on Perceived Quality of Advice about a Problem." *Human Communication Research* 26 (2000): 234–263.
47. "Sound and Fury." *PBS.org,* 2003. Retrieved 29 July 2006 from www.pbs.org/wnet/soundandfury/film/video.html. See also Desai, J. "Falling on Deaf Ears." *Science and Spirit Magazine,* 2002. Retrieved 13 July 2004 from www.science-spirit.org/article_detail.php?article_ed=467&pager=2.

Chapter 9

1. Katherine, A. *Boundaries: Where You and I Begin.* New York: Fireside, 1991.
2. Katherine, A. *Where to Draw the Line: How to Set Healthy Boundaries Every Day.* New York: Fireside, 2000.
3. Veroff, J., E. Douvan, T. L. Orbuch, L. K. and Acitelli. "Happiness in Stable Marriages: The Early Years." In *The Developmental Course of Marital Dysfunction.* Ed. T. N. Bradbury. New York: Cambridge University Press, 1998.
4. Elgin, S. H. *The Gentle Art of Verbal Self-Defense.* Upper Saddle River, NJ: Prentice-Hall, 1980.
5. Gross, M. "AP/Ipsos Poll: The Decline of American Civilization, or at Least Its Manners." *Ipsos.* 14 October 2005. Retrieved 14 October 2005 from www.ipsos-na.com/news/pressrelease.cfm?id=2827. See also "The Decline of Manners in the U.S." *CNN.com,* 14 October 2005. Retrieved 14 October 2005 from www.cnn.com/2005/US/10/14/poll.rude.ap/index.html.
6. Lauer, C. S. "The End of Civility?" *Modern Healthcare* 33 (2003): 28. See also Cronin, T. J. "Manners Matter." *American Catholic Newsletter,* July 2002. Retrieved 10 October 2005 from www.AmericanCatholic.org/newsletters/YU/ay0702.asp; and Carter, S. L. "Just Be Nice." *Yale Alumni Magazine,* May 1998. Retrieved 14 May 2005 from www.yalealumnimagazine.com/issues/98_05/Stephen_Carter.html.
7. Garcia, L. "Thank You." *Dallas Morning News,* 28 November 2002, 1C. See also Rand, R. "Why Manners Matter, Part I." *Focus over Fifty,* 2002. Retrieved 18 October 2005 from www.family.org/focusoverfifty/justforyou/a0020308; Isaacs, W. *Dialogue and the Art of Thinking Together.* New York: Currency, 1999; and Lauer.
8. Bolton, R. *People Skills.* New York: Touchstone, 1986.
9. Ibid. See also Spitzberg, B. H., D. J. Canary, and W. R. Cupach. "A Competence-Based Approach to the Study of Interpersonal Conflict." In *Conflict in Personal Relationships.* Ed. D. D. Cahn. Mahwah, NJ: Lawrence Erlbaum, 1994, 183–202; and Infante, D. A., A. S. Rancer, and F. F. Jordan. "Affirming and Nonaffirming Style, Dyad Sex, and the Perception of Argumentation and Verbal Aggression in an Interpersonal Dispute." *Human Communication Research* 22 (1996): 315–334.
10. Wood, A. F., and M. J. Smith. *Online Communication: Linking Technology, Identity, and Culture,* 2nd ed. Mahwah, NJ: Lawrence Erlbaum, 2005, 91.
11. Lea, M., T. O'Shea, P. Fung, and R. Spears. "Flaming in Computer-Mediated Communication: Observations, Explanations, Implications." In *Contexts of Computer-Mediated Communication.* Boston: Harvester Wheatsheaf, 1992, 89–112.
12. Kayany, J. M. "Contexts of Uninhibited Online Behavior: Flaming in Social Newsgroups on Usenet." *Journal of the American Society for Information Science* 49 (1998): 1135–1141. See also Burnett, G., and H. Buerkle. "Information Exchange in Virtual Communities: A Comparative Study." *Journal of Computer-Mediated*

Communication 9 (2004). Retrieved 5 June 2007 from http://jcmc.indiana.edu/vol9/issue2/burnett.html.

13. Alonzo, M., and M. Aiken. "Flaming in Electronic Communication." *Decision Support Systems* 36 (2004): 205–213.
14. Kayany, 1141.
15. Emmons, R., and M. Alberti. *Stand Up, Speak Out, Talk Back.* New York: Pocket Books, 1991.
16. Kim, M.-S. *Non-Western Perspectives on Human Communication: Implications for Theory and Practice.* Thousand Oaks, CA: Sage, 2002, 52.
17. Kim.
18. Lane, S. D. "Empathy and Assertive Communication." Western Speech Communication Association Conference, San Jose, CA, 1981. See also Bolton.
19. Lang, A. J., and P. Jakubowski. *Responsible Assertive Behavior.* Chicago: Research Press, 1976, 15. See also Lane.
20. Garner, A. *Conversationally Speaking.* Los Angeles: Lowell House, 1997.
21. "Home Page." *The First Amendment Center.* 2 May 2007. Retrieved 2 May 2007 from www.firstamendment center.org.
22. Willoughby, B. *10 Ways to Fight Hate on Campus.* Atlanta: Southern Poverty Law Center, 2003.
23. Leets, L. "Experiencing Hate Speech: Perceptions and Responses to Anti-Semitism and Antigay Speech." *Journal of Social Issues* 58 (2002): 341–361.
24. Ibid. See also Blezard, R. "We Don't Use That Language Anymore." *Teaching Tolerance* 23 (2003): 32–38; and Willoughby, *10 ways,* 9.
25. Willoughby, B. *Speak Up: Responding to Everyday Bigotry.* Atlanta: Southern Poverty Law Center, 2005. See also Fountain, J. "Telling It Like It Is." Boston: Intercultural Resource Corporation, 1996. Video Archive.
26. Katherine, *Where to Draw the Line,* 21.
27. Hofstede, G., and G. J. Hofstede. *Cultures and Organizations: Software of the Mind.* New York: McGraw Hill, 2005.
28. Yep, G. A. "From Homophobia and Heterosexism to Heteronormativity: Toward the Development of a Model of Queer Interventions in the University Classroom." *Journal of Lesbian Studies* 6 (2002): 163–176.
29. Samovar, L. A., and R. E. Porter. *Communication between Cultures,* 5th ed. Belmont, CA: Wadsworth, 2004.
30. Kim, 2002.
31. Wahloss, S. *Family Communication.* Boston: Macmillan, 1983.
32. Stafford, L., and M. Dainton. "The Dark Side of 'Normal' Family Interaction." In *The Dark Side of Interpersonal Communication.* Ed. W. R. Cupach and B. R. Spitzberg. Mahwah, NJ: Lawrence Erlbaum, 1994, 259–280.
33. Weger, H. "Disconfirming Communication and Self-Verification in Marriage: Associations among the Demand/Withdraw Interaction Pattern, Feeling Understood, and Marital Satisfaction." *Journal of Social and Personal Relationships* 22 (2005): 19–31.
34. Gottman, J. M. *Why Marriages Succeed or Fail.* New York: Simon & Schuster, 1994. See also Gottman, J. M., and N. Silver. *The Seven Principles for Making Marriage Work.* New York: Crown Publishers, 1999; and Gottman, J. M. *What Predicts Divorce?* Mahwah, NJ: Lawrence Erlbaum, 1994.
35. Hample, D. "Anti-Comforting Messages." In *Making Connections: Readings in Relational Communication,* 4th ed. Ed. K. M. Galvin and P. J. Cooper. New York: Oxford University Press, 2006, 222–227.
36. Hallowell, E. M. "The Human Moment at Work." In *Making Connections: Readings in Relational Communication,* 3rd ed. Ed. K. M. Galvin and P. J. Cooper. New York: Oxford University Press, 2003, 373–379.
37. Murphy, B. O., and T. Zorn. "Gendered Interaction in Professional Relationships." In *Gendered Relationships.* Ed. J. T. Wood. New York: Mayfield, 1996, 213–232.
38. Twenge, J. M. "Changes in Women's Assertiveness in Response to Status and Roles: A Cross-Temporal Meta-Analysis, 1931–1993." *Journal of Personality and Social Psychology* 81 (2001): 133–145.
39. "Men, Women, and the Brain." *Exploring Your Brain.* Television transcript, WETA-TV, February 1998. Retrieved 20 April 2006 from www.dana.org/books/radiotv/eyb_0298.cfm.
40. Gurian, M. *What Could He Be Thinking: How a Man's Mind Really Works.* New York: St. Martin's Press, 2003.
41. Ibid., 12
42. Taylor, S. E. *The Tending Instinct: Women, Men, and the Biology of Our Relationships.* New York: Times Books, 2002.
43. Cupach, W. R., and D. J. Canary. "Managing Conflict and Anger: Investigating the Sex Stereotype Hypothesis." In *Gender, Power, and Communication in Human Relationships.* Ed. P. J. Kalbfleisch and M. J. Cody. Mahwah, NJ: Lawrence Erlbaum, 1995, 233–252.
44. Archer, J., and S. M. Coyne. "An Integrated Review of Indirect, Relational, and Social Aggression." *Personality and Social Psychology Review* 9 (2005): 212–230.
45. Jones, C. J., and W. Meredith. "Patterns of Personality Change across the Life Span." *Psychological Aging* 11 (1996): 57–65.
46. McCrae, R. R., and P. T. Costa Jr. "Personality Trait Structure as a Human Universal." *American Psychologist* 52 (1997): 509–516. See also Wright, R., and S. Wright. "Trait Theory of Personality." *Raynet,* 2001. Retrieved 20 October 2005 from www.raynet.mcmail.com/behaviour.trait.shtml/ and Srivastava, S. "Measuring the Big Five." *Measuring the Big Five Personality Traits.* 2005. Retrieved 20 October 2005 from http://darkwing.uoregon.edu/~sanjay/bigfive.html.

47. Vissing, Y. M., M. A. Straus, R. J. Gelles, and J. W. Harrop. "Verbal Aggression by Parents and Psychosocial Problems of Children." *Child Abuse and Neglect* 13 (1991): 223–238.
48. Marshall, L. L. "Physical and Psychological Abuse." In *The Dark Side of Interpersonal Communication.* Ed. W. R. Cupach and B. H. Spitzberg. Mahwah, NJ: Lawrence Erlbaum, 1994, 281–311.
49. Lane, S. D., and G. A. Yep. "Verbally Abusive Communication in Intimate and Nonintimate Relationships: A Review and Critique." Speech Communication Association convention, Chicago, 1994. See also Ellis, A., and M. G. Powers. *The Secret of Overcoming Verbal Abuse.* Los Angeles: Wilshire Book Co., 2000.
50. Ellis and Powers, 29.
51. Marshall.
52. Evans, P. *The Verbally Abusive Relationship.* Boston: Bob Adams, 1993.
53. Wu, E. "Name Change May Be Sign of the Times." *Dallas Morning News,* 22 July 2004, 7B.

Chapter 10

1. Gross, M. "AP/Ipsos Poll: The Decline of American Civilization, or at Least Its Manners." *Ipsos,* 14 October 2005. Retrieved 4 October 2005 from www.ipsos-na.com/news/pressrelease.cfm?id=2827. See also "American Manners Poll: The Associated Press-Ipsos Poll on Public Attitudes about Rudeness." *USATODAY.com,* 14 October 2005. Retrieved 28 January 2006 from www.usatoday.com/news/nation/2005-10-14-rudeness-poll-method_x.htm.
2. Carter, S. L. *Civility: Manners, Morals, and the Etiquette of Democracy.* New York: HarperPerennial, 1998.
3. Sternberg, R. J. *The Triangle of Love: Intimacy, Passion, Commitment.* New York: Basic Books, 1988.
4. Duck, S. *Understanding Relationships.* New York: Guilford Press, 1991. See also Taylor, S. *The Tending Instinct: Women, Men, and the Biology of Our Relationships.* New York: Times Books, 2002; and Hargie, C. T. C., and D. Tourish. "Relational Communication." In *The Handbook of Communication Skills,* 2nd ed. Ed. O. D. W. Hargie. New York: Routledge, 1997, 359–382.
5. Kane, K., and K. Montgomery. "A Framework for Understanding Dysempowerment in Organizations." *Human Resource Management* 37 (1998): 263–275. See also Motowidlo, S. J., J. S. Packard, and M. R. Manning. "Occupational Stress: Its Causes and Consequences for Job Performance." *Journal of Applied Psychology* 71 (1986): 618–629.
6. Myers, S. A., M. M. Martin, and T. P. Mottet. "Students' Motives for Communicating with Their Instructors: Considering Instructor Socio-communicative Style, Student Socio-communicative Orientation, and Student Gender." *Communication Education* 51 (2002): 121–133. See also Myers, S. A. "Using Leader-Member Exchange Theory to Explain Students' Motives to Communicate." *Communication Quarterly* 54 (2006): 293–304.
7. Roloff, M. *Interpersonal Communication: The Social Exchange Approach.* Thousand Oaks, CA: Sage, 1981.
8. Altman, I., and D. Taylor. *Social Penetration: The Development of Interpersonal Relationships.* New York: Holt, Rinehart, & Winston, 1973.
9. Knapp, M. L., and A. L. Vangelisti. *Interpersonal Communication in Human Relationships,* 5th ed. Boston: Allyn & Bacon, 2005.
10. Hargie and Tourish. See also Baxter, L. A. "The Social Side of Personal Relationships: A Dialectical Perspective." In *Understanding Relationship Processes: 3. Social Context and Relationships.* Ed. S. Duck. Thousand Oaks, CA: Sage, 1993, 139–165.
11. Baxter, L. A. "Dialectical Contradictions in Relationship Development." *Journal of Social and Personal Relationships* 7 (1990): 69–88.
12. Baxter, L. A., and C. Bullis. "Turning Points in Romantic Relationships." *Human Communication Research* 12 (1986): 469–493. See also Bullis, C., C. Clark, and R. Sline. "From Passion to Commitment: Turning Points in Romantic Relationships." *Interpersonal Communication: Evolving Interpersonal Relationships.* Ed. P. J. Kalbfleisch. Mahwah, NJ: Lawrence Erlbaum, 1993, 213–236.
13. Nordenberg, T. "Pick-up Lines that Work . . . or Will They?" Love and Relationships. *Discovery Health,* 4 December 2005. Retrieved 5 December 2005 from http://health.discovery.com/centers/loverelationships/articles/pickuplines.html.
14. Rabby, M. K., and J. B. Walther. "Computer-Mediated Communication Effects on Relationship Formation and Maintenance." *Maintaining Relationships through Communication: Relational, Contextual, and Cultural Variations.* Ed. D. J. Canary and M. Dainton. Mahwah, NJ: Lawrence Erlbaum, 2003, 141–162. See also Shedletsky, L. J., and A. J. Baker. *Double Click: Romance and Commitment among Online Couples.* Cresskill, NJ: Hampton Press, 2005; Aitken, J. E. *Human Communication on the Internet.* Boston: Allyn & Bacon, 2004; and Madden, M., and A. Lenhart, *Online Dating.* Washington, DC: Pew Internet and American Life Project, 2006.
15. Duck, S. "The Essential Nature of Talk." In *Making Connections: Readings in Relational Communication,* 2nd ed. Ed. K. M. Galvin and P. J. Cooper. New York: Oxford University Press, 2000, 147–152.
16. Stafford, L., and D. J. Canary. "Maintenance Strategies and Romantic Relationship Type, Gender, and Relational Characteristics." *Journal of Social and Personal Relationships* 8 (1991): 217–242.
17. Stafford, L. "Maintaining Romantic Relationships: A Summary and Analysis of One Research Program." In

Maintaining Relationships through Communication: Relational, Contextual, and Cultural Variations. Ed. D. J. Canary and M. Dainton. Mahwah, NJ: Lawrence Erlbaum, 2003, 51–78. See also Canary, D. J., L. Stafford, K. S. Hause, and L. A. Wallace. "An Inductive Analysis of Relational Maintenance Strategies: A Comparison among Lovers, Relative, Friends, and Others." *Communication Research Reports* 10 (1993): 5–14.

18. Rosenberg, M. B. *Nonviolent Communication: A Language of Compassion.* Encinitas, CA: PuddleDancer Press, 2001.
19. Garner, A. *Conversationally Speaking,* 3rd ed. Los Angeles: Lowell House, 1997. See also Canary, D. J., and L. Stafford. "Preservation of Relational Characteristics: Maintenance Strategies, Equity, and Locus of Control." In *Interpersonal Communication: Evolving Interpersonal Relationships.* Ed. P. J. Kalbfleisch. Mahwah, NJ: Lawrence Erlbaum, 1993, 237–259.
20. Wilmot, W. W., and D. C. Stevens. "Relationship Rejuvenation: Arresting Decline in Personal Relationships." In *Uses of "Structure" in Communication Studies.* Ed. R. L. Conville. Portsmouth, NH: Praeger, 1994, 103–124.
21. Aune, R. K., S. Metts, and A. S. E. Hubbard. "Managing the Outcomes of Discovered Deception." *Journal of Social Psychology* 138 (1998): 677–689.
22. Baxter, L. A. "Trajectories of Relationship Disengagement." *Journal of Social and Personal Relationships* 1 (1984): 29–48.
23. Weber, A. L. "Losing, Leaving, and Letting Go: Coping with Nonmarital Breakups." In *The Dark Side of Close Relationships.* Ed. B. H. Spitzberg and W. R. Cupach. Mahwah, NJ: Lawrence Erlbaum, 1998, 267–306.
24. Baxter, L. A. "Strategies for Ending Relationships: Two Studies." *Western Journal of Speech Communication* 46 (1982): 223–241.
25. Patterson, B., and D. O'Hair. "Relational Reconciliation: Toward a More Comprehensive Model of Relational Development." *Communication Research Reports* 9 (1992): 119–129.
26. Lustig, M. W., and J. Koester. *Intercultural Communication: Interpersonal Communication across Cultures,* 4th ed. Boston: Allyn & Bacon, 2003. See also Martin, J. N., and T. K. Nakayama. *Intercultural Communication in Contexts,* 3rd ed. New York: McGraw-Hill, 2004.
27. Collier, M. J. "Communication Competence Problematics in Ethnic Friendships." *Communication Monographs* 63 (1996): 314–346. See also Gaines, S. O. "Relationships between Members of Cultural Minorities." In *Under-Studied Relationships: Off the Beaten Track.* Ed. J. T. Wood and S. Duck. Thousand Oaks, CA: Sage, 1995, 51–88.
28. Demo, D. "Children's Experience of Family Diversity." *National Forum* 80 (2000): 16. See also Huston, M., and P. Schwartz. "The Relationships of Lesbians and of Gay Men." In *Under-Studied Relationships: Off the Beaten Track.* Ed. J. T. Wood and S. Duck. Thousand Oaks, CA: Sage, 1995, 89–121; and Yep, G. A., K. E. Lovaas, and J. P. Elia. "A Critical Appraisal of Assimilationist and Radical Ideologies Underlying Same-Sex Marriage in LGBT Communities in the United States." *Journal of Homosexuality* 45 (2003): 45–64.
29. U.S. Census Bureau. *America's Families and Living Arrangements: Population Characteristics.* Washington, DC: U.S. Department of Commerce, Economics and Statistics Administration, 2000. See also West, R., and L. Turner. "Communication in Lesbian and Gay Families: Developing a Descriptive Base." In *Parents, Children, and Communication.* Ed. T. Socha and G. Stamp. Mahwah, NJ: Lawrence Erlbaum, 1995, 147–169.
30. Galvin, K. M., C. L. Bylund, and B. J. Brommel. *Family Communication: Cohesion and Change,* 6th ed. Boston: Pearson Education, 2004.
31. Hatfield, E., and R. L. Rapson. "Love and Attachment Processes." In *Handbook of Emotions,* 2nd ed. Ed. M. Lewis and J. M. Haviland-Jones. New York: Guilford Press, 2000, 654–662.
32. Sprecher, S., and D. Felmlee. "The Influence of Parents and Friends on the Quality and Stability of Romantic Relationships: A Three-Wave Longitudinal Investigation." *Journal of Marriage and the Family* 54 (1992): 888–900.
33. Fehr, B. *Friendship Processes.* Thousand Oaks, CA: Sage, 1996. See also Adams, R. G., and G. Allan. "Contextualising Friendship." In *Placing Friendship in Context.* Ed. R. G. Adams and G. Allan. Cambridge: Cambridge University Press, 1999, 1–17.
34. McPherson, M., L. Smith-Lovin, and M. E. Brashears. "Social Isolation in America: Changes in Core Discussion Networks over Two Decades." *American Sociological Review* 71 (2006): 353–375.
35. Cloud, J. "Sex and the Law." *Time,* 23 March 1998, 48–54.
36. Elsesser, K., and L. A. Peplau. "The Glass Partition; Obstacles to Cross-sex Friendships at Work." *Humen Relitions* 59 (2006): 1077–1100.
37. Pierce, C. A., and H. Aguinis. "A Framework for Investigating the Link between Workplace Romance and Sexual Harassment." *Group and Organization Management* 26 (2001): 206–229.
38. Willis, G. "Managing an Office Romance." *CNN-Money.com,* 9 February 2006. Retrieved 9 February 2006 from http://money.cnn.com/2006/02/08/pf/saving/willis_tips/index.htm.
39. Gurian, M. *What Could He Be Thinking?* New York: St. Martin's Press, 2003. See also "Scientists Uncover Neurobiological Basis for Romantic Love, Trust, and Self." *Science Daily,* 11 November 2003. Retrieved 14 April 2004 from www.sciencedaily.com/releases/2003/11/031111064658.htm; and Marazziti, D., and D. Canale. "Hormonal

Changes When Falling in Love." *Psychoneuroendocrinology* 29 (2004): 931–936.

40. Wood, J. T. *Gendered Lives: Communication, Gender, and Culture.* Belmont, CA: Wadsworth, 1994.
41. Knapp and Vangelisti. See also Parrott, L., and L. Parrott. *Relationships.* Grand Rapids, MI: Zondervan Publishing House, 1998.
42. Metts, S., and W. R. Cupach. "Responses to Relational Transgressions: Hurt, Anger, and Sometimes Forgiveness." In *The Dark Side of Interpersonal Communication,* 2nd ed. Ed. B. H. Spitzberg and W. R. Cupach. Mahwah, NJ: Lawrence Erlbaum, 2007, 243–274.
43. Metts, S. "Relational Transgressions." In *The Dark Side of Interpersonal Communication.* Ed. W. R. Cupach and B. H. Spitzberg. Mahwah, NJ: Lawrence Erlbaum, 1994, 217–239. See also Guerrero, L. K., P. A. Anderson, and W. A. Afifi. *Close Encounters: Communicating in Relationships.* New York: Mayfield, 2001; and Metts, S. "Face and Facework: Implications for the Study of Personal Relationships." In *Handbook of Personal Relationships,* 2nd ed. Ed. S. Duck. New York: John Wiley, 1997, 373–394.
44. Precker, M. "How Do I Love Thee? (Very Discreetly)." *Dallas Morning News,* 5 June 2005, 2E.

Chapter 11

1. Folger, J. P., M. S. Poole, and R. K. Stutman. *Working through Conflict: Strategies for Relationships, Groups, and Organizations,* 4th ed. Boston: Longman, 2001.
2. Cupach, W. R., and D. J. Canary. *Competence in Interpersonal Conflict.* Long Grove, IL: Waveland Press, 1997.
3. Geraghty, J. "It's Time to Act." *National Review,* 6 October 2004. Retrieved 26 March 2006 from www.nationalreview.com/kerry/kerry200410061538.asp. See also Pichaske, P. "Sign Burning Alert: Republican Campaign Signs Vandalized." *Howard County Times,* 1 October 2004. Posted on the Free Republic Web site. Retrieved 26 March 2006 from www.freerepublic.com/focus/f-news/1233242/posts.
4. Tannen, D. *The Argument Culture: Stopping America's War of Words.* New York: Ballantine Books, 1998. See also Forni, P. M. *Choosing Civility.* New York: St. Martin's Griffin, 2002.
5. Hobman, E. V., P. Bordia, B. Irner, and A. Change. "The Expressions of Conflict in Computer-Mediated and Face-to-Face Groups." *Small Group Research* 33 (2002): 439–465.
6. Zornoza, A., P. Ripoll, and J. M. Peiro. "Conflict Management in Groups That Work in Two Different Communication Contexts: Face-to-Face and Computer-Mediated-Communication." *Small Group Research* 33 (2002): 481–508.
7. Kilmann, R. H., and K. W. Thomas. "Developing a Forced-Choice Measure of Conflict-Handling Behavior: The Mode Instrument." *Educational and Psychological Measurement* 37 (1977): 309–325.
8. Cupach and Canary.
9. Roloff, M. E., and D. H. Cloven. "The Chilling Effect in Interpersonal Relationships: The Reluctance to Speak One's Mind." In *Intimates in Conflict: A Communication Perspective.* Ed. D. D. Cahn. Mahwah, NJ: Lawrence Erlbaum, 1990, 49–76. See also Cloven, D. H., and M. E. Roloff. "Sense Making Activities and Interpersonal Conflict: Communicative Cures for the Mulling Blues." *Western Journal of Speech Communication* 55 (1991): 143–158.
10. Wilmot, W. W., and J. L. Hocker. *Interpersonal Conflict,* 6th ed. New York: McGraw-Hill, 2000.
11. Takaku, S. "The Effects of Apology and Perspective Taking on Interpersonal Forgiveness: A Dissonance-Attribution Model of Interpersonal Forgiveness." *Journal of Social Psychology* 141 (2001): 494–508.
12. Bachman, G. F., and L. K. Guerrero. "Forgiveness, Apology, and Communicative Responses to Hurtful Events." *Communication Reports* 19 (2006): 45–56. See also Metts, S. "Face and Facework: Implications for the Study of Personal Relationships." In *Handbook of Personal Relationships,* 2nd ed. Ed. S. Duck. New York: John Wiley, 1997, 373–394; and Bennett, M., and C. Dewberry. "'I've Said I'm Sorry, Haven't I?' A Study of the Identity Implications and Constraints That Apologies Create for Their Recipients." *Current Psychology* 13 (1994): 10–21.
13. Metts, S., and W. C. Cupach. "Responses to Relational Transgressions: Hurt, Anger, and Sometimes Forgiveness." *The Dark Side of Interpersonal Communication,* 2nd ed. Ed. B. H. Spitzberg and W. R. Cupach. Mahwah, NJ: Lawrence Erlbaum, 2007, 243–274.
14. Takaku.
15. Bachman and Guerrero.
16. Guerrero, L. K., P. A. Anderson, and W. A. Afifi. *Close Encounters: Communicating in Relationships.* New York: Mayfield, 2001.
17. Worthington, E. C. *Forgiving and Reconciling: Bridges to Wholeness and Hope,* rev. ed. Downers Grove, IL: InterVarsity Press, 2003. See also Waldron, V. R., and Kelley, D. L. *Communicating Forgiveness.* Thousand Oaks, CA: Sage, 2008.
18. Kelley, D. L. "Communicating Forgiveness." In *Making Connections: Readings in Relational Communication,* 3rd ed. Ed. K. M. Galvin and P. J. Cooper. New York: Oxford University Press, 2003, 222–232.
19. Ting-Toomey, S. "Intercultural Conflict Competence." In *Readings in Cultural Contexts.* Ed. J. N. Martin, T. K. Nakayama, and L. A. Flores. New York: Mayfield, 1998.
20. Gudykunst, W. B., and Y. Y. Kim. *Communicating with Strangers: An Approach to Intercultural Communication,* 4th ed. New York: McGraw-Hill, 2003.

21. Kim, M. S. *Non-Western Perspectives on Human Communication: Implications for Theory and Practice.* Thousand Oaks, CA: Sage, 2002.
22. Gudykunst and Kim. See also Kurdek, L. A. "Areas of Conflict for Gay, Lesbian, and Heterosexual Couples: What Couples Argue about Influences Relationship Satisfaction." *Journal of Marriage and the Family* 56 (1994): 923–934.
23. Canary, D. J., W. R. Cupach, and S. J. Messman. *Relationship Conflict.* Thousand Oaks, CA: Sage, 1995.
24. Argyle, M., and M. Henderson. "The Rules of Friendship." *Journal of Social and Personal Relationships* 1 (1984): 211–237. See also Dainton, M., E. Zelley, and E. Lamgan. "Maintaining Friendships throughout the Lifespan." In *Maintaining Relationships through Communication: Relational, Contextual, and Cultural Variations.* Mahwah, NJ: Lawrence Erlbaum, 2003, 79–102.
25. Anderson, J. W., M. Foste-Kuehn, and B. C. McKinney. *Communication Skills for Surviving Conflicts at Work.* Cresskill, NJ: Hampton Press, 1996.
26. Dodd, C. H. *Managing Business and Professional Communication.* Boston: Pearson Education, 2004.
27. Papa, M., and W. Papa. "Competence in Organizational Conflicts." In *Competence in Interpersonal Conflict.* Ed. W. R. Cupach and D. J. Canary. Long Grove, IL: Waveland Press, 1997, 149–173.
28. Canary, Cupach, and Messman. See also Cupach, W. R., and D. J. Canary. "Managing Conflict and Anger: Investigating the Sex Stereotype Hypothesis." In *Gender, Power, and Communication in Human Relationships.* Ed. P. J. Kalbfleisch and M. J. Cody. Mahwah, NJ: Lawrence Erlbaum, 1995, 233–252; and Wood, J. T. "I Can't Talk About It Now." In *Making Connections: Readings in Relational Communication,* 4th ed. Ed. K. M. Galvin and P. J. Cooper. New York: Oxford University Press, 2006, 209–215.
29. Cupach and Canary. See also Canary, Cupach, and Messman; Gottman, J. M. *Why Marriages Succeed or Fail.* New York: Simon & Schuster, 2004 and Gottman, J. M. *What Predicts Divorce?* Mahwah, NJ: Lawrence Erlbaum, 1994.
30. Cahn, D. D. "Intimates in Conflict: A Research Review." In *Intimates in Conflict: A Communication Perspective.* Ed. D. D. Cahn. Mahwah, NJ: Lawrence Erlbaum, 1990, 1–22.
31. Infante, D. A., T. A. Chandler, and J. E. Rudd. "Test of an Argumentative Skill Deficiency Model of Interspousal Violence." *Communication Monographs* 56 (1989): 163–177. See also Sabourin, T. C. "The Role of Negative Reciprocity in Spouse Abuse: A Relational Control Analysis." *Journal of Applied Communication Research* 23 (1995) 271–283; and Sabourin, T. C. "The Role of Communication in Verbal Abuse between Spouses." In *Family Violence from a Communication Perspective.* Ed. D. D. Cahn and S. A. Lloyd. Thousand Oaks, CA: Sage, 1996, 199–217.
32. Spitzberg, B. H. "Violence in Intimate Relationships." In *Competence in Interpersonal Conflict.* Ed. W. R. Cupach and D. J. Canary. Long Grove, IL: Waveland Press, 1997, 175–201. See also Johnson, M. P. "Patriarchal Terrorism and Common Couple Violence: Two Forms of Violence against Women." *Journal of Marriage and the Family* 57 (1995): 283–294.
33. Holland, K. "Pixel This: Dad Tells Son to Switch to GOP or Else." *Dallas Morning News,* 11 March 2006, 1B, 8B.

Photo Credits

Chapter 1

page 2: AP Photo/Judi Bottoni; **page 8:** Lucidio Studio Inc./Corbis; **page 9:** Mario Anzuoni/Corbis; **page 11:** Reuters/Corbis; **page 17:** Randy Faris/Corbis; **page 21:** Comstock/Corbis;

Chapter 2

page 34: Newscom; **page 44:** Fancy Photography/Veer; **page 52:** Steve Sands/New York Newswire/Corbis;

Chapter 3

page 62: PEOPLE Magazine/Newscom; **page 65:** Michelle Bridwell/PhotoEdit Inc.; **page 75:** Corbis Royalty Free; **page 78:** Universal Pictures/Photofest;

Chapter 4

page 92: John McCoy/WireImage/Getty Images; **page 97:** Chris Faytok/Star-Ledger/Corbis; **page 101:** Purestock/Superstock Royalty Free; **page 110:** Francis Dean/Dean Pictures/The Image Works; **page 115:** AP Images/Will Kincaid;

Chapter 5

page 118: UNHCR/Handout/Reuters/Corbis; **page 122:** Lisa Peardon/Taxi/Getty Images; **page 136:** Javier Larrea/SuperStock, Inc.; **page 141:** WENN/Newscom;

Chapter 6

page 146: Tim Graham/Getty Images; **page 149:** Stuart Pearce/age fotostock/SuperStock, Inc.; **page 155:** Creatas/SuperStock; **page 157:** Courtesy of Paul Ekman's *Unmasking the Face*; **page 162:** Thomas Northcut/Photodisc/Getty Images; **page 162:** Rod Morata/Stone/Getty Images;

Chapter 7

page 178: Newscom; **page 182:** Rubber Ball/SuperStock, Inc.; **page 199:** WireImageStock/Masterfile;

Chapter 8

page 204: Newscom; **page 219:** ImageSource/SuperStock, Inc.; **page 222:** ThinkStock/Superstock Royalty Free; **page 225:** Darrin Klimek/Riser/Getty Images;

Chapter 9

page 230: Corbis/Bettmann; **page 242:** Mario Tama/Getty Images; **page 244:** Francesco Bittichesu/Taxi/Getty Images; **page 250:** Christopher Bissell/Stone Allstock/Getty Images; **page 252:** Color Day Production/Image Bank/Getty Images;

Chapter 10

page 256: AP Photo/Danny Moloshok; **page 259:** GoodShot/Superstock Royalty Free; **page 274:** ThinkStock/Superstock Royalty Free; **page 278:** Altrendo/Getty Images; **page 282:** Comstock Complete Royalty-Free;

Chapter 11

page 290: E. Ornelas/San Antonio Express-N/ZUMA/Corbis; **page 304:** Comstock/Superstock Royalty Free; **page 306:** Orbit/Masterfile; **page 312:** Carlos Serrao/Riser/Getty Images.

Glossary

ableism Messages that denigrate people on the basis of their physical or mental ability.

abstraction Concept that refers to levels of specificity in language. In general, highly connotative words also tend to be highly abstract.

accenting A function of nonverbal communication. Nonverbal communication can accent or emphasize the spoken word.

accents A particular way that words are pronounced. Accents vary according to ethnicity, age, and geographical location.

accommodating Tending to smooth over conflicts and not make waves in order to preserve relational harmony.

accounts Typically claim responsibility for behavior but minimize its undesirability or seriousness.

active listening Involves verbal and nonverbal responses to others that let them know we are paying attention and taking responsibility for understanding their meanings.

advice Suggesting a solution.

affect blends May be one emotion evidenced in one facial area and another emotion shown in a different area, two different emotions illustrated in one part of the face, or a facial display that results from muscle action that is associated with two emotions.

affection In terms of relational communication, the force to become close with a relational partner.

ageism Language that disparages people based on their age.

aggressive communication Standing up for our needs, rights, and wants at the expense of others.

allness Occurs when we believe that it's possible to know everything about a person, place, or thing and we draw conclusions based on evidence that is insufficient and biased.

amygdala An almond-shaped structure that is located in the emotional brain or limbic system.

analyzing Another term for *interpreting* or *reframing*.

anti-comforting messages Messages that are disconfirming because they discount, disregard, and/or diminish others' feelings.

apologies Serve to accept responsibility for a behavior and recognize its undesirability. Apologies can also help save the offended partner's face, appease the partner, and restore relational harmony.

appreciation Communicates that we feel grateful and that we are thankful for our relational partner and the relationship itself.

appreciative listening A type of listening in which we engage when we want to enjoy and appreciate the messages we listen to.

appropriateness Refers to conforming to the expectations or communication rules of a particular situation.

argumentative skill deficiency A model that suggests that individuals use verbal aggression to manage their conflicts because they lack the verbal skills to deal constructively with conflict.

artifacts These include clothing, jewelry, accessories, and personal objects such as briefcases and backpacks. Artifacts communicate about the person who wears them.

assertive communication Entails standing up for our needs, rights, and wants while respecting the needs, rights, and wants of others.

assurances A relationship maintenance strategy in which we can support, comfort, and communicate feelings for our relationship partner.

attraction theory A theory that predicts that we are drawn to and may initiate relationships with people who we believe are physically attractive, who are in physical proximity to us, and who are similar to us.

attribution theory A theory that explains exactly how we create explanations or attach meaning to our own or another's behavior.

attributions Reasons for or causes of behavior.

autonomy/connection dialectic Reflects the tension between wanting to be independent and wanting to feel connected. Sometimes we desire to spend time with friends, partners, family members, and coworkers; at other times, we want to be alone and prefer to emphasize our individuality.

avoiding We avoid conflict physically when we remove ourselves from a conflict, and we avoid conflict psychologically when we refuse to discuss an issue.

biased language Using words that fail to acknowledge and validate others. A subtle form of biased language is that which is gender-biased.

blind quadrant According to the Johari Window, this includes information about ourselves that we don't know but others do.

body orientation and posture Related to the extent to which we face or lean toward or away from others. Both body orientation and posture can indicate whether we are open to interaction.

bonding strategies Strategies that can strengthen and potentially change the meaning of a relationship. Asking questions about a potential or new relational partner and identifying ourselves as a "couple" are tactics associated with bonding strategies.

boundary An edge or limit that defines us as being separate from others. Emotional, relational, sexual, and spiritual boundaries let others know that we have limits to what we believe is safe and appropriate.

boundary violations Occur when others knowingly or unknowingly cross our emotional, relational, sexual, and spiritual limits. Such violations may be committed on the basis of malice, ignorance, or thoughtlessness, or even with the intention of kindness.

brainstorming In terms of collaborative conflict resolution, this is generating as many solutions as possible that can meet each partner's needs. The aim is quantity, not quality.

broken record An assertive skill that entails repeating the same words over and over again.

channel The pathway used to convey a message between the sender and the receiver.

chronemics Or time, is another environmental factor that influences nonverbal behavior.

civility Characterized as a sacrifice that we make for others. Civility can also be characterized as a code of behavior that is based on respect, restraint, and responsibility.

closed-ended questions Often evoke one-word responses and may not provide us with additional information we can use to keep a conversation going.

closure In terms of perception, a way we can organize stimuli by filling in the "missing pieces" to form a whole or complete picture.

co-cultures Groups with their own particular values, such as ethnic, racial, and religious groups. Co-cultural values and values associated with the dominant culture influence behavior.

coherence Refers to "making meaning" and is coordinated by the rules we use to manage talk and create our social realities.

collaborating A personal conflict style used when we attempt to satisfy both our needs and our partner's needs. This style is labeled "win-win" because the goals of both self and the other are attained.

collectivist cultures Focus is more on the group (e.g., the family, village, or organization) than on the individual. Decisions are made based on what is best for the group, and the group is expected to take care of its members.

commitment Refers to the decision to maintain and sustain a relationship based on love. Commitment is the intention to stay together, despite the difficult times that are an inevitable part of any romantic relationship.

communication The process of creating and sharing meaning.

communication apprehension (CA) An individual's level of fear or anxiety associated with either real or anticipated communication-related outcomes.

communication climate Refers to the emotional tone of a relationship.

communication competence Communication that is perceived as both effective and appropriate in an interpersonal context.

communication rules Prescriptions that tell us what we should or shouldn't say or do in certain situations.

communication style How people verbally and nonverbally communicate, the preferred amount of talk and silence, and the degree of familiarity with which conversational partners speak.

comparison level (CL) Entering relationships with an idea about rewards and costs based on our experiences in past relationships and on relationships we have observed among our friends, family, and the media. These expectations are called the comparison level (CL).

comparison level of alternatives (CLalt) Comparing the rewards we are receiving with those we may receive in alternative relationships.

competing To make use of the personal conflict style of competing, we attempt to meet our needs without concern for our partner's needs. We may use any type of tactic to achieve our needs, whether or not the tactic is considered appropriate.

complaints Negative comments aimed at specific actions and behaviors.

complementary relationship A relationship in which one partner has more power and control than the other.

complementing Similar to the accenting function of nonverbal communication, complementing nonverbal behavior adds meaning to verbal communication. We usually have less control of complementing nonverbal communication than we have of accenting nonverbal behaviors.

comprehensive listening When we want to learn, understand, and recall information.

compromising Parties in conflict give up part of what they want in order to achieve partial satisfaction in meeting their goals.

concrete words Words based on sense data.

confirming responses Verbal and nonverbal behaviors that validate others with expressions of affection, respect, and concern.

conflict The interaction of interdependent people who perceive incompatible goals and interference from each other in achieving those goals.

conflict rituals Patterns that reinforce specific ways to manage conflict.

confrontational listening Listening carefully for flaws in a message to refute them or attack the speaker in response.

connotative Meaning that is emotional, personal, and that engenders disagreement.

constructive criticism A type of judgment or evaluation meant to confirm others and that can call attention to problems, encourage growth, and promote learning.

contempt Based on long-simmering negative thoughts about a partner, it is evident in sarcasm, name-calling, hostile humor, and mockery. Nonverbally, contempt is communicated by eye-rolling, sneering, and "tsking." Contempt is described as the most poisonous disconfirming message because it communicates disgust with a partner.

content conflict Occurs when we disagree about information. These types of conflicts are sometimes labeled "simple" because we can turn to sources to verify the facts in dispute.

content paraphrase Rewords a speaker's message in terms of our understanding of its meaning. A content paraphrase can be used when we have listened to a lot of information, we have been given complex directions and/or instructions, and when the information is technical and laden with unfamiliar jargon.

content-level meaning A message that refers simply to the content of the words and sentences that are communicated.

context A synonym for *situation* and can be characterized as a physical location or environment that affects communication. Contexts also refer to cultures and co-cultures, relationships with significant others, gender, and individual characteristics.

control The force to gain dominance; communicated at the relational level.

conversation analysis The study of the order, the organization, and the orderliness of everyday interaction.

conversational coherence Refers to how talk is organized. Comments made by one person should directly relate to the comments made by others.

conversational dilemmas Occasionally we may experience conversations during which we feel that we can't say anything right; whatever we say creates a problem or some sort of undesirable outcome. Such types of difficult communication encounters are called conversational dilemmas.

conversations Locally managed and interactive sequential interchanges.

cooperative principle Suggests that conversation partners use their talk to facilitate understanding. Cooperative conversations are assumed to result when participants follow the quality, quantity, relevancy, and manner maxims which are associated with the cooperative principle.

coordinated management of meaning According to this theory, the application of syntactic, semantic, and pragmatic rules enable conversation partners to experience meaning based on coherence, coordination, and mystery.

coordination How meaning is created by the rules we use to manage talk and create our social realities.

costs Features of a relationship that are considered negative. Costs can take the form of anxiety, insecurity, and the investment of too much time and too much energy.

couple violence Physical pain inflicted because of an impulsive desire to express a state of heightened arousal. Common couple violence that may accompany relatively uncontrollable verbal outbursts isn't related to the desire to exert power over others.

covert verbal abuse May be more harmful than overt forms of verbal abuse because of its subtle nature and its resulting harmful consequences.

crediting sources A skill used to sustain a conversation. Crediting sources during a conversation is similar to including footnotes or references in a written paper.

critical thinking Refers to activities involved in analyzing and evaluating messages.

criticism Involves negative words about a partner's personality or character.

cues-filtered-out approach An approach taken in early computer-mediated communication (CMC) research that characterizes CMC as primarily verbal and without the benefit of nonverbal cues.

cultural patterns Particular beliefs and values associated with a specific culture.

culture The shared assumptions, values, and beliefs of a group of people that result in characteristic behaviors.

dating information Specifying a time that something was known to be true; can add precision to our comments.

debilitative emotions Emotions that detract from effective functioning. Debilitative emotions are characterized by their intensity and duration.

deception cues Behaviors that people typically associate with lying; includes fidgeting behaviors and throat-clearing.

decoding The mental process of interpreting the message.

decoding rules Tell people how to interpret emotions when they are displayed.

defensive listening Interpreting messages as criticism and personal attacks.

defensive reactions Defending your self-concept and public face when you are feeling threatened.

defensiveness A cognitive, emotional, and physiological state that occurs when we believe that our self-concept is under attack.

denotative Meaning that is considered to be "correct" and that is found in dictionaries.

dialectical tensions Suggest that relationships evolve and change over time because partners constantly reassess and redefine their needs.

disclaimers Used to prevent others from forming negative judgments about a speaker and to disassociate one's identity from her or his communication and behavior.

disconfirming communication Communication that invalidates and disrespects others. Disconfirming communication includes ignoring people, failing to acknowledge others' thoughts and feelings, and refusing to accept others' opinions and emotions.

disconfirming listening Listening that does not acknowledge and respect a speaker's verbal and nonverbal messages.

displacement messages Messages that occur when we are the target of emotions such as anger and frustration that result from situations and experiences in which we are not involved.

display rules Tell people how and when to display emotions, and are culturally influenced.

effectiveness Achieving one's goals; a component of communication competence.

ego conflict Can result when individuals believe that they must win at all costs to save face; the issue under discussion becomes secondary to the effort to maintain the perception of credibility or worth.

emblems Nonverbal behaviors that can be translated directly in a word or two of verbal communication. Nonverbal emblems are culturally specific.

emotion families Clusters of emotions that share common characteristics. Emotion families include unique characteristics as well as variations, which result from differences in biology, learning experiences, and specific situations.

emotional intelligence (EQ) Knowing how to manage our feelings and to read and respond effectively to the emotions of others.

emotions Feelings we experience that result from the interaction of physiology, cognition, and social experience. Emotions significantly affect how we communicate with others and interpret others' communication.

empathic assertion A type of communication that involves making a statement that conveys recognition of the other person's situation or feelings and is followed by another statement that stands up for the speaker's rights.

empathic listening Occurs when we want to understand and experience the feelings of a conversation partner.

empathy Occurs when we not only attempt to understand the thoughts and feelings of others but also vicariously experience the emotions of others.

encoding The process of translating thoughts, feelings, and ideas into symbols (words and nonverbal cues).

ethics Can be characterized as well based on standards of right and wrong that prescribe what humans ought to do.

euphemisms Replace words associated with unpleasant and negative connotations with those associated with pleasant or neutral connotations.

evaluative listening Used when we want to judge the soundness of a message.

exit lines Often focus on situations outside a conversation that may cause us to conclude that the conversation is nearing its end.

expectancy In terms of perception, our interpretation of stimuli is influenced by expectancy, or what we expect to perceive.

face Relates to our perceived self-concept but also involves how we want others to perceive us and our worth.

face-threatening acts (FTAs) Occur when messages are perceived as challenging someone's face needs.

facework Designed to prevent loss of face and restore face if lost; it is a fundamental aspect of communication competence.

facial expression and eye behavior Nonverbal communication that is involved in opening, closing, and regulating the channels of interaction and functions as the prime communicator of emotion.

facilitative emotions Emotions that contribute to effective functioning.

fact Something that is independently verifiable by others and typically based on sense data such as what we see, hear, taste, smell, and touch. Statements of fact are made after observation and don't go beyond what is observed.

familiarity Our interpretation of stimuli is influenced by how familiar we are with the stimuli.

family A group of people with a past history, a present reality, and a future expectation of interconnected, mutually influencing relationships. A network of people who share their lives over long periods of time bound by ties of marriage, blood, or commitment, legal or otherwise, who consider themselves as family and who share a significant history and anticipated future of functioning in a family relationship.

family rules Shoulds and oughts; they range on a continuum from explicit to implicit.

fast-track circuit emotions Emotional reactions and brain activity that occur before we have time to rationally analyze a situation.

feedback A response to the sender's message. The response can either be verbal, nonverbal, or both. It is through feedback that the sender learns whether his message has been received as intended.

feelings paraphrase Rewords a speaker's message in terms of our understanding of its meaning. A feelings paraphrase requires us to monitor a speaker's nonverbal communication for clues about what the speaker may be feeling.

fight-or-flight syndrome The crisis response that originates in the brain in response to a perceived physical or social threat (such as when we receive face-threatening communication in the form of criticism). The physiological changes that occur as a result of the fight-or-flight syndrome enable us to more easily flee from or fight in a threatening situation.

figure-ground organization In terms of perception, occurs when a portion of the stimuli selected from the environment is the focal point of our attention ("figure") and the rest is placed in the background ("ground").

flaming Computer mediated communication that is characterized by intense and/or negative language, swearing, and communication that is intended and perceived as hostile.

forgiveness The process (rather than the product) of overcoming resentment toward persons who have committed a transgression.

formal communication Communication within an organization that flows along official paths or networks that are prescribed by the organization.

free information Data beyond that which we request or expect in a conversation. The use of free information relates to the quantity maxim in that it enables us to offer information that is sufficient to keep a conversation going.

fundamental attribution error A tendency to overemphasize inherent characteristics or personality and underemphasize situational factors when we explain the reasons for others' behavior.

gender Refers to the influence of the environment and socially constructed meaning as it relates to femininity and masculinity.

gender-inclusive language Language that communicates respect for and includes meaning that relates to men and women.

general attractiveness and body shape We use appearance to judge others' backgrounds, characters, personalities, talents, and potential future behavior.

gestures Movements of the body used to communicate thoughts, feelings, and/or regulate communication. Our use of gestures may be intentional or unintentional.

gossip Talking about people (rather than talking against them).

haptics Another name for touch. Touch is related to the development of emotional and mental adjustment.

hate speech Speech that is based on prejudice and can be defined as "that which offends, threatens, or insults groups based on race, color, religion, national origin, gender, sexual orientation, disability, or a number of other traits."

heteronormativity Refers to the belief that everyone should be heterosexual and assumes that heterosexual experience is synonymous with human experience.

heterosexism Heterosexism includes derogatory terms used for lesbians, gays, bisexuals, and people who are transgendered.

hidden quadrant In terms of the Johari Window, this area includes information about ourselves that we know but that others do not.

high-context cultures Cultures in which communication is indirect, implicit, and derived from nonverbal communication.

human moment Refers to an encounter that happens only when people share their emotional and cognitive attention and the same physical space.

hyperpersonal approach Posits that CMC users strategically manipulate their identity and plan and edit their communication to achieve relational goals. The hyperpersonal approach can facilitate relational development because of visual anonymity; that is, CMC users don't have cues that demonstrate the physical attractiveness of their conversation partners.

hyperpersonal communication Internet communication that can be described as more sociable, personal, and intimate than what is found in face-to-face interaction.

idioms Words or phrases that are used with a specific meaning in a particular language and culture.

illustrators Typically gestures that are directly tied to speech. Pointing movements, those that depict spatial relationships, and rhythmic chopping gestures are examples of illustrators.

immediacy Refers to physical or psychological closeness between people involved in interaction.

impersonal communication Communication with others as if they are "objects" or roles; impersonal communication also occurs when we communicate in stereotypic ways.

indexing Acknowledges differences in thought and opinion in communicating and can prevent us from engaging in indiscriminant verbal communication. Indexing-related words and phrases include *maybe, it could be,* and *perhaps.*

indirect aggression A communication strategy that is used when the costs of direct aggression are too high. This strategy makes use of social exclusion and seeks to harm the social status of a target by manipulating her or his reputation.

indirect communication style Includes meanings that don't arise directly from the actual words used in communication. Indirectness can function to avoid conflict and can be a satisfying way to communicate when unstated meanings are shared, such as in irony, sarcasm, and figures of speech.

indiscrimination Occurs when we fail to make distinctions among similar but different persons, places, or things.

individualist cultures Cultures that focus more on the individual than on the group. Individual needs come before group needs, and people take care of themselves before they take care of others, if at all.

inference An interpretation based on a fact.

informal communication Flows via the grapevine and typically relates gossip or topics of personal interest but may also include rumors about an organization if a formal communication channel is ineffective in providing company-related information.

initiation phase Includes the first words we utter to a potential relationship partner. Pickup lines and a direct approach are ways we can engage in relationship initiation.

inner critic Intrapersonal communication messages that are typically critical or demanding.

interaction management The regulation of communication and how we control channels of communication.

internal dialogue A conversation that we have with ourselves (i.e., "talking to ourselves"). It's a natural and normal form of intrapersonal communication that helps us solve problems and work out our feelings.

interpersonal communication Involves at least two people who establish a communicative relationship. Partners have the power to simultaneously affect each other through their behavior, either positively or negatively.

interpretation Occurs when we assign meaning to stimuli that we have selected and organized from the environment. The interpretation of stimuli is influenced by both expectancy and familiarity.

intimacy Feelings of tenderness, connection, and closeness. Intimacy also includes warm feelings and affection for a romantic partner.

intimate distance Contact to 18 inches. This distance is sometimes called our "personal space bubble" and is used for touching and intimacy, as well as physical aggression and threat. People who communicate within the range of intimate distance may have close relationships and may communicate confidential information.

intrapersonal communication Communication that takes place within us. Internal dialogue and self-talk are examples of this form of communication.

jargon A specialized vocabulary shared and understood by members of particular occupational groups. Jargon often functions as a "shorthand code" or a quick method for sharing meaning.

Johari Window Comprised of four quadrants—the open, blind, hidden, and unknown areas—that change in size in terms of what, how much, or how little we disclose about the self and what, how much, or how little we know about the self in relation to others.

kinesics A category of nonverbal communication that includes body movement and position; specifically, gestures, body orientation and posture, touch, and facial expressions and eye behavior.

knowledge Related to communication competence and includes knowledge about ourselves, our conversation partner(s), our topic, the situation, and the communication process itself.

leading questions A type of closed-ended question that suggests the "correct" answer and/or attempts to guide a respondent's answer. Leading questions also communicate judgment and criticism.

listening Defined as a complex activity that involves the process of receiving, constructing meaning from, and responding to spoken and/or nonverbal messages.

literal listening Occurs when we overlook nonverbal communication and the emotional tone of a message. Literal listening also occurs when we focus on content level meanings and ignore the relational level meanings of messages.

loaded questions A type of closed-ended question that typically provides only two alternatives and presupposes something that has not been proven or accepted.

low-context cultures Cultures in which communication is direct, and most of the meaning comes from the spoken word.

maintenance skills Skills used to sustain the meaning of the relationship held by the relational partners.

manipulation In terms of relational termination, manipulation tactics are unethical and entail intentionally provoking a relational partner to initiate a breakup.

manner maxim States that we should be organized and specific when we speak. We cooperate with our conversational partners when we choose language and use it in a manner that is easy to understand.

many request messages These messages violate our boundaries, and the people who use them refuse to take "no" for an answer.

message Contains the information (e.g., thoughts, feelings, ideas) the sender wishes to convey to the receiver. Both verbal (words) and nonverbal communication (e.g., body language and vocal behavior) are used to convey meaning.

metacommunication Defined both as "communication about communication" and as "communication about relationships." We can metacommunicate about both the content of a message and the underlying relational message.

microexpressions These are extremely fast facial movements that last less than a fifth of a second, also can reveal emotions, especially those we are trying to conceal.

mindfulness Being aware of not only our thoughts but also the physical sensations of our body as we experience them.

mixed emotions A classification system that moves us beyond primary emotions and labels our complex feelings in terms of various blends of emotion. For example, the primary emotions "surprise" and "sadness" blend to form "disappointment," and the primary emotions "joy" and "acceptance" blend to form love.

mobbing A form of bullying that occurs at the workplace. Mobbing occurs when a person in authority, typically the perpetrator, creates a circle of allies, "the mob," that helps carry out the emotional abuse.

monochronic time Refers to time perceived as a commodity. Individuals who have a sense of urgency, believe that time shouldn't be wasted, and feel that people should do things one at a time adhere to a monochronic time system.

motivation In terms of communication competence, motivation refers to the desire to communicate. We are likely to be motivated if we are confident and interested in our conversation partners and if we see the interaction as potentially rewarding.

mystery Refers to the idea that coherence and coordination are arbitrary and are created by language; the words we use not only create and name things in our experience of reality but also limit them and can make them invisible.

negative politeness Strategies that confirm or protect someone's sense of independence or personal control.

neutralization Negotiating between the two extremes of a dialectic continuum. Neutralization entails a compromise between relationship partners who agree to give up some of what they need so that their desires can be partially fulfilled.

noise Any force that can interfere with the communication process in any communication context or situation. Noise can occur anytime during an interaction and can be external or internal.

nonverbal communication All forms of communication other than words themselves. This form of communication occurs via gestures, body orientation and posture, touch, facial expression and eye contact, vocal qualities and accents, body shape, clothing and artifacts.

nonverbal ritual Rituals helps to preserve and maintain a particular family's identity. Family rituals include private nonverbal codes, patterns, habits, and symbols.

novelty/predictability dialectic A dialectic that concerns the tension between wanting predictability and routine in a relationship and desiring novelty and newness.

open quadrant In terms of the Johari Window, this area includes information about ourselves that we and others know.

open-ended questions These questions encourage meaningful and thorough answers. Responses to open-ended questions tend to be descriptive and provide us with insight into what a conversation partner thinks and feels.

openness A relationship maintenance strategy that includes direct discussions about a relationship; giving and seeking advice; and demonstrating empathy.

openness/closedness dialectic Reflects the tension between wanting to self-disclose and engage in open communication and desiring privacy. Sometimes we feel the need to share our innermost thoughts and feelings with others; at other times we feel the need to be reserved.

organization Occurs when we categorize the stimuli we have selected from the environment to make sense of it.

owning thoughts Suggests that we realize that we don't know "everything" and that our perceptions are influenced by culture, social, gender, and individual contexts. Owning our thoughts also suggests that we realize that others may think differently than we do, acknowledges the validity of other viewpoints, and implies that we may be willing to change our opinions.

paralanguage How we say something rather than what we say.

paraphrase Rewords a speaker's message in terms of our understanding of its meaning.

passion Typically refers to the fireworks or sparks between people who are attracted to each other. In addition to sexual feelings, passion can entail an ardent desire for another based on emotional, intellectual, or spiritual attraction.

passive aggression Responses that appear to be submissive (i.e., they suggest we ignore our needs and rights) but actually ignore the needs and rights of others.

passive listening Practiced by those who believe that it's a speaker's responsibility to ensure that the listener understands. Because passive listeners merely absorb information, they believe that any misunderstanding is the fault of the speaker.

perception The process of selecting, organizing, and interpreting sensory information.

perception check A description of sense data, at least one interpretation (perception) of the sense data, and a request for feedback.

personal communication Occurs when we interact with others on the basis of their uniqueness.

personal conflict styles Our preferred ways of dealing with conflict situations. Five basic conflict styles indicate how much concern we have for the relationship with our conversation partner and how much concern we have for attaining our personal goals: avoiding, accommodating, competing, compromising, and collaborating.

personal distance Preferred for informal conversation and to keep people "at arm's length." Most Americans prefer personal distance when interacting with others (eighteen inches to four feet).

perspective taking When we use our imagination to "walk in another's shoes" and perceive the world as others perceive it.

pickup line A rehearsed question or comment designed to make the communicator appear attractive to a potential relationship partner.

polychronic time Refers to time perceived as limitless and not quantifiable. Individuals who believe that time should be adjusted to people's needs, that it's acceptable to change schedules and deadlines, and that people can do several things simultaneously adhere to a polychronic time system.

positive politeness Strategies that boost or protect someone's esteem or self-image.

positive tone Involves using direct communication that indicates a desire for the termination of a relationship yet demonstrates respect for and saves the face of a relational partner.

positivity A relationship maintenance strategy that attempts to make interactions pleasant by being cheerful, doing favors, and avoiding criticism of our partner.

pragmatic rules Rules that enable us to determine how to respond or behave within a given context.

prejudice A negative feeling toward and rejection of others who are not members of our group(s).

primary emotions There are eight primary emotions: anger, anticipation, joy, acceptance, fear, surprise, sadness, and disgust.

process That which is ongoing. Communication is a process because it is ongoing and dynamic.

process models Reflect the idea that relationships are ongoing and that relational meaning ebbs and flows, based on partners' attributions.

prompts These include silence, sounds ("Mmm" and "Uh-huh"), or words ("Go on" and "I'm listening") that let a speaker know that we not only are listening but also desire the speaker to continue.

proxemics Refers to how people use space and distance. Also labeled "personal space," proxemics can reveal how we feel about ourselves and how we feel about others.

proximity In terms of perception, we organize on the basis of proximity when we group stimuli that are physically close to each other.

pseudoconflict Occurs when we falsely believe that a relationship partner has incompatible goals or is interfering with our attainment of our own goals.

pseudolistening Pretending to listen even though we focus on our own thoughts and miss the speaker's message.

public distance This distance is used by instructors in their classrooms and for other public speaking situations. This distance is also sometimes used to communicate with strangers (twelve feet and beyond).

Pygmalion effect The way our significant others (people who are important to us) influence our self-concept.

quality maxim Tells us to refrain from lies, distortions, and misrepresentations.

quantity maxim States that we should offer information that is sufficient to keep a conversation going. We should refrain from offering too little or too much information in relation to our conversational partner(s).

racism Communication that places certain groups in inferior positions because of skin color, religious background, and/or ethnic background.

rational emotive behavior therapy (REBT) A clinical technique which teaches people how to reduce the intensity and duration of debilitative emotions. REBT directs us to identify and dispute our irrational thoughts that distort our emotions and actions.

receiver The person who receives the message conveyed by the sender.

receiving Involves selecting verbal or nonverbal stimuli from the environment and attending to the stimuli.

reconciliation strategies Include spontaneous development; third-party mediation; high affect/ultimatum; tacit/persistence; mutual interaction; avoidance; and vulnerable appeal.

reframing Engaging in perspective taking to redefine opposing dialectics as no longer threatening a relationship.

regulating Nonverbal communication can function to regulate the flow of verbal behavior; that is, subtle shifts in nonverbal behavior can signal that a speaker is finished with her or his turn and/or a listener desires a turn to speak.

relational communication Demonstrates that we not only interact about the content of communication but also interact about our association with a conversation partner.

relational feedback A brief description of a situation that parallels the speaker's and points to a connection between the speaker's experience and our own.

relational transgressions Behaviors and communication, such as cheating, lying, and keeping secrets, that violate relational expectations or rules.

relational-level meaning Typically unspoken meaning that can be ascertained, in part, from nonverbal communication. Relational-level meaning refers to our association with a conversation partner in terms of affection, control, and/or respect.

relevancy maxim States that we should provide information that pertains to the topic under discussion.

repair strategies Used to improve relationships that appear to be in decline and include neutralization, selection, separation, and reframing.

repeating A function of nonverbal communication; occurs when nonverbal communication repeats what is communicated verbally.

respect Valuing a person's right to life and expression. Respect (whether or not we are taken seriously) may be a relational-level message and is often a source of relational conflict.

rewards Features of a relationship that are considered positive. Relationship rewards can take the form of good feelings, need fulfillment, economic stability, and social status.

role Learned behaviors that we use to meet the perceived demands of specific situations.

salience In terms of perception, stimuli that are selected from the environment based on their interest, use, and meaning to us.

Sapir-Whorf hypothesis Suggests that culture influences language and that language influences cultural differences in thought.

schemas Mental templates that enable us to organize and classify stimuli into manageable groups or categories.

selection The first stage of the perception process; we select from the environment the stimuli to which we will attend.

selective attention Occurs when we ignore certain parts of a stimulus and attend to others.

selective listening Occurs when we attend to some parts of a message and ignore others.

selective perception Occurs when we see what we want to see, hear what we want to hear, and believe what we want to believe.

self-concept How we perceive ourselves. Our self-concept is based on our self-image and self-esteem.

self-disclosure The act of willingly sharing information about ourselves to others. The intimacy of our relationships is characterized not only by the depth of topics about which we self-disclose but also by the breadth or variety of topics about which we self-disclose.

self-efficacy The belief in our ability to manage prospective situations.

self-esteem In terms of our self-concept, it depends on what characteristics we perceive to be worthwhile and/or valuable.

self-fulfilling prophecies The expectations we have and the predictions we make for ourselves.

self-image A component of our self-concept; the characteristics we believe we possess.

self-serving bias Attributing inherent characteristics or our personality to successful behavior and situational factors to our unsuccessful behavior.

self-talk Intrapersonal communication within us that is specifically about ourselves.

semantic rules Rules refer to what symbols or words mean.

sender The person who conveys thoughts, feelings, or ideas to others.

separation Giving priority to a specific dialectical need in certain circumstances and placing emphasis on the opposing dialectical need in others.

sexism Language that disparages women or men.

sharing tasks Strategies that we can use to maintain our relationships. Through sharing tasks we can help equally with chores and other tasks that must be done.

significant others People who are important to us and who contribute to who we think we are and how we evaluate ourselves. Family members, friends, teachers, coaches, and bosses are examples of significant others.

similarity In terms of perception, the tendency to group elements together based on size, color, shape, and other characteristics.

skills Influence the perception of communication competence and can be characterized as goal-oriented actions or action sequences that we can master and repeat in appropriate situations.

slang A specialized vocabulary shared by people with similar experiences and interests. Slang functions to establish a sense of belonging and commonality among its users.

slow-track circuit emotions Emotional reactions that result from our thinking process. The thinking brain rationally analyzes a situation and then communicates with the emotional brain to produce slow-track circuit emotions.

social comparison Provides us with knowledge about ourselves in terms of how we measure up to others.

social distance The appropriate distance for business discussions and conversations that are neither personal nor private (four to twelve feet).

social exchange theory Suggests that we decide whether to form, sustain, or dissolve relationships based on rewards and costs.

social information processing (SIP) theory Suggests that computer-mediated communication groups can develop social rules similar to face-to-face groups if given enough time for an equal amount of message exchange.

social networks One of the strategic behaviors we can use to maintain our relationships; we can rely on and accept our relationship partner's friends and family.

social penetration theory States that relationships develop and change in terms of the breadth and depth of the self-disclosure between relational partners.

social presence Our perception of a receiver's involvement in an interaction.

speech acts Relate to what conversation "does." Speech acts include greetings, criticism, invitations, congratulations, insults, promises, requests, and warnings.

stage models These models suggest that relationships follow a trajectory and can be classified in terms of particular stages of integration, maintenance, or termination.

stalking A harmful course of conduct involving unwanted communications and intrusions repeatedly inflicted by one individual on another.

static evaluation We engage in static evaluation when we use verbal communication that ignores the idea that persons, places, and things change.

stereotypes Generalizations that are often based on only a few perceived characteristics. Stereotypes ignore individual differences.

stonewalling Occurs when a partner physically and/or mentally disengages from a situation. A stonewaller fails to give verbal and nonverbal feedback during a conversation and may act as if she or he doesn't care what a partner has to say.

submissive communication Entails failing to stand up for one's needs, rights, and wants.

substituting A function of nonverbal communication; occurs when nonverbal communication substitutes for verbal communication.

supportive communication A type of confirming response that is recognized within a culture as intending to convey assistance.

symbolic interactionism Posits that our view of self is shaped by those with whom we communicate.

symbols Verbal (i.e., words) and nonverbal communication that stands for something else.

sympathy Refers to feeling sorrow *for* another person rather than feeling *with* that person.

syntactic rules Rules that specify how symbols are arranged (e.g., grammar).

tag questions These questions are added to the end of declarative sentences. A tag question changes a sentence to a question.

talkaholic A person who talks too much consistently and compulsively.

termination strategies Strategies used to end a relationship.

territoriality A stationary area or fixed geographical location to which we lay claim and protect from invasion by others.

transaction When individuals who participate in face-to-face conversation simultaneously communicate and listen as a conversation unfolds.

turning points A specific feeling, event, or discussion that changes the intensity or definition of a relationship.

unknown quadrant In terms of the Johari Window, this area refers to the "unknown" information about ourselves that neither we nor others know about.

validating communication Involves listening and responding to others in a way that communicates that we acknowledge and respect them and their thoughts and feelings.

value conflict Results when people have differing opinions on issues that relate to their personal value systems and issues of right and wrong.

verbal abuse Characterized as verbal or nonverbal communication intended to and/or perceived as intending to cause psychological pain to another person. Such verbal abuse may take the form of public or private humiliation, name-calling, threats, criticism, insults, blame, and accusations.

vividness In terms of perception, refers to stimuli that are selected from the environment because they are noticeable. We tend to pay attention to stimuli that are intense, large, and repetitious and demonstrate movement.

vocalics A category of nonverbal communication that includes vocal qualities (such as volume, pitch, inflection, speed, and silence) and accents.

withdrawal/avoidance The withdrawal/avoidance strategy uses indirect tactics to terminate a relationship, such as reducing the frequency and/or intimacy of contact with a partner.

workplace bullying A type of emotional abuse that most often emanates from a powerful person such as a boss. Workplace bullying robs employees of their professional integrity, their reputation, and their competence.

Index

A

B

C

D

E

F

J

K

L

M

N

O

P

Q

R

S

T

U

V

W

Y